Multiple Intelligences

The Complete MI Book

Dr. Spencer Kagan
& Miguel Kagan

Kagan
COOPERATIVE LEARNING

Kagan Cooperative Learning
1160 Calle Cordillera
San Clemente, CA 92673
(949) 369-6310
Fax: (949) 369-6311
1 (800) WEE CO-OP
www.KaganCoopLearn.com

ISBN: 1-879097-45-1

Table of Contents

The Visions

The Intelligences

Matching Intelligences

Stretching Intelligences

Celebrating Intelligences

MI in Action

Testing and Assessment of MI

Evaluating MI Theory

Resources

The Eight Intelligences

Where to Find it!	Verbal Linguistic	Logical Mathematical	Visual Spatial	Musical Rhythmic	Bodily Kinesthetic	Naturalist	Interpersonal	Intrapersonal
The Intelligence								
• Overview Page	4.5	4.11	4.16	4.22	4.27	4.36	4.46	4.55
• Description	4.6	4.12	4.17	4.23	4.28	4.37	4.47	4.56
• Quotations	4.7	4.13	4.18	4.24	4.29	4.38	4.48	4.57
• Introducing to Students	12.4	12.5	12.6	12.7	12.8	12.9	12.10	12.11
Strategies & Activities								
• MI Strategies	7.5	7.12	7.18	7.21	7.22	7.28	7.30	7.36
• Activities to Match	8.6	8.14	8.22	8.30	8.38	8.44	8.52	8.60
• Activities to Stretch	10.6	10.14	10.22	10.30	10.38	10.46	10.54	10.62
• Activities to Celebrate	12.12	12.14	12.16	12.19	12.21	12.22	12.25	12.27
Additional Ideas								
• Mini-Curriculum	9.15	9.16	9.17	9.18	9.19	9.20	9.21	9.22
• Careers & Famous Folks	11.7	11.8	11.9	11.10	11.11	11.12	11.13	11.14
• More Activity Ideas	13.9	13.9	13.10	13.10	13.11	13.11	13.12	13.12
• Project Ideas	13.21	13.21	13.21	13.21	13.22	13.22	13.22	13.22
• Presentation Modes	13.25	13.25	13.25	13.25	13.25	13.25	13.25	13.25
• Stations and Centers	14.4	14.5	14.6	14.7	14.8	14.9	14.10	14.10
• Classroom Decorations	14.12	14.13	14.14	14.15	14.16	14.17	14.18	14.19
• Field Trips	14.22	14.22	14.22	14.23	14.23	14.23	14.24	14.24
• Classroom Resources	14.26	14.27	14.28	14.29	14.30	14.31	14.32	14.32
• School Environment	15.14	15.15	15.15	15.15	15.16	15.16	15.17	15.17
• Schoolwide MI Projects	15.25	15.25	15.25	15.25	15.26	15.26	15.26	15.26

Chart of MI Strategies
Intelligences

Key
● = Very Strong
◐ = Strong
○ = Also Involved

MI Strategy (pg.)	Verbal Linguistic	Logical Mathematical	Visual Spatial	Musical Rhythmic	Bodily Kinesthetic	Naturalist	Interpersonal	Intrapersonal
Agreement Circles (7.25)	○		●		●		○	●
Blackboard Share (7.33)	◐		●				○	
Blind Sequencing (7.17)	◐	●	◐		○	◐	◐	
Carousel Discussion (7.33)	◐				○		◐	
Carousel Feedback (7.33)	◐				○		◐	
Carousel Review (7.33)	◐				○		◐	
Cartoons & Picture Stories (7.20)	○	○	●					
Categorizing (7.28, 8.48)	○	◐	○		○	●	◐	
Circle-the-Sage (7.6)	◐				○		◐	
Corners (7.38)	◐		○		○		◐	●
Crack My Venn (7.14)	○	◐	◐			◐	○	
Debate (7.6)	●	◐					●	●
Dialogues (7.7)	●				○		○	
Discussion (7.7)	●						●	
Draw-What-I-Write (7.9)	●		●				◐	
Draw It! (7.21)	○	◐	●				○	
Fact or Fiction (7.15)	○	◐					◐	
Find My Rule (7.14, 8.14)	○	●	○			◐	◐	
Find Someone Who (7.27, 8.52)	◐				○		●	
Find the Fib (7.15)	○	◐					●	
Formations (7.26, 8.42)			●		●		●	
4S Brainstorming (7.8, 8.6)	●						○	
Gambit Chips (7.33)	●						◐	
Guided Imagery (7.20)	◐		●					
Inside/Outside Circle (7.27)	◐				○		○	
Jigsaw (7.30)	◐				○		●	
Jigsaw Problem Solving (7.17)	◐	●			○		◐	
Journal Reflections (7.36, 8.60)	●							●

Spencer & Miguel Kagan: *Multiple Intelligences*
Kagan Cooperative Learning • 1 (800) WEE CO-OP

Key
- ● = Very Strong
- ● = Strong
- ○ = Also Involved

Intelligences

MI Strategy (pg.)	Verbal Linguistic	Logical Mathematical	Visual Spatial	Musical Rhythmic	Bodily Kinesthetic	Naturalist	Interpersonal	Intrapersonal
Kinesthetic Symbols (7.23)			●		●			
Line Ups (7.26)	●	●	●		●	●	●	●
Lecture (7.7)	●							
Look-Write-Discuss (7.28)	●		●			●	●	
Lyrical Lessons (7.22, 8.30)	●			●			○	
Match Mine (7.18, 8.22)	●				○		●	
Metacognition (7.15)		●						●
Mind Mapping (7.19, 8.26)	○	●	●					●
Mix-Freeze-Group (7.26)		○	○		○			
Mix-Pair-Discuss (7.34)	●				○		●	
Numbered Heads Together (7.30)	●				○		●	
Observe-Draw-RallyRobin (7.29)	○		●			●		
One Stray (7.34)	●				○	●	●	
Pairs Check (7.31)	○						●	
Pairs Compare (7.15)		●				○	●	
Paraphrase Passport (7.32)	●						●	●
Poems for Two Voices (7.22)	●			●			●	
Proactive Prioritizing (7.32)	●						●	●
RallyRobin (7.7)	●						○	
RallyTable (7.10)					○		○	
RoundRobin (7.7, 8.10)	●						○	
RoundTable (7.10)					○		○	
Roving Reporters (7.35)	●				○	●		
Sages Share (7.35)	●				○		●	
Same-Different (7.29, 8.44)	●	●	●			●	●	
Send-A-Problem (7.17)	●	●					●	
Sequencing (7.15)	●	●	●		○	●	●	
Share & Compare (7.35)	●						●	

Chart of MI Strategies (continued)

Intelligences

Key:
● = Very Strong
◐ = Strong
○ = Also Involved

MI Strategy (pg.)	Verbal Linguistic	Logical Mathematical	Visual Spatial	Musical Rhythmic	Bodily Kinesthetic	Naturalist	Interpersonal	Intrapersonal
Similarity Groups (7.38)	◐	◐			◐	◐	◐	
Simultaneous RoundTable (7.12)					○		○	
Songs for Two Voices (7.22, 8.34)	◐			●			◐	
Spend-A-Buck (7.32)	◐	○			○		◐	●
Stand-N-Share (7.35)	◐				○			
Stir-the-Class (7.31)	◐				○		●	
Storytelling (7.8)	●						◐	
Talking Chips (7.33)	●				○		◐	◐
Team-Pair-Solo (7.32)	◐						◐	
Team Chants (7.22)	◐			●	◐		◐	
Team Charades (7.24, 8.38)	○	◐	●		●		○	
Team Inside-Outside Circle (7.34)	◐				○		◐	
Team Interview (7.36, 8.56)	●						●	
Team Statements (7.37)	●						●	●
Telephone (7.32)	●						◐	
Think Time (7.37)		◐						●
Think-Pair-Share (7.37)	◐						◐	●
ThinkPad Brainstorming (7.8)	●				○		◐	
Three-Pair-Share (7.8)	●						○	
Three-Step Interview (7.36)	●						●	◐
Timed Pair Share (7.37, 8.64)	●						○	●
Timelines (7.19)	○	●	●					
Total Physical Response (7.27)	◐		○		●			
Turn Toss (7.7)	◐		○					
Value Lines (7.26)	◐		◐		●		◐	●
Visualization (7.20)			●					●
Voting (7.32)								◐
Who Am I? (7.17, 8.18)	◐	●			○		◐	

Spencer & Miguel Kagan: *Multiple Intelligences*
Kagan Cooperative Learning • 1 (800) WEE CO-OP

Table of MI Activities

	Matching	Stretching	Celebrating

Verbal/Linguistic Activities

Matching	Stretching	Celebrating
• A Fairy Tale (8.7) • Aliens Abduct Student (8.13) • Book Report (8.12) • Descriptive Sentences (8.8) • Friendly Letter (8.11) • Mystery Story (8.9)	• Act It Out! (10.10) • Creative Sentences (10.6) • Describe the Castle (10.8) • Language & Me (10.13) • Letter Manipulatives (10.10) • The Antonym Song (10.9) • The Spotted Horse (10.11) • Why Share? (10.12) • Working Together Better (10.12) • Write the Instructions (10.7)	• Career Brainstorm (12.12) • I Am Smart (12.13) • Word Smart (12.4)

Logical/Mathematical Activities

Matching	Stretching	Celebrating
• Acute & Obtuse (8.17) • Rounding (8.16) • Symmetry (8.15) • What's My Number (8.21) • What's My Pattern (8.20) • What's My Time (8.19)	• Analyze the Graphs (10.15) • Building Relations (10.20) • Making Analogies (10.21) • Natural Taxonomy (10.19) • Numbers & Dots (10.18) • Symmetry & Asymmetry (10.16) • The Fraction Song (10.17) • What's the Cause? (10.14)	• Logic/Math Smart (12.5) • What Kind of Smart (12.14) • Who Am I? (12.15)

Visual/Spatial Activities

Matching	Stretching	Celebrating
• Color Mind Map (8.27) • Match My Tangram (8.23) • My Room Mind Map (8.28) • School Mind Map (8.29) • Shape Match Up (8.24)	• My Favorite Instrument (10.25) • Nature Scene (10.27) • Positive & Negative (10.26) • Self-Portrait (10.29) • Squaring Up (10.23) • Team Caps (10.28) • Upside Down Drawing (10.24) • Upside Up Drawing (10.24) • Writing About Shadows (10.22)	• Art/Space Smart (12.6) • Chart Your Smarts (12.16) • My Mind Map (12.18)

Musical/Rhythmic Activities

Matching	Stretching	Celebrating
• Hibernate (8.35) • Song For Two Voices (8.37) • Sounds All Around (8.33) • The Instrument Song (8.32) • Types of Music (8.31) • We're Democracy (8.36)	• A Song About Me (10.37) • Let the Music Move You (10.34) • Making Body Music (10.34) • Musical Expressions (10.30) • Music Note Math (10.31) • Music Symbols (10.36) • My Song Book (10.32) • Nature Songs (10.35) • Note Names (10.33)	• Lots of Ways to Be Smart (12.19) • Music Smart (12.7) • We're Smart (12.20)

Table of MI Activities

	Matching	Stretching	Celebrating
Bodily/Kinesthetic Activities			
	• Bodily Career Charades (8.40) • Formations Ideas (8.43) • Movie Charades (8.41) • Sports Charades (8.39)	• Animal Charades (10.43) • A Sporty Letter (10.38) • Balance Games (10.44) • Compare & Contrast (10.39) • Cooperative Juggling (10.44) • Mirror Mirror (10.44) • My Life As an Athlete (10.45) • Sign Language (10.42) • The Body Song (10.41) • The Sports Channel (10.40)	• Body Smart (12.8) • Career Charades (12.21)
Naturalist Activities			
	• Categorize Dinos (8.50) • Categorize Sea Life (8.51) • Categorizing Systems (8.49) • Shark & Dolphin (8.45)	• A Budding Artist (10.48) • A Natural Phenomenon (10.53) • Classify It! (10.47) • Describing Nature (10.46) • Natural Observations (10.50) • Recycling Sort (10.52) • The Mammal Song (10.49) • The Weather Log (10.51)	• Categorize Actions (12.22) • Nature Smart (12.9)
Interpersonal Activities			
	• Find Someone Who (8.53) • Find Someone Who (8.54) • Find Someone Who (8.55) • Personal Questions (8.59) • "You" Interviews (8.57) • Your Favorites (8.58)	• Being a Friend (10.54) • Close to Me (10.56) • People & Animal Relations (10.59) • People Person Plan (10.61) • Role Play (10.58) • Taking Turns (10.57) • Team Rules (10.60) • The Cause of Conflict (10.55)	• Find Someone Who (12.25) • People Smart (12.10) • Tell Us About You (12.26)
Intrapersonal Activities			
	• All About Me (8.65) • I Am (8.61) • The Complete Me (8.67) • What Do You Think? (8.66) • What I Learned Today (8.62) • When I Grow Up (8.63)	• A Poem About Me (10.65) • Group by Favorites (10.66) • "If" Questions (10.68) • Like or Unlike Me (10.67) • My Résumé (10.62) • My Time Line (10.63) • The Me Mobile (10.64) • What I Value (10.69)	• How I Was Smart (12.27) • Self Smart (12.11) • Share Yourself (12.28)

Index of MI Activities

(A to Z)

Index of MI Activities

Table of MI Strategies

Verbal/Linguistic Strategies (7.5)

Logical/Mathematical Strategies (7.12)

Table of MI Strategies (continued)

Visual/Spatial Strategies (7.18)

Musical/Rhythmic Strategies (7.21)

Bodily/Kinesthetic Strategies (7.22)

Table of MI Strategies (continued)

Interpersonal Strategies (7.30)

Naturalist Strategies (7.28)

Table of MI Strategies (continued)

Intrapersonal Strategies (7.36)

MI Learning Centers (7.38)

MI Project Strategies (7.41)

Index of MI Strategies

(A to Z)

Index of MI Strategies

Acknowledgments

We would like to express our appreciation to a number of people who made this book possible. First, of course, to Dr. Howard Gardner whose theory of multiple intelligences is transforming education. We, like so many others, fell into the grasp of the power of the theory — it has been the stimulus for our reevaluation upward of what is possible in our classrooms and schools. We are grateful for Dr. Gardner's input on an earlier book, out of which the present book grew.

Dr. David Lazear, in a formidable series of books (1991, 1991, 1994), articulated three visions — teaching with, for, and about multiple intelligences. The three visions at the heart of this book — matching, stretching, and celebrating students' intelligences — align well with Lazear's visions. Lazear's books remain a treasure trove of thoughtful theory and teacher tools for those who would like to take the journey from MI theory to MI implementation. This present book adds new tools and hopefully contributes to the ongoing conversation about the nature of human intelligences and how education should respond, now that it is established that there are many ways to be smart.

We gratefully acknowledge the kindness of Dr. Thomas R. Hoerr, director of New City School, who contributed a description of his school — one of our nation's most formidable MI schools. We appreciate Pat Wolfe's review and supportive comments on the portions regarding the relationship between MI theory and brain research.

We also appreciate the work of the numerous other authors and researchers — referenced throughout the book — that we draw on for inspiration and direction as we work toward our shared goal.

Many people read and gave useful feedback on parts or all of earlier versions. Laurie Kagan, always with a watchful eye toward what makes sense for teachers, has helped make sure the book went beyond theory to, hopefully, become a teacher-friendly resource. Laurie also created the Eight Intelligences Mind Map in Chapter 4 and the helpful framework for conceptualizing and organizing the intelligences used throughout the book. Dr. Liana Forest, Dr. Thomas Armstrong, Jill Carroll, Jeanne Stone, Dr. Micki McGuire, and Monica Kagan all read and made useful comments on earlier versions. La Vonne Taylor edited the entire manuscript. Her very thoughtful labor is a substantial and much appreciated contribution.

Karen Schumacher, graphic designer, contributed to layout, design, and data entry. Most of the art in the book was created by Celso Rodriguez. Celso continues to express in a few lines what we struggle to express in many. Miguel Kagan also contributed to design, art, and created the cover.

Brian Maas and Dave Sanders of The Multiple Intelligences Company compiled and provided Internet sites in the Resources chapter, providing another wonderful and rapidly expanding avenue for us and our students to explore and strengthen our multiple intelligences. Liz Warner also contributed her Internet skills to track down helpful resources.

Clint Klose and Larry Wolfe of Lyrical Lessons wrote (and also perform for students and teachers) a number of songs we've included throughout the book. Their songs add another dimension to this book as does music in general to the classroom environment and learning.

And finally, we wish to express our gratitude to the many teachers who waited so patiently for this expanded and updated version. We appreciate your understanding. We hope it was worth the wait.

Preface

"I have never let my schooling interfere with my education."
— *Mark Twain*

As is obvious from the size of this book, we like many other educators, have become engrossed in the educational implications of multiple intelligences (MI) theory. MI grips educators, we think, primarily because it validates what we know instinctively: Students are smart in different ways! Of course! The theory resonates so well because the basic premise aligns with our everyday experience in schools. We know the student who is withdrawn in language arts, but really comes alive in science. We see the student who is not particularly adept in math, but is an excellent illustrator. We witness the student who struggles in class, but is always the first pick on the field. And, yes, we marvel at some students who excel in just about everything. Indeed, each student is different. Each student is a unique gift!

Students are smart in different ways! Of course! The theory resonates so well with us as educators because the basic premise aligns so well with our everyday experience in schools.

We, as educators, readily embrace MI theory because it calls for us to do what we intuitively know is good for our students. We know our students become alert, become engaged, like class, like each other more, and learn more when we include movement, pictures, music, nature, introspection and interaction as part of our instruction and curriculum. MI is providing education with a rationale for doing what we know is good for kids. Characteristic of his wit, Mark Twain in the opening quote describes traditional schooling as an interference with education. A schooling based on MI does not interfere with students' education, it promotes it!

MI theory, though, goes beyond acknowledging individual differences and encouraging us to liven up our classrooms and instruction. The theory identifies eight specific ways of being smart. This theoretical framework for human intelligences has become a catalyst within the educational community, releasing a great deal of energy. As educators, we are seriously reexamining our teaching, our curriculum, our students, and ourselves. Acknowledging that students are smart in different ways, we are questioning our curriculum: If students are smart in many ways, shouldn't we align curriculum with the intelligences to nurture the development of every intelligence in every student? MI theory leads us to look anew also at our instructional strategies: If students learn in different ways, shouldn't we present our curriculum in different ways to provide greater access to the curriculum for every student? MI theory has us questioning, too, our own perspectives about our students and ourselves: We ask not if, but how our students are smart. We explore our own pattern of intelligences, asking if by developing our own weaker intelligences we can teach more effectively those students with a different intelligence pattern than our own.

The major impetus for our writing this book has been our dedication to the development and training of instructional strategies. One way to apply MI theory is to teach with a range of instructional strategies — strategies which engage the range of intelligences of each student. If we can engage all intelligences through the instructional strategies we use on a regular basis in our classrooms, we reach each student regardless of his or her particular pattern of intelligence, and foster the development of all facets of all intelligences in all students. It is to this application of MI theory — the development and dissemination of MI instructional strategies — we feel we have something very valuable to offer to the growing field of MI resources.

If we can engage all intelligences through the instructional strategies we use on a regular basis in our classrooms, we reach each student regardless of his or her particular pattern of intelligence, and foster the development of all facets of all intelligences in all students.

Over the last two decades, our focus in cooperative learning has been and continues to be to develop and popularize numerous cooperative learning instructional strategies. These strategies, it turns out, stimulate and engage students' multiple intelligences. For years, we have been developing and providing trainings in MI strategies, we just never knew it.

We have developed and provide books and trainings in strategies for each intelligence including specific strategies for: reading, writing, listening and discussing (verbal/linguistic strategies); questioning, thinking, problem solving (logical/mathematical strategies); spatial relations, visual imagery, visual communication (visual/spatial strategies); music and rhythm (musical/rhythmic strategies); hands-on strategies, movement, body communication and representation (bodily/kinesthetic strategies); classification, comparison and observation strategies (naturalist strategies); peer tutoring, decision making, communication and information sharing (interpersonal strategies); reflection, preference and value articulation (intrapersonal strategies). In the last few years, stimulated by the MI framework, we have added a number of strategies to our repertoire in order to more evenly reflect the different ways of being smart. MI theory has stimulated us to strengthen our own areas of weakness.

It is our philosophy that the more diverse learning experiences we provide our students, the more robust their education will be, the more ways they will learn each topic, hence the more they are prepared to succeed in a world marked by increasing diversity and an accelerating change rate. MI theory validates that philosophy. Our personal bias is toward the interpersonal intelligence. We feel that our success as a pluralistic, democratic nation hinges on our population's ability to work with and get along with each other. Therefore, many instructional strategies described in this

The more diverse learning experiences we provide our students, the more robust their education will be, the more ways they will learn each topic, hence the more they are prepared to succeed in a world marked by increasing diversity and an accelerating change rate.

book integrate cooperative student-to-student interaction. Cooperative learning strategies have a proven track record — research in cooperative learning has established it as the leading method for producing academic gains, improving ethnic relations, and fostering the development of a range of positive social and emotional outcomes. For those reasons you will find us leaning toward interactive MI strategies as our preferred application of the theory. Interaction is a powerful vehicle for students to explore the content as well as their own intelligences and those of others. Here too, though, MI theory has caused us to

reexamine our teaching — whereas a few years ago we trained only Team Mind Mapping, we now also train individual visual/spatial Mind Mapping (in which students work alone and use only pictures and icons to symbolize the content), correcting the general bias toward verbal/linguistic over visual/spatial instruction and our own bias toward interpersonal over intrapersonal instruction. MI theory has pushed us to develop a variety of new variations on old strategies (using Same-Different to foster visual memory; having students draw rather than write instructions to each other for Match Mine) and new strategies as well. Kinesthetic Symbols, Observe-Draw-RallyRobin, and Team Chants, are but three of many of our new favorite instructional strategies born from the energy released from the MI big bang.

Although we advocate and try to support as fully as we can all approaches to teaching with, for, and about multiple intelligences, it is in MI instructional strategies that we put our greatest faith. Why are we so in love with MI strategies? Let us say.

MI Strategies are Easy

The first thing we love about MI strategies is that they are so easy. As teachers we have a tremendous task. Educating our students to take their place as effective citizens in the twenty-first century is no minor undertaking, especially when we fully realize the uniqueness of each student. We do not realistically expect teachers, many of whom are overburdened as is, to completely redesign their curriculum, plan all new MI lessons, and restructure students' entire educational experiences based on MI. If MI theory is applied in a way which multiplies the difficulty of an already challenging task, it will not become common in classrooms across the nation. What a tragedy it would be if we failed to reach all students and failed to develop all intelligences because we made the task of implementing MI too difficult. To realize the MI visions, we must have realistic, practical, easy-to-use methods.

Using MI strategies is the easiest way to begin to integrate MI into the classroom. As teachers, we simply learn a few easy strategies to include as part of any lesson. Success breeds success. Having easily extended our ways of reaching more students and engaging more intelligences, we begin experimenting with additional MI strategies. Before long, almost without noticing, MI becomes a part of every lesson. Our classrooms are brimming with movement, song, visualization, art, thinking, discussing, analyzing, and naturalist observations. School becomes more fun, engaging, and meaningful for our students and ourselves.

MI Strategies Break the Replacement Cycle

MI strategies are the best bet we have for creating sustained implementation of MI. If we want long-term matching, stretching, and celebrating MI, all teachers need to adopt MI strategies.

What leads us to that conclusion? Experience. In thirty years of researching, fostering, watching, and analyzing the implementation of cooperative learning, we have discovered a simple truth: The greatest sustained change results from the smallest changes in instruction.

When cooperative learning was the rage, complete curriculum packages and complex lesson designs were designed to apply

Using MI strategies are the easiest way to begin to integrate MI into the classroom. Before long, our classrooms are brimming movement, song, visualization, art, thinking, discussing, analyzing, and naturalist observations.

the principles of cooperative learning to the classroom. The complex cooperative learning lessons which resulted improved achievement, ethnic relations, social skills, social relations, liking for class and subject matter, and self-esteem. But they didn't last. Complex cooperative learning lesson designs did not lead to sustained implementation.

In contrast, simple cooperative learning strategies did.

Today, few teachers even know what "Double Expert Jigsaw" is, let alone use it on a regular basis. Ten years ago it was quite popular. Many teachers, however, use Timed Pair Share on a daily basis, with dramatic improvement in engagement, achievement, social and ethnic relations, verbal listening and articulation skills, and liking for class and content.

This realization, that simple instructional strategies lead to dramatic gains and sustained implementation, was the most important force which led us to develop New Cooperative Learning — we stopped training teachers in methods to create complex cooperative learning lessons; we started developing and training simple techniques for releasing the power of cooperative learning as part of every lesson. The mantra of New Cooperative Learning: No more cooperative learning lessons; let's make cooperative learning part of every lesson.

If history repeats itself, as it has been known to do from time to time, MI will be another passing fad unless MI becomes incorporated as part of every teacher's basic repertoire of teaching methods. If we put our energy into creating complex MI lessons, they will become occasional events in the classrooms of inspired and talented teachers. If instead we use simple MI strategies as part of any lesson, MI instruction becomes part of the daily experience of all students. We want every teacher to find it as natural to ask students to respond to a question with a Timed Pair Share (intrapersonal strategy), Kinesthetic Symbol (kinesthetic strategy) or a RallyRobin (interpersonal strategy) as it once was for them to have students respond only to the teacher and only verbally.

Since MI theory — in its attempt to describe the incredibly complex and diverse topic of human intelligence — is such a far-reaching theory with no single educational application, many educational prac-

Since MI theory — in its attempt to describe the incredibly complex and diverse topic of human intelligence — is such a far-reaching theory with no single educational application, many educational practices will fall under the MI blanket. This is part of the power of the theory, and also a seed for its perversion.

tices fall under the MI blanket. This is part of the power of the theory, and also a seed for its perversion. Under the label of MI, there will be many wonderful, helpful applications; there will also be some questionable practices. We as educators must take caution to evaluate practices for their merits, not for their labels.

Music playing in the background is not matching students' musical intelligence; having students create Lyrical Lessons is. Having students move around the room is not matching students' kinesthetic intelligence, having them symbolize the content with a class formation is. Telling students to talk over the content with a partner does little to develop the interpersonal intelligence, having them complete a team statement does. This is not to say that we should not play background music, give students the opportunity to get out of their seats and move around, and allow students to talk in class from time to time; however, these practices do not ensure a quality MI education. A quality MI education is characterized by MI strategies that match and stretch the intelligences.

Education has been plagued by waves of "This Year's New Thing" replacing "Last Year's New Thing." Faced with wave after wave in educational reform's replacement cycle, the longer teachers stay in the field, the more jaded they become. Eventually they face each new innovation with the same comment, "this too will pass." Right now, MI is education's new darling. Accordingly, for a number of years there will be a tremendous amount of time, energy and resources invested in MI. Teachers, schools, and districts will make a variety of wonderful changes. Whereas the power of many of these changes cannot be doubted, their sustained implementation can. What will happen when next year's new thing comes along? Complex MI lessons, projects, centers, and theme units are a full-time job. If there is press to implement some new program, will MI be set aside, just one more educational innovation in the long list of innovations which have fed education's replacement cycle? Will this wave, too, crash?

When cooperative learning was the new kid on the block, teachers developed complex lessons to teach students about cooperation. For the most part, those lessons are no longer being taught. Complex cooperative learning lessons designed to teach about cooperation did not weather the replacement cycle. Teaching with cooperative learning strategies did. And, wonderfully, those teachers who use cooperative learning strategies have students who learn about the power of cooperation. Learning about cooperativeness and multiple intelligence can be a by-product of teaching with cooperative learning and multiple intelligences strategies. Just as students best learn about cooperativeness in the context of cooperation, they best learn about their intelligences in the context of engaging their intelligences.

Lessons which have as their objective learning about MI, layer one more task onto an overburdened curriculum. Lessons in which learning about MI is a positive by-product of the way the lesson is taught, accomplish as much or more, but make a teacher's job easier, not harder. MI instructional strategies realize the powerful MI visions in the process of reaching traditional curricular objectives. There is only so much time in the school day. MI instructional strategies, because they are an integrated approach, do not replace traditional content with MI content, they deliver any content while reaching all students and engaging all intelligences — they break the replacement cycle.

Breaking the replacement cycle, the MI strategies allow a building of competen-cies among teachers. Rather than replacing one proven educational innovation with another, teachers add more tools to their toolbox of instructional strategies. If we as teachers, repeatedly use Kinesthetic Symbols as part of any lesson, using that

If there is press to implement some new program, will MI be set aside, just one more educational innovation in the long list of innovations which have fed education's replacement cycle? Will this wave, too, crash?

strategy becomes as natural as it once was to pick a student to respond. When we as teachers reach that level of fluency with an instructional strategy, the strategy becomes a tool for life. It becomes part of the fabric of our daily classroom. And so when next year's new thing comes along, we will continue to use the MI tools we have stored in our toolbox. In this way we break the replacement cycle, and the wonderful visions springing from MI theory continue to be implemented. MI, then, is not a passing fad but a permanent, powerful, transformative force.

MI Strategies Sidestep the Testing Trap

MI strategies sidestep the pitfalls of testing, labeling and tracking based on MI. A lot of emphasis has been placed on assessing students' intelligences. Why? The idea is well-intended. Theoretically, if we know our students' intelligences, we are better able to teach with strategies which engage their strengths, and develop curriculum to address their weaknesses. Theoretically we could teach students differently depending on their intelligences and even provide courses tailored to their special skills. We're in favor of individual attention and a student-centered education, in theory. What is possible in theory, however, does not always exist in reality. In the reality of classrooms as they exist today, especially at the secondary level, there is not time enough to design special content or instruction for each individual student. We rarely have the opportunity to work with students independently; enriching individualized instruction is the exception, not the rule. Further, any move toward individualization is usually a move away from the power of heterogeneous interaction and away from full access to the range of curriculum and instruction for all students.

Testing usually serves the master of evaluation and often serves the master of sorting. It is seldom a tool for improved curriculum or instruction. While testing almost never leads to improved curriculum and instruction, it does almost always lead to a parade of unacceptable outcomes in-

The beauty of MI instructional strategies is that they sidestep all the pitfalls inherent in testing. Instead of testing and sorting students, we enrich learning simultaneously for all our students!

cluding labeling students, students labeling themselves, lowered teacher and student expectations, diluted content and instruction for some students, and worse of all, differential access to curriculum.

The beauty of MI instructional strategies is that they sidestep all the pitfalls inherent in testing. Instead of testing and sorting students, an instructional strategy approach allows teachers to use a wide range of MI strategies with the whole class. With each MI strategy, we always match the strength of some students and challenge others to overcome their weaknesses. We enrich learning simultaneously for all our students!

MI Strategies Realize Three MI Visions

This book is about ways to realize three powerful MI visions: matching, stretching, and celebrating MI. As we use any MI strategy, we make progress toward all three visions! For example, if we want to reach our kinesthetic learners as we teach about the different classes of animals, we may have them use Kinesthetic Symbols, one of the many MI strategies. Students make up hand gestures representing mammals, reptiles, fish, birds, amphibians, insects. Students who are strong in that facet of the kinesthetic intelligence (usually students who talk with their hands), learn the content better, enjoy the lesson more, and feel validated. The teaching strategy *matches* the way those students learn best; we match our instruction with students' intelligences.

The power of MI strategies, however, does not stop there. As we teach with a kinesthetic strategy, those students who are weak in kinesthetic symbolization and communication get a stretch. The more often we use our nondominant intelligences, the stronger they become. If we repeatedly used the simple MI strategy, Kinesthetic Symbols throughout the grades, all students become fluent in that symbol system. Thus, as we use an MI instructional strategy, we also *stretch* students' intelligences. By using a range of MI strategies, we can nurture the development of all facets of all intelligences.

But the power of MI strategies extends even further. Students who are strong in the kinesthetic intelligence, but not particularly strong in the linguistic intelligence, shine when they use Kinesthetic Symbols. MI strategies reveal the different strengths of each student. When students reflect on their learning, they come to understand their own pattern of intelligences and that of their classmates. Students come to celebrate their own uniqueness and honor the diversity they discover among themselves. Through metacognition, students recognize their weaknesses and overcome them through their strengths. They learn about MI theory not from a book or a lecture, but from their own immediate experience. As we use a range of MI strategies, students observe themselves and others as they engage their various intelligences. With MI strategies, we also *celebrate* MI; students discover MI theory. The more ways we teach, the more opportunities each student has to know himself or herself, and his or her classmates. Students come to honor their uniqueness and celebrate their diversity.

Beyond MI Strategies

Our love affair with MI strategies has not blinded us to the wonderful alternative ways to match, stretch, and celebrate MI. In this book, we explore and share possibilities inherent in MI curriculum, lessons, centers, theme units, field trips, and classroom and school environments. We have done our best to represent, not only our favorite approach to implementing MI in the classroom, but also other wonderful approaches that hold enormous potential for our students. What we have provided, we hope, is an elaborate MI buffet. Each teacher and each school will place different items on their table, creating their own

unique MI meals. In the spirit of MI, we have attempted to provide food for every taste.

We sincerely hope you will find this book a useful resource. We know there will be future editions, so if you have an MI strategy we have not included, or know of some other way we can make the book more comprehensive or more useful, please contact us. We would love to hear from you.

Sincerely.

Spencer and Miguel Kagan
San Clemente, California
April, 1998

A Peek Preview

…there is an alternative vision that I would like to present — one based on a radically different view of the mind, and one that yields a very different view of school (Gardner, 1993, p. 6).

This book is intended as a resource and guide to translate enthusiasm about the theory of multiple intelligences into educational practices.

Multiple intelligences theory is, at its root, quite simple. The central proposition is that there is not one or two ways to be smart. There are many ways to be smart. There are multiple intelligences. The implications of that simple idea, when explored, are enormously profound. When we as educators fully recognize that each one of us is smart in many ways and that each one of us has different ways to be smart, we end up transforming how we teach, what we teach, the way we think of students and the way students think of themselves and others. Our role as teachers changes; our very mission as educators is transformed. Multiple intelligences theory is as transformative as any educational innovation ever.

The central proposition of MI theory is that there is not one or two ways to be smart. There are many ways to be smart. There are multiple intelligences.

The Visions

Recognizing that different students have different ways to be smart, when a student "doesn't get it," we attempt to reach the student in a different way. If there are many ways to be smart, there must be many ways to teach. Teaching in more ways, we reach more students. We match students' range of intelligences. We transform our instruction.

Spencer & Miguel Kagan: *Multiple Intelligences*

We, as educators, have always recognized that as our students develop they become more and more skilled with words and numbers. Traditionally, we took it on as our very mission to foster that development. Traditional education is captured by the 3 R's: Reading, wRiting, and aRithmetic. With the flowering of multiple intelligences theory we recognize that skill with words and numbers does not necessarily foster skill with pictures, movement, nature, movement, people, or oneself. We outgrow Reading, wRiting, and aRithmetic. We foster the development of not two, but many intelligences. We transform our curriculum.

Multiple intelligences empowers us to be more successful. We begin to see ourselves and others in more differentiated ways. No one is smart or dumb; each of us has a unique pattern of intelligences. Of our students we stop asking, "How smart are you?" and begin asking, "How are you smart?" We find hidden treasures in students we might otherwise have dismissed. We are enriched by our understanding of multiple intelligences theory. As educators, we want to share the treasure we have discovered. We begin to teach about and celebrate the intelligences. We transform students' understanding of themselves and others.

Having, in the first section of the book, identified three visions for education: Matching, stretching, and celebrating multiple intelligences, most of the rest of the book is an exploration of ways to make those visions a reality. This book is dedicated to those who would make the three MI visions a reality — and to their students.

The Intelligences

The first step in reaching the MI visions is to fully understand the intelligences. The more fully we understand each of the intelligences, the more successfully we will be able to match, stretch, and celebrate the

Multiple intelligences empowers us to be more successful. We begin to see ourselves and others in more differentiated ways. No one is smart or dumb; each of us has a unique pattern of intelligences. Of our students we stop asking, "How smart are you?" and begin asking, "How are you smart?"

range of intelligences. Thus, in the second section of the book, we explore core questions: What is an intelligence? What are each of the eight intelligences so far identified in MI theory? Are there others? Our exploration leads us to conclude it would be presumptuous to conclude that the number eight fully captures the ways humans are smart. We have students who have become second-class citizens in our schools because we have failed to match, stretch, and celebrate the mechanical intelligence. We cannot with any seriousness defend the notion that it takes less genius to create a gourmet masterpiece than to make an oil painting. As we make the case for the mechanical and culinary intelligences, we are making the case for all intelligences. There are not eight, but many ways to be smart. If we are to fully realize our mission as educators, we must match, stretch, and celebrate all the intelligences.

Our exploration of the intelligences leads also to the conclusion that intelligence is more than the ability to solve problems and fashion products of value. In the real world, our intelligences cooperate in exquisite harmony to allow us to function in many different ways. Our intelligences allow us to survive, develop skills, communicate, be creative, be perceptive, solve problems, know the world, and make wise decisions.

Recognizing the range of functions of intelligences provides hints for those of us who would match, stretch, and celebrate the intelligences. Just as the intelligences operate in harmony to allow us to function in many ways, they are probably best developed by educational practices which allow them to operate in harmony. If we are to foster the development of the intelligences, we would do well to have our students use the range of intelligences in coordination as they create, communicate, develop skills, solve problems, hone their perceptiveness, acquire knowledge, and make decisions.

If we are to fully develop each intelligence, we must fully develop all of the intelligences. The intelligences are interdependent. If the intelligences evolved to function in harmony, almost certainly we will do well as educators to provide ample educational experiences in which the intelli-

> **Paradoxically, the intelligences may be best fostered not by programs to develop the intelligences separately, but by allowing the intelligences to function naturally in an integrated, contextual way.**

gences may work in harmony. Separate programs to develop each intelligence have their place, but those programs must be counterbalanced by integrated instructional experiences designed to allow the intelligences to function in coordination. Paradoxically, the intelligences may be best fostered not by programs to develop the intelligences separately, but by allowing the

intelligences to function naturally in an integrated, contextual way. The separate intelligences did not evolve to function separately, and if development of the intelligences in individuals is fostered in the same way intelligences developed in evolution, we would do well to have our students using their intelligences in coordination to accomplish real life functions.

Matching Intelligences

Having explored the intelligences, we turn to the heart of the book: Matching, stretching, and celebrating the multiple intelligences. Two chapters are provided for each vision — for each vision, one chapter explores the theory and methods, and the following chapter provides practical hands-on blacklines and ready-to-do sample activities. Here important choices have been made: In matching students' intelligences we emphasize instructional strategies that, once learned, can be used over and over on a daily basis in any classroom or educational setting. We are much more concerned about making multiple intelligences instruction part of every lesson than making multiple intelligences lessons. Thus, after describing the range of MI instructional strategies, we choose some that can be incorporated on a daily basis at any grade with any content. You will find step-by-step instructions and ready-to-use blacklines to get started. Our goal: to provide as much support as possible for classroom teachers who want to translate the theory into action by using simple MI strategies to make every lesson an MI lesson.

Stretching Intelligences

In stretching students' intelligences, we overview many facets of each intelligence and sketch the enormous task before us if we are to truly develop all facets of each intelligence. But then, in the activity chapter, we pick our favorite approach: Developing each intelligence through the others. The intelligences interact and can support each other. If a student is strong in say the kinesthetic intelligence but weak in the mathematical intelligence, we can provide a window onto the math content and skills by building on his or her kinesthetic intelligence. When we do, wonderful things happen. The student becomes more successful in the math, feels validated and accepted, and develops his or her strong kinesthetic intelligence even further. Thus in Chapter 10: Activities to Stretch Intelligences, we provide blacklines to teach each of the intelligences through each of the other intelligences. These blackline activities are provided not just as a support for the teacher who would translate theory into action; they are provided with the hope they will become a model of easy-to-create activities which any teacher can design to teach the content and skills of any intelligence through any of the other intelligences.

Celebrating Intelligences

In celebrating the intelligences, we identify two goals: First, each student should discover MI theory from the inside. That is, students are enriched and empowered to the extent they know and understand their own unique pattern of intelligences — their strengths as well as their areas needing development.

Second, each student should discover MI theory from the outside. That is, students are enriched and more successful to the extent they know and understand that each person is unique and that our strength lies in our collective diversity. Teaching about

the intelligences transforms students' self-concepts and their understanding of others. Our students, too, when faced with themselves and with another human being need to stop asking "How smart are you?" and begin asking, "How are you smart?"

Knowing one's own unique pattern of intelligences empowers a student to translate a difficult learning situation into an opportunity, to operate from strength.

Knowing one's own unique pattern of intelligences empowers a student to translate a difficult learning situation into an opportunity, to operate from strength. It also gives the student the resilience to admit weaknesses, and face rather than avoid challenging learning opportunities. Understanding and coming to celebrate the diversity among us prepares students to work well with others. Work relations and social relations are successful to the extent that we can honor the uniqueness in each individual; understanding MI theory is a prerequisite for success in the twenty-first century that will be marked by increasing interdependence and diversity. In Chapter 12: Activities to Honor Uniqueness and Celebrate Diversity, naturally we take an MI approach: Among the many ways to teach about the intelligences are to have students sing about their intelligences, interview each other, play "Career Charades," categorize MI actions, and reflect on "How I Was Smart." Again the blacklines are offered as samples of the myriad ways we can foster in our students the discovery of their own unique pattern of intelligences and that of others.

MI in Action

Although our bias is toward making MI part of every lesson rather than creating MI lessons, we provide as much support as we can for educators wishing to create MI lessons, classrooms, and schools. Thus in Chapter 13: MI Lessons, Centers, Projects, and Theme Units, we examine the various ways to set up MI lessons, centers, projects, and theme units. Here, again, you will find practical step-by-step supports including blackline activity generators, lesson planners, and evaluation forms. You also will find lists of dozens of ideas for activities to engage each of the intelligences.

In Chapter 14: Creating the MI Classroom, there are numerous ideas for creating a classroom environment that engages the multiple intelligences. Is a classroom really complete without a listening bar, a sequencing center, a recording station, image gallery, shop, nature station, lounge, or concentration station? You will find pages of classroom decoration ideas including

Any attempt to test the intelligences, to reduce the complexity of human intelligences to a set of numbers, especially if those numbers are to be used to decide that some students should receive different instruction or curriculum than others, should not occur.

posters, charts, class records, and motivational sayings. Field trip ideas from A to Z, and checklists of MI resources for each intelligence help us create fully engaging MI environments.

Just as we can transform our classrooms to make them MI compatible, we can transform our schools to engage all the intelligences. So in Chapter 15: Creating the MI School, you will find the ingredients for creating an MI school, including staff development and peer coaching, MI school resources, team teaching, MI clubs, and schoolwide MI projects. You will find here also a description of model MI schools and programs including Gardner's individual-centered school, Project Spectrum, the Key School, Green Tree East, and a description of New City School provided by its director, Dr. Tom Hoerr.

Testing and Assessment of MI

Assessment yes, testing no. That is the conclusion of our review of MI testing and assessment. Any attempt to test the intelligences, to reduce the complexity of human intelligences to a set of numbers, especially if those numbers are to be used to decide that some students should receive different instruction or curriculum than others, should not occur.

We provide our own Multiple Intelligence Test (The MIT), not as another tool for those who would label and/or differentially treat students based on their pattern of intelligences, but rather as a vehicle for exploring the pitfalls in MI testing. It is a test designed to help us question testing. We review the pitfalls of MI testing at some length, with the hope that we can add our voice to those who would warn against the trap of multiplying by eight the problems associated with the traditional IQ test.

We provide the Facet Tests as well, but again they are provided not to score individuals, but rather so, ultimately, individuals will not be scored. Through the Facet Tests we discover the meaninglessness of labeling a person strong or weak in an intelligence — most of us are strong in some facets of each intelligence and weak in other facets of the same intelligence. To speak of someone as strong or weak in an intelligence is almost always an over-generalization.

Although we say no to testing, labeling, and differential curriculum and instruction based on MI, we advocate authentic assessment of MI. Teachers do well to know as fully as they can the unique pattern of intelligences of their students. In Chapter 19: Authentic MI Assessment, we lay out the elements of authentic MI assessment — assessment which is representative, comprehensive, intelligence-fair, facet-sensitive, affect-weighted, meaningful, engaging, ipsative and developmental. This daunting list of prerequisites for authentic MI assessment is counterbalanced by practical approaches to understanding the pattern of intelligences of our students — and to fostering self-understanding among students. You will find here blacklines to create reflection responses, dialogue journals, and a host of ideas for creating authentic learning situations in which authentic assessment can occur as an integral part of the learning process.

Evaluating MI

Evaluation of MI theory can occur at many levels. In Chapters 20 through 23, we take a hard look at the evidence supporting the existence of separate intelligences. We look not just at how well the eight intelligences proposed by MI theory stack up to the eight criteria set forth in the theory, but we question the validity of the eight criteria themselves. On both counts we find the theory lacking.

MI theory takes brain localization to be the most important criteria of the existence of an intelligence, but the intelligences cannot be localized in the brain. As we draw a picture we use the left hemisphere to process details but the right hemisphere to process relations. Visual/spatial intelligence, like all the intelligences, does not

We discover the meaninglessness of labeling a person strong or weak in an intelligence — most of us are strong in some facets of each intelligence and weak in other facets of the same intelligence. To speak of someone as strong or weak in an intelligence is almost always an over-generalization.

reside in any one part of the brain; it is a by-product of an interaction among billions of neurons. Every one of the 100 billion neurons in the brain is in communication with every other neuron within a few synapses. Each of those 100 billion neurons is hungry for information, reaching out with electrochemical connections to up to 1,000 other neurons. The neurons are firing an average of 200 times each second. And they do not fire by simply adding up neural input from all their neuro-connections. They weigh the input! We are talking about 100 billion networked mini-microcomputers — computers so small 30,000 of them fit in a space the size of the head of a pin! The brain is nothing if not networked. In the face of this incredible interacting community of neurons, the very concept of brain isolation as a criteria of an intelligence breaks down. Upon analysis, the other criteria break down as well.

The person who is excellent at color-coordinating his or her outfits may or may not be good at parallel parking. When we take the Facet Tests we discover we are each strong in some visual/spatial intelligences but weak in others. What then can we mean by one visual/spatial intelligence? To claim the facets are but components of one intelligence would only make sense if the facets were related. But what, really, does flower arrangement have to do with navigational abilities? Does speed and accuracy of typing predict the ability to make a quality football tackle?

The data collected by Project Spectrum found no better correlation between one musical ability and another than the correlation of either musical ability with tests of other intelligences. Discrete unrelated abilities within the broad MI intelligences categories are the rule, not the exception.

Autistic children who can perform lightning calculations of prime numbers cannot give correct change from a five dollar bill. A student who can find the logical flaw in any verbal argument may have no skill at all with numbers. A student who delights and succeeds in geometry hates and fails algebra. To speak of one logical/mathematical intelligence flies in the face of brain physiology, psychometric data and common sense. Just as knowledge of skill with words does not tell us about skill with movement or music, knowledge of a skill with one facet of an intelligence does not tell us about skill with another facet of that same intelligence. There are not eight intelligences but a multiplicity.

That there are a multiplicity of ways to be smart and that there are serious problems both with how well the eight intelligences fit the eight criteria as well as problems with the criteria themselves, does nothing at all to subtract from the three powerful, positive visions which spring from MI theory. We need to match, stretch, and celebrate the intelligences — not because we can locate them in the brain, not because autistic children can do lightning calculations or play back lengthy conversations or musical compositions they have heard but once. We need to align our instruction and curriculum with the intelligences because it is good for our students. If there were not a shred of brain evidence in support of separate intelligences, and not a nickel's worth of evolutionary plausibility, we as educators would still find MI theory the most positive, powerful, and transformative of any visions for our field.

Howard Gardner shook the very roots of education by asking a simple question: What does it mean to be smart? As we ask that question, worlds open up. Embedded in that simple question are powerful levers to help us make positive transformations of our instruction, of our curriculum, and of student understanding of self and others. And for this we owe a great debt to Howard Gardner.

Let us begin our journey, then, with the three MI visions. For it is the three visions which provide inspiration and direction as we attempt to translate MI theory into educational practices.

Reference

Gardner, H. *Multiple Intelligences. The Theory in Practice.* New York: Basic Books, 1993.

Three Visions for Education:
Matching, Stretching, and Celebrating MI

What are possibilities of teaching FOR, WITH, and ABOUT multiple intelligences in the classroom? There are at least three different types of lessons that are needed: 1. Intelligence as a subject unto itself (teaching FOR multiple intelligences)…2. Intelligence as a means to acquire knowledge (teaching WITH multiple intelligences)…3. "Meta-intelligence" — intelligence investigating itself (teaching ABOUT multiple intelligences (Lazear, 1991, p. xviii).

Howard Gardner set forth his Theory of Multiple Intelligences as a conscious challenge to prevailing notions of intelligence. Gardner defines intelligences as "…ability to solve problems or fashion products that are of consequence in a particular cultural setting or community (Gardner, 1993, p. 15)."

It is a testimony to the value of MI theory that it is transforming how we conceptualize intelligence, our curriculum, our teaching methods, our students, and ourselves.

Central to the theory are three fundamental propositions: 1) Intelligence is not unitary, 2) Intelligence is not fixed, and 3) Intelligence is not fully measured by IQ tests. All three propositions are unquestionably true. Common experience aligns well with all three propositions: As teachers, we know students brilliant in math, but poor in English; we know some "late bloomers;" we have successes in teaching students to act and think smarter; and we know students who score low on standardized tests, but who are very intelligent in other ways. Turning to more scientific evidence, we find a variety of forms of support: factor analysis and subscales of intelligence tests; individuals who have shown remarkable gains in IQ and intellectual development (Feuerstein, 1980; Rymer, 1993); rats whose brains grow when afforded enriched experience (Diamond, 1988); a range of brain changes as a function of different types of experience (Kandel & Hawkins, 1992); and lack of predictive validity of IQ tests for success beyond school. There can be little argument with the fundamental assumptions of MI theory.

Howard Gardner's gift to education, MI theory, is creating a paradigm shift for the field. He has set in motion a revolution which will leave both our curriculum and our instruction transformed. It is rare for an academic to attempt a synthesis as broad as MI theory. It is a measure of Howard Gardner's power that he brought together into a coherent theory so much diverse research and theory. It is a testimony to the value of MI theory that it is transforming how we conceptualize intelligence, our curriculum, our teaching methods, our students, and ourselves. Gardner's work is as important as any there is in education. MI theory is facilitating a reexamination and enrichment of curriculum and instruction as well as an increased exploration, understanding and celebration of individual differences.

Perhaps the greatest gift Gardner has provided education is that MI theory is nourishing new visions of what education can be.

Three MI Visions
Vision 1. Matching

One of the most dramatic case studies in the Multiple intelligences literature is the case history of Paula (Campbell, Campbell, & Dickinson, 1992, Pp. 7-8). Early in school Paula was assessed as learning disabled; she developed a very low self-esteem, and a dislike for school. By fifth grade she was several grade levels behind her classmates.

Howard Gardner's gift to education, MI theory, is creating a paradigm shift for the field.

Paula attempted suicide in the summer before sixth grade. Her sixth grade teacher noticed Paula moved with poise and dignity. Following her hunch that Paula would benefit from kinesthetic instruction, Paula's teacher asked her to create a "movement alphabet" — movements to form the letters of the alphabet. Paula responded. Not only did she create letters, she sequenced them into a dance. Paula went on to dance her name, the words on the blackboard, spelling words, and even entire sentences. She performed for her class. Paula's self-esteem and liking for school increased; by the end of sixth grade, Paula reached grade level in reading and writing. In seventh grade, she was mainstreamed in all classes and received above-average grades!

Paula's story provides the basis for the first of three powerful MI visions of what education can be. This first vision involves a transformation of how we teach.

Theoretically, all we need do is develop instructional strategies for each of the intelligences, and teach with them to make an otherwise inaccessible curriculum accessible — doing wonders to boost self-esteem and liking for school in the process. In essence, we match the way we teach with the way students are smart. In Gardner's (1993, p. 33) words,

> In this way, the student is given a secondary route to the solution to the problem, perhaps through the medium of an intelligence that is relatively strong for that individual.

In this vision, the goal of maximizing academic success in all the areas of the curriculum is reached not by transforming the curriculum, but by changing the instructional methods with which the curriculum is taught. In short, academic success is reached by *matching* instruction to students' multiple intelligences. The belief is that all aspects of the curriculum can be made more accessible by delivering curriculum through instructional strategies which match the intellectual strengths of each student. It is important to note that this first vision calls for a shift not in curriculum, but in instruction. Paula's teacher

did not question the importance of teaching her spelling words, she made a shift only in the method to get there — to teach with kinesthetic rather than traditional methods.

Vision 2. Stretching

Gardner provided the basis for a second powerful MI vision with his glowing description of his visit in 1980 to the Suzuki Talent Education Center in Matsumoto, Japan.

> The performances were virtually incredible. Children as young as seven or eight were playing movements from violin concerti drawn from the concert repertoire; a pre-adolescent played a virtuoso piece of the Romantic ear; children hardly old enough to hold a violin performed in startling unison a number of pieces that any Western schoolchild would be proud to have mastered. The youngsters performed with style, gusto, and accuracy, clearly enjoying themselves and clearly giving satisfaction…(Gardner, 1983, p. 367).

Gardner describes ordinary preschoolers performing like exceptional prodigies. In his later work, Gardner (1993, p. 48) states,

> What Suzuki did for musical performance can, I think, be accomplished for every other intelligence, and indeed each intelligence may require its own specific educational theory.

Thus, we have springing from MI theory a second vision of what education can be.

Gardner (1993, p. 9) takes this second vision as the very purpose of school:

> In my view, the purpose of school should be to develop intelligences and to help people reach vocational and avocational goals that are appropriate to their particular spectrum of intelligences.

In this vision, the goal is to develop each human intelligence to its maximum by

---

Vision 1:

Matching

▼ *Goal:* Maximize academic success.

▼ *Method:* Match instructional strategies to students' intelligences.

▼ *Consequence:* Instruction is transformed.

▼ *Vision:* We eliminate or radically reduce school failure by teaching with instructional strategies that match each student's intelligences.

---

transforming the curriculum to focus on the development of each of the intelligences. In short, development of intelligences is reached through curriculum-intelligences alignment or *stretching* students' multiple intelligences. It is important to note that this second vision is primarily a call for a shift not in instruction, but in curriculum. The belief is that we can stretch each intelligence to its maximum, to create a population smarter in each of the intelligences, by aligning our curriculum with the intelligences, teaching for the development of each intelligence.

Vision 2:
Stretching

▼ *Goal:* Maximize development of all intelligences.

▼ *Method:* Use instructional strategies and curriculum that develop or stretch all intelligences in all students.

▼ *Consequence:* Curriculum is transformed.

▼ *Vision:* We make each student more intelligent in all ways.

Vision 3. Celebrating

The third vision for transforming education through the application of MI theory involves a shift in attitudes — attitudes of teachers toward students, students toward each other, and each student toward him or herself. Through the application of MI theory we can generate among teachers and students a renewed respect for the uniqueness of each individual. This enhanced understanding and respect for self and others is grounded in an understanding and celebration of the unique pattern of intelligences of each individual and the richness in our collective diversity.

Gardner (1993, p. 109) provides a moving example of how an understanding of the variety of ways to be smart can transform how a teacher views a student, and in turn how the student views himself. Donnie, as Gardner names him, was having great difficulty with first grade content. After two months into that year, Donnie's teacher reluctantly concluded he would have to be retained. After viewing a Project Spectrum videotape of Donnie's exceptional performance at a mechanical task, the teacher's view of Donnie was profoundly transformed.

> A thoughtful and dedicated person, she was overwhelmed. She had difficulty believing that this youngster, who experienced such trouble with school-related tasks, could do as well as many adults on this real-world endeavor. She told me afterwards that she could not sleep for three nights; she was distraught by her premature dismissal of Donnie and correspondingly eager to find ways to reach him. I am happy to report that Donnie subsequently improved in his school performances, possibly because he had seen that there were areas in which he could excel and that he possessed abilities that were esteemed by older people.

This third vision, in effect, treats MI theory itself as content for students and teachers. To the extent this vision is realized, a student can no longer think of herself as smart or dumb, but rather as having a unique blend of strengths and weaknesses. Students celebrate their own uniqueness and that of others.

School achievement improves when students know and accept their own unique pattern of intelligences because it is easier to improve once we admit a weakness, and

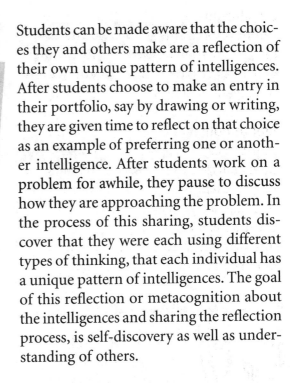

Vision 3:

Celebrating

▼ *Goal:* Understand and celebrate our own uniqueness and that of others.

▼ *Method:* Students discover MI theory through metacognition and sharing.

▼ *Consequence:* Understanding of self and others is transformed.

▼ *Vision:* We create a renewed respect in teachers for students and in students for themselves by fostering among students and teachers an understanding and celebration of their own unique patterns of intelligences and those of others. We prepare students to understand and work with diversity.

it is much easier to admit a weakness if we know we have other areas of strength. If we have but one yardstick for thinking about intelligence, each person stacks above or below each other person. When we break the single yardstick and replace it with many, no one is better than anyone else; we each possess a unique pattern of intelligences to be celebrated. We ask no longer how smart are we, but how are we smart.

In this vision, the goals of self-knowledge and self-acceptance, as well as knowledge and acceptance of others, are reached by teaching students about multiple intelligences, allowing them to discover their own unique pattern of intelligences and those of others. In short, self-understanding and social understanding is reached through metacognition and by allowing students to discover and celebrate the diversity in intelligences among them.

Students can be made aware that the choices they and others make are a reflection of their own unique pattern of intelligences. After students choose to make an entry in their portfolio, say by drawing or writing, they are given time to reflect on that choice as an example of preferring one or another intelligence. After students work on a problem for awhile, they pause to discuss how they are approaching the problem. In the process of this sharing, students discover that they were each using different types of thinking, that each individual has a unique pattern of intelligences. The goal of this reflection or metacognition about the intelligences and sharing the reflection process, is self-discovery as well as understanding of others.

It is important to note that this third goal does not involve a transformation of either curriculum or instruction, it creates instead, a transformation of how we view students, and how they view themselves and others. It involves structuring a time out from regular curriculum and instruction so students can reflect on and share how they are thinking and why they are choosing; in effect, students are encouraged through metacognition to discover the theory of multiple intelligences.

The following page, Three MI Visions for Education, summarizes the three MI visions for education: Matching, stretching, and celebrating students' multiple intelligences.

Three MI Visions for Education

1. Matching

- Matching instructional strategies with students' intelligences
- Providing access to the curriculum for all students
- Building multiple bridges onto the curriculum
- Teaching the curriculum through all intelligences
- Creating windows for learning for all learners
- Teaching *with* MI

The more ways we teach, the more students we reach — And the more ways we reach each!

2. Stretching

- Stretching students' multiple intelligences
- Nurturing the development of each intelligence
- Developing students' dominant and nondominant intelligences
- Fostering growth in all facets of all intelligences
- Enhancing students' capacities in each intelligence
- Teaching *for* MI

Helping students stretch every facet of every intelligence! — Making students smarter in many ways!

3. Celebrating

- Understanding and celebrating our own unique pattern of intelligences
- Improving ourselves through metacognition and reflection
- Respecting others' unique pattern of intelligences
- Appreciating differences
- Celebrating our collective diversity
- Teaching *about* MI

Honoring uniqueness and celebrating diversity! — Asking not how smart we are, but how we are smart!

References

Campbell, L., Campbell, B., & Dickinson, D. *Teaching and Learning through Multiple Intelligences.* Stanwood, WA: Campbell & Associates, Inc., 1992.

Diamond, M.C. *Enriching Heredity: The Impact of the Environment on the Anatomy of the Brain.* New York: Free Press, 1988.

Feuerstein, R. *Instrumental Enrichment. An Intervention Program for Cognitive Modifiability.* Glenview, IL: Scott, Foresman and Co., 1980.

Gardner, H. *Frames of Mind. The Theory of Multiple Intelligences.* New York: Basic Books, 1983.

Gardner, H. *Multiple Intelligences. The Theory in Practice.* New York: Basic Books, 1993.

Kandel, E. R. & Hawkins, R. D. *The Biological Basis of Learning and Individuality.* **Scientific American**, 1992, *267(3)*, 78-86.

Lazear, D. *Seven Ways of Teaching: The Artistry of Teaching with Multiple Intelligences.* Arlington Heights, IL: IRI/Skylight Training and Publishing, Inc., 1991.

Rymer, R. *Genie: An Abused Child's Flight from Silence.* New York: Cambridge University Press, 1989.

What Is an Intelligence?

To my mind, a human intellectual competence must entail a set of skills of problem solving — enabling the individual to resolve genuine problems or difficulties that he or she encounters and, when appropriate, to create an effective product — and must also entail the potential for finding or creating problems — thereby laying the groundwork for the acquisition of new knowledge. These prerequisites represent my effort to focus on those intellectual strengths that prove of some importance within a cultural context (Gardner, 1983, pp. 60-61).

What is an intelligence? This question is not only an interesting theoretical pursuit, but also holds profound implications for what we teach and how we teach. How we define an intelligence impacts which candidates we consider and which intelligences we settle on as bona fide intelligences. If we accept the definition of intelligence as linguistic and mathematical skills, our schooling reflects that definition, focusing on reading, writing, and mathematics. If we broaden our definition of intelligence, as does MI theory, we have a rationale to subsequently enrich our curriculum and our instruction. As part of the educational process, we include movement, art, rhythm, nature, interaction, and introspection. The definition we adopt influences which intelligences we choose to match, stretch, and celebrate in our classrooms and schools.

How we define an intelligence has profound implications for what we teach and how we teach. A broader definition enriches our instruction, the curriculum, and students' educational experiences.

In this chapter, we will attempt to capture the essence of a human intelligence as defined by MI theory. We will also forward another way for educators to conceptualize human intelligences — one based on an expanded set of functions for which intelligences are used. In the following chapter, we will explore MI theory's eight intelligences in more depth.

Entering a Restaurant

It is lunch time in an imaginary restaurant. At the entrance, there is a line of customers waiting to be seated. Let's peek inside the minds of a number of people as they wait to be seated. In a very important sense, each person enters a different restaurant.

Upon entering the restaurant, our first patron immediately notices the posted specials of the day, and begins to think about the prices. His thoughts go to calculating how much is saved if one buys the salad bar with the meal, as opposed to separately. This patron is strongly logical/mathematical in all life situations.

The second person to enter the restaurant is concentrating on the conversation she and her companions are having, and focuses on the word choice of her friend. Her friend has just said, "I wish they would serve 'fewer' mashed potatoes," and she is wondering if the word should have been "less." She often thinks about words and word choice — she is strong in the verbal/linguistic intelligence.

A third person does not think at all about sale prices or word choices, he is examining the arrangement of the tables and chairs in the restaurant. He has a highly developed visual/spatial intelligence, and immediately begins visualizing an arrangement of the restaurant which would be more attractive and allow customers more space.

Standing right next to him, his friend, who is strong in the musical/rhythmic intelligence, is listening to the music in the restaurant; he is thinking that a different type of music would create a more pleasant ambiance.

A party of three enters right behind them, and as they pause to take their place in line, a young lady in that party begins to stretch. She has just come from a racquetball game and is thinking about how good it feels to workout right before lunch. Her mind goes to a missed shot and how she might better position herself for that type of a shot in the future. She is exercising her bodily/kinesthetic intelligence.

We live in different worlds. We are attracted to, and in turn become skilled with different types of stimuli.

The plants in the restaurant have caught the eye of one of her two companions. Strong in the naturalist intelligence, she notices a philodendron with somewhat yellowish leaves, and is actually putting her finger in the pot to check if it has been overwatered.

The third member of their group is noticing the facial expressions of two people who are sitting at a table. As she reads the expressions, she is using her highly developed interpersonal intelligence. She is almost certain she has picked up some tension beneath their polite outward appearances.

Just then, one more person enters the restaurant. He is alone. As he takes his place in line, using his exceptional intrapersonal intelligence, his thoughts turn inward. He did not get the praise he hoped for that day upon completing a job, and he is trying to decide if he is angry, or just disappointed. He muses that perhaps disappointment is a mild form of anger.

Each student has a very different mind; each is attracted to, comfortable with, and in turn becomes skilled with different kinds of stimuli.

We live in different worlds. We are attracted to, and in turn become skilled with different types of stimuli. The individuals entering the restaurant did not choose which things would grab their attention. It was natural for each of them to think about different things; in fact, they gravitate to very different kinds of stimuli. The lady who notices plants has many plants in and around her home; she loves plants; her friends say she has a green thumb. The man who is musing about the relation of disappointment and anger often thinks about his inner states; he regularly makes entries into his dream diary — he has a rich inner life.

To some extent, each of our students enters our class in much the same way as the eight imaginary individuals entered our imaginary restaurant. Each student has a very different mind; each is attracted to, comfortable with, and in turn becomes

skilled with different kinds of stimuli. Each has a different pattern of intelligence.

Definition and Criteria
General Definition

As indicated in the lead quote of this chapter, MI theory defines human intelligences as abilities to solve problems, find or create new problems, and when appropriate, create products of value within a cultural context. This definition of intelligence makes it obvious that according to MI theory, intelligence is far more than a score on an IQ test, and that there may be many ways to be smart. This very general definition of intelligences, however, is far too broad to produce a workable set of intelligences. If we granted the status of intelligence to any set of skills which leads to problem identification and solution and the production of products of value in a culture, we would end up with a pottery-making intelligence, a water-finding intelligence, a fishing-lure designing intelligence, a ballet-performing intelligence, and a mask-making intelligence, along with countless others.

The general definition of intelligences, therefore, needs more specific criteria to produce a workable set of intelligences. MI theory attempts to discover a limited number of intelligences which alone or together identify and solve all important problems, and produce all valuable products. To select those intelligences, MI theory uses eight criteria.

The Eight Criteria

A candidate intelligence is deemed to qualify as a genuine intelligence if it meets eight criteria. The eight criteria are 1) Potential isolation by brain damage; 2) The existence of idiot savants, prodigies, and other exceptional individuals; 3) An identifiable core operation or set of operations; 4) A distinctive developmental history, along with a definable set of expert "end-state" performances; 5) An evolutionary history and evolutionary plausibility; 6) Support from experimental psychological tasks; 7) Support from psychometric findings; and 8) Susceptibility to encoding in a symbol system.

We will examine these eight criteria in some depth, especially in Chapters 20, 21, and 22. Our examination will reveal a number of problems with the criteria. For example, if brain localization is taken as a determinant of human intelligence, there are a multiplicity of human intelligences, not just eight. An incredible number of very specific skills have been linked to specific brain locations, not just eight, and the skills of any one intelligence are not all located in the same parts of the brain. The intelligences defined by MI theory also do not receive support from the available psychometric data: some psychometric data, including that collected by Project Spectrum, flatly fails to support the conclusion of eight intelligences. The story of the eight criteria, however, is to be told later. The most important point here is that none of the problems revealed in our examination of the criteria in any way subtracts from the validity of the three visions which flow from MI theory! Matching, stretching, and celebrating the intelligences remain among the most powerful sets of visions for education today.

The Eight Intelligences

Using the eight criteria, MI theory claims support for the existence of eight human intelligences (see box: The Eight Intelligences). We will examine these eight intelligences in depth in the next chapter. For now, we have a simpler task: understanding the essence of an intelligence. What is

---

The Eight Intelligences

▼ Verbal/Linguistic Intelligence .... Word Smart

▼ Logical/Mathematical Intelligence .... Logic/Math Smart

▼ Visual/Spatial Intelligence .... Art/Space Smart

▼ Musical/Rhythmic Intelligence .... Music Smart

▼ Bodily/Kinesthetic Intelligence .... Body Smart

▼ Naturalist Intelligence .... Nature Smart

▼ Interpersonal Intelligence .... People Smart

▼ Intrapersonal Intelligence .... Self Smart

---

a human intelligence? We will take two approaches to understanding the intelligences. First, we will look at characteristics of the intelligences — what they are, and what they are not. Second, we will look at how they function. By looking at the functions of intelligences, examining how they serve us, we gain further insight into their nature.

Characteristics of an Intelligence in MI Theory
Intelligences Are Not Linked to the Senses

According to MI theory, the intelligences evolved to deal with different types of information. They are not, however, linked to specific sensory input. There is not an auditory intelligence for example, because both music and language provide auditory information and a musical and linguistic intelligence are distinguished. Similarly, there is not a visual intelligence because both written words and spatial information come to us visually, but the linguistic and spatial intelligences are distinguished.

Intelligences Are Not Cognitive Styles

The intelligences are linked to specific types of information, and are associated with ways of thinking, but they are not cognitive styles. A person may think in numbers, in words, pictures, or even music depending on her or his most highly developed intelligence. The intelligences, though, are not cognitive styles. Many cognitive styles have been proposed. Among the researched dimensions of cognitive style are Reflective-Impulsive; Field Independence-Dependence; Analytic-Global; Analytic-Categorical-Relational; Feeling-Thinking, Acting-Reflecting; Repressors-Sensitizers; Conceptual-Perceptual/Motor; Broad-Narrow Attention; Levelers-Sharpeners; Augmenters-Reducers; and Right-Left Brained.

The claim for all of theses cognitive styles is that across a wide range of types of information, a person approaches information with a consistent style. For example, if a person is presumed to be analytic, they will focus on details in their approach to music, art, math, and even sports. If they have a global style, across those domains they will focus on the "big picture" — the forest, not the trees. Styles cut across domains. If a person is presumed to be impulsive, they are presumed to be impulsive across all kinds of activities. We all know, however, the student who is very impulsive when it comes to math (she quickly comes to an answer and is "done," not taking time to reflect on alternative approaches to the problem), but who is very reflective when it comes to a video game (she will spend hours trying to figure out the best strategy to get to the next screen). Gardner gives the example of the computer programmer who makes an interdigitated program with thousands of steps, who can't find his car in the parking lot (Gardner, 1997). The person is logical and organized in one domain, but not at all in another. Logic is not their style, although it may be a type of information with which they are comfortable and skilled.

Intelligences Are Not Nature or Nurture

When trying to grasp the notion of human intelligences, the question often comes up — are the intelligences learned or are they due to genetic differences? The answer: Neither. Neither nature or nurture alone determine intelligences — it is their interaction. All human intelligences are a function of genes and environment interacting, in different ways and in different proportions for each group and for each individual.

Heredity alone and environment alone cannot produce intelligence. Their interaction does.

The nature of this interaction is portrayed in a couple of thought experiments. First, let's imagine identical twins. They are born of the same egg and the same sperm, and share 100% of their genes in common. Yet on any test of any intelligence, they do not score the same. So, we have proof that genes alone do not determine individual differences in intelligences, at least as measured by all existing measures. Identical twins do not score identically on intelligence measures; all differences between them are due to environment, not genes.

Now let's engage in the second thought experiment. Imagine two quite different individuals. This next pair have different parents; and very few genes in common. They, however, have been brought up in an impossible world in which their environmental experiences are identical. They watch the same television programs, attend the same classes, are stimulated by the same peer interactions, and their parents treat them identically. This cannot happen, of course. But if it did happen we would find they too would score differently on every existing intelligence test. For this second pair, exposed to exactly the same environmental stimuli, the differences in intelligences would be entirely due to genes.

Thus, we have an answer to how much differences in intelligences between two individuals or groups is determined by genes or environment. The answer is different for different individuals and groups. The more similar the environment, the more intellectual differences are a function of genetic differences. The more similar the genes, the more observed intellectual differences are a function of environmental differences. Since environment and genes both differ for most individuals, observed differences are a function of both environment and genes.

> When trying to grasp the notion of human intelligences, the question often comes up — are the intelligences learned or are they due to genetic differences? The answer: Neither.

That differences in intelligences are determined by both genes and by environment is proven in a different thought experiment: If we deprive a normal child of significant intellectual stimulation, he or she will score low on tests of intelligences, and the low scores are due primarily to environmental factors. If a child is born with an extra chromosome, such as in Down's Syndrome, he or she will score low on certain tests of intelligences, and the low score is due primarily to genetic factors. Thus, both environment and genes influence intelligences.

Empirical studies also support the tremendous importance of both environmental and genetic factors in the development of the intelligences. Genetic factors underly-

The essence of the an intelligence in MI theory becomes clearer when we distinguish the "how" of thinking from the "what" of thinking. It is "what" we tend to think about that defines the intelligence we are using.

ing the exceptional intelligence patterns of autistic savants cannot be doubted: 82% of identical twins of autistics show intellectual impairment, in contrast to only 10% of fraternal twins (Folstein & Rutter, 1977). Environmental factors also cannot be doubted, as in the astounding intellectual gains obtained with certain kinds of remedial learning programs (Feurestein, 1980).

So, what are the implications of this environment-gene interaction for us as educators? The message is clear: The full realization of genetic potential is possible only in the presence of stimulating, enriching learning experiences which engage all the facets of all the intelligences. Our work is cut out for us!

Intelligences Are Attraction to and Skill With Specific Stimuli

The essence of the an intelligence in MI theory becomes clearer when we distinguish the "how" of thinking from the "what" of thinking. A student who is categorizing flora and fauna is exercising the logical intelligence on naturalist content. The "how" of her thinking is logical — categorization; the "what" of her thinking is

naturalist — flora and fauna. The what of the thinking defines the intelligence. Stimuli may be external (butterflies, paintings) or internal (feelings, thoughts), but it is the content, not the way the content is being dealt with, which defines the intelligence.

MI theory postulates that the brain evolved to deal with different types of content, and that different individuals are differentially developed in their attraction to and skill with the different types of content. If a student is attracted to and skilled with categorization itself and the logical relations among all matter of things, we would say she has a strongly developed logical intelligence. Logical relations is the content of her thoughts. If she is attracted to and skilled in thinking about flora and fauna, and other types of natural phenomena, we would say she has a strongly developed naturalist intelligence. It is *what* we tend to think about that defines the intelligence we are using.

A student who spends time categorizing acquaintances along different dimensions is exercising a logical intelligence on interpersonal content. If she enjoys categorizing not just people, but also music, books, paintings, flowers, stamps, and cars, and she is attracted to and skilled with analyzing relations, patterns, and sequences among all manner of things, we would conclude she has a strongly developed logical intelligence. If however, she enjoys categorizing only people and is attracted to and skilled in thinking about interpersonal relations, but is not especially interested in categorizing other things, we would conclude she has a highly developed interpersonal intelligence.

To determine a student's intelligence, we ask, rather simply, what is on his or her mind. It is not how he or she thinks about a particular content; it is his or her attraction to and skill with that particular content. What is the student attracted to and skilled in thinking about? Does he enjoy and is he skilled in thinking in numbers and relations, in words, or in pictures, about natural phenomena, interpersonal relations, or the meaning of life? When he tries to understand new material does he make an analogy to interpersonal relations, or does he form a mental picture? When we ask him to recall a party, does he remember who said what to whom, or does he remember the spatial organization of the room? When we ask him to plan a dinner party, does he focus on how to seat the individuals to create dynamic social relations, at what time the dinner should be served, or the meaning of the event? When we give him freedom to create any type of project, does he write his personal reactions, draw, create a dialogue between two characters, or create an experiment?

A student is a naturalist to the extent she or he is attracted to, skilled with, and thinks in terms of natural phenomena like flora and fauna. A student has a highly developed interpersonal intelligence if she or he is attracted to, skilled in, and thinks in terms of interpersonal relations. A student is logical to the extent she or he is attracted to, skilled with, and thinks in terms of logical relations. A student with strongly developed mathematical intelligence will tend to think in numbers and proportions and will feel at home with that kind of information. A student with strongly developed spatial intelligence will be comfortable with finding his or her way around, will think about and remember the spatial

arrangement of objects; presumably he or she thinks spatially. Gardner who himself spent a lot of time playing the piano and listening to music when he was young says, "I believe that I think musically (Gardner, 1997)."

To determine a student's intelligence, we ask, rather simply, what is on his or her mind.

The claim for separate intelligences rests on the idea that a person skilled in and comfortable with one kind of information may or may not be skilled in or comfortable with another. There is not one way to be smart, but many. Knowing that a person is skilled in one intelligence does not tell us if they are skilled in another. We all have all the intelligences, but each of us has differently developed our intelligences so each of us is unique and there is great diversity among us.

Stimuli, Skills and End States

Given that each intelligence deals with different kinds of information, the essence of each intelligence is best captured when we focus on the kinds of stimuli with which it deals. Further, skills with any one kind of stimuli will lead the individual toward different types of development or end-states. The linguistically skilled individual might become a poet, author, or orator. The logically skilled person might become a scientist, an accountant, or an efficiency expert. See the Multiple Intelligences: Stimuli, Skills, End State table. Examining the table helps us understand the differences between the intelligences, but more importantly for the focus of this chapter, helps us capture what is meant by an intelligence in MI theory.

Multiple Intelligences: Stimuli, Skills, End State

Intelligence	Stimuli	Skills	End State
Verbal/ Linguistic	Written & Spoken Words	listening, speaking, reading, writing, encoding and decoding language	Orator Journalist
Logical/ Mathematical	Patterns, Relations, Numbers, Symbols	problem solving, reasoning, logic, numerical skills	Scientist Mathematician
Visual/ Spatial	Color, Shape, Distance	sense of direction, architecture, painting, sculpting, arranging, decorating	Navigator Sculptor
Musical/ Rhythmic	Rhythm, Pitch, Timbre	composing, performing, appreciating, recognizing music	Composer Pianist
Bodily/ Kinesthetic	Bodily Cues	dancing, catching, throwing, jumping, handling objects, moving with grace, and precision	Athlete Dancer
Naturalist	Flora, Fauna, Rocks, Clouds	green thumb, animal husbandry, discriminating, recognizing, categorizing, analyzing	Biologist Gardener
Interpersonal	Desires, Motivation, Feelings of Others	accurate social map, empathy, organize and lead groups, understand and connect with others, conflict resolution and consensus seeking skills, good teammember	Counselor Salesman
Intrapersonal	Emotions, Impulses, Moods, Deeper Thoughts	self-knowledge, accurate self-concept, evaluation, self-direction, impulse control	Philosopher Religious Figure

Spencer & Miguel Kagan: *Multiple Intelligences*

Functions of Intelligences

Although we may understand the differences in intelligences by examining the different stimuli individuals focus on, the different types of skills associated with each intelligence, and the different end states aligned with each intelligence, it is equally important to understand that intelligences don't work in isolation. We integrate our multiple intelligences to perform every function. Every act of intelligence is a miracle of integration.

Everything that we do requires the use of many of our intelligences working simultaneously in harmony. As we sit and type these words, we use the bodily/kinesthetic intelligence to manipulate the keys and trackpad, the verbal/linguistic intelligence to formulate words for thoughts, the logical/mathematical intelligence to organize the subsections of this chapter. Later we will employ the visual/spatial intelligence to select fonts and a design for what, hopefully, will become a pleasing and useful page layout.

In MI theory, intelligence is defined in terms of certain functions for which intelligences are used. According to MI theory, we use our intelligences to solve problems, generate new problems, and to create products or services of value within a cultural setting. We consider "smart" anyone who can solve problems, generate new problems to solve, or create products or services of value.

Whereas problem solving, problem generation, and creativity are certainly important functions of intelligence, they do not capture the range of ways to be smart. We think of students as smart also if they can master new skills and learn new information. In fact, much of schooling is dedicated to producing lifelong learners, students who will attend to new information, store that information in ever-expanding knowledge bases, and reflect on new information to fashion ever-improving models of the world. Learning from experience, modifying one's information base and model of the world to best fit reality, is at the heart of intellectual progress — both for individuals and for the human race.

Thus, our view of intelligence would not be complete if it did not encompass the ability to perceive new information, acquire knowledge, and obtain skills. Being smart is bigger than problem solving and creativity. If as educators we are to fullfil the mission of fully developing the intelligences among students, certainly we must foster problem solving and foster creativity, but we must as well nurture perceptiveness, and the acquisition of skills and knowledge. Traditionally, schools too often have emphasized acquisition of skills and knowledge over problem solving and creativity.

By focusing on problem solving and creativity, MI theory corrects this imbalance. But we would not do well to use MI theory to foster a pendulum swing. Schools should not move away from knowledge and skill acquisition toward creativity and problem solving — we should foster all ways to be smart.

MI theory is serving education well by having us recognize and foster the development of all rather than just a few of the intelligences. In the same way education

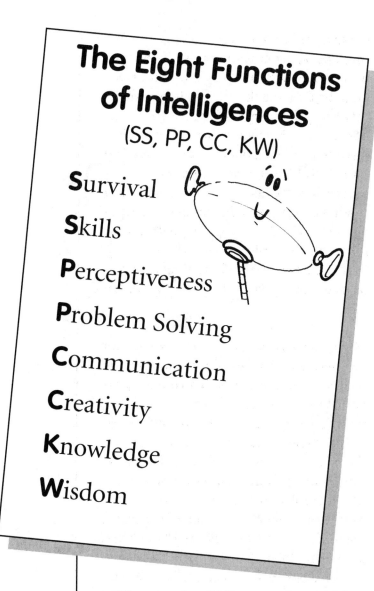

The Eight Functions of Intelligences
(SS, PP, CC, KW)

Survival

Skills

Perceptiveness

Problem Solving

Communication

Creativity

Knowledge

Wisdom

will be served well if it recognizes and fosters all rather than just a few of the functions of intelligences. What, then, are all the functions of intelligence?

In what follows, we outline and describe eight functions of intelligences. See box: Eight Functions of Intelligences. To be sure, this is but one way to categorize and describe the functions of intelligences, not necessarily the correct or only way.

We believe intelligence is more than the ability to solve problems, create problems, and create a product or service of value. Intelligences also function to allow us to

survive, perceive and retain knowledge about the world, acquire skills, solve problems, communicate, create, and make wise decisions. Not all intelligences serve all functions. For example, creating music does not necessarily function for survival, but does for creativity. Many intelligences serve many or all functions. For example, the bodily/kinesthetic intelligence helps us survive, acquire knowledge, solve problems, communicate, create, and acquire skills.

We forward this expanded set of the functions of intelligences as another window onto understanding the essence of human intelligences. Further, we believe that as educators, it is helpful to view intelligences from a functional perspective. It is only within the context of their functions that intelligences are best understood and fostered.

When we understand that everything we do depends on our intelligences working in concert, we no longer view students as "Word Smart," "Math Smart," or "Nature Smart." We realize we do more harm than good by labeling our students, and better serve our students and more accurately reflect the nature of intelligences by asking not what type of smart our students are, but for what ends are our students using their intelligences? We are all, with the exception of rare individuals perhaps, smart in many ways. We, and our students, are much more than the sum of our intelligences. We will examine this notion in greater depth in Chapter 6: Smart in Many Ways.

Understanding the functions of intelligences is helpful as we create learning experiences for our students, nurturing the development of their multiple intelligences. Just as the intelligences have evolved because they are functional, they are best developed in functional contexts.

For example, mathematical intelligence evolved in part to help us quantify things we needed to quantify, and to understand and communicate relations among things. It follows that acquisition of mathematical intelligence is probably best facilitated in contexts which have students quantify things they want to quantify, and understand and express relations among things they wish to understand and express. To give students mathematical problems out of a meaningful, functional context is more likely to alienate them from mathematics than to foster mathematical intelligence. By understanding the functions of intelligences and designing learning experiences which allow students to use their intelligences in meaningful, functional ways, we go with, rather than against, the natural way in which intelligences have evolved and are developed.

Schooling should attempt to establish natural learning environments in which students develop their various intelligences simultaneously in integrated, meaningful ways. Just as the intelligences enhance our ability to function — to understand, cope with, master, and appreciate the world — so too should schooling. Schooling should foster the development of the intelligences — to do for individual students what the evolution of the intelligences has done for the human race.

Let's look then at each of the functions of intelligences in a bit more depth, examining implications for our curriculum and instruction. It turns out that understanding the functions of intelligences provides an excellent blueprint for the design of curriculum and instruction.

Survival

Certainly the intelligences give us a survival advantage. If we can distinguish a poisonous from a palatable plant, a friendly from a hostile facial expression, or plead convincingly for help, we are more likely to survive. The case that intelligence evolved to promote survival is made by the late Carl Sagan in his provocative book, *The Dragons of Eden: Speculations on the Evolution of Human Intelligence* (Sagan, 1977).

The link to survival is not equally obvious for all intelligences. It is easy to see how a sense of direction, the ability to distinguish the path home from a path into new and dangerous territory, links to survival. It is harder to see how musical skills have their roots in survival. It is not clear how musical skills evolved in humans, how they increase our ability to survive or reproduce. Birds sing to guard their territory; wolves to call the pack to assembly; and gorillas sing from sheer joy. Chimps, however, the animals to whom we have the strongest genetic link, do not sing at all.

Nevertheless, it is clear that most of the intelligences increase our chances of survival. We are better able to survive to the extent that we are better able to move skillfully, find our way around, count, talk, and know our own needs and those of others. Mothers who do not understand the needs of their offspring are less likely to pass along their genes; their offspring is less likely to survive. Those with a better sense of direction are more to find their shelter, food, and water; they are more likely to survive and pass along their genes.

For teachers wishing to explore with their students how intelligences interact to allow survival, we recommend the astonishing account of Alicia, the teenager who by sheer wit survived time and again the ravages of the holocaust (Appleman-Jurman, 1990). On the night before she is to be marched to an open grave to be shot, Alicia is planning. She is visualizing a route to a hiding place, encouraging a companion to escape with her.

> "Eva, I know what will happen," I told her, holding her hand in both my own. "The Gestapo will probably take us all to the Fador in the morning to be shot. If they do, then I know how you and I can escape.
>
> She eyed me warily. "How?" she asked.
>
> "Remember the hill that leads down to the riverbank? Where the new pine trees were planted? Before the war we used to do cartwheels in the grass. Surely you remember! Once we reach that hill, it takes only a moment to reach the water."
>
> She listened somberly as I continued. "We have got to break away from the group and get to the river," I whispered. "Once we do, I know a place where we can hide." Then I told her about the hallowed tree in the water that I had discovered years before in my attempts to smuggle firewood down the Stripa. I explained how easy it was to enter the tree by diving down beneath the water's surface. "Don't you see?" I said. "From the outside it looks like an ordinary tree. And since it's in the water, the dogs won't smell us. It's perfect (Appleman-Jurman, 1990, p. 222)."

Time and again, Alicia exquisitely displays how the intelligences combine to allow survival. Alicia would not have survived without the abilities to visualize an escape route, knowledge about animal behavior, ability to infer the intentions of others, and, of course the ability to run and swim. Throughout her story we are repeatedly reminded of the intelligences most fundamental function — survival. Alicia knows which leaves to apply to a wound to draw out infection. She uses her knowledge of languages to distinguish safety from a death trap. The naked necessity of "if...then" logic is notched up to its most intense peak in the cat and mouse game of survival. Knowing how to make a horse buck; ability to run, swim, and dodge; humor; understanding of others; and ability to know and control one's own emotions all translate at different times for Alicia into the difference between life and death.

Even compassion and empathy reveal themselves as survival tools in Alicia's story. Time and again, Alicia risks her life for others — even going so far as refusing to leave prison to provide a companion she knew only an hour before imprisonment moral support so the companion would not expose the names of those on the outside. How, one might ask, can this level of compassion have its roots in survival? Would not survival be served better by leaving the prison? Alicia's story provides many examples of how concern for others is adaptive for one's own survival. He who does not stop to help a friend escape, even in the face of danger, later has no friend to stop for him.

Alicia has escaped a holding room after a train explosion. She is free. She could run away, but:

> As I was crawling away along the building wall I passed another window and looked inside. I could see men on the floor and heard what

sounded like moaning. I realized that they were probably wounded partisans who had been caught by the police. They will certainly be shot, poor men, I thought, probably after being tortured. I felt such compassion for the men in that room that I made up my mind to try to help them (Appleman-Jurman, 1990, p. 241).

She saves some of the Russian partisans. Later those same partisans are instrumental in her salvation. Could we ask for a clearer example of how empathy and compassion — components of the interpersonal intelligence — provide a survival advantage?

Because survival is such a core value, we would do well as teachers to include it as a theme throughout our units and use it as the basis for generating activities across the curriculum. If students see how a skill can give them survival advantage, they will be more motivated to acquire the skill. While studying reptiles, emphasis should be placed on distinguishing poisonous from harmless snakes. While studying nutrition, emphasis should be placed on longevity rates associated with a different diet, exercise, and drug usage. Survival can be a theme or a topic in a wide range of academic areas, including the study of economics, history, math simulations, word problems, essays, creative writing topics, and science studies.

Skills

Skills are usually acquired through practice. There are many skills associated with each of the intelligences. Skill development progresses in stages until it reaches automaticity or fluency. When we first learn a new language, we have to think about the language. Later, the language skills are so great we no longer have to think about them; they operate in the background and we concentrate only on what we want to

say. In a similar fashion, skills in the other intelligences progress toward fluency. The more we type, the faster we get. When we are really fluent in typing, we no longer think of the keys at all, the words appear as we think them. The skilled track and field star no longer has to think about foot position as he/she jumps the hurdles; the skilled swimmer no longer things of the steps of a flip turn. When fluency is reached, the flip turn becomes a single act which is performed without thoughts about its components. Skill development in drawing, painting, tying rebar wire, playing music, playing chess, and in countless other areas, with practice progresses toward fluency.

Important skills involve more than one intelligence. Skilled athletes might emphasize the interpersonal intelligence in team sports and the intrapersonal intelligence in individual sports, but a host of intelligences combine for any successful performance. The skilled surgeon uses visual/spatial, logical/mathematical, and naturalist intelligences in concert. The skilled musical conductor must have a keen interpersonal skills to complement his/her musical rhythmic skills. The skilled naturalist uses the musical/rhythmic intelligence in the study of bird song; and the spatial intelligence in the study of territoriality.

Traditionally, we have done a pretty good job of identifying and training for the skills within the verbal and mathematical areas, and to some extent physical education, art, and music. As we teach for the development of all intelligences, we will need to broaden our curriculum to include the many skills of each intelligence, including interpersonal skills, and self-development skills. The functional approach indicates skills of all the intelligences are best acquired in the context of accomplishing real-life goals. Aligning skill acquisition with how skills actually function in the real world enhances learning and later application of the learning. Students reject acquisition of skills unless they see applications to their own lives.

Perceptiveness

The intelligences help us attend to and distinguish different types of stimuli; as we develop the intelligences we become more perceptive. Perceptiveness is related to, but distinct from knowledge. If we are perceptive, we make observations which build up our storehouse of knowledge, but we can be perceptive in the moment and not store the perceptions in a way which builds up a solid knowledge base. Further, we can build up a large knowledge base, say by reading, but not be perceptive in the musical, or visual domains.

As we become more skilled in the visual/spatial intelligence, we become more perceptive. We see more as we look at paintings and architecture. We notice things we would not otherwise. Similarly, as we learn about music, we hear things we did not before. Our senses are sharper. We are more perceptive musically. As we learn more about geometry, we become more perceptive as we look at shapes. As we learn about defense reactions, we become more perceptive of others who protest too much, trying to convince themselves of something a part of them does not believe. It is not accidental that, for many, to say that someone is perceptive, is close to saying they are intelligent. Perceptiveness is a function of intelligence.

As we study any topic, the perceptiveness of students can be sharpened. For example, students can be given a photograph, drawing, or document related to the content of study, and be given an opportunity to find all they can in the object. They can listen to a piece of music, and attempt to perceive subtle cues regarding the musicians' intent and values. Students "wake up" when they are given an opportunity to sharpen their senses. When we teach our students facts and information we give them a fish; when we teach them how to be more perceptive, we give them tools with which to fish.

Problem Solving

The intelligences allow us to solve problems. Our visual/spatial intelligence allows us to pack more in the trunk of the car before the big trip, and to find the shortest route to our destination. Our mathematical intelligence allows us to figure how much we will save by buying the economy package rather than two regular size packages. Our interpersonal intelligence and our verbal intelligences team up to let us tell someone about a mistake they made without hurting their feelings. Our intrapersonal intelligence allows us to decode a dream. Our bodily/kinesthetic intelligence allows us pass through the barbed wire fence without getting our clothing snagged!

We are problem solving animals. The different intelligences allow us to solve different types of problems. If we develop in our students the various intelligences, we prepare them to solve problems, to be smarter. In the minds of many, to solve problems is synonymous with being clever or intelligent.

Traditionally, the development of problem solving skills have been the domain of the mathematics teacher. Taking seriously the idea that the goal of schooling should be the alignment of the curriculum with the functions of intelligences indicates that we would do well to include problem solving as part of all aspects of the curriculum. From color mixing to tone generation, from development of clever athletic plays to care of animals, all curriculum can be presented in formats which enhance problem solving.

Too often we have viewed our jobs as teaching solutions, rather than teaching problem solving. Again we give our students a fish when we should be teaching them how to fish. We give our athletes ready-made plays to learn and run off, rather than allowing them to team up to design solutions. We have our students memorize rather than discover formulas. We teach color mixing rules, rather than have our students encounter color mixing as a problem to solve. If we are to foster the development of the intelligences within our students, we must make problem solving an integral part of every aspect of the curriculum.

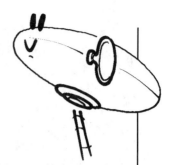

Communication

When we need to communicate, we use any intelligence that gets across the message. Far before the development of verbal language, infants communicate with facial expressions and gestures. Before elaborate linguistic systems evolved, primitive man communicated with gestures and simple sounds which represented objects or sounds in the environment — onomatopoeia in our language retains the primitive communicative function of representing something by its sound. The need to communicate has its roots in the advantages of coordinating efforts during a cooperative hunt. How else could relatively frail and defenseless humans dominate lions and elephants?

Although we can communicate through each of the intelligences, some of the intelligences almost seem "designed" for communication. Most of us communicate our thoughts and feelings easily through words (verbal/linguistic), but deeper feelings and life views can be communicated through mime (bodily/kinesthetic), playing or composing a piece of music (musical/rhythmic), or painting a picture (visual/spatial). The natural way to communicate discoveries about the relations among physical objects is mathematical formulas. With a stretch, we can think of the garden or well designed aquarium as a medium of communication, just like a painting, sculpture, or piece of music. Anything we do communicates to others about ourselves, but only some of the intelligences seem to have communication as a primary aim. Given a need to communicate, we will most likely turn to our strongest intelligences and those most suited to the message. We communicate our order to the waitress with words; directions with a map; and our mood with a tune.

The development of communication skills among students fosters the development of intelligences partly because it enhances communication of information and ways to think about information, and partly because in the process of communicating information, students sharpen their understanding. Only as our ideas bump into the ideas of others, only as we communicate with someone with different information or a different point of view are we forced to rethink and develop our conceptual frameworks. This is one of the reasons that cooperative learning is so powerful and consistently produces gains in higher-level thinking. Interaction produces thinking.

If we are to develop the intelligences, we need to work on developing communication skills across the curriculum. Every form of communication should be emphasized. Too often we emphasize verbal responses to an exclusion of other possibilities. Inclusion of communication via other modes would develop a greater range of intelligences. When we call on our students to respond, sometimes it can be a verbal answer, but we would do well to mix in other response modes such as writing on slates; drawing a picture, humming a tune, or making a movement. Communication

skills are extraordinarily predictive of success in the interdependent workplace of the 21st century. The more ways we ask our students to communicate, the more we develop the range of intelligences.

Creativity

Creativity involves making something, often by putting together existing elements in new and satisfying ways. Creativity is often driven by the desire to solve a problem which cannot be solved in familiar ways. We are driven to create a new solution. Creativity is motivated also often by the desire to express an intense experience.

Imagine for a moment you have had a very intense experience. Imagine further the experience is so intense you wish to capture it or express it. Depending on your pattern of intelligences you might turn to different mediums. If you are strong in the verbal/linguistic intelligence you might write a poem; if you are strong in the visual/spatial intelligence you might paint a picture, make a sculpture, create a photo or video; if you are strong in the musical intelligence, you might compose a song, tune, or even a concert; if you are strong in the bodily/kinesthetic intelligence you might create a dance or design a pantomime. If you are strong in several intelligences, you might write a play which conveys your message through dialog (verbal/linguistic), arrangements of props (visual/spatial), and movements of the actors (bodily/kinesthetic). Creativity to a large extent is self-expression through one or more intelligences. The dance, poem, sculpture, or painting is an outward expression of a subjective experience. A great deal of creativity is an attempt to objectify the subjective.

There is a link between communication and creativity: Every creative product, if perceived by others, communicates. Behind many creative works is the drive to communicate. To the extent artistic work is an attempt to communicate, the paint on the canvas, the moves on the stage, or the notes from the orchestra are simply alternative symbol systems or languages. Using the intelligences to communicate and to create, however, can be different phenomenologically. The difference centers around intent. The question is whether the primary intent of a creative act is to create, build, synthesize, or make something, or whether it is to communicate, touch or move others, to convey a message. If, while we are engaged in the creative process, there is no imaginary audience, we are involved in a creative act for the sake of creativity; if there is an audience, it may also be an act of communication. Fully immersed in creativity, we forget others. In that case, communication is a by-product of creativity, but not its aim. An interesting paradox: the most communicative works of art may be created when there is the least concern for communication. Is it true that when creativity is an end in itself, the product delivers the most profound message?

Too often creativity has been relegated primarily to our art and music classes. We teach "creative writing," but do not often enough teach "creative problem solving," "creative experimentation in science," and "creative thinking about social problems." Creativity should occur across all the intelligences and in every academic discipline. We can ask students for creative, alternative geometry proofs, creative solutions to math and science problems, creative solutions to social issues, to conceptualizing and categorizing historical events.

The emphasis should shift from solving the problem, to how many ways the problem can be solved, from knowing history facts, to creating novel ways to conceptualize the events of history. Creative expression should be an integral part of every academic topic. All the intelligences are fostered when creativity is allowed to flourish across the curriculum.

Knowledge

To capture the notion of "knowledge" we like the image of a house with rooms. The rooms represent areas of knowledge. What is in each room represents the knowledge base the person has amassed about that area. For example, if we have never heard of psychology, our house might not have a "psychology room." Two people who have both heard of psychology would both have a psychology room, but one might be very large and differentiated and the other rather small and barren. In the barren room, we might find a few books at best. In the other room we might find pictures on the walls of many great psychologists; well-stocked shelves of books by Freud, Rogers, Maslow, Perls, and Skinner; file drawers containing results of numerous experiments all well categorized; and even stacks of videos and audio tapes regarding behavior, brain, and therapy sessions. Knowledge is having many rooms, each of which is well stocked.

In this analogy, having a great deal of knowledge is having a mental house with many rooms, each elaborately furnished. It is one of the primary functions of the intelligences to help us construct our house

of knowledge. We gather different kinds of information with each of the intelligences, reading books, interviewing others, watching television and movies, looking at diagrams and maps, developing category systems, hearing songs, and manipulating objects, are all ways of gathering information to construct our house of knowledge. Each of the intelligences helps us construct more rooms, and to furnish them more lavishly.

The intelligences increase our skill with stimuli, which in turn helps us build our house of knowledge. Traditionally, as educators we have emphasized acquisition of knowledge, but unfortunately too often we have emphasized discrete bits of knowledge out of their broader context. Our students end up knowing Columbus sailed in 1492, but not who he was or why he was sailing! They can recite the formula for the area of a circle, but not use it in a meaningful context. Acquisition of knowledge, if it is to be learned and retained, must be part of a larger, meaningful context, and students must practice, or at least see, potential applications of the knowledge. Like skills, students often reject acquisition of knowledge unless they see it as potentially useful or helpful to them personally.

Wisdom

Wise decisions and wise ways to be in the world usually result from the combination of a highly developed introspective intelligence acting in concert with one or more of the other intelligences. Wisdom involves insight and foresight. We introspect to find our values, to know what we feel and what we want. Once we know what we want, where we want to go, we turn outward to ask which path will lead us there. Our knowledge of the way the world works

helps us make wise decisions, decisions which will obtain what we want. Only if we know both what we want and also which of the many possible courses of action will most likely lead us there, can we act with wisdom. Wisdom is a by-product of insight and foresight operating in concert.

For example, a student is misbehaving. Our impulse might be to reprimand the student. Wisdom involves insight — going inside and finding what we want (for the student to learn and not disrupt the class) and then foresight — knowing which kinds of behaviors are most likely to result in what we want. If the student is seeking attention, the wise decision might be to find appropriate ways to meet the student's need for attention, so the student will not need to act out. If instead the student is avoiding failure, the wise decision might be to minimize the potential for failure in the situation. Thus, in the case of the misbehaving student, introspection and interpersonal/social intelligences must conspire to produce the wise decision. To reprimand the student is to treat the symptom; wisdom involves having a clear vision of goals, and experience to select efficient paths to the goals.

Because wisdom depends on knowing how the world works, depending on the type of behavior involved, wisdom will depend on the development of different intelligences. Wisdom is not simply problem solving or skill development, it goes beyond, invoking values obtained through introspection.

What, Then, Is an Intelligence?

An intelligence is a sensitivity to and skill with certain kinds of stimuli. The intelligences differ in that they specialize in different kinds of stimuli. The intelligences act in concert to help us survive, perceive information, acquire knowledge and skills, create solutions to problems, communicate, and make wise decisions. We foster the intelligences to the extent we hone skills with and sensitivity to a range of stimuli, but also to the extent we align our curriculum with the functions of intelligences.

In the abstract we can define an intelligence as sensitivity to and skill with a specific type of stimuli. That abstract definition, however, does not further our understanding of specific intelligences. It is to that topic that we now turn. Let's meet the eight intelligences of MI theory.

References

Appleman-Jurman, A. *Alicia. My Story.* New York: Bantam, 1990.

Feuerstein, R. *Instrumental Enrichment. An Intervention Program for Cognitive Modifiability.* Glenview, IL: Scott, Foresman and Co., 1980.

Folstein, S. & Rutter, M. *Infantile autism: a genetic study of 21 twin pairs.* ***Journal of Child Psychology and Psychiatry***, 1977, *18*, 297-321.

Gardner, H. *Keynote Address. Is Musical Intelligence Special?* In Verna Brummett, (Ed.). Ithaca Conference '96: Music as Intelligence. A Sourcebook. Ithaca, NY: Ithaca College, 1997.

Gardner, H. *Frames of Mind. The Theory of Multiple Intelligences.* New York: Basic Books, 1983.

Sagan, C. *The Dragons of Eden: Speculations on the evolution of human intelligence.* New York: Ballantine, 1977.

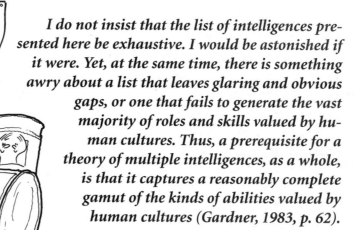

The Eight Intelligences

I do not insist that the list of intelligences presented here be exhaustive. I would be astonished if it were. Yet, at the same time, there is something awry about a list that leaves glaring and obvious gaps, or one that fails to generate the vast majority of roles and skills valued by human cultures. Thus, a prerequisite for a theory of multiple intelligences, as a whole, is that it captures a reasonably complete gamut of the kinds of abilities valued by human cultures (Gardner, 1983, p. 62).

Our attempts to develop intelligences among students, to deliver the curriculum through a range of intelligences, and to celebrate the unique pattern of intelligences of each student depends on our understanding of the different intelligences. There are different approaches we can take toward acquiring that understanding, and each approach deepens our understanding further. In this chapter, we will provide a summary page for each intelligence. The summary for each intelligence provides a brief description of the intelligence, the stimuli and symbols to which individuals are attracted, the types of skills and preferences associated with the intelligence, the end states (vocational and avocational roles) aligned with each intelligence, model individuals as archetypical examples of a high degree of some facet of the intelligence, and finally a brief description of some of the educational

If we as teachers are to fully respect the different ways to be smart in our class and school, we must first understand the different ways to be smart. Let us explore, then, the eight intelligences so far identified by MI theory.

implications for matching, stretching and celebrating each intelligence.

Additionally, we will explore each of the eight intelligences through anecdotes, examples, research, quotations, and interpretation. The intent is to explore each intelligence through a variety of media to enhance our intuitive understanding of the eight intelligences. The summary pages, anecdotes, and quotations provided in this chapter are all helpful tools you may use to introduce the eight intelligences to your students, students' parents, or colleagues.

Remembering the Eight

Four is easier to remember than eight, so Laurie Kagan, in her work in training teachers pairs the intelligences. She says it is easy to remember two disciplines we traditionally teach in school (Language Arts and Mathematics), two programs that are the first to go when monies get short (Art and Music), two things we often do outside (Physical Education and Nature Study), and the two personal intelligences (Interpersonal and Intrapersonal). See box: Remembering the Eight Intelligences. (School subjects usually associated with each intelligence are included in parentheses). With a nod to Laurie, in this chapter and throughout the book, we will examine each of the intelligences in the order she has found most helpful. Before doing so, however, a few words of caution are in order.

Intelligences Are Multidimensional and Interdependent

Before providing examples of individuals strong in each intelligence, it is important to warn against two misconceptions that

Remembering the Eight Intelligences

Traditional Intelligences
1. Verbal/Linguistic (Language Arts)
2. Logical/Mathematical (Mathematics)

Art and Music Intelligences
3. Visual/Spatial (Art)
4. Musical/Rhythmic (Music)

Outdoor Intelligences
5. Bodily/Kinesthetic (Physical Education)
6. Naturalist (Science)

Personal Intelligences
7. Interpersonal (Social Studies)
8. Intrapersonal

can result. By looking at the intelligences in isolation, we must be careful not to convey the impression that the intelligences work in isolation. They don't. We use all of the intelligences all of the time; they are interdependent. Also, we must be careful not to convey the notion that the intelligences consist of only a few skills as portrayed in the particular example we choose. By focusing on individuals who are strong in some aspects of an intelligence, we don't want to convey either that those aspects represent all the dimensions of the intelligence or that a person strong in some aspects of an intelligence is strong in all aspects of that intelligence. Each of the intelligences is multidimensional, and it is common for individuals to be strong in some aspects of an intelligence and not others.

Multidimensional

Each intelligence has many dimensions. Visual/spatial intelligence encompasses skills related to flower arranging, painting, sense of direction, and appreciation of architecture, to name but a few. Further, there is no established correlation for many of the skills within each intelligence. For example, a strong sense of direction (a visual/spatial skill) may be associated with weak or even no color sensitivity (another presumed visual/spatial skill). It is the very extraordinary person who is strong or weak on all dimensions within an intelligence. The multidimensionality of intelligences has important implications: usually if we say someone is strong or weak in an intelligence we are over-generalizing.

Real life examples cannot capture all the dimensions of any one intelligence. To get a better appreciation of the multidimensionality of the intelligences, examine or take the MI Facet Tests provided in Chapter 18: The MIT and the Facet Tests. If you are like most people, you will find that you score all over the map within each intelligence, scoring high on some facets of the intelligence and low on others. Thus the examples in this chapter are illustrative, not exhaustive. For each intelligence they give a peek at individuals strong in at least some dimensions of that intelligence, other examples would emphasize other dimensions of the intelligence. There is not just one way to be smart linguistically, or kinesthetically, and individuals smart in one way may not be smart in another.

Similarly, the icons we have created to represent each intelligence strive to capture the essence of the intelligence, but often do so by illustrating but one facet. Each intelligence is multifaceted as we will point out on the summary pages.

Interdependent

The intelligences do not develop in isolation from each other. For example, as we learn new vocabulary words for feelings (verbal/linguistic development), we become more sensitive to those feelings in ourselves (intrapersonal intelligence) and others (interpersonal intelligence). One of the clearest examples of the interdependence of intelligences is the intertwining of the development of interpersonal and intrapersonal intelligences, an interdependence Gardner recognized: As we come to understand others, we gain a better understanding of ourselves; as we gain a deeper understanding of ourselves, we can relate more fully to others. This intertwining of development occurs in many ways across all the intelligences. See Chapter 6: Smart in Many ways. For example, as we learn to appreciate or play a certain musical composition, we go deeper in contacting associated feelings and other internal states. As we understand the principle of parsimony in math, it deepens our appreciation of parsimony in a line drawing. Rhythmical development in music helps us become better poets, orators, and, perhaps even better architects.

Multidimensionality and Interdependence Are Brain-Based

The multidimensionality and interdependence of the intelligences correspond to brain structure and function. All neurons in the brain are linked by chemical and physical reactions — they are interdependent. In Chapters 20, 21, and 22 of this book we discover that for some purposes "community of neurons" is a better metaphor for the brain than is separate frames of mind. Brain researchers have documented incredible interdependence among the neurons of the brain, and they have also documented fantastic independence of certain neuron groups. Multidimensionality also corresponds to new findings from brain science: very discrete brain functions have been isolated. An individual very strong in certain aspects of an intelligence may preserve those strengths while completely losing other aspects of that same intelligence. The different dimensions of intelligence are physiologically independent so that for some purposes it is more useful to think of there being a multiplicity of intelligences than some small discrete number like eight. In sum, study of the brain leads us to the same conclusion as the study of individuals — the intelligences are both multidimensional and interdependent.

These two facts, the multidimensionality of intelligences and their interdependence have profound implications for curriculum and instruction. Those implications will be explored in depth later. For now, it is important to recognize that the following examples of the intelligences are merely illustrative: they cannot capture the range of skills associated with each intelligence or the relation among skills across intelligences.

Let's turn now to the eight intelligences so far identified by MI theory.

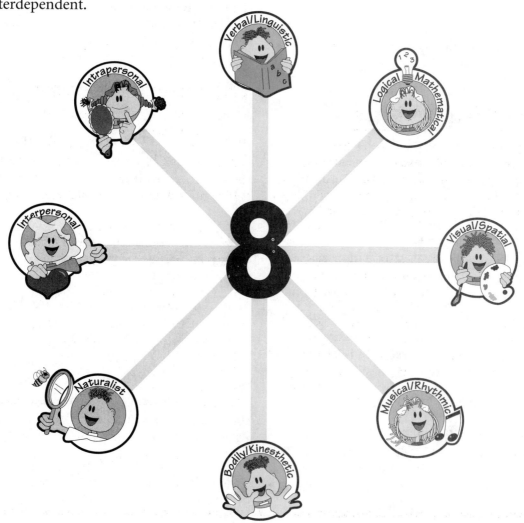

Verbal/Linguistic Intelligence

W̲e use our verbal/linguistic intelligence to think in, with, and about words. Oral and written language are symbols to think in and express this intelligence. Those strong in the verbal/linguistic intelligence enjoy reading, writing, speaking, and listening. Some forms this intelligence takes include telling jokes, discussing, writing poems, and passing notes.

Educational Implications

• **Matching:** Students strong in the verbal/linguistic intelligence learn best through listening to verbal presentations, reading, writing, and discussing. They benefit from audio tapes in the class listening bar. They enjoy strategies such as Draw-What-I-Write, RoundTable, and Brainstorming.

• **Stretching:** We develop the verbal/linguistic intelligence as we have students create oral presentations, written essays, poems, debates, dialog journals, book reports, and summaries of lectures. The verbal/linguistic intelligence is stretched also as students learn foreign languages, and hone traditional language arts skills such as vocabulary, syntax and grammar, and the various genres of writing. We may stretch students' linguistic intelligence through the other intelligences as when we have them write word problems, discuss their artwork, share their goals.

• **Celebrating:** Students celebrate their word smarts through positive peer response groups, self-validation following oral and written presentations, writer's journals, and written entries in their portfolios.

Attracted To

• Words; Oral and Written Language

Skills & Preferences

• Communicating (oral and written)
• Creating stories
• Debating, discussing
• Learning foreign languages
• Playing word games
• Reading with comprehension
• Remembering quotes, sayings
• Spelling easily
• Telling jokes, puns, rhymes
• Using correct grammar
• Using rich vocabulary
• Writing (descriptive and humorous)

End States & Models

• **Attorney:** Marcia Clark, Johnny Cochrane, Clarence Darrow
• **Comedian:** Bill Cosby, Jerry Seinfeld
• **Educational theorist:** John Dewey, Howard Gardner, Jean Piaget
• **Inspirational speaker:** Joan of Arc, Anthony Robbins
• **Journalist:** Walter Cronkite, Barbara Walters
• **Novelist:** Louisa May Alcott, Jane Austen, James Baldwin, Pearl Buck, James Joyce, John Steinbeck, Harriet Beecher Stowe
• **Orator:** Winston Churchill, Frederick Douglass, Dr. Martin Luther King, Jr.
• **Playwright:** Carol Churchill, William Shakespeare, Wendy Wasserstein, Tennessee Williams
• **Poet:** Elizabeth Barrett Browning, Emily Dickinson, T.S. Eliot, Langston Hughes, Ezra Pound, Shel Silverstein, Phillis Wheatley, Walt Whitman
• **Publisher:** Henry R. Luce, Joseph Pulitzer
• **Salesperson:** Phineas Taylor Barnum
• **Satirist:** Jonathan Swift, George Orwell
• **Short Story Writer:** Ernest Hemingway, Edgar Allan Poe

Verbal/Linguistic Intelligence

One type of attraction to and skill with language is exemplified by Jean-Paul Sartre. Sartre showed remarkable verbal fluency at five and wrote whole books before the age of ten. Writing for Sartre was an end in itself; through writing he manifested his essence. Describing this process, at age nine Sartre wrote:

> By writing I was existing.... My pen raced away so fast that often my wrist ached. I would throw the filled notebooks on the floor, I would eventually forget about them, they would disappear.... I wrote in order to write (Sartre, 1964, p. 81).

Verbal/linguistic intelligence can take many forms, including sensitivity to and ability to create poetry and prose of many types as well as debate, oratory, discussion, dialogue, and word play. Like all of the many skills within each broad MI category, we cannot assume that skill in one area (say, verbal debate) is necessarily associated with skill in another (say, ability to write poetry). Different linguistic competencies are expressions of combinations of intelligences — success in debate depends on logic skills; genius in poetry depends on rhythm; artful discussion depends on interpersonal skills. Further, many discrete types of linguistic skills are associated with specific, different, identifiable parts of the brain. See Chapter 20: Is MI Theory Brain Based?

Among the Japanese, there are two different reading systems: Kana, which is based on the sound of syllables and Kanji, which is based on pictures which symbolize words. Accordingly, Kana is associated with the left hemisphere portions of the brain that are linked to processing verbal information; Kanji, with the right hemisphere areas, associated with decoding pictorial information.

Oprah Winfrey's attraction to and skill with verbal/linguistic stimuli took a very different form than did Sartre's. Oprah was the child of unmarried parents. Her mother worked as a maid and left Oprah to the care of Oprah's grandparents who lived on a farm. With no children to play with, Oprah was extremely lonely and took to making up plays in which her corncob doll as well as the farm animals — chickens, pigs, and cows — all had parts. During long church services Oprah would make up questions she wanted to ask of people from the bible stories. Oprah's grandmother, Hattie Mae, read to Oprah every day and taught her to recognize the sounds of letters. By three years of age Oprah was reading, memorizing poems, and performing them at church, teas, recitals, and Sunday school programs! By four she had a nickname: "The Little Speaker." Oprah loved to recite the poems and stories she had memorized,

> I would just get up in front of her [grandmother's] friends and start doing pieces I had memorized. Everywhere I went, I'd say, "Do you want to hear me do something (Johnson, 1997, p. 48)?"

Whenever a program director would announce, "Little Miss Winfrey will now do her recitation," became one of her favorite childhood moments. Asked what she wanted to do when she grew up, Oprah replied, "I want to be paid to talk (Buffalo, 1993, p. 32)."

Words of Wisdom
on the Verbal/Linguistic Intelligence

Language is the light of the mind.
— *John Stuart Mill (1806-1873)*

Language as well as the faculty of speech was the immediate gift of God.
— *Noah Webster (1758-1843)*

He who cannot read is worse than deaf and blind, is yet but half alive, is stillborn.
— *Henry David Thoreau (1817-1862)*
    in Journal

No one ever told me I was loved. Ever, ever, ever. Reading and being able to be a smart girl was my only sense of value, and it was the only time I felt loved.
— *Oprah Winfrey (1954-)*

I no more thought of style or literary excellence than the mother who rushes into the street and cries for help to save her children from a burning house, thinks of the teaching of the rhetorician or the elocutionist.
    — *Harriet Beecher Stowe (1811-1896),*
    on writing Uncle Tom's Cabin

A room without books is like a body without a soul.
— *Marcus Tullius Cicero (106-43 B.C.)*

To speak of "mere words" is much like speaking of "mere dynamite."
— *C.J. Ducasse*

Words can bruise and break hearts, and minds as well. There are no black and blue marks, no broken bones to put in plaster cast, and therefore no prison bars for the offender.
— *Marlene Dietrich (1901-1992)*

A word is not a crystal, transparent and unchanging, it is the skin of a living thought and may vary greatly in color and content according to the circumstances and time in which it is used.
— *Oliver Wendell Holmes, Jr. (1841-1935)*

Reading makes a man full, conference a ready man, and writing an exact man.
— *Francis Bacon (1561-1626)*

Words are, of course, the most powerful drug used by mankind.
— *Rudyard Kipling (1865-1936)*

Speech is civilization itself. The word, even the most contradictory word, preserves contact — it is silence that isolates.
— *Thomas Mann (1875-1955)*

I can write better than anybody who can write faster, and I can write faster than anybody who can write better.
— *A. J. Liebling (1904-1963)*

The man who does not read good books has no advantage over the man who cannot read them.
— *Mark Twain (1835-1910)*

Some editors are failed writers, but so are most writers.
— *T. S. Eliot (1888-1965)*

The difference between the right word and the almost right word is the difference between lightning and the lightning bug.
— *Mark Twain (1835-1910)*

A good listener is not only popular everywhere, but after a while he gets to know something.
— *Wilson Mizner*

A word is dead when it is said, some say. I say it just begins to live that day.
— *Emily Dickinson (1830-1886)*

Language is not only the vehicle of thought, it is a great and efficient instrument of thinking.
— *Sir H. Davy (1778-1829)*

Oprah was writing before she entered school. On the first day of kindergarten she wrote a note to her teacher: "Dear Miss New, I do not think I belong here." She was placed in first grade, but advanced to third grade before the end of her first school year. Oprah became an avid reader. Her favorite book from childhood was *A Tree Grows in Brooklyn* about Francie, who was a loner whose only friends were on the pages of books. Oprah could not put the book down ("my first all-night book"). Today Oprah has an enormous library and has formed a national book club which has encouraged millions to read. She says reading is what she loves most.

Verbal/linguistic intelligence is the least easily categorized or described intelligence because there are so many dimensions and functions to language. We encode (put thoughts into words) and decode (make meaning of the words of others). We use words in so many different ways: as part of a song, to shout a warning, as part of a syllogism, to create a sonnet, to chat with a friend, to talk ourselves into or out of the tempting dessert, to describe the nuances of color, to label our feelings, to write a book. To an important degree, with words we create our world. The Eskimo growing up in a culture with dozens of words for snow lives in a more differentiated world. Once we name an object it springs into existence in a new way and can be thought about in new ways. The words our culture gives us molds the way we conceptualize reality: For many, language is the primary medium of thinking. Language is the universal intelligence, with more links to the other intelligences than any other. Feelings can be merely amorphous arousal until they are given a name; syllogisms and other forms of logic are language dependent; much of music is song; interpersonal

skills are acquired and expressed through language. Language can be seen (written language), heard (oral language), touched (braille), and expressed through movement (signed). A nod of a head up and down means yes in some cultures and no in others. Written forms can be phonetic or pictorial, with correspondingly different parts of the brain involved. PET scans show that very different parts of the brain are active when we are saying words, seeing words, hearing words, or generating words. Language can be very specific and concrete (proper nouns) or general and abstract (common nouns). Language can be the vehicle for expression of our most cold and calculating thoughts or our most intimate and romantic feelings.

Linguistic skills are a passport to much of the traditional academic content. Most input is provided through lectures or written material. Most of traditional academic curriculum is dependent on reading. Thus it is not surprising that elementary school reading skills predict achievement in all other academic subjects far better than any other single academic skill.

Language is the dress of thought. — Samuel Johnson (1709-1784)

Linguistic skills not only provide critical input, they provide a voice to thoughts generated by the other intelligences. The development of and expression of the interpersonal intelligence is dependent on verbal communication, and although there are other vehicles by which we can communicate, language is common and natural. Whereas the mathematical and musical intelligences can operate in relative isolation, the linguistic intelligence seems intertwined with the other intelligences. Interpersonal intelligence is intimately linked to verbal communication: very social students are often very verbal, and it is hard to say whether they talk to socialize or socialize to talk. For the verbal-social students, the need to express oneself with others is, to an important extent, the need to

Language most shows a man; speak that I may see thee; it springs out of the most retired and inmost part of us.
— Ben Jonson (1573-1637)

know what one is thinking. They say, "I love to interact with others because I get to talk, and as I talk, I listen to my own thoughts and discover what I am thinking!" Contrast the verbal-social student with the introspective student who says, "I wish everyone would stop talking for a while. Only when it is quiet can I listen to myself think." Many introspective students discover what they are thinking only if they and others stop talking, so they can get into contact with their own emotions, nonverbal visual images, or bodily sensations.

Although we may make our most important discoveries at a deep, nonverbal level, we are later driven to translate them and express them in words. Often this translation into words is associated with a struggle. Much of the work of therapy is a struggle to translate visual dream images and nonverbal impulses and emotions into words. Gestalt therapy works on the assumption of an inverse relation between words and feelings. A person stays out of contact with his or her feelings by talking about feelings; they experience the feelings when they stop talking. The poet struggles to capture and express experience in words in the same way as a painter struggles to capture and express experience with col-

ors and forms. Scientists of various specialities make important discoveries in nonverbal modes, struggling later to translate those truths into words or numbers. As Einstein described it:

> The words of the language, as they are written and spoken, do not seem to play any role in my mechanisms of thought. The psychical entities which seem to serve as elements in thought are certain signs and more or less clear images which can be voluntarily reproduced or combined.... The above mentioned elements are, in my case, of visual and some of muscular type (Gardner, 1983, p. 190).

Some of our thinking is most naturally conducted at a nonverbal level, only later to be translated into words. Other thinking is conducted at a purely verbal level. It is at those times, when the most natural medium for our thoughts is words, that we are in a pure form exercising our verbal/linguistic intelligence.

Great authors and poets have a message. The message is almost always generated by a combination of intelligences; the verbal/linguistic intelligence is merely the means through which that content is conveyed. Let's take a simple poem by Thomas Moore:

> I've oft been told by learned friars,
> That wishing and crime are one,
> And heaven punishes desires
> As much as the deed were done.
>
> If wishing damns us, you and I
> Are damned to all our heart's content;
> Come, then, at least we may enjoy
> Some pleasures for our punishment!

Moore has used his logic to have us praying to be damned! Clearly Moore's verbal/linguistic intelligence is involved in giving voice to his logic, but the content of the poem is primarily a logical argument more than an expression of a love for rhyme, meter, rhythm, or the other elements of poetry. To think of poetry (or any other expression) as a function of just one intelligence is to oversimplify. Moore's poem expresses content generated by the logical/mathematical, interpersonal, and intrapersonal intelligences. Content aside, in writing a poem (or any piece of literature) the author must consider organization (logical/mathematical), reader reaction (interpersonal), and how well the tone matches the author's feelings and thoughts (intrapersonal). To view, then, any piece of writing as a function solely of the verbal/linguistic intelligence shortchanges the complexity of the act of writing. A similar argument can be made for any expression of any of the intelligences; the intelligences, like the parts of the brain, act as an integrated, cooperative community.

Some animals, notably chimpanzees and parrots have demonstrated remarkable abilities with language. Chimps have been taught American Sign Language and have been taught to use computer boards to press symbols which allow them to compose sentences. Some have acquired vocabularies approaching 200 words, and compose remarkable, meaningful sentences. For example, Washoe, the most famous signing chimp, upon seeing for the first time a duck land on a pond signed "waterbird," a word he had never seen or been taught. Similarly, upon tasting a watermelon, Lucy, another chimp, signed "drink fruit," a word close to our English word "water melon."

Having learned to sign, Washoe was observed alone reading. That is, while slowly turning the pages of a magazine, studying the pictures, he would make appropriate signs, such as "cat" while looking at a photograph of a tiger, and "drink" when examining a Vermouth advertisement. Lan-

guage became for the chimps a natural mode of expression. They taught their offspring who with no human intervention acquired extensive vocabularies. Language allowed the chimps "to give voice to" emotions which they otherwise would only feel or express through facial expressions. For example, when Jane, Lucy's foster mother left the lab, Lucy gazed after her and signed, "Cry me. Me cry."

The finest words in the world are only vain sounds, if you cannot comprehend them. — Anatole France (1844-1924)

The world's most famous talking parrot, Alex, an African gray parrot, has been extensively trained by psychologist Irene Pepperberg. Alex knows the names of fifty objects, seven colors, and five shapes. He can say which of two objects is smaller. Most remarkably, Alex uses language appropriately in a functional context. For example, when Alex is scolded, his trainers might say, "No! Bad boy!" But when they then begin to walk out, Alex will say, "Come here! I'm sorry!" He was never 'trained' to say "I'm sorry," he picked up the phrase by hearing humans say it, much as human children pick up many phrases. Alex's most poignant speech came without prompting one day when his trainer, Irene Pepperberg turned to leave Alex in a veterinarian's office because he needed lung surgery. As Irene began to leave, Alex called out, "Come here. I love you. I'm sorry. I want to go back." (Masson & McCarthy, 1996, p. 229).

Logical/Mathematical Intelligence

W e use our logical/mathematical intelligence to think in, with, and about numbers and relations. Numbers and symbols representing relations express this intelligence. Those strong in the logical/mathematical intelligence enjoy solving problems, quantifying outcomes, and determining relations such as cause-effect and if…then relations. Some forms this intelligence takes include creating, thinking about and solving problems; analyzing objects and situations for their components; using abstract symbols; and discovering and using algorithms and logical sequences.

Educational Implications

• **Matching:** Students strong in the logical/mathematical intelligence learn best through problems and opportunities to analyze. They benefit from asking questions, experimenting, and analyzing results in an attempt to solve problems and understand reality. They enjoy strategies such as Find My Rule and Jigsaw Problem Solving.

• **Stretching:** We develop the logical/mathematical intelligence as we have students solve problems, perform experiments, learn and develop algorithms, make predictions, discover relationships, categorize information, and engage in inductive and deductive reasoning. Skills with patterns and functions, probability, statistics, measurement, and logic can be developed across the curriculum. We may stretch students' logical intelligence through the other intelligences as when we have them write the steps, graphically depict the sequence, discuss the rationale.

• **Celebrating:** Students celebrate their number smarts by sharing and appreciating their different approaches to problem solving, analyzing their own progress in math and science, and including samples of their problem solving skills in their portfolios.

Attracted To

• Numbers, Relations, Problems

Skills & Preferences

• Analyzing
• Computing
• Deducing
• Discovering functions, relations
• Estimating, predicting
• Experimenting
• Figuring things out
• Finding, creating patterns
• Inducing
• Organizing, outlining, sequencing
• Playing strategy games
• Questioning
• Reasoning abstractly
• Selecting, using algorithms
• Sequencing
• Solving logic problems
• Using abstract symbols

End States & Models

• **Accountant:** H. R. Block
• **Computer programmer:** Bill Gates, Grace Murray Hopper
• **Mystery writer:** Agatha Christie, Michael Crichton, Sir Arthur Conan Doyle
• **Engineer:** Alexandre Gustave Eiffel, Lillian Moller Gilbreth, Judith Resnick
• **Inventor:** Alexander Graham Bell, Thomas Edison, Sybilla Masters
• **Judge:** Oliver Wendell Holmes, Thurgood Marshall, Sandra Day O'Connor
• **Logician:** Aristotle, Réne Descartes, Bertrand Russell, Socrates
• **Mathematician:** Lady Augusta Ada Byron, Francis Galton, Hypatia, Anna Pell Wheeler
• **Scientist:** Marie Curie, Albert Einstein, Isaac Newton, Chien-Shiung Wu

Logical/ Mathematical Intelligence

The logical/mathematical intelligence is epitomized by a school days incident in the life of Karl Friedrich Gauss (1777-1855). Gauss, was to become a famous mathematician and astronomer known for his contributions to algebra, differential geometry, probability theory, and number theory. As a schoolboy, Gauss along with his classmates, had misbehaved. For a punishment, their headmaster gave them the task of summing the numbers from one to one hundred. In a few minutes, Gauss turned in his paper with an answer: 5050. The headmaster reprimanded him for not doing the assignment, believing he had simply guessed rather than working through the problem. The headmaster, however, had to reassess his interpretation. By the end of the hour, when other students who had worked through the problem with laborious calculations began turning in their papers, the better students had the same answer: 5050. After the correctness of Gauss' answer was revealed, he was asked how he had arrived at his answer.

Gauss had used logical/mathematical intelligence rather than rote calculations. He reasoned: if we sum the largest number (100) with the smallest (1) the result is 101. Eliminating those numbers and summing the new largest number (99) with the new smallest number (2), the result is again 101. Since the string of 100 numbers consists of 50 such pairs which all equal 101, the answer is 50 x 101 or 5050. Using the logical/mathematical intelligence, Gauss could obtain the answer in his head!

Playing with numbers, a joy in combining and recombining them, finding relationships — these are the signs of the logical/mathematical intelligence at work. Ordering, counting, comparing, categorizing objects as well as determining patterns and relations among them are all marks of the logical/mathematical intelligence. Notice, the logical/mathematical intelligence in an important way is different from the verbal and the musical intelligences. Whereas the verbal/linguistic and musical/rhythmic intelligences each deal with a specific type of external stimuli (words and sounds respectively), the logical/mathematical intelligence can be applied to words, sounds, cars, goats, or even ideas. The logical/mathematical intelligence is not linked to a specific type of external stimuli, but rather to a type of internal stimuli, thinking about patterns, relationships, numbers. Logical/mathematical thinking can be applied to any kind of external stimuli and some of the highest forms of logical and mathematical skills are not linked at all to specific stimuli as in the cases of higher math or abstract logic.

That logical and mathematical skills are not linked to specific external stimuli may explain why they are less localized in the brain than the skills associated with other intelligences. Electrophysiological studies show complex, rapidly changing patterns of many areas in front and back of both sides of the brain during mathematical

Figuring Out
the Logical/Mathematical Intelligence

Cogito, ergo sum (I think, therefore I am.)
— *Réne Descartes (1596-1650)*

Logic is the anatomy of thought.
— *John Locke (1632-1704)*

The trouble with the world is that the stupid are cocksure and the intelligent are full of doubt.
— *Bertrand Russell (1872-1970)*

That vast book which stands forever open before our eyes, the universe, cannot be read until we have learned the language and become familiar with the character in which it is written. It is written in mathematical language, without which means it is humanly impossible to comprehend a single word.
— *Galileo Galilei (1564-1642)*

If people are taught how to think and not always what to think, a false concept will be guarded against.
— *George Christoph Lichtenberg*

It is not the answer that enlightens, but the question.
— *Eugène Ionesco (1909-1994)*

As far as the laws of mathematics refer to reality, they are not certain; and as far as they are certain, they do not refer to reality.
— *Albert Einstein (1879-1955)*

Not everything that can be counted counts, and not everything that counts can be counted.
— *Albert Einstein (1879-1955)*

Each problem that I solved became a rule which served afterwards to solve other problems.
— *Réne Descartes (1596-1650)*

Logic is in the eye of the logician.
— *Gloria Steinem (1934-)*

Most people would sooner die than think; in fact, they do so.
— *Bertrand Russell (1872-1970)*

The opposite of a correct statement is a false statement. The opposite of a profound truth may well be another profound truth.
— *Niels Bohr (1885-1962)*

When I am working on a problem I never think about beauty. I only think about how to solve the problem. But when I have finished, if the solution is not beautiful, I know it is wrong.
— *Buckminster Fuller (1895-1983)*

Anyone who considers arithmetical methods of producing random digits is, of course, in a state of sin.
— *John von Neumann (1903-1957)*

A man may die, nations may rise and fall, but an idea lives on.
— *John F. Kennedy (1917-1963)*

"Contrariwise," continued Tweedledee, "If it was so, it might be; and if it were so, it would be; but as it isn't, it ain't. That's logic."
— *Lewis Carroll (1832-1898)*

Do not worry about your difficulties in Mathematics. I can assure you mine are still greater.
— *Albert Einstein (1879-1955)*

Pure mathematics do remedy and cure many defects in the wit and faculties of individuals; for if the wit be dull, they sharpen it; if too wandering, they fix it; if too inherent in the sense, they abstract it.
— *Francis Bacon (1561-1626)*

$E = MC^2$.
— *Albert Einstein (1879-1955), Theory of Relativity*

operations (Gardner, 1983, p. 159) in contrast to more focal activity for music.

Mathematical skills appear early and peak early. There are many documented cases of early love of, proclivity toward, and skill with math. Bertrand Russell stated,

> I began Euclid, with my brother as my tutor, at the age of eleven. It was one of the greatest events of my life, as dazzling as first love.... From that moment until...I was thirty-eight, it was my chief interest and my chief source of happiness...(Gardner, 1983, p. 152).

The development of the mathematical intelligence for some is a powerful driving force which proceeds even in the absence of outside instruction.

> Befitting a mathematical prodigy, Kripke went forth quickly on his own and had reached the level of algebra by the time he was in fourth grade. For instance, he discovered that, in multiplying the sum of two numbers by the difference between them, he got the same answer as he did when he subtracted the square of the smaller one from the square of the larger number. Once he realized that this pattern applied to any set of numbers, he had arrived at the core of algebra. Kripke once mentioned to his mother that he would have himself invented algebra if it had not already been invented, because he came upon its insights so naturally (Gardner, 1983, p. 153).

The major work of most mathematicians is over by the age of thirty and productivity drops after that.

There are important links between math and science. Scientists, like mathematicians, are driven to solve problems and look for simple, certain solutions. Many areas of science are dependent on math, and advances in math can create revolutions in scientific thought. Further, attempts to understand relations of things in the real world have driven advances in

> ## It was a saying of the ancients, that "truth lies in a well"; and to carry on the metaphor, we may justly say, that logic supplies us with steps whereby we may go down to reach the water.
> ## — Isaac Watts (1674-1748)

math. Some extraordinary scientists have been extraordinary mathematicians as well; for example, Isaac Newton (who in his earliest years in school spent so much time building intricate mechanical toys that he scored lowest in his class) discovered fundamental laws of physics, gravitation, light, and invented calculus as well.

While there are links between math, logic, and science, it is possible to overemphasize them. Science usually deals with the discovery of relations among things in the real world, especially cause-effect relations, and is based on observations. In contrast,

> ## In science, we must be interested in things, not in persons.
> ## — Marie Curie (1867-1934)

math and logic can proceed purely in the abstract. We can find students who are quite logical and very preoccupied with the "Why?" questions who are not particularly oriented toward or skilled with numbers. Keen observers of behavior, for example, may induce core attributes of their peers or deduce reasons for their behavior without resorting to math in any form. No matter how much math we teach students, they will not thereby discover cell biology; no matter how much time students spend looking through a microscope or telescope, they will not thereby discover calculus.

The development of early math skills and of early scientific skills share a dependence on careful, repeated observations under controlled conditions, but further development of math and science skills are fostered by different kinds of experiences. Science attempts to know the external world; math and logic explore the relations among symbols. To foster a scientific mind-set we must provide experiences in intense observation and thought about the world, including repeated observations under controlled conditions and the extending of one's senses by use of technology. In contrast, advanced logic and math, in important ways, do not look outside themselves; while early development is fostered in part by repeated experience of representing objects with symbols and manipulation of those objects, advanced development involves mental manipulation of abstract symbols without ties to a specific external reality. Following this reasoning, we can ask whether early training in math or early training in representational painting and or mechanical models better predicts later success in science.

It may well be doubted whether human ingenuity can construct an enigma of the kind which human ingenuity, by proper application, cannot resolve.
— Edgar Allan Poe (1809-1849)

Visual/Spatial Intelligence

We use our visual/spatial intelligence to think in, with, and about visual images. We think in and express this intelligence through pictures, sculpture, arranging objects, and navigating through space. Those strong in the visual/spatial intelligence enjoy doodling, designing, drawing, combining colors, arranging objects, and often have a good sense of direction. Some forms this intelligence takes include map interpreting and making, decorating, page layout and design, and making collages.

Educational Implications

• **Matching:** Students strong in the visual/spatial intelligence learn best through visual input such as charts, graphs, models, drawings, photographs, computer animations, films and videos. They benefit from opportunities to express themselves or create reports in visual formats and create icons to represent content. They enjoy strategies such as Match Mine, Mind Mapping, and Guided Imagery.

• **Stretching:** We develop the visual/spatial intelligence as we have students create maps, diagrams, charts, two-dimensional and three-dimensional models, pictures, and videos. To develop this intelligence we explore elements of art including color, light and shading, lines and shapes, patterns and designs, texture, and various mediums. We may stretch students' spatial intelligence through the other intelligences as when we have them make rhythms corresponding to patterns, write about their art, and use as a nature as the subject.

• **Celebrating:** Students celebrate their picture smarts through posting and displaying visual products. They give and receive feedback to each other on their models and art projects. They celebrate also by drawing in their journals, and selecting and commenting on drawings, videos, and other visual products they place in their portfolios.

Attracted To

• Spatial Relations, Shape, Size, Color

Skills & Preferences

• Appreciating, creating architecture
• Appreciating, creating page layout
• Arranging, decorating
• Building models
• Charting, Graphing
• Coordinating colors
• Creating, interpreting graphic organizers
• Decorating, interior design
• Doodling
• Imagining in vivid detail, visualizing
• Navigating, sense of direction
• Painting, sketching, drawing
• Playing spatial games
• Reading, creating maps
• Remembering visual details
• Rotating figures mentally
• Sculpting, molding, designing
• Seeing another person's perspective
• "Seeing" solutions to problems
• Solving jigsaw puzzles
• Thinking in pictures and images

End States & Models

• **Architect:** Gian Lorenzo Bernini, Frank Lloyd Wright
• **Chess Master:** Bobby Fischer, Gary Kasparov
• **Decorator:** Laura Ashley, Martha Stewart
• **Explorer:** Admiral Richard E. Byrd, Leif Ericson, Robert Edwin Peary
• **Geometrician:** Euclid
• **Marksperson:** Frank Butler, Annie Oakley
• **Navigator:** Christopher Columbus, Ferdinand Magellan, Amerigo Vespucci
• **Painter:** Vincent van Gogh, Georgia O'Keeffe
• **Photographer:** Ansel Adams, Anne Geddes
• **Sculptor:** Camille Claudell, Frederic Remington, Auguste Rodin
• **Topologist:** Mathew Fontaine Maury

Visual/Spatial Intelligence

Michael Jennings, a fifth-grader began complaining of headaches and dizziness. Dr. John Duncan, 39, a pediatric neurosurgeon confirmed Michael had a tumor on his brain stem. Michael would die if the tumor were not removed. To prepare for the operation Duncan used three-dimensional holograms. He watched Michael's brain rotate before him. "Twenty years ago I wouldn't have believed these images were based on reality. The data is exquisite in detail. The tumor surrounds the brain stem like petals of a flower."

The next morning the first incision is made at 10:45. By 1:30 Duncan has uncovered the tumor. "It looks like three-day-old porridge. It's growing right out of the brain stem. It doesn't get any harder than this." The surgeon assisting Duncan says it is too risky to proceed. Given his practice with the holographic images, however, Duncan feels confident he can remove the tumor without damage to healthy tissue. With a hologram of Michael's brain floating on a light box in the operating room, Duncan, operating under a microscope delicately breaks up the tumor with ultrasound and sucks the pieces away through an instrument called a cavitron. At 5:00 p.m. the operation is over.

"The fear that he is not going to wake up, or that he will be injured, never really leaves me until I assess the child afterward," says Duncan. Michael could open his eyes. He could see. He could move his feet and legs. He was going to be okay. Relieved after the operation, Duncan comments:

> Visualizing the tumor is crucial. You have to decide where to stop cutting. If you take out too much, the kid is left with devastating injury. Too little, you don't get the job done. There is no room for error. The 3-D rendition gave me confidence…. Very few surgeons take on this type of tumor and go for broke…. If my mental image had been wrong, Michael would be dead now (Life Magazine, February 1997, pp. 72-76).

Visual/spatial intelligence varies dramatically among individuals. Some of us cannot create realistic mental images; others can do so with vivid detail. The inventor Nikola Tesla created mental images of the machines he was designing. He could see them in detail. He claimed to be able to test them by visualizing them, having them run for weeks — and then examining them visually for signs of wear (McKim, 1972, p. 8).

It would seem that some people are born sensitive to and skilled with visual stimuli. British art historian Kenneth Clark describes his own attraction to and skill with the visual arts as a "freak aptitude," likening the awakening in himself to the visual arts to the joy of a young mathematician upon discovering a Euclid proof. He recalls that as a young child, upon entering an art gallery, he was "immediately transported."

> On either side were screens with paintings of flowers of such ravishing beauty that I was not only struck dumb with delight, I felt that I had entered a new world. In the relationship of the shapes and colors a new order had been revealed to me, a certainty established (Gardner, 1983, p. 199).

Other Perspectives
on the Visual/Spatial Intelligence

I found that I could say things with color and shapes that I had no words for.
— *Georgia O'Keeffe (1887-1986)*

Thinking in pictures precedes thinking in words.
— *Immanuel Kant (1724-1804)*

Imagination is more important than knowledge.
— *Albert Einstein (1879-1955)*

Some of my best ideas come to me in my dreams.
— *Norman Alexander (1825-1888)*

Every child is an artist. The problem is how to remain an artist once he grows up.
— *Pablo Picasso (1881-1973)*

I visualized where I wanted to be, what kind of player I wanted to become. I knew exactly where I wanted to go, and I focused on getting there.
— *Michael Jordan (1963-)*

Beautiful buildings are more than scientific. They are true organisms, spiritually conceived; works of art, using the best technology by inspiration rather than the idiosyncrasies of mere taste or any averaging by the committee mind.
— *Frank Lloyd Wright (1869-1959)*

I choose a block of marble and chop off whatever I don't need.
— *Francois-Auguste Rodin (1840-1917), when asked about his sculptures*

Give me a museum and I'll fill it.
— *Pablo Picasso (1881-1973)*

The artist is nothing without the gift, but the gift is nothing without work.
— *Emile Zola (1840-1902)*

Art is either plagiarism or revolution.
— *Paul Gauguin (1848-1903)*

Every artist dips his brush in his own soul, and paints his own nature into his pictures.
— *Henry Ward Beecher (1813-1887)*

Art is not a handicraft, it is the transmission of feeling the artist has experienced.
— *Leo Tolstoy (1828-1910)*

The eye that directs a needle in the delicate meshes of embroidery will equally well bisect a star with the spider web of the micrometer.
— *Maria Mitchell (1818-1889)*

Art is the only way to run away without leaving home.
— *Twyla Tharpe (1942-)*

Painting is poetry that is seen rather than felt, and poetry is painting that is felt rather than seen.
— *Leonardo da Vinci (1452-1519)*

May I repeat what I told you here: treat nature by the cylinder, the sphere, the cone, everything in perspective?
— *Paul Cézanne (1839-1906)*

The greatest artists are those who impose their peculiar illusion on the rest of mankind.
— *Guy de Maupassant (1850-1893)*

The painter is, as to the execution of his work, a mechanic; but as to his conception and spirit and design he is hardly below even the poet.
— *Johann Christoph Friedrich von Schiller (1759-1805)*

The learned understand the reason of art; the unlearned feel the pleasure.
— *Quintilian (35-95)*

Similarly, the Renaissance art historian Giorgio Vasari commented that Leonardo da Vinci,

> was so pleased whenever he saw a strange head or beard, or hair of unusual appearance that he would follow such a person the whole day and so learn him by heart, that when he reached home he could draw him as if he were present (Gardner, 1983, p. 197).

What better way to describe the essence of the visual/spatial intelligence — attraction to and skill with visual spatial stimuli?

Visual/spatial stimuli comes in many forms and the visual/spatial intelligence can manifest itself in everything from navigating a ship, to painting a painting, to selecting a winning race horse. In *Frames of Mind* Gardner refers to a "spatial" intelligence rather than a "visual/spatial" intelligence because he wanted to emphasize the intelligences are not tied to the senses. Spatial intelligence is not dependent on visual stimuli: a blind person can have very strong spatial intelligence, and a master chess player can win playing blindfolded. The master chess player does not think in terms of concrete visual stimuli. Further, visual stimuli are associated with other intelligences: Verbal/linguistic (printed words), naturalist (sight of flora and fauna); bodily/kinesthetic (sight of gestures, movements). Nevertheless, in his chapter on spatial intelligence Gardner discusses the ability to draw pictures, imagine pictures, and sensitivity to size, shape, color, contour and visual patterns (Gardner, 1983, pp. 178-204).

In whether or not to view both visual and spatial skills as one intelligence, the theory of multiple intelligences hits a snag: Shall we maintain that the spatial intelligences is distinct from the visual intelligence (a conclusion supported by the fact that the congenitally blind develop the spatial intelligence), in which case we would need to invent another intelligence to account for skills with purely visual material? Or shall we lump the two and end up with an intelligence which encompasses skills as diverse as sense of direction and ability to capture the play of light in a painting? The empirical relations between visual and spatial skills have not been established. It is doubtful that the training in esoteric navigational systems of the Puluwat people of the Caroline Islands in the South Seas will enhance ability to paint pictures more than it enhances ability to solve logic problems. If we are good at mentally rotating figures in space, are we more likely to combine colors in an artful way? Are children who can see what the world looks like to the other person, better able to appreciate the use of light in a painting? Our informed guess in answer to these questions: no. It is far easier to believe there are a multiplicity of human intelligences than to believe eight intelligences explain all human skills. This question of the correlation of specific visual and spatial skills, within and across the visual and spatial domains, can be established only with empirical work. In the absence of that work, however, it is not safe to simply assume, for example, that ability to arrange flowers in an artistic way is correlated with sense of direction. This topic —

**Art is a creative effort of which the wellsprings lie in the spirit, and which brings us at once the most intimate self of the artist and the secret occurrences which he has perceived in things by means of a vision or intuition all his own, and not to be expressed in ideas and in words — expressible only in the work of art.
— Jacques Maritain (1882-1973)**

are there really a multiplicity of intelligences — will be explored in depth in Chapter 22: Beyond Multiple Intelligences — A Multiplicity! For now, it is sufficient to take the eight intelligences as useful categories, and in order to not multiply the number of categories, let's treat in one section, as does Gardner, the discussion of visual and spatial skills.

Spatial skills are often assessed by tasks that ask the subject to identify which of several alternatives best represents a figure that has been rotated in space. We must be careful, however, because most spatial problems of that sort can be solved by logic rather than spatial skills. Spencer, for one, can almost always figure out the right response to that type of problem, but he has very poor spatial skills. To solve that type of problem, he does not mentally rotate the objects, but rather eliminates the noncorrect alternatives by examining each alternative for analytic details. He uses a strength (logical intelligence) to compensate for a weakness (lack of spatial skills). Critical in assessing spatial skills is not asking *if* a student has solved a problem, but rather *how* they have solved the problem. Similarly, it is often assumed that skill in chess is a function of highly developed spatial skills. It is probable, however, that different players reach success in quite different ways and that for some logic is a far better predictor of skill in chess than spatial skills. The IBM computer that defeated Gary Kasparov did not visualize; it tested millions of alternatives in terms of which led to the greatest advantage. It used logic, not spatial skills to become the best chess player in the world.

A girl blind from birth, demonstrated various spatial skills: At two-and-a-half years of age she could determine the correct path (angle and distance) between two objects in a room when she had gone to each object only from a third location. At four years of age she was for the first time presented with a tactile map; she found it easy to understand and use the map to find a prize in a room (Landau, et. al, 1981). Clearly spatial intelligence can be developed without visual intelligence.

In the art of design, color is to form what verse is to prose, a more harmonious and luminous vehicle of thought.
— Anna Jameson (1794-1860)

Researchers and theoreticians have distinguished a number of distinct visual and spatial skills, many of which have links to other intelligences. Some skills in this category are more visual than spatial (sensitivity to and ability to match colors) and others are more spatial than visual (sense of direction). Some skills are quite specific. For example, attention to, recognition of, and memory of faces has been linked to the functioning of specific neurons. Others involve an integration of many intelligences, such as expressive painting. Different skills in this domain link to different other intelligences, for examples, recognition of faces has links to the interpersonal intelligence; sculpting to the bodily kinesthetic, whereas both facility with geometric shapes and understanding of maps link to mathematical intelligence.

Between 1973 and 1990 Monty Roberts and his wife Pat purchased 195 yearling Thoroughbreds for $6.9 million dollars at public auctions, and sold the young racehorses within a year for $13.3 million, a process called pinhooking. During those years the Roberts were ranked first in the business ten times, and among the top three in the industry for sixteen out of eighteen years! To what does Roberts attribute this phenomenal success? A visual/spatial skill he learned observing one of Pat's painting teachers.

> To get a sense of what I saw that day, imagine a horse seen from the side, and over that horse lay a triangle, its apex sitting as high as the horse's head and midway between head and tail. From that high point, one line angled down at forty-five degrees through the shoulder; another angled down at forty-five degrees through the hip, and the baseline ran horizontally through both knees and hocks.
>
> In a well-balanced horse, the apex is right in the middle. In a Thoroughbred racehorse, the two sides of the triangle are equal, but the baseline is considerably longer.
>
> Using triangles to judge conformation is so simple, yet so profound. Pat still works in bronze and it's rare not to have one of her equine sculptures taking shape in our kitchen. And when I look on as she subtly molds and adjusts, I think of that day by the paddock when an artist's sketch reduced the tangled business of horse conformation to a bit of basic geometry (Roberts, 1996, pp. 164-5).

In 1970 Roberts bought a registered Thoroughbred yearling stallion.

> A bay horse with two rear white patterns, he was in horrible condition and not many people gave him a second glance. Precisely because he was so thin, I could see that he had the best skeletal balance of any Thoroughbred I had every seen. And history would suggest I was right.

The horse was Alleged, twice winner of the Arc de Triomphe, the greatest possible achievement for a racehorse. Thus what appears to be an almost mystical, uncanny ability to see the future of a racehorse has its underpinnings in a fundamental visual/spatial skill!

Vincent van Gogh revolutionized treatment of color in paintings. At the age of thirty he had been a painter for three years when, in his words, "I have felt a certain power of color awakening in me." Van Gogh began piano lessons, but his teacher thought Vincent was mad and discontinued the lessons when Vincent said the musical notes ranged from dark blue to yellow! In his letters to his brother Theo, Vincent made it clear that his extraordinary skills with color were in part due to his sensitivity to that stimuli, but in part due to application of his logical intelligence to the analysis of color.

> He developed a rigorous system, based on the "laws of simultaneous contrast and complementary colors" described by Michel-Eugene Chevreul, a 10th-century French chemist.

In van Gogh's words,

> The laws of the colors are unutterably beautiful.… If one combines two of the primary colors, for instance yellow and red, in order to produce a secondary color — orange — this secondary color will attain maximum brilliancy when it is put close to the third primary color not used in the mixture (van Gogh in letter to Theo, quoted by Swerdlow, 1997, p. 112).

People vary dramatically in the distinct visual and spatial abilities. For example, take just one skill, ability to remember visual details. Students with very strong eidetic imagery can actually look at a comb, close their eyes, and then from the visual image in their heads count the number of teeth on the comb! Others of us can barely picture the comb. It is not safe to assume that a strength in one of the visual/spatial skills means a general strength across those skills. Some students excel, for example, in expressive painting, but are not exceptional in illustrating or even representational painting. Others are able to produce extraordinary reproductions, but incapable of creating unique works.

Musical/Rhythmic Intelligence

We use our musical/rhythmic intelligence to think in, with, and about music. Melodies and rhythms can be symbols to think in and express this intelligence. Those strong in the musical/rhythmic intelligence enjoy listening to and creating music in many forms. Some forms this intelligence takes include playing instruments, singing songs, reading music, composing melodies and lyrics, and appreciating music.

Educational Implications

• **Matching:** Students strong in the musical/rhythmic intelligence learn and remember best through musical input such as songs, raps, and chants. They enjoy a classroom in which music is played in the background. They benefit from opportunities to express themselves musically through musical and rhythmic products. They enjoy strategies such as Songs for Two Voices, Team Chants, and Lyrical Lessons.

• **Stretching:** We develop the musical/rhythmic intelligence as we have students sing, play, react to, analyze, and compose music. A wide range of musical genre stretch different facets of the intelligence so we include humming, singing, tapping, clapping, snapping, and playing a range of electronic, string, percussion, and wind instruments. A differentiated musical rhythmic curriculum includes development of specific skills such as recognizing and producing pitches, rhythms tempos, and timbre. We may stretch students' musical intelligence through the other intelligences as when we have them write lyrics, draw their reaction to a song, discuss their interpretation.

• **Celebrating:** Students celebrate their music smarts through recitals of various types and recorded entries into their portfolios.

Attracted To

• Rhythms, Melodies, Lyrics, Pitch, Timing, Timbre

Skills & Preferences

• Composing melodies, lyrics
• Humming, chanting, whistling,
• Identifying instruments
• Keeping time, recognizing rhythm
• Learning through lyrics
• Listening to, appreciating music
• Playing by ear
• Playing instruments
• Reading and writing music
• Recognizing melodies, songs, composers
• Singing, rapping
• Singing with perfect pitch
• Tapping feet, hands
• Understanding structure of music

End States & Models

• **Composer:** Anna Magdalena Bach, Ludwig van Beethoven, Irving Berlin, Wolfgang Amadeus Mozart, Richard Wagner, Andrew Lloyd Weber
• **Conductor:** Sarah Caldwell, Arthur Fiedler, Zubin Mehta
• **Instrumentalist:** Louis Armstrong, Ray Charles, Benny Goodman
• **Instrument maker:** David Gomes, Edwin Medeiros, Antonio Stradivari
• **Improvisers:** Duke Ellington, Thelonius Monk
• **Singer:** Marian Anderson, Ray Charles, Billie Holiday, Ella Fitzgerald, Julio Iglesias, Mario Lanza, Luciano Pavoratti, Diana Ross, Frank Sinatra, Barbara Streisand, Joan Sutherland
• **Songwriter:** Burt Bacharach, Bob Dylan, John Lennon, Neil Sedaka

Musical/Rhythmic Intelligence

Musical skills can be taught and developed to a high degree in most people, as the Suzuki Talent Education program demonstrates. Advanced musical composition and extreme development of the musical intelligence, however, appears to be a natural endowment, reserved for only a few. As Gardner (1983) points out, Wagner said he "composed like a cow producing milk;" Saint-Saens likened the process to "an apple tree producing apples." Gardner himself has a highly developed musical intelligence and states:

> I believe that I think musically…. I need music to work. I also hear music all the time in my head…. I think that my major activities — to think and to read and to write — occur in a very musical way. My literary work reflects the sorts of organization that I observed in compositions I studied and played (i.e., the development of themes, the effects that something introduced at one point has much later back and forth) (Gardner, 1997, p. 10).

That a highly developed musical intelligence is a gift is supported by the number of composers who where child protégées and by the extent to which those with extreme musical talents seem to live in a world different from the ordinary. "Arthur Rubinstein, when he ate breakfast, would turn on a record in his own mind and hear it, scratches and all (Gardner, 1997, p. 10)." Stravinsky at only two years of age remembered and later repeated a song he heard country women sing on their way home from the fields (Gardner, 1983, p. 121).

Although we make music by arranging sounds of various pitch, loudness, timbre, and pace, the music itself transcends the sounds in the same way that a painting can not be reduced to the arrangements of colors and forms on the canvas. The whole is qualitatively different than the sum of its parts. One measure of the quality of the musical composition and performance is the extent to which the music (or any other form of art) transcends its components. The components of music combine to create an illusion.

> Music also presents us with an obvious illusion, which is so strong that despite its obviousness it is sometimes unrecognized because it is taken for a real physical phenomenon: that is the appearance of *movement*. Music flows; a melody moves; a succession of tones is heard as a progression. The differences between successive tones are steps, or jumps, or slides. Harmonies arise, and shift, and move to resolutions. A complete section of a sonata is quite naturally called a "movement"…(Langer, 1957, p. 36).

Just as language exists in part to give voice to thoughts, music exists in part to give expression to certain elements of experience which are only poorly expressed in words. Music, perhaps more than any other medium, allows us to express our experience of existence. Existence is marked by cycles and rhythms, by mounting tensions and their resolution or transformation. We wake each day seeking stimulation, but having had enough, having taken in as much stimulation as we can deal with, we retreat. In our dreams we sort out the day's stimuli, and then, having sorted and stored the new stimuli, we are ready to wake, to seek new stimuli. We struggle to maintain homeostatic balances, physically, mentally,

Getting In Tune
with the Musical/Rhythmic Intelligence

Every time you take up the instrument you are making a statement, your statement! And it must be a statement of faith that this is the way you want to speak!
— *Isaac Stern (1920-)*

Making music is another way of making children.
— *Friedrich Nietzsche (1844-1900)*

If you have to ask what jazz is, you will never know.
— *Louis Armstrong (1900-1971)*

The notes I handle no better than many pianists. But the pauses between the notes — ah, that is where the art resides!
— *Artur Schnabel (1882-1951)*

Singing was a serious business with me, and I had a deep sense of responsibility about my work with the choirs. Singing in the presence of other people seemed to me a normal activity all through the years of growing up. I loved to sing. My heart was filled when I sang, and I wanted to share what I felt.
— *Marian Anderson (1897-1993)*

Wagner's music is better than it sounds.
— *Mark Twain (1835-1910)*

Too many pieces of music finish too long after the end.
— *Igor Stravinsky (1882-1971)*

A musicologist is a man who can read music but can't hear it.
— *Sir Thomas Beecham (1879-1961)*

An agreeable harmony for the honour of God and the permissible delights of the soul.
— *Johann Sebastian Bach (1685-1750), definition of music*

Don't play the saxophone. Let it play you.
— *Charley Parker (1920-1955)*

Music is the mediator between the spiritual and the sensual life. Although the spirit be not master of that which it creates through music, yet it is blessed in this creation, which, like every creation of art, is mightier than the artist.
— *Ludwig van Beethoven (1770-1827)*

Let me have music dying and I seek no more delight.
— *John Keats (1795-1821)*

If music could be translated into human speech, it would no longer need to exist.
— *Ned Rorem (1923-)*

If I don't practice one day, I know it; two days, the critics know it; three days, the public knows it.
— *Jascha Heifetz (1901-1987)*

It is in learning music that many youthful hearts learn to love.
— *Dominique Ricard (1741-1803)*

Yea, music is the prophet's art; among the gifts that God hath sent, one of the most magnificent.
— *Henry Wadsworth Longfellow (1807-1882)*

The meaning of song goes deep. Who is there that, in logical words, can express the effect music has on us? A kind of inarticulate, unfathomable speech, which leads us to the edge of the infinite, and lets us for moments gaze into that!
— *Thomas Carlyle (1795-1881)*

I shall hear in heaven.
— *Ludwig van Beethoven (1770-1827), last words*

and socially, in the moment, in the day, and over our lives. Life is the rise and fall of stimulation over time.

> If music is indeed time made audible, then that is what the auditor ought to hear: virtual movement, motion that exists only for the ear. No tangible thing is actually going from one place to another. But the listener hears musical figures that move through a definite tonal range, from points of origin to points of relative rest; he hears tonal qualities as intense as colors, steadily or briefly holding places in the stream. Melodies and harmonic masses within it build up tensions like growing emotions, and resolve them or merge them into new tensions. Also, in the clearest demonstration of the difference between materials and elements, we hear something in music that does not exist outside of it at all: sustained rest. If a figure ascends to a resting tone, the actual motion of the air is faster on that resting tone than anywhere else in the passage; but what we hear is changeless continuity in time, sustained rest (Langer, 1957, pp. 38-39).

There is something marvelous in music. I might almost say it is, in itself a marvel. Its position is somewhere between the region of thought and that of phenomena; a glimmering medium between mind and matter, related to both and yet differing from either. Spiritual and yet requiring rhythm; material and yet independent of space.
— Heinrich Heine (1797-1856)

The need is strong. It drives us to fashion musical instruments from everything: hollow bamboo, two sticks, stretched hide, cat gut, forged brass. We blow into hollow tubes, pluck strings, strike things together. We tap our feet and slap our thighs. Wherever we find people, in primitive tribes to sophisticated cultures, from unclad children to tuxedo- and-gown-adorned adults, we find music. What drives people to make music?

From the point of view of evolution, music is a puzzle. It is obvious how there is a survival advantage to being able to find one's way around, throw a stone accurately, communicate with one's companions, distinguish poisonous from nonpoisonous plants and animals, count, know what one wants, and be able to coordinate actions with others. But how did music evolve? We hear the tones and patterns of raindrops as a sort of music, and experience the call of some birds and even some insects as music, but what survival advantage might that have? Birds, frogs and some insects use their tunes — either to defend their territory or to call for a mate. But of what ultimate use is humankind's music?

Our closest genetic matches among the primates do not sing or make music. So it seems misdirected to seek the origins of human music in bird song. We do find some pleading for a mate in some country music, but reducing human's need to make music to a need to attract mates, in the face of the range and quality of music seems preposterous. Bird song functions to defend territory, but we humans do not burst into song to warn off territorial intruders!

Unless the need to make music is a genetic throwback, a refined expression of the primitive need to call for a mate, we need to look elsewhere for the evolutionary advantages of music. From where then comes man's need to make music? Could music be genetically linked to some other skill which provides a selective advantage? Or does music itself increase the probability of survival of a group? The music we make expresses our common human experience and so bonds us to others. As we sway in unison to the beat of music, we lose our individuality and become part of a group. Making music together we mystically become one voice. In that melding may be our answer — anything which strengthens our collective bonds provides an advantage, a willingness to sacrifice for others of the same collective, thus increasing the probability of survival among tribes with strongly developed musical genes. Sad it would be if our gift for music had it roots among warriors marching in rhythm, off to do battle. But perhaps the experience of music increases our willingness to tend the wounded or come to the aid of another in distress.

We prefer to think that people make music to express their essence. Perhaps chimps do not make music (and other art) because their inner lives are not marked by the ebb and flow of rising and falling harmonies and disharmonies, rhythms, tones, tunes, tensions and their resolution. Or perhaps they do not reflect on their being as we do. We like to think we make music for the same reasons we paint, and sculpt, and dance — not as a way of surviving but as a way of expressing our joy and wonder in the miracle of life. We make music because we are human.

Music moves us, and we know not why; we feel the tears, but cannot trace their source. Is it the language of some other state, born of its memory? For what can wake the soul's strong instinct of another world like music?
— Letitia Elizabeth Landon (1802-1838)

Bodily/Kinesthetic Intelligence

We use our bodily/kinesthetic intelligence to think in, with, and about movement and gestures. Facial and hand gestures and movements are symbols to think in and express this intelligence. Those strong in the bodily/kinesthetic intelligence enjoy physical activities, hands-on activities, acting, and developing physical skills.

Educational Implications

• **Matching:** Students strong in the bodily/kinesthetic intelligence learn best through movement and hands-on activities. They learn well when there is movement to symbolize the content. They benefit from opportunities to express themselves or create reports which include acting, mime, or movement. They enjoy strategies such as Kinesthetic Symbols, Formations, Folded Value Lines, and Agreement Circles.

• **Stretching:** We develop the bodily/kinesthetic intelligence as we have students communicate through body language, dance, develop fine and gross motor skills, learn the art of various physical activities, sports, and performances. Speed, strength, flexibility, agility, coordination, and endurance are keys to stretching the bodily kinesthetic intelligence. We may stretch students' kinesthetic intelligence through the other intelligences as when we have them reflect on their acting, write about a physical activity, or interact with nature.

• **Celebrating:** We celebrate being body smart by keeping records of bodily/kinesthetic accomplishments and progress: students move their names up the appropriate chart as they can juggle more items or in more ways, can do more pull-ups, or master another dance step. Live performances by teams and individuals offer opportunities to receive feedback and to celebrate. Students learn to accept winning with humility and accept losing with grace. Video recordings of dance and performances are possible portfolio entries.

Attracted To

• Movement, Body Language, Hands-on Activities, Athletics

Skills & Preferences

• Acting, mime
• Athletic performances
• Dancing, choreographing
• Exercising, working out
• Fine motor skills, hand-eye coordination
• Gross motor skills, endurance, strength
• Juggling
• Learning through "hands-on" activities
• Manipulating things
• Mimicking
• Moving with grace and coordination
• Playing Sports
• Using gestures, body language

End States & Models

• **Athletes:** Chris Evert, Michael Jordan, Carl Lewis, Joe Montana, Pele, Mary Lou Retton, Babe Ruth, Tiger Woods
• **Actors/Actresses:** Lucille Ball, Jim Carrey, Katherine Hepburn, Grace Kelly, Steve Martin, Demi Moore, Sylvester Stallone, John Wayne, Robin Williams
• **Ballet:** Mikhail Barishnikov, Evelyn Cisneros, Anna Pavlova
• **Boxer:** Mohammed Ali, Oscar de la Hoya
• **Choreographer:** Gower Champion, Martha Graham
• **Dancer:** Fred Astaire, George Balanchine, Katherine Dunham, Ginger Rogers
• **Fitness enthusiast:** Jane Fonda, Arnold Schwarzenegger, Richard Simmons
• **Juggler:** Anthony Gatto, Albert Luca
• **Magician:** David Copperfield, Harry Houdini
• **Mime:** Charlie Chaplin, Marcel Marceau
• **Surgeon:** Christiian Barnard, Jessica Gray
• **Typist:** Barbara Blackburn
• **Yoga:** Beryl Bender Birch, B. K. S. Lyengar

Bodily/Kinesthetic Intelligence

No one had ever won three straight U.S. Junior amateur titles before Tiger Woods. Nor had anyone won three straight U.S. Amateur titles. And, of course, no one before had won the Masters at such a young age. At twenty-one, Tiger Woods not only won the prestigious Masters Tournament, but broke the records for the largest win margin and lowest score ever! For those of us outside the world of golf, Tiger Woods appeared to break onto the scene. But this, of course, was as far from the truth as possible. Tiger Woods' story is a wonderful example of how extraordinary bodily/kinesthetic intelligence is a by-product of natural talents, environmental support and challenge, mental and physical training, and intense drive.

Tiger's father, Earl Woods, played catcher for Kansas State University baseball team, becoming the first African-American baseball player in the Big Eight Conference (then called the Big Seven Conference). He was a natural athlete. After he returned from serving as a Green Beret in the Vietnam War he took up golf. He shot a remarkable 91 for 17 holes the very first time he played (Gutman, 1997). By the time Tiger was born two years later, Earl was hooked on golf. Tiger got his first training at six months of age.

> Tiger would sit in his high chair in the garage and watch his father practice his golf swing. He seemed fascinated by the movement. So it wasn't surprising that soon after he began walking, Tiger began picking up the clubs. He was barely a year old when his father sawed off one of his old clubs to Tiger's size. The boy immediately began trying to copy his father's swing (Gutman, 1997, p. 14).

"When he was eighteen months old I would take him to the driving range at the Navy Golf Course," Earl Woods said. "And when he was done hitting, I would put him back in the stroller and he'd fall asleep."

By 1978, when Tiger was just over two years old, he was filmed by a television film crew as he played a complete hole. At that time sportscaster Jim Hill finished the broadcast with the following prediction: "This young man is going to be to golf what Jimmy Connors and Chris Evert are to tennis (Gutman, 1997, p. 15)." Shortly after, still at two years of age, Tiger appeared on the *Mike Douglas Show* in a driving contest with Bob Hope. By five he was a star on *That's Incredible*. At six years of age he shot his first hole in one! At fourteen he played a round of eighteen holes with twenty-one touring pros in Fort Worth, Texas. Tiger shot 69, beating eighteen of the twenty-one pros!

Citing the incredible performances of Tiger Woods would make it appear that he was simply a born golfer. That would miss the tough mental and physical training underpinning Tiger's success. Knowing that golf depends on extraordinary concentration, Tiger's father set out on a course to train those skills.

> Using part of his Green Beret training as a guide, Mr. Woods decided he would be the one to create an unshakable mental toughness in his son....

"I pulled every nasty, dirty, obnoxious trick on him, week after week," Mr. Woods admitted.

Moving To
the Bodily/Kinesthetic Intelligence

Great ideas originate in the muscles.
— *Thomas Alva Edison (1847-1931)*

Iron rusts from disuse, stagnant water loses its purity and in cold weather becomes frozen; so does inaction sap the vigors of the mind.
— *Leonardo da Vinci (1452-1519)*

Genius is one percent inspiration and ninety-nine percent perspiration.
— *Thomas Alva Edison (1847-1931)*

"Why," said the Dodo, "the best way to explain it is to do it."
— *Lewis Carroll (1832-1898),*
   in Alice's Adventures in Wonderland

Among those many things most of us do as well as we can — without once considering them acts of intelligence — are athletics and art. The nonathlete has long derided sports as the doltish domain of mental laggards and meatheads, but there is at least inferential evidence that such surpassing motor skills are in the truest sense intelligent. The finest sort of spatial and kinesthetic intelligence may not be limited to dance and sculpture but may also be tautly at work on a circus tightrope, in the pert of muscularity of an Olga Korbut, in the crack of Hank Aaron's bat against baseball, in the fifty-yard "bomb" a football quarter-back lays in the outstretched arms of a racing flanker.
— *Jack Fincher*

[on dance]…the loftiest, the most moving, the most beautiful of the arts, because it is no mere translation or abstraction from life; it is life itself.
— *Havelock Ellis (1859-1939)*

All I need to make a comedy is a park, a policeman and a pretty girl.
— *Charlie Chaplin (1889-1977)*

A good education is usually harmful to a dancer. A good calf is better than a good head.
— *Agnes de Mille (1905-1993)*

Dance is the only art of which we ourselves are the stuff of which it is made.
— *Ted Shawn (1891-1972)*

Two or three weeks will put anyone in perfect condition if he is willing to work out properly. My own system at Carlisle was to go out on a few warm days, jog and exercise for two or three hours in the morning under a hot sun in heavy sweat clothes, come in and take a nap, and then go back in the afternoon and repeat the performance. During this period I did not eat very much food and drank practically no water. To stay right, all you have to do is get plenty of rest and know what you are going to do before you do it, and then act.
— *Jim Thorpe (1888-1953)*

Get up and do something useful, the work is part of the koan!
— *Hakuin*

It is not the same to talk of bulls as to be in the bullring.
— *Spanish Proverb*

I hear and I forget. I see and I remember. I do and I understand.
— *Confucius (551-479 B.C.)*

Well done is better than well said.
— *Benjamin Franklin (1706-1790)*

Never mistake motion for action.
— *Ernest Hemingway (1899-1961)*

Acting is not being emotional, but being able to express emotion.
— *Kate Reid*

That included dropping a bag of clubs just before the impact of Tiger's swing. Imitating the sounds of birds or other animals just as Tiger was getting ready to putt. He would sometimes toss a ball right in front of Tiger's line of vision just as he was getting ready to hit. He would stand in his line of sight and then move just as he was about to hit his shot. He would cough, rattle keys, play mind games by telling him he better not hit the ball into the water when they were near a water hazard.

Sometimes Tiger would become so exasperated that he would stop his swing and glare at his father who would then bark, "Don't look at me. Are you gonna hit the ball or not?"

"I taught him every trick an opponent could possibly pull, and some I invented myself," Mr. Woods said. "I'm not really proud of this, but I even cheated, just to get a reaction from him. Let's face it. Somewhere down the

line somebody was going to do that, too. I made sure he was exposed to every devious, diabolical, insidious trick. It was a very difficult thing for me to do, and it didn't really fill me with pride and joy. But if he was going to continue in golf, I felt it was necessary (Gutman, 1997, pp. 25-26)."

Repeatedly this tough mental training paid off. As Tiger said with thirty-six holes of match play between him and his third straight U.S. Amateur title, "All I have to do is stay strong up here (pointing to his head with a finger)." In perhaps his most remarkable exhibition of mental strength, Tiger reversed an almost disastrous start on his way to win the masters. He was shooting poorly — the first nine holes in 40. No golfer in history had won the Mas-

Athletes Who Transformed and Transcended Their Sports

Baseball	Jackie Robinson, Babe Ruth
Basketball	Wilt Chamberlain, Magic Johnson, Michael Jordan, Pete Maravich, Bill Russell
Boxing	Muhammad Ali
Figure Skating	Sonja Henie
Football	Jim Brown, Red Grange, Jim Thorpe
Golf	Jack Nicklaus, Arnold Palmer, Tiger Woods
Hockey	Wayne Gretzkey, Maurice Richard
Martial Arts	Bruce Lee
Mountain Climbing	Sir Edmund Hillary
Soccer	Pele
Tennis	Arthur Ashe, Maureen Connolly, Jimmy Connors, Chris Evert
Track & Field	Babe Didrikson Zaharias, Jesse Owens, Wilma Rudolph, Jim Thorpe
Surfing	Mark Richards, Tom Curren, Kelly Slater
Swimming	Gertrude Ederle, Duke Kahanamoku, Mark Spitz, Johnny Weissmuller, Ester Williams

ters with that poor a start. Tiger, however, kept cool. He analyzed his swing, realized a mistake he was making, adjusted it, and made a night-to-day change in performance. To everyone's amazement he hit the back nine in a six-under-par 30, for a 2 under par 70 for the round! This process, bringing analytic skills to bear on bodily/kinesthetic performance, should give pause to anyone who thinks of the intelligences as operating in isolation. Listen to Tiger's words: "I was bringing the club almost parallel to the ground on my backswing," he said later. "That was way too long for me. I knew I had to shorten the swing." Having analyzed the fault, he corrected it, and transformed his game.

Understanding the success of any great athlete is not really possible. We stand in awe of an athletic performance just as we are awed by a great painting or great symphony. The drive for excellence, to be the very best one can, however, is common to greatness in any field. After Tiger had won his first junior title, Earl Woods became aware of how his son was always talking about lowering his score.

Finally, Mr. Woods told his son to stop worrying about his score and just start enjoying himself. The reply he got surprised him.

"That's how I enjoy myself" Tiger said. "Shooting low numbers makes me happy (Gutman, 1997, p. 24)."

Great Moments in Sports

Upon being presented with two gold medals for the pentathlon and decathlon by the King of Sweden who stated, "Sir, you are the greatest athlete in the world," Jim Thorpe, a Sauk and Fox Indian replied, "Thanks, King."

It was the 1932 world series. Babe Ruth had been spit on by hostile Cubs fans. When they threw lemons at him, he tossed them back. He stepped up to the plate, purportedly pointed to a place in the stands, and hit a home run to that spot. His comment, "I never had so much fun in all my life."

In 1924 Red Grange scored four touchdowns in the first twelve minutes of a game against the undefeated Michigan Wolverines.

Hundreds of men and women had tried to cross the English Channel by 1926. Only five men had succeeded. It was considered impossible for a woman. Gertrude Ederle beat the existing men's record by two hours. Her record stood for twenty-four years.

In a three hour span in the 1932 Olympic tryouts, Babe Didrikson Zaharias won five events, tied one, and finished fourth in one. She alone scored more

points than the second place team of twenty-two women!

Jesse Owens in a track meet in Ann Arbor, Michigan in 1935 competed in four events at 3:15, 3:25, 3:34, and 4:00 p.m. He broke three world records and tied another!

The Berlin 1936 Olympics were to be a testimony to the views of the Nazi white supremacist, Adolph Hitler. With Hitler watching, Jesse Owens, from Oakville, Alabama, disproved Hitler's views, winning four gold medals!

Maurice Richard was knocked unconscious and was carried off the hockey rink in the 1952 Stanley Cup play-offs. Stitched up, he returned to the ice to score the tie breaker which won the cup.

In 1958, seventeen-year-old Pele returned from an injury to score the only goals in Brazil's World Cup victory — one of which was an amazing backward bicycle kick.

— *Adapted from Krull, 1997*

Just as extraordinary gross motor skills are to a large extent a function of mental processes, so too are fine motor skills. I (Spencer) was in the seventh grade, at Walter Reed Junior High School. I signed up for Typing I as one of my electives. (It would be decades before I discovered I was really about to take a class in beginning "Keyboarding"). We each sat at a big bulky black Underwood typewriter and, after mastering the correct way to insert the paper, set the margins, and throw the carriage, we advanced to the base keys. For endless repetitions we produced lines of "jkl;" and "fdsa." We were excited when our fingers finally were allowed to explore new territory on the home row — we could hit an "h" and a "g!" After weeks we, with wonder, explored the world beyond the base keys and began to produce a "u" and even a "y."

My friend in the class was Danny Kaufman. If I remember correctly, he was a fairly ordinary student — except in typing. When the rest of us were proud to get up to about 25 words a minute on our weekly timed test, Danny was hitting around 60. One day we were standing by the bleachers during P.E. and I asked him his secret. He said, "It is easy. I just type all the time. You don't need a typewriter to practice. Look at my fingers now." As I looked down, I saw that Danny's fingers were on the bleachers and he was typing the words he was speaking! He confessed that he often kept his fingers in his desk during a dull class so he could practice typing what his teachers were saying! In Typing II when the rest of us were thrilled to hit 50 words a minute, Danny went well beyond one hundred. When I asked him again about his secret, he told me something strange had happened. He said, "I am practicing all the time, whether I want to or not." As people talked, he

would no longer move his fingers. He would simply feel himself typing.

Danny was well before his time. Today it does not seem strange to require athletes to spend hours sitting quietly, visualizing their performances. The best athletes probably always have. Today millions are spent on neuromuscular training videos which help athletes and amateurs improve their games without moving a muscle, by visualizing themselves performing like the experts. We do not need to carry out an action to strengthen the connection between the impulse and the muscles which do the work.

The false duality of mind and body is a relatively recent cultural invention, an illusion which is shattered when we look at any of the many ways in which activity effects emotion and thought and the many ways emotion and thought determine activity. Harmonious interaction of mind and body was an ideal among the Greeks. Part of Zen training is to "Chop wood, carry water." Morita therapy in Japan successfully treats mental depression by a program of progressive engagement in simple work activities. When I (Spencer) was on the swim team as an undergraduate at U.C. Berkeley, during the swim season, when we had to take several hours a day from busy academic schedules for practice and swim meets, our grades were always better than during off season.

It is a puzzle why the stereotypes of the dumb jock and the awkward geek persist when the data as well as our common experience tell us exactly the opposite — those students who are the best coordinated and athletically talented, on the average do the best academically. When we set the stereotypes aside and honestly examine our reactions, we discover the link between movement and intelligence. Graceful movement is an expression of intelligence. We see an awkward movement and wonder if the child is immature or "slow;" we see a graceful, coordinated action and it reinforces our impression that the student is bright. Intelligence does not stop at the borders of the brain. The brain is designed as much for skillful action as for skillful perception. Intricate neural systems are dedicated to allowing us to perceive our own actions and to correct them as we perform them.

In multiple intelligences theory the bodily/kinesthetic intelligence involves two related components: mastery over one's own body, and skillful manipulation of objects. The range of activities dependent on development of the bodily/kinesthetic intelligence is enormous: from kick boxing to brain surgery, from ballet to knitting. The bodily/kinesthetic intelligence is exemplified by both the athlete and the artisan. Both sets of skills are directly linked to survival and advancement of civilization. As we evolved, the difference between avoiding a predator or being eaten, having a dinner or going hungry depended on our ability to craft and more skillfully use a well-weighted stone ax, run more quickly, leap a higher hurdle, or throw a stone more accurately. To defeat another in battle or to escape the battle allowed one to pass on one's genes. In today's sports we see thinly disguised expressions of our most basic evolutionary past. See box: Sports and Games: Not So Thinly Disguised Combat.

Sports and Games: Not So Thinly Disguised Combat

I am not an animal in my personal life. But in the ring there is an animal inside me. Sometimes it roars when the first bell rings. Sometimes it springs out later in a fight. But I can always feel it there, driving me forward. It is what makes me win. It makes me enjoy fighting.
— *Roberto Duran*

I like the moment when I break a man's ego.
— *Bobby Fischer*

Serious sport has nothing to do with fair play. It is bound up with hatred, jealousy, boastfulness, disregard of all rules, and sadistic pleasure in witnessing violence.
— *George Orwell*

Pitching is…the art of instilling fear.
— *Sandy Koufax*

Described variously as the knockdown pitch, the beanball, the duster and the purpose pitch — the Pentagon would call it the peacekeeper — this delightful stratagem has graced the scene for most of the 109 years the major leagues have existed. It starts fights. It creates lingering grudges. It sends people to the hospital.
— *Melvin Durslag*

Pro football is like nuclear warfare. There are no winners, only survivors.
— *Frank Gifford*

It's just a job. Grass grows, birds fly, waves pound the sand. I beat people up.
— *Muhammad Ali*

People don't seem to understand that it's a damn war out there.
— *Jimmy Connors*

It is not an accident that we spend far more money on fishing and hunting than on any of the other sports. What else besides our biology would have us spend countless hours crafting a fishing fly when we could easily purchase a trout at the supermarket for far less the price? The drive to craft a more powerful or accurate golf club or baseball bat, hit a ball farther or more often, or outmaneuver another individual or team is as fundamental as our biology.

The need for competitive and combative sports and the release of the intense emotions by spectators of those sports finds an explanation in Paul McLean's triune theory of the brain: Below the neocortex of the human brain is the limbic system, and below that is a reptilian complex (For a layman's introduction to the McLean's theory, see Carl Sagan's well written popular book, *The Dragons of Eden: Speculations on the Evolution of Human Intelligences*). The neocortex is responsible for functions which have evolved most recently, functions unique to humans such as the elaborate symbol systems of language and math. Buried beneath the neocortex is the limbic system which controls among other things intense emotions — including rage, fear, and attachment. Beneath the limbic system lies the reptilian complex which consists of the hindbrain (brainstem), midbrain, and forebrain. This reptilian complex with its three major divisions is found in all animals and existed in fish-like creatures swimming 500 million years ago. Evolution works not by replacing older parts of the brain, but by adding to them. So this primitive reptilian complex exists in all humans today. This complex controls our most fundamental bodily process, walking, running, and partially controls aggressive behavior, territoriality, and

Grown Men Flinging Stones

As I (Spencer) was writing this section of this book, I pushed away from the computer to take a morning jog. Coming toward the beach by a route I seldom take, I discovered an underpass to cross the coast highway. As I passed under the highway, to my right was a stream of water making its way to the ocean. Just as I emerged from the dark underpass I heard a large splash in the water.

At first I thought it was a large fish, but then saw and heard another large splash. I looked up to see the source: Two beach workers, both at least in their late thirties. They were playing a game. They were each armed with one of those sticks with claws on the end — the kind that allow you to squeeze a lever at the top to close the claw at the bottom so you can pick up trash without bending down.

These men were using their tools, not to clean the beach, but to grab rocks from the beach to then fling them into the water. After watching for awhile I realized the goal of the game: there was a small round drainage hole on the far wall, and the men were competing to see who could get closest to the hole, or, for a really big score, to get a rock into the hole.

The beach workers were completely absorbed in the game; they hardly gave me notice. As I continued to jog I wondered about how many sports in the history of humankind, like baseball and cricket, involved sticks or, like basketball and archery, involved aiming a projectile toward a target. And then I wondered the extent to which those sports have their roots in our prehistory when our ancestors honed their "batting average" to improve their chances of survival. Was I witnessing not just two grown men playing in the sun, taking a break from work, but also the expression of one of the deepest needs of humankind, rooted in the recesses of our brains?

behaviors which maintain social hierarchies. All parts of the brain are intimately interconnected, and many functions are controlled in part by all parts. Nevertheless, some kinds of sports activities seem designed expressly as an outlet for and expression of our limbic and reptilian complex functions. Our competitive and combative sports allow expressions of needs to dominate, attack, avoid, and outmaneuver. When Roberto Duran speaks of the animal in him released in boxing, he seems to be talking about the need to allow expression for those parts of the brain which evolved earlier, parts we share with other animals.

It is important, however, not to equate bodily/kinesthetic intelligence with release of primitive animal instincts. In some cases extraordinary athletes do not have a drive to dominate others — they are just gifted athletes. For example, take Duke Kahanamoku, the legendary Hawaiian swimmer, surfer, and water polo player. At age 20 he broke two long-standing world swimming records and went on to win Olympic swimming medals in 1912 and 1920 and compete in water polo on the Olympic team in 1932. Nevertheless, he seemed to have little drive to beat others. He found it painful to embarrass an opponent and preferred to swim just fast enough to touch them out (Brennan, 1994)!

Combat and competition is but one of many functions of the bodily/kinesthetic intelligence. We perform the fine and delicate actions and craft creative and artistic solutions to problems — actions with roots not in survival but in the need to express oneself, communicate, and solve problems.

The bodily/kinesthetic intelligence is an enabling intelligence, allowing the flowering of unique artistic styles in dance, mime, pottery, music, painting, sculpting, and calligraphy. Ability to exercise the other intelligences is dependent in a variety of ways on the bodily/kinesthetic: painting pictures, playing music, exploring nature, writing, and manipulating counting blocks are but a few examples. Could we imagine a successful architecture program which did not have students build models, or a successful physics or chemistry course which did not include a "hands-on" component? Singing and oration depend on breath control, whether it is learned intuitively or from training. Less obvious connections exist between interpersonal and intrapersonal, but we should not underestimate the power of the handshake, gesture, and even proper sitting during mediation. In Zen there is no distinction between enlightenment expressed in words and enlightenment expressed in action.

Movement is the most fundamental art form and appears in exquisitely developed forms in tribes which in other respects appear primitive.

> Societies limited to savage living, primitive sculpture, primitive architecture, and as yet no poetry, quite commonly present the astonished ethnologist with a highly developed tradition of difficult, beautiful dancing. Their music apart from the dance is nothing at all; in the dance it is elaborate. Their worship is dance. They are tribes of dancers (Curt Sachs, *World History of Dance*, as quoted in Langer, 1957, p. 11).

Langer argues that in the primitive world which contains demonic powers, subhuman and/or superhuman gods and spooks, magic forces, the natural form of objectification of human experience is dance. In dance we express our emotions and our sense of the forces which move us.

Naturalist Intelligence

We use our naturalist intelligence to think about plants, animals, clouds, rocks, and other natural phenomena. Those strong in the naturalist intelligence enjoy collecting, analyzing, studying, and caring for plants, animals, and environments. They are sensitive to interdependence within plants/animal ecologies, and to environmental issues.

Educational Implications

• **Matching:** Students strong in the naturalist intelligence learn best through presentations involving natural phenomena, by bringing natural phenomena into the classroom, and by having students interact with nature through field trips. They learn best when the content may be sorted and classified or related to the natural world through analogies. They enjoy strategies such as Look-Write-Discuss, Same-Different, Observe-Write-RoundRobin, and Categorizing.

• **Stretching:** Students stretch their naturalist intelligence as they study flora and fauna, regions and habitats, weather and climate, rocks and minerals, and hone their observational and recording skills. We may stretch students' naturalist intelligence through the other intelligences as when we have them record or draw their observations in a log, develop classification systems, learn about nature through music.

• **Celebrating:** Students celebrate their nature smarts through harvesting the fruits of their gardens, demonstrating their care for animals, and recording positive interactions with the environment such as steps to counter pollution. Portfolio contributions may include excerpts from their nature log.

Attracted To

• Plants, Animals, Natural Phenomena, the Environment

Skills & Preferences

• Analyzing similarities and differences
• Appreciating plants, flowers, trees
• Caring for plants, gardens, pets, wild animals
• Classifying flora, fauna, natural phenomena
• Collecting plants, insects, rocks
• Discovering patterns in nature
• Enjoying animal antics
• Observing details
• Predicting the weather
• Protecting the environment
• Recognizing species, rocks, stars, and clouds
• Taming, training animals
• Understanding environmental interdependence

End States & Models

• **Agricultural chemist:** George Washington Carver
• **Animal protector:** Henry Bergh, Henry Wood Elliott
• **Animal trainer:** Monty Roberts
• **Astronomer:** Annie Jump Cannon, Nicholas Copernicus, Galileo Galilei, Maria Mitchell, Carl Sagan
• **Biologist:** Jewel Plummer Cobb, Sylvia Earle, Louis Pasteur, Jonas Edward Salk
• **Botanist, horticulturist:** Luther Burbank, Asa Gray
• **Doctor:** Elizabeth Blackwell, Benjamin Spock
• **Ecologist:** Aldo Leopold, Henry David Thoreau
• **Environmentalist:** Rachel Carson, John Muir
• **Herbalist:** Andrew Weil
• **Naturalist:** Charles Darwin, Jane Goodall
• **Oceanographer:** Jacques Cousteau
• **Ornithologist:** John James Audubon
• **Veterinarian:** James Herriot

Naturalist Intelligence

Attraction to and skill with flora and fauna can take many forms, from growing orchids to bird- or horse-watching, from studying the clouds to noticing interesting rock formations. The naturalist may be attracted to any type of natural stimuli, including plants, animals, clouds, minerals, rocks, land formations, or chemicals. Associated with the naturalist intelligence is the ability to discriminate and classify. Clearly the ability to discriminate poisonous plants and snakes from those which are nonpoisonous has an evolutionary advantage. Our ancestors who were quicker and more accurate in distinguishing that which was good to eat from that which was not, had a better chance of survival. In today's safer environment, the naturalist intelligence can take many forms. Gardner has indicated that the ability to discriminate and classify stimuli, rooted in the naturalist intelligence, may extend to man-made objects such as tennis shoes or compact discs.

We get a glimpse of the inner world of a naturalist as Jane Goodall describes her own reactions observing the plight of old Gregor, an old chimpanzee whose legs were crippled by polio and who was shunned and even attacked by younger, healthier chimps. Observing two fellow chimpanzees in a tree grooming each other, old Gregor laboriously dragged himself up the tree in an apparent attempt to receive some grooming as well. As he finally approached them,

With a loud grunt of pleasure he reached a hand towards them in greeting — but even before he made contact they both swung quickly away and, without a backward glance, started grooming on the far side of the tree. For a full two minutes, old Gregor sat motionless, staring after them. And then he laboriously lowered himself to the ground. As I watched him sitting there alone, my vision blurred, and when I looked up at the groomers in the tree I came nearer to hating a chimpanzee than I have ever done before or since (Goodall, 1971, p. 202).

The passage is remarkable in several respects. For a brief moment we see the world through Goodall's blurry eyes, feel her love for old Gregor as well as her anger toward those who would deprive him of a simple pleasure. Having experienced Goodall's empathy and love for the object of her study, we have for a moment entered the world of a naturalist. To devote a life to studying a species or an insect or a flower makes sense once we feel the love, fascination, pleasure, or awe with which the naturalist regards aspects of nature.

Monty Roberts has devoted his life to horses. He has tamed them, bred them, cured them physically and psychologically, been an advocate for them, and worked with them in many capacities including riding them in numerous championship rodeo performances of many types. Throughout his autobiography, Roberts lets us see horses through his eyes, through the eyes of a naturalist. Time and again he communicates a powerful empathy for his animals, for all horses. Monty Roberts looks not so much at the horse, as at the world through the point of view of the horse. Roberts does not look at horses as animals in the way many of us do; he looks

The Nature
of the Naturalist Intelligence

• •

Back of my workshop there is a little grove of trees. One has been cut down. It makes a good seat. I have made it a rule to go out and sit on it at 4 o'clock every morning and ask the good Lord what I am to do that day. Then I go ahead and do it. Alone there with the things I love most, I gather my specimens and study the lessons Nature is so eager to teach us all. Nothing is more beautiful than the loveliness of the woods before sunrise.
— *George Washington Carver (1864-1943)*

Nature, to be commanded, must be obeyed.
— *Francis Bacon (1561-1626)*

I never for a day gave up listening to the songs of birds or watching their ways or drawing them in the best way I could. During my deepest troubles I would often take myself away from the people around me and return to some hidden part of the forest to listen to the wood thrush's melodies.
— *John James Audubon (1785-1851)*

Nothing is rich but the inexhaustible wealth of nature. She shows us only surfaces, but she is a million fathoms deep.
— *Albert Einstein (1879-1955)*

We need another and a wiser and perhaps a more mystical concept of animals…. In a world older and more complete than ours they move finished and complete, gifted with extensions of the senses we have lost or never attained, living by voices we shall never hear. They are not brethren, they are not underlings; they are other nations, caught with ourselves in the net of life and time, fellow prisoners of the splendor and travail of the earth.
— *Henry Beston*

My green thumb came only as a result of the mistakes I made while learning to see things from the plant's point of view.
— *H. Fred Ale*

There is that in the glance of a flower which may at times control the greatest of creation's braggart lords.
— *John Muir (1838-1914)*

The goal of life is living in agreement with nature.
— *Zeno of Citium (335-263 B.C.)*

How various are the talents of men! From the brook in which one lover of nature has never during all his lifetime detected anything larger than a minnow, another extracts a trout that weights three pounds, or an otter four feet long. How much more game he will see who carries a gun, i.e. who goes to see it! Though you roam the woods all your days, you never will see by chance what he sees who goes to purpose to see it.
— *Henry David Thoreau (1817-1862)*

When we no longer look at an organic being as a savage looks at a ship, as something wholly beyond his comprehension; when we regard every production of nature as one which has had a long history; when we contemplate every complex structure and instinct as the summing up of many contrivances, each useful to the possessor, in the same way as any great mechanical invention is the summing up of the labour, the experience, the reason, and even the blunders of numerous workmen; when we thus view each organic being, how far more interesting — I speak from experience — does the study of natural history become!
— *Charles Darwin (1809-1882)*

The most incomprehensible thing about the world is that it is comprehensible.
— *Albert Einstein (1879-1955)*

at them as brothers. Let's try to see the world through Roberts' eyes.

Roberts' point of view comes through clearly as he describes Brownie. Brownie had been captured in the wild and then broken in the traditional way by Roberts' father. Breaking the horse included "sacking-out," a procedure in which horses are tied up for days and repeatedly, intentionally thrown into a panic by their handler, who tosses a sack on their back. The goal: break the horse's will to resist, teaching them resistance is futile and that man is to be feared and obeyed. Often the horses are badly injured in this process; ropes burn through their hide, leaving bloody tracks

> **Nature is the armory of genius. Cities serve it poorly, books and colleges at second hand; the eye craves the spectacle of the horizon; of mountain, ocean, river and plain, the clouds and stars; actual contact with the elements, sympathy with the seasons as they rise and roll.**
> **— Amos Bronson Alcott (1799-1888)**

on their pasterns. As a young man, reflecting on this, Roberts (1996, p. 91) saw the world through Brownie's eyes:

> During my trips to Nevada, I had become acutely aware that Brownie was due an apology from us. In the high desert, I had seen how he must have been brought up. Predators aside, it had looked to me to be idyllically happy. Brownie would have been (sic) raised in a close family group, with affection tempered by discipline, and with all the security of a large extended family communicating effectively with one another.
>
> He had then been wrenched into an alien environment, and right away beaten and frightened into submission. I had taken it upon myself to try to make up for the sacking-out procedure. I talked to him all the time, listened to him, gave him the best possible care; I

wanted to do everything right for him. His health was always good; I thought carefully about his diet, I read his every mood. And he had responded. He had become as close as a brother to me.

Empathy, then, is one critical attribute of a naturalist, or at least leads some to love, study, communicate, and care for animals. A second critical attribute is being a careful observer. This passion for observation appeared early in Monty Roberts and stayed with him his whole life. On his first roundup, upon finding a herd of wild mustangs, his partners wanted to "press on and simply drive the horses back toward the ranch."

> I, on the other hand, wanted to stop and simply observe the horses. There was something compelling about seeing them as a family, the alpha male or breeding stallion circling and lifting his tail, stepping out with a high, proud action, and acknowledging our presence. It made me want to melt into the background and see what could be seen, without subjecting them to our interference. It was almost as if I wanted to be a horse myself, so thoroughly had I taken their side. These horses were not only Brownie's brothers and sisters, they were mine too (Roberts, 1996, p. 9).

Years later his passion for understanding horses expressed itself in quite another way. He was dealing with a famous race horse, Prince of Darkness, who had become phobic of starting gates. To cure the horse Roberts had to know what frightened it. Roberts, by then past middle age and with a severely injured spine, repeatedly stood in the starting gate with the 1,400 pound horse to try to figure out what frightened it. Repeatedly the horse panicked and knocked Roberts down.

> This was no game for a man of my age with a part of his spinal column missing, but I was determined to go in yet a little closer.
>
> Once again he jumped forward and bowled me over, stepping on my leg, side, and ear. Then

he ran to the end of my come-along, turned, and stood there looking at me from twenty feet away. I was hurting badly, but in a flash, it came to me. Though my brain was muddled by this time, I had noticed something: just before he jumped up and ran over the top of me, Prince of Darkness had rolled his eye back to look at his off flank and his attention seemed to be focused on the off-side rail.

I stood there, bruised, battered, with a trickle of blood running into my collar, but I had found the source of the fear. The rail itself, of course (Roberts, 1996, p. 223)!

Out of this insight came a Monty Roberts invention: a blanket which has protected over 1,000 race horses, "blanket horses" as they are now called, from a rail phobia. Monty's passion for understanding, for decoding the mysteries of animals is what he shares with all born naturalists — they are in love with and have a passion for understanding some aspect of nature.

It is unswerving desire to observe and understand horses which has led to Roberts' most fundamental contribution — the ability to communicate with horses. This ability eliminates the need to break a horse; because of Roberts' work "horse gentlers" will replace "horse breakers." The title of his autobiography (Roberts, 1996), *The Man Who Listens to Horses*, captures the essence of his story. That title grasps the essence of every naturalist's story. The naturalist listens to, observes, tunes into nature. Just as the bibliophile cannot resist a book, the naturalist cannot resist the messages of nature. As part of a film documenting his taming a wild mustang in the wild, Roberts had to ride day and night. Asked how he could follow the mustang through the night Roberts replied, "If you can listen to your own horse, he can be your compass and your guide (Scanlan, 1996, p. 253)."

In the following incident, Roberts demonstrated his uncanny ability to communicate with horses — as well as with humans. He was in Dublin doing a demonstration with a supposedly "mad horse." Watching the horse's reactions as he made certain hand motions, Monty read the nonverbal communication:

> "I am going to tell you what the horse is saying," he told the audience through his lapel microphone…. "He's saying he's been kicked in the belly and head, and had a whip across the hocks. This horse if full of stories."

The owner, a handsome woman, stood frozen.

> She was looking across the ring to her husband, and when I spotted him I knew the horse was telling the truth. Horses, in fact, never lie, and this horse was no exception. The horse comes to me, I saddle him and get a rider on, and the horse is moving around like a million dollars. By now both the man and his wife are extremely distraught.

After the demonstration people left the arena but the woman approached Monty.

> "You're in danger," he told her.

> "I can't talk about that," she replied. "I'd rather give up my life."

> When her husband joined them, Monty told them that their lives would be a shambles until they got a handle on the violence. Monty had cut to the quick, and the response was immediate and emotional. The man threw his arms around Monty, and pleaded, "I need help, I need help." It must have been a riveting scene: in the ring where a mad horse had been proven sane, three people, their arms entwined, linked by a common history of pain (Scanlan, 1996, pp. 245-246).

**There is no other door to knowledge than the door Nature opens; and there is no truth except the truths we discover in Nature.
— Luther Burbank (1849-1926)**

The skills of the naturalist are evident in Monty's behavior both toward the horse and toward the couple. Keen observation is motivated not just by interest, but by love. Yes, the naturalist may use logic to "figure out" nature, but it is not cold logic. It is logic born of fascination, awe, and love of the content.

Nature does not capriciously scatter her secrets as golden gifts to lazy pets and luxurious darlings, but imposes tasks when she presents opportunities, and uplifts him whom she would inform. The apple that she drops at the feet of Newton is but a coy invitation to follow her to the stars.
— Edwin Percy Whipple (1819-1886)

The skills of the naturalist seem almost mystical to those of us who do not share them. I (Spencer) am not a naturalist, and compared to those who are gifted in that area, my sensitivity to plants and animals is not particularly strong. Nevertheless, for years I developed fifty acres of land in rural Mexico. I loved time at our ranch. My primary love was the solitude (it was so quiet in our isolated valley that the silence was practically audible — sometimes I would just sit and listen to the sound of no sound) and the change of roles (I left the college professor outside the gates of the ranch, becoming instead an architect, construction worker, engineer, farmer, and rancher). I loved the challenge of building a self-sustaining ecology: I found extreme pleasure in the logic of designing self-operating irrigation systems so the trees would flourish under gravity flow drip systems. I did love planting trees and I raised rabbits for years, but cannot claim particular sensitivity to flora and fauna. I raised the rabbits as an experiment to raise meat

in a rural, poor part of Mexico — and was more intrigued by designing feeding and watering systems for the rabbits than by observing them or their habits. In the language of MI theory we would say the logical/mathematical and the introspective intelligences were much more highly developed in me than the naturalist intelligence. My love of the solitude and the logic of design exceeded my love of the flora and fauna the ranch provided.

Raising rabbits is trickier than the stereotype would have it; a successful breeding program demands extreme sensitivity to the cycles of the rabbits: You cannot leave the rabbits together too long after they mate, or the male will upset the female and she will lose her babies. If you don't leave her with the male long enough though, you decrease the chances of their successful mating. Similarly, you cannot leave the new mother too long with her young or she will eat them. Separate her from the young too soon, however, and they will not do well. Timing is everything. Over the time I raised rabbits, I had various helpers. With some we had almost no luck; with others the rabbits were prolific. My best helper was my brother-in-law, Carlos. Carlos knew exactly when to put a female rabbit in with a male, when to take her out, when to put in nesting materials, when to separate her from her young, when to change or supplement their diet. The rabbits under Carlos' care were healthy; they did what the proverbial rabbits are supposed to do — they multiplied. Under my care or that of others, the rabbits did not fare nearly as well. Repeatedly I would try to get coaching from Carlos. Time and again he would point out subtle signs. Finally, reluctantly, I had to conclude that I just could not see what Carlos saw;

he lived in a world apart from mine. He lived in the world of the naturalist. Or at least, he was sensitive to animals. It seemed that any animal did well under his care.

On the other hand, Carlos did not have any particular gift with plants or trees. I was far more sensitive to whether a tree was over- or under-watered than he was, and I do not claim for myself especially strong skills in that area. Under Carlos' care trees withered, and the garden and crops saw lean years. If I wanted good vegetables and healthy trees, I found, I needed to find a different helper. My rancher was not a farmer! Skill with fauna does not predict skill with flora. Or at least so it appeared in my limited experience running my ranch/farm in rural Mexico.

Sensitivity and skills with flora can seem almost mystical — we speak of a green thumb as if it were a sort of extrasensory skill. It is not. For example, Susan has a green thumb. Plants do very well for her. Susan and others, though, don't know why. They take it to be a mystical gift and just say, Susan has a "green thumb." It turns out there is nothing mystical at all about Susan's green thumb. The explanation: Susan, unlike Carlos, is the kind of naturalist who is sensitive to plants. Each person is sensitive to a certain kinds of stimuli.

As I enter a room, my eye is caught by a painting, someone else's ear is caught by the music playing, a third person focuses on the spatial relation of the furniture in the room. Susan immediately notices a plant, walks over to the plant, looks at it, feels a leaf, notices the earth, comments, "This plant would do better with a little more water and may be catching too much afternoon sun through that window." Su-

san is unaware she has chosen one alternative among many; her choice to attend to the plant is unconsciously propelled by her unusual attraction to that kind of stimuli. The explanation of Susan's green

Nature is man's teacher. She unfolds her treasures to his search, unseals his eye, illumes his mind, and purifies his heart; an influence breathes from the sights and sounds of her existence.
— Alfred Billings Street (1811-1881)

thumb is her intense attraction to and sensitivity to plants. There is nothing more mystical in having a green thumb than in being sensitive to paintings or being moved by music. The person with the green thumb cannot let a plant go too long over or under-watered because they see the deleterious effects in the plant. It hurts them to see a plant suffer; they have empathy for plants. The plant speaks to Susan in the same way the rabbits speak to Carlos, books speak to the verbal/linguistic person, and a poorly adjusted motor speaks to a mechanic.

This is not to say that the skills of a naturalist cannot be learned. They can be. They are learned from tutors and from the constant contact with the natural phenomena toward which the naturalist is attracted.

We hear of both types of learning from Lynn Rogers who has devoted his life to the study of black bears. One day Lynn and his professor, Albert Erikson, were attempting to obtain a blood sample from an anesthetized wild bear. The bear suddenly woke and lunged at Erikson. Erikson lunged back! The bear then turned to Rogers. Erikson commanded: "Lunge!" Rogers did. The bear ran away. Erikson was teaching Rogers to respond not to his own fear but that of the bear. Rogers eventually came to know bears well enough that he could sleep a few feet from their den and even handle their cubs. How could he become so intimate with the bears? Rogers had to learn to *read* bears.

> You can be very close to a bear and have things be calm, until some little unidentified noise happens far off in the forest. Then the bear is suddenly keyed up, wary.... Whenever there's anything that makes the bear take a deep breath, which is the first sign of their fear, and then you see its ears prick up, you think, "Better give the bear a little bit more room, don't be standing right on top of it, because there's a good chance it'll whack you...." It feels threatened by some other thing and it wants room and the peace of mind from you to deal with that. After being told in no uncertain terms by bears to get away in that situation, after a while I learned (Lynn Rogers, quoted in Masson & McCarthy, 1995, p. 46).

There is a connection between the naturalist intelligence and the intrapersonal intelligence. Both involve cutting away from the usual demands of the social, interpersonal world, tuning away from words

Nature hath nothing made so base, but can read some instruction to the wisest man.
— Aleyn (1590-1640)

and toward a different kind of stimuli, in one case internal stimuli and in the other case the stimuli associated with nature. Being in nature helps one find and develop the inner self. It is not an accident that when we think of "finding ourselves" we conjure up the image of going into the woods, or getting "back to nature." Back to nature means back to plants and animals, but it also means a return to our own, deeper nature.

In many places in his journals, Thoreau makes the connection between finding oneself and finding nature.

> It is well to find your employment and amusement in simple and homely things. These wear best and yield most. I think I would rather watch the motions of these cows in their pasture for a day, which I now see all headed one way and slowly advancing — watch them and project their course carefully on a chart, and report all their behavior faithfully — than wander to Europe or Asia and watch other motions there; for it is only ourselves that we report in either case, and perchance we shall report a more restless and worthless self in the latter case than in the first. (Thoreau, *Journal*, October 5, 1856)

> The week that I go away to lecture, however much I may get for it, is unspeakably cheapened. The preceding and succeeding days are a mere sloping down and up from it.

> In the society of many men, or in the midst of what is called success, I find my life of no account, and my spirits rapidly fall. I would rather be the barrenest pasture lying fallow than cursed with the compliments of kings.... But when I have only a rustling oak leaf, or the faint metallic cheep of a tree sparrow, for variety in my winter walk, my life becomes continent and sweet as the kernel of a nut. I would rather hear a single shrub-oak leaf at the end of a wintry glade rustle of its own accord at my approach, than receive a shipload of stars and garters from the strange kings and peoples of the earth (Thoreau, *Journal*, February 8, 1857).

Henry David Thoreau is often cited as the prototypical naturalist. He was before his time in his concern for preservation of the wilderness, values which sprang from his sensitivity to plants, animals, and ecology.

> Each town should have a park, or rather a primitive forest, of five hundred or a thousand acres, where a stick should never be cut for fuel, a common possession forever, for instruction and recreation (Thoreau, *Journal*, October 15, 1859).

Thoreau's concern for the preservation of the wilderness was rooted in his sensitivity to the beauty of natural phenomena and the wonder it inspired in him.

> When the question of the protection of birds comes up, the legislatures regard only a low use and never a high use; the best-disposed legislators…never study their dispositions, or the beauty of their plumage, or listen and report on the sweetness of their song. The legislature will preserve a bird professedly not because it is a beautiful creature, but because it is a good scavenger or the like (Thoreau, *Journal*, April 8, 1859).

In Thoreau, the naturalist, introspective, and verbal/linguistic intelligences are exquisitely intertwined. He was in demand to give lectures; he wrote books. But the content of these verbal/linguistic accomplishments were his introspections and his appreciation of nature. We can ask about the relative strengths of the introspective versus the naturalist intelligences in Thoreau. Did he leave the company of men more to approach nature or to avoid the artificial social values he deplored? He spends more space in his journal writing against the errors of society and the superficiality of man than the beauty of nature. At times he expresses disgust for his fellow man and the institutions of society "Wherever a man goes, men will pursue and paw him with their dirty institutions (Thoreau, *Journal*, 1850)."

> The vast majority are men of society. They live on the surface; they are interested in the transient and fleeting; they are like driftwood on the flood. They ask forever and only the news, the froth and scum of the eternal sea. They use policy; they make up for want of matter with manner…. They swell, they are ever right in my face and eyes like gnats; they are like motes, so near the eyes that, looking beyond, they appear like blurs; they have their being between my eyes and the end of my nose. The terra firma of my existence lies far beyond, behind

them and their improvements (Thoreau, Journal, April 24, 1852).

Thoreau, however, is not a misanthrope. He simply sees so clearly the beauty in nature and the need to live in harmony with it that he is offended by those who would live by other, to him, false values. Man can use two different yardsticks: he can measure worth with a dollar (the value others place on something) or measure worth with his own senses and feelings. Living in harmony with nature man is uplifted; allowing the dollar to dictate value, man is downtrodden.

Future generations are unlikely to condone our lack of prudent concern for the integrity of the natural world that supports all life. This is an era of specialists, each of whom sees his own problem and is unaware of or intolerant of the larger frame into which it fits.
— Rachel Carson (1907-1964)

As Thoreau contrasts handcrafted pail making with factory production of pails, we glimpse the naturalist extending his appreciation of nature to an appreciation of living in harmony with nature, including one's own nature. Thoreau takes this line of reasoning further, generating a basis for a critique of society which creates a cleavage between man and nature.

> They may make equally good pails, and cheaper as well as faster, at the pail factory compared with the home-made ones, but that interests me less, because the man is turned partly into a machine there himself. In this case the workman's relation to his work is more poetic; he also shows more dexterity and is more of a man. You come away from the great factory saddened, as if the chief end of man were to make pails; but in the case of the countryman who makes a few by hand, rainy days,

the relative importance of human life and of pails is preserved, and you come away thinking of the simple and helpful life of the man — you do not pale at the thought — and would fain to making pails yourself. We admire more the man who can use an adz skillfully than him who can merely tend a machine. When labor is reduced to turning a crank, it is no longer amusing nor truly profitable; but let this business become very profitable in a pecuniary sense, and so be "driven," as the phrase is, and carried on a large scale, and the man is sunk in it, while only the pail or tray floats…(Thoreau, *Journal*, October 19, 1858).

As Thoreau plays with words and paints verbal images ("we pale, man sinks, pails float") we marvel at the power released when the verbal/linguistic, introspective, and naturalist intelligences join forces. Thoreau cannot resist playing every which way with the contrast between the river banks which support him, and those banks which house money.

> Was there ever such an autumn? And yet there was never such a panic and hard times in the commercial world. The merchants and banks are suspending and failing all the country over, but not the sandbanks, solid and warm, and streaked with bloody blackberry vines. You may run upon them as much as you please — even as the crickets do, and find their account in it. They are the stockholders in these banks, and I hear them creaking their content…. In these banks, too, and such as these, are my funds deposited, a fund of health and enjoyment. Their (the crickets) prosperity and happiness and, I trust, mine do not depend on whether the New York banks suspend or no. We do not rely on such slender security as the thin paper of the Suffolk Bank. To put your trust in such a bank is to be swallowed up and undergo suffocation. Invest, I say, in these country banks. Let your capital be simplicity and contentment. Withered goldenrod (*Solidago nemoralis*) is no failure, like a broken bank, and yet in its most golden season nobody counterfeits it. Nature needs no counterfeit-detector. I have no compassion for, nor sympathy with, this miserable state of things. Banks built on granite, after some Grecian or Roman style, with their porticoes and their safes of iron, are not so permanent, and cannot give me so good security for capital invested in them, as the heads of withered hardhack in the meadow. I do not suspect the solvency of these. I know who is their president and cashier (Thoreau, *Journal*, September 30, 1857).

The naturalist provides a corrective to society; nourishing our connection with our roots. When we lose the naturalist within us we are lost — subject to forces beyond our control, floating on the surface, driftwood on the flood.

Nature is no sentimentalist — does not cosset or pamper us. We must see that the world is rough and surly, and will not mind drowning a man or a woman, but swallows your ships like a grain of dust. The cold, inconsiderate of persons, tingles your blood, benumbs your feet, freezes a man like an apple. The diseases, the elements, fortune, gravity, lightning, respect no persons.
— Ralph Waldo Emerson (1803-1882)

Interpersonal Intelligence

We use our interpersonal intelligence to know and interact successfully with others. Those strong in the interpersonal intelligence enjoy working with, caring for, and learning with others. Some forms this intelligence takes include leadership skills, friendship skills, and ability to understand points of view different from one's own.

Educational Implications

- **Matching:** Students strong in the interpersonal intelligence learn best interacting with others over the content. They benefit from opportunities to interact with points of view different from their own. They enjoy strategies such as Jigsaw, Telephone, Paraphrase Passport, Mix-Pair-Discuss, Team Interview, and Numbered Heads Together.

- **Stretching:** We develop the interpersonal intelligence as we have students debate, use cooperative learning, interview others, and do surveys. The interpersonal intelligence is stretched as students learn leadership skills, negotiation, peacemaking, empathy, role-taking, communication skills, respect, honesty, teamwork skills. We may stretch students' interpersonal intelligence through the other intelligences as when we have them reflect on their interaction with others, create creative cooperative projects, explore nature together, compose songs and sing together in harmony.

- **Celebrating:** Students celebrate their people smarts as they share what they have learned from and about others. They celebrate their increasing teamwork and leadership skills, and include pages from their peer dialog journals as entries in their portfolios.

Attracted To

- Other People, Interaction

Skills & Preferences

- Caring for, teaching others
- Communicating with others
- Interacting with others
- Empathizing and sympathizing with others
- Leading and organizing groups and events
- Making and maintaining friends
- Resolving conflicts, mediating
- Respecting rights, point of view of others
- Seeing things from another's perspective
- Showing sensitivity to the moods and motives of others
- Understanding thoughts, values, needs of others
- Working as team member

End States & Models

- **Anthropologist:** Claude Levi-Strauss, Margaret Mead
- **Doctor:** Elisabeth Kubler-Ross, Albert Schweitzer
- **Educator:** Leo Buscaglia, John Dewey, Maria Montessori, Sequoia, Anne Sullivan, Horace Mann
- **Humanitarian:** Princess Diana, Mother Teresa
- **Nurse:** Clara Barton, Florence Nightingale
- **Philanthropist:** Andrew Carnegie, Elizabeth Browning Scripps
- **Politician:** William Clinton, John F. Kennedy
- **Prime Minister:** Winston Churchill, Golda Meir, Margaret Thatcher
- **Social consultant:** Ann Landers, Emily Post
- **Social reformer:** Jane Addams, Susan B. Anthony, Cesar Chavez, Mother Jones, Eleanor Roosevelt, Margaret Sanger, Sojourner Truth, Harriet Tubman, Malcom X
- **Sociologist:** Karl Marx, Mary Wollstonecraft
- **Talk show host:** Johnny Carson, Oprah Winfrey

Interpersonal Intelligence

When Princess Diana died, there was an unparalleled outpouring of sympathy and grief. Thousands of people stood in line for more than twelve hours for the opportunity to write a few lines in a condolence book. The initial funeral route had to be tripled to accommodate the millions who wanted to view the procession. TV feeds went out to 187 countries in 44 languages. An estimated two billion viewers, the largest television audience in history, viewed the funeral. Some 50 million Americans got up in the wee hours to watch the funeral live. An outpouring of literally acres of flowers, notes, poems, and gifts were placed outside the Kensington Palace, Diana's former home, and at other spontaneous monuments around the world.

> People who had never met her cried openly as if they had lost a close friend. Complete strangers embraced on the lawn of Hyde Park as Elton John sang his tribute to her at Saturday's funeral, and the hearse bearing her body was so strewn with flowers thrown by admirers that it had to stop to have them removed (*USA Today*, September 8, 1997, p. D1).

People themselves were baffled by the intensity of their own grief.

> "She touched people's hearts, even people down in Hackney," said Diana Campbell, referring to her mostly black East London neighborhood. "When I heard the news, I broke down and cried. I'd shaken her hand once, when she opened the housing projects I live in. It's not like I knew her, but why do I feel this way (*USA Today*, September 2, 1997, p. 3A)?"

How had this simple school teacher from a noble family so captured the heart of citi-zens around the world? How had she become so very much more popular than any member of the royal family?

The world had watched Diana develop. The shy, awkward young girl played her part perfectly in a fairy-tale wedding ceremony. When she found no love or support in her marriage or from her new family, she turned to the world and the world adopted her. Without asking for sympathy she evoked it. When she struggled bravely with her loveless marriage, infidelity, an eating disorder, and ostracism, we rooted for her like we do for any underdog who has moxie enough to stand up to overwhelming odds. When she beat her tough odds and in turn began to help others beat their tough odds (cancer, homelessness, AIDS, land-mines) we found in Diana a symbol for the hero in each of us. Not a Prince Charming to the rescue, rather a Princess Charming. Diana became ours — a hero for all of us. How did she so completely achieve her goal of becoming the "Queen of Hearts?"

The answer to these questions resides in understanding the interpersonal intelligence. Diana knew how to win hearts because she let her own be known. She was open to receive the feelings of others and to share her own. "Diana wasn't like the other royals," said medical secretary Dawn Winter, 35, as she placed a bouquet of lilies at Kensington Palace. "She was one of us (*People Magazine*, September 15, 1997, p. 74)."

Diana admitted her problems publicly, never asking for sympathy but winning it completely.

Just Between Friends
the Interpersonal Intelligence is...

Small things with great love. It is not how much we do, but how much love we put in the doing. It is not how much we give, but how much love we put in the giving.
— *Mother Teresa (1910-1997)*

Let us endeavor so to live that when we come to die even the undertaker will be sorry.
— *Mark Twain (1839-1910)*

If you judge people, you have no time to love them.
— *Mother Teresa (1910-1997)*

There is no exercise better for the heart than reaching down and lifting people up.
— *John Andrew Holmer*

The simplest and shortest ethical precept is to be served by others as little as possible, and to serve others as much as possible.
— *Leo Tolstoy (1828-1910)*

What do we live for if it is not to make life less difficult for each other.
— *George Eliot (1819-1880)*

Be ashamed to die until you have won one victory for humanity.
— *Horace Mann (1768-1859)*

This is the final test of a gentleman: his respect for those who can be of no possible value to him.
— *William Lyon Phelps (1865-1943)*

The time is always right to do what is right.
— *Martin Luther King, Jr. (1929-1968)*

After all, the only proper intoxication is conversation.
— *Oscar Wilde (1854-1900)*

Nonviolence is a weapon of the strong.
— *Mahatma Gandhi (1869-1948)*

The greatest tragedy is indifference.
— *Red Cross slogan*

The worst sin toward our fellow-creatures is not to hate them but to be indifferent to them; that's the essence of inhumanity.
— *George Bernard Shaw (1856-1950)*

Treat all people as though they were related to you.
— *Navajo Nations*

I've decided to stick with love. Hate is too great a burden to bear.
— *Martin Luther King, Jr. (1929-1968)*

The service we render others is really the rent we pay for our room on earth.
— *Wilfred Grenfell (1865-1940)*

Grief can take care of itself, but to get the full value of a joy you must have somebody to divide it with.
— *Mark Twain (1839-1910)*

A teacher affects eternity, he can never tell where his influence stops.
— *Henry B. Adams (1838-1918)*

Above all nations is humanity.
— *Goldwin Smith (1823-1910)*

A community is like a ship, everyone ought to be prepared to take the helm.
— *Henrik Ibsen (1828-1906)*

Children need models rather than critics.
— *Joseph Joubert (1754-1824)*

If it is very painful for you to criticize your friends — you're safe in doing it. But if you take the slightest pleasure in it — that's the time to hold your tongue.
— *Alice Duer Miller (1874-1942)*

When she responded to a request to visit a young lady diagnosed with cancer and given only two years to live, Diana knew intuitively exactly what to say to shatter any formality or pretense, to relate person-to-person. She asked, "Aren't you just terribly angry?" From that moment it was no longer a princess calling on a patient, it was two young ladies having a chat.

In 1987, when many still feared that AIDS could be contacted by casual contact, Diana offered her ungloved hand to touch an AIDS patient. As she touched that patient she touched the world, returning the word "royalty" to a finer meaning. Once again there was meaning in the traditional British saying "the monarchy is a mirror to our better selves."

Goodbye England's Rose

Goodbye England's rose,
from a country lost without your soul,
who'll miss the wings of your compassion
more than you'll ever know.
— *Elton John, September 5, 1997*

Royalty before Diana had come to mean formality, aloofness, and distance. White gloves separated royalty from the commoners; the proverbial stiff upper lip separated the British from the world of emotions. Diana took off the starchy white gloves which distanced generations of royals from commoners; she donned a sweatshirt. She went on national television to discuss emotional problems. Royalty was suddenly associated with warmth, closeness, and compassion. Di was communicating in the way that to her came most naturally, she was using her emotional intelligence.

People understood her feelings. Whether she was holding a wounded child, touching a patient, or opening her arms to hug her boys, we knew exactly what she was feeling. We could relate. She was like us. The new name we gave her told the story. She was no longer Lady Diana Spencer or Princess Diana, she became simply Di. Elton John was to eulogize her as "the princess next door."

Di became a hero for the world. Not a distant hero to look up to, but a hero each of us knew we could emulate. Diana became a shining symbol for the caring and vulnerable side within each of us. She traveled to Bosnia to help rid the world of landmines; while in Nepal she touched lepers; she dropped in unannounced at AIDS hospices to volunteer help and support. Diana's message was most powerfully conveyed with pictures, as when she held and hugged Angolan children wounded by landmines. She did not need to say a word to project and communicate her message; hers was not a verbal intelligence — it was an interpersonal message born of an highly developed interpersonal intelligence. Di not only projected, she received. She did not need words from the children, to receive their message. As she said, "I looked into their eyes and saw it all (People Magazine, September 15, 1997, p. 73)."

Diana articulated the type of intelligence she wanted to build in her sons. In a globally televised interview for the BBC's Panorama in 1995 Diana described her vision for her sons,

> I want them to have an understanding of people's emotions, people's insecurities, people's distress and people's hopes and dreams...I take them around homelessness projects. I've taken William and Harry to people dying of AIDS, albeit I told them it was cancer.

She Made Royalty of Commoners

My wife and I were fortunate to meet the princess in July 1991 at London's Savoy Hotel, at a luncheon benefiting Rainbow House, a proposed children's hospice. As Diana made her way down the long line of well-wishers, my wife and I were like children at Christmas, barely containing our excitement. Diana spoke softly but directly to each of us — a moment that was irreplaceable.

When our "turn" came, she laughed gently at our Texas accents and asked us to use the word "y'all" correctly. We did, and Diana smiled broadly. Then she moved on.

Clearly on a cloud, my wife said it was she who felt like the princess. It occurred to me that this was Diana's magic; if only for a moment, she could make commoners feel like royalty.
— Gene Dickey, Irvine Texas,
    USA Today, September 5, 1997

I have taken the children to all sorts of areas where I'm not sure anyone of that age in this family has been before, and they have a knowledge. They may never use it, but the seed is there and I hope it will grow because knowledge is power (Princess Diana, in BBC's Panorama Telecast, 1995, quoted in USA Today, September 2, 1997).

Why did Diana insist on breaking the ancient mold? Why did she insist in taking her boys to Disney World and to McDonald's and having them stand in line like commoners? Diana was teaching her sons, as she put it, "to lead from the heart, not the head." She said she was not out to destroy the 1,000-year-old monarchy, she made it clear, though, that she intended to rear a new kind of king.

And the people understood. Upon Diana's death, Londoner Nita Agyemen summed up the feelings of a nation:

In the past, the monarchy was very discreet, closed and secretive. But she opened them up. I hope when the sons take over, they will have her same qualities (*USA Today*, September 2, 1997).

Diana had won the hearts of the world. As tea salon waitress Pascale Tremblay said,

Diana was a truly magnificent woman, a super human being. She knew how to give something to everyone, and she was as good as she was beautiful (*USA Today*, September 2, 1997, Front Page).

It appears that the seeds that Diana sowed took root and will some day have their impact on the monarchy and the nation. It was William who suggested she auction off her gowns for charity! The boys insisted on following Diana's casket on foot, following her example, leading from the heart.

Part of the interpersonal intelligence, is the ability to understand the feelings of others, and to communicate one's own feelings. Diana demonstrated the power of this intelligence — she used it to transform a nation and touch the world.

We may ask from where compassion and caring spring. Certainly empathy, the ability to put oneself in the place of another and feel what it is like to be them, is part of the answer. This intelligence is often strongly developed in those who have suffered. Having felt our own pain deeply, it is easier to understand and feel that of others. Diana herself, two years before her death, in a famous BBC interview linked her own status as an outcast in the royal family to her discovery of her mission.

> I was very confused by which area I should go into. Then I found myself being more and more involved with people who were rejected by society…and I found an affinity there (Princess Diana, in BBC's Panorama Telecast, 1995, quoted in *People Magazine*, September 15, 1997, p. 73).

We forget that there is no hope of joy except in human relations. If I summon up those memories that have left me with an enduring savor, if I draw up the balance sheet of the hours in my life that have truly counted, surely I find only those that no wealth could have procured me. True riches cannot be bought.
— Antoine de Saint Exupéry (1900-1944)

The life of another very powerful woman, Oprah Winfrey, supports the view that intense suffering can translate to empathy and compassion, which in turn may touch and transform millions. The September 15, 1997 issue of *LIFE* magazine carried Oprah's picture with the tag line, "The secret inner life of America's most powerful woman." How did Oprah come to earn that title? How did a rural girl who was sent from family to family to live as a child, by 43 years of age become the world's highest-paid entertainer, amassing half a billion dollars? How does she so control her daily audience of 20 million fans that she has the power to launch any book of her choosing straight to the top of the *New York Times* best-seller list, merely by telling her audience they should read it?

Oprah by her own account, was raped at nine, sent away by her mother as a child, pregnant as a teenager; and smoking cocaine in her twenties. "My most vivid memory of growing up is a sense of loneliness, of being alone (Oprah, as quoted in *LIFE*, September 15, 1997, p. 53)." Did Oprah's suffering lead to intense empathy? An essential clue about the intensity of Oprah's empathy is how she lost her job as a newscaster: While interviewing those with tragic stories she would lose her objective "newsperson composure;" she would break down and cry!

Oprah's ability to be affected by the stories of others is witnessed daily on her television program, but is not limited to face-to-face encounters. Oprah, who early showed extraordinary verbal/linguistic skills, has always been moved by stories she reads.

> I remember not being able to sleep, literally not sleep, without the lights on for three years after that [reading Truman Capote's *In Cold Blood*].

Oprah's addiction to books began early; it was not just an escape from her difficult life, but a chance to enter another. As she says,

> What a difference it makes in your world to go into some other life. It's what I love most. I'm reading always to leave myself, always to leave myself behind. That's what reading is. You get to leave (*LIFE*, September 15, 1997, p. 60).

Each day viewers tuning in to the Oprah Show learn what it is to "go into some other life." We come to understand those Oprah interviews in part by what they say, but in part by seeing Oprah's reaction to them — sharing her empathy. Oprah has become a symbol for the empathy within each of us; part of our addiction to her show is a desire to connect to the caring, compassionate, empathetic side of ourselves.

When first presenting his theory of multiple intelligences, Gardner described both the interpersonal and the intrapersonal intelligence under one heading, the personal intelligences. Both were linked to emotional awareness, but the intrapersonal intelligence was rooted in the ability to know one's own feelings whereas the essence of the interpersonal intelligence was the ability to understand the feelings of others. In Gardner's words:

> In this chapter, I shall examine the development of both of these aspects of human nature. On the one side, there is the development of the internal aspects of a person. The core capacity at work here is *access to one's own feeling life* — one's range of affects or emotions: the capacity instantly to effect discriminations among these feelings and, eventually, to label them to enmesh them in symbolic codes, to draw upon them as a means of understanding and guiding one's behavior....
>
> The other personal intelligence turns outward, to other individuals. The core capacity here is the *ability to notice and make distinctions among other individuals* and, in particular, among their moods, temperaments, motivations, and intentions.... In an advanced form, interpersonal knowledge permits a skilled adult to read the intentions and desires — even when these have been hidden — of many other individuals and, potentially, to act upon this knowledge — for example by influencing a group of disparate individuals to behave along desire lines (Gardner, 1983, p. 239).

Gardner recognized that the interpersonal and intrapersonal intelligences are interdependent.

> In the course of development, these two forms of knowledge are intimately intermingled in any culture, with knowledge of one's own persona perennially dependent upon the ability to apply lessons learned from the observation of other people, while knowledge of others draws upon the internal discriminations the individual routinely makes. Our two forms of personal intelligence could, in fact, be described separately; but to do so would involve unnecessary duplication as well as artificial separation. Under ordinary circumstances, neither form of intelligence can develop without the other (Gardner, 1983, p. 241).

The ability to impact on and lead others is a function of both interpersonal and intrapersonal intelligences, often exquisitely intertwined. Sensitivity to the feelings of others is enhanced to the extent we are open to our own feelings; pity, compassion, and empathy are key interpersonal skills based on intrapersonal sensitivity. We see this intertwining of the interpersonal and intrapersonal intelligences in both Di and Oprah (notice how we relate to them on a first name only basis). They both have an extraordinary ability to read the emotions of others — interpersonal intelligence. For example, Di relates to the anger in the young cancer patient; someone with less interpersonal intelligence would not even be aware of the anger. And on a daily basis, Oprah holds millions in her grasp because of her extraordinary ability to understand and relate to the feelings of her guests and audience.

But these two powerful women have the ability to influence others also because of their sensitivity to their own feelings, and their ability to communicate them — intrapersonal intelligence. Oprah was nominated for an Oscar in her acting debut because of her ability to project her feelings into her character. When Princess Diana and Prince Charles went on national television, each to tell their side of the story in an attempt to win the hearts of the nation, the audience had more sympathy for Di than Charles. Why did they side with Di over the future King of England? In part because she was better able to communicate from the heart. She had better access to and ability to show her feelings. Impact on and even power over others, leadership skills, skills we think of as related to interpersonal intelligence, are based in part on ability to know and communicate one's own feelings, forms of intrapersonal intelligence. The two intelligences, as Gardner indicated, are intertwined.

The war for the nation's heart in Great Britain was played out on television again following Princess Diana's death, with the same result: The subdued reaction to the reserved statement made by the Queen (many said it was "too little and too late") was in stark contrast to the tumultuous,

> **Love is a thing to be learned. It is a difficult, complex maintenance of individual integrity throughout the incalculable processes of inter-human polarity.**
> **— D. H. Lawrence (1885-1930)**

spontaneous applause in response to the passionate eulogy for Di by her brother, Earl Charles Spencer. Why was there such a passionate reaction to his speech? In part because it was laden with the vocabulary of the heart. He spoke of protecting the boys from the "anguish" and "despair" Diana experienced. Diana's brother picked up the sword from his fallen sister, to continue the battle to develop in her sons the interpersonal and intrapersonal intelligences. Standing before her casket, he spoke to Diana and to the hearts of the nation as he made his heartfelt promise:

> On behalf of your mother and sisters, I pledge that we, your blood family, will do all we can to continue the imaginative and loving way in which you were steering these two exceptional young men so that their souls are not simply immersed by duty and tradition, but can sing openly as you planned.

Intense contact with one's own feeling, one aspect of intrapersonal intelligence, allows one to reach others, an aspect of interpersonal intelligence.

A number of school programs recognize the interdependence of social and emotional development and have been called SEL or Social Emotional Learning programs (Elias, et al., 1997; Berreth & Berman, 1997; Weissberg et al., 1997). Goleman's (1995) popular book, *Emotional Intelligence*, is based on the work of Salovey (1990) who defines emotional intelligence as abilities in five domains: Knowing one's own emotions; managing emotions; motivating oneself; recognizing emotions in others; and handling relationships. The first three of these domains fall neatly into the intrapersonal intelligence and the last two fall neatly into the category of interpersonal intelligence.

Not all aspects of interpersonal and intrapersonal intelligences are interdependent; a highly developed intrapersonal intelligence does not ensure high development of interpersonal intelligence. Most of us have encountered a person so preoccupied with themselves that they talk endlessly about themselves, discussing the nuances of their own inner life, unaware they are boring or irritating their audience.

People who spend a great deal of time preoccupied with their inner states may or may not use that knowledge to further an understanding of others. Conversely, people who are very social and even quite sensitive to the needs and feelings of others may or may not be deeply grounded in their own inner life. Most of us are familiar with a very gregarious person who is truly interested in others, but who has little inner life. Those of us who have led therapy groups have been often struck by the individuals who can see in others what they cannot see in themselves. They are the opposite of those who are highly attuned to their own needs and inner states, but in-sensitive to those of others.

These individuals prove that interpersonal and intrapersonal intelligences are partially independent. Further, the development of interpersonal intelligence does not ensure its use for the benefit of others. The sales-person who knows how to hook a poten-tial buyer, or worse, a Hitler, may use his or her interpersonal skills to harm rather than help others. But, hopefully, these are exceptions. Normally, as we become more sensitive to our own feelings, we become more empathetic. And, as we tune in to the feelings of others, we recognize parts of ourselves.

Someone with very highly developed in-terpersonal intelligence picks up and can later use extremely subtle cues from oth-ers. It is fascinating that while the person offering the cues may be unconscious that they are doing so and the person receiving the cues may not be aware they have re-ceived those cues, those unconscious non-verbal messages nevertheless become part of the "impression" of that person.

We perceive peculiarities in the features and bearing and movements of others that help to make the impression we receive without our observing or attending to them. We remem-ber details of another person's dress and pe-culiarities in his gestures, without recalling them; a number of minor points, an olfactory nuance; a sense of touch while shaking hands, too slight to be observed; warmth, clamminess, roughness or smoothness in the skin; the man-ner in which he glances up or looks — of all of this we are not consciously aware, and yet it influences our opinion. The minutest move-ments accompany every process of thought; muscular twitchings in face or hands and movements of the eyes speak to us as well as words. No small power of communication is contained in a glance, a person's bearing, a bodily movement, a special way of breathing.

Signs of subterranean motions and impulses are being sent silently to the region of every-day speech, gesture, and movement (Reik, 1948, p. 135).

Gardner has taken as one measure of in-terpersonal intelligence the ability to cre-ate an accurate picture of the preferences of others. Some children are able with a great deal of accuracy to indicate the friendship choices and preferred activities of their classmates; they have highly de-veloped interpersonal intelligence. Others, while knowing their own feelings and pref-erences quite well, may be relatively igno-rant of those of others. There are many di-mensions of interpersonal intelligence, some involving a correct cognitive picture of the feelings of others, others involving empathy, and yet others involving leader-ship and other relationship skills. Devel-opment of one interpersonal skill does not ensure skill in another. For example, as stu-dents learn to appreciate a point of view different from their own they do not nec-essarily improve their conflict resolution skills to any significant degree. All of the intelligences are multifaceted. We will deal with that topic extensively in Chapter 22: Beyond Multiple Intelligences — A Multi-plicity. For now, let's turn to the eighth and last of the intelligences, intrapersonal in-telligence.

**Love sought is good,
but given unsought is better.
— William Shakespeare (1564-1616)**

Intrapersonal Intelligence

W e use our intrapersonal intelligence to think in, with, and about internal feelings, moods, and states of mind. Dream images and feelings are symbols to think in and express this intelligence. Those strong in the intrapersonal intelligence enjoy solitude, contemplation, and an opportunity to explore inner states and thoughts including preferences, plans, fantasies, memories and feelings.

Educational Implications

• **Matching:** Students strong in the intrapersonal intelligence learn best through introspection, reflection, and individual think time. They benefit from alone time to write, draw, doodle, or allow their thoughts to incubate. They enjoy strategies such as Journal Reflections, Timed-Pair-Share, Corners, and Think Time.

• **Stretching:** We develop the intrapersonal intelligence as we have students engage in metacognition and/or free association on their own behavior and feelings. The intrapersonal intelligence is stretched as students attempt to determine their own patterns of intelligences, examining their strengths and weaknesses and exercising intrapersonal skills such as introspection, planning, metacognition, reflection, value clarification, prioritizing, self-discipline, and time management. We may stretch students' linguistic intelligence through the other intelligences as when we have them write journal reflections, relate problems to personal experience, choreograph personally relevant movements.

• **Celebrating:** Students celebrate their self smarts through sharing interpretations of their dreams, analyzing internal strengths and weaknesses, setting and checking progress on self-determined goals, and weighing their own products to select those most representative of themselves as contributions to their portfolios.

Attracted To

• Internal experiences: Moods, Memories, Intuitions, Values, Feelings, Fantasies

Skills & Preferences

• Attending to memories, fantasies, dreams,
• Clarifying own values and beliefs
• Controlling impulses
• Developing differentiated opinions, beliefs
• Enjoying think time, alone time, quiet time
• Introspecting, intuiting
• Knowing and managing moods and feelings
• Knowing own strengths and weaknesses
• Motivating oneself
• Setting realistic goals
• Thinking about one's own thinking
• Understanding inner conflicts, motivations

End States & Models

• **Philosopher:** Friedrich Wilhelm Nietzsche, Jean Paul Sartre
• **Poet:** Emily Dickinson, Walt Whitman
• **Political leader:** Indira Gandhi, Thomas Jefferson, Barbara Jordan, Abraham Lincoln, Margaret Chase Smith, Gloria Steinam
• **Psychologist/psychiatrist:** Deepak Chopra, Sigmund Freud, Karen Horney, Carl Jung
• **Religious figure:** Buddha, Jesus Christ, Confucius, Dalai Lama, Pope John Paul II, Joseph Smith
• **Theologian:** St. Thomas Aquinas, Thomas Moore, Mary Baker Eddy
• **Visionary:** Edgar Cayce, Black Elk

Intrapersonal Intelligence

Intrapersonal intelligence is the ability to focus on and understand internal stimuli. Gardner's focus in defining the intrapersonal intelligences shifted over the years. When looking back at the evolution of MI theory a decade after *Frames of Mind*, Gardner indicated his original conception of intrapersonal intelligence focused on the "feeling life" of the individual, but that he had come to stress instead,

> the importance of having a viable model of oneself and of being able to draw effectively upon that model in making decisions about one's life (Gardner, 1993, p. xviii).

This statement reflects the "cognitive" leaning in Gardner's theory of intelligences; intelligences are in this view, ways of thinking associated with different types of information. Gardner points out that the intrapersonal intelligence is unique in that it is the only "human-only" intelligence: Primates do not brood about themselves. More recently, however, evidence indicates a far more extensive world of feelings within nonhumans than previously recognized (Masson & McCarthy, 1995), but certainly other animals are not as self-reflective as humans, and do not discriminate among nearly as great a number and range of internal states.

Extraordinary development of intrapersonal intelligence can take many forms. One form is described in detail by Theodore Reik in his classic work, *Listening with the Third Ear* (Reik, 1948). Reik, a student of Freud, describes the inner life of a psychoanalyst and recommends to as-piring therapists and others ways to develop the intrapersonal intelligence. It is not just attention to inner stimuli that is key — it is the way in which one attends to inner stimuli that opens the door to developing the intrapersonal intelligence.

Freud described the free associative process which allows the patient to set aside all inhibitions, experiencing and describing anything which comes to mind. In the process, unconscious, repressed material emerges, entering consciousness. Reik went further, developing a theory of attention which helps us understand and even develop the intrapersonal intelligence.

Reik's theory of attention is simple. It involves only two factors: the content of attention, and the quality of attention. With regard to the content of attention, it may be focused either on internal or on external stimuli. When we focus on a cloud, a person, a painting or some other object in the world outside ourselves, our attention is on external stimuli. When we focus on a thought, a feeling, a sensation, a dream, a mental image, or a memory, our attention is on internal stimuli. Thus, as we all know, our attention can be internal or external.

But it is the quality of attention too, not just whether it is focused inward or outward, which determines what we perceive, what we learn, and to a remarkable extent who we are. Attention can be voluntary or involuntary. We can control it, keeping it focused on an object of study. Or we can let it drift, allowing it to go to whatever stimuli attracts it. It can be like the narrow beam of a spotlight focused on just one object, casting everything else in darkness.

To Know Thyself
is to Know the Intrapersonal Intelligence

What lies behind us and what lies before us are tiny matters compared to what lies within us.
— *Oliver Wendell Holmes (1809-1894)*

My being alone like this has given me something tremendous, and it's just what I need.... My mind is so serene, but concentrated and I am watching it like a cat a mouse.
— *J. Krishnamurti (1895-1986)*

I never found the companion that was so companionable as solitude.
— *Joseph Addison (1672-1719)*

You can never have a greater or lesser dominion than that over yourself.
— *Leonardo da Vinci (1452-1519)*

Believe nothing, no matter where you read it, or who said it, no matter if I have said it, unless it agrees with your own reason and your own common sense.
— *Buddha (563-483 B.C.)*

Silence is a true friend who never betrays.
— *Confucius (551-479 B.C.)*

Many a time I have wanted to stop talking and find out what I really believed.
— *Walter Lippmann (1889-1974)*

Self-reverence, self-knowledge, self-control: These three alone lead life to sovereign power.
— *Alfred Tennyson (1809-1892)*

Illusions commend themselves to us because they save us pain and allow us to enjoy pleasure instead. We must therefore accept it without complaint when they sometimes collide with a bit of reality against which they are dashed to pieces.
— *Sigmund Freud (1856-1939)*

Be good enough to remember that your morals are only your habits ; and do not call other people immoral because they have other habits.
— *George Bernard Shaw (1856-1950)*

The purpose of life is to know one's self.
— *Gandhi (1869-1948)*

Ful wys is he that can himselven knowe!
(Very wise is he that can know himself.)
— *Geoffrey Chaucer (1340-1400)*

Consider what thou wert, and make it thy business to know thy self, which is the most difficult lesson in the world. Yet from this lesson thou will learn to avoid the frog's foolish ambition of swelling to rival the bigness of the ox.
— *Miguel de Cervantes (1547-1616)*

A friend is a present you give yourself.
— *Robert Louis Stevenson (1850-1894)*

Have patience with all things, but first of all with yourself.
— *St. Francis of Sales (1567-1622)*

Act only on that principle whereby you can at the same time want that it should become a universal law.
— *Immanuel Kant (1724-1804)*

It is not who is right, but what is right, that is important.
— *Thomas Huxley (1825-1895)*

The only upright man is he who knows his shortcomings.
— *Titus Maccius Plautus (254-184 B.C.)*

Think for yourselves and let others enjoy the right to do the same.
— *François Marie de Voltaire (1694-1778)*

Attention as a 2 x 2 Matrix

These two qualities of attention — its content and its quality — can be symbolized as a two-by-two matrix: Our attention can be either intentionally focused on internal stimuli (thinking about a mental math problem) or intentionally focused intensely on external stimuli (examining the pattern in the wings of a butterfly); it can be undirected, but oriented toward external stimuli, (noticing whatever catches your eye in a room) or undirected, but oriented toward internal stimuli (noticing whatever thought, feeling, or image comes to mind). Time spent in one of the four cells, undirected attention to internal stimuli, is a powerful way to develop intrapersonal intelligence.

Content

	External	Internal
Voluntary	Focused Study	Metacognition
Involuntary	Responsiveness	Free Association

Quality

Or it can be like a searchlight, scanning, looking only for specific things, as when we are looking only for the car keys among a clutter of objects. Or it can be like the glow of a lantern, casting a dim light all around. Attention can be highly selective, attending only to a specific type of object; or it can be nonselective, spending much time or little time on any object to which it is drawn. Attention can be fleeting, skipping from one thing to another; or it can be sustained. Attention can be vigilant, as when we sit up in bed at night, listening for the sound of an intruder. Or it can be relaxed, like the time just before we allow ourselves to drift off to sleep. Of all of the qualities of attention, it is the voluntary vs. involuntary dimension on which Reik focuses. Much is revealed when we cease controlling our attention, allowing it to flow of its own accord.

It is a certain combination of the content of attention and the quality of attention which allows us to develop the intrapersonal intelligence. Intrapersonal intelligence is developed, in part, by carving out time for involuntary attention to internal stimuli.

> It can be demonstrated that the analyst, like his patient, knows things without knowing he knows them. The voice that speaks in him, speaks low, but he who listens with a third ear hears also what is expressed almost noiselessly, what is said in *pianissimo* (Reik, 1948, p. 145).

How can we get access to this inner knowledge? How does one learn to listen with the third ear?

When we are intently looking through a microscope or examining the brush strokes in a painting, we are controlling our attention, focusing it on an object we wish to study. This voluntary, external attention allows us to learn a great deal about the object of our study, but it keeps us from attending to the other things in the environment, and from internal stimuli. Voluntary, external attention is like the beam of a flashlight keenly focused on things outside ourselves. Voluntary, focused attention can be turned inward, as when we concentrate with focused effort, trying to remember a name. Focusing our attention

What a man really has, is what is in him. What is outside of him, should be a matter or no importance. — Oscar Wilde (1854-1900)

inward, however, does little to develop intrapersonal intelligence. Intrapersonal intelligence is developed only when we allow our inward attention free reign, to move of its own accord to the stimuli toward which it gravitates. If we control our attention, even inward attention, it remains like the spotlight which illuminates some things while casting others in darkness. It is precisely those things which voluntary

attention cast into darkness that hold the key to intrapersonal intelligence. Just as we are more likely to remember that forgotten name when we stop trying, only when we stop directing our attention do we open the door to the most profound intrapersonal discoveries.

Voluntary attention sheds a bright light on selected objects, but leaves much in the dark. When we give up control, when we allow our attention to flow in any direction which attracts it, we become aware of many things we cannot know by maintaining voluntary, focused attention.

> Voluntary attention, which brings so much into a clear light, causes so much more to sink or lose its clarity. While raising the significance of some things vigorously and definitely, it degrades others to insignificance. To return to our former analogy, the searchlight, which casts a brilliant light upon a small area, plunges the greater part of the field into profound darkness. The proverb, "Where there is much light, there is also much shade," is true of the phenomena of attention, too (Reik, 1948, p. 165).

The development of intrapersonal intelligence is partially a function of the ability to allow involuntary, internal attention. By not controlling our attention, by allowing it to be drawn to whatever internal stimuli seem to call to it, we tune in to a rich inner life. Involuntary, internal attention is the royal road to certain kinds of self-knowledge. We do not become aware of our feelings by looking for them; we become aware of our feelings by allowing them to surface. In fact, thinking about our feelings can be a way to prevent discovery of their true nature.

Involuntary attention to internal stimuli can be practiced, learned. Once practiced regularly, it opens a process in which a rich inner life is discovered and developed.

When we give up control of our attention, and it is turned inward, we enter the free associative process. If we simply let our attention turn inward and go where it will, we might attend first to a tension in a muscle, then to an itch, then perhaps, to a fleeting thought, then to a memory, then to a link between that memory and something that bothered us yesterday. In this process we are led to a feeling we did not know was there, perhaps frustration in a relation. A link is discovered between the muscle tension and the memory. A resolve emerges to act differently in the relation. Values are clarified. Involuntary, internal attention flows, often leading to realizations which cannot be made through voluntary, focused attention. People who regularly engage in sustained involuntary attention to internal stimuli discover and develop a rich inner life; they develop an openness to feelings and a strong core of values.

While Reik's simple two-factor theory of attention appears obvious, the implications are profound. Reik provides evidence that when we learn how to maintain an uncontrolled sustained attention on internal stimuli, a very remarkable process results. We open the door to learning about ourselves and others — we develop the intrapersonal and interpersonal intelligences.

Reik provides many examples of the power of this process. One of the most remarkable occurred during a psychoanalytic session in Holland in 1935. It is best presented in Reik's own words:

> I was treating a young German woman who had been a member of the Socialist party. Despite the fact that she came of an old gentile family, she had to flee Hitler's Third Reich. In Holland she had come to psychoanalysis because serious disturbances interfered with her work. Among them was the memory of a love affair that had lasted for several years and had ended before she left Germany. The man had been a prominent physician. He was married and he had promised to divorce his wife and marry my patient. When Hitler came, he did not have the moral courage to sacrifice his career. He had broken off the relationship with her and returned to his wife. It was obvious that my patient had suffered more from this disappointment than from the other blows of destiny and that she still loved the man to whom she had been devoted for so long and who was lost to her.

Learn to be quiet enough to hear the sound of the genuine within yourself so that you can hear it in others.
— Marion Wright Edelman (1939-)

> We had been discussing the problem for a few months and she still had not overcome her grief. At a certain point the analysis reached a deadlock. One session at this time took the following course. After a few sentences about the uneventful day, the patient fell into a long silence. She assured me that nothing was in her thoughts. Silence from me. After many minutes she complained about a toothache. She told me that she had been to the dentist yesterday. He had given her an injection and then had pulled a wisdom tooth. The spot was hurting again. New and longer silence. She pointed to my bookcase in the corner and said, "There's a book standing on its head."

> Without the slightest hesitation and in a reproachful voice I said, "But why did you not tell me that you had an abortion?" I had said it without an inkling of what I would say and why I would say it. It felt as if, not I, but something in me had said that. The patient jumped up and looked at me as if I were a ghost. Nobody knew or could know that her lover, the physician, had performed an abortion on her. The operation, especially dangerous because of the advanced state of her pregnancy, was, of course, kept very secret because abortion in the case of gentiles was punishable by death in Germany. To protect the man she still loved, she had decided to tell me all except this secret (Reik, 1948, pp. 263-264).

If intelligence is the ability to solve problems, Reik's ability to figure out his patient's secret has to be ranked as sheer genius! There are a number of remarkable aspects to this case (and other similar cases presented by Reik), but let's focus first on the way in which Reik knew with certainty the woman's secret — a secret he could not know with certainty using only the logical intelligence. Reik says, "I had said it without an inkling of what I would say and why I would say it. It felt as if, not I, but something in me had said that."

If our minds were only logical and conscious, Reik would be right in saying "Not I...said that." The logical mind cannot make that kind of leap. In fact, though, it was not Reik's logical, conscious intelligence which had solved the puzzle; it was, rather, his intrapersonal intelligence.

Like water which can clearly mirror the sky and the trees only so long as its surface is undisturbed, the mind can only reflect the true image of the Self when it is tranquil and wholly relaxed.
— Indra Devi

What is this intrapersonal intelligence? How can it have knowledge not accessible to the rational mind? Can it be developed? How?

Reik's theory of attention provides a powerful explanation of the nature of intrapersonal intelligence, as well as hints to those wishing to develop it in themselves and their students. It is accessed and developed by sustaining inward, involuntary attention, not by trying to direct one's mind, but allowing it to go to the places it wants to visit. In fact, the logical mind interferes

with certain kinds of problem solving which occurs only when we suspend logic and allow the mind free reign.

In the free associative process of psychoanalysis, the patient lies on his or her back, looks only at the ceiling, in a room with muted colors and subdued light, and is instructed to say anything which comes to mind. The patient undergoing psychoanalysis soon tires of attending to the boring external environment and begins to explore his or her internal world. Memories with strong emotions, unresolved conflicts, misunderstood behaviors all become natural candidates for attention. The patient pushes toward expressing deep, forgotten memories.

Which memories were forgotten? Those most painful. In the safe environment of the analysis, given sustained involuntary internal attention, the mind struggles to become whole — to recover the lost memories, to cope with that with which at an earlier time it could not cope.

Given internal, involuntary attention, the mind of the patient again approaches that which is unresolved. Further, if the psychoanalyst allows his or her attention to float freely, and if it is not too preoccupied with resolving its own internal conflicts, the mind of the analyst gravitates to receiving the messages the patient is struggling to express. An unconscious conversation occurs.

One of the peculiarities of this third ear is that it works two ways. It can catch what other people do not say, but only feel and think; and it can also be turned inward. It can hear voices from within the self that are otherwise not audible because they are drowned out by the noise of our conscious thought-processes. The student of psychoanalysis is advised to listen to those inner voices with more attention than to what "reason" tells about the unconscious; to be very aware of what is said inside himself…and to shut his ear to the noise of adult wisdom, well-considered opinion, conscious judgment. The night reveals to the wanderer things that are hidden by day (Reik, 1948, pp. 146-7).

The meaning is conveyed to him by a message that might surprise him much like a physical sensation within his organism. Again, the only way of penetrating into the secret of this language is by looking into oneself, understanding one's own reactions to it (Reik, 1948, p. 147).

The patient without knowing is pushing to express his/her deepest self; the analyst through involuntary, inward attention allows that self to be received. If the analyst tries to figure out the patient, he or she is using the rational/logical mind, and is likely to miss or misinterpret the patient's message. To receive the message, the analyst must suspend the rational mind, receiving the message in the free associative mode in which it is being sent. It is possible later to put the process into a logical framework, but the process itself is not a logical, sequential process. The analyst who is unwilling to suspend logic will never receive the deepest messages of his patients. In Reik's words:

When I look back on the psychological situation, I can, of course, realize what brought me to my surprising statement. I must have felt for some time that the patient was keeping something secret when she spoke of the physician. Then came the session with the long pauses. I can follow the subterranean thread between her few associations now. Toothache, the injection by the dentist, the pulling of the wisdom tooth, the book that stands on its head. If I had followed this train of associations logically, I might perhaps — have come to the same conclusion. Here was a displacement from below to above, from the genital region to the mouth…an operation…pain…the position of

the book and embryo on it head. I did not, however, use my logical powers and I can only warn my students against using them in such situations. Logical operation subjects the analyst to errors and mistakes he would not make if he trusted his psychological rather than his logical gifts. An understanding of the process and the insertion of the logical links in the chain can and sometimes should be attempted afterward but not during the process (Reik, 1948, p. 264).

It is not by chance that so many powerful discoveries are made during dreaming. During dreaming the mind attends only to internal stimuli, and is free to focus on any stimuli in any order, allowing the dreamer to make connections the logical mind would reject as irrational. Erich

You cannot teach people anything. You can only help them discover it within themselves. — Galileo Galilei (1564-1642)

Fromm, in one of the most important and readable books on dreaming, *The Forgotten Language*, details examples of how the unconscious mind can "know" things which the logical, mind rejects as irrational. One of many examples provided by Fromm:

A prediction of a different kind occurs in the following dream: A, who has met B to discuss a future business association, was favorably impressed and decided that he would take B into his business as a partner. The night after the meeting he had this dream:

I see B sitting in our common office. He is going over the books and changing figures in them in order to cover the fact that he has embezzled large sums of money.

A wakes up and, being accustomed to paying some attention to dreams, is puzzled. Being convinced that dreams are always the expression of our irrational desires, he tells himself that this dream is an expression of his own hostility and competitiveness with other men, that this hostility and suspicion lead him to a fantasy that B is a thief. Having interpreted the dream in this fashion, he leans over backwards to rid himself of these irrational suspicions. After he started the business association with B, a number of incidents occurred which re-aroused A's suspicion. But recalling his dream and its interpretation, he was convinced that again he was under the influence of irrational suspicions and feelings of hostility and decided to pay no attention to those circumstances which had made him suspicious. After one year, however, he discovered that B had embezzled considerable sums of money and covered it by false entries in the books. His dream had come true almost literally.

The analysis of A's association showed that his dream expressed an insight into B which he had gained at the first meeting, but of which he had not been aware in his waking thought. Those many and complex observations which we make about other persons in a split second without being aware of our own thought processes had made A recognize that B was dishonest. But since there was no "evidence" for this view and since B's manner made it difficult for A's conscious thinking to believe in B's dishonesty, he had repressed the thought completely, or rather the thought had not even registered with him while he was awake (Fromm, 1951, pp. 41-42).

Just remember, we're all in this alone.
— Lily Tomlin (1939-)

The ability to gain insights and solve problems during the dream state may be related to the suppression of the left (logical, linear, sequential) hemisphere relative to the right (apperceptive, global, simultaneous) hemisphere during dreaming. The left hemisphere can be likened to a digital computer, processing one bit of information at a time whereas the right hemisphere can be likened to an analog computer, simultaneously synthesizing a great deal of input. The right hemisphere deals better with relations among different things, making a whole from the discrete parts in contrast

to the left hemisphere which deals better with analyzing a whole into its parts. Both types of functioning are important for insight and understanding, but during waking hours the left hemisphere is usually dominant whereas the right hemisphere takes over during dream states. Carl Sagan (1977, pp. 178-179) interprets this reversal of dominance as a possible explanation of insights obtained during dreaming; dream discoveries and insights often involve creatively synthesizing apparently discrete bits of information and/or spatial information — tasks at which the right hemisphere excels. Sagan interprets the most classic of all dream discoveries, the discovery of the organization of the benzene molecule:

> Perhaps the most famous is the dream of the German chemist Friedrich Kekule von Stradonitz. In 1865 the most pressing and puzzling problem in organic structural chemistry was the nature of the benzene molecule. The structure of several simple organic molecules had been deduced from their properties, and all were linear, the constituent atoms being attached to each other in a straight line. According to his own account, Kekule was dozing on a horse-drawn tram when he had a kind of dream of dancing atoms in linear arrangements. Abruptly the tail of a chain of atoms attached itself to the head and formed a slowly rotating ring. On awakening and recalling this dream fragment, Kekule realized instantly that the solution to the benzene problem was a hexagonal ring of carbon atoms rather than a straight chain. Observe however, that this is quintessentially a pattern-recognition exercise and not an analytic activity. It is typical of almost all of the famous creative activities accomplished in the dream state: they are right-hemisphere and not left-hemisphere activities.

The underlying brain mechanisms, common to both dreaming and to psychoanalysis, in which intrapersonal insights can be gained, is the turning away from external stimuli and allowing the mind to go where it will — involuntary, internal attention.

If personal and even scientific insights are gained though this involuntary, internal attention, then learning the process of attending to internal stimuli, development of intrapersonal intelligence, has a proper place in our classrooms. Certainly we are not preparing all our students to become psychoanalysts. Although it is only the very extraordinary individual who will develop his/her intrapersonal intelligence to the extent Reik describes, every individual can benefit from some development of that intelligence. Recent evidence indicates the development of intrapersonal intelligence is fundamental for academic success. In his recent book, *Emotional Intelligence,* Daniel Goleman (1995) has summarized a mountain of evidence indicating the importance of emotional intelligence for school and life success. Knowing and controlling one's own emotions, two facets of emotional intelligence, are among the skills developed with intrapersonal intelligence.

Implications for Education

That there is not one but at least eight ways to be smart has revolutionary implications for education. If students do not understand a concept, we no longer have the luxury of continuing to teach in the same way, rationalizing our action by saying the student is not very bright. We have an obligation to ask if the student might get the concept better if we taught it another way. We need to use a variety of instructional strategies if we are to match students' multiple intelligences. The more ways we teach, the more students we reach. Further, if there are eight ways to be smart, all students can be smarter in eight ways. We have

an obligation to ask if we have designed our curriculum and instruction to foster growth in all intelligences. We need not only match all students' intelligences, but also to stretch all intelligences. Learning another fact or skill will not serve a student as powerfully as learning another way to learn, another way to think, another way to be smart. Finally, if there are eight ways to be smart, we have an obligation to teach students about how they, and others, are smart in different ways. In doing so, we honor the uniqueness of every student and celebrate our collective diversity. Only then can all students shine, regardless of their particular pattern of intelligences. To do less is to buy self-esteem and success for some at the expense of others. Unless we honor all intelligences, we cannot be true to the most fundamental principle of education in a democracy — equal educational opportunity for all students.

In the chapters that follow, we will examine ways to make these three visions a reality — matching, stretching, and celebrating multiple intelligences. But before we do, let's examine a prior question: Are there other intelligences? If we are to match, stretch, and celebrate students' intelligences, if we are to deal with a full deck, we must ask if there are intelligences beyond the eight named in MI theory. To ignore an intelligence would be to fail to reach all of our students as fully as we could, fail to develop the full potential of our pupils, and fail to validate the unique giftedness of some. The question of whether there are other intelligences is fundamental to our mission as educators in a democracy. It is to that question, then, that we next turn.

The Eight Intelligences Mind Map

Created by Laurie Kagan

References

Berreth, D. & Berman, S. *The moral dimensions of schools.* **Educational Leadership**, 1997, *54(8)*, 24-27.

Brennan, J. L. *Duke: The Life Story of Duke Kahanamoku.* Honolulu, HI: Hu Pa'a Publishing Inc., 1994.

Buffalo, A. *Oprah Winfrey. A self-made woman of many talents.* New York: Random House, 1993.

Elias, M. J., Bruene-Butler, L., Blum, L. & Schuyler, T. *How to launch a social and emotional learning program.* **Educational Leadership**, 1997, *54(8)*, 15-19.

Fromm, E. *The Forgotten Language.* New York: Grove Press, 1951.

Gardner, H. *Is Musical Intelligence Special? Keynote Address.* In V. Brummett, (Ed). *Ithaca Conference '96: Music as Intelligence. A Sourcebook.* Ithaca, New York: Ithaca College, 1997.

Gardner, H. *Frames of Mind. The Theory of Multiple Intelligences.* New York: Basic Books, 1983.

Goleman, D. *Emotional Intelligence.* New York: Bantam Books, 1995.

Goodall, J. *In the Shadow of Man.* London, England: Collins, 1971.

Gutman, B. *New York: Pocket Books,* 1997

Johnson, M. *Oprah Winfrey: A Life in Books.* **LIFE**, September 1997, 45-60.

Krull, K. *Lives of the Athletes.* San Diego, CA: Harcourt Brace & Co., 1997.

Langer, S. K. *Problems of Art.* New York, Charles Scribner, 1957.

Masson, J. M. & McCarthy, S. *When Elephants Weep. The Emotional Lives of Animals.* New York: Dell Publishing, 1995.

McKim, R. H. *Experiences in Visual Thinking.* Belmont, CA: Brooks Cole, 1972.

Reik, T. *Listening with the Third Ear.* New York: Noonday Press, 1948.

Roberts, M. *The Man Who Listens to Horses.* New York: Random House, 1996.

Sachs, C. *World History of Dance,* as quoted in Langer, 1957, 11.

Sagan, C. *The Dragons of Eden: Speculations on the evolution of human intelligence.* New York: Ballantine, 1977.

Salovey, P. & Mayer, J. D. *Emotional Intelligence.* **Imagination, Cognition and Personality**, 1990, *9*, 185-211.

Sartre, J.P. *The Words: The Authorbiography of Jean-Paul Sartre.* New York: George Braziller, 1964.

Swerdlow, J. L. *Vincent van Gogh: Lullaby in Color.* **National Geographic**, October 1997, 101-129.

Scanlan, L. *Afterword.* In Roberts, M. *The Man Who Listens to Horses.* New York: Random House, 1996.

Thoreau, H. D. *Journal.* In Meltzer, M. (Ed.) *Thoreau: People, Principles, and Politics.* New York: Hill and Wang, 1963.

Weissberg, R. P. Schriver, S. B. & DeFalco, K. *Creating a districtwide social development project.* **Educational Leadership**, 1997, **54(8)**, 37-39.

Winfrey, O. as quoted in *LIFE*, September 15, 1997, 53.

Are There Other Intelligences?

Perhaps there are candidates that I have not considered (Gardner, 1993, p. 39).

Are there other intelligences than the eight so far identified by MI theory? A full ten years after publishing his theory, the original list of seven intelligences had not grown, but Gardner stated perhaps there were candidates that he had not considered. Indeed there was one, the naturalist. Are there others? Should we expect more intelligences to be canonized? In this chapter, we will evaluate claims for four additional intelligences: culinary, mechanical, existential, and emotional. We will find sufficient evidence to support all four.

As educators attempting to build curriculum and instruction based on MI theory, we would do well to ask some tough questions of this process: Are the eight criteria the best criteria for selecting human intelligences? Are they objective? Are there other intelligences?

Eight intelligences sounds somewhat manageable. Why are we arguing for the existence of four additional intelligences? Our intent is twofold. First, it is good for students. Just as students benefited when we expanded our singular notion of intelligence into multiple intelligences, students will benefit even more as we recognize and validate additional ways to be smart. If we know our students are smart in eight ways rather than one, we strive to match our instructional strategies with how students are smart in order to build more bridges onto the curriculum. If we know there are eight ways to be smart, we broaden our curriculum to help stretch students' eight intelligences to maximize their personal potential and to enrich our diverse society. If we know there are eight intelligences, in our class and school we honor the eight ways our students are smart and celebrate our collective diversity. However, as concerned educators, we must ask: Even with the broader definition of intelligence offered by MI theory, are there students who still fall through the cracks because we have failed to respect how *they* are smart? Are there additional intelligences we should match, stretch, and celebrate?

Second, we investigate claims for additional intelligences as a further exploration of MI theory itself. We believe it is a healthy process for educators to question educational theories that determine what and how we teach, especially those as influential as MI theory. It is important to question whether the criteria proposed by MI theory are objective. Would we all, using the same criteria identify the same intelligences, or is a degree of subjectivity involved? Are the eight criteria set forth by MI theory the only, or the best way to select human intelligences? Is "frames of mind" the best metaphor for the mind? Finally, we must ask whether, even if the criteria can be applied objectively and the eight intelligences are those which best fit the criteria, to what extent should we base curriculum and instruction on those eight — are there other considerations which might override matching, stretching, and celebrating those intelligences? If, for example, computer intelligence cannot pass the test to become a verifiable intelligence (computers were not around thousands of years ago, so a "computer intelligence" can-

not pass the test of evolutionary plausibility), does that mean we should put any less weight on designing computer instructional strategies and teaching to develop computer literacy?

We believe these are important questions for the educational community. We will suspend our evaluation of MI theory for the latter portion of the book (Chapters 20-22). For now, let's focus on the search for additional intelligences.

The number of intelligences we identify depends on the candidates we consider and the criteria we use to evaluate the candidates. MI theory set forth eight criteria for evaluating a candidate intelligence. Briefly stated, the criteria are as follows:

1. Brain Isolation

The intelligence is linked to specific sites in the brain. For example, injury or surgery to those sites effects the intelligence.

2. Exceptional Individuals

Exceptional individuals show early or extraordinary development of the intelligence in contrast to other intelligences. For example, autistic savants may show extraordinary development of math skills but not other skills.

3. Core Operations

A set of operations core to the intelligence can be identified. For example, ability to orient oneself in space is a core operation of the visual/spatial intelligence and operates among the blind as well as the sighted.

4. Developmental History

A unique developmental history for the intelligence can be identified. For example, math skills peak far earlier than do music skills.

5. Evolutionary Plausibility

Development of the skill improves genetic fitness — the ability to survive and reproduce — and the skill can be identified in nonhuman animals. For example, sense of direction allows one to find food and return home; this visual/spatial skill is strongly developed in all animals.

6. Experimental Support

Experiments isolate the intelligence. For example, interference studies show music in the background does not interfere with writing, but the sound of random words does.

7. Psychometric Support

Factor analysis and other psychometric tests show the intelligence to have unique correlations. For example, tests of spatial skills correlate well with other tests of spatial skills, but not as well with tests of verbal skills.

8. Symbol System

The intelligence can be encoded and decoded with a unique symbol system. For example, we have words for the verbal/linguistic; numbers for the logical/mathematical intelligence; and musical notes for the musical/rhythmic intelligence.

To ask then, whether there are additional intelligences, we must ask how well additional candidates fare in the MI criteria crucible. For fun, let's first propose two candidates — a mechanical intelligence and a culinary intelligence — and put them to the test. Let's compare how well they hold up to the eight criteria compared to some of the accepted intelligences. On the surface the mechanical and culinary intelligences appear likely candidates; certainly they fit MI theory's basic definition of intelligence as the ability to solve problems and fashion products valued by the society. Do we not pay (sometimes too well) for a well-tuned car and a gourmet meal? Additionally, the mechanical and culinary intelligences are plausible candidates because we readily can identify stimuli, skills, and end states for each, and certainly have been blessed with gifted individuals in each domain. Before we evaluate these two candidates, let's take brief look at the description and rationale for each.

Culinary Intelligence

Skillful selection, preparation, and preservation of food is as essential to human survival as any other set of skills. Those who more acutely detected and responded to the odor and taste of foods had an increased biological fitness. We do not know when human precursors first discovered that meat of an animal killed in a forest fire tasted better and was easier to digest than raw meat. Nor do we know exactly when this discovery led to roasting spitted meats over fires. We do know that by the Paleolithic Period the Aurignacian people of southern France were steaming their food over hot embers by wrapping it in wet leaves, and that well before the introduction of pottery during the Neolithic Period, our ancestors were toasting wild grains on flat rocks and using shells, skulls, and hollowed stones to heat liquids.

Culinary Intelligence

We use our culinary intelligence to think about and solve food related problems, including production, selection, storage, preparation, cooking, and presenting foods. Those strong in the culinary intelligence are attracted to food related topics such as preferences, cultural differences in preparation, and the various culinary arts.

Educational Implications

• **Matching:** Students strong in the culinary intelligence enjoy learning through food related activities. They benefit from links between food and the curriculum such as cultural differences, historical trends, dietary needs of different regions and different species, impact of geography on food growth and food customs.

• **Stretching:** We develop the culinary intelligence as we have students follow and create recipes. We may stretch students' culinary intelligence through the other intelligences as when we have them draw, write, measure, feel, taste, talk, and think about foods.

• **Celebrating:** Students celebrate their food smarts through feasts which they prepare. Teams or individuals prepare items for a meal on a theme, such as Chinese Food, Wagon Train Food, or Space Food.

Attracted To

• Foods: Taste, Texture, Odor, Chemistry, Color, and Shape of Edible Plants and Animals

Skills & Preferences

• Baking, barbecuing, braising
• Canning, pickling, preserving, presenting
• Marinading, microwaving, roasting
• Sautéing, seasoning, selecting, smoking
• Steaming, stewing, sun and freeze drying
• Tasting, toasting

End States & Models

• **Chef:** John Ash, Mario Batali, Dean Fearing, Susan Feniger, Emeril Lagasse, Michael Lomonaco, Mary Sue Milliken, Wolfgang Puck
• **Cook book author:** Betty Crocker, Fannie Merritt Farmer, Irma Rombauer
• **Cookie maker:** Wally "Famous" Amos
• **Cooking educator:** James Beard, Julia Child, Simone Beck, Louisette Bertholle
• **Food franchiser:** "Colonel" Harlan Sanders
• **Food processing, preservation:** Clarence Birdseye, Gail Borden
• **Food reformer:** John Harvey Kellogg, Samuel Cate Prescott, Harvey Washington Wiley
• **Food technologist:** Charles Olin Ball, Bernard Emerson Proctor
• **Health food expert :** Curtis Aikens
• **Home economist:** Helen Woodard Atwater, Isabel Bevier
• **Ice cream designer:** Ben Cohen, Jerry Greenfield
• **Nutritionist:** Katharine Blunt
• **Wine expert:** David Rosengarten, Ernest Gallo, Pierre Gallo, Steve Olson
• **Pie Master:** Marie Callender
• **Restaurateur:** Michael Romanoff
• **Restaurant reviewer:** Bill Boggs, Nina Griscom, Alan Richman

Cooking Up
the Culinary Intelligence

Progress in civilization has been accompanied by progress in cookery.
— *Fannie Farmer (1857-1915)*

A good cook is like a sorceress who dispenses happiness.
— *Elsa Schiaparelli (1907-1973)*

A good dinner sharpens the wit, while it softens the heart.
— *John Doran (1807-1878)*

The turnpike road to most people's hearts, I find, lies through their mouths, or I mistake mankind.
— *John Wolcot (1738-1819)*

They are sick that surfeit with too much, as they that starve with nothing.
— *William Shakespeare (1564-1616)*

One should eat to live, not live to eat.
— *Benjamin Franklin (1706-1790)*

Simple diet is best; for many dishes bring many diseases; and rich sauces are worse than even heaping several meats upon each other.
— *Pliny (23-79)*

Eat with moderation what you know by experience agrees with your constitution. Nothing is good for the body but what we can digest.
— *François Marie de Voltaire (1694-1778)*

All courageous animals are carnivorous, and greater courage is to be expected in a people whose food is strong and hearty, than in the half-starved of other countries.
— *Sir William Temple (1628-1699)*

There is no sincerer love than the love of food.
— *George Bernard Shaw (1856-1950)*

A good cook is the peculiar gift of the gods. He must be a perfect creature from the brain to the palate, from the palate to the finger's end.
— *Walter Savage Landor (1775-1864)*

A house is no home unless it contains food and fire for the mind as well as for the body
— *Margaret Fuller (1810-1850)*

We may live without poetry, music and art;
We may live without conscience,
         and live without heart;
We may live without friends;
         we may live without books;
But civilized man cannot live without cooks.
— *Lord Lytton (1801-1872)*

The proof of the pudding is in the eating
— *Miguel de Cervantes (1547-1616),*
   in **Don Quixote**

Let the salad maker be a spendthrift for oil, a miser for vinegar, a statesman for salt, and a madman for mixing.
— *Spanish Proverb*

The discovery of a new dish does more for the happiness of mankind than the discovery of a star.
— *Anthelme Brillat-Savarin (1755-1826)*

Of course, huge advances in the culinary arts had to await the formation of settled farming villages with their associated introduction of domesticated livestock, cultivation of edible plants, a more stable supply of milk and its derivatives, and the ability to efficiently manufacture tools for cooking, including fired clay vessels and various utensils. The form of cooking to a large extent is a function of available resources (chronic fuel shortages of China led to emphasis on foods which can be cooked in a few seconds, and the development of the wok). Nevertheless, regardless of the form it takes, every culture makes an art of cooking. That cooking is a universal artform is evidence for a deeply rooted intelligence which supersedes mere survival. Can we consider a gourmet masterpiece any less the product of an intelligence than a painting, dance, or sonata?

As a testimony to, if nothing else, the pervasiveness of the culinary intelligences, consider the following quotation from *Grolier's Encyclopedia* on popular cookbook, *Joy of Cooking*:

> *Joy of Cooking* has clarified American cooking techniques and considerably enlarged the American cuisine. Written in 1931 by Irma Starkloff Rombauer and her daughter Marion Rombauer Becker (who also provided the original illustrations), the work — now in its 13th edition — is an encyclopedic compendium of classic American and European recipes, lucid explanations of culinary techniques, and detailed discussions of every important aspect of food preparation. A perpetual bestseller, the book to date has sold about 8,000,000 copies.

Mechanical Intelligence

The history of humankind's progress can be traced as the history of crafting more and more sophisticated tools. We love our tools. People decorate tools and fashion them into elegant works of art. Tools are the crystallization of intelligence. As we examine a tool, we are looking at the solution to a problem. And, of course, as tools are used to fashion ever more sophisticated tools, civilization advances at an exponential rate. Evolution is slow. The radical, ac-

Can we consider a gourmet masterpiece any less the product of an intelligence than a painting, dance, or sonata?

celerating advances with which we are daily bombarded have their roots not in biological evolution, but in the evolution of tool making. Through the fashioning of tools we have learned to bypass the slow, accidental pace of evolution.

Long ago our ancestors acquired skills like those practiced today among diverse chimpanzee groups who break or bite sticks to fashion them as better tools to increase success in termite fishing. The chimps use their sticks as tools to coax termites from their mounds. Termite fishing is taught through modeling: Chimps who do not observe other chimps using tools in the process of termite fishing are less likely to make those tools and acquire skills in their use. Tools allow an accelerated, extra-genetic inheritance of intelligence. The repair of the Hubble telescope was but one step in a series of steps to fashion tools which extend our senses, our power, and our efficiency. Toolmaking and tool use are

Mechanical Intelligence

We use our mechanical intelligence to think in, with, and about tools and mechanical relations and apparatus. Those strong in the mechanical intelligence enjoy making, using, and repairing tools, making models, hands-on activities, assembly, disassembly, using manipulatives, and designing machines and mechanical systems. Some forms this intelligence takes include designing, building, improving, tools and mechanical apparatuses.

Educational Implications

• **Matching:** Students strong in the mechanical intelligence learn best through exploring and creating models, tinkering with manipulatives, building mechanical apparatuses. They benefit from opportunities to fashion their own models related to the content of study.

• **Stretching:** We develop the mechanical intelligence as we have students engage in assembly, disassembly, and a variety of mechanical tasks. We may stretch students' mechanical intelligence through the other intelligences as when we have them write about and draw machines, discuss tools, and create songs about mechanics.

• **Celebrating:** Students celebrate their tool smarts through creating and sharing mechanical products and selecting models and mechanical products as entries in their portfolios.

Attracted To

• Tools, Mechanical Apparatus

Skills & Preferences

• Analyzing, designing machines and mechanical systems
• Disassembling and assembling machines
• Experimenting, testing, recording
• Inventing, building, tinkering
• Learning via manipulatives
• Making and using tools
• Making models
• Repairing broken objects
• Solving mechanical problems
• Working with wheels, gears, levers, pulleys, springs

End States & Models

• **Builder, architect:** Nora Stanton Barney, Natalie de Blois, Thomas Jefferson, Julia Morgan, Louis Henry Sullivan, Robert Venturi, Frank Lloyd Wright
• **Inventor:** John Logie Baird, Alexander Graham Bell, Karl Benz, Paul Cornu, George Eastman, Thomas Edison, Benjamin Franklin, Buckminster Fuller, Robert Fulton, Johan Gutenberg, Sir John Harington, Elias Howe, Kirkpatrick Macmillian, Guglielmo Marconi, Cyrus Hall McCormick, Samuel F. B. Morse, Joseph Niepce, Valdemar Poulsen, Christopher Scholes, Stanley Brothers, George Westinghouse, Eli Whitney, Wright Brothers
• **Engineer:** Octave Chanute, Bill Gates, Lillian Moller Gilbreth, James McDonnell, David Packard, Judith Resnick, Stephen Wozniak
• **Machinist:** Joseph Brown, David Macaulay
• **Mechanic:** John Deere, Henry Ford, James Watt

Constructing
the Mechanical & Craft Intelligences

Mechanical Intelligence

A bird is an instrument working according to mathematical law, which instrument it is within the capacity of man to reproduce with all its movements.
— *Leonardo da Vinci (1452-1519)*

There was too much hard hand labor on our own and all the other farms of the time. Even when very young I suspected that much might somehow be done in a better way. That is what took me into mechanics — although my mother always said that I was born a mechanic. I had a kind of workshop with odds and ends of metal for tools before I had anything else. In those days we did not have the toys of today; what we had were homemade. My toys were all tools — they still are! And every fragment of machinery was a treasure.
— *Henry Ford (1863-1947)*

Intelligence ... is the faculty of making artificial objects, especially tools to make tools.
— *Henri Bergson (1859-1941)*

Every tool carries with it the spirit by which it has been created.
— *Werner Karl Heisenberg (1901-1976)*

Man is a tool-using animal.... Without tools he is nothing, with tools he is all.
— *Thomas Carlyle (1795-1881)*

And now I see with eye serene
The very pulse of the machine.
— *William Wordsworth (1770-1850)*

Shining and free; blue-massing clouds; the keen
Unpassioned beauty of a great machine
— *Rupert Brooke (1887-1915)*

The greatest invention of the nineteenth century was the invention of the method of invention.
— *Alfred North Whitehead (1861-1947)*

Craft Intelligence

In response to the question, "Do you consider what you do a craft, or an art, or both (Diamonstein, 1995)?"

It is a craft up to a certain limit. And then it becomes an art, according to the steps you take to pursue the highest skill in your craft.
— *Jacques Francais, Master violin maker and restorer*

I describe myself as a craftsman....An artist need only be concerned with making something beautiful. A craftsman must make it beautiful and functional. I take great pride in calling myself a craftsman.
— *Sandi Fox, Quilter*

To experience the image, you have to move all the way around the bowl and into it, so you have to experience the whole object before you get a complete sense of the image. I'm not interested in just presenting a kind of picture but in giving the viewer some feelings of moving through time and space.
— *Wayne Higby, Ceramist*

Weaving is slow. I think one learns patience, and it's as close as I get to mediation, I guess. It's a mechanical process of drawing yarn through treadles or pushing the shuttle through the webs and watching something grow in front of you.
— *Jack Lenor Larsen, Weaver*

What I'm concerned with, though, is how one perceives one's own reality. If you're alive and aware, the work goes on twenty-four hours a day. So many people work and then have leisure time and play or whatever. This does not seem to be the pattern for me....To me, it's all the same thing. The excitement and the release and the experimentation and the newness and the freshness and the regeneration and everything — all that happens in the work, in the vision.
— *Albert Paley, Metalsmith*

close to the pure expression of human intelligence.

The invention of tools, however, is almost always not an end in itself. The creation of a tool is usually a by-product of the desire to solve a problem: to see further, move faster, become stronger, operate more delicately. Tool use is associated with every aspect of human functioning, from word processing to cutting toenails; from making wire hangers to making artificial hearts. The use of tools is not in itself the hallmark of the mechanical intelligence. The sign of a strong mechanical intelligence is an attraction to and love for tools per se; attraction to the mechanical as an end in itself, not just as a means. The mechanic loves tools.

It is important to distinguish the mechanical intelligence from the logical/mathematical intelligence. Both involve solving problems. The design, creation, and repair of tools and mechanical apparatus is a type of problem solving which involves a type of logic, but the mechanic who loves and is skilled with all sorts of tools may show no particular skill or interest at all in syllogisms or equations and a person who loves and is skilled with syllogisms, equations and all sorts of logic problems may show no interest whatsoever in tools. The mechanical intelligence cannot be reduced to the logical intelligence. Similarly, mechanics may or may not be strong in the bodily/kinesthetic intelligence. There are those who design tools who are not particularly inclined to work with them, and there are gifted athletes or dancers who are not particularly attracted to or skilled with tools.

Craft Intelligences

It is important also to distinguish the mechanical intelligence from the intelligences of the crafters. Craftmaking is enormously popular in the United States: one out of every two American households is involved in crafts, either professionally or through hobbies or leisure-time activities (Diamonstein, 1995). Involvement in crafts, however, usually springs from a different intelligence than involvement in mechanics. The mechanic is attracted to machines and mechanical apparatus of all sorts, including tools. The mechanical is the intelligence strongly developed in the master car mechanic or machinist. It is what drives the young child to take apart the toaster and the clock, to figure out how they work. In the mechanic there is an attraction to machines, mechanical apparatus and tools (which are another kind of machine) per se.

The intelligence of the craftmasters is different. Underlying the intelligence of the crafter is an attraction to a certain kind of medium. Out of the desire to work with and manipulate that medium springs tool use, whether it is to tools of the glassmaker, weaver, quilter, ceramist, woodworker, basketmaker, metalsmith, jeweler, or violin maker. The use of tools here, however, is secondary; tools are the means to more fully or more efficiently manipulate the medium. What is primary for the crafter is the attraction to, love for, and desire to work with the medium itself.

What emerged from in-depth interviews from America's most gifted and influen-

> Are There Craft Intelligences Too?

tial craftmasters (Diamonstein, 1995) was that regardless of their particular craft, the craftmasters had a passionate attraction to and desire to manipulate, form, mold, transform a particular medium.

While the craftsmakers included in this book are all special people leading special lives, few generalizations can be made to explain their interest in the crafts. Some were trained in the so-called fine arts; some were influenced by childhood experiences; some were guided by a remarkable teacher or mentor. All, however, seem continually inspired and nurtured by the aspect of their medium that initially attracted them to it — the material itself. "I don't know of anyone I would consider a real master who doesn't have a deep feeling for materials," say Wayne Higby. "Even for those people who use commercial glazes, because of the way they use them, an intensive understanding of materials is critical. That takes a long time. I think it probably takes longer for a ceramic artist to mature than for any other kind because of the tremendous amount of technical information that you have to assimilate. I've been working with the same glazes for ten years."

The wood the Sam Maloof uses is itself unending nourishment. Says Maloof of the widely imitated exposed joinery technique he invented years ago: "When I first started I thought, 'What a shame to cover something so beautiful.' I just didn't feel that joinery should be covered; it should be there for people to see. After all the hard work of making beautiful joints, to then cover them over took something away." For glassmaker Dale Chihuly, "The material itself is a continuing source of inspiration. The heat and the gravity continually inspire new ideas. I usually have an idea and begin to work on a concept that might be intellectual, but then it is taken over to a large extent by the process itself." For metalworker and former painter Mary Ann Scherr, "The blank canvas is a frightening wall, but a foot square of metal is another kind of canvas, loaded and exploding with ideas and solutions. I feel as though I've used miles of metal and still feel a rich source of inspiration just below the surface (Diamonstein, 1995)."

End States and Models for the Craft Intelligence

- **Basketmaker:** John McQueen
- **Carpenter:** Jocasta Innes
- **Ceramic maker:** Wayne Higby, Gordon Lee, Randy Morehouse, Ron Nagle
- **Furniture, cabinet maker:** Peter Blackwell, Tai Lake, Duncan Phyfe, Leopold Stickley
- **Glassmaker:** Dale Chihuly, Mary Shaffer, Wilfred Yamazawa
- **Metalsmith:** Daniel Hurwitz, Mary Ann Scherr
- **Quilt maker:** Sharon Balai, Tafi Brown, Kaye Wood
- **Seamstress, tailor:** Sandra Betzima, Nancy Zieman
- **Woodworker:** Wendell Castle, Dan Deluz, Sam Maloof

If intelligence is defined as attraction to and skill with a particular type of stimuli, we would have to conclude that each craft corresponds to a different intelligence, because each craftsmaster is passionately attracted to, and becomes skilled with a different medium. Some crafts (clockmaking) are clearly aligned with the mechanical intelligence; others (the fabric arts) are linked to the visual/spatial intelligence. All involve the bodily/kinesthetic intelligence. But none of the crafts can be reduced to some combination of those three intelligences. They each involve an attraction to, and, a love of, a particular medium. Although analysis of the unique intelligences associated with each type of craft is very important, examination of each craft intelligence is beyond the scope of this book.

Curriculum and Instruction Are Value Judgements

In what follows, we will focus on mechanical and culinary intelligences. We will test them against the eight criteria of MI theory to see if they, too, can be considered intelligences.

Before testing the mechanical and culinary intelligences, we offer one caveat: It should be made clear that there is no necessary relation between how well an intelligence fits the criteria and how much emphasis should be placed on developing that intelligence or using it as an instructional strategy. For example, if synthesis of more skills is involved when the mechanic exercises her skills, than when the musician exercises hers, musical ability would be more tightly localized in the brain than mechanical skills. But that would in no way make mechanical skills any less brain-based. Even if more potential lesion areas in the brain could incapacitate a mechanic than a musician, that would not indicate mechanical skills are less deserving of emphasis as we develop curriculum and instruction. It might indicate only that the art of the mechanic involves synthesis of many types of brain functioning.

That mechanical skills are less specific than musical skills in terms of brain localization, in no way makes it less essential that we teach mechanical skills than musical skills. On what basis can we defend the notion that as educators we should devote more of our resources to functions that are more narrowly brain localized? Integration of greater amounts of input is the function of neurons further removed from sensory input, neurons associated with "higher level," more abstract functioning. There is nothing in brain research, nor can

there be, which allows us to place a higher value on musical than mechanical talents. To teach music over mechanics or any set of skills over another is a value judgment, not a necessary conclusion which springs from brain science.

Testing the Mechanical and Culinary Intelligences

Having established the credentials of the culinary and mechanical intelligences as likely candidates to be considered for anointment along with the other intelligences, let's put them to a somewhat more rigorous, criterion-by-criterion test to see how well they fare.

Criterion 1.
Brain Isolation

There is as much evidence for the localization of taste and smell in the brain as there is for localization of music. Score one for the chef.

When we turn to the mechanic, the story is different. The essential brain functioning upon which the mechanic relies cannot be localized as well as the brain functioning essential to the musician or the cook. The mechanic integrates a wide range of kinesthetic, spatial, and logical skills directed to tool making, repair, and use. Mechanical skills are not narrowly localized. There is, however, one aspect of the mechanical intelligence which has been clearly located: The words for tool-related concepts tend to be found in the rear of the left temporal lobe (Calvin, 1996). Overall, though, we must fail to score one for the mechanic.

But wait. If we are to reject the mechanic because we cannot isolate the brain functioning upon which her skills are based, we must reject most or all of the MI theory broad intelligences. If brain isolation is the criterion, we must conclude there are linguistic intelligences, not a single linguistic intelligence. See Chapter 22: Beyond Multiple Intelligences — A Multiplicity! Similarly, there is no single site in the brain for intrapersonal, interpersonal, or most of the other intelligences. The mechanic passes this first test as well as most of MI theory intelligences. If we are to bar mechanical intelligence from the list of the chosen, on the same grounds we must bar the linguistic, interpersonal, intrapersonal, naturalist, and spatial intelligences as well, because there is not one well-localized brain site for any of these intelligences.

In sum, with regard to this first criteria, the chef scores better than most; the mechanic does as poorly as most.

Criterion 2.
Idiot Savants, Prodigies, Exceptional Individuals

A number of cases document autistic savants with extraordinary specific mechanical skills (Treffert, 1989). Consider Earl who had an IQ of 45.

> Earl had a mechanical talent out of proportion to his intellectual and speech limitations. At one point, without suggestion or help from anyone, he took a clock apart and rigged it up as a windmill, which ran very well. His perfor-

mance on all subtests for language and comprehension placed him inferior to 99 percent of 10 year-old boys. However, on tests of mechanical ability, dexterity, and mechanical comprehension, he did unexpectedly well — in one of those subtests, which often gave college students difficulty, he placed in the upper 99 percent of persons his age.

> Earl was able to make a model ferry boat out of wood after seeing a picture in a newspaper. He could draw blueprints of airplanes and boats with excellent coordination and detail, and he had an uncommon amount of knowledge about the parts and the operation of such vehicles (Treffert, 1989, p. 92).

If MI theory would have us take the existence of exceptional musical skills in some savants as evidence for a "musical intelligence," is not the existence of exceptional mechanical skills in some savants equally valid evidence of a "mechanical intelligence?"

If MI theory would have us take the existence of exceptional musical skills in some savants as evidence for a "musical intelligence," is not the existence of exceptional mechanical skills in other savants equally valid evidence of a "mechanical intelligence?"

Exceptional mechanical skills are found also in nonsavants. Most of us know the average student who is mechanically talented. In Gardner's own work (1993, p. 108) we find evidence of exceptional mechanical skills. Donnie, a six-year-old child performed so poorly in school, his teacher with regret concluded he would have to be retained.

> In Project Spectrum, however, Donnie excelled at the assembly tasks. He had greater success in taking apart and putting together common objects, like a food grinder and a doorknob, than any other student his age (Indeed, most teachers and researches failed to match

Donnie's skilled and seemingly effortless achievements in these mechanical tasks).

Some case studies of autistics suggests some support for the culinary intelligence as well — support like that which Gardner claims for math, music, and linguistic skills. Because autistic skills are often found near the concrete/perceptual range of the continuum, seldom at the abstract range, it is not surprising to find exceptional taste and olfactory proclivities and skills among autistics. George and Charles, two of the most celebrated savants, both frequently approached people and sniffed them. They would pick out their own slippers or clothes by smelling them (Treffert, 1989, p. 37). They did not, however, perform better than average on quantitative smell tests (Horwitz, et al. 1969). This would represent a proclivity toward smell rather than exceptional ability. Some savants have rituals of smelling everything about them, extreme sensitivity to and love of perfumes, and unusual abilities to discriminate tastes (Bergman and Escalona, 1949).

To our knowledge there are no examples of autistic children manifesting extraordinary culinary skills — probably because cooking demands a balancing of attention between many things at once. If our attention is like a laser beam rather than a lantern, we burn the bacon while watching for the toast to pop up.

A meal is like music: The chef and the musician both create beauty by arranging a different set of variables, foods in one case and sounds in the other.

There is a suggestion, however, that a proclivity toward food-related activities may have some consistency over time. Gardner (1993, p. 104) parenthetically notes,

> One girl, who identified "snack" as the activity she enjoyed the most during Year One of Spectrum, reported to her mother that one of the activities she did best two years later was "eating lunch."

If we are to take consistency over time in the other intelligences as evidence for their existence, can't we take this girl's consistency over time as support for at least a "culinary proclivity" which might, with proper nurturing, blossom into a full-scale culinary intelligence?

More seriously, the existence of exceptional individuals in the culinary arts is a matter of common experience. We do not have to dig up the biographies of famous chefs to prove our point here — to each of us comes the memory of the aroma and taste of a dish prepared with love by a favorite grandmother, aunt, husband, brother, or neighbor.

In sum, both the chef and the mechanic score well here.

Criterion 3.
Core Set of Operations

There is a remarkable parallel between the chef and the musician. One deals primarily with sounds, the other primarily with tastes and smells. The chef must be sensitive to the taste and smell of foods. A meal is like music: The chef and the musician both create beauty by arranging a different set of variables, foods in one case and sounds in the other.

Just as a deaf musician can still compose, a person with lesions eliminating taste and smell can still cook. Just as not all of us who love music can compose

it, not all of us who love a good meal can cook it. There are an infinite number of ways to combine and recombine sounds to create ever new musical masterpieces. And, of course, there are an infinite number of ways to combine and recombine foods and seasonings to cook ever new gourmet masterpieces. Can we seriously say the core operations of the chef are any less defensible than the core operations of the musician?

The mechanic must be sensitive to the arrangement, interdependence, and function of parts. Mechanical skills are in some ways more analogous to interpersonal skills, they each deal at a more abstract level with a range of information from a variety of perceptual domains. Recognizing the parts of a clock is a rather specific set of skills close to the perceptual domain, analogous to recognizing facial expressions. Creating a new machine for a new function, demands a great deal more integration of diverse variables, calling upon abstractions further from the perceptual domain. This type of higher-level mechanical activity is analogous to higher-level interpersonal skills, say the leadership skills necessary to bring a squabbling group into harmony.

There is no more support on the basis of "core operations" for a musical intelligence or an interpersonal intelligence than there is for a culinary intelligence or a mechanical intelligence.

Score more for the chef and the mechanic.

Criterion 4.
Developmental History and "End States"

With a bit of effort it would not be hard to define critical developmental stages for both the chef and mechanic. First, the chef learns to distinguish different flavors and odors, later to follow simple recipes, later yet, to follow and modify complex recipes, and finally, to create from scratch fantastic gourmet masterpieces. Again, we move from recognition to production, from concrete to abstract, toward development of the ability to integrate greater and greater experience.

With the mechanic, there is the often disconcerting (especially to parents) first stage of disassembly. It is followed (hopefully quickly) by reassembly — of progressively complex apparatuses. Later comes repair. Later yet, minor improvements on existing machines. Finally, mechanical skills merge into engineering skills as the budding mechanic gains the ability to generalize from concrete experiences to formulate abstract rules, applying them to solve new problems.

Once again the chef and the mechanic score as well as those gifted in other intelligences.

Criterion 5.
Evolutionary Plausibility

The chef and the mechanic are on especially strong ground with regard to this criterion. What could have its roots more deeply in evolution than toolmaking and sensitivity to the sight, odor, and taste of foods? Primates use tools to gather food, placing sticks into ant hills. The evolution of humankind is a story told by the evolution of toolmaking.

No arguments here. Having passed the halfway mark through the eight criteria, the chef and mechanic are looking strong!

The chef and the mechanic are on especially strong ground with regard to evolutionary plausibility. What could have its roots more deeply in evolution than toolmaking and sensitivity to the sight, odor, and taste of foods?

Criterion 6.
Experimental Psychological Tasks

The same kind of evidence which MI theory takes in support of the independence of linguistic and musical intelligences can be taken as support of the existence of culinary and mechanical intelligences. Music playing in the background in no way interferes with cooking or mechanics.

In general, though, the chef and the mechanic are on weak ground with regard to experimental examination of the processing involved in their skills. This is so, not because there are not definable unique types of processing going on with culinary and mechanical skills, but because mechanical and culinary skills have been so little studied. Perhaps if we elevate mechanical and culinary skills to the status of "intelligences," their neglect by experimental psychology will be remedied.

Criterion 7.
Psychometric Findings

To obtain psychometric support for a culinary intelligence and a mechanical intelligence, we would need to find valid measures of those intelligences which were independent of the other intelligences.

In Project Spectrum activities there is no cooking task, but there is an assembly activity designed to measure a child's mechanical ability. The Assembly Activity Task in fact shows splendid independence (lack of correlation) from activities presumed to reflect other intelligences. In fact, all measures in Project Spectrum, save the math tests, showed isolation from each other — even those which were presumed measures of the same intelligence. We can only assume that if the Spectrum battery included culinary activities, they, like the other measures, would demonstrate independence.

Tests, however, of mechanical and culinary intelligence must be careful to distinguish mechanical and culinary aptitudes from mechanical and culinary skills — just as we need to distinguish musical skills from musical aptitude. We can teach students to play music, cook, or use a socket set; a proclivity toward choosing those activities, however, will not necessarily follow.

A systematic, psychometric approach would need to distinguish three factors: skills, interests, and natural strengths. A student who is naturally weak in an intelligence can become quite skilled in that intelligence with enough training. That does not make him naturally strong. Further, someone who is naturally gifted in an intelligence may not be interested in exercising that intelligence.

One girl who had demonstrated both interest and ability in art while in the Spectrum classroom, in kindergarten became much more interested in learning how to read and avoided the art area (Gardner, 1993, p. 104).

In sum with regard to the seventh criteria, the chef and the mechanic score as poorly as the other intelligences.

Criterion 8.

Symbol System

Is it more of a stretch to say cooking is encoded and decoded by recipes and mechanical operations are encoded and decoded by blueprints and assembly diagrams than to say spatial intelligence is encoded and decoded by maps? Musical notation captures well the sounds of music; it is possible that we could develop equally well a notation system which would capture the range of flavors? Perfume manufacturers demand precision; consequently fragrances are precisely symbolized by chemists; chefs usually do not demand that degree of precision, so some chefs are satisfied with a pinch of oregano.

All of this is a bit silly: There is no more of a precise symbol system for the interpersonal intelligence or intrapersonal intelligence than there is for mechanical intelligence or culinary intelligence. In any case, whether or not a set of skills is too broad to be captured by a single symbol system should not be a determinant of whether those skills should become part of our curriculum and instruction.

● ● ● ● ● ● ● ● ● ● ● ● ● ● ● ● ● ● ● ●

What Do the Chef and the Mechanic Tell Us?

Consideration of the chef and the mechanic reveal that the intelligences selected by MI theory's eight criteria are subjective. The difference between subjective and objective statements lies, as we all learned early in school, in the independence of the

Is it more of a stretch to say cooking is encoded and decoded by recipes and mechanical operations are encoded and decoded by blueprints and assembly diagrams than to say spatial intelligence is encoded and decoded by maps?

statement from the speaker. "This is beautiful" is subjective because some will say it is beautiful and some will not; the truth of the statement depends on who states it. "This butter weighs one pound," is an objective statement because, presumably, there is an external reality to which it refers; the truth of the statement does not depend on who states it.

Multiple intelligence theory postulates a specific number of discrete intelligences. It appears to be an objective statement, one which can be verified against criteria external to the speaker. It is, however, a subjective statement. How many intelligences we end up with depends on the values of the speaker. Different results will be obtained depending on which criteria we choose, which candidate intelligences we choose to hold up to those criteria, how we weigh the various criteria, and who does the weighing. If we choose brain isolation

Are There Culinary and Mechanical Intelligences?

1. Brain Isolation

▼ **Chef:** "Smells" can be located in the brain just as well as can "sights," and far better than "leadership skills" or "intuition."

▼ **Mechanic:** Mechanical abilities, like linguistic and other complex abilities, cannot be localized in only one site in the brain.

2. Exceptional Individuals

▼ **Chef:** Master chefs, savants with proclivities for taste and smell, and exceptional individuals all make a strong case for a culinary intelligence. If you are not convinced, you should have seen our Daddy Julie (Miguel's great grandfather) cook brunch.
End State: Gourmet Chef

▼ **Mechanic:** Mechanical savants make the case. If you are not convinced, you should have seen Simón (Miguel's brother), build a Chevy practically from scratch.
End State: Master Mechanic

3. Core Operations

▼ **Chef:** Sensitivity to sights, smells, and tastes and ability to synthesize those elements into mouth-watering delights are more specific core operations than those for interpersonal skills.

▼ **Mechanic:** Sensitivity to arrangement and function of objects, ability to assemble parts from diagrams, and ability to modify and create arrangement of parts to serve specified function are more specific core operations than those for intrapersonal skills.

4. Developmental History

▼ **Chef:** Early sensitivity to tastes, smells, and arrangement of foods develop into the ability to follow and then modify recipes.

▼ **Mechanic:** Early sensitivity to arrangement of parts in mechanical apparatuses develop into ability to disassemble, reassemble, and invent.

5. Evolutionary Plausibility

▼ **Chef:** Where would humans be if we were not genetically predisposed to react to taste. Biological preparedness and taste aversion experiments demonstrate a strong, genetically determined proclivity to react to and remember tastes.

▼ **Mechanic:** Primates use tools to more efficiently gather food, to threaten each other, and kill prey. Where would our thumb be if our biological ancestors were not toolmakers and users?

6. Experimental Support

▼ **Chef:** Music does not interfere with cooking just as it does not interfere with writing. Cooking skills learned at breakfast transfer to preparing lunch; they do not transfer to long division.

▼ **Mechanic:** Music does not interfere here either, and repair of a clock produces skills which can be transferred to auto repair, but not singing.

7. Psychometric Support

▼ **Chef:** Intelligence-fair culinary aptitude tests involve cooking a breakfast. They predict quality of cooking a dinner better than any known tests.

▼ **Mechanic:** Mechanical aptitude tests have at least as much validity as tests of most of the other intelligences.

8. Symbol System

▼ **Chef:** Recipes are the symbol system of the chef. It is as strong as any single symbol system for the intrapersonal intelligences.

▼ **Mechanic:** Assembly diagrams are one of the symbol systems of the mechanic. It is as strong as any symbol system for interpersonal intelligence.

as a sole criterion, we are forced to conclude there are too many intelligences to count, and none of the MI theory candidates fit — they are all too multifaceted to be located in any specific site in the brain. See Chapter 20: Is MI Theory Brain-Based?

If we choose MI theory's eight criteria, but weigh them differently than does Gardner, or choose different candidate intelligences than those examined in MI theory, we end up with a different set of "intelligences" than the original seven. Two new intelligences — culinary and mechanical — taken primarily as foils, prove to qualify as well as any of the originally selected intelligences and far better than some. The culinary intelligence shows far greater brain isolation than do the interpersonal and intrapersonal intelligences. Primates don't play music, but they do use tools and prepare food. We find mechanical savants and savants with a proclivity toward smell and taste; we do not find interpersonal savants. An autistic with exceptional interpersonal skills is an oxymoron. The two most important defining characteristics of autism are lack of reciprocal social interaction and impairment of communication (American Psychiatric Association, 1987; World Health Organization, 1987).

If we can so easily defend new intelligences, why should the educational community focus so narrowly on the intelligences selected in MI theory? Given the subjectivity in selecting intelligences, we might decide to look freshly at which intelligences we should be fostering, and which we should use as primary instructional strategies.

In almost every high school in the nation there is a subset (shall we say "underclass") of students who hang around auto shop.

They are often considered not very bright academically. Those students, however, are very intelligent — their intelligence expresses itself in the mechanical domain. If we had used mechanical instructional strategies and developed in all students the mechanical intelligence throughout school, those students would have been integrated into the mainstream of schooling. If for example, our unit on the civil war included the opportunity to build a model cannon, their interest in the war would have been intensified dramatically. If our unit on grammar included the opportunity to build a physical, working model of a sentence, their understanding of, and retention of grammar would have been enhanced. If we were to declare the existence of a mechanical intelligence, we would foster the development of their mechanical intelligence, academic achievement, self-esteem, and social status.

Generalizing from this argument, we can conclude that as educators we should teach with as broad a range of instructional strategies as possible — attempting to match all of the many intelligences — attempting to stretch the development of every intelligence we can identify. Every intelligence should be honored.

Existential Intelligence

Gardner has joked about there being eight and a half intelligences, the existential intelligence being the intelligence which only partially qualifies. As educators, what do we gain by saying some intelligences are less qualified than others, and presumably therefore less important as we design cur-

Existential Intelligence

We use our existential intelligence to think about ultimate questions such as the meaning of life, ultimate ends, and our place in the universe. Those strong in the existential intelligence enjoy meaning and value-related issues and an opportunity to place any content in it's broadest context. Some forms this intelligence takes include search for meaning, questioning or defining values, and viewing everyday experience from an ageless or timeless perspective.

Educational Implications

• **Matching:** Students strong in the existential intelligence learn best through links between academic content and questions of meaning and value. They benefit from opportunity to take alternative perspectives and view content through the filters of philosophical, moral, and value issues. They enjoy strategies such as Folded and Split Value Lines, Agreement Circles, and Team Statements.

• **Stretching:** We develop the existential intelligence as we have students discover, think about, and express their deepest values. We may stretch students' existential intelligence through the other intelligences as when we have them write about, draw, and discuss the meaning of life, or create mimes, dances, or music to express ultimate ends.

• **Celebrating:** Students celebrate their existential smarts through expressing and reflecting on their value stances and personal and team meaning statements. They can select entries for their portfolios which reflect their values and thoughts about the meaning of life.

Attracted To

• Cosmic Perspectives, Transcendental States, Ultimate Questions, Underlying Meanings, Value Issues

Skills & Preferences

• Concern with cosmos, microcosms
• Finding meaning
• Guiding self and others toward ultimate ends
• Reducing questions to their essence
• Thinking about life, death, birth, pain, joy, compassion
• Understanding, analyzing issues
• Wrestling with philosophical issues

End States & Models

• **Existentialist:** Friedrich Wilhelm Nietzsche, Jean Paul Sartre
• **Philosopher:** Plato, Socrates
• **Religious Leader:** Buddha, Christ, Confucius, Hillel, Mohammed
• **Theologian:** Saint Thomas Aquinas
• **Thinker:** Albert Einstein, Carl Sagan

The Existence
of the Existential Intelligence

Rules to Live By

What is hateful to you, do not do unto your neighbor.
— *Hillel (1st century B.C-1st century A.D.)*

What is hurtful to you, do not do to any other person.
— *Moses (15th-13th century B.C.)*

What you do not want done to yourself, do not do to others.
— *Confucius (551-479 B.C.)*

Fear to do ill and you need fear nothing else.
— *Benjamin Franklin (1706-1790)*

On Forgiveness

Love your enemies, bless them that curse you; do good to them that hate you.
— *Christ (6 B.C.-30 A.D.)*

Let go. Why cling to the pain and the wrongs of yesterday? Why hold on to the very things that keep you from hope and love.
— *Buddha (563-483 B.C.)*

Bitterness imprisons life; love releases it.
— *Harry Emerson Fosdick (1878-1969)*

Where there is hatred, let me sow love.
— *St. Francis of Assisi*

On Giving

If you want others to be happy, practice compassion. If you want to be happy, practice compassion.
— *Dalai Lama*

There is joy in transcending self to serve others.
— *Mother Teresa (1910-1997)*

Get outside your suffering and into the suffering of others and you will soon find that you do not have any.
— *Virginia Henderson*

One thing I know: the only ones who will be really happy are those who have sought and found how to serve.
— *Albert Schweitzer (1875-1965)*

What is the essence of life? To serve others and to do good.
— *Aristotle (384-322 B.C.)*

Doing nothing for others is the undoing of ourselves.
— *Ben Franklin (1706-1790)*

Do all the good you can, to all the people you can, for as long as you can.
— *John Wesley (1703-1791)*

We make a living by what we get. We make a life by what we give.
— *Winston Churchill (1874-1965)*

Life's most persistent and urgent question is: What are you doing for others?
— *Martin Luther King, Jr. (1929-1968)*

Only a life lived for others is a life worthwhile.
— *Albert Einstein (1879-1955)*

The greatest source of happiness is in forgetting yourself and trying seriously and honestly to be useful to others.
— *Millicent Fenwick*

The way to heaven is to benefit others.
— *Lao Tzu (604-531 B.C.)*

A man's true wealth hereafter is the good that he does in this world for his fellow man.
— *Mohammed (570-632)*

When one reaches out to help another he touches the face of God.
— *Walt Whitman (1819-1892)*

The Existence
of the Existential Intelligence

On Knowing

We know the truth, not only by the reason, but by the heart.
— *Blaise Pascal (1623-1662)*

It is only with the heart that one can see rightly; what is essential is invisible to the eye.
— *Antoine de Saint-Exupéry (1900-1944)*

God conceals himself from the mind of man, but reveals himself to his heart.
— *The Book of Zohar*

On Love

There is none more lonely than the man who loves only himself.
— *Abraham Ibn Esra*

Love is the ultimate and highest goal to which a man can aspire. The salvation of man is through love and in love.
— *Viktor Frankl (1905-)*

Love possess not, nor would it be possessed, for Love is sufficient onto Love.
— *Khalil Gibran (1883-1931)*

It is futile to love in order that we be loved in return. As soon as it is recruited to some other purpose it ceases to be love.
— *Hugh Downs*

We should love others truly, for their own sakes rather than our own.
— *St. Thomas Aquinas (1225-1274)*

Love is God; that is the only God that I really recognize. Love equals God.
— *Mahatma Gandhi (1869-1948)*

Where love rules, there is no will to power; and where power predominates, there love is lacking. The one is the shadow of the other.
— *Carl Gustav Jung (1875-1961)*

Happiness

He is richest who is content with the least; for content is the wealth of nature.
— *Socrates (469-399 B.C.)*

To be content with what we possess is the greatest and most secure of riches.
— *Marcus Tullius Cicero (106-43 B.C.)*

It is the chiefest point of happiness that a man is willing to be what he is.
— *Desiderius Erasmus (1466-1536)*

If you want to be happy, be.
— *Aleksei Konstantinovich Tolstoy (1817-1875)*

The secret of contentment is knowing how to enjoy what you have, and to be able to lose all desire for things beyond your reach.
— *Lin Yutang*

A happy person is not a person in a certain set of circumstances, but rather a person with a certain set of attitudes.
— *Hugh Downs (1921-)*

If you can't change your fate, change your attitude.
— *Amy Tan (1952-)*

Happiness is not having what you want, but wanting what you have.
— *Hyman Judah Schuctel*

riculum and instruction? If we can identify students who gravitate to existential thought or who manifest any other kind of intelligence, we should be teaching with and teaching for that kind of thinking, celebrating their unique talents. Let's take a moment to validate the existentialist.

The existentialist is concerned with ultimate issues: What is the meaning and purpose of life? What is man's place in the universe? What is truth? What are the rules by which to live? Clearly there are people who are attracted to and skilled at thinking about those issues.

We can hold the existential intelligence up to brain research and ask if temporal-lobe involvement in certain kinds of religious and transcendental experiences helps it qualify as an intelligence. We can note that identical twins raised apart show similar scores on psychometric measures of religiosity. Gardner notes that the existential intelligence scores reasonably well on his criteria for an intelligence, but he has shied away from proclaiming it a ninth intelligence. He hints that he might in the future name it a ninth intelligence depending on brain research:

> If there should be neurological work on the human capacity to pose big questions (like existential questions), it would have implications for my theory (Gardner, 1997).

In our view it is simpler to examine the deepest thoughts of thinkers who have inspired generations, and on that basis determine if it is worth while to stretch the existential intelligence in all students, and to develop instructional strategies to match existentialist thinkers. As we look at the great existentialist thought, we must conclude: If intelligence did not produce those thoughts, there is no such thing as intelligence. Yes, we need to develop ways of delivering curriculum which will match the existentialist in all students, and to develop the existential intelligence as much as possible.

As we read the great thinkers on the meaning of life, we cannot but be struck by the overwhelming convergence of thought across the centuries (see box: The Existence of the Existential Intelligence). It is interesting to speculate: is there such tremendous convergence among the great thinkers across the centuries on the answers to life's existential questions because they have thought deeply about life and have discovered the universal truths, or is there convergence because the brain is wired in a way to lead to those conclusions and not others? It would be adaptive for the species to be selected for the ability to transcend selfishness; it would be adaptive also for the brain to be wired in a way which leads one beyond caring for oneself. In any case, clearly there is a drive for meaning, and some of us gravitate toward existential thinking just as others gravitate toward music, and yet others gravitate toward numbers, words, movement, food, or mechanical apparatuses.

● ● ● ● ● ● ● ● ●
▶ Emotional Intelligence

Emotional intelligence stands in a different relationship to MI theory than do the culinary, mechanical, and existential intelligences. So far we have been asking the question if intelligences in addition to the MI theory eight exist. Emotional intelligences raises a different question: Are there other valid ways to cut the MI pie?

Emotional Intelligence

We use our emotional intelligence to think about and control the world of feelings, in ourselves and others. Those strong in the emotional intelligence become aware of their own feelings and those of others, and are skillful in dealing with their own feelings and with relationships.

Educational Implications

• **Matching:** Students strong in the emotional intelligence learn best through opportunities to relate content to their own emotions and those of others. They benefit from reflection time and attunement — knowing their own feelings and those of others are received. They enjoy the opportunity to reflect on and share their personal emotional reactions to stories, poems, historical events, current events, field trips, difficult problems, and classroom events.

• **Stretching:** We develop the emotional intelligence as we have students deal with the affective component of the curriculum. The emotional intelligence is stretched also as students learn about their own emotions, how to control their emotions, how to motivate themselves, empathy and social skills. We may stretch students' emotional intelligence through the other intelligences as when we have them write about, draw, and discuss feelings, and when they create songs and dances about feelings.

• **Celebrating:** Students celebrate their feeling smarts through opportunities to express their feelings, share their knowledge about their feelings and those of others, and make emotional reaction entries in their portfolios.

Attracted To
• Emotions in Self and Others

Skills & Preferences
• **Awareness of One's Own Emotions**
(Self-Knowledge)
  • Metacognition
  • Understanding inner conflicts
  • Recognizing, discriminating own emotions
• **Controlling One's Own Emotions**
(Self-Control)
  • Controlling impulses
  • Delaying gratification
  • Interrupting escalating emotions
• **Motivating Oneself**
(Self-Motivation)
  • Setting realistic goals
  • Analyzing tasks into doable components
  • Managing time
• **Knowing the Emotions of Others**
(Empathy)
  • Taking role of others
  • Interpreting nonverbal cues
  • Recognizing, discriminating others' emotions
• **Relationship Skills**
(Social Skills)
  • Leading others
  • Friendship skills
  • Managing conflicts

Feelings
About the Emotional Intelligence

• •

A competent and self-confident person is incapable of jealousy in anything. Jealousy is invariably a symptom of neurotic insecurity.
— *Robert Heinlein (1907-1988)*

An ounce of emotion is equal to a ton of facts.
— *John Junor*

Expressing anger is a form of public littering.
— *Willard Gaylin*

Exuberance is beauty.
— *William Blake*

Man is the only animal that blushes — or needs to.
— *Mark Twain (1835-1910)*

Emotion turning back on itself, and not leading on to thought or action, is the element of madness.
— *John Sterling (1806-1844)*

By starving emotions we become humorless, rigid and stereotyped; by repressing them we become literal, reformatory and holier-than-thou; encouraged, they perfume life; discouraged, they poison it.
— *Dr. Joseph Collins (1866-1950)*

Ride your emotions as the shallop rides the waves; don't get upset among them. There are people who enjoy getting swamped emotionally just as, incredibly, there are people who enjoy getting drunk.
— *Mary Austin (1868-1934)*

Our feelings were given us to excite to action, and when they end in themselves, they are cherished to no good purpose.
— *Daniel Sanford (1766-1830)*

Hatred does not cease by hatred, but only by love; this is the eternal rule.
— *Buddha (568-488 B.C.)*

Thought is deeper than all speech; feeling deeper than all thought; soul to souls can never teach what unto themselves was taught.
— *Christopher Cranch (1813-1892)*

Feeling in the young precedes philosophy, and often acts with a better, more certain aim.
— *William Carleton (1794-1869)*

Strong feelings do not necessarily make a strong character. The strength of a man is to measured by the power of the feelings he subdues, not by the power of those which subdue him.
— *Jean Paul Richter (1763-1826)*

A true history of human events would show that a far larger portion of our acts are the results of sudden impulses and accident, than that of reason of which we so much boast.
— *Peter Cooper (1791-1883)*

The fire you kindle for your enemy often burns yourself more than him.
— *Chinese Proverb*

Our instinctive emotions are those that we have inherited from a much more dangerous world, and contain, therefore, a large portion of fear than they should.
— *Bertrand Russell (1872-1970)*

Joys are our wings; sorrows our spurs.
— *Jean Paul Richter (1763-1826)*

Love and you shall be loved. All love is mathematically just, as much as the two sides of an algebraic equation.
— *Ralph Waldo Emerson (1803-1882)*

Emotional intelligence includes knowledge of and ability to control emotions in oneself and understanding of emotions in others. It cuts across MI theory's interpersonal and intrapersonal intelligences. If it is as valid as the other intelligences, it demonstrates that the MI theory eight are but one way to conceptualize human intelligences and that other, equally valid, ways are possible.

We will not attempt here to present the topic of emotional intelligences in any detail. It is one of the most important recent developments in education, and is a very complex and important topic — far too large to be covered comprehensively in this book. What we can do here is provide a brief summary of some critical points on emotional intelligence as it relates to additional ways to be smart.

Dr. Peter Salovey of Yale University and John D. Mayer of University of New Hampshire first developed and researched the concept of emotional intelligence (Salovey and Mayer, 1990; Mayer & Salovey, 1997). Daniel Goleman (1995) has popularized and extended Salovey's work with his extremely readable and informative book, *Emotional Intelligence.* Goleman provides numerous case studies as well as summaries of experimental and correlational data which indicate that people high in traditional IQ act dumb if they are lacking emotional intelligence, and that emotional intelligence is associated with school achievement and superior performance in a range of life situations, especially interpersonal relations.

On first hearing the term emotional intelligence, many of us do a double-take.

It sounds like an oxymoron. We have so long thought in terms of a mind/heart dichotomy, that to put the two words together sounds like a contradiction of terms. Much of Western thought has placed emotions and intellect in opposition. We speak of judgment or reason being clouded by or warped by emotions. Did not Freud teach us that we struggle with our conscious intellect to rationalize the powerful emotional forces which drive us? Emotions have been depicted as the wild horse which the mind (the rider) tries to tame. Much of our literature, philosophy, and psychology is the attempt to reconcile these presumed warring opposites.

> The very essence of literature is the war between emotion and intellect.
> — Isaac Bashevis Singer (1904-1991)

What then does it mean to talk of emotional intelligence?

There is another stream of Western thought very compatible with the notion of "emotional intelligence." Rather than placing emotion in opposition to intelligence, this stream of thought would place emotion as the ultimate basis for intelligent action. For centuries some philosophers have placed the heart (emotion) above mind as a more dependable guide for decision making and knowing:

> We know the truth, not only by the reason, but by the heart.
> — Blaise Pascal (1623-1662)

> It is only with the heart that one can see rightly; what is essential is invisible to the eye.
> — Antoine de Saint Exupéry (1900-1944)

The mind is not our ultimate resource in making life's decisions. The mind determines possibilities; certainty is a feeling: The mind can place a thousand paths before us, but only the heart can choose one.

What Is Emotional Intelligence?

There are contradictory definitions of emotional intelligence being proposed. According to Goleman (1995) there are five dimensions of emotional intelligence, see box: Five Dimensions of the Emotional Intelligence.

Viewed through the lens of multiple intelligences theory, the first three of these sets of skills are dimensions of intrapersonal intelligence; the latter two are aspects of interpersonal intelligence. To the extent that it is valid and useful to conceptualize emotional intelligence in terms of these five sets of skills, the concept demonstrates MI theory is but one of many possible conceptual frameworks for human intelligences. The advent of a crosscutting intelligence, emotional intelligence, indicates it is meaningful and useful to think in terms of other intelligences.

Within the field of emotional intelligence itself, there is debate over how best to conceptualize the topic. Some definitions of emotional intelligence are narrower than Goleman's; others are broader. Salovey and Mayer who did the original work on the concept take issue with the inclusion of motivation in the definition of emotional intelligence, proposing a more focused definition. They prefer motivation be considered a separate intelligence, motivational intelligence (Mayer and Geher, 1996). They propose the following definition of emotional intelligence:

> Ability to perceive emotions, to access emotions and generate emotions so as to assist thought, to understand emotions and emotional knowledge, and to reflectively regulate emotions so as to promote emotional and intellectual growth (Mayer and Salovey, 1997, p. 9).

Five Dimensions of the Emotional Intelligence

1. **Self-Knowledge**
   Awareness of one's own emotions

2. **Self-Control**
   Controlling ones own emotions

3. **Self-Motivation**
   Motivating oneself

4. **Empathy**
   Knowing the emotions of others

5. **Social Skills**
   Relationship skills

They point out that their definition captures the notion that intelligence is enhanced by the ability to understand and control emotions, and that one can think intelligently (as opposed to irrationally) about emotions, but they do not want to include in the definition such things as persistence and the ability to motivate oneself. Other broader definitions of emotional competence have been proposed. They include such things as awareness of the importance of the quality of emotional communication, and ability to feel the way one wants to feel. (See for example Saarni, 1997.)

All of the definitions of emotional intelligence place emotions and cognition on the same side rather than opposed to each other. There is a growing recognition that the ability to recognize and understand emotions in oneself and others as well as the ability to control and harness one's own emotions are all extremely important components of what it means to be smart. For us as teachers, it remains an academic question whether to carve out "motivational intelligence" as separate from "emotional intelligence" — we know all the skills which come under both those labels are crucial for academic, social, and life success.

Why Is Emotional Intelligence Important?

Goleman (1995) summarizes a variety of studies which indicate the inability of traditional IQ tests to predict school, career, and life success and the importance of emotional intelligence. He demonstrates that traditional IQ tests, with their narrow focus on a few types of cognitive skills, do not really tell us if someone will do well in school or life, or even if they will act smart or dumb.

Lack of emotional intelligence explains how someone so smart can do something so dumb.

The National Center for Clinical Infant Programs points out that the facts a child knows and even early ability to read are not as predictive of school success as are factors like self-assurance, impulse control, ability to seek help from teachers, and social skills (National Center, 1992). In study after study, IQ is not the critical determinant of academic and life success. For example, Goleman (1995) cites the following:

> IQ offers little to explain the different destinies of people with roughly equal promises, schooling, and opportunity. When ninety-five Harvard students from the classes of the 1940's — a time when people with a wider spread of IQ were at Ivy League schools than is presently the case — were followed into middle age, the men with the highest test scores in college were not particularly successful compared to their lower-scoring peers in terms of salary, produc-

tivity, or status in their field. Nor did they have the greatest life satisfaction, nor the most happiness with friendships, family, and romantic relations (Original Source: George Vaillant, 1977).

A similar follow-up in middle age was done with 450 boys, most sons of immigrants, two thirds from families on welfare, who grew up in Somerville, Massachusetts, at the time a "blighted slum" a few blocks from Harvard. A third had IQ's below 90. But again IQ had little relationship to how well they had done at work or in the rest of their lives; for instance, 7 percent of men with IQ's under 80 were unemployed for ten or more years, but so were 7 percent of men with IQ's over 100. To be sure, there was a general link (as there always is) between IQ and socioeconomic level at age forty-seven. But childhood abilities such as being able to handle frustrations, control emotions, and get on with other people made the greater difference (Original Source: Felsman & Vaillant, 1987).

The most extreme example of the discrepancy between emotional and cognitive intelligence provided by Goleman is the case of Jason H., a straight-A high school sophomore. He dreamed of going to Harvard. When his physics teacher gave him an 80 on a quiz, which Jason believed would destroy his chances of going to Harvard, Jason took a butcher knife to school and stabbed his teacher in the collarbone. Jason was found innocent by reason of temporary insanity, but his teacher stated, "I think he tried to completely do me in with the knife (Goleman, 1995. p. 33)." Jason went on to graduate from a private school with a 4.614 grade-point average, but never apologized to his teacher. Goleman asks the question: How can someone so smart do something so dumb? The answer: a person can have cognitive intelligence but lack emotional intelligence.

Emotional Intelligence: A Challenge for MI Theory

There is a difference in focus between the focus in MI theory and the focus in the field of emotional intelligence. MI theory emphasizes the cognitive aspects of the interpersonal and intrapersonal intelligence — having an accurate picture of oneself and an accurate social map are core to the intrapersonal and interpersonal intelligences in MI theory. In contrast, the work in the field of emotional intelligence, as the term would suggest, focuses primarily on ability to know, control, and channel emotions. Gardner's work is more cognitive; the work in the field of emotional intelligences broadens the concept of intelligence to include not just knowledge of emotions in oneself and others, but ability to deal effectively with those feelings as well.

For us as educators, the field of emotional intelligences is broadening our concept of intelligences to include some of the most vital skills our students must know if they are to succeed. It points out that our curriculum, if it is to fully prepare students, must include things once thought to be topics only for research psychologists. Let's examine the importance of but one of the many skills of emotional intelligence: Delay of gratification.

Walter Mischel of Stanford designed the now famous marshmallow experiment. Four-year-old children were put to a simple test of their ability to control their impulses and delay gratification: They were taken into a room with a one-way mirror and shown a marshmallow. They were told the experimenter had to leave and that they could have the marshmallow right away, but if they waited for the experimenter to return from an errand, they could have two marshmallows. The one marshmallow was left on a table in front of them. Some children grabbed the available marshmallow within seconds of the experimenter leaving. Others waited up to twenty minutes for the experimenter to return. In a follow-up study (Shoda, Mischel, & Peake, 1990), the children of the original experiment were tested at 18 years of age. Comparisons were made between the third of the children who most quickly grabbed the marshmallow (the "impulsive") and the third who delayed gratification the longest in order to receive the enhanced reward ("impulse controlled").

As adolescents the impulse controlled preschoolers were rated as more socially competent in a variety of ways including personal effectiveness, self-assertiveness, and ability to cope with frustration. They worked better under pressure, less often gave up when faced with difficulties, were self-reliant and confident, trustworthy and

Gobbling a marshmallow now or waiting in order to obtain two later, at four years of age is twice as good a predicator of later SAT scores than is IQ at that age.

dependable, and took initiative and were more likely to delay gratification in pursuit of goals. Those who as preschoolers did not delay gratification, were more often stubborn and indecisive, easily upset by frustrations, lower in self-image, overwhelmed more easily by stress, prone to jealousy and envy, overreacted to irritations, had a sharp temper, and provoked arguments and fights. They showed less ability to delay gratification.

The impulsive children were poorer students. Those who delayed gratification were rated as more academically competent. They were better able to put their ideas into words, to use and respond to reason, to concentrate, to be eager to learn, and to create and follow through on plans. Hard evidence for the profound differences between the impulsive and impulse controlled comes from their SAT tests. The third of the children who were most impulsive at four years of age, scored 524 verbal and 528 math, compared to the impulse controlled who scored 610 verbal and 652 math! This astounding 210 point total score difference on the SAT was predicted on the basis of a single observation at four years of age! The 210 point difference is as large as the average differences between that of economically advantaged versus poor children, and is larger than the difference between children from families with graduate degrees versus children whose parents did not finish high school! Gobbling a marshmallow now or waiting in order to obtain two later, at four years of age is twice as good a predicator of later SAT scores than is IQ at that age. Poor impulse control is also a better predictor of later delinquency than is IQ (Block, 1995).

Impulse control is but one of the five dimensions of emotional intelligence. It provides a good example of the intertwining of interpersonal and intrapersonal intelligences: a child who is poor in impulse control has not developed sufficient knowledge and skills with internal states, but in turn will not be as skilled socially. If we cannot control our emotions, our emotions drive rather than inform our behavior. We will then act out our emotions, rather than reflect on them. As a result we will have less self-knowledge (intrapersonal intelligence), but also will be far less effective socially (interpersonal intelligence). Understanding and ability to control emotions leads to social skills (talking through a conflict rather than hitting) as well as life success in many domains (studying for the test or planning the project, rather than following one's impulses).

Emotional intelligence provides an excellent example of why it is meaningful to think in terms of other intelligences. It partially explains the intertwining of interpersonal and intrapersonal intelligences, and provides us insights not available if we think only in terms of separate intelligences.

Other Intelligences: Implications for Educators

Yes, there are other intelligences. Intelligences such as the culinary, craft, motivational, attentional, mechanical, existential, and emotional intelligences cannot and should not be reduced to mere combinations of the eight intelligences. There are many ways to be smart. All the ways for humans to be intelligent do not fit neatly into one or another of the eight categories. There are many possibilities for conceptualizing human intelligences in ways other than the eight posited by MI theory, as illustrated by emotional intelligence. Emotional intelligence is crosscutting intelligence, but emphasizes skills not included in MI theory's description of interpersonal and intrapersonal intelligences.

The call to split motivational intelligence from emotional intelligence is another example of a call to cut the human intelligence pie yet another way. Future brain and experimental research will reveal discrete attentional intelligences. Dividing human intelligence into only eight neat categories cannot tell the whole story.

That there are other valid ways to conceptualize human intelligence, other intelligences, has profound implication for education. The most important implication for educators is that we cannot limit our thinking to just eight intelligences. Unless we teach for the development of the full range of intelligences, and design curriculum and instruction to teach with the full range of intelligences, we cannot fully realize our mission as educators in a democracy. Our mission is to maximize the potential of all individuals. To choose some intelligences over others is to choose the development of fewer rather than more skills, less rather than more effective teaching, and preferential treatment of some students over others. Education in a democracy demands we examine and teach with and for all intelligences — even those not included in MI theory.

Well, then, do we abandon MI theory because there are other intelligences and other ways to conceptualize intelligence? Not at all. MI theory is a living, evolving theory. The eight intelligences are not etched in stone; we should not take them as limits, but as lamp posts. MI theory is showing us that there are many ways to be smart. Only recently an eighth intelligence was declared, the naturalist. What happened when educators focused on this additional way to be smart is a shining example of the power of recognizing an ad-

ditional human intelligence. When the naturalist was declared, there was a flurry of activity — teachers began scrambling for instructional strategies which match the naturalist intelligences and ways to develop that intelligence, workshops at national conferences sprang up as did new publications dedicated just to that intelligence (See, Roth, 1998). Curriculum and instruction is enriched to the extent we recognize each additional way to be smart.

There are other intelligences. All the ways for humans to be intelligent do not fit neatly into one or another of the eight categories. There are many other possibilities for conceptualizing human intelligences than the eight posited by MI theory.

We take a pragmatic stance: MI theory is moving us in the right direction, motivating us to reexamine and broaden our curriculum and instruction. It provides a very useful category system, but it is not the only category system possible. As educators we would do well to take the broad categories of intelligences provided by MI theory as suggestive, knowing there are other ways to categorize human intelligences, and knowing the eight categories cannot capture all the ways humans are smart.

Yes, we should match, stretch, and celebrate the eight intelligences, but we should not limit ourselves to only eight intelligences. We should match, stretch, and celebrate all the ways our students are smart. Because some students are gifted in humor, for example, our instruction should teach in ways which engages humor and develops the comedian in every student (along with knowledge of when it is and is not appropriate to exercise that intelligence!). Humor, like all of the intelligences can be a window onto the curriculum, curriculum in itself, and a window onto oneself. If we recognize humor as an intelligence, we are more likely to present curriculum through humor and develop in our students the ability to appreciate and create humor. To the extent we recognize that additional intelligence, our curriculum and instruction is further enriched. Similarly, to the extent we recognize a culinary intelligence, mechanical intelligence, craft intelligences, existential intelligence, emotional intelligences, and attentional intelligences, we further broaden and enrich our curriculum and instruction and help students more fully understand themselves and others.

MI theory is moving us in the right direction, motivating us to reexamine and broaden our curriculum and instruction. It provides a very useful category system, but it is not the only category system possible.

Focus on the various facets of each intelligence has similar benefits for our students. For example, we cannot develop the logical/mathematical intelligence as a whole, but we can develop instructional strategies to match and attempt to stretch only one facet of any intelligence at a time. Matching and stretching student's deductive thinking skills does not necessarily improve their inductive thinking skills. As we recognize and focus on any one facet of an intelligence, our curriculum and instruction is enriched. As we recognize the core importance of organizational skills, for example, we are more likely to have students organize their writing, sort objects, develop organizational frames, prioritize outcomes, organize academic content in various ways and even develop their personal organizational skills. In the process our students benefit. Although organizational skills might be thought of as a manifestation of the logical/mathematical intelligence, it is only when we recognize organizational skills as important in their own right that we begin to develop new instructional strategies and curriculum which benefit students. Developing organizational skills, however, does not fully develop inductive skills, analytic skills, patterning skills, and scores of other facets of the logical/mathematical intelligence. For our students to develop their full potential we need to explore curriculum instruction which matches, stretches, and celebrates all facets of all intelligences.

While we recognize the multiplicity of ways to be smart, we recognize too the need for practical, usable guideposts in this process of aligning curriculum and instruction with the range of intelligences. As guideposts the eight intelligences provided by MI theory are extremely useful. In this book, we adhere to MI theory's present eight intelligences. Exploring what it means to match, stretch, and celebrate just those eight intelligences is a daunting task! Our hope, though, is that with time teachers as individuals and education as a field will outgrow the notion of eight intelligences, embracing instead curriculum and instruction which matches, stretches, and celebrates a multiplicity of ways to be smart.

Our examination of intelligences beyond the eight named in MI theory leads us to conclude that our students are not smart in eight ways — they are smart in many ways. It is to that topic, then, that we now turn: What does it means to say our students are smart in many ways?

References

American Psychiatric Association. *Diagnostic and Statistical Manual of Mental Disorders, 3rd Rev. Ed. (DSM-III-R).* Washington, DC: American Psychiatric Association, 1987.

Bergman, P. & Escalona, S. *Unusual sensitivities in very young children.* The Psychoanalytic Study of the Child, 1949, *3*, 333-352.

Block, J. *On the relation between IQ, impulsivity and delinquency.* **Journal of Abnormal Psychology**, 1995, 104.

Calvin, W. H. *How Brains Think. Evolving Intelligence, Then and Now.* New York: HarperCollins, 1996.

Diamonstein, B. *Handmade in America. Conversations with 14 Craftmasters.* New York: Harry N. Abrams, Inc., 1995.

Felsman, J. K. & Vaillant, G. E. *Resilient children as adults: a 40-year study.* In E. J. Anderson and B. J. Cohler, eds., The invulnerable child. New York: Guilford Press, 1987.

Gardner, H. *Keynote Address. Is Musical Intelligence Special?* In Verna Brummett, editor. Ithaca Conference '96: Music as Intelligence. A Sourcebook. Ithaca, New York: Ithaca College, 1997.

Gardner, H. *Multiple Intelligences. The Theory in Practice.* New York: Basic Books, 1993.

Goleman, D. *Emotional Intelligence.* New York: Bantam Books, 1995.

Horwitz, W. A., Deming, W. E., and Winter, R. F. *A further account of the idiot savants: experts with the calendar.* American Journal of Psychiatry, 1969, *126*, 160-163.

Mayer, and Geher, G. *Emotional intelligence and the Identification of Emotion.* **Intelligence**, 1996, **22**, 89-113.

Mayer, J. D. & Salovey, P. *What Is Emotional Intelligence?* In P. Salovey & D. J. Sluyter, Emotional development and emotional intelligence: Educational Implications. New York: Basic Books, 1997.

National Center for Clinical Infant Programs. *Head Start: The emotional foundations of school readiness.* Arlington, VA: National Center for Clinical Infant Programs, 1992.

Roth, K. *The Naturalist Intelligence. An Introduction to Gardner's Eighth Intelligence.* Arlington Heights, IL.: Skylight Publishing, 1998.

Saarni, C. *Emotional competence and self-regulation in childhood.* In P. Salovey & D. J. Sluyter, *Emotional development and emotional intelligence: Educational Implications.* New York: Basic Books, 1997.

Salovey, P. & Mayer, J. D. *Emotional Intelligence.* Imagination, Cognition and Personality, 1990, **9**, 185-211.

Shoda, Y., Mischel, W. & Peake, P. K. *Predicting adolescent cognitive and self-regulatory competencies from preschool delay of gratification.* **Developmental Psychology**, 1990, **26(6)**, 978-986.

Treffert, D. A. *Extraordinary people. Understanding "Idiot Savants."* New York: Harper & Row, 1989.

Vaillant, G. *Adaptation to life.* Boston: Little, Brown, 1977.

Smart in Many Ways

MI theory is not a "type theory" for determining one intelligence that fits. It is a theory of cognitive functioning, and it proposes that each person has capacities in all seven intelligences. Of course, the seven intelligences function together in ways unique to each person (Armstrong, 1994, p. 11).

The theory of multiple intelligences has taken us a long way toward broadening our concept of intelligence. We no longer ask whether or not a student is smart, but how the student is smart. The answer, it turns out, is that every student is smart in many ways.

We no longer ask whether or not a student is smart, but how the student is smart. The answer, it turns out, is that every student is smart in many ways.

There are four different meanings for the phrase "smart in many ways." First, while each of us has all of the multiple intelligences, our profiles of strengths differ. No one is just body smart or just people smart — we are all smart in many ways. Second, there are more than eight ways to be smart — human intelligence is complex, and there are many ways to be smart. Third, some kinds of smartness seem to cross the boundaries of the eight intelligences — they express themselves naturally in more than one way. Fourth, there are some individuals who show extraordinary development of several or even all of the intelligences — they are exceptionally smart in many ways.

We All Have All the Intelligences

It is important that we do not attempt to pigeonhole ourselves or our students. With the popularity of the theory of multiple intelligences has come a popularity of phrases like, "he is body smart" and "she is musical/rhythmic." While a person may have developed their bodily/kinesthetic intelligence more than any other, this tells us nothing about the development of their other intelligences. There is not a limited amount of "smartness" which flows either into one or another intelligence. Being smart in one intelligence in no way implies poor development of another.

This obvious point bears emphasizing because it is an antidote against labeling ourselves or others in terms of any one intelligence. For teachers to think of a student as bodily/kinesthetically smart or musically/ rhythmically smart prevents appreciation of the whole student and the student's potential to grow in all of the intelligences. Worse, for a student to think of themselves as particularly strong in any one intelligence can be an excuse for not developing the other intelligences. The phrase "smart in many ways" is a reminder that we can all develop each of our intelligences more.

As I (Spencer) am writing this, I am sitting in an attic room in The Camel Crossing, a bed and breakfast in Warrensburg, Missouri, a few blocks from Central Missouri State University. After Ed, the innkeeper, got me settled, I began to read some of the many framed sayings on the highly decorated walls. As I read a framed sixteenth century schoolbook prayer, I realized the idea of teaching students to be smart in many ways has been with us for centuries. The text is as follows:

Sixteenth-Century Primer

*God be in my head
and in my understanding;
God be in my mind and in my thinking;
God be in my eyes and in my seeing;
God be in my tongue and in my speaking;
God be in my heart and in my loving;
God be in my hands and in my doing;
God be in my ways and
in my walking.*

More Than Eight Ways to Be Smart

As we have seen by looking at emotional, existential, culinary, mechanical, and other intelligences, there are more than eight ways to be smart. It is possible to come up with a variety of category systems for human intelligences. Emotional intelligence cuts across interpersonal and intrapersonal, but has integrity as an intelligence on its own. In the same way, mechanical intelligence draws on, but cannot be reduced to logical, bodily/kinesthetic, and visual/spatial skills. There is added meaning in describing someone as high in mechanical intelligence. Two individuals can be equally skilled on measures of logic, bodily/kinesthetic intelligence, and visual/ spatial skills, but one is attracted to and skilled with mechanical stimuli of all sorts and the other has no interest in that type of stimuli.

Not only is it possible to identify additional intelligences and intelligences which cut across the eight specified in MI theory, it is possible as well to distinguish independent intelligences within each of the eight MI categories. Let's take the visual/spatial intelligence as an example: There are a host of skills related to sense of direction which have little or no correlation with sensitivity to and skill in mixing and matching colors in artful ways. And knowing someone's skill with sense of direction and skill with colors does not tell us anything about their ability to close their eyes and visualize and recall from memory an array of objects they have just seen. Visual recall, skill with color, and sense of direction are but three of many sets of skills within the visual/spatial intelligence; many more can be identified. Whether we call them facets, subintelligences, skills, dimensions, or even intelligences, it is important we recognized that within each of the broad categories called intelligences in MI theory, there are many discrete skills, many of which are independent of each other. There is a multiplicity of intelligences — we are smart in many ways.

Why make a relatively workable concept like multiple intelligences so complex by recognizing there really are a multiplicity of intelligences? Because only when we recognize the full range of human intelligences will we be sensitive to the unique strengths of each individual and foster full development of each individual. Our students are smart in many ways, and when we recognize that, we create more bridges

Our students are smart in many ways, and when we recognize that, we create more bridges to the curriculum and more opportunities to develop the whole student.

to the curriculum and more opportunities to develop the whole student.

Intelligences Cross MI Boundaries

Most of us know someone who is rhythmic. That person moves with rhythm, talks with rhythm, and enjoys or creates poetry and song with rhythm. Describing that person as "rhythmic" tells us more about them than by saying the person is strong in certain aspects of the bodily/kinesthetic, musical/rhythmic, and verbal/linguistic intelligences.

Similarly, we have all encountered students who are exceptionally observant. They are observant of others — what others wear and how they speak and move, of natural phenomena, of their visual surroundings, and of relations and connections among things. They pick up on motivation of others as well as why things work. We understand those students better by noting that they are exceptionally observant than by saying they are strong in certain aspects of the bodily/kinesthetic, verbal/linguistic, visual/spatial, interpersonal/social, and logical/mathematical intelligences.

Most of us as teachers have been blessed (some would use a different word) by yet another type of child: the mimic. This child seems to carry a recorder in his/her brain. But the recorder does not record just sound, or just body movements, or just facial expressions; she seems to be able to reproduce everything. She is able to mimic not just people, but animals, and even inanimate objects — how they move, how they talk, and the feelings they have. To say that the student is a great mimic seems to capture her intelligence better than to say she is exceptional in certain aspects of the bodily/kinesthetic, interpersonal, visual/spatial, and verbal/linguistic intelligences. We could multiply these examples. Some types of intelligence simply cross the MI boundaries.

Interestingly, quite a few of the intelligences seem to operate in pairs more often than one would expect by chance. Some intelligences seem to go together. There are many of these pairs. To name a few:

Interpersonal & Intrapersonal

Gardner (1983) originally noted the connection between these two intelligences in *Frames of Mind*, calling them the personal intelligences. Goleman (1995) makes the case for an Emotional Intelligence which cuts across the interpersonal and intrapersonal domains. People and animals who have the connections to their amygdala severed lose the ability to recognize not just their own feelings, but the feelings of others. Psychotherapists skilled in interpreting dreams also do relationship therapy; understanding feelings in depth helps understand interpersonal relations. We can hardly understand a feeling in someone else if we have never experienced it.

Bodily/Kinesthetic & Musical/Rhythmic

It seems to be more than a mere coincidence that musicians tap their feet as they play, we sway our bodies and are moved to dance to music, and that good dancers more than the rest of us can sing the words to the songs as they dance, and good sing-

ers move their whole bodies to express their song. We almost never see a good singer motionless while she or he sings.

Naturalists & Logical/Mathematical

Darwin did not make his enormous contributions to understanding animals and humans by simply observing nature; he relentlessly applied logic to figure out the relations among variables. The child who collects and sorts butterflies is more likely to collect and sort coins than is the average child. Collecting and sorting involves logic, but it seems to go hand-in-hand with the naturalist intelligence. It is hard to imagine someone very attracted to plants who is not also concerned with distinguishing variations among species, and creating a mental category system. Environmentalists focus on relations among species; we cannot destroy one part of an ecosystem without (sometimes disastrous) impact on all parts of the system. The naturalist intuitively understands the logic of nature. In addition to logical thinking, mathematics is a prerequisite for much of modern science.

Naturalist & Interpersonal

The naturalist uses acute observation skills to gain insights into animals and plants. These same skills, however, do not stop at the boundaries of nonhuman animals; often they are turned toward people. After all, aren't people animals? Monty Roberts is a fine example. Roberts gained fuller understanding of horses than any human before him, revolutionizing our understanding of horses. Throughout his autobiography, Roberts describes people in great detail, using the same keen observational skills he applied to the understanding of animals. For example, in describing

Horseman, an English butler, Roberts writes:

> Horseman was probably no more than sixty, but he looked eighty-five. Stooped and gray, he had a sad, droopy face with big watery eyes. He was dressed properly, but his collars and cuffs had seen a lot of wear. His method was to move quickly, wobbling on his feet as if his joints were suspect. With each step he mumbled, and occasionally the mumbles got louder and took on a strangled quality (Roberts, 1996, Pp. 198-199).

As we read Robert's description of Horseman (and many other characters in his book), we cannot help but see the link between the naturalist and interpersonal intelligences. In this light, it is a bit less mysterious that Roberts was foster father to 47 children, and would immediately pick up on subtle interpersonal cues, sometimes leading to spontaneous therapy.

Naturalist & Bodily/Kinesthetic

Although animals can be taught to respond to and even use forms of human speech, the natural way for us to understand them is in the way they communicate with each other — through nonverbal facial expressions, gestures, and body movement. A person more "into" bodily/kinesthetic signs and symbols is more likely to "read" animals correctly. Monty Roberts provides an excellent example. A star athlete since the age of three, it was natural for Roberts to respond to nonverbal communication signals in animals.

> I learned that in the equine universe, every degree of a horse's movement has a reason. Nothing is trivial, nothing is to be dismissed…. I would learn, much later, while starting horses in a round pen, a rich code of signs and subsigns. Keeping my mouth closed invited the horse's discomfort, opening it slightly was fine. Opening a fist on the side of my body away from the horse drew him in, while opening a fist close to him sent him away. Fingers open stirred one response, fingers closed another. Hands above my head with fingers splayed provoked true panic (perhaps it triggers pri-

mordial memories of cat claws). Whether I am moving, standing still, facing the horse, or away: all this matters as the horse reads my body language and I read his. I can now enumerate about one hundred or more signs the horse will respond to, and the vocabulary is still growing.

> The key ingredient in the equine language is the positioning of the body and its direction of travel…. (Roberts, 1996, p. 23).

The examples of intelligences which go hand in hand can be multiplied:

Logical/Mathematical & Verbal/Linguistic

Much of what is written and spoken is an expression of logic; syllogisms are most often expressed in sentences. There is an internal logic to a good poem, essay, or debate.

Bodily/Kinesthetic & Visual/Spatial

We throw a spear and throw a pot. Great sculptors and great painters are talented not just with their eyes, but with their hands.

Musical/Rhythmic & Visual Spatial

Can it be a mere coincidence that we speak of "The Arts," and that the person deeply moved by a painting is more likely than not to be deeply moved by a symphony? Vincent van Gogh exquisitely expressed this connection when he made the statement: "Whether I really sang a lullaby in colors, I leave to the critics."

What are we as educators to make of these connections? Perhaps little. But knowing the relations among intelligences cannot but help us in our understanding of our pupils. We would do well to be sensitive to the links. Our job is not to develop intelligences so much as to foster development of whole pupils. And if we are alert to the many ways in which an intelligence can express itself and the links among the intelligences, we are more likely to see the whole student, not just separate skills.

For those of you who would like to muse over the connections among the intelligences in far more depth, see Appendix A: Categories of Intelligences.

Smart Across the Intelligences

In the process of writing this book, while we were reviewing the biographies of famous people to look for exceptional development of each of the intelligences, we were struck by the number of people who have shown extraordinary development in several or even most of the intelligences. Looking for a model of linguistic intelligence, we moved in our library to the poetry section. Noticing Shel Silverstein's book, *Where the Sidewalk Ends*, we pulled it down. As we did, we hesitated. He did both the poetry *and* the drawings for the book. Should we list Shel Silverstein as a model of verbal/linguistic intelligence or as a model of visual/spatial intelligence? As we were about to write down Winston Churchill's name as a great orator, we again took pause. Churchill was an orator, yes, but he was also an extraordinary leader of others, and a prize-winning painter. Lewis Carroll wrote *Alice in Wonderland*, but was a fine mathematician and logician. Oprah Winfrey has extraordinary interpersonal skills, exceptional verbal/lin-

guistic skills, and award winning acting skills as well.

The lives of great athletes put to rest the stereotype of the dumb jock. Pele, the single most watched athlete in the world, scores at a genius level on traditional IQ tests. He claims that honing his skills in geometry and chess have been especially helpful in developing his soccer game (Arnold, 1992; Krull, 1997)!

We know of Roberto Clemente, the Puerto Rican wonder boy who started his baseball career playing with a stick and rags, but who went on to become the most valuable player in the 1971 world series. Perhaps we read of his extraordinary charitable contributions — building San Juan Sports City, a 600 acre sports complex for poor kids to have a chance to learn with real equipment and real coaches. But it is important to note Clemente loved to read, taught himself how to play the electric organ, and in his spare time loved to make ceramic lamps!

Our job is not to develop intelligences so much as to foster development of whole people. And if we are alert to the many ways in which an intelligence can express itself and the links among the intelligences, we are more likely to see the whole student, not just separate skills.

Red Grange is remembered for his electrifying feats on the football field: In 1924 he scored four touchdowns in the first twelve minutes of a game against the undefeated Michigan Wolverines. In high school he was a star in football, basketball, baseball, and track. But, Grange showed a wide range of exceptional talents, including: public speaker, author, actor, mechanic,

Smart In Many Ways

If intelligences are relatively independent, why are intelligent people so often intelligent in many ways?

Aristotle	384-322 B.C.	Philosopher, Logician, Scientist, Author
Cicero	106-43 B.C.	Historian, Poet, Orator, Lawyer, Legislator, Governor, Judge
Marcus Aurelius Antoninus	83-30 B.C.	Emperor, Author, Philosopher, Philanthropist
Leonardo da Vinci	1452-1519	Painter, Sculptor, Architect, Engineer, Scientist
Michelangelo Buonarroti	1475-1564	Sculptor, Painter, Architect, Poet
Francis Bacon	1561-1626	Scientist, Lawyer, Author, Philosopher
Ben Franklin	1706-1790	Author, Philosopher, Diplomat, Inventor, Scientist
Thomas Jefferson	1743-1826	Scientist, Inventor, Architect, Musician, Philosopher, Statesman, Author
Johann Wolfgang Von Goethe	1749-1832	Poet, Dramatist, Philosopher, Scientist
Winston Churchill	1874-1965	Soldier, Correspondent, Orator, Author, Prime Minister, Painter
Albert Schweitzer	1875-1965	Musician, Philosopher, Physician, Minister, Author
Albert Einstein	1879-1955	Scientist, Author, Ethicist
R. Buckminister Fuller	1895-1983	Inventor, Scientist, Architect, Philosopher, Poet, Educator
Red Grange	1903-1991	Athlete, Mechanic, Actor, Speaker, Author, Architect, Naturalist
Yousuf Karsh	1908-	Photographer, Author, Orator, Philanthropist
Hugh Downs	1921-	Television Personality, Author, Navigator, Philosopher, Composer, Scientist, Race Car Driver
Monty Roberts	1935-	Naturalist, Athlete, Entrepreneur, Author, Lecturer, Teacher, Researcher, Inventor, Foster Parent, Therapist

and designer of a remarkable estate where he personally tended the gardens and befriended the wildlife he loved, including alligators, quail, rabbits, and cranes. He designed a lagoon so he could be closer to nature and beauty (Grange, 1993)!

Monty Roberts is world famous for having learned to communicate with horses. He knows their language so well that he can tame and ride a wild horse within a half hour — without using force. He extended his research into animal-human communication, taming deer in the wild. But Monty Roberts' intelligence expresses itself in many ways; besides being a naturalist he is an author, lecturer, researcher, entrepreneur, inventor, and athlete. As a child he was a film extra and stunt rider. As a youngster he devised and executed money-making plans that awed adults. As a teen and young man he won world titles in numerous equestrian events, was a champ football player, wrestler, and body builder. As a researcher he discovered the proper angle at which to position horses for travel in trailers. He invented a protective blanket that has saved the career of skittish race horses. His extraordinary interpersonal skills have enabled him to be a successful foster parent to dozens of disturbed children, and even to offer therapy to those in abusive relations (Roberts, 1996).

It is almost as if some individuals are bursting at the seams to express the range of their intelligences. "Babe" Didrikson Zaharias at age 21 tried out for the Olympics. In a three hours span she won five events, tied another, and finished fourth in another. Her performance "as a team of one" beat the second place team — which consisted of twenty-two women! But her Olympic gold medals do not tell the whole story. She was a musician, typed a hundred words a minute, won first place at the Texas State Fair in sewing by creating an original dress design, was extraordinary at crossword puzzles, ballroom dancing, and cooking (Krull, 1997)! Time and again, what stands out in the biographies of great individuals is their contributions in many domains.

> **To look at individuals as a collection of semiautonomous intelligences demeans the person. It is to see the separate branches, but miss that they are all part of one tree. There is a self pushing for expression, a self which transcends any one intelligence.**

Is remarkable performance across the intelligences evidence that intelligence is something far beyond the mere semiautonomous action of discrete parts of the brain? One must be struck by the obvious parallel between the poems and the drawings of Shel Silverstein. They both express the same lighthearted wit. The intelligences do not function as an end in themselves, they function in service of a self struggling to express itself. Shel Silverstein's poems and drawings do not simply compliment each other; they are both expressions of one deeper intelligence — oneself. This does not mean there is only one thing called smart — there are many ways to be smart. For us to gain a deep understanding of our students, however, we must look not just at what they do within an intelligence, but what they do across them.

To look at individuals as a collection of semiautonomous intelligences demeans the person. It is to see the separate branches, but miss that they are all part of one tree. There is a self pushing for expression, a self which transcends any one intelligence. The intelligences are to some extent voices which give expression to a deeper self. Making contact with that deeper self in ourselves and in our students provides the climate for growth. The person harnesses any and all intelligences to express him or herself in every way possible. How we walk, how we dress, how we move, the car we choose, the way we drive it, the kinds of music and movies we are attracted to, our handwriting, the friends we choose, the kind of art we create and with which we decorate our homes, and the philosophy of life we create for ourselves are all related. Our intelligences do not operate in isolation, they serve and are an expression of one self.

In this context, to say we are smart in many ways takes on a different meaning: We express ourselves, our essence, through all of the intelligences. As a clinical psychologist, while offering therapy it became obvious to Spencer (as it did to every other clinical psychologist with whom he worked), that as a person begins to be liberated through the therapy process, to emerge, changes occur simultaneously on many dimensions. The person's social skills and relations improve, his work improves, he seeks more exercise, he moves with more poise and dignity, he dresses better, and he be-

when we feel accepted by ourselves and others, all the intelligences function at a higher level. Happiness is associated with expression of all our intelligences more freely and creatively — not just one intelligence, but all. We do not liberate one intelligence in isolation; we liberate an underlying self which is expressed through all available avenues. We are smart in many ways.

There is yet another way in which we are smart in many ways. When we learn a skill, there is a yearning to transfer it across intelligences. When we learn about primary colors and color mixing, we are driven to ask if there are primary emotions, and if there are rules for predicting what happens when we mix (experience) two emotions at once. When we learn about parsimony in math proofs, we ask ourselves if we can write with fewer words. Gothic architecture was but one expression of a world view which influenced art, music, dress, and social relations. When enlightenment hit Europe, it did not influence the expression of one or another intelligence, but all of them. This transfer occurs at many levels. When we obtain an enhanced sense of rhythm it influences not just our music, but our art, speech, and even our negotiations. See box: We Are Smart in Many Ways on page 6.10.

> ## Perfection is achieved, not when there is nothing left to add, but when there is nothing left to take away.
> ### — Antoine de St. Exupéry (1900-1944)

comes more sensitive to the music, art, plants, and animals in his environment. Normally the intelligences do not grow or get blocked independently. When we are depressed, they all shut down together;

If a sense of rhythm cuts across all of the intelligences and is essential to each of them, the development of the intelligences is not entirely independent. But rhythm is not unique; there are many crosscutting skills such as sense of parsimony, proportion, identification of patterns and relations, relation of parts to whole, focus, and analogical thinking. The existence of these crosscutting skills knits the intelligences.

We Are Smart in Many Ways: Rhythm Across the Intelligences

When we look up "Rhythm" in the *American Heritage Dictionary* we find (bold added):

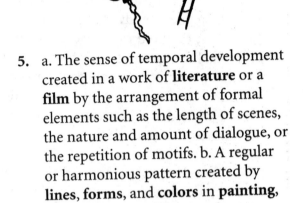

Rhythm n.

1. **Movement** or variation characterized by the regular recurrence or alternation of different quantities or conditions: the rhythm of the tides.
2. The patterned, recurring alternations of contrasting elements of sound or **speech.**
3. **Music.** a. A regular pattern formed by a series of notes of differing duration and stress. b. A specific kind of such a pattern: a waltz rhythm. c. A group of instruments supplying the rhythm in a band. "Rhythm was described by Schopenhauer as melody deprived of its pitch" (Edith Sitwell).
4. a. The pattern or flow of sound created by the arrangement of stressed and unstressed syllables in accentual **verse** or of long and short syllables in quantitative verse. b. The similar but less formal sequence of sounds in **prose.** c. A specific kind of metrical pattern or flow: iambic rhythm.
5. a. The sense of temporal development created in a work of **literature** or a **film** by the arrangement of formal elements such as the length of scenes, the nature and amount of dialogue, or the repetition of motifs. b. A regular or harmonious pattern created by **lines, forms,** and **colors** in **painting, sculpture,** and other **visual arts.**
6. The pattern of development produced in a **literary** or **dramatic work** by repetition of elements such as **words, phrases,** incidents, themes, **images,** and **symbols.**
7. Procedure or routine characterized by regularly recurring elements, activities, or factors: the rhythm of **civilization;** the rhythm of the lengthy **negotiations.**

If we are to fulfill our mission as educators, we must teach students to be smart not just within intelligences, but across the intelligences.

Every intelligent behavior is really an expression of all the intelligences. As we interact, we use all our intelligences — not just an isolated interpersonal intelligence.

See box: Encoding and Decoding Interpersonal Information.

What does all this mean? It indicates that while the intelligences are to some extent located in different parts of the brain and have evolved to deal with different kinds of stimuli, they cannot be understood fully in isolation. Students who delayed gratification at four years of age still delayed

Encoding and Decoding Interpersonal Information

All of the intelligences combine to create what we observe as interpersonal intelligence. The intelligences, like the neurons of the brain, function as a cooperative community. Interpersonal skills are a function of all the intelligences, all the parts of the brain interacting.

▼ **As we attempt to remember a name…**
We use a rhyme (musical/rhythmical).

▼ **As we try to decode the feelings of others…**
We make facial expressions like those of the other (bodily/kinesthetic).

▼ **As we try to lead a group toward consensus…**
We analyze the arguments of the members, creating a mental Venn Diagram hoping to find things in the center (visual/spatial).

▼ **As we try to understand another person's perspective…**
We mentally get inside them, looking out through their eyes, trying to see what they see (visual/spatial).

▼ **As we try to win a card game…**
We try to figure what our opponent will think if we discard a certain card, playing a mental game of "If…Then" (logical/mathematical).

gratification twelve years later and they used that intelligence to study for both their math and their language arts exams (Shoda, Mischel, & Peake, 1990). They showed superior performance in **both** math and language arts. Their smarts, delaying gratification, applied across the intelligences — as do many kinds of smarts.

Let's take the drive for parsimony as one example. It cuts across the intelligences. It would be foolish (and unparsimonious) to think that the separate disciplines somehow independently evolved to value parsimony. Why is it that we value essays and songs without the wasted word, geometry proofs and ballets which involve no extra steps, drawings and poems which express the most with the fewest lines, and scientific hypotheses which explain phenomena in terms of the fewest basic principles? Isn't it more parsimonious to think there is one intelligence pushing for parsimony than many?

Does this mean there is but one way to be smart? No. But it does indicate the various smarts serve one master. When we come to appreciate parsimony, we appreciate it across domains. In the same way, appreciation of honesty, compassion, expression of truth and beauty, self-expression, ability to break prior sets, creative synthesis, detailed analysis, wit, and countless other forms of intelligence do not halt at the borders of any one intelligence. Those qualities cut across the intelligences.

The whole is more than the sum of the parts. If we ever lose sight of the whole by studying the parts, we will fail to be teachers in the noblest sense. Our mission is to teach students, not intelligences. When we reach the student, not just this or that intelligence — that is when the student blossoms in many ways. Intelligence (solving problems, fashioning products of value) is not simply a product of this or that part of a person, but rather of the whole person. Discovering the separateness of the intelligences, we must not forget their unity. The brain is a community of interacting neurons. We will turn to that issue in depth in Chapters 20 and 22. For now, let's take a deeper look at the first of the three MI visions, matching the intelligences.

References

Armstrong, T. *Multiple Intelligences in the Classroom.* Alexandria, VA: Association for Supervision and Curriculum Development, 1994.

Arnold, C. *Pele: The King of Soccer.* New York: Franklin Watts, Inc., 1992.

Gardner, H. *Frames of Mind. The Theory of Multiple Intelligences.* New York: Basic Books, 1983.

Goleman, D. *Emotional Intelligence.* New York: Bantam Books, 1995.

Grange, R. *The Red Grange Story: An Autobiography.* Urbana, I: University of Illinois Press, 1993.

Krull, K. *Lives of the Athletes.* San Diego, CA: Harcourt Brace & Co., 1997.

Roberts, M. *The Man Who Listens to Horses.* New York: Random House, 1996.

Shoda, Y., Mischel, W. & Peake, P. K. *Predicting adolescent cognitive and self-regulatory competencies from preschool delay of gratification.* **Developmental Psychology**, 1990, **26(6)**, 978-986.

MI Instructional Strategies

MI theory suggests that no one set of teaching strategies will work best for all students at all times. All children have different proclivities in the seven intelligences, so any particular strategy is likely to be highly successful with one group of students and less successful with other groups (Armstrong, 1994, p. 65).

In Chapter 2: Three Visions for Education, we looked at Paula's Dance (Campbell, Campbell, & Dickinson, 1992). Paula was assessed learning disabled. By sixth grade, her spelling skills were approximately at the second grade level. Her teacher noticed that she moved with grace and asked her to create a "movement alphabet." She formed letters with her body and sequenced the letters of the alphabet into a dance. Paula went on to dance her name, words, and sentences. Her self-esteem and liking for school increased and in four months of kinesthetic learning, Paula overcame a four-year deficit!

By aligning "how" we teach with how all students learn, we give all students an equal opportunity to excel.

Paula's story is a compelling argument for using multiple intelligences instructional strategies. Paula's teacher had the insight to see one of Paula's strengths (the bodily/kinesthetic intelligence) and to use a teaching strategy (movement and dance) to help Paula learn the content (spelling). In an important way, all students are like Paula. Each student has his or her intelligence profile. Students strong in the verbal/linguistic intelligence often excel with traditional lectures, reading, and writing. But if we only lecture, we

Matching Intelligences

inadvertently advantage some of our students while others with different intelligence profiles slip through the cracks. By aligning "how" we teach with how all students learn, we give all students an equal opportunity to excel.

In each classroom, there is a great diversity of intelligences. Multiple intelligences makes major strides toward acknowledging diversity by breaking intelligences into eight separate categories. But the eight intelligences are just broad generalizations. It's nice to think that we have eight kinds of students; it sounds more or less manageable. It's not true, though. Each student is unique and has his or her unique profile. Just as there are differences across intelligences, there are also differences within each intelligence.

Let's stretch the Paula example a little further to make the case for individual differences. Seemingly similar students rated high in the bodily/kinesthetic intelligence may be very different upon closer inspection. A bodily/kinesthetic strategy that reaches one student will not suffice for all students considered body smart.

Imagine another student, Paul, whose strongest intelligence is the bodily/kinesthetic intelligence. Unlike Paula, however, Paul is not big on, or especially talented with, expressive movement. Paul is a "hands-on" learner. For learning to be motivating and meaningful, Paul must play with and manipulate concrete materials. Creating an alphabet dance may not interest Paul in the least. Working with magnetic letters and spelling out words and phrases with manipulatives may be absolutely fascinating for Paul. Hands-on exploration may be the teaching or learning

strategy most appropriate for Paul — and his ramp into the content (spelling).

Let's imagine another student, Pauline. Pauline is very athletic and is also considered high in the bodily/kinesthetic intelli-

> **It's nice to think that we have eight kinds of students; it sounds more or less manageable. It's not true, though. Each student is unique and has his or her unique profile. Just as there are differences across intelligences, there are also differences within each intelligence.**

gence. Sitting still at her desk is a struggle for Pauline. She needs action; she needs movement; she needs to get out of her seat and move around. Pauline displays no graceful or expressive movements like Paula. For Pauline, the most suitable teaching strategy may be one that harnesses her physical energy in a productive way. Maybe Pauline would be better served making a cheerleader chant for each spelling word, spelling out each letter with her body, "Give me an M, give me an I…."

What does this mean? If there are not eight but a multiplicity of ways to learn, is not our job as teachers impossible? Can we as teachers assess the intelligences of every student and tailor every learning experience to each students' strengths? Of course not. Perhaps if we had infinite planning time, we could individualize instruction to make the same curriculum more relevant and accessible to each student. But the daily reality is, there are simply too many students and not enough time.

So, how then do we reach all students with all intelligence profiles? The answer is simple. We use a wide range of MI instructional strategies in our classes. With each

MI strategy we *match* some students' intelligences. With a large array of strategies we can match all students' intelligences. With each strategy we make the curriculum attractive and engaging to students strong in the corresponding intelligence. We provide that student access to the curriculum through a natural medium.

But wait. We do more. As we engage each intelligence, we develop it for all students — those strong and those weak in the intelligence. By using MI strategies, students become smarter in many ways. With MI strategies we also *stretch* students' intelligences.

But wait. We do even more yet. As we use a range of instructional strategies, students get to know their strengths, their weaknesses, their likes, their dislikes. And they become aware of their unique intelligence profiles of their peers as well. Sure, sometimes their peers flounder. But sometimes they do unbelievably well. The more instructional strategies we use, the more opportunities we provide for each student to shine. Students learn to *celebrate* their own uniqueness and the diversity among them.

Yes, as we teach with a range of instructional strategies, we make all three MI visions a reality — matching, stretching, and celebrating MI. Through the MI strategies, we do miracles. Without losing a moment from our academic curriculum, we enrich that curriculum while reaching more students, developing their multiple intelligences, promoting self-esteem and fostering social acceptance and harmony.

In this chapter, we will explore a variety of practical multiple intelligences strategies to match, stretch, and celebrate MI. The instructional strategies are divided into three

categories: 1) Strategies for MI Lessons, 2) MI Learning Centers, and 3) MI Projects. Strategies for MI lessons are instructional tools we can integrate as part of any lesson to transform the lesson into an MI lesson. MI centers involve establishing locations in the classroom where students go to engage different intelligences. MI projects are events in which students integrate their multiple intelligences as they plan, prepare and present projects and products to the class. Note: This chapter is written as a reference chapter and is not intended to be read from start to finish. With that said, let's turn first to strategies that can transform any lesson into an MI lesson.

Strategies for MI Lessons

As a community of teachers and researchers, we have developed a wide range of instructional strategies that we may use to deliver our lessons. In this section we will present numerous strategies. One question you might ask: Why so many strategies?

Why So Many MI Strategies?
The answer is easy. Each strategy is particularly useful for achieving some educational objective. However, no single instructional strategy can achieve all educational objectives nor match, stretch, and celebrate all intelligences. To reach our diverse range of educational objectives and to match, stretch, and celebrate each intelligence, we need many different strategies.

Think about it this way: If there are at least eight intelligences we are striving to develop and each is comprised of many sub-intelligences, we need quite a few strategies to reach and teach our diverse population of students.

Let's take the verbal/linguistic intelligence as an example. It is comprised of many facets including reading, writing, listening, speaking, discussing. To develop speaking and listening skills, we could use Timed Pair Share. This is a simple strategy that involves partners taking turns, each sharing their ideas on a topic for a duration of time. One student speaks uninterrupted and the other listens, then they switch roles. Each student in the class is actively involved speaking and listening. All students get an equal opportunity to develop speaking skills, to share their ideas on the topic, and to listen. Timed Pair Share is an easy, powerful strategy for developing certain aspects of the verbal/linguistic intelligence.

If we want to develop students' descriptive writing skills — another facet of the verbal/linguistic intelligence — a Timed Pair Share simply would not be the strategy of choice. Draw-What-I-Write, another instructional strategy, is better suited.

In Draw-What-I-Write, students draw a simple picture, then describe it in writing. They switch written descriptions with a partner. The partner's task is to recreate the drawing based on the description. When done, students pair and compare the original illustration with the one produced by the writing. They discuss how the descriptions could be improved to be more effective.

With Draw-What-I-Write, students acquire descriptive writing skills in the process of writing something meaningful and functional. This is not to say Draw-What-

I-Write is a better verbal/linguistic instructional strategy than Timed Pair Share. Each strategy has its usefulness in the classroom. It takes different strategies to develop different facets of the same intelligence.

Across intelligences, the differences in instructional strategies for achieving our diverse educational objectives is even more obvious. To teach with logic and develop students' logical thinking skills, writing, speaking and listening may not be as helpful as strategies focusing on sequencing, inductive reasoning, and higher-level thinking. There is a spectrum of instructional strategies available to match and stretch students' spectrum of intelligences.

MI instructional strategies are powerful tools to make multiple intelligences come alive in the classroom.

A major thrust of our work in cooperative learning is to develop and train cooperative learning strategies or "cooperative structures." As we train teachers how and when to use the various cooperative learning strategies, we use a toolbox analogy. Instructional strategies are tools in a teacher's toolbox. The more tools we have in our toolbox, the more efficient we are in building meaningful learning experiences for our students.

If we hired a carpenter to build us a house, but the carpenter only knew how to use a hammer, we would end up with a poor excuse for a house. The same would be true if the carpenter could use only a saw. But if the carpenter had a toolbox full of tools, and could switch artfully from the hammer, to the saw, to the wrench, we would be much more likely to end up with an interesting, luxurious, beautiful, and functional house. To the extent we as teachers rely on but a few instructional strategies, we are less likely to build meaningful, engaging learning experiences for our students.

As teachers, the better equipped we are with a wide range of strategies for each intelligence, the more likely we will reach students dominant in each intelligence, and the more likely we will stretch students in all intelligences. Each student has different proclivities in the various intelligences. Any single strategy may be very successful with some students, yet less successful with others. Using a range of teaching strategies makes learning more accessible to all students.

With Paula, using a strategy that engaged her bodily/kinesthetic intelligence made all the difference. However, we cannot realistically expect one strategy to be a watershed for all students. As we teach MI lessons, we use a range of instructional strategies that stimulate the multiple intelligences. Over time, we provide students many opportunities to engage their bodily/kinesthetic intelligence as well as their other intelligences. With MI lessons that integrate a variety of instructional strategies, we give all students the opportunity to learn and to excel.

How the Strategies Are Presented

Presented below are a number of instructional strategies to make any lesson a motivating and meaningful MI lesson. The list is not complete. There are numerous strategies that can be added to this section.

We have organized the instructional strategies in this section by primary intelligence. The MI strategies are arranged alphabetically in subcategories within each intelligence. For example, in the verbal/linguistic strategy section, the strategies are divided into Listening and Discussing Strategies, Reading Strategies, and Writing Strategies. Variations of an MI strategy are bulleted.

Many strategies integrate several intelligences and facets simultaneously. In Draw-What-I-Write, for example, students use their visual/spatial intelligence as they create the original drawings and try to match their partner's drawing; they use their verbal/linguistic intelligence as they write the description of their drawings and read their partners description; and they use their interpersonal intelligence as they pair up to improve each other's writing. Since many strategies are multifunctional, there are many ways they may be organized. We have attempted to place strategies according to one intelligence they strongly engage. Let's loot the treasure chest of MI strategies.

Verbal/Linguistic Instructional Strategies

The verbal/linguistic intelligence is engaged by the written and spoken word. Teaching strategies for the verbal/linguistic intelligence require the use of language in the processes and products of learning such as: reading, writing, speaking, discussing and listening. Verbal/linguistic strategies are far and away the most common pedagogical tools. Below you may find some strategies that you may want to add to your toolbox, as well as some strategies you may use every day.

Verbal/Linguistic Strategies

▼ Listening and Discussing Strategies

- Circle-the-Sage
- Debate
- Dialogues
- Discussion
- Lecture
- RoundRobin
    RallyRobin
    RallyToss
    Think-Write-RoundRobin
    Turn Toss
  - Storytelling
  - Three-Pair-Share

▼ Writing Strategies

- Brainstorming
    A-Z Brainstorming
    4S Brainstorming
    ThinkPad Brainstorming
- Compositions
- Draw-What-I-Write
    Build-What-I-Write
    Find-What-I-Write
- Journals
    Buddy Journal
    Character Journal
    Dialogue Journal
    Double Entry Journal
    Draw & Tell Journal
    Electronic Journal
    Home-School Journal
    Learning Log
    Literature Response Journal
    Personal Journal
    Writer's Journal
- RoundTable
    RallyTable
    Simultaneous RoundTable

▼ Reading Strategies

- Reading
    Independent Reading
    Oral Reading
    RallyRobin Reading
    RoundRobin Reading
    Teacher Reading

Listening and Discussing Strategies

Circle-the-Sage

Students who know the answer to the teacher's question become "Sages." Sages stand up and students gather around the Sages to listen to the Sage's explanation or answer. When working in teams, each teammate circles a different Sage, then they return to their team to compare notes.

Debate

A debatable issue is presented to the class. For example, the issue may be, "Drug testing should be mandatory for all students." Students may be assigned to agree or disagree, or, in an alternative version, students may decide whether they agree or disagree. Agree students go to one side of the room and Disagree students go to the other side. In their sides, they discuss their perspectives and arguments supporting their view.

A teacher may facilitate and direct the discussion. Students may take notes. Then, teams are formed, usually with two Agree and two Disagree students per team. In teams, students debate the issue.

As an extension, students may write an essay on the topic. For big issues, students can simulate a court case with a judge, attorneys, jury, defendant, plaintiff.

Dialogues

Dialogues, also known as narratives, are a common strategy for teaching a second language. In pairs or small groups, students read a dialogue between characters. Students learn vocabulary and conversational skills while engaging in the dialogue. When done, students process the dialogues with a series of questions relating to who was talking and what was going on.

Discussion

Discussions are open-ended verbal exchanges on any topic. Any member of the discussion is free to contribute at will. The discussion may be an argument or debate exploring the pros and cons of the given issue. Discussions work well in pairs, small groups or as an entire class.

Class Discussion

Lecture

The lecture is one of the most common teaching strategies. The teacher verbally shares information or imparts knowledge. Additional verbal/linguistic extensions in-clude students taking notes, and or verbally discussing shared information with teammates or classmates.

RoundRobin

RoundRobin is a simple turn-taking strategy for talking. In teams, one student shares with teammates, then the next student shares. Sharing may go one round with long discussion topics, or many rounds to create a verbal list of short answers. See sample activities 8.10 - 8.13.

RoundRobin

• **RallyRobin.** Individuals in pairs take turns talking. RallyRobin is the verbal counterpart of a Ping-Pong rally in which two players rally back and forth.

• **RallyToss.** Partners toss a ball (paper wad) while doing RallyRobin.

• **Think-Write-RoundRobin.** Students are given a discussion topic and extended think time. They write down the ideas they'd like to share before the RoundRobin. Using the think and write time before RoundRobin allows students to articulate their thoughts before they are asked to share them.

• **Turn Toss.** Students in any order toss a ball (paper wad) while talking, visually indicating whose turn it is to talk. A "no toss backs" rule prevents a pair from dominating.

Storytelling

Storytelling is the time-honored tradition of passing along information in the form of a story. Stories can revolve around a theme, have a moral and can be allegories. Students can write and share stories on a topic or the teacher may present information in the form of a story.

Three-Pair-Share

A topic is presented by the teacher. Students share on a topic three times, once with each of their teammates. By repeatedly sharing their ideas on the same topic, each time with a new audience, students hear multiple perspectives and articulate their own ideas on the topic.

Writing Strategies

Brainstorming

Brainstorming is a method used to generate ideas quickly, the perfect prewriting tool. Students can brainstorm alone by listing all ideas that pop into their heads. Students can brainstorm in pairs, teams or as a class with a chosen or rotating recorder.

• **A-Z Brainstorming.** Students write the letters A through Z vertically down the left side of a piece of paper. In teams, the first student brainstorms a word or idea that starts with A about the theme or topic. The next student comes up with a B idea. For example, if the topic is possible desserts, A might be "apple pie;" B might be, "banana nut bread."

• **4S Brainstorming.** In teams of four, each student has a different role: 1) Sultan of Silly: encourages silly ideas; 2) Synergy Guru: asks teammates to expand or combine ideas; 3) Sergeant Support: affirms all ideas and ensures judgment is suspended during brainstorming; 4) Speed Captain: encourages many ideas to be generated quickly. Each idea is recorded on a separate slip of paper and teammates attempt to "cover the table with ideas" in a brief, predetermined amount of time. See sample activities 8.6 - 8.9.

• **ThinkPad Brainstorming.** To generate many ideas quickly, try using ThinkPad Brainstorming as a class. Announce a topic and have each student quickly record as many ideas as possible on small slips of paper. All ideas are collected and a category system may be devised to sort the ideas.

4S Brainstorming

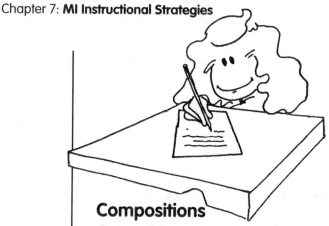

Compositions

Compositions are expression, creative or functional, through writing. A written composition can be as simple as students writing a sentence about a topic or can proceed step-by-step through the writing process: prewriting, writing, proofing/editing, conferring/rewriting, publishing. Some types of compositions include:

- Autobiographies
- Biographies
- Book reports
- Creative writing
- Debates
- Descriptive writing
- Editorials
- Essays
- Fiction
- Instructions and directions
- Letters
- Narratives
- News articles
- Nonfiction
- Paragraphs
- Persuasive writing
- Poems
- Research reports
- Sentences
- Speeches
- Stories

Draw-What-I-Write

Students draw a simple picture. For example, students may draw a simple robot using only geometric shapes. Then, students write instructions to a partner as clearly as possible, so their partner can produce an identical picture. Students trade written descriptions with their partners. It is crucial that students do not show each other their drawings. Students then attempt to use the written description to re-create the original illustration. When done, partners compare their drawings with the original and discuss how the author can edit to do a better job of describing the drawing. Sometimes edited versions are traded with a new partner to test the effectiveness of editing. Pictures can be line drawings, graphs, patterns, color schemes.

- **Build-What-I-Write.** Students use building materials such as Legos, building blocks, pattern blocks, Lincoln logs, tangrams, to make a construction. Students describe their construction in writing as clearly as possible, then switch written descriptions with a partner. Partners attempt to recreate the original construction using just the written description. Partners compare their constructions with the original and discuss how to improve their written descriptions.

- **Find-What-I-Write.** Students hide an object like an eraser somewhere in the classroom. They describe in writing how to locate the object. Students switch descriptions and locate each other's hidden objects. A good visual/spatial adaptation is to have students draw a map to find the object.

Journals

In their most basic format, journals involve a student recording her or his ideas in a booklet. Students can record their answers, ideas, thoughts, correspondence, progress. Journals are a multifunctional teaching tool. Karen Bromley (1993) identifies a variety of journals and provides ideas and samples for each type.

• **Buddy Journal.** A buddy journal is a dialogue journal except students, instead of the teacher, read and respond to each other's entries.

• **Character Journal.** Students assume the role of a character and make a journal entry in role. Character journals are a good exercise to develop the ability to take the role of another.

• **Dialogue Journal.** A dialogue journal is an interaction between the writer and the reader. Students write in their journal as in partaking in dialogue. The teacher reads each new entry and responds. Dialogue journals are a great forum to answer questions, elaborate ideas, give opinions, share observations. Dialogue journals and buddy journals integrate the interpersonal intelligence. Dialogue Journals also work well for authentic MI assessment as an open conversation between the student and the teacher. See Dialogue Journal blackline on page 19.28.

• **Double Entry Journal.** Students make two entries on the same topic. The first entry is objective. It is a report of information, summary of events, quotation, facts. The second entry is subjective. It is the student's feelings, personal observations, and interpretations of the first entry.

• **Draw & Tell Journal.** These journals integrate the linguistic and visual intelligences. Students make a drawing and describe it in their journal. See blackline on page 7.11.

• **Electronic Journal.** Students communicate with other students in a neighboring or distant school via E-mail.

• **Home-School Journal.** Parents respond to their child's entry with a written journal response.

• **Learning Log.** Students record what they learned from a lesson, project, center, trip.

• **Literature Response Journal.** Students write or draw their responses to books they are reading, read or heard on tape.

• **Personal Journal.** Personal journals are private diaries used to record events, feelings, emotions, ideas, reflections. Personal journals or Journal Reflections integrate the intrapersonal intelligence. See activities on pages 8.60 - 8.62.

• **Writer's Journal.** Students journal information. For example they may make entries in their writer's journal as prewriting for a subsequent written composition.

RoundTable

RoundTable is a simple strategy with many applications. In teams, students pass one piece of paper and one writing utensil around the table, each making a contribution in turn. RoundTable is used for making a list or writing a collaborative story.

• **RallyTable.** Pairs take turns writing down ideas or answers, using one piece of paper per pair.

Draw & Tell Journal

Name _____ Date _____

Title _____

Draw

Tell _____
_____
_____
_____
_____
_____
_____
_____
_____
_____
_____
_____
_____

• **Simultaneous RoundTable.** In teams of four, four papers are passed around the table, with students each simultaneously making a contribution, then simultaneously passing the paper clockwise.

Reading Strategies
Reading

There are many forms of reading possible in the classroom. The content of reading can be anything from textbooks to magazines to cereal boxes.

• **Independent Reading.** Students read quietly to themselves. Also called Sustained Silent Reading and SQUIRT: Sustained Quiet UnInterrupted Reading Time.

• **Oral Reading.** A student reads aloud to the class or group.

• **RallyRobin Reading.** In pairs, students take turns reading. They may read a sentence, paragraph, or page each depending on ability level. Often they are required to ask their partner one comprehension and one thought question before passing the book for the partner to read.

• **RoundRobin Reading.** In small groups, students take turns reading.

• **Teacher Reading.** The teacher reads to the class, small group or to an individual student.

Logical/Mathematical Instructional Strategies

There are many facets to the logical/mathematical intelligence. Some strategies engage students' logical minds. Questioning strategies foster higher-level thinking and guide students to elaborate on their own thinking. Metacognitive strategies build students' awareness of their own thinking. Strategies can be used to enhance specific thinking skills such as sequencing, inductive reasoning, and team problem solving.

Questioning Strategies
Question & Answer

Another commonly used, overused, teaching strategy is Question and Answer. The questions vary from class to class, but the procedure is remarkably common. Usually after direct input, the teacher poses a question. One student is selected to share with the class. The teacher provides evaluation, feedback, or redirects the thinking of students.

Questions can be for comprehension, review, or to generate higher-level thinking about a subject. Benjamin Bloom (1977) classified different types of thinking into what is commonly known as Bloom's Taxonomy. The levels of thinking in Bloom's Taxonomy are: 1) Knowledge, 2) Comprehension, 3) Application, 4) Analysis, 5) Synthesis, 6) Evaluation. High-consensus recall questions stimulate the knowledge and comprehension levels of thinking while low-consensus questions stimulate application, analysis, synthesis and evaluation.

Logical/Mathematical Strategies

▼ Questioning Strategies
• Question & Answer
• Question Matrix
• The Socratic Method
• What If?

▼ Thinking Skills Strategies
• Find My Rule
  Crack My Venn
  Two Box Induction
  What's My Line
• Find the Fib
  Fact or Fiction
• Metacognition
• Pairs Compare
• Sequencing
  Blind Sequencing
• Who Am I?

▼ Problem-Solving Strategies
• Jigsaw Problem Solving
• Send-A-Problem
  Trade-A-Problem

Different types of thinking are involved in analysis than in synthesis. Each type of thinking involves discreet skills: A student skilled in analysis may or may not be skilled in acquiring knowledge and vice versa.

Research indicates that using an average of three seconds of "wait time" or "think time" after a question is posed and before a student is called on, significantly enhances quality of responses (Rowe, 1978). Students provided wait time give longer responses, have more confidence in responding. Further, wait time is associated with decreased failure to respond, and decreased discipline problems. With greater wait time more students respond, including those who were otherwise thought to be poor students. Think time is also beneficial after the student response and before the teacher evaluation.

Question Matrix

Charles Wiederhold (1995) developed the Question Matrix or the Q-Matrix. There are six question starters vertically on the matrix: 1) What, 2) Where/when, 3) Which, 4) Who, 5) Why, 6) How, and six question endings horizontally: 1) Is? 2) Did? 3) Can? 4) Would? 5) Will? 6) Might? The combination of the horizontal and vertical words forms 36 question prompts that span the range of questioning and thinking: Who is? What did? When will? What might? How would? The question prompts are a powerful tool to turn students' natural curiosity into higher-level thinking questions about the curriculum. The questions have been formatted as attractive hands-on manipulatives to stimulate higher level thinking among students. Students can generate and answer their own questions about any content. These question prompts can also be used by teachers to ensure a wide variety of questioning.

The Socratic Method

This questioning strategy takes its name from Socrates, the Greek scholar. The teacher uses skillful questions to help students uncover, elaborate and clarify their own thinking about a topic. Socratic questioning can be used as an assessment measure.

What If?

A great way to stimulate the logical/mathematical intelligence is to ask "What if?" questions. Students must think about the hypothetical question and report on all of the logical consequences. What If? works well as a group activity where students take turns coming up with consequences. Teams can compare their responses.

Jackie Scott (1997) applies this approach to popular childrens' stories, changing one important dimension, and leading students through all the changes: "What if the dwarfs in the story of *Snow White* were giants? What if the ugly duckling was an ugly caterpillar? What if the three pigs were three fishes? This approach can easily be applied to any content area: What if Martin Luther King Jr. was never assassinated? What if there was no such thing as a circle? What if algebra was never invented? What if sharks became extinct? What if gold was never discovered?"

Thinking Skills Strategies

Find My Rule

Find My Rule promotes inductive thinking. The teacher presents to the class many items that follow a rule. It is up to students to induce the rule. There are a number of variations for Find My Rule. See sample activities 8.14 - 8.17.

• **Crack My Venn.** Objects are placed in one of the two circles of a Venn diagram, the intersection, or outside the circles. Students induce the names of the circles of the Venn diagram. For example, the Venn circles may be, "numbers divisible by 2," and "numbers divisible by 3" numbers that are divisible by 2 and 3 placed in the intersection, numbers not divisible by 2 nor 3 are placed outside the circles.

Find My Rule

• **Two Box Induction.** Students induce the rule for why items are placed in two different boxes. For example, if the rule is symmetry, the teacher places symmetrical shapes in one box and nonsymmetrical shapes in the other box. After each item is placed in the box, students discuss the differences until they can name the rule. If a student or team thinks they have found the rule, they provide the next examples for the two boxes, in order to test the rule. Two box induction can be used with the range of MI content as students induce rules about different types of melodies, rhythms, movements, color, feelings, plants or animals.

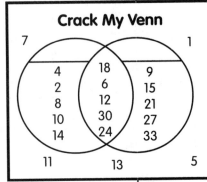

• **What's My Line?** Students induce the poles of a continuum line. For example the

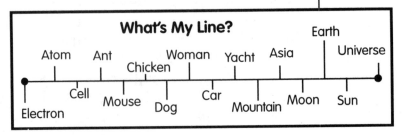

poles of the line may be large and small. To make it more challenging, start near the middle of the continuum where items are similar, working out to the poles.

Find the Fib

Students write three statements: two true, one a fib. In teams, students take turns reading their statements. After a teammate shares her statements, teammates discuss the statements and try to determine which of three statements is a fib. In the class version, the teacher or a student reads three statements. After a team discussion, students hold up a number card or finger(s) corresponding to the "fib," to indicate their best guess.

• **Fact or Fiction.** A variation of Find the Fib; classmates or teammates try to determine if a statement is true or false.

Metacognition

Metacognition is thinking about one's own thinking. As students think about how they think, evaluate why they think the way they do, question what they know, don't know and would like to learn, they develop a deep understanding of their own logical minds, a deeper understanding of the content, and direct their own learning in acquiring knowledge and constructing meaning.

Sequencing

Robin Fogarty (1994) identifies three areas for self-reflection: 1) Planning, 2) Monitoring, 3) Evaluating. Planning involves standing outside of a situation or learning experience and making predictions, formulating hypotheses, and preparing for what is to follow. Monitoring occurs once students are actually in the process. Students again stand outside of themselves and look clearly at what's going on. Monitoring allows for modifications of behavior or thinking while in the course of action. And finally, evaluating is the stage after an experience where students reflect on what they learned, how they interacted, what went well and what needs improvement. Fogarty provides numerous specific techniques for each stage of metacognition.

Pairs Compare

Students work in pairs to generate a list of ideas. Pairs pair up and compare their lists. For example, students work with a partner to come up with math equations that equal 24. The two partners in each pair take turns writing each new equation. After generating a list of equations, pairs group with another pair to form a group of four. Pairs compare their equations using a Venn diagram to see which equations only one pair came up with and which equations both pairs produced. As a team of four, students then work together to see if they can come up with additional responses neither pair alone had. Pairs Compare stretches the logical intelligence through comparing answers and challenging pairs to come up with new ideas. See Pairs Compare blackline on page 7.16.

Sequencing

Sequencing involves placing events, dates, numbers or steps in the proper sequence. It can be done independently, in small

Pairs Compare

Team Challenge

Pair 1

_____ _____
_____ _____
_____ _____
_____ _____
_____ _____

Both

_____ _____
_____ _____
_____ _____
_____ _____
_____ _____

Pair 2

_____ _____
_____ _____
_____ _____
_____ _____
_____ _____

_____
_____
_____
_____
_____
_____
_____
_____
_____
_____
_____
_____
_____
_____
_____
_____
_____
_____
_____
_____
_____
_____
_____
_____
_____
_____
_____
_____

groups or as a class. Two formats are most common: 1) students come up with their own sequence of events or steps; or 2) the events or steps are provided and the students' task is to organize them in the proper sequence, working individually or as a team.

• **Blind Sequencing.** In teams, each student receives cards often with pictures of events or steps. Students do not show each other their cards. They must describe their events and work together as a team to sequence the events, placing them face down on the table. When completed, they flip over the cards and check the sequence. Teammates discuss how effective they were in sequencing and then create strategies to improve sequencing.

Who Am I?

Students attempt to determine their secret identity (taped on their back) by circulating and asking "yes/no" questions of classmates. They may be allowed three questions per classmate, or unlimited questions until they receive a no response. They then find a new classmate to question. When the student guesses his/her identity, he/she becomes a consultant to give clues to those who have not yet found their identity. Who Am I develops inductive reasoning, problem-solving skills, and effective questioning strategies. See sample activities on pages 18.18 - 18.21.

Jigsaw Problem Solving

Each teammate receives a clue to solve the team problem. Teammates must put all the information together to solve the problem. For example, to uncover the arrangement of a star, circle, square and triangle, each student may receive one clue card:
1) The circle is not in the middle.
2) The triangle is on one end.
3) The star is to the left of the square.
4) The square is to the right of the circle.
Each student on the team reads his or her clue card and independently decides what can be concluded from the clue. The teammates then check to see if they all agree before the next person acts on his or her clue. Jigsaw Problem Solving ensures all students are included in problem solving. See Goodman (1992, 1997), and Erickson (1989, 1996).

Send-A-Problem

Send-A-Problem

Send-A-Problem allows students to generate their own problems to solve and practice team problem solving. Teammates work together to come up with their own problems. For example, if students are learning division, teams may come up with a word problem that requires division for the solution. Each team makes a problem or list of problems. Problems are "sent" to other teams to solve.

• **Trade-A-Problem.** Teammates make problems which are traded with another team to solve. When done, students can check answers against a key or with the problem creators. Problems can be traded many times.

Visual/Spatial Instructional Strategies

We can use a range of instructional strategies to promote the visual/spatial intelligence. Some strategies access and develop students' spatial relations, others lead students in visual imagery, other strategies present the content in a visual format, and others develop students' skills in communications via visual mediums.

Spatial-Relations Strategies

Graphic Organizers

Graphic organizers are frames used to visually depict the interrelation of information. Graphic organizers can be used by teachers in lectures and demonstrations to visually illustrate to students how information is related. Graphic organizers can also be used by students to organize their own information or graphically depict how the learning material is related.

Some graphic organizers include: Venn Diagram, Ladder, Word Web, Mind Map, Fish Bone, Sequence Chart, Flow Chart, Target, Compare and Contrast Chart, Spectrum, T-Chart, Know-Wonder-Learn Form, Five W Chart, Matrix, Tree Diagram, Cause and Effect Chart, Cyclical Diagram. See Categorizing Systems on page 8.49 for some sample graphic organizers. (For more on graphic organizers, see Bellanca, 1990, 1992; Buzan & Buzan, 1994; Bromley, Irwin-De Vitis & Modlo, 1995; Margulies, 1991; and Parks & Black, 1990, 1992).

Mapping Space & Modeling

Students can represent spatial relations with their own maps and models. Maps and models may be drawn or constructed with manipulatives or building materials. Some examples: For geography, given state names, students draw their own relief map of the United States; for math, students draw a proportional map of their own homes; for fun, students map out the classroom seating arrangement; for social studies, students build a model of a mission, or state.

Match Mine

In pairs, students sit on each side of a barrier. The barrier can be a file folder barrier, book, or binder. Each member of a pair receives an identical game board and game pieces. One student, the Sender, sets up her pieces on her game board. For instance, the game pieces can be geometric pieces and the game board can be graph paper. Without seeing how the Sender arranged her pieces, the Receiver must match the layout. To do this, the Sender must describe the layout as well as possible, paying close attention to visual cues. To succeed, the Receiver must visualize what is being described. The Receiver places her pieces accordingly. Partners check the design when done, then switch roles so the Receiver gets a chance to be the Sender. Match Mine is great for developing directionality and spatial relations.

The content of the game board and game pieces can vary depending on curriculum.

Visual/Spatial Strategies

▼ **Spatial-Relations Strategies**
- Graphic Organizers
- Mapping Space & Modeling
- Match Mine
- Mind Mapping
- Timelines

▼ **Visual Input Strategies**
- Graphs & Charts
- Modeling & Demonstrations
- Visual Aids

▼ **Visual Imagery Strategies**
- Guided Imagery
- Visualization
- Visualize-Write-RoundRobin

▼ **Visual Communication Strategies**
- Cartoons & Picture Stories
- Draw It!
- Representational Art

For example, for the simple concept of inside and outside, the game board may have a large circle drawn in the center. The game pieces are placed either inside or outside of the circle. For order, the game board may be a sequence of boxes and the game pieces may be put in the first, second, third box and so on. Analytical visual skills and verbal skills can be enhanced with game pieces that are very similar, with minor alterations. See sample activities on pages 8.22 - 8.24.

Match Mine is a very strong visual/spatial strategy as it engages spatial relations, visual input, visual communication, and visual imagery.

Mind Mapping

Mind Mapping, developed by Tony Buzan (1994), involves students creating a visual "map" of their ideas. The teacher announces a topic such as Geometry. Students write the word or draw a representational picture of the word in the center of a sheet of paper. Radiating from the main idea are related ideas, bridges, colors, icons, arrows, symbols and codes used to represent the main idea and the interrelation of related ideas. For Mind Mapping activities, see pages 8.26 - 8.29. For more on Mind Mapping, see Margulies (1991).

Timelines

Students arrange events on a timeline. Timelines allow students to visually see how events are related in time.

Visual Input Strategies

Graphs & Charts

Students create graphs and charts to quantify and symbolize data in a visual format. The teacher poses the topic for graphing. A simple example: "Make a graph indicating the number of boys and girls in the class." As a first step, students collect the data. They count the number of boys and the number of girls. They use their data to form their graph. Bar, line, and pie graphs are the most common. Students can make large poster displays and use color for their graphs.

Modeling & Demonstrations

The effectiveness of modeling and demonstrations cannot be overstated. Both translate information, usually directions, into a visual symbol system. Students who do not understand a description often readily understand if they can *see* what is desired. If a picture is worth a thousand words, modeling and demonstrations speak volumes.

Visual Aids

Teachers may use a wide variety of visual aids with any content to reach visual students. Film, TV, slides, multimedia, the internet, art, charts, graphs, bulletin boards, overhead projectors, the chalkboard, and signs are all effective visuals that can be used to present any content in a visual format.

Visual Imagery Strategies

Guided Imagery

With Guided Imagery students close their eyes to the world outside and focus on visualizing what is being described by the teacher. The teacher reads a script or creates the guided tour by describing a scene. The voyage should be rich with visuals and sensations. For example, for teaching about the Gold Rush, the teacher may take students through a westward journey, the toil of the search, the excitement of discovery or despair of the harsh reality. Guided Imagery works well as a set for many types of lessons and is especially powerful as a prewriting activity.

Visualization

Visualization produces such dramatic performance gains that it has become a regular part of training for athletes, dancers, actors, and even musicians. It is a form of mental rehearsal. World Class pentathlete Marilyn King was able to remain fit through a hospital stay by repeatedly visualizing her performance (Rose & Nicholl, 1997). The method is easy: Students close their eyes to see with their mind's eye the topic of visualization. Unlike Guided Imagery, Visualization is not scripted. Students visualize the content for themselves.

Visualize-Write-RoundRobin

The teacher presents a scenario or topic to the class, then leads the students through guided imagery on the topic. For example, "You are in Costa Rica. You step out of your car into the lush jungle. What do you see?" After some silent time for visualization, the teacher takes them further, "You see a plant. You walk over to it. What color is it? You reach over to feel a leaf. How does it feel? Is it moist or dry, fuzzy or silky? After the class visualizes, students write down what they "saw." In their small groups, students take turns reading what they wrote. Students can close their eyes and visualize what their teammates saw. Visualize-Write-RoundRobin is an effective visualization technique, promoting equal participation that allows students to share their visions, and hear teammates visions as well.

Visual Communication Strategies

Cartoons & Picture Stories

Cartoons and picture stories are effective strategies to have students translate any content into a visual symbol system. Students draw single or multiple cell cartoons to represent an event, the steps of a problem, the events in a story, a time line sequence.

With picture stories, students draw pictures, use photographs, use clip art, or cut pictures out of magazines to tell a story. Picture stories can be integrated with language, but don't have to be. Cartoons and picture stories also promote the logical intelligence, depicting a logical sequence.

Draw It!

This strategy is similar to the game Pictionary. It may be played in small groups or as an entire class. For the small group version, objects or events relating to the topic of study are written on slips of papers and stacked upside down in the middle of the table. One student picks one slip and reads it silently without showing it to anyone else. He or she draws the object or event and teammates try to guess what is drawn. Draw It! can be played in turns, or the student who guesses correctly can be next up to draw. For the class version, a student goes to the chalkboard to draw the item the teacher whispers in his or her ear. The student who guesses the item is next up to the chalkboard.

Representational Art

Art (and crafts) can be used in the classroom to develop artistic skills, enhance visual communication skills, and give visual students an insight into the content.

Students develop art skills as they paint, draw, sculpt, make collages. Students can use a range of media to translate any content into visual images. "Symbolize the poem in a painting." "Make a collage representing the importance of geometry." "Draw a picture that captures the essence of the Vietnam War." Students can gain insight to historical times, movements and events by studying art of the time, or art capturing the event. To create excitement

Musical/Rhythmic Strategies

- Background Music
- Lyrical Lessons
- Songs for Two Voices
  Poems for Two Voices
- Team Chants

about a lesson on snakes, students can draw a colorful picture of a snake or mold one from clay. While reading a descriptive novel, students can illustrate a particular scene or build a diorama. After a lesson on the human skeleton, through illustration students can try to depict their knowledge of the structure of the human skeleton, or construct a pipe cleaner model.

Musical/Rhythmic Instructional Strategies

Music isn't only for the music class. Music and rhythm may be introduced to liven up any lesson. Music is used effectively to create a tone, for mastery of information, and to stretch students' sense of rhythm. Research supports the beneficial impact of music on cognitive performances of many types (Campbell, 1997).

Background Music

There is research suggesting that music reduces stress, and increases learning and long-term retention (Campbell, 1997; Jensen, 1995). Different types of music may be used to calm students down, to introduce a time period, celebrate a culture, explore a theme, set a mood, and, of course, energize students.

Lyrical Lessons

Lyrical Lessons (Klose & Wolfe, 1997) engage students in writing and/or performing songs based on the curriculum. Many fine cassettes are available to teach the range of curriculum through all genres of music from biology raps to rocking phonics. An effective technique for having students ease into writing their own Lyrical Lessons is to have students first brainstorm content ideas, phrases, and words, and then place the phrases into a popular tune like: *Twinkle Twinkle Little Star, Have You Ever Seen a Lassie, When the Saints Go Marching In.* Students can perform their songs solo, duet, trio, quartet, or as a class. See sample activities on pages 8.30 - 8.34.

Songs for Two Voices

In Songs for Two Voices, students pair up to sing a song. Some lines are marked "A," others "B," and others "AB." One student sings the A lines; her or his partner sings the B lines; in unison, they sing the AB lines creating a rhythmic, dynamic duo. Songs for Two Voices can also be sung as a class.

Half of the class sings the A lines; the other half sings the B lines; and the entire class sings the AB lines. Usually the teacher formats the first songs, but with subsequent songs students decide which lines are A lines, B lines, and AB lines.

When academic content is the focus of the songs, students master important concepts as they harmonize. For sample activities, see pages 8.34-8.37.

• **Poems for Two Voices.** Students recite poems in pairs, alternating reading some lines, and reading some lines in unison.

Team Chants

Students work in small groups to make Team Chants related to the content. First, students come up with the words and phrases related to the content. Then they come up with a rhythmic chant that highlights the important words or phrases. Finally, they add rhythm to their chant, usually in the form of stomping, clapping, pounding or snapping. Movements may be integrated with Team Chants to engage the bodily/kinesthetic intelligence.

Bodily/Kinesthetic Instructional Strategies

The bodily/kinesthetic strategies include bodily communication, hands-on learning, and bodily representational strategies. There are also a number of learning strategies incorporating movement that do not symbolize the content kinesthetically. These strategies do not necessarily teach with the kinesthetic intelligence, but they sure do energize the class.

Bodily/Kinesthetic Strategies

▼ Bodily Communication Strategies
- Acting
- Kinesthetic Symbols
- Puppet Show
- Role Playing & Impersonating
- Team Charades

▼ Hands-On Learning Strategies
- Experiential Learning
- Hands-On Learning
- Inventing, Designing, & Building

▼ Body Representational Strategies
- Agreement Circles
- Body Graphs
- Dance & Movement
- Formations
- Line Ups
    Folded Line Ups
    Split & Slide
    Value Lines
- Mix-Freeze-Group
- Total Physical Response (TPR)

▼ Movement Strategies
- Find Someone Who
    Fact Bingo
    People Hunt
- Inside/Outside Circle

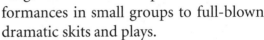

Bodily Communication Strategies

Acting

Students can act out vocabulary words, natural phenomena, historical events, story events and much more. Acting can range from individual performances in small groups to full-blown dramatic skits and plays.

Kinesthetic Symbols

Kinesthetic Symbols are hand gestures to translate learning material into a kinesthetic symbol system. For example, when studying natural disasters, a kinesthetic symbol for an earthquake may be interlocking the fingers of both hands and making a rolling and shaking motion. A twister may be quick rotating motion with one hand. Students may make Kinesthetic Symbols for vocabulary words. The entire class can learn the same Kinesthetic Symbols or students can generate and share their own symbols relating to the content. Using Kinesthetic Symbols is a powerful strategy to connect the content with movement or body position. Students may sequence a series of Kinesthetic Symbols into one fluid motion as when they symbolize the eight intelligences as hands in front of their eyes symbolizing an open book (verbal), fingers punching a calculator (mathematical), hand to their forehead as if looking (visual), hands playing a violin (musical)…

Puppet Show

Students work in groups to make puppets and create a short puppet show around an event or topic. For example, after hearing the story, *Three Little Pigs*, students make puppets for the three pigs, the mother, and the wolf. Students can also make props or a puppet stage with cardboard. Students rehearse their show and perform for another team or the class.

Role Playing & Impersonating

Students acquire insights to individual's lives and perspectives as they role play or impersonate that figure. Some applications include: inventors, explorers, pilgrims, civil rights activists, presidents, athletes, musicians, artists, story characters. A role-play party or meeting is always a hit. Students research, then role play celebrities at a party or gathering. As they act out their character's role, often in costume, students share pertinent information with others. Students may develop a form beforehand with questions they need to ask other celebrities.

Team Charades

Charades is a popular game that is successfully applied to the classroom to reach and teach the bodily/kinesthetic intelligence. Playing in small teams increases active participation. To play, each student is given an item, say for example, a vocabulary word. In small teams, one student acts out his or her word. It is up to teammates to guess what word is being acted out. Students take turns acting, in a RoundTable fashion, or

using a student selector spinner to see who is next to act. If students are given multiple words, they can play many rounds. Charades works well with a wide range of academic content. See sample activities on pages 8.38 - 8.41.

Hands-On Learning Strategies
Experiential Learning

In the tradition of constructivist education comes Experiential Learning. Experiential Learning is perhaps more of a philosophy of teaching than a specific strategy. The basic philosophy espoused by constructivists is that students learn best by doing and experiencing. The teacher should strive less to impart knowledge and more to create situations or experiences from which students discover and construct meaning. The learning experiences may be actual experiences or well-crafted simulations. Experiences often involve many of the intelligences, but rely heavily on hands-on interaction with the content. Simulations that evoke feeling, sensations, and movement are most poignant.

Hands-On Learning

Thomas Edison said, "Great ideas originate in the muscles." The idea with hands-on learning is to give students the opportunity to interact with the learning material in a concrete form rather than just learn about it in the abstract. As students build, explore, play with, assemble, disassemble and manipulate physical objects, they develop a deeper understanding and appreciation of the content. Students can learn about magnets in the abstract, but they can arguably never achieve the level of understanding as they can by playing with magnets, seeing how much they can pick up, seeing how they attract and repel, testing what they stick to and what they don't. Hands-on learning requires hands-on classroom resources. A detailed list of classroom resources for each intelligence is provided in Chapter 14: Creating the MI Classroom.

Inventing, Designing, & Building

Students invent and build their own objects or design and build objects related to the content. For example, studying Native Americans, student teams design their own teepee on paper, then build it using sticks and cellophane. Studying airplanes, individual students or pairs of students design and build their own model airplane. Studying simple machines, students build their own catapult, and have accuracy and distance contests firing tennis balls or water balloons. As students design and create inventions and models, they develop the visual/spatial and bodily/kinesthetic intelligences while learning about the content or theme.

Body Representational Strategies
Agreement Circles

The class stands in one large circle. The teacher states a stance on a value issue such as, "Capital punishment should be abolished." Students physically locate themselves in relation to their agreement or disagreement with the given response. If a student strongly agrees, he stands very close to the teacher. If he strongly disagrees, he remains on the perimeter of the circle. Students pair with others close to them to discuss the issue.

At a glance, students can see how others feel about a particular topic. After a number of rounds on different issues, students may come to the center to make a statement with which the rest of the class agrees or disagrees. Agreement Circles is a good basis for discussion, debate, and mutual support.

Body Graphs

Body Graphs involve students actually forming the graph with their bodies. For example, students might stand in twelve lines to represent their birthday bar graph. The bar graph is converted into a line graph as students at the ends of the bars hold string or yarn. To form a pie graph, students in the bar graph hold hands, then join with other bars to form one large circle. Yarn is stretched from the center of the circle to the end points of each pie segment.

Dance & Movement

Creative movement and dance helps students gain knowledge through the body and grasp concepts from within, directly connecting students to the content. Dance and movement can take many forms in the class and can be performed with almost any curriculum. Students can make their own movements to symbolize events, phenomena, words. Movements can be performed with the fingers, hands, arms or the entire body. Dances evolve as movements become more elaborate. Students can make up their own personal movements and dances, or they can choreograph a movement or dance for a small group or for the class.

Formations

The teacher presents the class or teams with a challenge. For example, "Form the capital letter 'A.'" Or, "Use your bodies to form the solar system." Students coordinate efforts, deciding who should stand or move to meet the class or team challenge. See ideas on pages 8.42 - 8.43.

Line Ups

In Line Ups, the teacher announces a dimension upon which students may vary: "Line up by birthday." Or, "Line up by the number of pockets you have on you." Or, "Line up by how many times your family has moved." Students line up according to where they stand relative to classmates on the characteristic.

• **Folded Line Ups.** To have students discuss their values or a characteristic with someone with a different opinion or trait, have one end of the line up walk around so the students on one end of the line meet with the students on the other end. Students discuss their differences.

• **Split & Slide.** Folded Line Ups are great for the poles, but students who don't feel strongly about an issue may not have much to discuss. With Split & Slide, the line up is split in half and one half slides up so that the students who don't have a strong opinion are faced with students who feel very strongly about the issue. This is a great way to have students interact with others with a different point of view, characteristic, or estimate.

• **Value Lines.** Students line up according to where they stand on a given value issue. For example, "Do you agree or disagree with school uniforms?" Students who feel strongly either way line up at the poles. Have students discuss their feelings with

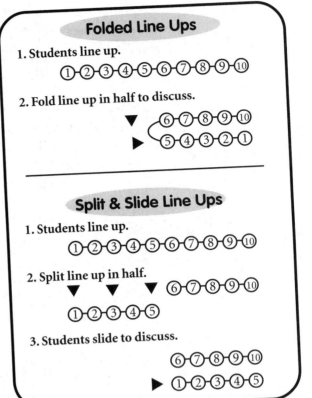

someone next to them. This is an excellent intrapersonal strategy as students clarify their own values on issues.

Mix-Freeze-Group

Everyone gets out of their seat, pushes in their chair, and starts to randomly circulate or "Mix" around the classroom. The teacher calls, "Freeze" and everyone stops in their tracks, ready to form a group. The teacher asks a question that requires students to get into groups depending on the answer. For example, the teacher may ask, "How many letters are in the words 'Verbal?'" Students rush to form groups of six by holding hands. Students who don't join a group become part of the lost and found, leftover students who stand in front of the classroom. As a rule, no students can be in the lost and found two turns in a row. Another way to form groups is to have a key. For example, with geography the following key may be posted on the chalkboard or overhead: "North = 2, East = 3, South = 4, West = 5." The question might be something like: "California is what direction from Nevada." Students rush to form groups of five. Generally Mix-Freeze-Group works better if students are not expected to get into groups larger than six. Music may be integrated: When the music stops, students freeze, then form groups.

Total Physical Response (TPR)

This method was developed by James J. Asher (1993) and has been most successfully applied to language learning, but also can be used across the curriculum. The method is based on how infants naturally acquire a language. Infants can comprehend language and respond physically well before they can actually talk: "Smile for daddy." In this strategy, the teacher gives commands that require a physical response, sometimes modeling the response. TPR can be thought of as a nonelimination Simon Says. For language learning, the applications are obvious: "Stand up, turn around, take two steps forward..." Other examples include: expressing different emotional expressions, acting out animal movements, forming numbers, letters and shapes.

Movement Strategies
Find Someone Who

Students each receive a worksheet with questions or problems on any content. Students mingle in the classroom until they find a partner. Partners ask each other one question from their worksheet. If a partner knows the answer or can work out the problem, he or she answers. The student asking the question records the answer given

by the partner. Partners sign each others' worksheet next to the problem to verify they have done it correctly or recorded their response accurately. Students circulate again and find a new partner to answer the next question. When done, students become helpers for students who have not finished. Find Someone Who is also a great interpersonal strategy, especially when the content involves finding classmates who fit the description or using each other as resources to solve problems students could not solve independently. See sample activities on pages 8.52 - 8.55.

• **Fact Bingo.** Find Someone Who played on bingo worksheet.

• **People Hunt.** Students fill out a form regarding personal characteristics, "eye color, favorite dessert, birthday..." or values, "How do you feel about affirmative action?" Students circulate through the class to find others who match their own characteristics. A variation is to find others who are different for discussion or debate.

Inside/Outside Circle

For Inside/Outside Circle, the class is divided in half. Half the class becomes the inside circle, and the other half the outside circle for two large concentric circles. Students in the inside circle face students in the outside circle. The teacher announces a topic, asks a question, or students ask each other questions on sheets or flashcards. After partners from the inside and outside circle have shared or answered each other's questions, one circle is rotated so students face new partners for a new question or topic.

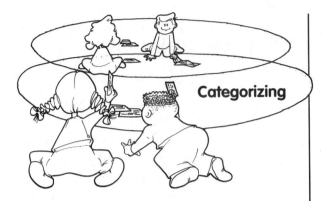

Categorizing

Naturalist Instructional Strategies

The naturalist intelligence is engaged as students observe, analyze, compare and classify, natural phenomena such as flora, fauna, rocks, clouds, and land formations. The naturalist intelligence may be directed toward cultural artifacts as when students make observations, recordings, and categorizations of shoes, litter, trash, and consumption patterns. Strategies which sharpen observational, comparison, and categorization skills are especially useful in engaging the naturalist intelligence.

Classification Strategy

Categorizing

Categorizing is an excellent strategy to develop classification and categorization skills, primary traits of the naturalist intelligence. Either the students or the teacher may develop the category system and/or the items to categorize. In the most structured version, students are given the items to categorize and a labeled categorization system or graphic organizer such as 2 x 2 matrix, or a Venn diagram. Students work independently or in small groups to categorize the items.

In the least structured version, students generate their own content to categorize and their own categorization system. Students or teams can compare their systems with other students to see novel ways to categorize the content.

Categorizing works well with natural content like: animals, plants, shells, rocks,

clouds, food. Yet, nearly any content can be put into category systems: list of words, pictures, places, shapes, numbers, problems, actions, music, cars. See sample activities and Category Systems on pages 8.48 - 8.51.

Observation and Comparison Strategies

Look-Write-Discuss

Each team is presented an object or specimen such as a flower, kitchen tool, or old shoe. They are given time, say two minutes, to examine it without talking. Their objective is to commit every detail to their visual memory. Then, the object is placed out of sight. Students write a description of the object as well as they can from memory. Finally, students use their descriptions of the object as the basis for a discussion about its characteristics. After the discussion, students can bring the object back into sight to see how accurate they were, or what they missed.

• **Listen-Write-Discuss.** Students listen to an animal sound, a sound from a musical instrument, or some other recording of some sound produced by something out of sight. This structure sharpens students' auditory observation skills.

• **Smell-Write-Discuss.** Students sharpen their olfactory observation skills by being presented foods and other objects to smell while blindfolded.

Naturalist Strategies

▼ **Classification Strategy**
• Categorizing

▼ **Observation and Comparison Strategies**
• Look-Write-Discuss
  Listen-Write-Discuss
  Smell-Write-Discuss
  Taste-Write-Discuss
  Touch-Write-Discuss
• Observe-Draw-RallyRobin
• Observe-Write-RoundRobin
• Same-Different

• **Taste-Write-Discuss.** To sharpen gustatory observation skills, the students cannot see something they are tasting, and make detailed observations and/or guesses

• **Touch-Write-Discuss.** Sharpens students kinesthetic observation skills. Works well if the object to be touched is not also seen, as when the object is placed in a large paper bag.

Observe-Draw-RallyRobin

Students observe a specimen such as a leaf through a magnifying glass, a cell through a microscope, a star or distant tree through a telescope or simply a worm with the calibrated naked eye. While observing the object, students draw what they see. Afterwards, two students who have observed and drawn the same object pair up. They take turns listing characteristics of the object. Pairs may compare their observations with another pair.

Observe-Write-RoundRobin

Students investigate objects or specimens independently and keep a log of their observations. For example, students go to the playground and all observe the behavior of ants. They keep a detailed description of their observations. When they return to the classroom, they transcribe their log into a detailed written description. Students unite with teammates and in turn share their observations.

An alterative format is to have each teammate observe a different object or specimen. One student observes the behavior of ants, another the variations of grass on the field, another the flowers around the school, and another the trees. Students record their observations, write a description, then share what they learned with teammates. In this way, students learn both observational strategies and about other natural phenomena from peers.

Same-Different

Each pair of students is given two items that are similar in some respects and different in other respects. Examples with naturalist content include a moth and a butterfly, a rose and a daisy, an oak tree leaf and a sycamore tree leaf. Students use a file folder, book or binder to create a barrier between them so they can not see each other's item. Partners work together to describe and record all the similarities and all the differences between the two objects. When students are done, they compare their objects to see what other similarities and differences they can find. Same-Different is a strong technique for attention to detail, a primary trait of the naturalist intelligence.

Same-Different can also be used effectively with almost any content. Students can work to discover what's the same and different about writing samples, news reports covering the same event, illustrations or paintings of the same subject matter, picture pairs with missing or changed elements, or historical characters. Kagan (1994, 1997) provides ready-made holiday and fairy tale same-different content. See sample activities on pages 8.44 - 8.45.

Interpersonal Instructional Strategies

There are many facets to the interpersonal intelligence. People-smart students are often good helpers and teachers, are capable of achieving group consensus, communicate well with others, and know how to share information with others. Instructional strategies to engage the interpersonal intelligence include peer tutoring, decision making, communication skills, and information sharing.

Peer Tutoring Strategies

Jigsaw

Elliot Aronson (1978) popularized the Jigsaw approach for the classroom. In Jigsaw, each student specializes in one specific part of the learning task. For example, if students are learning about Ben Franklin, one student might become an expert on his early life, another his political life, a third his innovations, and a fourth the time when he lived. Students master their part of the material, reunite as a team and teach teammates what they learned. This form of Jigsaw creates a very strong positive interdependence among teammates because

no student can succeed without the help of teammates. There are now many forms of Jigsaw. For a presentation of many Jigsaw formats see Kagan (1994). Caution is in order: it is inappropriate to use Jigsaw activities in which the sole access to important curriculum is via the presentation of a teammate; teammates of a very weak or unmotivated student will suffer.

Jigsaw

Numbered Heads Together

This strategy creates active participation and engages the interpersonal intelligence as students work in teams to answer teacher questions. The teacher asks a question. The question may be recall, "Who assassinated Martin Luther King, Jr.?" Or, the question may be open-ended to generate higher-level thinking, "What impact did his assassination have on the civil rights movement?" Students put their heads together to make sure everyone knows the correct answer or to discuss their ideas as a team. The teacher calls a number between 1 and 4, then picks the team. The student with the corresponding number shares the team's answer or idea.

Numbered Heads Together

Interpersonal Strategies

▼ Peer Tutoring Strategies

- Jigsaw
- Numbered Heads Together
    - Paired Heads Together
    - Stir-the-Class
    - Traveling Heads Together
- Pairs Check
- Team-Pair-Solo
- Telephone

▼ Decision-Making Strategies

- Proactive Prioritizing
- Spend-A-Buck
- Voting

▼ Communication Skills Strategies

- Affirmation Passport
- Paraphrase Passport
- Talking Chips
    - Gambit Chips
    - Response Mode Chips

▼ Information-Sharing Strategies

- Blackboard Share
- Carousel
    - Carousel Discussion
    - Carousel Feedback
    - Carousel Review
- Gallery Tour
- Mix-Pair-Discuss
- One Stray
- Presentations
    - Team Inside-Outside Circle
- Roving Reporters
- Sages Share
- Share & Compare
- Stand-N- Share
    - Individual Stand-N-Share
    - Team Stand-N-Share
- Team Interview
- Three-Step Interview
- Three Stray

• **Paired Heads Together.** Students in pairs huddle to make sure they both can respond. The teacher calls "A" or "B." The student with that letter responds.

• **Stir-the-Class.** Teams stand in a circle around the perimeter of the room. The teacher asks a question. Students huddle to discuss the question. When they have the answer or are done discussing, they stand shoulder to shoulder. The teacher calls a number. The student with the corresponding number rotates to the next team to share their answer. Students remain in their new team for the next question.

• **Traveling Heads Together.** The teacher asks a question. Students put their heads together to make sure everyone knows the answer or has an idea to share. The teacher calls a number. The students with the corresponding number "travel" to a new team to share their answer.

Pairs Check

Pairs Check is an excellent strategy for mastering information or skills with the help of peer tutors. In teams of four, students form two pairs. One student in each pair works on a given problem or task while his or her partner, the coach watches, checks, and helps if necessary. When done, the coach offers affirmation. Partners switch roles to work on the next problem. After the pair has done two problems, they check with the other pair on their team. If they all agree, they celebrate as a team. If they don't agree, they work on solving the problem or reaching consensus as a team.

Team-Pair-Solo

Students solve a problem or work on a given task first as a team of four. Then, the team splits in half and both pairs work on a similar problem. If they have questions, they can consult with the other pair on their team. Finally, students work on a similar problem independently or "solo." Team-Pair-Solo allows students to solve independently a problem they could only solve with help.

Telephone

One student from each team is selected to leave the classroom, or go to another part of the classroom. The teacher teaches or shares information with the remaining students. The absent students return to their teams. Teammates teach them what was missed during their absence. Quizzing the absent student motivates teammates to teach the material well, and allows assessment of how well students taught each other the given material. Quizzes in telephone, however, are to motivate and appreciate accomplishment; they do not count as part of individual student grades.

Proactive Prioritizing

Students may choose among and prioritize alternatives with Proactive Prioritizing. Each student gets a turn at making a case for his or her preference among a list of alternatives. Students try to make their case as well as they can to persuade teammates to see things their way. Their statements can be only positive statements in favor of their preference. They cannot make negative comments toward the other alternatives. If students succeed in getting consensus on their top choice, they attempt to reach consensus on their next top choice. They continue until they have prioritized the list.

Spend-A-Buck

Each student gets four tokens to represent quarters. Students may spend their quarters on any of the alternatives, but they must spend their quarters on more than one alternative. The alternative with the most quarters is deemed the class or team decision. Alternative: Students are given ten tokens representing dimes. Spend-A-Buck works well when the alternatives are each represented by a word, phrase, or picture on separate cards.

Voting

Many times in the classroom, students must make a choice. Maybe the whole class must choose between kickball and basketball for P.E., or maybe a small group must choose between writing an essay or doing a team presentation. Whatever the case, voting, the old democratic standby usually does the trick. The alternative with the most votes wins. If their is a tie, students may discuss the alternatives and vote again.

Affirmation Passport

A strategy to promote the tone in discussions and team work is Affirmation Passport. Students must give each other a positive affirmation before they contribute to the task or discussion: "I appreciate the way you used yellow to make the name stand out more. I'm going to try to use orange to..."

Paraphrase Passport

Paraphrase Passport can be used in any discussion to enhance active listening. Before a student may contribute to the discussion, she must paraphrase the student who spoke before her: "You feel that students should not be let off campus for lunch because it increases tardiness." Students must check to ensure the speaker feels adequately paraphrased. If so, they have the passport to express their own ideas. If not, they must try again to paraphrase more accurately.

Talking Chips

Talking Chips

Each student has one talking chip. Students place their chip in the center of the team table each time they talk. They can speak in any order, but they cannot speak a second time until all chips are in the center. When all chips have been placed (everyone has spoken), the chips are all collected and anyone in any order can speak again. Talking Chips regulates the communication, giving each person an equal opportunity to express her ideas.

• **Gambit Chips.** As they talk, students use Gambit Chips which contain gambits (things to say or do): For examples, Affirmation Chips contain praisers; Paraphrase Chips contain gambits for paraphrasing, such as, "If I hear you correctly…."

• **Response Mode Chips.** As they talk, students use Response Mode Chips which contain responses like: Summarizing, Giving an Idea, Praising an Idea.

For more on Talking Chips, Gambit Chips and Response Mode Chips, see Kagan (1994).

Information Sharing Strategies
Blackboard Share

As students are generating ideas in their teams, if they have an idea to share with the class, one student from the team goes to the board or chart paper to post his or her team's idea or answer. There may be several students at a time posting ideas, each from a different team. If a second idea is generated by a team and it is not yet posted, a second student from the team goes to the front of the class to post the idea. Blackboard Share allows teams to continue working while the ideas are posted, and for the ideas of one team to impact on the discussions of others.

Carousel

Students as teams or individuals rotate around the class in order to view the products of other teams or individuals which are posted or at desks. There are various forms of Carousel, as follows:

• **Carousel Discussion.** Team products are posted or displayed on tables. Each team has a predetermined time to view and discuss each product before rotating as a group to the next product.

• **Carousel Feedback.** As in Carousel Discussion teams rotate to view each product, but they also record feedback on a feedback sheet which stays with the product. When a team returns to their team table, waiting for them is feedback from each of the other teams.

• **Carousel Review.** Review topics are posted, usually on chart paper around the room. Each team stands by one chart. They have a minute to discuss the topic. Then they have a minute to record (list or mind map) their thoughts about the topic. Then they rotate to the next topic. Following their discussion of the topic and the notes left by the prior team, a recorder adds to the notes. A new team recorder writes the team thoughts each time the team rotates to a new topic.

Gallery Tour

In Gallery Tour, also sometimes called Roam the Room, students' products are displayed, often at their desks. Students as individuals, pairs, or teams tour the room to view and/or discuss the products, in no specified order and with no limit on how much or little time is spent viewing each product. A gallery tour might be followed by an opportunity for students as individuals or teams to write affirmative letters to those who created the projects.

Mix-Pair-Discuss

Students mix in the classroom until signaled by the teacher to pair with the nearest classmate. In pairs, students discuss a question posed by the teacher.

One Stray

One Stray gives students experiences in reporting back to the team, like an independent consultant. One student from a team of four visits another team while the three teammates stay behind. After visiting another team, the reporter returns to explain what he or she has seen. This strategy may include rounds. On round one, each reporter visits the next team. On round two a different reporter is chosen, and this time the reporter visits a different team, and so on.

Presentation

Presentations

Presentations are an excellent way for students to share information or their projects or products with each other. There are two variable group sizes with presentations: the number of presenters and the number of students in the audience. Individuals, pairs, or small groups can present to the entire class or to other individuals, pairs or small groups. As a general rule, there is much more active participation when pairs or small groups present to other pairs or small groups. Whole class presentations are good for practicing public speaking and to disseminate information. Student teams are always far more successful in whole class presentations if they first practice with a team-to-team presentation and have the opportunity to revise based on reflection and feedback.

• **Team Inside-Outside Circle.** One favorite team presentation mode is Team Inside-Outside Circle. Two teams go to each corner of the room. One team presents to the other, and then receives feedback. The teams switch roles, with the second team presenting to the first and then receiving feedback. Teams pull apart and discuss how to improve their presentations. One team from each corner then rotates clockwise to give and receive a presentation with another team. Having just given their presentation and having just received feedback and planning time, often the second presentation is dramatically improved.

Roving Reporters

While students are working on projects, one student from each team may for a certain amount of time be a "Roving Reporter," wandering the room gathering information such as discoveries of other teams which might be useful. This role is sometimes called "Scout," and sometimes called "Spy."

Sages Share

Students brainstorm ideas on a given topic, writing each idea on a separate thinkpad slip. Students initial the ideas they feel they can explain to their teammates. Students take turns interviewing the "Sages" — those who have initialed the ideas. The sages explain ideas as the interviewer asks questions. This strategy works well for review of events, main ideas, principles, algorithms.

Share & Compare

Teams simultaneously share their best answer with the team next to them. All teams are actively involved in sharing at once. They compare the similarities and differences between their ideas.

Stand-N-Share

Students as individuals or teams share one item each with the class or share a list of items. Because of the structure of Stand-N-Share, no items are repeated and all items are shared.

• **Individual Stand-N-Share.** In this version individuals share either a list or one or two items, each sitting down when her items have been shared. When seated, the individuals record the other items shared. Often Individual Stand-N-Share is preceded or followed by a team discussion

• **Team Stand-N-Share.** Teams first RoundRobin or Brainstorm a list of ideas or items, such as ways to keep the playground more clean or how to end world hunger. When time is called (usually when teams have generated between six and a dozen ideas), all teams stand. The teacher points to a team. The student with the list reads his or her favorite item from the team list. All other students in the classroom who have the team list check it off if they have it or an item which is similar, or add it to their list if they don't have it. All students then pass their lists to the teammate to the left. The teacher picks another team to share. The student with the list reads her favorite unchecked idea. This continues until all items on a team's list have been shared. The team then sits down and continues to take turns adding each new shared item. When all teams are seated, all ideas have been shared. The method is attractive because all students feel their ideas are represented, but the process does not take a long time.

In a much quicker version, before standing each team decides on one or two favorite ideas, and only those are shared.

Three Stray

Three members of the team rotate to the table of the next team to view a product or project, while Student One stays back to explain the product to the visiting team. After the students return, Student Two stays back while the other three rotate forward two teams. Then Students Three and Four each in turn stay back while the teams rotate three and four teams ahead.

Intrapersonal Instructional Strategies

Instructional strategies which engage the intrapersonal intelligence include those which foster reflection, and value clarification.

Team Interview

In Team Interview, students practice their questioning and sharing skills. In small groups, each student gets a turn at being "in the spotlight" and "on the spot." One student stands up. Teammates take turns asking him or her questions. The questions can be content-related as when the student plays a character from history or literature, or the questions can be personal. With personal questions, students have the right to pass, or answer a question they wish they received. Teammates are each interviewed for an allotted time. See sample activities on pages 8.56 - 8.59.

Three-Step Interview

Three-Step Interview can be used with any content, but works especially well to relate the content to personal experiences. The teacher presents the interview topic such as: "What problem did you find most difficult and why?" Or, "Do you like the story so far?" Or, "Have you ever been in an earthquake?" In teams of four, students break into pairs. One is the interviewer and the other the interviewee. The interviewee shares with the interviewer, then they switch roles and share again. The team reunites and in turn, each teammate shares what they learned from their partner.

Reflection Strategies
Journal Reflections

Journal Reflections, or Personal Journals, are a wonderful way to engage the intrapersonal intelligence. Personal Journals can be used by students to record their feelings, events, stories, poems, drawings, reflections and goals. With less structure, personal journals become more personal. Students express what they want to express, rather than what they feel they must. Personal journals can remain personal or they can be shared with classmates. See sample activities on pages 8.60 - 8.63.

Intrapersonal Strategies

▼ **Reflection Strategies**
- Journal Reflections
- Think-Pair-Share
    Think-Pair-Square
- Team Statements
- Think Time
- Timed Pair Share

▼ **Preference Articulation Strategies**
- Corners
- Free Time
- Similarity Groups

"An intelligence is..." Students think about the topic for at least 20 seconds, then discuss with a partner what they think is a good statement. Then, individuals write down their own statement in their own words and in turn share it with teammates. The team then works together to come up with a team statement that captures the essence of all individual statements. The team statement may be very different from all individual statements. Teams share their statements with other teams.

Think-Pair-Share

Think-Pair-Share is a simple, yet powerful strategy that can be integrated at any point in a lesson. The teacher poses a question and asks students to think about their response. After ample think time, students pair up to discuss their answers. Some students are selected to share their own or partner's answer with the class.

• **Think-Pair-Square.** This strategy is the same as Think-Pair-Share except in the final step, pairs turn to the other pair on their team and share their answers or ideas with teammates. This version creates more active participation than having just a few students share.

Team Statements

Team statements allow students to explore what they think about a topic and what their teammates think. First, the teacher announces a topic or statement starter like:

Think Time

Think Time is a powerful teacher tool. It's simple too: Think Time, also called Wait Time (Rowe, 1978) is merely a silent 3 to 15 seconds for students to think about their response to a question before students share with the class, a partner, write their answer. Think time allows reflective students to collect their thoughts before they are asked to share them or write them down. A quick Think Time used for reflection after a response or action is also a powerful tool. Students think about their own thinking or actions and learn to better direct their thinking and actions.

Timed Pair Share

After a topic is presented by the teacher, students share with a partner for a predetermined amount of time, say one minute. Then, their partner shares with them for the same amount of time. Timed Pair

Timed Pair Share

Share allows for equal speaking opportunities and ensures that all students actively participate. Because partners do not interrupt while they share, students reach deeper intrapersonal levels as they share, especially if the content is personal. See sample activities on pages 8.64 - 8.67.

See sample activities on pages 8.64 - 8.67.

Preference Articulation Strategies

Corners

The teacher announces a topic and gives students a choice of four alternatives. Any preference can be the focus, such as favorite season, profession, holiday, line from a poem, design, sport, animal. The corners are often indicated with a posted word or picture. Students think about their favorite alternative and write it down on a slip of paper. Students then go to the corner of the classroom corresponding to their choice. In pairs in the corners students share the reasons for choice (often using a RallyRobin). Students from each corner may be called on to share their reasons for making their decisions. They may be asked to paraphrase their partner, or to pair up with someone from a different corner to appreciate different values.

Free Time

Occasional free time allows students the freedom of personal choice and expression. It works well to break up a long block schedule or a transition period. Free time is an easy strategy, because teachers don't have to do anything for ten to fifteen minutes. Some students choose to talk with each other about what happened that day or what will happen the coming weekend; some students sit alone at their desk and doodle; some students choose to read their books; some students choose to play a board game; some students choose to fin-

ish or start their homework. The enhanced energy and focus with which students tackle academics following Free Time compensates for the time off.

Similarity Groups

The teacher poses a question upon which students should vary, but not too greatly (preferably no more than eight or so groups). For example the question may be: "If you could be any movie actor, who would you be?" Students form groups based on their commonality. In groups of two or three within the similarity groups, students discuss their similarities. Later they may share their reasons with the class or individually with students with other choices. With Similarity Groups, students get to know themselves better by exploring their favorites and sharing them with others. Similarity Groups, like Corners, can be used with any MI content: favorite music, art, artist, sport, book, type of puzzle, plant, pet, hobby.

MI Learning Centers

Learning centers are physical environments established in the classroom where students go to interact with the content and often with each other. MI learning centers are a recent adaptation of the time-honored learning center approach. With MI centers, the learning centers are set up based on the multiple intelligences. Each classroom is unique, and how you design your MI centers will depend on your students and your teaching philosophy. Let's

Naming MI Centers

Intelligence	Famous Person	Simple
Verbal/Linguistic	Emily Dickinson	Word Smart
Logical/Mathematical	Albert Einstein	Math or Logic Smart
Visual/Spatial	Georgia O'Keeffe	Art or Space Smart
Musical/Rhythmic	Ludwig van Beethoven	Music Smart
Bodily/Kinesthetic	Thomas Edison	Body Smart
Naturalist	Jane Goodall	Nature Smart
Interpersonal	Martin Luther King, Jr.	People Smart
Intrapersonal	Sigmund Freud	Self Smart

look at some common questions and issues regarding MI centers.

How Many MI Centers?

MI theory identifies eight intelligences. This is a good number of learning centers in the classroom, one corresponding to each intelligence. However, if by some stroke of luck, we have a small class, eight centers may be too many. We can always have fewer centers. If we think six centers is more appropriate for our class, we may decide to rotate intelligences from week to week. We may leave out the musical and intrapersonal centers one week, then include them the next week while leaving out the visual and kinesthetic centers.

The eight intelligences are great content for centers, but there is nothing to say that we cannot set up a center based on another intelligence that we value, say the emotional, or mechanical, or even culinary intelligence.

How MI Centers Look

Centers can be integrated with different stations in the classroom. At each center there are usually materials associated with the intelligence of focus. For example, students go to a corner of the classroom colorfully labeled, "Theater." Inside the Theater, a center based on the bodily/kinesthetic intelligence, there is a little stage and boxes filled with costumes and props.

If students are seated in cooperative clusters, or at small tables, their desks may double as MI centers.

MI Center Names

Each center has a name, often indicated by a mobile above the center or by placard. The center may be named after the eight intelligences (e.g. the Verbal/Linguistic Center) or after a well-known individual who displays expertise in the particular intelligence (e.g. the William Shakespeare Center). Some teachers name their centers according to the intelligence being developed such as The Word Smart Center. See box: Naming MI Centers. There are many famous individuals for each intelligence listed that may be used as center names (See Chapter 11: Honoring Uniqueness; Celebrating Diversity).

Center names do not have to always remain the same. MI center names can change as often as the activity changes. For example, if the activity at the verbal/linguistic center for the day or week is a foreign language exercise, the center may be called the Berlitz or Spanish or French Center.

How Many Students Per Center?

We recommend four. If we have thirty two students in the class and set up eight centers, four students can visit each center at once. Four students is an ideal group size for cooperative work: It is large enough for ensure a diversity of views and skills; it is evenly divisible for breaking students into pairs; it is small enough for active participation.

Cooperative or Independent?

MI centers can be either cooperative or independent. In cooperative learning centers, students often have specific roles in working on the cooperative task. For example, at the Naturalist (Charles Darwin) learning center on dinosaurs, each student may be in charge of finding information about a different dinosaur, or each student may have a different task with the same dinosaur such as: eating habits, size and weight, time and place, natural habitat. Students share their information with their teammates at their center.

Cooperative structures such as Pairs Check, RallyTable, and Timed-Pair-Share, may be included in center task cards, ensuring more equal participation. Centers may center around projects so that by the end of a visit to a center, a team has completed a project.

Independent centers allow students to work independently and at their own pace. Activities at the intrapersonal center will

usually be independent and those at the interpersonal center will usually be cooperative. The other centers will depend on your teaching philosophy.

Assigned or Free Choice?

Students can be assigned to their centers or can be given free choice to attend the centers they wish in the order they wish. If students are given a free choice, it is helpful to have a name pocket chart by the center with a limit of students indicated, so when the pocket chart is full other students do not join the center. Assigning students to centers works well when using heterogeneous cooperative teams. Each team is assigned one center, and teams rotate to the other centers in a determined order.

Using free choice gives students some autonomy. Students may have a job card or a portfolio to create by end of the week. They may attend any center they wish in the order they choose as long as they complete their tasks or portfolio. Free choice can be a little more difficult to manage when too many students want to work at the same center at once or very social friends go to the same centers together and are difficult to keep on task.

Exploratory or Structured?

The activities at each center can be loosely structured, exploratory activities so students engage and develop their intelligences through discovery. At an exploratory center, students play with the material at the center such as building materials, pattern blocks, or fraction manipulatives. Exploratory centers can be used with younger students and when centers are first set up for students to freely explore the resources available at the center.

Center activities can also have more structure, leading to specific learning objectives. A more structured center may include a task card with prescribed procedures and roles. For example, the task card may instruct students to use the fraction manipulatives to find as many combinations as possible to build one. An answer sheet may be provided at the center. A helpful hint for managing centers is assigning the same time length to each task and providing a sponge activity relating to the intelligence or content for students or teams that finish early.

MI Projects

- Commercial
- Co-op Co-op
- Co-op Jigsaw
- Event Planning
- Experiment
- Group Investigation
- Partners
- Plays
- Research Report
- Survey
- Video

MI Theme Centers

MI centers can revolve around a theme. For example, if the theme is transportation, at the Musical/Rhythmic (or the Louis Armstrong) center, students may write an airplane rap, integrating learned facts about airplanes. At the Visual/Spatial (Pablo Picasso) center, students draw or paint pictures of travel by air, land, or sea.

How Often Do Students Visit MI Centers?

Some teachers use MI learning centers all day long. Every student visits all eight learning centers every day. Some teachers have a specific time of the day when students visit one or two learning centers. Over a week or two week period, students visit all eight MI centers. We believe centers are an excellent teaching strategy, but a mixture of MI instructional strategies, MI lessons, centers and projects gives students a healthy balance of learning experiences.

Planning MI Centers

In Chapter 13: MI Lessons, Centers, Projects, and Theme Units, we look at the steps for planning MI centers and provide a number of practical planning forms.

MI Projects

MI projects are powerful instructional strategies to teach with and for the multiple intelligences. Some favorite MI projects include: conduct an experiment, research a topic, create a video, direct a play, build a model, write a report, design a work of art, plan an event. As students engage in the process, create products, and present their projects, they use a number of their intelligences in a meaningful way.

In Chapters 13: MI Lessons, Centers, Projects, and Theme Units, we examine the steps of planning MI projects, provide a range of project ideas spanning the intelligences, and have practical forms for facilitating MI projects in the classroom. Here, we will look at a few different types of projects and some strategies to prepare and present MI projects.

Commercial

In small groups, students plan, create, rehearse, and perform a commercial for the class. The commercial can be on any topic, from selling the planet Jupiter to advertising the artwork of a famous artist to selling a book the class has read. Students can do a quick 30-second commercial or they can do an extended "infomercial." Commercials usually integrate a jingle (musical/rhythmic), acting (bodily/kinesthetic), visual aids (visual/spatial), a script (verbal/linguistic), and most importantly, a coordination of efforts (interpersonal). Videotaping the commercials is helpful for self-evaluation and reflection (intrapersonal) as well as assessment.

Co-op Co-op

Co-op Co-op (Kagan, 1994) is a cooperative strategy well suited for preparing and presenting MI projects. The essence of Co-op Co-op is structuring the classroom so students cooperate within and between teams to reach the class-determined learning objectives. Co-op Co-op provides an excellent forum for students to explore any content area in a self-directed manner while developing their intelligences, especially their interpersonal abilities to cooperate and communicate. There are ten basic steps to Co-op Co-op.

On MI Projects

When I began teaching through the Multiple Intelligences in the mid-1980's I thought the highlight of my program was the seven learning centers. On a daily basis, students approached content and skills in seven ways. Over the years, however, I have found that the independent project work is the most valuable feature of my program. The projects enable students to apply and further develop the concepts and skills they have gained at the centers. While students enjoy their active, center-based learning, they even more eagerly pursue their independent projects. It is the projects which teach my students how to direct their own learning.

— *Bruce Campbell, 1994*

1. Student-Centered Class Discussion

A topic is presented to the class in the form of a stimulating lecture, readings, experience, demonstration or presentation. Students are then encouraged to discover and express their own interests relating to the topic. Students, with artful questioning from the teacher, determine the content for Co-op Co-op.

2. Selection of Student Teams

Students may be assigned to mixed ability, sex, ethnicity, and intelligences teams or may select their own teams based on interest.

3. Teambuilding and Cooperative Skill Development

When students are assigned to new teams, some time is spent to establish a positive team environment to ensure successful cooperation and communication. See Teambuilding (Kagan, Kagan, & Kagan, 1997).

4. Team Topic Selection

Students divide the learning unit into topics so that each team is responsible for one aspect of the learning unit, and the work of teams will complement each other in moving toward the class objective of covering the various aspects of the topic.

An MI variation is to have each team be in charge of one of the intelligences relating to the topic. So for example, if the topic was careers, one team is word-smart careers, the next logic/math-smart careers and so on.

5. Mini-Topic Selection

In groups, students further divide their topic into mini-topics. Student select the mini-topic that interests them most. Continuing with the MI example, in the word-smart careers team, one student may select journalist, another novelist, another speech writer.

6. Mini-Topic Preparation

Each student becomes an expert in his or her own mini-topic. Students investigate their mini-topic through any variety of sources. Students engage their multiple intelligences as they read, watch videos, interview, conduct surveys and experiments to learn as much as they can about their selected area of interest.

7. Mini-Topic Presentation

Students present to their teammates what they learned on their mini-topic. Teammates give feedback. Students may then delve deeper into their mini-topic and present new information to teammates.

8. Preparation of Team Presentations

After students each present their mini-topic, the team discusses how they want to present all of the information to the class in an integrated way. Students make their presentations as multimodal and stimulating as possible. Straight lectures are discouraged. Presentations that integrate movement, art, music, statistics, graphic organizers, reflection, and audience participation are encouraged.

9. Team Presentations

Each team presents their topic to the class.

10. Reflection and Evaluation

Students reflect on the process of the project and the final product and presentation. Students receive feedback on: 1) their team presentation to the class, 2) their individual contributions to the presentation, and 3) an individual product such as a report based on their mini-topic. A group grade, however, should not feed into a student's report card grade.

Co-op Jigsaw

A variation of Co-op Co-op is Co-op Jigsaw, described in detail by Kagan (1994). In Co-op Jigsaw the students from each team leave the team to work with members of other teams to become experts on some skill which will be applied as the team prepares its research and presentation. MI presentation skills are an obvious candidate for the expert topics, so one student on the team may become an expert on how to integrate music into a presentation, another teammate may become the movement expert, a third the visual/spatial expert, and a fourth the interpersonal expert. The experts work with corresponding experts from other teams to learn skills they later bring back to their own teams. In one form of Co-op Jigsaw the expert groups report out to the whole class; in another form they simply bring back skills to share with their teammates who then create an enriched, integrated MI presentation for the class.

Event Planning

Planning an event requires a great coordination of efforts, engaging and developing people smarts. Have the entire class pick an event they want to do, plan it, and carry it through. Often, the event is divided into components and students or teams assume responsibility for different aspects. Some events for students to plan include: field trips, guest speakers, pizza party, pool party, parade, sporting event, and celebrations of the various intelligences.

Experiment

Although experimentation is most common in the natural and social sciences, and involves generating, analyzing, and interpreting data, experiments are by no means entirely the products of the logical/mathematical and naturalist intelligences. Experiments and their products actually require a great integration of students' multiple intelligences. Experiments usually require organizational and leadership skills (interpersonal skills), the ability to set aside biases in analysis and look objectively at the data (intrapersonal skills), write factual report of procedures, results and implications (verbal/linguistic skills), conduct the experiment (bodily/kinesthetic skills), and create charts graphs and visuals to present the experiment (visual/spatial skills).

The procedure for using an experiment as an MI project often follows the scientific method. First, students select a topic of interest, say testing the absorbancy of different types of paper towels. They then formulate a hypothesis (towel x will soak up more water than towel y). Next, students design an experiment to test their hypothesis, often controlling variables. They might determine the absorbancy of the towels for different types of liquids, or passive versus active absorbancy. They perform the experiment, and collect data. Students then analyze their data, make interpretations and draw conclusions.

Group Investigation

Group Investigation (Sharan & Sharan, 1992) is a complex cooperative learning lesson design integrating cooperation and communication with student-directed inquiry. It may also be easily adapted to develop the multiple intelligences. In Group Investigation, students coordinate efforts within small groups and between groups in the classroom. Students progress through six stages as they do Group Investigation.

Stage 1: Class Determines Subtopics and Organizes into Research Groups

The teacher presents a problem to the class such as, "What is the importance of space exploration?" Students' interest may be stimulated with associated books, magazines, a film, lecture. Students work independently or in small groups to select subtopics related to the investigation. The whole class settles on a number of subtopics and students sign up for the subtopic that interests them most.

Stage II: Groups Plan Their Investigations

In their groups, students discuss what they want to investigate relating to their subtopic, the resources they have available, who will do what.

Stage III: Groups Carry Out Their Investigations

Students locate the information they will need for their inquiry, research their topic, organize and interpret the information, and finally work together to integrate their findings.

Stage IV: Groups Plan Their Presentations

Students work in their groups to plan their presentations, what they are going to present and how they will present it. It is important that everyone is active in the group presentations. Students can use a variety of presentation modes spanning the intelligences. They can use charts, graphs, slides, video, music, drama, movement.

Stage V: Groups Make Their Presentations

Groups take turns presenting their information to the class. The audience shows appreciation, asks questions, then gives the group written feedback.

Stage VI: Teacher and Students Evaluate Their Projects

Students may be evaluated on the information or application of their knowledge. Students reflect on their own projects.

Partners

Partners is another excellent cooperative learning strategy that works well with MI projects. It has been detailed at length (Kagan, 1994) in ten steps. Essentially, partners are formed within teams. The class then divides so that one pair from each team sits on one side of the room and the other pair sits on the other side of the room. Pairs on one side of the room all work on one project; pairs on the other side, work on a different project. Pairs can consult with like-project pairs sitting near them. When the projects are completed, the teams reunite and each pair presents its project to the other pair. If the project involves learning objectives, each pair may teach and tutor the other pair.

Plays

A play is an excellent MI project integrating many intelligences. Students write and/or read scripts (verbal/linguistic), create stage designs and props (visual/spatial), act (bodily/kinesthetic), and interact to plan and present their play to an audience (interpersonal). Students can perform plays in small groups or as an entire class. Students can write their own plays or enact existing plays.

Research Report

A research report is a good project to stimulate the verbal/linguistic intelligence as it involves reading and writing. Research reports also usually emphasize the logical skills of organization, induction and analysis. For reports, students pick a topic or are assigned a topic. They write a paper making an argument or summarizing their learning. Reports can integrate the visual/spatial intelligence (integration of graphics, illustrations, or design), the interpersonal intelligence (students work collaboratively or do peer conferences for their independent report), and the intrapersonal intelligence (students relate the topic to themselves personally and include their personal perspective on the topic).

Survey

A survey is a relatively easy project that focuses primarily on the logical/mathematical, interpersonal, and intrapersonal intelligences. Surveys may be conducted as team projects or independently.

Simple surveys may be conducted within the class in an hour as students interview each other to determine things like how many classmates have pets of various kinds, favorite foods, average number of hours a night spent watching TV, or doing homework. Students conduct their surveys, then often chart or graph the results and present them to a partner or to the class.

More complex surveys may be conducted following experimental methodology. Students formulate a hypothesis about a topic, then come up with a question or series of questions to test their hypothesis. For example, one student may test her hypothesis that weather affects people's moods by asking subjects questions relating to their moods during different types of weather. Another student may test his hypothesis that there is a correlation between grades and study time by collecting students' grades and the number of hours a day they study. After students collect their data, they analyze it and make charts and graphs. They draw conclusions on what they found out. The final step of the Survey is to present it to the class.

Video

The Video is an exciting project based on the visual/spatial intelligence. Small groups each plan, make and present their videos to the class.

Here's one format for a Video project: The class is given or chooses a topic of interest. For younger students the topic may be one that may be covered during schooltime. Older students may venture into the community to explore their topic. Let's say, for instance, the topic is the Five Senses. The topic is divided into a number of subtopics. In this case, the topic may be divided into sight, sound, smell, touch, taste. The topic could also be divided into at school, at home, in a restaurant, in a store. Students are assigned to small groups, each focusing on one subtopic. A target duration for the video may be assigned depending on students' level.

Students work together in their group and plan how they are going to capture the essence of their subtopic with a video. An initial meeting with students is helpful to make sure they're on the right track. Ideally, each team gets their own video camera. With the popularity of video cameras, this is becoming more feasible. Parents are often willing to lend their cameras. If not enough video cameras are available, groups sign up for the use of a camera for a specific time slot. Editing equipment is a nicety, but definitely not a requirement.

After students have their videos prepared, they watch them in the class. Often, groups present the video to the class and provide closure after the video. Each group may make up a quiz on the content of their video for the rest of the class. The audience asks questions after each video and provides feedback.

Videos are a great visual/spatial project. They also integrate a range of intelligences as students plan their videos, cooperate, write their scripts, make props, conduct interviews, design signs, act.

Summary

In this chapter, we looked at dozens and dozens of strategies that can transform any lesson into an engaging MI lesson; we examined MI centers in the classroom; and finally, we explored projects to engage students' multiple intelligences. These MI strategies are tools for every teacher's toolbox. The more skilled we are with each tool and the more artfully we integrate them in our daily teaching, the more we match, stretch, and celebrate each intelligence. With a wide range of strategies, we

reach all students, develop the many facets of each intelligence, and our classrooms come alive, making that place called school a fun, challenging, engaging place for everyone!

References

Armstrong, T. *Multiple Intelligences in the Classroom.* Alexandria, VA: Association for Supervision and Curriculum Development, 1994.

Aronson, E. *The Jigsaw Classroom.* Beverly Hills, CA: Sage Publications, 1978.

Asher, J. *Learning Another Language through Actions.* Los Gatos, CA: Sky Oaks Productions, Inc., 1993.

Bellanca, J. *The Cooperative Think Tank I & II.* Arlington Heights, IL: IRI/Skylight Training and Publishing, Inc., 1990, 1992.

Bloom, B. S., et al. *A Taxonomy of Educational Objectives: Handbook 1: Cognitive Domain.* New York, NY: Longman, 1977.

Bromley, K. *Journaling.* New York, NY: Scholastic Inc., 1993.

Bromley, K., Irwin-De Vitis, L. & Modlo, M. *Graphic Organizers.* New York, NY: Scholastic, Inc., 1995.

Buzan, T. & Buzan, B. *How to Use the Mind Map Book: Radiant Thinking to Maximize Your Brain's Untapped Potential.* New York, NY: NAL-Dutton, 1994.

Campbell, L., Campbell, B. & Dickinson, D. *Teaching and Learning Through Multiple Intelligences.* Needham Heights, MA: Allyn & Bacon, 1992.

Campbell, D. *The Mozart Effect.* New York: Avon, 1997

Erickson, T. *United We Solve: 116 Math Problems for Groups (Grades 5-10).* Oakland, CA: eeps media, 1996.

Erickson, T. *Get It Together: Math Problems for Groups (Grades 4-12).* Berkeley, CA: Equals, 1989.

Fogarty, R. *How to Teach for Metacognitive Reflection.* Palatine, IL: IRI Skylight, 1994.

Goodman, J. *Group Solutions. Cooperative Logic Activities.* Berkeley, CA: Lawrence Hall of Science GEMS, 1992.

Goodman, J. with Kopp, J. *Group Solutions, Too!* Berkeley, CA: Lawrence Hall of Science GEMS, 1997.

Jensen, E. *The Learning Brain.* Del Mar, CA: The Brain Store, 1995.

Kagan, M., Robertson, L., & Kagan, S. *Classbuilding.* San Clemente, CA: Kagan Cooperative Learning, 1995.

Kagan, L., Kagan, M., & Kagan, S. *Teambuilding.* San Clemente, CA: Kagan Cooperative Learning, 1997.

Kagan, S. *Cooperative Learning.* San Clemente, CA: Kagan Cooperative Learning, 1994.

Kagan, S. *Same-Different, Holidays.* San Clemente, CA: Kagan Cooperative Learning, 1994.

Kagan, S. *Same-Different, Fairy Tales.* San Clemente, CA: Kagan Cooperative Learning, 1994.

Klose, C. & Wolfe, L. *Lyrical Lessons.* San Clemente, CA: Kagan Cooperative Learning, 1997.

Margulies, N. *Mapping Inner Space. Learning and Teaching Mind Mapping.* Tucson, AZ: Zephyr Press, 1991.

Parks, S. & Black, H. *Organizing Thinking, Book I.* Pacific Grove, CA: Critical Thinking Press & Software, 1992.

Parks, S. & Black, H. *Organizing Thinking, Book II.* Pacific Grove, CA: Critical Thinking Press & Software, 1990.

Rose, C. & Nicholl, M. *Accelerated Learning for the 21st Century.* New York, NY: Dell, 1997.

Rowe, M. *Teaching Science as a Continuous Inquiry.* New York, NY: McGraw Hill, 1978.

Scott, J. *Story Switchers.* San Clemente, CA: Kagan Cooperative Learning, 1997.

Sharan, Y. & Sharan, S. *Expanding Cooperative Learning through Group Investigation.* New York, NY: Teachers College Press, 1992.

Wiederhold, C. *Cooperative Learning and Higher-Level Thinking: The Q-Matrix.* San Clemente, CA: Kagan Cooperative Learning, 1995.

Activities to Match Intelligences

Each of the intelligences can be used as a means to gain knowledge in areas beyond itself: using body movement to learn vocabulary words, music to teach math concepts, art (drawing, painting, and sculpture) to bring to life different periods of history and different cultures, debate to explore various perspectives on current events, and the skill of comparing and contrasting to analyze characters in a Shakespearean play (Lazear, 1991, p. xviii).

Having explored a number of MI strategies for each of the eight intelligences, we will now take a closer look at some of our personal favorites, and provide some sample activities to illustrate how each strategy looks in the classroom.

Multiple intelligences instructional strategies are tools in our toolbox that we may pull out time and time again to create powerful and engaging learning experiences for our students.

For each intelligence, we have selected two MI strategies to examine in some detail. Each strategy has a single-page overview containing a basic description, how it relates to the intelligence, and a step-by-step procedure to implement the strategy in your class. After each one page description of the MI strategy, there are some sample activities. These MI strategies are tools in our instructional strategy toolbox to pull out time and time again to create powerful and engaging learning experiences for our students.

We must admit, because of our emphasis on cooperative learning, we are biased toward the interpersonal intelligence. It is our belief that one of the primary functions of education in a democratic society, in addition to passing along the knowledge and thinking skills to make wise, informed decisions, is to foster the interpersonal values and skills necessary to prepare our students to become productive workers and citizens in an increasingly pluralistic and interdependent society. Therefore, many of the strategies you'll find in this chapter involve cooperative effort. Many of the strategies are based on cooperative learning teams of four. For more information regarding cooperative learning or for dozens of cooperative learning strategies, please see *Cooperative Learning* (Kagan, 1994).

For the visual/spatial intelligence, you will find Match Mine, and for the naturalist intelligence, you will find Same-Different. The two strategies are very similar. They both involve two students on opposite sides of a barrier, coordinating efforts. In the case of Same-Different, students are working to uncover similarities and differences in two natural objects such as sharks and dolphins. In the case of Match Mine, one student arranges objects such as geometric shapes on a board and must communicate his or her arrangement to a partner to match the design.

As students coordinate efforts to find similarities and differences in Same-Different, they are using their interpersonal and verbal/linguistic intelligences. They learn to take the role of the other — a key interpersonal skill — and learn to articulate their perception unambiguously — a key verbal/linguistic skill. The logical/math-ematical intelligence is developed as well: To be successful, students must analyze the Same-Different pictures into their components, developing their analytic capabilities.

One of the primary functions of education in a democratic society is to foster the interpersonal values and skills necessary to prepare our students to become productive workers and citizens in an increasingly pluralistic and interdependent society.

The same is true with Match Mine — it involves a number of intelligences. Why, then, have we chosen to place Match Mine in the visual/spatial intelligence section and Same-Different in the naturalist intelligence section? We have attempted to match up the core operation of the strategy with the core operation or facet of the intelligence. The core operation of Match Mine is spatially arranging objects, an operation central to the visual/spatial intelligence; the core operation of Same-Different is comparing and contrasting two samples, an indispensable operation of the naturalist intelligence.

Because of their inherent design, different MI strategies stimulate different intelligences. However, because of the relation of intelligences, it is rare that a strategy stimulates only a single intelligence.

Also, the type of learning that results from using an MI strategy heavily depends on the academic content being delivered. As students engage in Same-Different, they will develop the naturalist intelligence if we use natural content; if we use musical selections to compare and contrast, students will also develop their musical intelligence; if we use two works of art, students will also develop their visual/spatial intelligence.

Similarly, if we use Match Mine with different content, a different learning experience results. Instead of using geometric shapes (visual/spatial content) as gamepieces, we can have students arrange parts of a face such as a smile, frown, angry eyebrows on an outline of a face (interpersonal content); we can have students arrange eighth notes, quarter notes, half notes on a staff (musical/rhythmic intelligence); we can have students arrange a python, macaw, ocelot, and chameleon on an illustrated picture of a lush rainforest (naturalist intelligence); or we can have students arrange internal organs on a skeleton (bodily/kinesthetic intelligence).

The type of learning experiences we create depends on both the strategy we select and the content being taught. Teaching is the art of skillfully selecting and sequencing the appropriate strategies to deliver the academic content. The more strategies we have in our instructional strategy toolbox, the more likely we will be able to create learning experiences to effectively teach our content and fully develop students' intelligences. The more ways we teach, the more students we reach — and the more intelligences we develop!

The more ways we teach, the more students we reach — and the more intelligences we develop!

The sample activities you'll find in this chapter are an attempt to match the content with the strategy. For example, 4S Brainstorming, one of the strategies selected for the verbal/linguistic intelligence,

is used to have students brainstorm morals for writing an original fairy tale, adjectives for writing descriptive sentences, and opening sentences for writing a mystery story. 4S Brainstorming can just as easily be used for having students brainstorm emotions they've felt (intrapersonal) names for a song (musical/rhythmic), and activities involving fine motor skills (bodily/kinesthetic).

RoundRobin, the second structure selected for the verbal/linguistic intelligence, involves students taking turns talking. The activities again are based on verbal/linguistic content: writing and reading a letter to a friend, writing and reading a book report, and writing and reading an article on an alien abduction. We can just as easily use RoundRobin to develop the other intelligences: students can RoundRobin count by threes (mathematical intelligence), RoundRobin share their feelings about a topic (intrapersonal), or RoundRobin share their reaction to a piece of music (musical).

Feel free to use the strategies provided here to teach for any intelligence. One of the benefits of these strategies is they can be used across the curriculum and across the intelligences. Try some sample activities provided in this chapter. They are intended to get you started with MI strategies. Once you are familiar with the strategies, try them with your own curriculum. Play with them to teach different content and develop different intelligences. Experiment with the strategies to see when they work best, what your students enjoy, what challenges your students. Make these MI strategies your own!

Table of MI Strategies and Activities

Table of MI Strategies and Activities

(continued)

MI Strategy | 1

4S Brainstorming

Speed | *Silly*

Synergy | *Support*

The team becomes a think tank as each student — each with a special role — contributes to the team's "storm" of ideas. 4S Brainstorming is a strong strategy for the verbal/linguistic intelligence as students generate and record verbal responses. Brainstorming also serves as a wonderful prewriting exercise to prime the pump for subsequent writing.

S t e p s . . . .

1 Teacher Assigns Roles

Assign each student on each team one of the roles below. As you assign each role, have students generate and record associated gambits — things for that person to say and do. Students can make role cards by folding a sheet of paper in half lengthwise and writing the name of their role on the front and their gambits on the back (e.g. on the back of Sergeant Support's role card it may say, "Great idea!" and "Wow!").

2 Teacher Announces Prompt

Announce a topic which prompts students to generate creative ideas. A prompt should have no right or wrong answers; rather it should be open-ended enough for students to come up with loads of creative ideas. "You find an old lamp and when you polish it, a genie pops out and says she'll grant you three wishes. What are some of your wishes?"

3 Students Generate Ideas

In teams, students generate ideas. Students take turns recording each on a sheet of paper, or each on a separate slip of paper (for categorizing). When done brainstorming, students can use the ideas they generated for a writing assignment.

4S Roles for Brainstorming

• **Speed Captain** ensures that teammates work fast, to come up with as many ideas as possible. "We only have one minute left." "Let's hurry!" "Let's get quicker with our responses."

• **Sultan of Silly** encourages silly ideas. "Let's have a crazy idea!" "Can anyone think of something funny?"

• **Sergeant Support** makes sure all ideas are encouraged with no evaluation of ideas. "All ideas are great!" "That's an excellent idea!" "I really like that!"

• **Synergy Guru** encourages teammates to build on each others' ideas. "Let's build on that." "Let's combine these ideas."

A Fairy Tale

Fairy tales often have lessons or morals in them. For example, what does the "Three Little Pigs" teach us? As a team, you will write a fairy tale with a moral to your story. First, brainstorm possible morals your team should consider. After brainstorming, as a team, select your favorite moral. Write a fairy tale that expresses the moral.

Morals:

_____

_____

_____

_____

_____

_____

_____

_____

_____

_____

_____

_____

_____

_____

_____

_____

Activity 2

4S Brainstorming

Descriptive Sentences

In teams, brainstorm adjectives for each of the objects below. On a separate sheet of paper, independently write a paragraph that best describes each object including the adjectives you brainstormed. Share your descriptions with a partner.

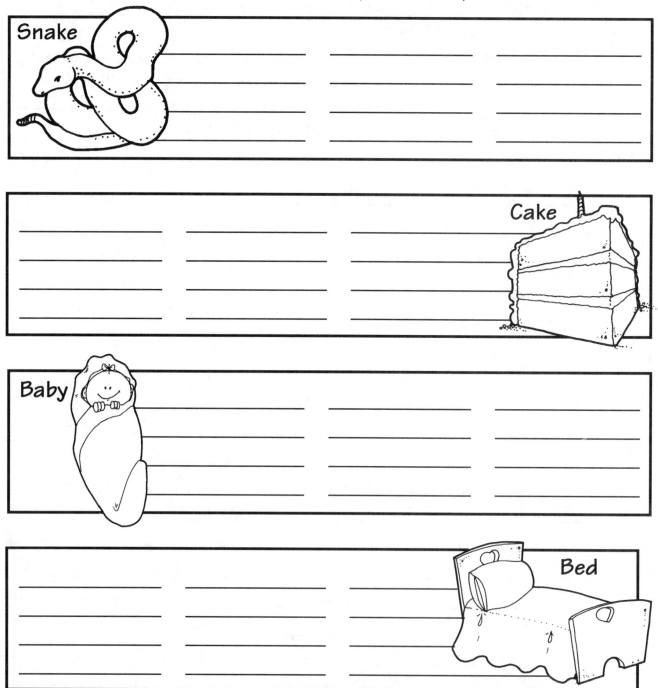

Snake

Cake

Baby

Bed

3   *Activity*

4S Brainstorming

Mystery Story

Brainstorm possible opening sentences for a mystery story. As a team, select your favorite opening sentence. Independently write a mystery story using your selected sentence. Share your stories in turn with teammates and compare how similar or different they are.

MI Strategy 2

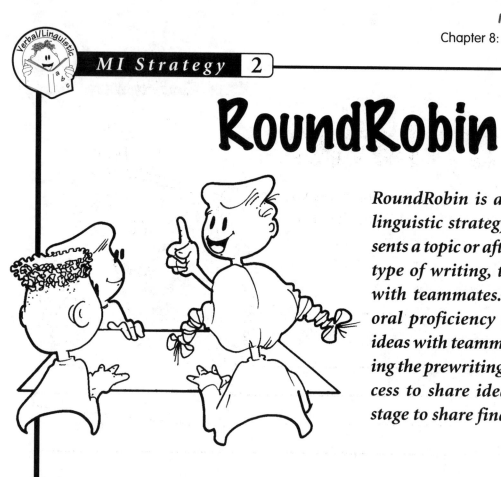

RoundRobin

RoundRobin is an indispensable verbal/ linguistic strategy. After the teacher presents a topic or after students complete any type of writing, they each share, in turn with teammates. RoundRobin promotes oral proficiency as students share their ideas with teammates. It may be used during the prewriting stage of the writing process to share ideas or as the publishing stage to share final written work.

Steps ....

1 Teacher Announces Topic

Announce the topic on which students are to share with the team. The topic can be from the linguistic domain such as sharing one idea on the use of symbolism in the story. Students can also share their completed writing: "In turn, read your paper on the symbolism to your teammates."

2 Students Take Turns Sharing

One student shares her or his ideas to teammates or reads aloud to teammates. The student to the left of him or her shares next. RoundRobin may be completed in one round of sharing or may continue for many rounds.

4 *Activity*
RoundRobin

Friendly Letter

Write a letter to your best friend describing what you did over the weekend. When done, use RoundRobin to share your letter with your teammates.

Dear _____

_____

_____

_____

_____

_____

_____

_____

_____

_____

_____

_____

_____

_____

_____

_____

_____

_____

_____

_____

_____

Activity 5

RoundRobin

Book Report

Write a brief summary of a book you read and your evaluation of the book. Use RoundRobin to share your book report with teammates.

Title _____

Author _____

Synopsis _____

_____

_____

_____

_____

_____

_____

_____

_____

_____

_____

_____

Evaluation _____

_____

_____

_____

_____

6 **"Activity**
RoundRobin

Verbal/Linguistic

Aliens Abduct Student

Read All About It

A UFO lands on the school and abducts a student. Write an article describing the incident. Draw an illustration and include a caption for your article. Use RoundRobin to share your article with teammates.

_____
_____
_____
_____

caption

MI Strategy 3

Find My Rule

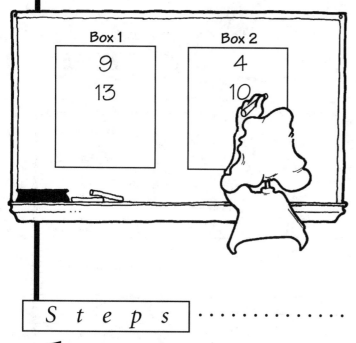

Box 1

9
13

Box 2

4
10

In Find My Rule, the teacher draws two boxes on the overhead or on the blackboard. Different items are drawn or written in the two boxes based on a "rule." For example, the rule may be odd and even; odd numbers are written in one box and even numbers written in the other. The class' task is to "find the rule." Find My Rule is a strong logical/mathematical strategy used for concept development, team problem solving and inductive reasoning.

S t e p s . . . .

1 Teacher Introduces the Rule

Draw two boxes on the chalkboard and label them Box 1 and Box 2. Add one item to each box. For example, draw a concave shape in one box and a convex shape in the other.

2 RallyRobin

Students in pairs take turns stating possible rules with their partner.

3 Add More Items

When pairs are done mentioning possible rules, add another pair of items to the boxes and have students do a RallyRobin on possible rules, this time with a different partner. Then add more items and allow students to discuss possible rules as a team.

4 Team Tests Rule

When the team thinks they have "found the rule" all hands go up on the team. Select a representative from the team to go to the blackboard and add an item to the two boxes. If incorrect, the teacher tells the class that it is incorrect and erases the team guess. If correct, the team receives a round of applause. This is repeated until all teams know the rule.

7 *Activity*

Find My Rule

Symmetry

Teacher: Draw two boxes on the chalkboard and label them Box 1 and Box 2. Add one symmetrical shape to Box 1 and one asymmetrical shape to Box 2. Have pairs take turns naming possible rules for placing the items in Box 1 or 2. Continue adding symmetrical shapes to Box 1 and asymmetrical shapes to Box 2, until a team knows the rule. Select one student to draw the next shape in each box to test the rule.

Activity **8**

Find My Rule

Rounding

Teacher: Draw two boxes on the chalkboard and label them Box 1 and Box 2. Add one number to round up to the nearest hundred in Box 1 and one to round down to the nearest hundred in Box 2. Have pairs take turns naming possible rules for writing the numbers in Box 1 or 2. Continue adding numbers until a team thinks they know the rule. Select one student to write a number in each box to test the rule.

Box 1	Box 2
152	249
489	522
763	708
276	439
855	246
398	318
553	821
682	934
974	602

9 | *Activity*
Find My Rule

Acute & Obtuse

Teacher: Draw two boxes on the chalkboard and label them Box 1 and Box 2. Add one obtuse angle in Box 1 and one acute angle in Box 2. Have pairs take turns naming possible rules for the difference in the angles in Box 1 or 2. Continue adding angles until a team thinks they know the rule. Select one student to draw a new angle in each box to test the rule.

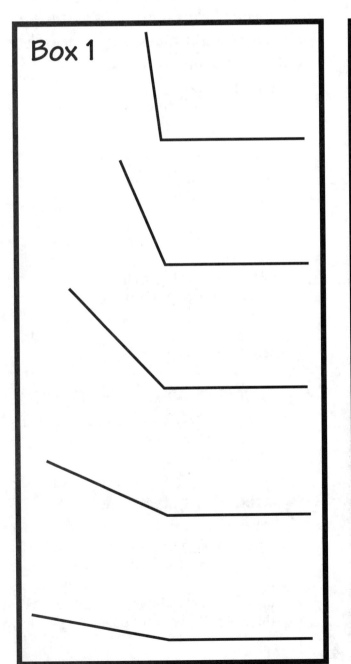

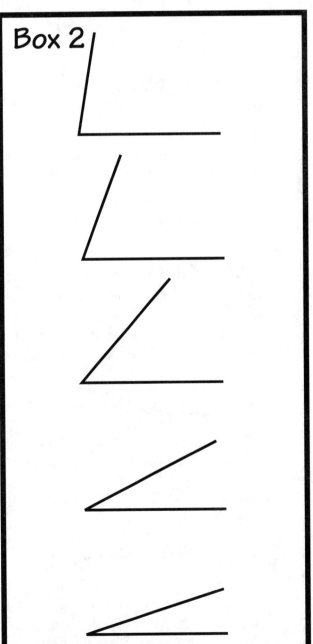

MI Strategy 4

Who Am I?

A card is taped on each students' back. The card may be a person, place, object, number. Students can not see their cards so their challenge is to mingle in the room and find out "who they are" by asking each other questions. Students must use their logical/mathematical skills to uncover their secret identity.

Steps

1 Cards Placed on Backs

A card is placed on each student's back. The card can have a picture, object, famous person's name, number, shape, time. It is essential that students do not see what is placed on their backs.

2 Students Mix & Pair

Students walk around the room until they find a partner. Partners check each other's back. "Walk around the room until you find a partner. After you shake hands, look at each other's pictures."

3 Students Question Partner

In pairs, Student One asks his/her partner a question trying to find out what or is on his/her back. For example, if the secret identity is a number, Student One may ask,

"Am I over 100?" Student One may continue to ask questions until he or she gets a negative response. Student Two then asks questions to find out his or her secret identity: "Am I odd or even?"

4 Students Mix & Pair Again

Students mix and pair up with a new partner, continuing the process until they guess who they are.

5 Students Become Helpers

When a student guesses who she is, her partner takes the card off her back and gives it to her to tape on her chest. She is now a "helper" and can answer questions or drop subtle hints such as: "You have three digits in your number."

10 *Activity*
Who Am I?

What's My Time

Draw the hour hand and minute hand on your clock. Cut out your clock. Without letting your partner see your clock, tape it on his or her back. He or she will tape his or her clock on your back. Get out of your seat and find a different partner. You can ask each other yes or no question until you receive a "No" answer. Then, find a new partner and ask more questions to find out what time your clock says. See how quickly you can discover your time.

Activity 11
Who Am I?

What's My Pattern

In the box below, draw a circle, square, triangle and star on the lines, but in a different order than the sample. Cut out the box. Without letting your partner see the order of your shapes, tape it on his or her back. He or she will tape his or her box on your back. Get out of your seat and find a new partner. You can ask your partner yes or no questions until you receive a negative response. Find another new partner to question. See how quickly you can uncover your hidden pattern order.

Sample Order

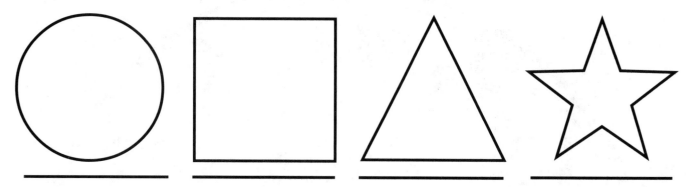

What's My Pattern

Spencer & Miguel Kagan: *Multiple Intelligences*
Kagan Cooperative Learning • 1 (800) WEE CO-OP

12 *Activity*
Who Am I?

What's My Number

In the box below, write a six-digit number, three before the decimal and three after the decimal. Cut out the box. Without letting your partner see the your number, tape it on his or her back. He or she will tape his or her box on your back. Get out of your seat and find a new partner. You can ask your partner yes or no questions until you get a "No" response. Find another new partner to question. See how quickly you can discover your number. Don't forget to use place value terminology. See sample below.

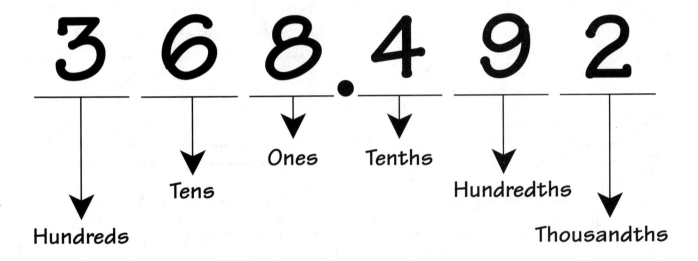

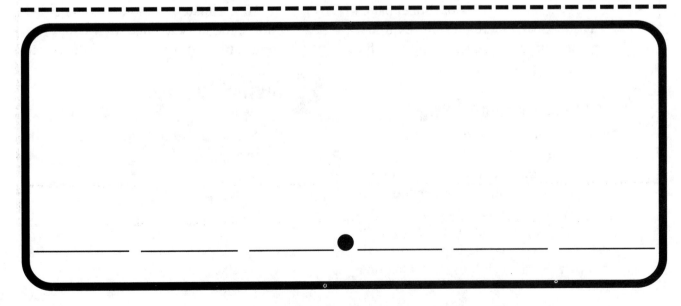

MI Strategy | 5

Match Mine

In pairs, one partner, the "Sender," arranges objects. The objects can be game-pieces on a gameboard, shapes, colors. The other partner, the "Receiver," cannot see the arrangement. The pair works together to try to get the Receiver's arrangement to "match" that of the Sender. Both the Sender and Receiver must use their visual/spatial skills to successfully create a match.

Steps · · · · · · · · · · · · ·

1 Senders Create Design

In pairs, one partner is a Sender and the other is the Receiver. Both partners have identical materials to create a design (tangrams, pattern blocks, crayons, card stock cut-outs, color tiles, or rubber bands on a geoboard). The Sender creates his design without the Receiver seeing it. A file folder barrier works well.

2 Receivers Match Design

When the Sender has created his design or arranged his pieces, the Receiver attempts to match it. Since the Receiver cannot see the Sender's design, the Sender must describe the arrangement well. For example: "My blue circle is centered on the page. The base of my red triangle is placed directly on top of the circle. It looks like a hat on a head."

3 Partners Check Design

When partners think that the Receiver has accurately matched the Sender's design, they compare their work. If the designs are identical, they celebrate their success. If they don't match, they congratulate their efforts, then discuss how they could have communicated better to make the match.

4 Switch Roles

Partners play again. The Receiver becomes the Sender and the Sender becomes the Receiver.

13 *Activity*
Match Mine

Visual/Spatial

Match My Tangram

Cut out your Tangram pieces below. Pair up with a partner and sit on opposite sides of a barrier. Without letting your partner see, create a design with your shapes. Describe your design so your partner can match it. When you think you have a match, check your partner's design. Let your partner make a design and try to match it.

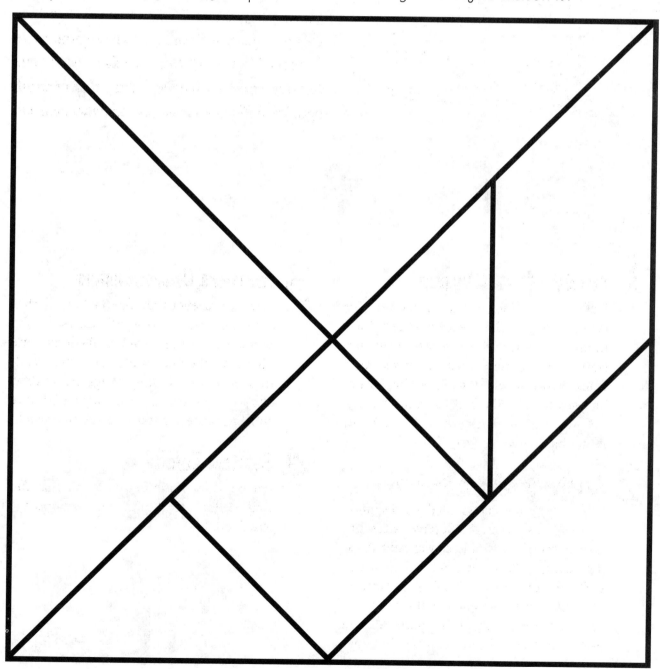

Activity 14

Match Mine

Shape Match Up

Pair up with a partner. Cut the sheet in half so you get Set 1 and your partner gets Set 2. Cut out the individual shapes along the dotted line. Sit on opposite sides of a barrier and arrange your shapes on the Shape Match Up board. Don't let your partner see your arrangement. Describe your design so your partner can match it. When you think you have a match, check your partner's design. Let your partner make a design and try to match it.

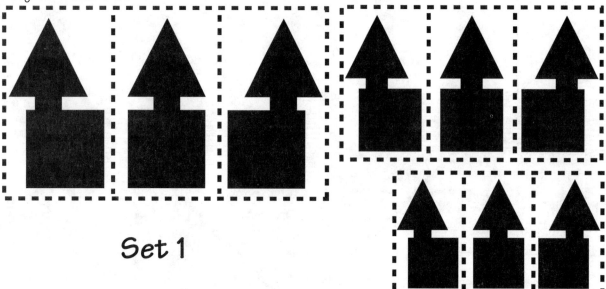

Set 1

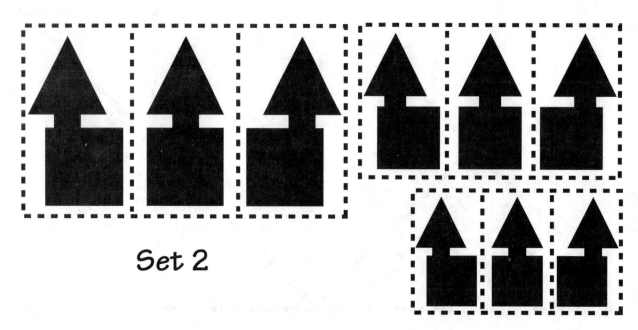

Set 2

14 *Activity*
Match Mine

Shape Match Up

Arrange your shapes in the boxes below. Describe your
arrangement and see if your partner can make a match.

MI Strategy 6

Mind Mapping

Students draw a "map" of their ideas. They start with the main idea in the center. Radiating from the main idea are related ideas, bridges, colors, icons, arrows, symbols, and codes used to represent the main idea and related topics. Mind Mapping is a wonderful visual/spatial strategy. As students visually depict their understanding of a concept or issue, they explore the interrelations of related ideas.

Steps

1 Teacher Assigns Topic

Assign the class a topic to mind map. Students can create a mind map before a lesson to explore what they already know about the topic; students can use mind mapping as visual note-taking during the lesson; or students can build mind maps after a lesson to represent and reflect on connections in the content, or to assess what they know or have learned.

2 Students Draw Main Topic

Students write the topic in the center of the page. They can use colors, graphics, symbols to visually represent the main topic.

3 Students Draw Related Topics

Around the main topic, students write or draw pictures of related topics. They use size, colors, and graphics to represent topics related to the central topic.

4 Students Make Connections

Students are free to add arrows, bridges, branches, supporting details to best map their understanding of the main concept and related topics.

15 *Activity*
Mind Mapping

Visual/Spatial

Color Mind Map

Think of all the different colors, the uses of colors, and where you find colors. Make a mind map of color. Use colors, arrows, bridges, symbols and text to map your image of color and related topics.

Mind Mapping

My Room Mind Map

Make a mind map of your bedroom. Use colors, size, arrows, bridges, symbols and text to map your image of the contents and locations of your room.

School Mind Map

Make a mind map of your school. Use colors, size, arrows, bridges, symbols and text to map your image of school and related topics.

School

MI Strategy 7

Lyrical Lessons

Students write new lyrics with information pertaining to the curriculum to familiar tunes. Students sing their lyrical lessons to classmates. Lyrical lessons promote musical/rhythmic skills, mastery of content and long-term retention.

Steps . . . .

1 Teacher Assigns Topic

Assign the class a topic about which they will write a song. Students can write songs on just about any content. Decide if students will work independently, in pairs or in small groups. You may select a familiar tune for students or allow them to choose their own such as: *Twinkle Twinkle Little Star, Three Blind Mice, Have You Ever Seen a Lassie,* or *Jingle Bells.*

2 Students Brainstorm Ideas for Lyrics

Students generate many words, phrases, and ideas related to the topic. For example, if the topic is food, on slips of paper students might write, "watermelon," "lunch," "carbos," "hungry," "snacks," "dinner is served."

3 Students Write Lyrics

Students write the lyrics to their curriculum songs. They may play with the ideas on the slips of paper they brainstormed, arranging them to fit the tune. If they are in pairs or teams, allow students some time to rehearse before sharing with others.

4 Students Perform Songs

Students share their song with a partner, teammates or with the entire class. For sharing, it is best for the audience to have a copy of the lyrics so they see as well as hear the song.

18 *Activity*
Lyrical Lessons

Types of Music

In a team of four, write a song about all the different types of music. Use the tune: "I've Been Working on the Railroad." When done, sing your song to another team.

Title

Activity 19

Lyrical Lessons

The Instrument Song

Write a song about the different types of instruments and the sounds they make. Write to the tune of "Old MacDonald Had a Farm." Share your song with a partner.

Spencer & Miguel Kagan: *Multiple Intelligences*
Kagan Cooperative Learning • 1 (800) WEE CO-OP

20 *Activity*
Lyrical Lessons

Sounds All Around

Pair up with a partner. Write a song about the sounds you hear all around you. Use the tune "You Are My Sunshine." Sing your song to another pair.

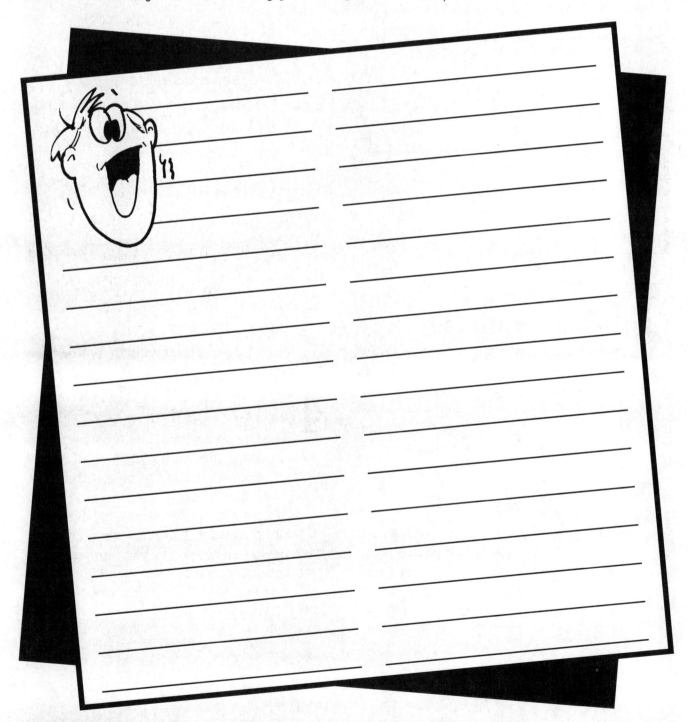

MI Strategy 8

Songs For Two Voices

In pairs, students alternate singing some parts of a song, and sing some parts together. Students develop an enhanced rhythmical sense and create a beautiful duet.

Steps . . . .

1 Teacher Prepares Song

Select a song related to the topic of study. By each line of the song write A, B, or AB corresponding to who is to sing which line. Lines marked with A are sung by one partner; lines marked with B are sung by the other; lines marked AB are sung together as a duet.

2 Pairs Rehearse

Students pair up to rehearse. One is A and the other B. A's sing lines marked A; B's sing lines marked B; A's and B's sing lines marked AB.

3 Pairs Perform

Pairs perform their song to another pair and receive appreciation.

4 Class Performs

The class as a whole sings the song. All A's sing their lines; all B's sing their lines. The whole class sings in unison for AB lines.

After students have learned to sing songs and poems for two voices scripted by the teacher, they move up to scripting existing poems and songs, and finally to creating their own original songs and poems for two voices.

21 **Activity**
Songs For Two Voices

Hibernate

To the tune of "Frère Jacques"

Pair up with a partner. One of you is A, the other is B. When the line starts with A, A sings the line. When it starts with B, B sings the line. When the line starts with AB, you both sing the line together in unison. Rehearse your song. When you're ready to perform, sing your song to another pair.

A	I'm a woodchuck		B	Snowflakes blowing
B	Ready to bunk		A	Time for going
A	I'll sleep long		B	In my nest
B	I'll sleep late		A	Time to rest
A	Curled up 'n cozy		B	Underground and happy
B	Always feeling "dozey"		A	Time for "winter nappy"
AB	Hibernate!		B	My heart will
AB	Hibernate!		B	Beat much less!
B	I'll go "downtown"		AB	Hibernation!
A	Way underground		AB	Hibernation!
B	I'll go deep		A	I'll sleep long
A	Into sleep		B	I'll sleep late
B	In my nest I'll stay warm		A	Sleeping through the snowfalls
A	Through the coldest snowstorm		B	Won't be making snowballs
B	In my "bed"		AB	Hibernate!
A	Kinda dead		AB	Hibernate!

Lyrics by Clint Klose and Larry Wolfe
K-6 Lyrical Lessons across the curriculum are available
from Kagan Cooperative Learning

A c t i v i t y   22

Songs For Two Voices

We're Democracy

To the tune of "I've Been Working on the Railroad"

Pair up with a partner. A sings lines that start with A; B sings lines that start with B; you both sing lines that start with AB.

A	I'm a local politician
A	Down at City Hall
B	If you have a "public problem"
B	Grab the phone and make a call
A	I'm your voice in city council
A	Through me you'll be heard
B	We can make the rules together
B	Together we'll be heard

Chorus

AB	**We're democracy**
AB	**Together you and me**
AB	**"We the people" govern our country**
AB	**We can have a voice**
AB	**We can have a choice**
AB	**We're a "peopleocracy"**

A	Your vote put me here in Congress
A	Washington, that is,
B	All the "Reps" from every state are
B	The House of Representatives
A	Some states have more people in them
A	Needing more "Reps," too
B	And the states with fewer people
B	Only need a few!

Repeat Chorus

B	Representatives in Congress
B	Must live in your state
A	We are twenty-five or older
A	(Younger "Reps" will have to wait!)
B	We're elected every two years
B	We can be "replaced!"
A	Must be citizens a long time
A	And mustn't be "two-faced!"

Repeat Chorus

B	I'm a senator in Congress
B	Your vote put me here
A	I'm a senator in Congress
A	Write a letter — "bend my ear!"
B	It's my job to represent you
B	I work many hours
A	You can help me make some choices
A	Spending our tax dollars

Repeat Chorus

B	Senators work in the Senate
B	Six-year terms they serve
A	Senators are over thirty
A	Some are spenders, some conserve
B	Must be citizens for nine years
B	Can't think "out-of-date"
A	Senate has a hundred workers—
A	Two from every state!

Repeat Chorus

Lyrics by Clint Klose and Larry Wolfe
K-6 Lyrical Lessons across the curriculum are available from Kagan Cooperative Learning

23 **Activity**
Songs For Two Voices

Song for Two Voices

Fill in the topic of your song in the box below. Write the song. When done, sing your song to another pair. Partner A sings A lines; Partner B sings B lines; Sing AB lines together in unison.

Our Song About _____

A _____   A _____
B _____   B _____
A _____   A _____
B _____   B _____
AB _____   AB _____

A _____   A _____
B _____   B _____
A _____   A _____
B _____   B _____
AB _____   AB _____

A _____   A _____
B _____   B _____
A _____   A _____
B _____   B _____
AB _____   AB _____

MI Strategy **9**

Team Charades

In teams, students take turns acting out words, ideas, concepts, events as teammates attempt to guess what is being acted. Charades activate the bodily/kinesthetic intelligence: Students practice creating and interpreting body language, gestures, movement and expressions. Team Charades is an exciting strategy that makes learning literally come to life.

S t e p s . . . .

1 Teacher Prepares Roles

For charades, students need their "roles" to act out. The roles can be anything that can be acted out: vocabulary words, concepts, historical events, characters, processes, algorithms. Fold a sheet of paper into fourths (for teams of four). In each quadrant, write an equal number of roles for students to act out. For one round only, write one role in each quadrant. Make a copy of the sheet for every team and hand it to them face down so they can't read the roles.

2 Teammates Divvy Roles

One teammate folds their role sheet in fourths, cuts it in fourths and without peeking at the content, randomly distributes one quadrant to each teammate.

3 Teammates Act Out Roles

Students flip over the quadrants and read through their role(s). Student One then stands in front of teammates and acts out his or her first role. When a teammate guesses correctly, Student Two acts out his or her first role. Teammates continue taking turns until all the roles have been acted out and correctly guessed.

24 | *Activity*
Team Charades

Sports Charades

Teacher: Give each student on a team of four one of the sports cards below. Have students take turns acting out their sports while teammates guess the sport.

Sports Card 1

1. Soccer
2. Water Polo
3. Snowboarding
4. Tennis
5. Skiing
6. Pole Vault
7. Boxing

Sports Card 2

1. Javelin Throw
2. Volleyball
3. Hockey
4. Bowling
5. Swimming
6. Long Jump
7. Basketball

Sports Card 3

1. Wrestling
2. Surfing
3. Football
4. Shot Put
5. Figure Skating
6. Bicycling
7. Racquetball

Sports Card 4

1. Archery
2. Baseball
3. Diving
4. Gymnastics
5. Badminton
6. Skateboarding
7. Weight Lifting

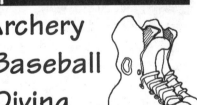

MI Strategy 25
Team Charades

Bodily Career Charades

Teacher: Give each student on a team of four one of the career cards below. Each career involves skillful use of the bodily/kinesthetic intelligence. Have students take turns acting out their career while teammates guess the career.

Career Card 1

1. Surgeon
2. Dancer
3. Electrician
4. Actor
5. Athlete
6. Chef
7. Engineer

Career Card 2

1. Acrobat
2. Carpenter
3. Lumberjack
4. Sculptor
5. Masseuse
6. Inventor
7. Roofer

Career Card 3

1. Plumber
2. Choreographer
3. Weight Trainer
4. Jeweler
5. Magician
6. Gardener
7. Hair Stylist

Career Card 4

1. Car Mechanic
2. Bricklayer
3. Chiropractor
4. Manicurist
5. Doctor
6. Locksmith
7. Shipping Clerk

Movie Charades

Teacher: Give each student on a team of four one of the movie cards below. Have students take turns acting out a movie from their card while teammates guess the movie.

Movie Card 1

1. E.T.
2. Rocky
3. Star Wars
4. The Lion King
5. Sixteen Candles
6. Ghostbusters
7. Batman

Movie Card 2

1. Top Gun
2. Grease
3. King Kong
4. Indiana Jones
5. Titanic
6. Little Mermaid
7. Men In Black

Movie Card 3

1. Jaws
2. Speed
3. True Lies
4. 101 Dalmations
5. Ace Ventura
6. Sleeping Beauty
7. Forrest Gump

Movie Card 4

1. Superman
2. Airplane
3. Toy Story
4. Rain Man
5. Jungle Book
6. Schindler's List
7. Jurassic Park

MI Strategy 10

Formations

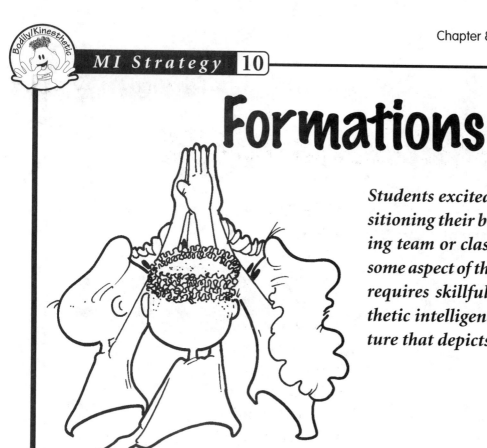

Students excitedly coordinate efforts, positioning their bodies to create a challenging team or class formation representing some aspect of the curriculum. Formations requires skillful use of the bodily/kinesthetic intelligence to create a body sculpture that depicts the content.

Steps · · · · · · · · · · · · · ·

1 Teacher Assigns Formations

Assign each team a different formation, all teams the same formation, or a formation for the entire class. The formation can be any word, date, event, object, or process that can be represented by students using their bodies. For example, a team may be asked to form the number 5. The class may be asked to form a happy face or the solar system.

2 Team or Class Discussion

Teams or the class take some time to plan how they are going to use their bodies to create their assigned formation. They decide who will do what and how to include everyone.

3 Students Create Formations

Select a team to create their formation for the class. The team gets in the middle of the class and makes their formations. If each team is assigned a different formation, classmates can guess what their body sculpture represents. Alternatively, the whole class works together to create the class formation.

Formations Ideas

Mathematics

- Geometric figures
- Numbers (1, 5, 9, 13)
- Operations (+, -, X, ÷)
- Shapes
- Number sentences (8+1=9)
- Algebraic equation
- People graphs
- Patterns (tallest to shortest)
- Fractions
- Number groups

Science

- Tree
- Fish
- Solar System
- Parts of a plant
- Land formations
- Animals
- Water cycle
- Dinosaur
- Simple machine
- Chemicals (H_2O)
- Elements in Periodic Table
- Chemical reactions
- Parts of an airplane
- Skeletal structure
- Digestive system
- Body parts

Social Studies

- Flag
- Covered wagon
- Words
- Shape state
- Spell city live in
- President's name
- Geographical formations
- States
- Countries
- Seas
- Rivers
- Mountains

Language Arts

- Letters: upper and lower case
- Book
- Abbreviations
- Words
- Scene of a story
- Parts of sentences
- Punctuation

MI Strategy 11

Same-Different

Students work in pairs to discover what is the same and what is different between two leafs, rocks, flowers, pictures, species. The challenge: Neither partner can see the other's specimen. Through discrimination of detail and communication, students uncover and record the commonalities and peculiarities of flora, fauna or other objects. As students play Same-Different, they develop keen observational skills, and sharpen their ability to make discriminations and comparisons, primary traits of the naturalist.

Steps . . . .

1 Teacher Prepares Material

Each pair needs two objects that are similar in some aspects and different in others. For example, a rose and daisy share many characteristics, but also vary on many dimensions. A boot and a shoe are two non-natural items that share some characteristics and differ on others. Partners can not see each other's objects or pictures as they play. A file folder barrier works well. Pairs also need a recording sheet to record all the similarities and differences.

2 Students Discover Similarities & Differences

Partners work together to discover everything that is the same and everything that is different about the two items. They can not tell each other what their object or picture is, but must instead focus on the specific characteristics. As they discover similarities and differences, they take turns recording them.

3 Pairs Compare Objects

When partners have uncovered all the similarities and differences or can't find any more, they compare their objects or pictures. They go over all the similarities and differences they recorded and make sure they are accurate. Then, they continue to find more similarities and differences.

Recording Sheet

Use this sheet to record everything that is the same and different.

Same

1. _____
2. _____
3. _____
4. _____
5. _____
6. _____
7. _____
8. _____
9. _____
10. _____
11. _____
12. _____
13. _____
14. _____
15. _____
16. _____
17. _____
18. _____
19. _____
20. _____

Different

1. _____
2. _____
3. _____
4. _____
5. _____
6. _____
7. _____
8. _____
9. _____
10. _____
11. _____
12. _____
13. _____
14. _____
15. _____
16. _____
17. _____
18. _____
19. _____
20. _____

A c t i v i t y **28**
Same-Different

Dolphin

The dolphin is actually a whale, the smallest whale in the family. Like whales, the dolphin is a mammal. Baby dolphins are born alive and they feed on their mother's milk until they are ready to hunt for themselves. Dolphins have lungs and breathe air through their blowhole on top of their head. They close their blowhole to dive underwater. They are warm-blooded and have a steady body temperature. There are 25 kinds of saltwater dolphins and 6 kinds of freshwater dolphins. The largest dolphin is up to 12 feet and weighs 1,500 pounds. Dolphins have no sense of smell, but have the best hearing of any animal. Dolphins use echoes to find food. They make clicks and when the clicks return, they know about the size, shape, speed, and direction of the object their sonar detected. Dolphins have a skeleton made of bones, and slick rubbery skin to propel them through the water. Dolphins have a strong tail that spreads into two wide flukes, a dorsal fin on their back and two flippers, one on each side. Dolphins have round, cone-shaped teeth.

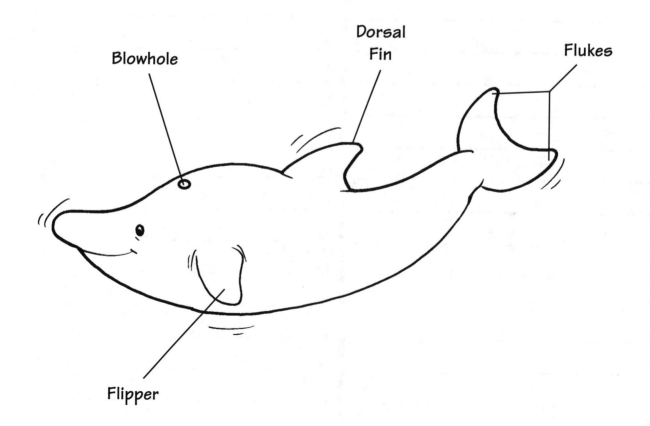

Blowhole

Dorsal
Fin

Flukes

Flipper

Spencer & Miguel Kagan: *Multiple Intelligences*
Kagan Cooperative Learning • 1 (800) WEE CO-OP

28 A c t i v i t y

Same-Different

Shark

Although sharks are different from most fish, they are still considered a fish. Most sharks are born alive, but some are hatched out of eggs. When born, sharks are independent and ready to hunt. Sharks breathe underwater by drawing water into their mouths and letting it pass over their gills. The gills take the oxygen out of the water. There are more than 350 different kinds of sharks today. Whale sharks are the largest of all sharks and can be 45 feet long and 40,000 pounds. Most sharks are saltwater fish, but some can survive in the freshwater too. A shark's skeleton is made of cartilage and their skin is covered by tiny teeth, called denticle which makes their skin very rough. The shark has two dorsal fins, two pectoral fins on each side, two pelvic fins on the bottom, an anal fin near the tail, and a tail, called the caudal fin. Sharks have a very good sense of hearing and a highly developed smell. In fact, up to two-thirds of a shark's brain is devoted to smell. They use their noses to sniff out their prey. Sharks have rows of sharp teeth. Their teeth fall out easily and a new tooth takes it place. Sharks can grow a new tooth in as little as 24 hours!

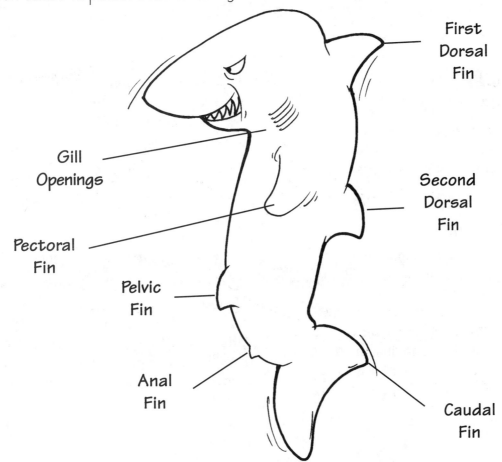

First Dorsal Fin

Gill Openings

Second Dorsal Fin

Pectoral Fin

Pelvic Fin

Anal Fin

Caudal Fin

MI Strategy 12

Categorizing

Teams discuss and create a system to categorize items (shells, leafs, buttons, bolts). After categorizing the items, teams share their systems with other teams. Classifying and categorizing are core operations of the naturalist intelligence. Categorizing promotes the ability to recognize patterns and characteristics in natural (plants, minerals, animals) and cultural artifacts (cars, sneakers).

Steps

1 Teacher Prepares Items to Categorize

For Categorizing, each team needs a set of items to categorize. The items can be anything from different animals to assorted buttons.

2 Team Discussion

Teammates look at their items and create a category system to organize the items they have. It is a good idea to explore category systems with students before categorizing. Some teams may decide on a two-by-two matrix, some a Venn diagram. For younger students, it may be necessary to provide students with the category system.

3 Teammates Categorize Items

Once students have their category system, they evenly divide the items among themselves. Teammates take turns placing each item into their system. Students check to make sure all teammates agree with the placement before the next teammate proceeds.

4 Teams Compare Systems

When done categorizing their items, teams share their category systems with other teams. To share, teams may visit with another team, draw it on the blackboard, or send a representative to another team to learn about the system and return to teach it to teammates.

29 *Activity*

Categorizing

Categorizing Systems

Here are five categorizing systems to consider when categorizing items.

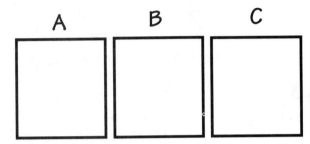

A   B   C

Categories

Separate items into different categories.
Example: A) Roses, B) Daisies, C) Tulips

Continuum

Organize items in sequence along one
dimension. **Example:** A) Docile to Z) Dangerous

A   Z

Plot

A continuum along two dimensions. Items are
plotted in the intersection. **Example:** A) Docile
to Z) Dangerous; 1) Large to 2) Small. Large
Docile animals plotted at A1; Small Dangerous
animals plotted at Z2...

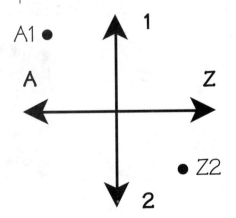

A1 •

A   Z

• Z2

Venn Diagram

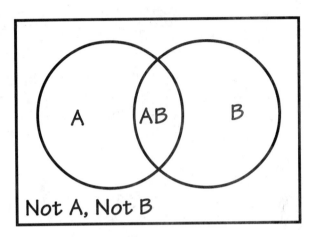

Not A, Not B

Separate items into categories based on
commonalities or differences.
Example: A) Blue, B) Red, AB) Red & Blue
Not A, Not B) Neither Red nor Blue.

Matrix

Separate items into categories based on
two dimensions. **Example:** Size: 1) Large, 2)
Small; Weight: A) Heavy, B) Light. Large and
Heavy items in A1, Small and Light items in
B2...

	1	2
A	A1	A2
B	B1	B2

Activity 30

Categorizing

Categorize Dinos

Cut out the dinosaur pictures below. Evenly divide them among your teammates. Come up with a category system for the dinosaurs, then take turns placing your dinos into the category system. When done, compare your category system with another team.

Spencer & Miguel Kagan: *Multiple Intelligences*

Kagan Cooperative Learning • 1 (800) WEE CO-OP

Categorizing

Categorize Sea Life

Cut out the sea life pictures below. Evenly divide them among your teammates. Come up with a category system for the sea creatures, then take turns placing your creatures into the category system. When done, compare your category system with another team.

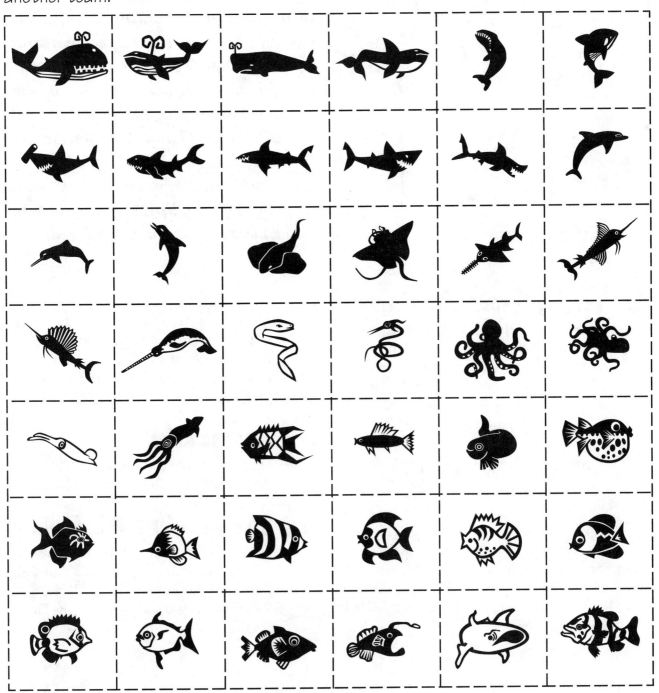

MI Strategy 13

Find Someone Who

Students excitedly circulate through the classroom, forming and reforming pairs, trying to "find someone who" can help them fill out their worksheet. Find Someone Who is a strong interpersonal strategy for a number of reasons. Students are out of their seats, interacting with a number of classmates in a positive context. Classmates who "know" become resources for others as they help and share information. The message: Even if you don't know the answer, with a little help and cooperation from a friend, you can succeed.

Steps . . . .

1 Teacher Prepares Worksheet

Create a worksheet that has problems to be solved (348 ÷ 56), specialized information (find someone who can define a supernova), or information to be learned about classmates (find someone who plays the guitar in a band).

2 Students Mix & Pair

With worksheets in hand, students circulate through the room until they find a partner. Student A asks B one question on the worksheet. If B knows the answer, she shares it with A. Student A writes the answer in his own words. B checks the answer for correctness and signs near the answer for agreement.

If B is the person described on the worksheet, she signs the worksheet. Student A can probe for more information: "What type of music does your band play? How long have you played the guitar?"

3 Reverse Roles

Students switch roles. Student B asks student A one question on the worksheet.

4 Students Mix & Pair Again

Students may ask each other one question only, then continue to mix and pair until they finish the Find-Someone-Who form. When they are done, they become "helpers" for students who are not yet done.

32 | *Activity*
Find Someone Who

Interpersonal

Find Someone Who...

Get out of your seats and find someone who fits each description. When you find someone who fits a description, ask him or her the question. Have him or her sign his or her name next to the description, and put a check in the box. Try to find a different classmate for each question. When you are all done, help classmates find each other.

❑ Is an only child. Do you like being an only child?

❑ Plays sports. Which sports do you play?

❑ Is short. What are some advantages of being short?

❑ Listens to music. What is your favorite kind of music?

❑ Likes to draw. What do you draw?

❑ Has a pet. What kind of pet(s) do you have?

❑ Has been out of the country. Where have you been?

❑ Is good at fixing things. What kind of things have you fixed?

❑ Likes to cook. What's your favorite dish?

❑ Has been to a concert. What concert have you been to?

❑ Is very tall. How do you like being tall?

❑ Keeps a diary. What do you write in your diary?

❑ Likes to write poems. What kind of poems have you written?

❑ Exercises regularly. What is your exercise routine?

❑ Likes to dance. When and where do you dance?

Activity **33**
Find Someone Who

Find Someone Who...

Get out of your seats and find someone who fits each description. When you find someone who fits a description, ask him or her the question. Have him or her sign his or her name next to the description, and put a check in the box. Try to find a different classmate for each question. When you are all done, help classmates find each other.

❏ Knows how to surf the net. What's your favorite site?

❏ Likes to play video games. What's your favorite game?

❏ Knows how to play the piano. What songs can you play?

❏ Gets all A's in school. How do you do so well?

❏ Wants to be a politician. What attracts you to politics?

❏ Knows how to ride a horse. How did you learn?

❏ Can speak another language. What other language(s)?

❏ Is a member of a club or group. What club?

❏ Likes to build models. What kind of models have you built?

❏ Can sing well. What do you sing?

❏ Rides the bus to school? Where do you live?

❏ Wants to be famous? How do you plan to get famous?

❏ Has been to another state. What state(s) have you been to?

❏ Has won a trophy or award. What did you win it for?

❏ Likes math. Why do you like math?

34 | *Activity*
Find Someone Who

Find Someone Who...

Get out of your seat and find the classmate who fits each description. When you find someone who fits a description, write his or her name next to the description. Try to find a different classmate for each question. When you are all done, help classmates find each other.

Find Someone Who...	Name

Teacher: Have students turn in one unique fact about themselves that they would like every classmate to know. Fill in the facts on this form. For more space, first whiteout or cover up these instructions and make two copies of this form, then fill in the facts. Make the student worksheet double-sided.

MI Strategy 14

Team Interview

Each teammate experiences both sides of the interview coin: They are interviewed by three teammates at once, and also act three times in the role of interviewer. The ability to communicate effectively is an instrumental aspect of the interpersonal intelligence. Team Interview provides the forum for students to acquire and practice interviewing skills as well as the opportunity to share personal or content-related information.

Steps

1 Teacher Announces a Topic

Announce a topic on which students are to interview each other. The content can be personal: "Find out what your teammates did over the weekend." Or, the content of the interview can be related to the topic of study: "Find out what your teammate knows about osmosis."

2 Students Interview Teammate

One student stands up. He or she is the first interviewee. Teammates can ask the teammate any question they want. The questions should be framed to "pull" information from the interviewee. After a predetermined amount of time has elapsed or when teammates have no more questions, the next teammate is up.

3 Interviews Continue

After the first student is interviewed, he or she sits down. The student to the left stands up and becomes the interviewee. The interviews continues until all students have been interviewed.

Helpful Hint

Have one student on the team act as the Timekeeper to make sure all teammates are interviewed for the same amount of time.

35 *Activity*
Team Interview

"You" Interviews

What would you like to know about your teammates? Write four questions to ask each teammate. Have one teammate stand up. Everyone asks him or her their interview questions. When done, the next teammate stands to be interviewed. Continue until every teammate has been interviewed.

Teammate Name _____

- Question 1_____
- Question 2_____
- Question 3_____
- Question 4_____

Teammate Name _____

- Question 1_____
- Question 2_____
- Question 3_____
- Question 4_____

Teammate Name _____

- Question 1_____
- Question 2_____
- Question 3_____
- Question 4_____

Activity 36
Team Interview

Your Favorites

Cut out the four cards below. Everyone on your team of four gets one card. One teammate stands up to be interviewed. Everyone asks their questions including the interviewee. When done, the next teammate stands to be interviewed. Everyone passes their interview cards to the person on the right. Continue until every teammate has been interviewed about their favorites and each person has had each card.

Interview Card 1

- What is your favorite color? Why?
- What is your favorite hobby? Why?
- What is your favorite kind of car? Why?
- What is your favorite animal? Why?

Interview Card 2

- Who is your favorite band? Why?
- What is your favorite dessert? Why?
- Who is your favorite artist? Why?
- What is your favorite sport? Why?

Interview Card 3

- What is your favorite cartoon? Why?
- What is your favorite subject? Why?
- What is your favorite movie? Why?
- What is your favorite dinner? Why?

Interview Card 4

- What is your favorite game? Why?
- What is your favorite holiday? Why?
- What is your favorite time of the day?
- What is your favorite drink? Why?

Spencer & Miguel Kagan: *Multiple Intelligences*
Kagan Cooperative Learning • 1 (800) WEE CO-OP

37 *Activity*
Team Interview

Personal Questions

Cut out the question strips below. Shuffle them face down. Have one teammate stand up. Teammates each draw and read one question. After the interviewee answers all questions, the next teammate stands up to be interviewed.

What is the most exciting thing you've ever done?

What would you do with one thousand dollars?

What was your most embarrassing moment?

Where would you like to go for vacation?

What is the biggest mistake you ever made?

What is one thing you haven't done, but really want to do?

What is one thing you've done that you are most proud of?

What did you wish for on your last birthday?

What is the most beautiful thing you've ever seen?

What is one thing that you never want to do again?

What was your last New Year's resolution?

What is the craziest thing you've ever done?

MI Strategy 15

Journal Reflections

Students write their reflections in their journals about their likes, values, beliefs, emotions, thinking processes, goals, ambitions, self-assessments. The intrapersonal intelligence is engaged and developed as they tune into the world within. What better way to get in tune with oneself than taking silent time to reflect? Journal Reflections also builds personally relevant bridges to the content.

Steps . . . .

1 Teacher Announces a Topic

Announce a journal topic. The topic can be on virtually any subject, but should allow for personal insight: "How do you feel about...? What does it remind you of...? Do you agree...? What are your plans...? What do you think...?

2 Students Write Journal Entries

Give students plenty of silent time to make their journal reflections. Since the journals are for personal reflections and growth, students can customize their entries. In addition to writing their responses, they can write poems, write free verse, draw pictures, or even doodle.

3 Students Share Reflections

Select a few students to share their reflections with the class. For more intimate sharing environments, have students share their entries with teammates or with a partner. If a student deems the content too personal to share, this is an indication that the journal is being taken seriously and the request to pass should be respected.

(38) *Activity*
Journal Reflections

I Am...

Write ten "I am..." statements about yourself.

1. I am _____
   _____

2. I am _____
   _____

3. I am _____
   _____

4. I am _____
   _____

5. I am _____
   _____

6. I am _____
   _____

7. I am _____
   _____

8. I am _____
   _____

9. I am _____
   _____

10. I am _____
    _____

What I Learned Today

Describe what you learned today and how you feel about it.

What I Learned

_____
_____
_____
_____
_____
_____
_____
_____
_____
_____
_____

How I Feel About It

_____
_____
_____
_____
_____
_____
_____
_____
_____
_____

40 *Activity*
Journal Reflections

When I Grow Up

What do you want to be when you grow up? Describe
what actions you must take to achieve your goal.

When I grow up...
_____
_____
_____
_____
_____
_____
_____
_____
_____
_____

Things I need to do...
_____
_____
_____
_____
_____
_____
_____
_____
_____
_____
_____

MI Strategy 16

Timed Pair Share

In pairs, students each share without interruptions for a predetermined amount of time. As students talk without interruption they increasingly focus toward inner thoughts, feelings, and/or memories, accessing and developing their intrapersonal intelligence. A discussion repeatedly brings a speaker to focus outward, on the comments of the other. A monologue brings the speaker to greater inner depth.

Steps

1 Teacher Announces a Topic

Announce a topic for students to share their ideas or feelings with a partner: "What was your reaction to the poem?" "What is one of the happiest moments in your life?" "What is something you have lost?" "Is there something you would be willing to die for?" "What is the most important thing you learned today?"

2 Student A's Share

Have students pair up. One is Student A and the other Student B. Give A's a minute (time will vary depending on the topic and grade level) to share their feelings, ideas, insights about the topic with no interruptions from B's. Student B's job is to listen carefully, but not comment.

3 Student B's Share

After the allotted time is up, announce that it is Student B's turn to share. Student A's listen attentively, but again, can not interrupt.

Spencer & Miguel Kagan: *Multiple Intelligences*
Kagan Cooperative Learning • 1 (800) WEE CO-OP

41 *Activity*
Timed Pair Share

All About Me

Pair up with a partner. Cut out the cards below, and shuffle them face down. Pick the top card and share your answer with your partner for one minute. Let your partner pick the next card and share with you for one minute.

If you could be any animal for a day, which would it be? Why?	What is your all-time favorite movie? Why?	What color best describes you? Why?
If you could jump into any book, what book would it be? Why?	Who is your hero? Why?	If you could go anywhere in the world for vacation, where would you go? Why?
What are your three most treasured material possessions? Why?	If you could do anything you wanted tomorrow, what would you do?	If you could be any famous person, who would it be? Why?
What is your favorite outfit? Why?	What makes you unique?	What is your favorite holiday? Why?

Intrapersonal

Activity 42

Timed Pair Share

What Do You Think?

Pair up with a partner. Cut out the cards below, and shuffle them face down. Pick the top card and share your answer with your partner for one minute. Let your partner pick the next card and share with you for one minute.

Should cloning humans be legal? Why or why not?	Should criminals ever be sentenced to death? Why or why not?	Should the government censor movies, books, music? Why or why not?
Should drugs be legalized? Why or why not?	Should euthanasia be legal? Why or why not?	Should police or government be allowed to spy on citizens? Why or why not?
Should abortion be legal? Why or why not?	Should the rich be taxed more than the poor? Why or why not?	Should citizens be allowed to carry guns? Why or why not?
Should we do medical testing on animals? Why or why not?	Should colleges and universities use affirmative action? Why or why not?	Should illegal aliens be denied medical treatment and education? Why or why not?

(43) *Activity*
Timed Pair Share

The Complete Me

Pair up with a partner. Read a sentence starter out loud and complete the sentence. Continue speaking on the topic for one minute. Then, let your partner complete a sentence and talk for one minute on the topic. Take turns talking first.

1. One thing I'm really *good* at is...

2. What really bugs me is...

3. My family...

4. My biggest hobby is...

5. My friends are...

6. I think a lot about...

7. What really makes me happy is...

8. My best subject in school is...

9. I like people who...

10. Something I hate to do is...

11. What really scares me is...

12. One thing I'd like to improve on is...

13. What really makes me sad is...

14. I think school is...

15. If I could change one thing about the world...

Teacher: Make a transparency of this page. For a short activity, have pairs pick one sentence to share about. For a longer activity, have pairs pick five or more sentences to share about.

Developing the Multiple Intelligences

Let's take the "extra" out of extracurricular and make everything curricular (David Lazear, 1991)!

In *Frames of Mind* (1983), Howard Gardner described in detail his visit to the Suzuki Talent Education Center in Matsumoto, Japan. Children hardly old enough to hold the violin were performing like prodigies. Through a rigorous program starting at a very young age, the Talent Education Center highly developed students' musical/rhythmic intelligence. Gardner later states,

What Suzuki did for musical performance, can, I think, be accomplished for every other intelligence, and indeed each intelligence may require its own specific educational theory (Gardner, 1993, p. 48).

If we truly believe that a singular notion of human competencies does not adequately capture students' full range of abilities and potential, and that students' multiple intelligences can be improved, then shouldn't education strive to enhance all of students' intelligences?

MI theory makes two tremendous contributions to education. First, it breaks the singular construct of intelligence into multiple intelligences. There was, and still to a large degree is, a prevailing notion that each individual has a measurable level of intelligence, reducible to a score. But this IQ-type thinking does not jibe with what we see in the classroom. Some of our students are skillful mathematicians, but really could use some work with spelling. Others may not do so well in math or language arts, but really come alive in social studies, where real people and relationships are the focus of study. Some students don't care much for traditional academics at all, but can create brilliant works of art, construct fantastic representational models, use their bodies to communicate meaning, or play music like prodigies. MI theory, and our experience as educators, tells us that students are not just dumb or smart. MI theory is a step forward in broadening our perspective on human intelligence. There are many intelligences and thus many measures of intelligences. We are smart in a variety of ways.

The second contribution MI theory makes is to help dispel the myth that intelligence is a fixed entity. Often as a corollary to the singular view of intelligence is the idea that individuals are born with a certain amount of intelligence and that's that. The belief is that people are given the gift (or curse) of their level of intelligence. However, again as teachers, we know that this antiquated notion of a fixed intelligence does not accurately describe what happens in the classroom. We, perhaps more than anyone, know how malleable individual competencies can be. We've seen students labeled "at-risk" turn on to a subject and completely turn around in the course of year. We've seen students grapple with a concept or struggle with a problem…and then AHA…the epiphany! We know students can learn to develop their intelligences. That's why we're in the business of education; we know we can help make students become smarter.

If we truly believe that a singular notion of human competencies does not adequately capture students' full range of abilities and potential, and that students' multiple intelligences can be improved, then shouldn't education strive to enhance all of students' intelligences? Why do we choose to explicitly develop students' lin-

guistic skills and not their interpersonal skills? The ability to understand others, work together cooperatively, and motivate others is a tremendously valuable skill that students will use throughout their lives. Have we as educators looked at the wide range of capacities, prioritized them, and made a conscious decision to focus on some intelligences and not others? No! What we teach and the intelligences we develop in our students are largely determined by the weight of tradition. MI theory gives us a framework to look anew at what we teach and why.

In this chapter, we will first explore the rationale for developing the multiple intelligences, why we should strive to develop students' full range of intelligences. Then, we will examine what it means to develop the multiple intelligences and how we may go about making students smarter in many ways.

What we teach and the intelligences we develop in our students are largely determined by the weight of tradition. MI theory gives us a framework to look anew at what we teach and why.

Why Should We Develop the Multiple Intelligences?

There are two arguments we can make supporting the development of the multiple intelligences. The first is to enrich our diverse society. The second is to maximize the potential of each individual.

Enriching Our Diverse Society

As a pluralistic society, we value the capabilities, products, and end-states of each intelligence. We appreciate and enjoy the products of the musical/rhythmic intelligence: we purchase countless CD's, listen to the radio for hours on end, and frequently attend concerts of all types.

The same is true for the visual/spatial intelligence: colorful artwork fills our houses and brightens our lives; architects design our homes, layout our schools, and plan cities and transportation systems.

The ubiquitous products of the verbal/linguistic intelligence are treasured: we cling to every word of our favorite authors; lawyers battle it out in court using words as their weapons; the fate of the country rests in the hands of word-crafting politicians.

Individuals highly skilled in the logical/mathematical intelligence send rovers to study the rocks of Mars; put technology in our hands with sophisticated computer hardware and software, and account for every nickel spent in our market economy.

In tribute to the bodily/kinesthetic intelligence, we rally around our favorite athletic team; spend millions watching actors and actresses strut their stuff on the silver screen; and watch awe-inspired as gymnasts flip their way into our hearts.

Individuals equipped with the naturalist intelligence fortify our cereal with essential vitamins and minerals; tell us when to prepare for a tornado or flood; and preserve endangered flora and fauna.

People with the personal intelligences are highly valued: teachers shape the future as they touch the lives of students; our daily lives are influenced by spiritual and political leaders who guide, legislate, and enforce behaviors.

We do indeed value each intelligence; people who possess each intelligence perform a valuable func-

It is of the utmost importance that we recognize and nurture all of the varied human intelligences, and all of the combinations of intelligences…. If we can mobilize the spectrum of human abilities, not only will people feel better about themselves and more competent; it is even possible that they will also feel more engaged and better able to join the rest of the world community in working for the broader good. Perhaps if we can mobilize the full range of human intelligences and ally them to an ethical sense, we can help to increase the likelihood of our survival on this planet, and perhaps even contribute to our thriving (Gardner, 1987).

tion in our society. Where would we be without music or art? Without the capacity to know ourselves or care for others? Without the ability to think logically or to communicate verbally? Without the capacity to use our bodies or commune with nature? We would be lost.

Maximizing Our Students' Potential

Another reason to develop students' full spectrum of intelligences is to help students reach their unique potential, whatever that may be. Gardner takes this vision to be the very purpose of schooling:

> In my view, the purpose of school should be to develop intelligences and to help people reach vocational and avocational goals that are appropriate to their particular spectrum of intelligences (Gardner, 1993, p. 9).

Schooling should maximize students' intelligences and help students reach appropriate goals for themselves. This is not to say that we should test and stream our students based on their proclivities at a young age; but by the same token, we should not shut them off to the world of possibilities. Here's a frightening thought: There is evidence that there is a critical period for the acquisition of a variety of skills. If we do nothing to stimulate the multiple intelligences for our students in school, inadvertently we may be limiting their potential. As educators, our goal is to open doors for our students, not shut them. We give students a wide range of experiences across the intelligences to stretch all their intelligences.

As discussed in Chapter 3: What Is an Intelligence?, intelligences serve a number of functions. As we develop students' intelligences, we make them smarter on many

fronts: We give them a survival advantage; a range of skills they will draw on throughout their lives; greater perceptiveness in many domains; problem-solving skills; creativity and the ability to communicate through many channels; the gift of accumulated cultural knowledge; and the insight and foresight to make wise decisions. Striving to develop students' multiple intelligences is among the most honorable of aims for education.

If we really value all intelligences in society and want to help maximize students' range of capacities, we cannot afford to elevate the status of certain intelligences in our classrooms while disregarding others. MI theory challenges the nature of our current curriculum as well as the very function of education.

If we really value all intelligences in society and want to help maximize students' range of capacities, we cannot afford to elevate the status of certain intelligences in our classrooms while disregarding others. MI theory challenges the nature of our current curriculum as well as the very function of education.

MI theory opens up a world of possibilities in the classroom. Since we cannot predict what the future holds for each student or for us as a rapidly changing society, the more opportunities we give our students to experience different instructional strategies and the more differentiated our curriculum, the better we prepare our students for lifelong success. As educators, we *should* strive to explicitly develop each intelligence to its fullest. We should develop all eight intelligences identified in MI theory as well as all other ways students can develop their limitless potentials. As David Lazear states in the opening quote of this chapter, "Let's take the 'extra' out of extracurricular and make everything curricular!"

How Do We Develop the Multiple Intelligences?

We've all heard that we only use about 10-% of our brains. Another favorite is that the brain is like a skyscraper, yet we live in the lobby. How do we develop the other 90% of our brain? How do we inhabit those multitudes of uninhabited floors? How do we tap those untapped reserves of competence and creativity? How do we unleash our students' limitless potential? How do we fully develop students' multiple intelligences?

The Implicit MI Curriculum

One way to further develop students' multiple intelligences is to use a range of instructional strategies in our classrooms, see Chapters 7 and 8. By using a variety of multiple intelligences instructional strategies, we teach in ways that match the strengths of each student. With each instructional strategy there is an implicit curriculum. As students create mind maps, all students in the classroom strengthen their visual/spatial skills. Students who do not have a strongly developed visual/spatial intelligence get the opportunity to work on stretching their skills. Students who are art or space smart, get the opportunity to develop an area of weakness. Using the strategy Lyrical Lessons, students of all musical abilities engage and stretch their musical intelligence as they write and sing songs.

Drawing mind maps and singing songs may seem perfectly natural to some students. They are already fluent with the symbol system of the intelligences. Perhaps they have had many experiences creating and performing music or constructing representational maps. Other students may be uncomfortable drawing mind maps and singing songs at first. They may feel incompetent. For them, it is the equivalent of asking an illiterate student to read a passage in front of the class. However, if students, starting at an early age, draw mind maps and sing songs, they become comfortable with the symbol systems of the intelligences. They become more fluent songwriters, singers, mind mappers, illustrators. They develop those intelligences.

Using a wide range of instructional strategies allows us not only to reach more students, and to stretch all the intelligences, it allows students to make links across the intelligences. If a student not only develops a set of verbal/linguistic symbols (words) for some content, but also develops kinesthetic symbols (hand gestures), the meaning of the content is more fully developed, and associative links are made across the intelligences, enriching the learning and students' intellectual development.

We, as teachers, each have our own profile of intelligences and repertoires of instructional strategies. Using some strategies in our classroom may feel uncomfortable at first until we, too, become fluent with the symbol systems of the intelligences. One of the most important insights to spring from MI theory is that the best method we have to develop our students' full range of intelligences is to use instructional strategies with which we are least comfortable! If we are strong in, say, the visual/spatial intelligence, we will draw on the blackboard and overhead, we will create colorful, interesting bulletin boards, we will arrange our rooms artfully. Students strong in the visual/spatial intelligence will be comfortable and learn well in our class. All students in our class will develop the visual/spatial intelligence. But what of the other students and the other intelligences? If we are weak in the kinesthetic intelligence, we will lose kinesthetic students and fail to develop our students' body smarts. Thus, if we wish to develop all the intelligences in all of our students, it is precisely those strategies which we are least comfortable with that we most need to use!

We overcome our teaching bias when we stretch ourselves to use a wide range of strategies across the intelligences. Within each instructional strategy there is an implicit curriculum. Over time, we and our students become fluent with the symbol systems of each intelligence and thus develop our multiple intelligences. Using an array of instructional strategies, we and our students become smarter in many ways.

Using a wide range of instructional strategies goes a long way toward developing the multiple intelligences. Realistically, in the current state of education, using a diverse collection of MI teaching strategies is our best bet for making students smarter in many ways. All of us can easily learn a number of multimodal teaching strategies and begin to slowly integrate them into our classroom. Over time, students will receive a wide range of experiences in many do-

mains. And this will be a major stride toward matching, stretching, and celebrating all the intelligences.

To have students perform like Mozart, paint like Monet, write like Dickinson, compute like Einstein, and analyze like Freud, would, as Gardner says, require its own specific educational theory for each intelligence.

However, to develop each intelligence to its fullest, we would need to completely retool education. We would need to design a new MI curriculum. No matter how often we use Lyrical Lessons, our students will not then be able to pick up the violin and play like prodigies. Even if we used Mind Mapping every day, our students will not pick up a brush and paint like Monet.

To have students perform like Mozart, paint like Monet, write like Dickinson, compute like Einstein, and analyze like Freud, would, as Gardner says, require its own specific educational theory for each intelligence. Designing an educational curriculum appropriate to develop each intelligence to its fullest is well beyond the scope of this book. We don't claim to be curriculum specialists. We do, however, based on our experiences and understanding of intelligences and learning, have a notion what an MI curriculum might look like and how the process of developing the intelligences may proceed.

An MI Curriculum

Each intelligence is multifaceted, has its own unique developmental pathway, and serves an important function. Any curriculum designed to fully develop each intelligence needs to take into account the many dimensions of each intelligence, its developmental trajectory, and integrate its development with the functions for which the intelligence is being developed.

A Multifaceted Curriculum

Each intelligence is multifaceted. For example the visual/spatial intelligence consists of many subintelligences or skills such as: the ability to create mental maps, rotate figures mentally, read maps, remember spatial details, estimate distance, create art, appreciate art, arrange objects, coordinate colors, create models, interpret diagrams.

Even though they fall under the visual/spatial category, facets do not necessarily hang together. Even closely related skills may not be linked. Someone who has a highly developed appreciation for art may be lost when given a palette, brush, and canvas. Someone who is an excellent illustrator may be a terrible colorist and vice versa. Skill with one facet of the same intelligence does not predict skill with another facet.

We must not confuse developing one facet of an intelligence with developing the entire intelligence. Expertise in one area may transfer, but then again, it may not.

Therefore, any curriculum that aims to fully develop an intelligence must identify the whole gamut of facets and develop each facet. Let's look again at our Suzuki example. These students would undoubtedly score extremely well on an authentic assessment of their violin playing skills. They may even do very well on an assessment of many associated skills such as reading music, recognizing pitch, timbre. However, they may score poorly on an assessment of their ability to play the cello or piano, or compose a song, or sing. We must not confuse developing one facet of an intelligence with developing the entire intelligence. Expertise in one area may transfer, but then again, it may not.

A Developmental Curriculum

Gardner (1983) traces the developmental pathway of each intelligence. For example, the roots of the spoken aspect of the linguistic intelligence begins with a child's babbling in the first months of life. By the beginning of their second year they start uttering single words, then meaningful pairs of words. By their third year, they start asking simple questions, making negations, and constructing sentences with clauses. By four or five, children can speak with remarkable fluency.

Gardner (1993, p. 27-29) calls this natural growth of an intelligence a developmental trajectory. All humans, with the exception of exceptional individuals, possess core abilities in each of the intelligences. Regardless of education or cultural support, all intelligences are universally manifested at some basic level.

Gardner states that the natural trajectory begins with *raw patterning ability*. He uses the example of making tonal differentiations for the musical/rhythmic intelligence and appreciating three dimensional arrangements in the visual/spatial intelligence.

The next stage of the intelligence is encountered through a *symbol system*. For music, the symbols are songs, for language symbols are stories and sentences, for the bodily/kinesthetic intelligence symbols are gestures and dance.

The next developmental stage involves a *notational system* which is a recorded version of the symbol system. Gardner gives the examples of mathematical notation, mapping, written words, and musical notation. The notational system is mastered in an educational setting.

The final stage of the developmental trajectory is *vocational and avocational pursuits*. During adolescence and adulthood individuals fill roles in society. An appropriate end-state for one skilled in the logical mathematical intelligence, according to Gardner is a mathematician, accountant, scientist, cashier. For the visual/spatial intelligence the roles may be a navigator, chess player, topologist.

David Lazear (1991, 1994) developed a helpful guideline outlining the hierarchical development of intelligence and relating it to formal schooling. The development of an intelligence, according to Lazear, is the movement from the basic, to complex, to coherence level. The *basic level* of learning occurs in infancy and early childhood. This level of development is secured by cultural socialization and biological heritage. The *complex level* occurs in the elementary school years. At this level, Lazear claims we should be concerned not only with increasing the number of skills, but the faculty in using strategies for problem solving, meeting challenges, and mastering knowledge. The *coherence level* occurs at the secondary level. At this level, our goal is to prepare students for the "real world." The skills students acquire are applied outside of schooling.

Given that the growth of an intelligence is a developmental process, it follows that a systematic attempt by education to maximize intellectual capacity should also be

---

Developmental Trajectory of an Intelligence

▼ *Raw Patterning Ability:* The ability to recognize patterns (e.g. tonal differentiations for the musical/rhythmic intelligence; appreciating three dimensional arrangements in the visual/spatial intelligence).

▼ *Symbol System:* Representation of meaning through symbols (e.g. for music, the symbols are songs, for language symbols are stories and sentences, for the bodily/kinesthetic intelligence symbols are gesture or dance).

▼ *Notational System:* Second-order, recorded symbol system (e.g. mathematics, mapping, reading, music notation).

▼ *Vocational and Avocational Pursuits:* Role in society, end-state (e.g. logical mathematical intelligence: mathematician, accountant, scientist, cashier; visual/spatial intelligence: navigator, chess player, topologist.)

— *Adapted from Gardner, 1993*

---

developmental. To a large extent our current curriculum in the existing disciplines is developmental.

For example, the Washoe County School District in Reno, Nevada prints a Mathematics Objectives for grades 1-6. Most districts or schools have something comparable for each subject. The Objectives tells teachers exactly what minimum competencies are expected for each strand of mathematics.

In the number strand, by the end of the first grade, students should be able to:

count, write, identify numbers from 0 to 100, identify place value of any digit in a two digit number, identify a set of whole numbers from least to greatest through 100, read and recognize number words 0 through 10. By the end of the sixth grade, students should be able to: read and write numerals from 0 to 999,999,999, identify place value of any digit in nine digit numbers, identify the period value for nine digit numbers, round numbers to the nearest ten, hundred or thousand, read and write decimals and fractions and so on. For every strand of mathematics, there is a similar developmental progression from basic to more complex mathematical skills.

The same developmental approach holds for language skills. Students usually begin their writing skills program by mastering their name, then writing the alphabet, then spelling simple words, forming simple sentences, learning more complex words and finally forming complex compositions.

Language skills like mathematical skills are multifaceted. Math strands include: problem solving, numbers, measurement, geometry, patterns and functions, statistics, probability, logic, algebra. Language skills include: phonology, syntax, semantics, mechanics, reading.

By the time students leave high school they are usually at least proficient with many facets of language and mathematics. A curriculum to develop the other intelligences should mirror the curriculum of the existing disciplines. It should be developmentally appropriate and sequentially build on skills from year to year moving students from what Gardner would call raw patterning to vocational and avocational pursuits.

An Integrated, Functional Curriculum

Years ago, when one of the authors was sitting on a bus, a father told him the following story:

My son is only four years old, but he can add any two numbers up to six plus six. The interesting thing is that I did not teach him. We play Chutes and Ladders. He loves the game. At first when he played, to advance he would roll the dice and then count the numbers on one die, one at a time, and move his marker that many spaces, one at a time, counting them off. Then he would count the numbers on the other die and move his marker that many spaces. After we had played many times, he changed. He would not count the numbers on the face of the die, he would just look at one die, and say three or five or whatever was on the face of the die. For him the three dots on the face of the die were no longer three dots, it was just a three. He would see it as one number and move that many spaces, then glance at the other die and move that many spaces. Later, he advanced so that he would add the numbers on each die before moving. He would roll a three and a five and say, "three and five…eight," and then move eight spaces. Now when he rolls the three and five he does not see the three and the five as separate dice, he just knows he has rolled an eight. He sees the two dice as an eight the same way he sees the four dots one die as a four, not four separate dots. The way he counts the moves on the board has changed too: if he rolls a seven, say, he seems to just see where seven spaces ahead will be and moves his marker there without counting each move.

In the context of playing the game of Chutes and Ladders this child had developed addition skills. Had his father set out to teach him to add by presenting him with addition worksheets, not only would the boy have not learned to add, but probably he would have grown to dislike math and thought he was poor in math. He had learned to add partly because it was functional for him to learn — adding helped him go where he wanted to go. He had learned to add also because addition was not presented to him in a decontextualized form — it was presented in a meaningful context. It was natural for the boy to acquire the math facts, they were an integral part of playing Chutes and Ladders. Had the boy been presented with abstract worksheets, learning the math facts would have felt unnatural; the math would have been divorced from a meaningful context.

Let's take another example. Within a few years of birth, almost all little children perform a miracle — they master a foreign language. They acquire their parents' language with little or no formal instruction. Our high school students, in the same amount of time, fail to become fluent in a foreign language — yet they have had the benefit of already having mastered one language. Why is it that very young children consistently do what our high school students fail to accomplish? At workshops, we have asked thousands of teachers to raise their hands if they have taken a foreign language in high school. Almost all teachers raise their hands. We then ask them to keep their hands up if they are fluent in that language, and almost all hands drop. What is wrong with this picture? Why are we as a nation investing the time and resources of our teachers and students in courses which year after year fail to reach their objectives?

Part of the reason that young children consistently outperform students in formal language courses is that the young children are learning an integrated, functional curriculum. The high school student in a foreign language course spends Thursday night memorizing a vocabulary list. On the list is the word "cup." The next day when the teacher says "cup" during the exam, the student correctly writes the foreign language word for "cup." Week after week the student correctly memorizes additional vocabulary words. Then, say a year later, the student is in a situation where he or she wants to speak the language. The words do not come. There is no fluency.

In contrast, in the same time-frame the young child who memorized no vocabulary lists, has become quite fluent. What has happened? When the mother handed the child a cup for the first time, the mother said, "cup." When the mother handed the child a cup for the second time, the mother said, "cup." This process was repeated a number of times until one day the child wanted the cup, reached for the cup, and said, "cup."

Within a few years of birth, almost all little children perform a miracle — they master a foreign language. In the same amount of time, high school students fail the same task. Why?

What is the critical difference between the language acquisition approach used with the child and the approach used with the high school student? The high school student is learning a nonfunctional, decontextualized curriculum. The student may memorize the list of vocabulary words for the test, but later when the student wants to speak they are not there. The mind does not function well that way: In the middle of a sentence, the learner cannot go back and picture week three's vocabulary list, pull off the word "cup," and plug it into a sentence. In contrast, the child has learned the word "cup" in a context very similar to the context in which the word will be used. Psychologically, the word is not back on a vocabulary list, it is right there in the situation. The word is helping the child survive, to get the liquid he wants; the word is functional. The word is integrated into the context. All the associations of sitting, eating, drinking, tasting, and feeling hungry and feeling full are linked to the word "cup" for the child; the word is integrated.

> **Language, numbers, and every other kind of learning are best acquired as an integrated, functional context. Learning is less likely to occur if it does not help the learner reach a goal towards which the learner is striving... Learning also is less likely to occur to the extent it is divorced from the context of performance.**

Language, numbers, and every other kind of learning are best acquired as an integrated, functional context. Learning is less likely to occur if it does not help the learner reach a goal towards which the learner is striving, or at least toward which the learner can imagine himself or herself striving. *Learning is accelerated to the extent that it is functional.* Learning also is less likely to occur to the extent it is divorced from the context of performance. *Learning is accelerated to the extent that it is integrated.*

When the high school student is memorizing the vocabulary list, he or she is attempting to acquire the language out of the context in which it will be performed. The more dissimilar the situation of acquisition from the situation of performance, the greater the transference gap. When the dissimilarity of the situation of acquisition and performance are great enough, the transference gap becomes so great that it cannot be bridged. Integrated learning is contextual learning; it reduces or eliminates the transference gap.

When the high school student is memorizing the vocabulary list, he or she may see little connection between memorizing the words and actually speaking the language. If no connection is even imagined, as when the student is memorizing the words for a grade, fluency will not result. Language fluency, and every other kind of learning, occurs to the extent that the learning is functional — that it functions to help the learner reach a valued goal.

In Chapter 3: What Is an Intelligence? we presented eight functions of intelligence, symbolized by the mnemonic SSPPCCKW. Learning is accelerated to the extent that the learner perceives it as fostering the SSPPCCKW functions. Learning occurs in the context of the functions of intelligence:

- Surviving;
- Skill development, developing skills students' perceive as helpful toward achieving relevant goals;
- Problem solving, solving problems students' want to solve;
- Perceiving interesting stimuli;
- Creating something the learner wishes to create;
- Communicating personally meaningful information;
- Knowing, understanding personally relevant information;
- Wisdom, making decisions of which the student is proud.

Just as the intelligences evolved to foster the SSPPCCKW functions, learning also is accelerated in the context of the SSPPCCKW functions. In the context of the SSPPCCKW functions, learning is both integrated and functional. In the real world the intelligences do not function in isolation, they work in harmony to allow us to function. All parts of the brain, as we will see in Chapter 20: Is MI Theory Brain-Based?, are remarkably integrated. The brain consists of a community of interdependent, integrated neurons. When we develop the intelligences through integrated instruction, in meaningful contexts which engage all aspects of the brain, we are designing brain-based learning. Integrated instruction, brain-based instruction, occurs in the context of the SSPPCCKW functions and involves the intelligences acting in concert.

If our goal is to teach a foreign language, we can have students memorize vocabulary lists and verb conjugations. If so, they learn about the language, but do not acquire the language. Formal, decontextualized curriculum leads to learning of isolated facts and skills which are soon forgotten.

Instead of using a formal, decontextualized approach we will be more successful if we create and deliver an integrated, functional curriculum. Applying the SSPPCCKW functions, we could have students listen, speak, read, and write in the language as they solve problems, communicate, make decisions, describe nuances of stimuli, and attempt to order items in a real or simulated store — using the language to survive. In a natural, functional context, the language is associated to many stimuli, so

One implication of this analysis is that we will not be successful in developing the intelligences if we attempt to develop them only in isolation. Spelling is best learned in the context of writing, and writing is best learned in the context of communicating. When we teach spelling out of the context of the student's own expressive writing (communication), not only does motivation go down, but a transference gap is created. Most elementary teachers have seen the student who spells a word correctly for the spelling test, but fails to spell it correctly while writing a report. Sensitivity to tone and timbre is more readily acquired in the context of singing a meaningful song, communicating, than if we introduce those skills only as ends in themselves. Color mixing is more enduringly, and meaningfully acquired in the context of expressive painting than as an end in itself.

> **One implication of this analysis is that we will not be successful in developing the intelligences if we attempt to develop them only in isolation.**

it is not easily forgotten, and it is acquired and practiced in situations similar to those in which it will be used, sidestepping the transference gap. An integrated, functional approach is a real-world approach. The apprenticeships advocated by Gardner are one of a number of wonderful ways to deliver an integrated, functional curriculum to develop the intelligences.

We are not arguing that formal, decontextualized instruction should never occur. It can compliment the integrated, functional curriculum. Memorizing grammar rules, multiplication facts, names of plants, states and capitals, names of musical notes, rules of soccer, modes of conflict resolution, or steps of decision making is at best part of teaching for the intelligences. Unless students also practice correct grammar in the context of communicating personally meaningful information, use the multiplication facts in the context of solving meaningful problems, and use the plant information in creating a garden or surviving a nature adventure, enduring learning is not likely. Memorizing the modes of conflict resolution is, at the very best, part of our curriculum to develop the interpersonal intelligence; if those conflict resolution modes are not applied in the context of solving important interpersonal conflicts, if they are not part of an integrated, functional curriculum, we will not have reached the goal of developing the intelligence. Formal, decontextualized instruction alone will not lead us to our goal of teaching for the intelligences. Learning all facets of all of the intelligences is accelerated to the extent we present them as an integrated, functional curriculum.

In sum, an MI curriculum would be multifaceted, developmental, and functional and integrated. Let's now take a look at what an MI curriculum might look like.

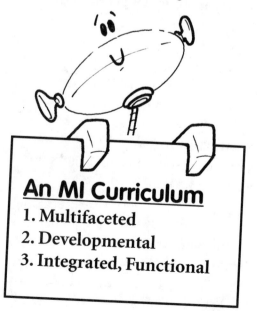

An MI Curriculum
1. **Multifaceted**
2. **Developmental**
3. **Integrated, Functional**

Mini-Curriculums

On the following pages, you will find a mini-curriculum for each intelligence. Each mini-curriculum lists some of the fundamental skills and information central to each intelligence. By no means do we claim these mini-curriculums are comprehensive or complete. In fact, they are a bit arbitrary. They are provided here merely as an illustration of the breadth of each intelligence. We have made no effort to organize the content developmentally. For ease, we have organized the skills and content alphabetically. If we are to fully develop students' multiple intelligences, an elaborate, multifaceted MI curriculum for each intelligence would have to be developed. Again, a differentiated, developmentally-appropriate curriculum for each intelligence is far beyond the scope of this book.

These mini-curriculums, however, serve as helpful references as we stretch each intelligence. As we stretch the visual/spatial intelligence, we integrate activities that teach about the elements of art such as: lines and shapes, texture, color, and art of various mediums. We enhance students' spatial awareness, with activities on: size, distance, shape, perspective, directionality, magnitude, rotation. See the eight mini-curriculums on the following pages.

Perhaps these mini-curriculums may be the starting point for a school- or district-wide effort to create a more systematic MI curriculum with goals and objectives at each grade level. When the intelligences neglected (or made extracurricular) by education become systematically developed — as do our programs for language and math — then we will truly be stretching the multiple intelligences to their potential.

Courses Across the Multiple Intelligences

So far, we have explored the notion of "infusion" quite extensively. Multiple intelligences is infused into existing subjects or classes. This approach works well at all grade levels. At any grade level, we can infuse MI into the classes by offering opportunities for students to engage their multiple intelligences as they learn the content.

At the middle, secondary, and college levels, developing the multiple intelligences can occur across courses as well as within a class. This approach involves providing students an array of courses relating to the multiple intelligences. Establishing MI courses is a school-wide decision rather than a choice made by individual classroom teachers. Many middle schools, secondary schools, colleges and universities already have a fantastic curriculum range, offering courses that span the range of intelligences, developing students' unique skills from painting to water polo. The school staff or administration may or may not be aware of MI theory, but the school provides a wonderful "multiple intelligences" curriculum nonetheless.

Courses Across the Multiple Intelligences on page 9.23 lists some traditional courses and categories of courses which address the multiple intelligences. An MI program for developing the multiple intelligences ideally includes a variety of courses in each intelligence.

Visionary MI schools may expand their required or elective course offerings to align them with the multiple intelligences and more fully develop students' range of intelligences. Applying MI theory, a school or college may add a number of MI-inspired courses. See box: Courses Inspired by Multiple Intelligences.

Courses Inspired by Multiple Intelligences

▼ Verbal/Linguistic
- Speed Reading With Comprehension
- Writing A Screenplay

▼ Logical/Mathematical
- Everyday Math Skills
- Logical Thinking

▼ Visual/Spatial
- Art for Nonartists
- Home Design

▼ Musical/Rhythmic
- Exploring Musical Instruments
- Making Music With Your Computer

▼ Bodily/Kinesthetic
- Getting In Tune With Your Body
- Yoga

▼ Naturalist
- Communing With Nature
- Survival in Nature

▼ Interpersonal
- Conflict Resolution and Negotiation
- Teamwork Skills

▼ Intrapersonal
- Setting and Reaching Goals
- Exploring Your Values

A Mini-Curriculum for Developing the

Verbal/Linguistic Intelligence

▼ **Foreign Language**
  • Reading, speaking, writing

▼ **Library Skills**
  • Card catalogue, databases, Dewey decimal system, microfiche, reference books, search engines

▼ **Phonology** (word sounds)
  ★ **Articulation/enunciation/pronunciation**
  • Digraphs and blends
  • Final sounds
  • Silent e, single consonant beginnings, vowel clusters, vowels
  • Homophones
  • Syllables

▼ **Reading**
  • Comprehension
  • Speed

▼ **Semantics** (word meanings)
  ★ **Figurative speech**
  • Multiple meanings
  • Hyperbole, simile, metaphor
  ★ **Vocabulary**
  • Affixes, prefixes, suffixes
  • Antonyms, synonyms
  • Dictionary, thesaurus skills
  • Etymology

▼ **Speaking/Discussing/Listening**
  • Active listening, conversation, debate, explaining, speech, storytelling

▼ **Spelling/Mechanics**
  • Abbreviations
  • Capitalization
  • Compound words
  • Contractions
  • Homonyms
  • Rules/exceptions

▼ **Syntax/Grammar**
  ★ **Parts of Speech**
  • Adjective, adverb, article, conjunction, interjection, noun, preposition, pronoun, verb
  ★ **Punctuation**
  • Apostrophe, colon, comma, ellipsis, end marks, hyphen, parenthesis, quotation mark, semicolons
  ★ **Sentences**
  • Structure - subject, predicate
  • Types - simple, compound, fragments, run-ons
  • Variety

▼ **Technological Skills**
  • Word processing

▼ **Writing**
  ★ **The Writing Process**
  • Prewriting, writing, proofing/ editing, conferring/rewriting, publishing
  ★ **Types of Writing**
  • Articles, autobiography, biography, book report, creative, description, essay, explanations, letters, narrative, paragraph, play/skit, persuasive, poetry, reports

A Mini-Curriculum for Developing the

Logical/Mathematical Intelligence

▼ **Logic/Higher-Level Thinking**
★ **Generating Information**
  • Brainstorming
  • Drawing conclusions
  • Evaluating
  • Exaggerating/elaborating
  • Inventing
  • Making analogies
  • Making decisions
  • Predicting
  • Questioning
  • Synthesizing
★ **Transforming Information**
  • Analyzing
  • Applying
  • Associating
  • Combining
  • Comparing/contrasting
  • Deciphering
  • Deducing
  • Determining cause/effect
  • Eliminating/reducing
  • Hypothesizing/predicting
  • Inducing
  • Prioritizing
  • Problem Solving
  • Rearranging/organizing/classifying
  • Reversing
  • Separating
  • Sequencing
  • Substituting
★ **Understanding Information**
  • Categorizing
  • Describing

  • Recalling
  • Role taking
  • Summarizing
  • Symbolizing

▼ **Mathematics**
★ **Algebra**
★ **Geometry**
  • Angles
  • Shapes
  • Proofs
★ **Logic**
★ **Measurement**
  • Time
  • Money
  • Distance
  • Weight
  • Volume
★ **Number**
  • Addition, subtraction, multiplication, division
  • Fractions, percents, decimals
  • Place value
  • Sequence/order
★ **Patterns & Functions**
★ **Probability**
★ **Statistics**
  • Graphs - line, bar, pie, scatter

▼ **Technology**
★ **Computers**
  • Hardware
  • Programming
  • Software

A Mini-Curriculum for Developing the

Visual/Spatial Intelligence

▼ **Art Appreciation & Art History**
- Artists and their works - van Gogh, Monet, Picasso…
- Art movements - impressionism, surrealism, cubism, pop art, Renaissance…
- Art of different cultures
- Art of different times

▼ **Elements of Art**
★ **Color**
- Black and white
- Color contrasts
- Color for positive and negative space
- Color values
- Complementary colors
- Cool and warm colors
- Primary colors
- Secondary colors
- Tertiary colors

★ **Light & Shading**
- Dimension
- Highlights
- Hue
- Shading, shadows
- Tint

★ **Lines & Shapes**
- Contour
- Curves and angles
- Different types of lines
- Outline Shapes

★ **Pattern & Design**
- Contrasting, repetitive, varied patterns

★ **Mediums**
- Animation
- Collage

- Drawing - pencil, ink, charcoal, pastels, color pencil, crayon
- Mixed, crafts
- Paint - oil, acrylic, gouache, watercolor, airbrush
- Sculpture

★ **Texture**
- Awareness of texture
- Creating texture

▼ **Spatial Relations**
★ **Size and Scale**
- Dominance, balance,
- Emphasis, magnitude

★ **Arrangement/Direction**
- Congruence, relationships
- Directionality, rotation
- Interpreting diagrams/maps
- Graphic organizers
- Maps, charts, graphs, coordinates
- Order, sequence, pattern
- Perspective, distortion, focus, illusion
- Shape, model
- Symmetry, reflection, similarity

▼ **Technology**
- Animation
- CAD, 3-D modeling, rendering
- Digital illustration/paint
- Graphic design, page layout

▼ **Visualization**
- Imagination/fantasy/pretend
- Film and video
- Organization

A Mini-Curriculum for Developing the

Musical/Rhythmic Intelligence

▼ **Body**
- Clap, hum, snap, stomp, tap

▼ **Conducting/Composing**

▼ **Instruments**
★ **Electric & Electronic**
- Electric bass guitar
- Electric guitar
- Electronic drums
- Electronic keyboards

★ **Percussion**
- Castanets
- Drums - Drum kit, congas, steel, kettledrum, talking drum
- Glockenspiel
- Guiro
- Maracas
- Piano

★ **String**
- Cello
- Banjo
- Bass
- Guitar
- Harpsichord
- Violin

★ **Wind**
- Bagpipes
- Flute
- Oboe
- Organ
- Recorder
- Saxophone
- Trombone
- Trumpet

▼ **Lyrics/Songwriting**
- Meaning
- Rhyme
- Song structure

▼ **Music Appreciation**
- Musicians and their works
- Music of different times
- Music of different cultures

▼ **Notation/Reading Music**
- Expressions
- Notes
- Symbols
- Tablature

▼ **Sensitivity**
- Pitch
- Rhythm
- Structure
- Tempo
- Timbre

▼ **Technology**
- Composition software

▼ **Voice**
★ **Singing**
- Solos, duets, trios quartets, chorus, choir
★ **Sounds**
- Effects
- Rhythm

A Mini-Curriculum for Developing the

Bodily/Kinesthetic Intelligence

▼ Body Awareness
- Meditation
- Relaxation
- Yoga

▼ Communication
- Body language
- Posture
- Facial expressions
- Gestures
- Sign language

▼ Expressive/Artistic
- Acting
- Impersonation
- Dancing - ballet, ballroom, break dancing, country, Latin
- Pantomime

▼ Fine Motor Skills
- Tool manipulation
- Precise hand movement
- Eye-hand coordination

▼ Physical Fitness/Skills
- Agility
- Balance
- Coordination
- Endurance
- Flexibility
- Speed
- Strength
- Timing

▼ Scientific Awareness
- Anatomy
- Biology
- Chemistry
- Physics
- Health
- Nutrition

▼ Sports/Physical Activities
- Aerobics
- Archery
- Badminton
- Baseball
- Basketball
- Bowling
- Boxing
- Football
- Golf
- Gymnastics
- Handball
- Jogging
- Juggling
- Lacrosse
- Ping-Pong
- Skateboarding
- Skiing
- Snowboarding
- Soccer
- Softball
- Stretching
- Surfing
- Swimming
- Tennis
- Track & field
- Volleyball
- Weight lifting
- Wrestling

A Mini-Curriculum for Developing the

Naturalist Intelligence

▼ **Nature**

★ **Animals/Insects/Sea Life**
- Identification
- Habitat/adaptations
- Characteristics/behavior
- Taxonomy
- Relations - predator/prey

★ **Flora/Fauna**
- Identification
- Habitat
- Characteristics
- Taxonomy

★ **Landforms**
- Mountain, plateau, isthmus, island
- Habitat

★ **Natural Phenomena**
- Natural disasters - earthquake, volcano, hurricane, tornado, flood, monsoon

★ **Regions/Habitat**
- Types - desert, grassland, mountain, polar, rainforest, tundra

★ **Rocks/Minerals**
- Fossils, seashells

★ **Space**
- Solar system
- Universe

★ **Water**
- Ocean/sea
- Lakes/rivers
- Water cycle

★ **Weather/Climate**
- Clouds
- Rain/sleet/snow
- Seasons
- Wind

▼ **Natural Sciences**
- Anatomy
- Animal physiology
- Astronomy
- Biology
- Chemistry
- Ecology/conservation
- Geology
- Meteorology
- Oceanography
- Physical geography
- Physics

▼ **Natural Skills**
- Animal husbandry/care
- Gardening/farming
- Hunting/fishing
- Hiking/camping
- Nature appreciation

▼ **Science Processes**
- Classifying
- Communicating
- Experimenting
- Identifying
- Inferring
- Measuring
- Model-making
- Observing
- Organizing data
- Predicting

▼ **Scientific Method**
- Analyzing data
- Collecting data
- Hypothesizing
- Interpreting data

A Mini-Curriculum for Developing the

Interpersonal Intelligence

● ●

▼ **Leadership Skills**
- Assertiveness
- Build consensus
- Communicating/articulate vision
- Organizing others
- Planning events
- Motivating others
- Negotiating
- Mediating
- Reading intentions/motives of others

▼ **Relationship Skills**
★ **Conflict Resolution**
- Compromise
- Role play
- Reach consensus

★ **Friendship/Prosocial Skills**
- Caring
- Compassion
- Empathy
- Forgiveness
- Honesty
- Humor
- Liking
- Listening
- Loving
- Loyalty
- Respect
- Tolerance
- Unity

▼ **Teamwork Skills**
- Appreciation of diversity
- Compromise
- Helping/tutoring/teaching
- Knowledge of group dynamics
- Mutual support
- Problem solving
- Role taking
- Sensitivity to individual differences
- Sharing
- Synergy
- Trust

A Mini-Curriculum for Developing the

Intrapersonal Intelligence

▼ **Emotions/Feelings**
  • Awareness of emotions
  • Control of emotions

▼ **Knowing Oneself**
  • Accurate picture of strengths/weaknesses
  • Awareness of cultural heritage
  • Awareness of family roots
  • Awareness of hopes/fears/dreams/desires
  • Developed sense of personal identity
  • Personal history
  • Tastes/preferences

▼ **Making Decisions**
  • Thinking/evaluation skills

▼ **Reflection/Metacognition**
  • Concentration/focus
  • Introspection
  • Metacognition
  • Planning
  • Self-observation

▼ **Self-Esteem**
  • Appreciation of uniqueness
  • Feeling of competence/ability
  • Liking/respect for self
  • Security/confidence

▼ **Setting Goals/Priorities**
  • Aspirations/ambitions
  • Determination
  • Motivating/inspiring self
  • Planning
  • Perseverance
  • Prioritizing
  • Responsibility
  • Self-discipline/will power
  • Time management

▼ **Self-Esteem**
  • Celebrating uniqueness
  • Feeling of competence/ability
  • Liking/respect for self
  • Security/confidence

▼ **Values/Beliefs**
  • Ethics/morality
  • Religion

Courses Across the Multiple Intelligences

▼ Verbal/Linguistic
Communications
Creative Writing
English
Journalism
Literature
Foreign Language
Play Writing
Poetry
Reading
Speech & Debate

▼ Logical/Mathematical
Accounting
Algebra
Business Math
Business
Calculus
Computers
Economics
Engineering
Geometry
Precalculus
Statistics
Trigonometry

▼ Visual/Spatial
Animation
Architecture
Art
Art Appreciation
Art History
Ceramics
Drawing
Fashion
Film/Video
Graphic Arts
Painting
Photography
Sculpting

▼ Musical/Rhythmic
Band
Choir
Instruments
Music Appreciation
Music History

▼ Bodily/Kinesthetic
Acting
Auto Shop
Dance
Driver's Education
Martial Arts
Metal Shop
Physical Education
Sports
Theater
Wood Shop
Yoga

▼ Naturalist
Anatomy
Animal Husbandry
Astronomy
Biology
Chemistry
Earth Science
Genetics
Geology
Horticulture
Nutrition
Oceanography
Physics
Physiology

▼ Interpersonal
Anthropology
Civics
History
Home Economics
Humanities
Political Science
Public Relations
Social Studies
Sociology

▼ Intrapersonal
Meditation
Psychology
Theology

Activities to Stretch Intelligences

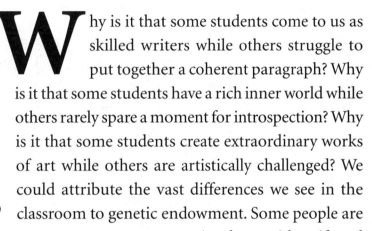

The human mind, once stretched to a new idea never goes back to its original dimensions.
— *Oliver Wendell Holmes*

Why is it that some students come to us as skilled writers while others struggle to put together a coherent paragraph? Why is it that some students have a rich inner world while others rarely spare a moment for introspection? Why is it that some students create extraordinary works of art while others are artistically challenged? We could attribute the vast differences we see in the classroom to genetic endowment. Some people are just born with a gift and some aren't. Alternatively, we could attribute different levels of intelligences to socialization or education. Some people are reared and educated in an environment that nurtures the development of an intelligence or intelligences while others are not so fortunate. As we have seen in Chapter 3: What Is an Intelligence?, both explanations have validity.

To help students become a little smarter in each broad category of intelligence, we give students the opportunity to develop their weaker intelligences through their strengths.

Intelligences are the product of the interaction between genetic constitution and environmental circumstances, different for each individual. But no matter what that interaction may be, our mission as educators is clear: Our job is to help every student realize his or her full potential. In our class and school we endeavor to build on students' inherent strengths and to develop students' less dominant intelligences. And to a large extent, we are successful. We do contribute to students' intellectual development in many ways. Glancing at our students' portfolios near the end of the school year, we see great progress. We see not only increased academic achievement, but also a flowering of intellectual development — our students become smarter in many ways.

Stretching Through Strengths

How, then, do we go about making students smarter in many ways? In Chapter 9: Developing the Multiple Intelligences, we explored implicit and explicit approaches to stretch students' intelligences. In this chapter, we will illustrate one of the simplest and most promising explicit approaches to stretching the multiple intelligences: developing each intelligence through the other intelligences. In this approach, we stretch weaker intelligences by providing access to them through intellectual strengths: Stretching through strengths.

An example of stretching through strengths is a musical activity to teach students about mathematics; in Activity 14 students sing a song about fractions (see page 10.17). Students who have a highly developed musical sense pick up important fraction terminology as they engage in what for them is a meaningful and motivating activity — an activity which matches a dominant intelligence. Similarly, we may develop a facet of the logical intelligence via the intrapersonal intelligence: We may have students make analogies re-

lating geometric shapes to themselves personally (see page 10.21). For example, students complete analogies such as: "I am like a circle because…" Students who have highly developed intrapersonal intelligence find the task engaging, but at the same time stretch their analogical thinking, one facet of the logical/mathematical intelligence, and their awareness of shapes, another facet of the logical/mathematical intelligence. If over time we teach content through each intelligence, we provide for each student access to the curriculum through their strongest intelligences.

The rationale for stretching through strengths is the same as that for our first MI vision, matching students' intelligences. In the process of delivering traditional academic curriculum, as we use instructional strategies which match the strengths of each student, we provide greater access to the curriculum for each student. Wise teachers stretch academic skills through strengths, as when they take reading assignments from *Popular Mechanics* for students with poor reading skills but strong mechanical skills. The same principle holds when we want to stretch the intelligences.

In the last two decades, a variety of researchers have demonstrated success with at-risk students by teaching basic skills in the context of higher-level skills, rather than by making proficiency in the basic skills a prerequisite to access to the higher-level skills (Means, Chelemer, & Knapp, 1991). Much of this work can be interpreted as stretching through strength. The poor reader willingly tackles decoding when the message is from a friend — linguistic intelligence stretched through the interpersonal intelligence. Low income black students engage in sophisticated writing and editing when the content is rap lyrics (Griffin & Cole, 1987) — linguistic intelligence stretched through the musical intelligence. A low-level reader given the opportunity to analyze a story in which a bear fell from a tree stated,

> You know it kind of told you what time of year was because it told you it went "splash," because if it was this time of the year [February], I don't think he'd splash in the water; I think he'd crack (Palincsar & Klenk, 1991, p. 119)

— linguistic intelligence stretched through the logical and naturalist intelligences.

By developing students' intelligences through the other intelligences, we engage students' less dominant intelligences through their more dominant intelligences. We also integrate students' multiple intelligences. Logical/mathematical skills are acquired in part through the other intelligences. We break down the artificial partitions. As students develop intelligences through other intelligences, they develop connectivity and cognitive flexibility. As we stimulate more parts of the brain at once, we are developing a brain-based curriculum. Students can relate art to language, math, music, movement. By developing each intelligence through the other intelligences, we match our students strengths, stretch their weaknesses through strengths, and increase connectivity among intelligences. Our students are, after all, much more than the sum of their isolated skills or intelligences.

In this chapter, we have provided a number of sample activities to illustrate the approach of developing each intelligence through the other intelligences. The activities are organized by intelligence. There are at least eight activities to develop each intelligence, stretching each intelligence through each of the other intelligences. These activities by no means are intended to be an MI curriculum for stretching the

intelligences. They are just a sampling to illustrate our favorite approach to developing intelligences: stretching through strengths.

It should be noted, the following are sample activities; they are acontextual. They are not sequential or integrated with any content. As they stand, they are just fun intelligence stretchers that can be used at any point. To the extent possible, however, efforts to develop students' multiple intelligences in the classroom should be rooted in a meaningful and developmentally appropriate context. A table of activities for this chapter follows.

References

Griffin, P., & Cole, M. *New technologies, basic skills, and the underside of education: What is to be done?* **In J. A. Langer** (Ed.) *Language, Literacy, and Culture: Issues of Society and Schooling.* Norwood, NJ: Ablex, 1987.

B. Means, C. Chelemer, & M. S. Knapp (Eds.) *Teaching Advanced Skills to At-risk Students. Views from Research and Practice.* San Francisco, CA: Jossey-Bass, 1991.

Palincsar, A. S. & Klenk, L. J. *Dialogues promoting reading comprehension.* **In B. Means, C. Chelemer, & M. S. Knapp** (Eds.) *Teaching Advanced Skills to At-risk Students. Views from Research and Practice.* San Francisco, CA: Jossey-Bass, 1991.

Table of Activities

Developing the Verbal/Linguistic Intelligence

Developing the Logical/Mathematical Intelligence

Developing the Visual/Spatial Intelligence

Developing the Musical/Rhythmic Intelligence

Table of Activities (continued)

Developing the Verbal/Linguistic Intelligence 1

Verbal/Linguistic Activity

Creative Sentences

Use the provided words to make a creative sentence. Make sure to include all words provided. Share your sentence with a partner.

SAMPLE

Nouns: Fox, Fence
Verb: Jumped
Adjectives: Brown, Lazy, Quick

The quick, brown, lazy fox jumped over
the fence.

Sentence 1

Nouns: Ocean, Shark, Fish, Bait
Verbs: Catch, Bite
Adjectives: Humongous, Ferocious

_____
_____
_____
_____

Sentence 2

Nouns: Mall, Car,
Verbs: Bought, Returned, Drove
Adjectives: New, Broken

_____
_____
_____
_____

Sentence 3

Nouns: Witch, Moon, Broom, Cat
Verbs: Stirred, Flew, Jumped
Adjectives: Fat, Ugly, Fast, Black

_____
_____
_____
_____

Sentence 4

Nouns: Museum, Art, Man
Verbs: Stared, Walked, Ate
Adjectives: Beautiful, Colorful, Hungry

_____
_____
_____
_____

Spencer & Miguel Kagan: *Multiple Intelligences*
Kagan Cooperative Learning • 1 (800) WEE CO-OP

Logical/Mathematical Activity

Write the Instructions

A UFO landed in your back yard. The aliens are hungry, and want to make something to eat. They don't understand spoken language but can read well. Write the instructions to make a peanut butter and jelly sandwich. When done, have a partner act out your instructions.

Peanut Butter & Jelly Sandwich

Instructions: _____

_____

_____

_____

_____

_____

_____

_____

_____

_____

_____

_____

_____

_____

_____

_____

_____

Developing the Verbal/Linguistic Intelligence `3`

Visual/Spatial Activity

Describe the Castle

Describe the castle as well as you can. When done, cut the castle out and hide it. Give your paper to a partner. He or she will attempt to draw the castle from your description. When done, compare castles and discuss how the description could have been better.

Your Partner's Drawing Here

_____

_____

_____

_____

_____

_____

_____

_____

_____

_____

4 *Developing the Verbal/Linguistic Intelligence*

Musical/Rhythmic Activity

The Antonym Song

Work with a partner to write a song about antonyms to the tune of "Jingle Bells." Sing your song to another pair.

Developing the Verbal/Linguistic Intelligence **5**

Bodily/Kinesthetic Activity

Act It Out!

Sample Vocabulary Words

- aghast
- bisect
- ceremony
- eccentric
- fiendish
- hobble
- investigate
- jangle
- knead
- languid
- migrate
- nauseous
- obstruct
- periodic
- reign
- slither
- tattle
- undulate

Pick one of your vocabulary words or use a word from the sample list below. In your team, take turns acting out your words. See if teammates can guess which word you are acting out. See if you can guess the words your teammates are acting out.

6 *Developing the Verbal/Linguistic Intelligence*

Bodily/Kinesthetic Activity

Teacher: Give students these letter manipulatives to spell out their spelling words.

Letter Manipulatives!

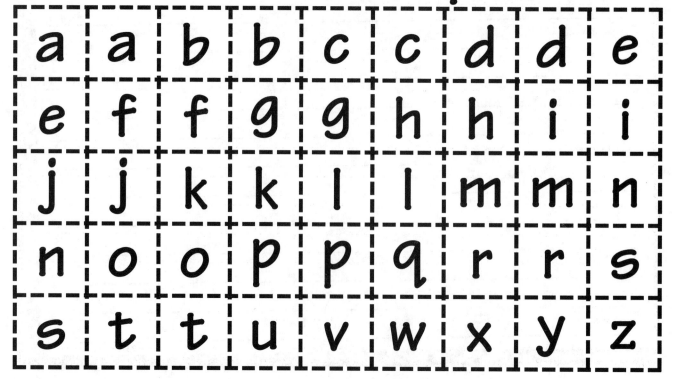

a	a	b	b	c	c	d	d	e
e	f	f	g	g	h	h	i	i
j	j	k	k	l	l	m	m	n
n	o	o	p	p	q	r	r	s
s	t	t	u	v	w	x	y	z

Naturalist Activity

The Spotted Horse

Write a creative story about the spotted horse.

C. RODRIGUEZ

Developing the Verbal/Linguistic Intelligence 8

Interpersonal Activity

Working Together Better

How can you and your teammates work together better? Write down your ideas, then share them with your teammates.

_____

_____

_____

_____

_____

_____

_____

9 **Developing the Verbal/Linguistic Intelligence**

Interpersonal Activity

Why   Share?

List 8 reasons why it is important to share with others.

1 _____

2 _____

3 _____

4 _____

5 _____

6 _____

7 _____

8 _____

10 *Developing the Verbal/Linguistic Intelligence*

Intrapersonal Activity

Language & Me

With a partner, read the following questions about language and you. Read the first question and share your answer with your partner. Have your partner share his or her answer with you. Then, your partner reads the next question and shares his or her answer. Then you share your answer. Alternate reading each question. The reader goes first sharing.

Reading

1. Do you enjoy reading?
2. Do you consider yourself a good reader?
3. Who is your favorite author? Is he or she like or unlike you?
4. What is your favorite book? Why?
5. Name a poem that you really like. Why do you like it?

Writing

1. Do you enjoy writing? Why or why not?
2. What have you written that you are most proud of?
3. Do you consider yourself a good writer? Why or why not?
4. What is one thing you'd like to improve about your writing?
5. Do you keep a journal or diary?
6. Are you a good speller? Why or why not?

Speaking

1. Do you prefer speaking one on one or in large groups?
2. Do you have a good vocabulary? Why or why not?
3. Can you speak another language?
   If not, which language would you like to learn?
4. How do you feel about giving speeches?

Developing the Logical/Mathematical Intelligence **11**

Verbal/Linguistic Activity

What's the Cause?

Let's make up causes. A boy laughs (effect) because he is watching a funny movie (cause). For every effect, describe a cause. See how creative you can make the causes. Compare your causes with a partner.

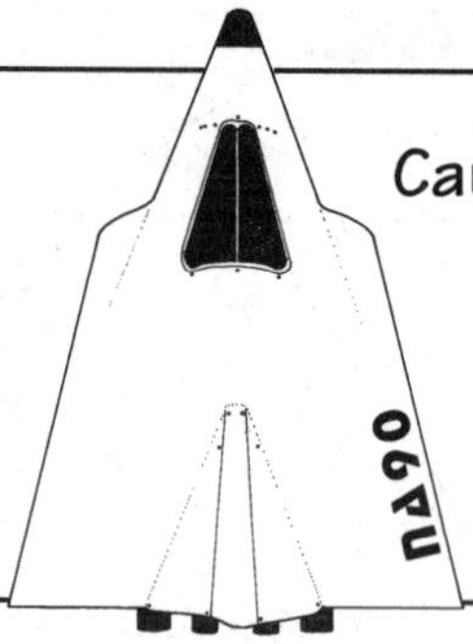

Cause: _____

_____

_____

Effect: The rocket ship blasted off and headed for outer space.

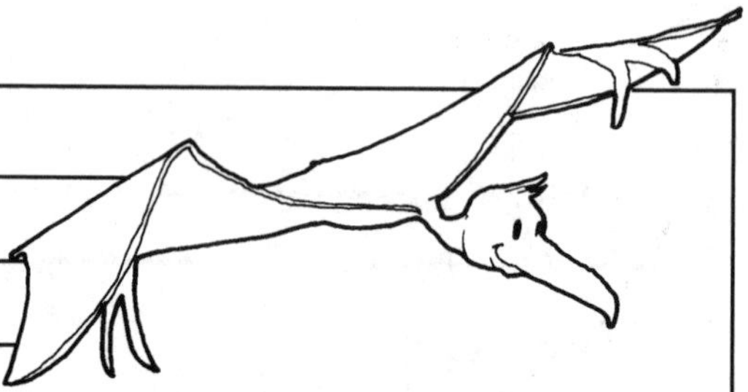

Cause: _____

_____

_____

Effect: The pterodactyl flew away with a big smile on his face.

Cause: _____

_____

_____

Effect: Sitting at his desk, Danny was scared stiff.

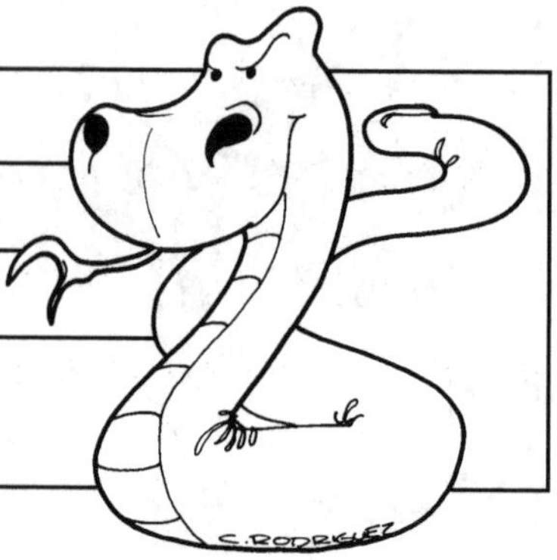

Cause: _____

_____

_____

Effect: The snake prepared to strike.

12 *Developing the Logical/Mathematical Intelligence*

Logical/Mathematical Activity

Analyze the Graphs

Mr. Stats sells math supplies at his store, Stat's Math Supplies. Take a look at his sales graphs and answer the questions below.

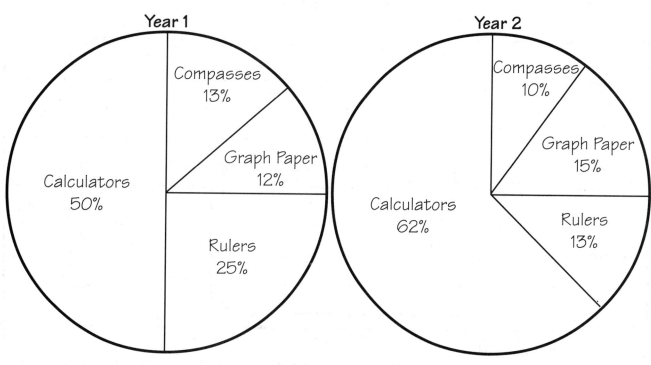

1. What was Mr. Stat's best-selling item year 1?_____

2. What was Mr. Stat's worst-selling item year 1? _____

3. Did the best-seller remain the best-seller year 2?_____

4. Did the worst-seller remain the worst-seller year 2?_____

5. For what item did sales increase the most? _____

6. For what item did sales decrease the most?_____

7. What two items had a 3% increase or decrease?_____

8. Rulers lost what percent of sales year 2?_____

9. What gained as much of sales as rulers lost year 2?_____

10. If you were going to make one suggestion to Mr. Stat, what would it be?_____

Developing the Logical/Mathematical Intelligence **13**

Visual/Spatial Activity

Symmetry & Asymmetry

Symmetry is the similarity of form or arrangement on either side of a dividing line. When a shape with symmetry is symmetrical; a shape without symmetry is asymmetrical.

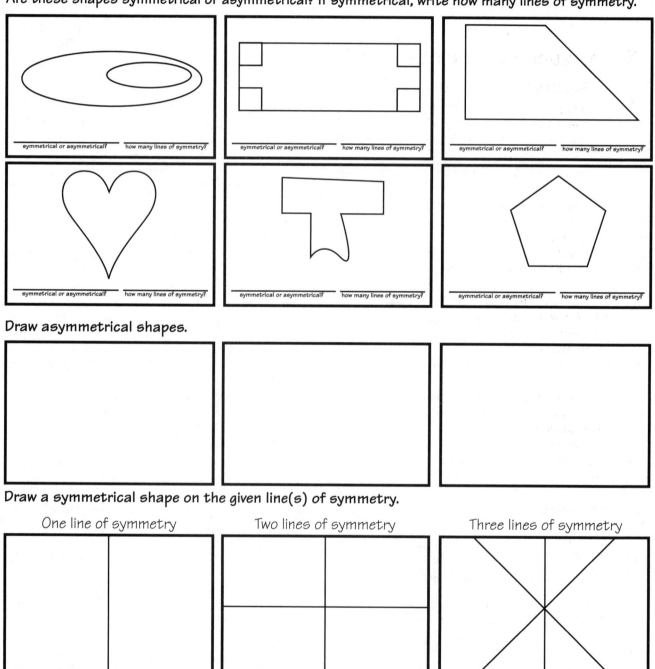

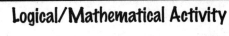

14 *Developing the Logical/Mathematical Intelligence*

Logical/Mathematical Activity

The Fraction Song

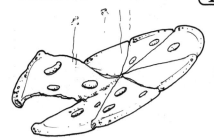

Sing "The Fraction Song" together as a class. Then, work in teams to write, "The Decimal Song." Sing your decimal song to the class.

To the tune of "She'll Be Comin' 'Round the Mountain"

(1) Kinda like the sky and kinda like the ground
(2) Fractions have two parts: an "upstairs" and a "down"
(3) " 'Upstairs' are the **numerators**"—
(4) Says my teacher, Mr. Slater—
(5) So I guess **denominators** must be "down"!

(6) Mr. Slater teaches fractions **"quarterly"**
(7) He is really into **"part equality"**
(8) He will slice a larger pizza
(9) Into equal parts to "eatsa"
(10) So that all will get the same amount—you see?

(11) Now the **total equal parts** that make a whole
(12) And **denominators**—they're the ones **"below"**
(13) Numerators up above 'em
(14) Tell the fractional part of 'em
(15) Of, that is, denominators "down below"!

(16) So the separate equal parts **less than a whole**
(17) Are shown **"upstairs"**—that's where **numerators** go
(18) Very often they are lower
(19) Often making them less "wholer"
(20) Than "denomineighbors" living down below!

(21) When your mother and your father disagree
(22) Over who gets how much from the lottery
(23) And your mother says "Now honey,
(24) We'll each get one-half the money"
(25) She is "fractioning" the money equally!

(26) When your three friends want the same piece of candy
(27) Cut the one piece into three parts equally
(28) Why should good friends take a beating
(29) When each one could do some eating?
(30) Just like magic you can turn **"one"** into **"three"**!

(31) Once a mother cooked up spinach from the store
(32) And it wound up in **one pile** on the floor
(33) The four children barely tried it
(34) And their father said "Divide it!"
(35) So they **halved it twice** and ended up with **four!**

(36) There were **six** more **children** waiting to be fed
(37) There was only **one** more **piece** of whole wheat bread
(38) But the clever mother fixed it
(39) She just took the **"whole"** and **"sixed"** it
(40) So each ate one **sixth** and then went off to bed!

(41) Eat a fraction of a cake—like **7/8**
(42) Meaning **seven of eight** equal parts you take
(43) **Seven** is the **numerator**
(44) **"Eight"** is the **denominator**
(45) So to eat the **"whole"** you'd eat exactly **eight!**

(46) My friend told me fractions can get **"over"** weight
(47) "For example," he said, "look at **20/8**!
(48) I can make **'two wholes'** from twenty,
(49) Using 'eighths' I'll still have plenty
(50) To make half a whole; or, in this case, **4/8**! "

(51) I've been taught **fractions** can be **equivalent**
(52) They're the same although they look quite different
(53) **One third's** very much like **two sixths**
(54) **One half** equals **fifty hundredths**
(55) They look different but they're **equivalent!**

(56) **Big denominators** could mean less to eat
(57) **Big denominator** "parts" are more petite
(58) Sometimes **fractions** can be stinky
(59) Cuz they really make ya "thinky"
(60) 'Bout the size of your "**denominator** treat"!

(61) Mr. Slater brought a candy bar to school
(62) We could eat a **fraction** of it—I was "cool"!
(63) **1/100** sounded thrilling
(64) I signed up for my huge "filling"
(65) Poor Rose signed up just for **1/2!** (What a fool!)

Lyrics by Clint Klose and Larry Wolfe
K-6 Lyrical Lessons across the curriculum are available from Kagan Cooperative Learning

Developing the Logical/Mathematical Intelligence **15**

Bodily/Kinesthetic Activity

Numbers & Dots

Teacher: Give each pair in the class matching numbers and dots. Then have all students mix in the class and trade cards until you call "Freeze." Have students find their matching number or dot partner as quickly as possible. Repeat numerous times.

1	2	3	4	5
•	• •	• • •	• • • •	• • • • •

6	7	8	9	10

11	12	13	14	15

16	17	18	19	20

Spencer & Miguel Kagan: *Multiple Intelligences*
Kagan Cooperative Learning • 1 (800) WEE CO-OP

16 *Developing the Logical/Mathematical Intelligence*

Naturalist Activity

Natural Taxonomy

Cut out the animal cards. Divide them evenly among teammates. As a team, create a classification system on a large piece of paper. Teammates take turns placing one of their cards in the classification system until all of the cards are placed. No cards are placed until all teammates agree. Share your system with another team.

Bat 	Ant
Snake	 Cat
 Horse	Grasshopper 
Bird	Lizard
Bee	 Cow
 Frog	Pig
Dog	Duck 
 Fish	Goat

Developing the Logical/Mathematical Intelligence 17

Interpersonal Activity

Building Relations

Work with a partner to write connections between two seemingly different objects.
Take turns writing your answers. Compare your answers with another pair.

Love is like tennis because...

School is like the beach because...

A car is like a bagel because...

A fire hydrant is like a clock because...

A song is like a butterfly because...

An oak tree is like a river because...

A dog is like lemonade because...

A computer is like a giraffe because...

Spencer & Miguel Kagan: *Multiple Intelligences*
Kagan Cooperative Learning • 1 (800) WEE CO-OP

18 *Developing the Logical/Mathematical Intelligence*

Intrapersonal Activity

Making Analogies

Write how you are like the shapes below. Share your answers with a teammate.

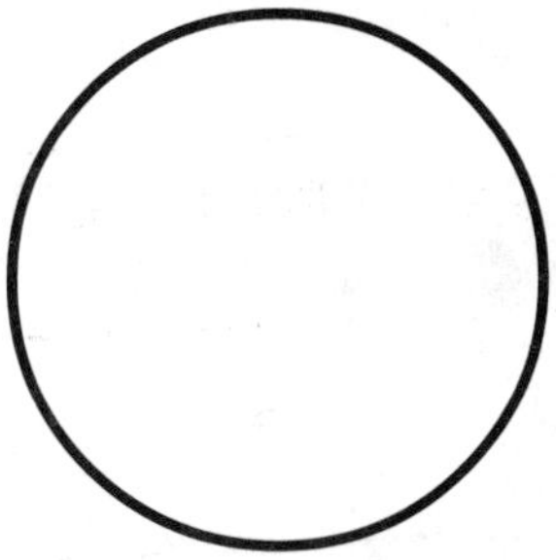

I am like a circle because _____

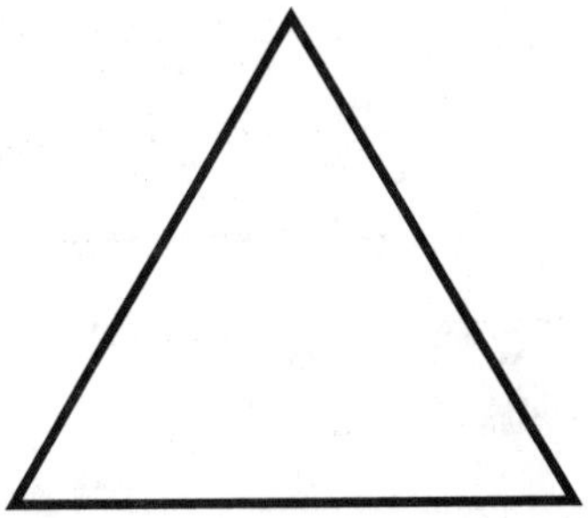

_____

_____

_____

I am like a triangle because _____

_____

_____

_____

I am like a square because _____

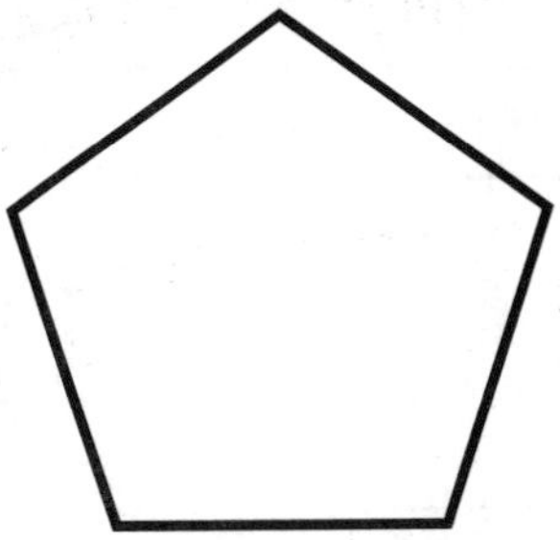

_____

_____

_____

I am like a pentagon because _____

_____

_____

_____

Developing the Visual/Spatial Intelligence 19

Verbal/Linguistic Activity

Writing About Shadows

Light and shadow are important elements of art and design. Below are three types of shadows. Describe how they were created and where the light source is. See if you can do the effect with the letter B.

The Drop Shadow

How was the effect created?_____

_____

_____

_____

Where is the light source?_____

Try the letter B

The Cast Shadow

How was the effect created?_____

_____

_____

_____

Where is the light source?_____

Try the letter B

The Floating Effect

How was the effect created?_____

_____

_____

_____

Where is the light source?_____

Try the letter B

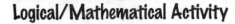

20 *Developing the Visual/Spatial Intelligence*

Logical/Mathematical Activity

Squaring Up

Squaring up is a technique used by artists to proportionally increase the size of an image. To "square up" a picture, draw a grid around the original. Then, draw a larger grid keeping the proportions the same. In this example the larger grid is twice as big, or a 1:2 ratio. Redraw the eye using your grid as a guideline.

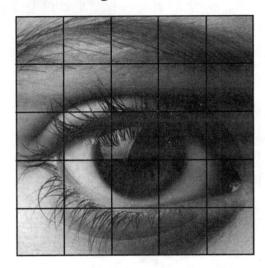

Developing the Visual/Spatial Intelligence 21

Visual/Spatial Activity

Upside Up Drawing

Copy the bird in the empty box as well as you can.

22 *Developing the Visual/Spatial Intelligence*

Visual/Spatial Activity

Upside Down Drawing

Upside down drawing is a technique many artists use to copy images. They turn the image upside down so the image becomes less recognizable. That way they can focus on the lines, curves and shapes. Copy the bird in the empty box upside down as you see it. When done, compare your upside down drawing to your upside up drawing.

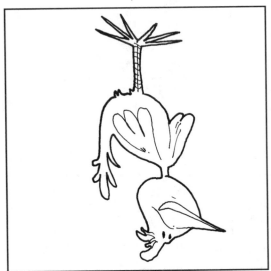

23 *Developing the Visual/Spatial Intelligence*

Musical/Rhythmic Activity

My Favorite Instrument

Draw and color a picture of your favorite instrument. Write a paragraph describing your favorite instrument. Share your drawing and paragraph with a partner.

Instrument Name

Bodily/Kinesthetic Activity

Positive & Negative

Below is a study on positive and negative space. Draw a picture of someone doing a sport in box 1. Convert the sport into a positive image in box 2. Convert the sport into a negative image in box 3.

1. Original Illustration

2. Positive

3. Negative

Spencer & Miguel Kagan: *Multiple Intelligences*

25 *Developing the Visual/Spatial Intelligence*

Naturalist Activity

Nature Scene

Draw a beautiful natural scene in the space below. Your drawing can be of a beautiful day at the beach with the waves crashing on the shore, underneath the ocean teeming with life, high atop a snowy mountain, a rainforest full of wild animals and plants, or anything you chose. Use crayons or colored pencils to bring your scene to life.

Developing the Visual/Spatial Intelligence 26

Interpersonal Activity

Team Caps

Everyone on the team gets one cap. Write your name on your cap and decide as a team whether you want to decorate your caps the same or want to make each one unique. After decorating your caps, cut them out. Paste your team's caps on a large sheet of paper. Write and decorate your team name across the top.

Team Green

27 *Developing the Visual/Spatial Intelligence*

Intrapersonal Activity

Self-Portrait

A self-portrait is an artist's representation of how he or she sees himself or herself. In the space below, draw your self-portrait. Describe why you drew yourself the way you did.

_____

_____

_____

_____

_____

_____

Developing the Musical/Rhythmic Intelligence 28

Verbal/Linguistic Activity

Musical Expressions

Musical expressions are Italian words that describe how music is to be played. Write the Italian expression on the front of a flashcard and the meaning on the back. Learn the expressions as vocabulary words. Quiz a partner with your flashcards.

presto = **very fast**

vivace = **lively, quick**

allegro = **fast**

moderato = **moderate**

andante = **walking tempo pace**

adagio = **medium slow (between lento and andante)**

lento = **slow**

largo = **very slow**

accel. = **accelerando (gradually becoming faster)**

rit. or ritard. = **ritardando (gradually becoming slower)**

ff = **fortissimo (very loud)**

f = **forte (loud)**

mf = **mezzo forte (medium loud)**

mp = **mezzo piano (medium soft)**

p = **piano (soft)**

pp = **pianissimo (very soft)**

or decresc. = **decrescendo (gradually becoming softer)**

or cresc. = **crescendo (gradually becoming louder)**

sfz = **sforzando (sudden strong accent)**

subito = **suddenly**

poco a poco = **little by little**

staccato = **short and detached**

legato = **smooth and connected**

dolce = **sweetly**

molto = **very**

29 *Developing the Musical/Rhythmic Intelligence*

Logical/Mathematical Activity

Music Note Math

Using the key, answer the questions below.

KEY

o = Whole Note (4 beats)

♩ = Half Note (2 beats)

♩ = Quarter Note (1 beat)

♪ = Eighth Note (1/2 beat)

♬ = Sixteenth Note (1/4 beat)

Value

In the circle, write greater than >, less than <, or equal to =.

Addition

In the circle, write the number of beats per line.

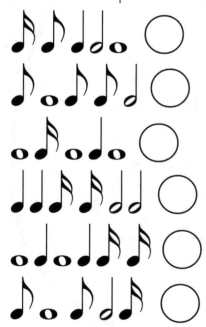

Patterns

In the circle, draw what note comes next.

Challenge Problems

Solve the problem.

$$(o\,♪ \div ♪\,♩\,♪) + o = \bigcirc$$

$$(♩ \times ♩) + (o\,♩ \times ♬\,♪) = \bigcirc$$

$$((o \times ♩) \div ♪)) + ♬ = \bigcirc$$

Developing the Musical/Rhythmic Intelligence 30

Visual/Spatial Activity

Color your song book cover. Put 5-10 sheets of writing paper behind the front cover and a construction paper for the back cover. Staple the book on the left side where indicated and cut out the pattern. Use your song book to collect your songs.

31 *Developing the Musical/Rhythmic Intelligence*

Teacher: Using the treble and bass staffs below, have students make flashcards, drawing the note on the staff and writing the note name on the back of the flashcard. Students may work in pairs to quiz each other. The may use the key until they can read the notes.

Musical/Rhythmic Activity

Note Names

Treble

Bass

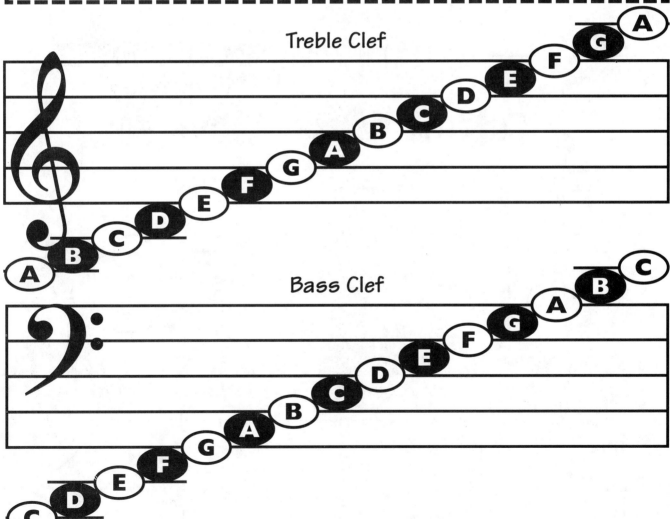

Treble Clef

Bass Clef

Developing the Musical/Rhythmic Intelligence **32**

Bodily/Kinesthetic Activity

Making Body Music

In groups of four, each student is in charge of one sound. Work together to come up with a song. When you perfect your song, share it with the class.

Student 1 - Snap
Student 2 - Clap
Student 3 - Stomp
Student 4 - Hum

33 *Developing the Musical/Rhythmic Intelligence*

Musical Rhythmic

Let the Music Move You

As a team, choreograph a dance or movement to a song.

What are some different dances or movements for different types of music?

- **Country Music**
- **Rap**
- **Rock 'n' Roll**
- **Electronica**
- **Blues**
- **Jazz**
- **Reggae**

34 *Developing the Musical/Rhythmic Intelligence*

Naturalist Activity

Nature Songs

Sing "When a Bird Comes Hatchin' Out" together as a class. Then, work in teams to write your own song about a natural phenomena.

To the tune of "When the Saints Go Marching In"

(1) Oh when a bird comes hatchin' out
(2) Oh when a bird comes hatchin' out
(3) Its mom and dad won't leave
(4) They'll stay by
(5) Until the bird can fly about!

(6) A mama bird, or papa bird
(7) Will feed its young 'til they get strong
(8) And then it's time for them
(9) To "take-off"
(10) It's time for them to say, "so long!"

(11) When younger birds must leave the nest
(12) When younger birds must leave the nest
(13) They have to try to fly
(14) Each day now
(15) They've got a pair of wings to test!

(16) Geronimo!! Away they go!
(17) Good thing bird bones don't weigh them down
(18) With hollow bones
(19) It isn't easy
(20) For gravity to pull them down!

(21) Oh when a bird begins to fly
(22) Oh when a bird begins to fly
(23) It will stay warm
(24) In rainy weather
(25) Its oily feathers keep it dry!

Lyrics by Clint Klose and Larry Wolfe
K-6 Lyrical Lessons across the curriculum are
available from Kagan Cooperative Learning

Developing the Musical/Rhythmic Intelligence 35

Interpersonal Activity

Music Symbols

Work in pairs to learn the music symbols. Cut out the music symbols below on the dotted lines. To quiz each other, fold back and hide the answers.

𝅝	Whole Note	𝅗𝅥.	Dotted Half Note	𝅗𝅥	Half Note
𝅘𝅥.	Dotted Quarter Note	𝅘𝅥	Quarter Note	𝅘𝅥𝅮	Eighth Note
𝅘𝅥𝅮𝅘𝅥𝅮	Pair of Eighth Notes	𝅘𝅥𝅯	Sixteenth Note	♯	Sharp (raises the pitch one-half step)
♭	Flat (lowers the pitch one-half step)	♮	Natural (cancels sharps and flats)	𝄞	Treble Clef or G-Clef
𝄢	Bass Clef or F-Clef	▬	Whole Rest	▭	Half Rest

36 *Developing the Musical/Rhythmic Intelligence*

Intrapersonal Activity

A Song About Me

What makes you YOU? On the lines below, brainstorm qualities that make you unique.

_____   _____
_____   _____
_____   _____
_____   _____

Include your personal qualities in your song about YOU.

Developing the Bodily/Kinesthetic Intelligence 37

Verbal/Linguistic Activity

A Sporty Letter

Pair up with someone in your class. Pretend your partner has never heard of your favorite sport. Write your partner a letter describing your sport, then trade letters.

38 *Developing the Bodily/Kinesthetic Intelligence*

Logical/Mathematical Activity

Compare & Contrast

Compare and contrast soccer and football. Write all the things unique to soccer in the soccer box. Write all the things unique to football in the football box. Write all things in common in the intersection.

Soccer

Both

Football

Developing the Bodily/Kinesthetic Intelligence **39**

Visual/Spatial Activity

The Sports Channel

Channel 34, The Sports Channel, has commissioned you to make a poster advertising their new show, Sport Shorts on Saturday evenings at 8:00pm. Their graphics department has given you six silhouettes to use in your poster. Use construction paper, scissors, glue and crayons to make your poster. Don't forget to label each sport.

Spencer & Miguel Kagan: *Multiple Intelligences*

Kagan Booperative Liearning • 1 (800) WEE CO-OP

40 *Developing the Bodily/Kinesthetic Intelligence*

Musical/Rhythmic Activity

The Body Song

Work with a partner to write a song about the wonders of the human body to the tune "Twinkle Twinkle Little Star." Sing your song to another pair.

Developing the Bodily/Kinesthetic Intelligence 41

Bodily/Kinesthetic Activity

Sign Language

Sign language uses hand gestures rather than written or spoken words. American Sign Language has hand gestures corresponding to the alphabet. Write a brief written message below. Then sign it to your partner, using the illustrated gestures below. Let your partner decode your message, then sign you his or her message.

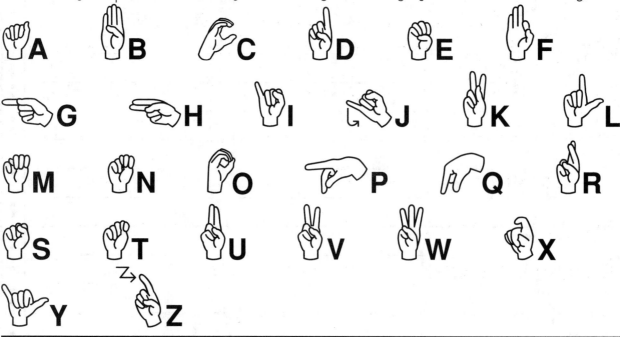

Message to My Partner

_____

_____

_____

_____

_____

_____

_____

_____

_____

42 *Developing the Bodily/Kinesthetic Intelligence*

Naturalist Activity

Animal Charades

Work in teams of four. Cut apart the animal cards below. Shuffle them face down on a desk. Take turns picking one card each until there are no more cards. Student 1 picks one of his or her animals and acts it out, no noises allowed. Teammates try to guess what animal he or she is acting out. Take turns acting out your animal cards.

	Shark	Anteater
Gorilla	Turtle	Hawk
Rattle Snake	Horse	Pig
Butterfly	Squirrel	Beaver
Cheetah	Swallow	Giraffe
Elephant	Cat	Mouse
Owl	Monkey	Dog

Developing the Bodily/Kinesthetic Intelligence **43**

Interpersonal Activity

Balance Games

Work with a partner. Come up with a position that alone you would fall without support, but together your are balanced. Share your balance position with the class. Pair up with another pair and come up with a four-person balance position.

44 *Developing the Bodily/Kinesthetic Intelligence*

Interpersonal Activity

Mirror Mirror

Find a partner and face each other. Pretend you are looking into a mirror and your partner is your mirror image. Make movements in front of the mirror. It is up to your partner to make corresponding mirror images. After a while, switch roles and you are the mirror image of your partner.

Developing the Bodily/Kinesthetic Intelligence **45**

Interpersonal Activity

Cooperative Juggling

In a team of four, stand in a small circle facing each other. Get one bean bag, tennis ball, or balloon and pass it around. When you get quick with one object, try two. See how many objects you can get going at once.

In pairs, face each other and try juggling three objects at once.

Spencer & Miguel Kagan: *Multiple Intelligences*

46 *Developing the Bodily/Kinesthetic Intelligence*

Intrapersonal Activity

My Life As an Athlete

In each of the five spaces below, write the name of a sport, or physical activity that you have done. Write a description of your history with each activity.

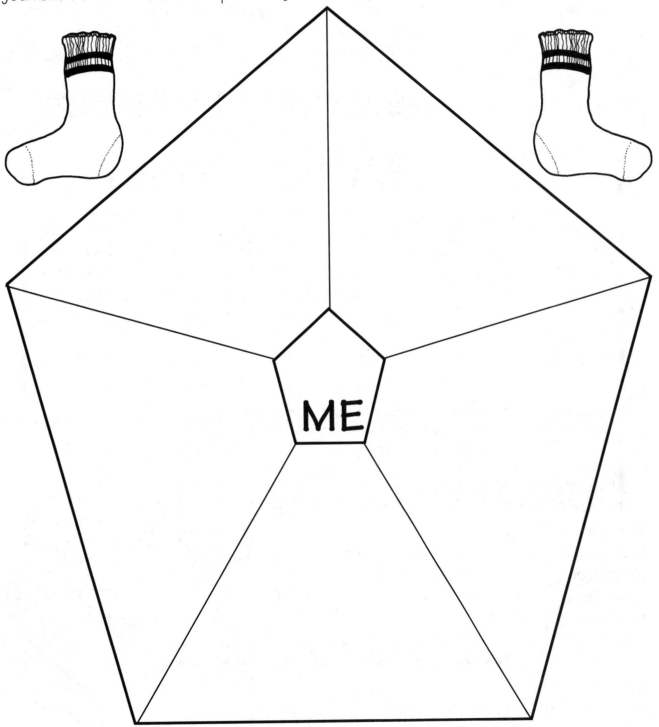

Developing the Naturalist Intelligence 47

Verbal/Linguistic Activity

Describing Nature

Go outside and find a leaf that has fallen from a tree. Describe your leaf as well as you can. Describe the color, texture, shape and all other details you can. Give your leaf to a partner and read him or her your description.
How could you make your description better?

Spencer & Miguel Kagan: *Multiple Intelligences*
Kagan Cooperative Learning • 1 (800) WEE CO-OP

48 *Developing the Naturalist Intelligence*

Logical/Mathematical Activity

Classify It!

Cut out the fictitious plant life below. Divide the plants evenly among teammates. On a separate sheet of large paper, come up with a system to classify your plant life. Only you can put your plant in the classification system. When you are happy with your classification system, paste down the plants and share your system with another team.

Developing the Naturalist Intelligence **49**

Visual/Spatial Activity

A Budding Artist

Flowers are one of Mother Nature's most beautiful creations.
Go outside and find a beautiful flower. Do the best you can
to draw the flower below. Pay special attention to color and detail.

Spencer & Miguel Kagan: *Multiple Intelligences*

50 *Developing the Naturalist Intelligence*

Musical/Rhythmic Activity

The Mammal Song

Sing "The Mammal Song" together as a class. Then, work in teams to write, "The Reptile Song." Sing your reptile song to the class.

(1)   I'm a *mammal*
(2)   Just a camel
(3)   Got two *lungs*
(4)   And lots of *hair*
(5)   And it's no jive
(6)   I was born live
(7)   Now I'm busy *breathin' air!*

(8)   When I'm thirsty
(9)   Mom'll *nurse* me
(10) Giving *milk*
(11) And lots o' care
(12) Till I'm older
(13) And can shoulder
(14) All the burdens camels bear!!

(15) I'm a *mammal*
(16) Just a camel
(17) Got two *lungs*
(18) And lots of *hair*
(19) And it's no jive
(20) I was born live
(21) Now I'm busy *breathin' air!*

(22) When I'm thirsty
(23) Mom'll *nurse* me
(24) Giving *milk*
(25) And lots o' care
(26) Till I'm older
(27) And can shoulder
(28) All the burdens camels bear!

Lyrics by Clint Klose and Larry Wolfe
K-6 Lyrical Lessons across the curriculum are
available from Kagan Cooperative Learning

Developing the Naturalist Intelligence 51

Bodily/Kinesthetic Activity

Natural Observations

Go outside and collect one rock, one leaf, one flower petal, and one twig of your choosing. Paste your specimens on the sheet below in the space provided. Observe your specimen carefully and write your observations. Give each of your specimens a name. When done, share your observations with a partner.

| paste **ROCK** here | Specimen Name_____
Observations_____
_____
_____ |

| paste **LEAF** here | Specimen Name_____
Observations_____
_____
_____ |

| paste **FLOWER PETAL** here | Specimen Name_____
Observations_____
_____
_____ |

| paste **TWIG** here | Specimen Name_____
Observations_____
_____
_____ |

52 *Developing the Naturalist Intelligence*

Naturalist Activity

The Weather Log

Observe the weather at the same time every day for one week. Keep track of your observations on the daily log below. After the week is over, summarize your observations.

Daily Log 	Monday	Tuesday
Wednesday	Thursday	Friday

Summary of Observations _____

_____

_____

_____

_____

Developing the Naturalist Intelligence 53

Interpersonal Activity

Recycling Sort

Step 1: Getting Ready

Get in teams of four. You will need 1 pen or pencil for your team. Everyone gets one sheet of blank paper. Fold it in eighths as illustrated at left and cut or rip it into little slips of paper.

Step 2: Brainstorm Trash

Student One is the recorder. Everyone brainstorms ideas of things that you would throw away or find in your trash. Be specific. Student One records one idea on one slip of paper and puts the paper in the middle of the desk for all to see. Then, Student One passes the pen or pencil to Student Two to record the next idea. Continue generating ideas until you have used up all slips of paper.

Yes	No
Coke Can	Rotten Cheese
Milk Carton	
Plastic Bag	

Step 3: Sort the Trash

Sort all your ideas into two piles: 1) Recyclable; 2) Non-Recyclable. To do this, Student One picks up the first item and says, "Recyclable." If everyone agrees it goes in the recycle pile. If anyone disagrees, vote on it. Student Two does the next one, and so on.

Step 4: Sort the Recyclables

Sort all your recyclables into different categories. Don't forget to sort the aluminum from the rest of the metals and the glass by color. Take turns sorting each item.

Metal	Paper	Plastic	Glass
Aluminum	Milk Carton	Plastic Bag	
Coke Can			

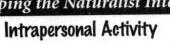

54 *Developing the Naturalist Intelligence*

Intrapersonal Activity

A Natural Phenomenon

Have you ever been in an earthquake, flood, hail storm, hurricane, lightning storm? Have you ever seen a forest fire, tornado, volcano, or any other natural disaster? Describe the event from your perspective. What did you see, what happened, how did you feel? What thoughts or feelings did you have after the event? How about now, as you remember the event?

The Event

_____

_____

_____

_____

_____

_____

_____

_____

_____

_____

_____

_____

_____

_____

_____

_____

_____

_____

Developing the Interpersonal Intelligence 55

Verbal/Linguistic Activity

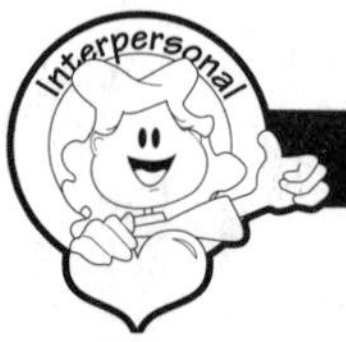

Being a Friend

Write what you think it means to be a friend. Take turns sharing your writing with teammates. After everyone has read their ideas, as a team, discuss what you wrote that was similar and what was different.

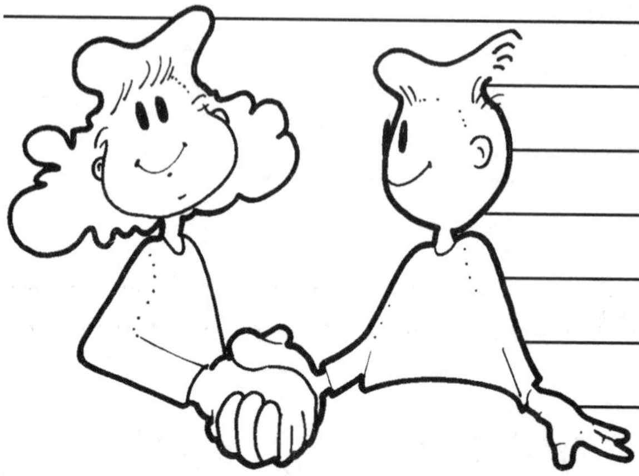

56 *Developing the Interpersonal Intelligence*

Logical/Mathematical Activity

The Cause of Conflict

There are usually many steps that lead to a conflict. See if you can come up with steps that lead to this type of conflict. Start at the bottom and work your way up.

Sheila said, "I hate you" to Joe and Karen. She angrily turned around and stormed away.

Sheila, Joe, and Karen were walking to school together.

Developing the Interpersonal Intelligence 57

Visual/Spatial Activity

Close to Me

Draw yourself inside the circle that says "Me." Draw people all around you who you know and with whom you are in contact. Draw people closest to you (like your family) nearest you. Draw people with whom you are not as close farther away.

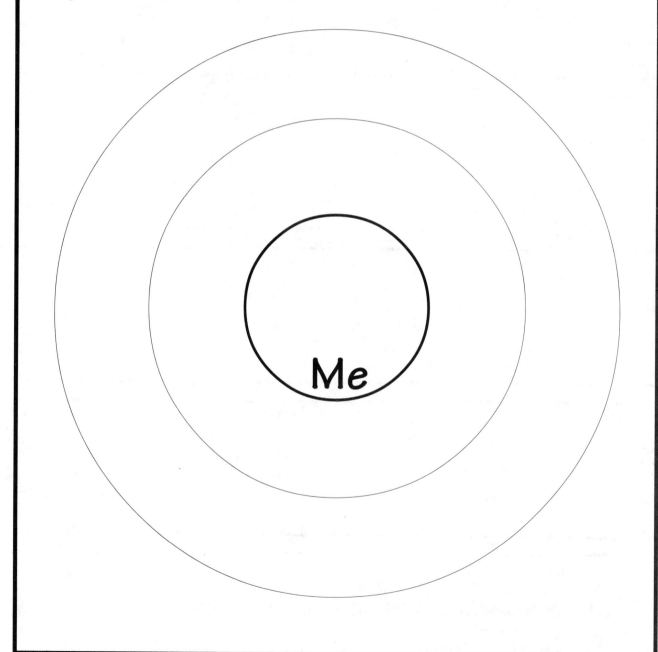

Me

58 *Developing the Interpersonal Intelligence*

Musical/Rhythmic Activity

Taking Turns

In teams of four, write a song about taking turns and why it is important. Write your song so there are some parts everyone sings together and some parts that you take turns singing. Sing your song to the class. You can write your song to a familiar tune.

Developing the Interpersonal Intelligence 59

Bodily/Kinesthetic Activity

Role Play

In pairs, pick a scenario to act out. Discuss possible solutions to the problem, then act out your favorite solution.

Gary and Sandi are sitting together and only have one pair of scissors between them. They both have 10 shapes they have to cut out. Gary grabs the scissors and says to Sandi, "Sorry. You snooze, you lose."

Carla is about to sit down. Michelle pulls away Carla's chair and Carla falls on the floor. Michelle starts laughing.

Jason and Isaac are on opposite basketball teams. Isaac's team is winning. Jason purposely pushes Isaac down on the ground and says, "You suck, you little twerp."

Erika and Sherri are supposed to be coming up with ideas together. Sherri keeps giving Erika ideas to write down, but Erika is not listening. She is only recording her own ideas.

Sang and Carlos are sitting next to each other at lunch. Carlos has chocolate chip cookies that really look good. Sang grabs Carlos' cookies and says, "Thanks, I love cookies."

Jeanne is working on a drawing. Sabrina walks by and accidentally bumps Jeanne, causing her to mess up. Jeanne is mad and says, "Watch out, fatso!"

60 *Developing the Interpersonal Intelligence*

Naturalist Activity

People & Animal Relations

How are relations among people like relations among animals? How are they different? In pairs, list your answers below. Then get together with another pair and take turns sharing your answers.

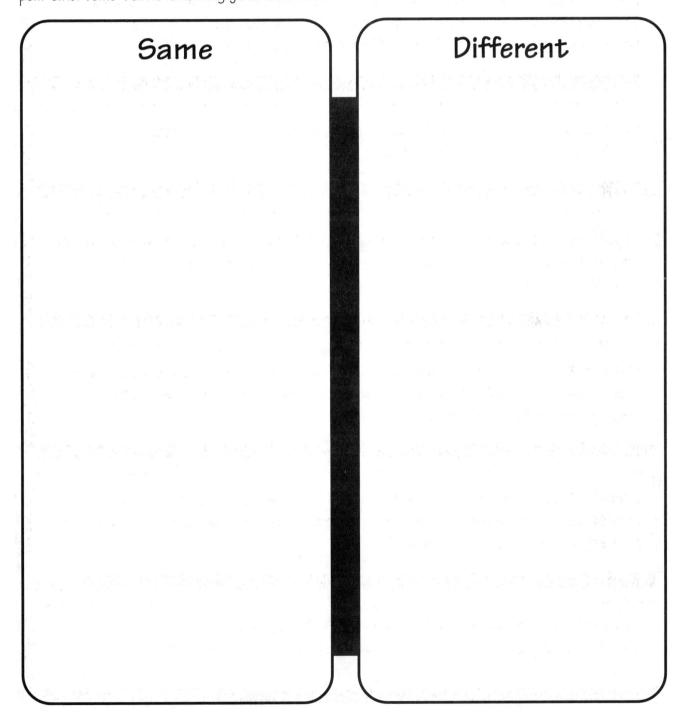

Same	Different

Team Rules

As a team, come up with five team rules to work together better. Make sure everyone agrees on each rule before you write it down. Keep your rules handy so you can refer to them if you run into trouble.

1 _____

_____

2 _____

_____

3 _____

_____

4 _____

_____

5 _____

_____

62 *Developing the Interpersonal Intelligence*

Intrapersonal Activity

People Person Plan

A People Person is someone who gets along with others well, likes others, and is liked by others. Describe three things you can do to be more of a People Person.

1

2

3

Developing the Intrapersonal Intelligence **63**

Verbal/Linguistic Activity

My Résumé

A résumé is a paper that job applicants give to employers to show their education, skills, and previous employment history. Make your own résumé. Make yourself seem as attractive as possible, but be honest. When you are done, work with a partner and see if you can make improvements to your résumé.

Name_____

Address_____

City_____State____Zip_____Phone (____)_____

Goals:_____

Education:_____

Related Experiences:_____

Special Skills:_____

Interests:_____

64 *Developing the Intrapersonal Intelligence*

Logical Mathematical Activity

My Time Line

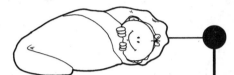

Fill out your personal time line below. Sequence the major events from birth until now. Illustrate or write about each important event. When done, share your time line with your team-mates.

Now

Developing the Intrapersonal Intelligence 65

Visual/Spatial Activity
The Me Mobile

Make a mobile all about yourself. Color in the illustrations below, write your favorites on the back and cut each one out. Using string and a clothes hanger, make a mobile out of your favorites. Cover both sides of the hanger with your name, and a drawing or decorations.

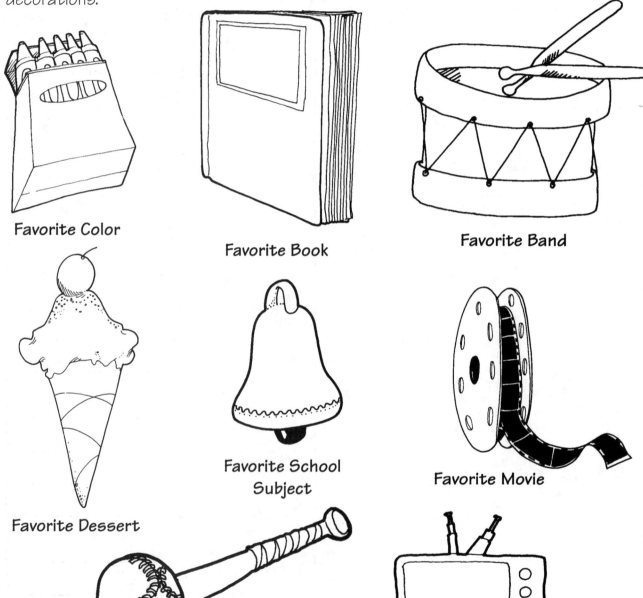

Favorite Color

Favorite Book

Favorite Band

Favorite Dessert

Favorite School Subject

Favorite Movie

Favorite Sport

Favorite TV Show

66 *Developing the Intrapersonal Intelligence*

Intrapersonal

Musical/Rhythmic Activity

A Poem About Me

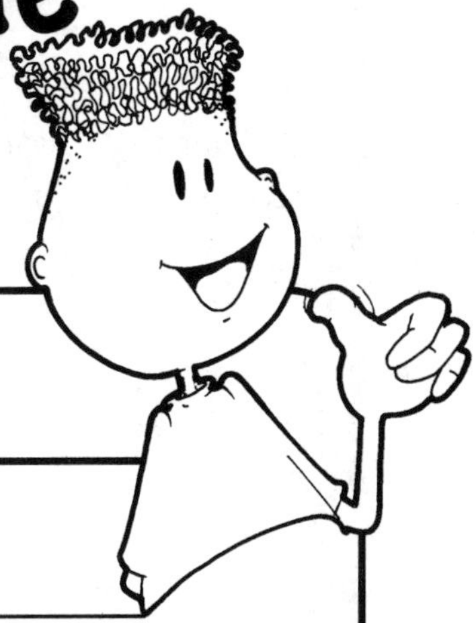

Write a poem about yourself. Write the poem alternating rhyme patterns. Make "A" lines rhyme and "B" lines rhyme. Share your poem with a partner.

____

title

A ____
A ____
B ____
B ____

A ____
B ____
A ____
B ____

A ____
A ____
B ____
B ____

A ____
B ____
A ____
B ____

Developing the Intrapersonal Intelligence 67
Bodily/Kinesthetic Activity

Group by Favorite

Similarity Groups allow students to form groups to learn more about themselves and their favorites.

Step 1: Teacher Asks "Favorite" Question

"What is your favorite dessert? Think about your favorite dessert. (Pause) Think about the last time you had it. (Pause) Where were you? How did it taste as you took your first bite? Write down your favorite dessert on a slip of paper."

Step 2: Students Form Groups

Students get up out of their seats and move about the classroom, finding others who share the same favorite. Unique responses can form together as the "unique" group.

Step 3: Pairs Discuss

Students break into pairs in their similarity groups and take turns sharing why they chose the favorite they did.

Other Favorites

- School subject
- Color
- Pizza toppings
- Restaurant
- Animal
- Movie

- TV show
- Cartoon
- Flower
- Artist
- Athlete
- Movie star

- Band
- Car
- Vacation spot
- Soft drink
- Hobby
- Author

68 *Developing the Intrapersonal Intelligence*

Naturalist Activity

Like or Unlike Me

Fill out the worksheet below. In the blank, write if you are like or unlike the animal or insect and why or why not? When done, share your answers with your teammates.

I am _____
a bee because
_____
_____
_____

I am _____
a goat because
_____
_____
_____

I am _____
a lamb because
_____
_____
_____

I am _____
a butterfly
because _____
_____
_____

I am _____
an owl because
_____
_____
_____

I am _____
an ostrich because
_____
_____
_____

Interpersonal Activity

"If" Questions

Pair up with a partner. Take turns reading each question. For the first question, you answer first, then your partner answers. For the next question, your partner answers first, then you answer.

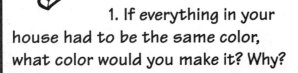

1. If everything in your house had to be the same color, what color would you make it? Why?

2. If you had to watch one movie every day, what movie would it be? Why?

3. If you could go anywhere on vacation, where would you go? Why?

4. If you could be in the Olympics, what event would you choose? Why?

5. If your house was burning and you could only save one personal belonging, what would you save? Why?

6. If you were granted one wish, what would you wish? Why?

7. If you could have anything for dinner tonight, what would it be? Why?

8. If you had to describe yourself with one word, what word would you choose? Why?

9. If you only had one CD, which one would it be? Why?

10. If you could be a famous artist, what would you create? Why?

11. If you could have any kind of pet, what pet would you choose? Why?

12. If you could change something about school, what would it be? Why?

13. If you were given ten thousand dollars, what would you do? Why?

14. If there is one thing about yourself that you could change, what would it be? Why?

15. If you could be any animal for a day, what animal would you be? Why?

70 *Developing the Intrapersonal Intelligence*

Intrapersonal Activity

What I Value

Below are 20 qualities or accomplishments. Rank order them based on what you value most. 1 = Value Most, 20 = Value Least.

- ☐ Spending time with my family.
- ☐ Making a lot of money.
- ☐ Being happy.
- ☐ Living a long, healthy life.
- ☐ Having lots of friends.
- ☐ Being an accomplished musician.
- ☐ Enjoying my work.
- ☐ Taking good care of my pet(s).
- ☐ Making others happy.
- ☐ Practicing my religion.
- ☐ Being loved by others.
- ☐ Having a successful relationship.
- ☐ Excelling at a sport.
- ☐ Being good at reading and writing.
- ☐ Having a keen, analytical mind.
- ☐ Helping others.
- ☐ Making a contribution to the environment.
- ☐ Being a talented artist.
- ☐ Having quality alone time.
- ☐ Being a hard worker.

> **Extension:** On a separate sheet of paper, write what your ranking of values tells you about yourself.

Honoring Uniqueness, Celebrating Diversity

I have seen students who have experienced failure in their studies for years suddenly experience success. I have seen countless teachers experience a renewed excitement for their chosen profession. I have experienced dramatic shifts in both students' and teachers' levels of self-esteem as they discover ways to affirm their unique ways of knowing and discover that they are not "weird" or "strange" just because they do not excel in verbal/linguistic or logical/mathematical intelligence capacities (Lazear, 1994, p. 214).

E ach student in our classroom has a unique pattern of intelligences. One might be high in logical and low on linguistic intelligence; another might be high on linguistic skills, but low on the logical. A third student may be low on both, but have extraordinary visual/spatial skills. By developing instructional strategies to match all intelligences and by creating curriculum to stretch all intelligences, we maximize the probability of reaching

Multiple intelligences transforms our perspective on how we view ourselves, our students, and how students view themselves and others. We are each a unique gift, with our own pattern of intelligences. When we acknowledge our individuality and focus on our strengths, not shortcomings we gain a renewed respect for ourselves and for the abilities of others. We don't condemn others for their differences, but rather celebrate our shared diversity.

each student, and developing all the intelligences. There remains, however, another vision which springs from MI theory: Celebrating our intelligences.

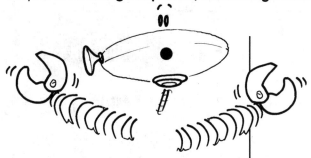

Why is it important that our students understand MI theory? Why should MI theory be treated not just as a basis for developing instructional strategies and curriculum, but also as important curriculum in itself? Why have our students understand and celebrate their own unique pattern of intelligences and that of others?

Why Honor Uniqueness and Celebrate Diversity?

It turns out there are a number of benefits which result when students know MI theory — when they understand that there are many ways to be smart and that each individual has his or her own unique pattern of intelligences. Just as we as teachers become more differentiated in dealing with others once we understand MI theory, so too do students become more differentiated and successful in dealing with others once they understand and use MI theory.

The theory is useful to students in many ways.

Students need to know there are many ways to be smart, and they need self-knowledge of their own unique pattern of intelligences. Once students understand MI theory, they can take ownership for the process of developing all the intelligences. They become actively engaged in fostering their own developmental process. Knowledge of MI theory empowers students in a number of other ways; it fuels a powerful transformation in the learning community.

If we know there are many ways to be smart and we know which intelligences are our strongest and which are our weakest, we can make wiser decisions. If we are unsuccessful mastering content or a skill, given our knowledge of MI theory and ourselves, we can attempt to learn it through another intelligence. Rather than saying, "We are dumb," We simply say, "We need to learn that in another way." Conversely, when someone does not understand us, we do not provide them the information a second time in the same way, or give up trying to communicate, concluding they are dumb. Instead, we provide them the information through a different intelligence.

Knowledge of MI theory empowers students. It helps them feel better about themselves, make wiser decisions, and become more effective in interpersonal relations. Our students need to know, understand, and apply MI theory in their daily lives.

Each student, to maximize her potential, needs to know and accept her own unique pattern of intelligences, her own strengths and weaknesses. She needs also to feel known and accepted by others. In a positive learning community, each person feels secure and accepted because they are honored for the unique gifts they bring to the community. Each person feels the community is enriched by every member, by the diversity among them.

To the extent we are successful in having students know their own unique pattern

United States Population:

We Are Becoming More Diverse

	Asian	Black	Hispanic	White
1995	3%	12%	10%	74%
2050	8%	14%	24%	53%

1995: Three out of four White
2050: One half White
After 2050: Whites become a smaller and smaller minority each year.

Source: US Census Bureau

of intelligences and the diversity among them, a range of positive benefits result. Creating an accepting learning community in which each student knows and accepts his own unique pattern of intelligences, and appreciates the diversity among them, establishes a community in which students:

- **Have enhanced pride, self-esteem, and confidence**
- **Feel accepted; waste less energy in the struggle for social status and acceptance**
- **Accept and work well with diversity**
- **Understand others better; are more successful in interpersonal relations**
- **Accept their own limits, and face failure with less defensiveness**
- **Take appropriate risks**
- **Persist in the face of failure; less often avoid tasks for fear of failure**
- **Redefine learning situations to maximize success; know and work from their own unique strengths**
- **Work to fully develop their strongest, as well as their weakest, intelligences**

As students come to know and understand that each of us has a unique pattern of intelligences, and that our uniqueness allows each of us to make a different contribution to the community, students realize diversity empowers us.

If we were all very strong in linguistic intelligence, but all weak in mathematical intelligence, our world would be impoverished in many ways. Think of the gifts which logic and math have given us. But, if we were all strong in mathematical intelligence, but weak in linguistic intelligence, our world would be impoverished also, just in different ways. Think of the many gifts which language brings. If our community is lacking any intelligence, it is weakened. Since we cannot all be equally strong in all the intelligences, diversity brings strength to our community. The more patterns of intelligences represented in our community, the stronger we are. We honor each individual's unique pattern of intelligence, not just out of respect for the individual, but to become stronger as a community.

Knowing and Celebrating Our Unique Pattern of Intelligences

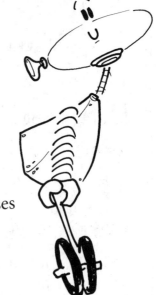

If I Know My Pattern of Intelligences...

...I can work from strengths

...I can work on weaknesses

...I understand interdependence

...I honor and celebrate my uniqueness

If I Know Patterns of Others...

...I respect their strengths and accept their weaknesses

...I accept others more

...I understand interdependence

...I celebrate our collective diversity

Students of today will face increasing diversity in their social lives and workplaces in the twenty-first century. Students will become more prepared for the workplace of the future, if today they have opportunities to know and work with diversity in their classrooms. Activities in which students explore and share their unique patterns of intelligences are part of that preparation process. The population in the United States is shifting dramatically; diversity is increasing; learning to appreciate the power of diversity is preparation for a more harmonious and successful society in the future. See box: We are Becoming More Diverse.

If we think there is but one way to be smart, we interpret all our successes and failures as a reflection of our intelligence. For ex-

ample, if we fail on a math quiz, we are likely to say to ourselves, "We are not very bright." Once we understand there are many ways to be smart, when we fail on that math quiz, we are more likely to say to ourselves, "We are not strong in that type of math problem, but there are other intelligences and other facets of math in which we are quite strong." Given the more robust sense of identity provided by knowledge of MI theory, any failure is not as devastating.

Knowledge of MI theory provides each of us multiple alternative sources for a positive intellectual identity. Empowered by the knowledge of MI theory, we can accept our weakness in one area without taking it as a reflection of a low general intelligence. It becomes easier, then, to make a plan to strengthen an area of weakness, rather than avoiding that area and rationalizing our failures. Critical in this process is knowing there are many ways to be smart, and that we each have our own unique pattern of intelligences. As teachers, we facilitate learning as we teach about the intelligences. Thus we take it as a goal for each student to better understand, appreciate, and even celebrate his or her own unique pattern of intelligences.

How to Honor Uniqueness & Celebrate Diversity

Once we accept that one outcome of education should be that each student understand his or her intellectual uniqueness and that of others, there remains a question: How do we foster that knowledge?

There are many ways to have students learn MI theory, to discover their own unique patterns of intelligences, and to understand and appreciate the diversity of patterns among us. In addition to direct instruction in MI theory, a wide range of activities can be structured so students discover the theory, and in the process better understand their pattern of intelligences and that of others.

Among the powerful approaches available to facilitate this discovery process are reflection time, journal writing, and discussions in which students share their preferences and strengths. Following any classroom activity, students can be asked to think about the intelligences they employed during the activity, and alternative intelligences which they might have used.

Students can be asked to share and discuss with teammates and classmates their own discoveries about their intelligences, including which intelligences they found themselves using during different activities, which intelligences they most enjoy using, which kinds of activities come easy for them, and which do not because of their own pattern of intelligences. As they engage in metacognition and share with others, they come to appreciate better their own uniqueness and the diversity among them.

Activities directly designed to help students know their own pattern of intelligences can occur within the context of regular academic lessons, so there is little or no time off task. This integrated approach to the discovery of MI theory sidesteps the trap of teaching about MI theory as a tack-on curriculum. If deepening student's understanding of MI theory is an integral part of our lessons, it is learned in a meaningful context and is less likely to be dropped when time runs short.

Cooperative learning teambuilding (Kagan et al., 1997) and classbuilding (Kagan et al., 1995) strategies are particularly powerful for understanding and appreciating diversity because students can interview each other on their intelligences (Team Interview; Three-Step Interview), play guessing games regarding their favorite intelligences (Find the Fib), group according to their intelligences (Similarity Groups, Line-ups), and find others who enjoy activities associated with certain intelligences (Find-Someone-Who). As students explore and appreciate their similarities and differences in patterns of intelligences, they come to more fully appreciate their diversity. The simple teambuilding and classbuilding strategies can be incorporated as part of any lesson. When they are used with MI content, they serve well the twin goals of honoring uniqueness and celebrating diversity.

In our next chapter, we highlight some strategies and activities designed to have students explore, share, and understand their patterns of intelligences. In the process, they discover MI theory — a discovery which is a tool for life.

Another excellent way to honor uniqueness and celebrate diversity is to learn about the end states of the multiple intelligences and famous folks who possess expert skills in an intelligence. When we explore the end states of each intelligence, students learn that musicians have expert skills in the musical/rhythmic intelligence. Artists are exceptionally talented with the visual/spatial intelligence. Politicians have a way with people and authors a way with words. By studying careers in the classroom, we make a connection between the intelligences and the vocational and avocational purposes for which they are used. Students learn about the great diversity of career opportunities and the types of intelligences they will need to succeed.

Students can also explore the biographies of famous figures who draw on their intelligences to make positive contributions to the world. By studying famous individuals with expert skills in the intelligences, we honor each intelligence. We teach students of the wonderful contribution Mozart made to music and communicate to our students that their musical skills are valued. We examine Escher's breakthroughs in perspectives, and tell our students that their drawing skills are appreciated. We learn about Darwin's attraction and attention to flora and fauna and how

he made remarkable contributions to how we see ourselves and the world. By studying famous folks, we communicate a message to our students: We value people with unique gifts and we value you for who you are.

Studying careers and famous individuals is an excellent vehicle for validating the uniqueness of every student in our class as well as celebrating the great diversity of intelligences in our larger society. It also serves as a inspiration for students to succeed in their own educational pursuits.

In Chapter 3: What Is an Intelligence? we explored a number of different biographies of famous individuals. These biographies can be shared with the class. We can also have students learn about famous people and careers by inviting guests into the class, having assemblies, having students explore and present biographies or careers as an MI project, creating a center based on each intelligence. On the following pages, there are lists of careers and famous folks we may investigate with our students to honor each intelligence and celebrate our diversity.

References

Kagan, L., Kagan, M., & Kagan, S. *Teambuilding*. San Clemente, CA: Kagan Cooperative Learning, 1997.

Kagan, M., Robertson, L., & Kagan, S. *Classbuilding*. San Clemente, CA: Kagan Cooperative Learning, 1995.

Lazear, D. *Seven Pathways of Learning: Teaching Students and Parents about Multiple Intelligences*. Tucson, AZ: Zephyr Press, 1994.

Careers & Famous Folks

Explorations to Celebrate the Verbal/Linguistic Intelligence

Careers	Famous Folks
• Actor/Actress	• Maya Angelou
• Attorney	• Jane Austen
• Author	• James Baldwin
• Comic	• Judy Blume
• Editor	• Winston Churchill
• Journalist	• Agatha Christie
• Librarian	• Frederick Douglass
• Marketing	• T. S. Eliot
• Newscaster	• Robert Frost
• Novelist	• Ernest Hemingway
• Orator	• Rudyard Kipling
• Playwright	• Martin Luther King, Jr.
• Poet	• Abraham Lincoln
• Politician	• Edgar Allen Poe
• Publicist	• William Shakespeare
• Publisher	• Shel Silverstein
• Religious Leader	• John Steinbeck
• Salesperson	• R. L. Stine
• Speaker	• Mark Twain
• Speech Writer	• E. B. White
• Teacher	• Walt Whitman
• Writer	• Oprah Winfrey

Careers & Famous Folks

Explorations to Celebrate the Logical/Mathematical Intelligence

Careers	Famous Folks
• Accountant	• Alexander Graham Bell
• Astronomer	• H.R. Block
• Banker	• Copernicus
• Bank Teller	• Marie Curie
• Buyer	• René Descartes
• Cashier	• Thomas Alva Edison
• Computer Programmer	• Albert Einstein
• Doctor	• Benjamin Franklin
• Detective	• Bill Gates
• Economist	• Galileo Galilei
• Engineer	• Francis Galton
• Entrepreneur	• Stephen Hawking
• Inventor	• Oliver Wendell Holmes
• Investor	• Grace Mary Hooper
• Judge	• Thurgood Marshall
• Mathematician	• Barbara McClintock
• Mystery Writer	• Alfred Nobel
• Philosopher	• Sir Isaac Newton
• Physicist	• Sally Ride
• Real Estate Agent	• Socrates
• Scientist	• Bertrand Russell
• Stock Broker	• Marilyn Savant

Careers & Famous Folks

Explorations to Celebrate the Visual/Spatial Intelligence

Careers	Famous Folks
• Art Director	• Ansel Adams
• Art Teacher	• Mary Cassatt
• Artist	• Paul Cézanne
• Architect	• Christopher Columbus
• Builder	• Salvador Dali
• Cartographer	• Leonardo da Vinci
• Cartoonist	• M. C. Escher
• Curator	• Anne Geddes
• Decorator	• Édouard Manet
• Driver	• Claude Monet
• Engineer	• Julia Montgomery
• Fashion Designer	• Grandma Moses
• Florist	• Georgia O'Keeffe
• Graphic Designer	• Pablo Picasso
• Illustrator	• Camille Pissarro
• Navigator	• Pierre-Auguste Renoir
• Painter	• Diego Rivera
• Pilot	• Auguste Rodin
• Photographer	• Charles Schulz
• Printer	• Vincent van Gogh
• Sculptor	• Andy Warhol
• Topologist	• Frank Lloyd Wright

Careers & Famous Folks

Explorations to Celebrate the Musical/Rhythmic Intelligence

Careers	Famous Folks
• Composer	• Louis Armstrong
• Conductor	• Johann Sebastian Bach
• Dancer	• Ludwig van Beethoven
• Disc Jockey	• Leonard Bernstein
• Foley Artist	• Garth Brooks
• Instrumentalist	• Ray Charles
• Instrument Maker	• Frédéric Chopin
• Music Critic	• Duke Ellington
• Music Teacher	• Ella Fitzgerald
• Musician	• Aretha Franklin
• Music Instructor	• Dizzy Gillespie
• Piano Tuner	• Jimi Hendrix
• Producer	• Billie Holiday
• Rapper	• Whitney Houston
• Singer	• Michael Jackson
• Songwriter	• B. B. King
• Sound Engineer	• Madonna
• Sound Mixer	• Wolfgang Amadeus Mozart
	• Luciano Pavarotti
	• Carlos Santana
	• Andrés Segovia
	• Igor Stravinsky

Careers & Famous Folks

Explorations to Celebrate the Bodily/Kinesthetic Intelligence

Careers	Famous Folks
• Acrobat	• Lucille Ball
• Actor	• Jim Carrey
• Athlete	• Charlie Chaplin
• Calligrapher	• Oscar de la Hoya
• Carpenter	• Martha Graham
• Choreographer	• Wayne Gretzky
• Circus Performer	• Michael Jordan
• Construction Worker	• Jackie Joyner Kersee
• Dancer	• Bruce Lee
• Electrician	• Lisa Lesley
• Gymnast	• Carl Lewis
• Inventor	• Tara Lipinski
• Jeweler	• Jesse Owens
• Juggler	• Jim Thorpe
• Martial Artist	• Lily Tomlin
• Magician	• Marcel Marceau
• Massage Therapist	• Joe Montana
• Mechanic	• Babe Ruth
• Physical Therapist	• Pete Sampras
• Plumber	• Summer Sanders
• Surgeon	• Tiger Woods
• Sculptor	• Kristi Yamaguchi

Careers & Famous Folks

Explorations to Celebrate the Naturalist Intelligence

Careers	Famous Folks
• Animal Trainer	• John James Audubon
• Archaeologist	• Luther Burbank
• Astronomer	• Rachael Carson
• Biologist	• Robert Chandler
• Botanist	• Jacques Cousteau
• Conservationist	• George Washington Carver
• Docent	• Charles Darwin
• Doctor	• Ralph Waldo Emerson
• Ecologist	• Asa Gray
• Environmentalist	• Jane Goodall
• Explorer	• James Herriot
• Farmer	• Galileo Galilei
• Fisher	• Sarah Hrdy
• Geologist	• Aldo Leopold
• Guide	• Gregor Johann Mendel
• Hunter	• John Muir
• Meteorologist	• Louis Pasteur
• Oceanographer	• Charles Richter
• Photographer	• Monty Roberts
• Scientist	• Carl Sagan
• Veterinarian	• Jonas Edward Salk
• Zoologist	• Henry David Thoreau

Careers & Famous Folks

Explorations to Celebrate the Interpersonal Intelligence

Careers	Famous Folks
• Arbitrator	• Madeline Albright
• Actor	• Cesar Chávez
• Counselor	• Winston Churchill
• Doctor	• Bill Clinton
• Entrepreneur	• John Dewey
• Human Resources	• Princess Di
• Manager	• Jaime Escalante
• Nurse	• Anne Frank
• Politician	• Mahatma Gandhi
• Principal	• Thomas Jefferson
• Psychiatrist	• John F. Kennedy
• Psychologist	• Martin Luther King, Jr.
• Public Relations	• Horace Mann
• Receptionist	• Margaret Mead
• Religious Leader	• Luisa Moreno
• Salesperson	• Ronald Reagan
• Social Worker	• Nelson Rockefeller
• Sociologist	• Franklin Roosevelt
• Supervisor	• Norman Schwartzkopf
• Teacher	• Anne Sullivan
• Therapist	• Mother Teresa
• Travel Agent	• Harriet Tubman

Careers & Famous Folks

Explorations to Celebrate the Intrapersonal Intelligence

Intrapersonal

Careers	Famous Folks
• Artist	• Mortimer Adler
• Autobiographer	• St. Thomas Aquinas
• Counselor	• Buddha
• Essayist	• Roslyn Carter
• Entrepreneur	• Jesus Christ
• Explorer	• Confucius
• Judge	• Emily Dickinson
• Lawyer	• Sigmund Freud
• Philosopher	• L. Ron Hubbard
• Poet	• Carl Jung
• Political Leader	• Dalai Lama
• Psychiatrist	• Abraham Lincoln
• Psychologist	• Mohammed
• Spiritual Leader	• Pope John Paul, II
• Teacher	• Anthony Robbins
• Theologian	• Eleanor Roosevelt
• Writer	• Jean Jacques Rousseau
	• Jean Paul Sartre
	• Albert Schweitzer
	• Henry David Thoreau
	• Harry Truman
	• Virginia Woolf

Activities to Honor Uniqueness and Celebrate Diversity

Once we become aware of something in our lives, our self-consciousness gives us the power to change it, if we so desire. This self-reflective dimension is at the heart of helping students understand their own multiple intelligences, how to improve those intelligences, and how to use them consciously to enhance the students' own and others' lives (Lazear, 1994, p. 1).

In this chapter you will find a number of activities that span the range of intelligences. The activities are designed to help students learn about MI. By learning MI theory, students deepen their understanding of their own unique pattern of intelligences, as well as that of others. By singing songs about the different types of intelligences, reflecting on their own intelligences, exploring the intelligences of other people and various professions, and classifying different actions associated with the multiple intelligences, students get to know themselves, and their classmates for who they truly are.

By honoring the uniqueness of every student, we establish a nurturing classroom atmosphere in which our students are free to blossom. Celebrating the diversity of others gives students an appreciation of the wonderful qualities other individuals possess.

When we see there are many ways to be smart; we develop a greater sense of self-esteem; we see what makes us each unique. School is a place we feel accepted and have something valuable to contribute. We are turned on to school, not turned away. When we see that fellow classmates and people in society at large also possess different intelligences, we come to appreciate the uniqueness of others as well. People are not smart or dumb. Everyone possesses a unique set of skills and qualities. Together we are smarter; together, we achieve the extraordinary.

Sample activities are provided in this chapter for honoring uniqueness and celebrating diversity. These activities are provided to enrich students understanding of themselves, others and MI theory. In the first activity, Introducing the Eight Intelligences, each of the intelligences are described in understandable language, each on a separate page. Use the eight intelligences cards to introduce students to MI and the eight intelligences. Some possible formats to introduce students to the eight intelligences include: Read, discuss, and share the cards with the whole class; have students take turns reading each card in teams; have each team present an intelligence to the class. This introductory activity familiarizes students with the eight different types of intelligences.

In Chapter 4: The Eight Intelligences, the intelligences are presented in more detail. The one-page introductions to each intelligence in Chapter 4 may be used as blacklines when teaching older students (as well as teachers and parents) about MI.

In the spirit of MI, each remaining activity in this section teaches about MI theory through a different intelligence. We match students' intelligences as they learn to honor their uniqueness and celebrate their diversity. The remaining activities in this chapter (activities 2-15) are all based on the MI strategies presented in Chapter 8: Activities to Match Intelligences.

For example, in the thirteenth activity, Tell Us About You, students learn about MI using the MI strategy Team Interview. Students interview each other about their own intelligences and the intelligences of others with questions such as: What is your strongest intelligence? Would the world be better or worse if everyone had the same pattern of intelligence? Students process MI in an interpersonal context.

In the ninth activity, We're Smart, students use the musical strategy, Songs For Two Voices to sing a song about MI. Students engage their musical skills as they learn about MI.

The Table of MI Strategies and Activities on the following page lists the strategies and activities in this chapter. They are organized by intelligence. There are one or two activities for each intelligence. These activities are a small sampling of the types of activities we can do with our students to teach them about our individual uniqueness and shared diversity.

Table of MI Strategies and Activities

Activity 1

Word Smart

When we use our verbal/linguistic intelligence, we are being "Word Smart." We show we are word smart when we are good at reading, writing, listening and speaking. Other ways to show we are word smart are to read frequently, have a good vocabulary, tell stories, play with words. When we are word smart, we think in words and often learn best through verbal presentations, reading, writing and discussing. People who put their word smarts to work include authors, poets, public speakers, attorneys, salespeople. Famous folks include William Shakespeare, John Steinbeck, Jane Austen, Emily Dickinson.

We are Word Smart when we:

★ **Learn through reading, writing, listening, and discussing**

  ★ **Communicate effectively**

   ★ **Have a good vocabulary**

    ★ **Write clearly**

     ★ **Spell easily**

      ★ **Think in words**

Logic/Math Smart

When we use our logical/mathematical intelligence, we are being "Logic/Math Smart." We show we are logic/math smart when we are good with numbers, computations. If we are logic/math smart, we quantify, sequence, analyze, evaluate, synthesize, and apply. When we are logic/math smart, we think in numbers, abstract symbols, algorithms and logical sequences. We often learn best when logic, numbers, or math are involved. People who put their logic/math smarts to work include accountants, scientists, computer programmers, mathematicians, detectives. Famous folks include Albert Einstein, Bertrand Russell, Marie Curie, Isaac Newton.

We are Logic/Math Smart when we:

★ Think in numbers, patterns, and algorithms

★ Think clearly and analytically

★ Learn by appeal to logic

★ Use abstract symbols

★ Solve logic problems easily

★ Are good in math

Activity | **1**

Art/Space Smart

When we use our visual/spatial intelligence, we are being "Art/Space Smart." We show we are art/space smart when we have good artistic capabilities, an eye for detail and color, spatial awareness, and when we enjoy painting, drawing, sculpting. When we use our art/space smarts, we think in pictures and can "see" through visualization and imagination. If we are art/space smart, we easily learn with guided imagery, films, videos and visual aids. People who put their art/space smarts to work include artists, decorators, designers, architects, photographers. Famous folks include Georgia O'Keeffe, Pablo Picasso, Claude Monet, M. C. Escher.

We are Art/Space Smart when we:

★ Think in pictures and images

  ★ Are good with spatial relations

    ★ Have a good eye for detail and color

      ★ "See" solutions to problems

        ★ Learn through visuals

          ★ Like to draw and create

Music Smart

When we use our musical/rhythmic intelligence, we are being "Music Smart." We show we are music smart when we have the ability to communicate or gain meaning from music, listen to music frequently, play an instrument or sing, are sensitive to pitch, timbre, timing, tone and rhythm of sounds.

When we are music smart, we often think in rhythms, melodies or lyrics and learn best through music or while music is played in the background. People who put their music smarts to work include musicians, composers, conductors, singers. Famous folks include Ludwig van Beethoven, Madonna, Louis Armstrong, Wolfgang Amadeus Mozart.

We are Music Smart when we:

★ Have a good sense of rhythm and melody

★ Like to sing, hum, chant, and rap

★ Enjoy listening to music

★ Read and write music

★ Learn through music and lyrics

★ Enjoy creating music

Body Smart

When we use our bodily/kinesthetic intelligence, we are being "Body Smart." We show we are body smart when we unite body and mind to perfect physical performance, have good motor skills, use our bodies to communicate, are good at dancing, athletics, acting, and use our body in highly differentiated and skilled ways. When we use our body smarts, we think in movements, gestures, body language. We often learn best when there is movement or the content is presented in a "hands-on" form. People who put their body smarts to work include athletes, surgeons, dancers, carpenters, gymnasts. Famous folks include Charlie Chaplin, Mary Lou Retton, Michael Jordan, Jim Carrey, Babe Ruth, Monica Seles.

We are Body Smart when we:

★ Are highly coordinated

  ★ Use gestures and body language

    ★ Take things apart and fix them

      ★ Learn through "hands-on" activities

        ★ Enjoy acting and role-playing

          ★ Enjoy dancing and athletics

Nature Smart

When we use our naturalist intelligence, we are being "Nature Smart." We show we are nature smart when we have a keen awareness of the natural world and phenomena, discriminate natural items like: animals, insects, birds, fish, rocks, minerals, plants, trees, flowers, stars, planets. We often learn best when the content may be sorted and classified or is related to the natural world. People who put their nature smarts to work include ecologists, oceanographers, zoologists. Famous folks include Charles Darwin, Carl Sagan, Jane Goodall, Jacques Cousteau, Henry David Thoreau.

We are Nature Smart when we:

★ Are aware of their natural surroundings

★ Discriminate different flora and different fauna

★ Are good at sorting and classifying

★ Have keen observational skills

★ Understand natural phenomena

★ Garden or care for pets or animals

Activity [1]

People Smart

When we use our interpersonal intelligence, we are being "People Smart." We show we are people smart when we make and maintain friends easily, are sensitive to the feelings moods and motives of others, are good mediators, leaders and organizers, put ourselves in the role of the other and see things from their perspective. When we are people smart, we learn best when we can interact with others over the content. People who put their people smarts to work include politicians, teachers, actors, sociologists, philanthropists. Famous folks include Mother Teresa, Winston Churchill, Martin Luther King, Jr., John F. Kennedy.

We are People Smart when we:

★ Make and maintain friends easily

　★ Understand and respect others

　　★ Lead and organize others

　　　★ Resolve conflicts

　　　　★ Learn by interacting with others

　　　　★ Like to work and be with others

Self Smart

When we use our intrapersonal intelligence, we are being "Self Smart." We show we are self smart when we are introspective, aware of our own feelings, strengths, ideas, values and beliefs, set and meet goals, enjoy private time to think and reflect. If we are self smart, we learn well when we are given time to process information, formulate ideas and reflect on our learning. People who put their self smarts to work include theologians, philosophers, psychologists, psychiatrists. Famous folks include St. Thomas Aquinas, Sigmund Freud, Confucius, Mahatma Gandhi.

Intrapersonal

We are Self Smart when we:

★ Need time to process information

★ Think about our own thinking

★ Have strong opinions and beliefs

★ Are introspective

★ Know ourselves well

★ Like quiet time alone

Activity 2

4S Brainstorming

Career Brainstorm

In a team of four, brainstorm careers that use the multiple intelligences. Take turns recording your ideas below.

Verbal/Linguistic

Bodily/Kinesthetic

Logical/Mathematical

Naturalist

Visual/Spatial

Interpersonal

Musical/Rhythmic

Intrapersonal

3 *Activity*
RoundRobin

I Am Smart

We are all smart, in different ways. Fill in one of the ways you are smart in the blank below. Describe how you know you are smart in this way. When done, share how you are smart with your teammates.

I am smart!

I Am _____ Smart!

I know because...

_____

_____

_____

_____

_____

_____

_____

_____

_____

_____

_____

_____

_____

_____

_____

_____

_____

_____

ACTIVITY 4

Find My Rule

What Kind of Smart?

Teacher: Draw two boxes on the chalkboard and label them Box 1 and Box 2. Write the name of one famous person known for his or her word smarts in Box 1. Write the name of one famous person known for his or her math/logic smarts in Box 2. Have teams discuss the rule for writing these people's names in Box 1 or 2. Continue adding people's names until a team thinks they know the rule. Select one student to write another famous person's name in each box to test the rule.

Box 1	Box 2
• Agatha Christie	• Albert Einstein
• E. B. White	• Alfred Nobel
• Edgar Allen Poe	• Alexander Graham Bell
• Ernest Hemingway	• Aristotle
• James Baldwin	• Benjamin Franklin
• John Steinbeck	• Bertrand Russell
• Judy Blume	• Bill Gates
• Mark Twain	• Carl Sagan
• Martin Luther King, Jr.	• Copernicus
• Oprah Winfrey	• Galileo
• R. L. Stine	• Sir Isaac Newton
• Robert Frost	• Marie Curie
• Rudyard Kipling	• René Descartes
• Shel Silverstein	• Sally Ride
• T. S. Eliot	• Thomas Edison
• Walt Whitman	• Thurgood Marshall
• William Shakespeare	• Voltaire

5 Activity

Who Am I?

Who Am I?

Teacher: Students familiarize themselves with the expert states of each intelligence with this fun activity. Cut apart the famous people cards below. Hand one to each student in the class. Without letting their partners see, students tape the famous people on each other's back. Students ask each other questions to try to find out who they are and what kind of smart they are.

William Shakespeare	John Steinbeck	Mark Twain
Albert Einstein	Ernest Hemingway	Thomas Edison
Benjamin Franklin	Sir Francis Bacon	Leonardo da Vinci
Vincent van Gogh	M. C. Escher	Georgia O'Keeffe
Ludwig van Beethoven	Whitney Houston	Ray Charles
Madonna	Charlie Chaplin	Lucille Ball
Bruce Lee	Muhammad Ali	Charles Darwin
Jane Goodall	Jacques Cousteau	Martin Luther King, Jr.
Mother Teresa	Mohandas Gandhi	Harriet Tubman
Sigmund Freud	Henry David Thoreau	Confucius

Activity | 6

Match Mine
Chart Your Smarts

Pair up with a partner. Cut the sheet in half so you get Set 1 and your partner gets Set 2. Cut out the intelligences icons. Sit back-to-back and arrange your intelligences icons on your Chart Your Smarts board. Arrange them spatially in a design that best describes you. Describe your arrangement to a partner and why you put each intelligence where you did. See if your partner can match your design. When you think you have a match, check your partner's design. Let your partner make a design and try to match it.

Set 1

Set 2

6 *Activity*
Match Mine

Chart Your Smarts

The "Me" box in the center represents you. Arrange your intelligences around you to best describe yourself. Describe your arrangement and see if your partner can make a match.

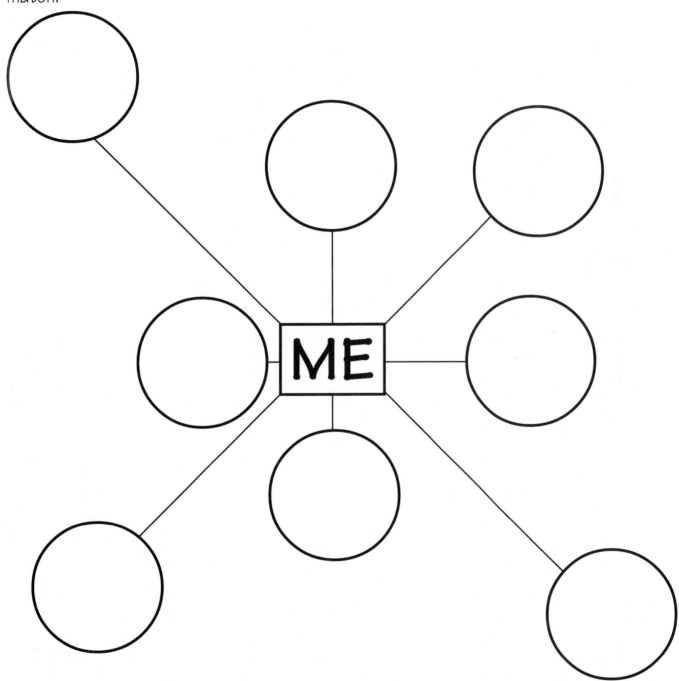

Activity **7**

Mind Mapping

My Mind Map

Draw a picture of yourself in the center box. Use words, colors, size, arrows, bridges, symbols and text to make a map of your different intelligences.

```
┌─────────────────┐
│      Me         │
│                 │
│                 │
│                 │
│                 │
└─────────────────┘
```

8 *Activity*

Lyrical Lessons

Lots of Ways to be Smart!

Pair up with a partner. Decide on a familiar tune. Write a song that describes the different ways. You can use some of the ideas in the box at right. When you're done with your song, sing it to the class.

Some ways to be smart include...
- Word Smart
- Logic Smart
- Math Smart
- Art Smart
- Space Smart
- Music Smart
- Body Smart
- Nature Smart
- People Smart
- Self Smart

A C T I V I T Y **9**
Songs For Two Voices

We're Smart

Pair up with a partner. Decide who is A and who is B. A sings lines that start with A; B sings lines that start with B; you both sing lines that start with AB.

To the tune of "My Bonnie Lies Over the Ocean"

A   Some people learn best when they solo.
B   Some people learn best when they talk.
A   Some people learn better in groups.
B   And some learn the best when they walk.

AB   We're smart, We're smart
AB   All kinds of people are smart
            (are smart)

AB   We're smart, We're smart
AB   All kinds of people are smart
            (are smart)

A   Some people can learn best with music.
B   Some people learn best by art.
A   Some people learn best by using numbers.
B   But all kinds of people are smart.

AB   We're smart, We're smart
AB   All kinds of people are smart
            (are smart)

AB   We're smart, We're smart
AB   All kinds of people are smart
            (are smart)

Spencer & Miguel Kagan: *Multiple Intelligences*

Career Charades

Teacher: Give each student on a team of four one of the career cards below. Have students take turns acting out their careers while teammates guess the career. After teammates guess the career, have students discuss the intelligences used for the profession.

Career Card 1

1. Teacher
2. Nurse
3. Architect
4. Carpenter
5. Veterinarian
6. Doctor
7. Philosopher
8. Disc Jockey

Career Card 2

1. Pilot
2. Fisher
3. Banker
4. Theologian
5. Conductor
6. Salesperson
7. Mechanic
8. Psychiatrist

Career Card 3

1. Receptionist
2. Accountant
3. Dancer
4. Explorer
5. Sculptor
6. Hunter
7. Actor
8. Politician

Career Card 4

1. Singer
2. Photographer
3. Lawyer
4. Counselor
5. Farmer
6. Astronomer
7. Poet
8. Gymnast

Activity | 11
Categorizing

Categorize Actions

Cut out the intelligences category headers below and on the following page. Paste them on a large sheet of butcher paper, leaving about 5" of space under each category header. Then, cut out the actions on the next two pages and evenly divide them among your teammates. Take turns categorizing the actions into the eight intelligences categories. When you're done, glue the categories and the skills to the butcher paper. No actions get glued down until everyone agrees. Compare your chart with another team.

Verbal/Linguistic

Bodily/Kinesthetic

Logical/Mathematical

Naturalist

Visual/Spatial
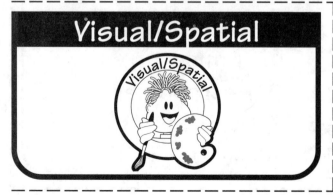

Interpersonal

11 *Activity*
Categorizing

Musical/Rhythmic	Intrapersonal

Musical/Rhythmic	Intrapersonal
Help others...	Drive a car...
Raise pets...	Listen to music...
Meditate...	Observe animals...
Read a book...	Write a poem...
Decipher codes...	Make a team project...
Dance ...	Chart a route...
Go camping...	Create a slogan...
Take photographs...	Set goals...
Write a jingle...	Sing a song...
Discuss an issue...	Give a speech...
Analyze data...	Play a sport...
Act in a skit or play...	Speak Spanish...
Design a brochure...	Make associations...

Activity **11**

Categorizing

Play an instrument...	Grow flowers...
Work together...	Resolve conflicts...
Solve math problems....	Organize others...
Build a 3D model...	Reflect...
Do an experiment...	Spend time alone...
Draw a pattern...	Decorate the house...
Garden...	Paint pictures...
Make friends...	Play video games...
Stretch...	Watch TV....
Clap in rhythm...	Listen to the radio...
Use sign language...	Go to the movies...
Draw a design...	Classify objects...
Watch nature videos...	Fix things...
Make a sculpture...	Make priorities...
Watch videos...	Create visuals...
Compose a melody...	Write a letter...
Collect specimens...	Use body language...

12 *Activity*
Find Someone Who

Find Someone Who...

Get out of your seat and find a partner. Give your partner a high five. Then, see if your partner fits one of the descriptions below. If he or she does, write your partner's name in the blank. Ask your partner the questions. Then, find a new partner that fits another description.

...can play a musical instrument.
Name_____
• What instrument do you play?
• Would you like to be a musician?
• What kind of music do you like to play?

...has a pet.
Name_____
• What kind of pet do you have?
• What is his or her name?
• What do you do together?

...likes to paint or draw.
Name_____
• What do you paint/draw?
• Describe your favorite work.
• What do you do with completed works?

...keeps a journal or diary.
Name_____
• What do you put in it?
• Why do you keep a journal/diary?
• How long have you done it?

...recently read a book.
Name_____
• What book did you read?
• Describe the plot.
• Did you like the book?

...likes math.
Name_____
• Why do you like math?
• What are your favorite types of math problems?

...belongs to a group or club.
Name_____
• What is the name of the group/club?
• Describe the activities you do.
• Do you get along well with the people in the group/club?

...plays a sport.
Name_____
• What sport do you play?
• Describe your best feat.
• What are your goals?

Interpersonal

Activity (13)

Team Interview

Tell Us About You

Cut out the four interview cards below. Place them in a stack upside down in the center of your table. One teammate draws the first card. Each teammate asks him or her one question on the card. The next teammate picks the next card and is interviewed . Continue until every teammate has been interviewed.

Interview Card 1

- What is your strongest intelligence? Why do you think so?

- Did it come naturally, or did you have to work at it?

- What do you think is your weakest intelligence? Why?

Interview Card 2

- What could you do to develop your weakest intelligence?

- If you could have expert skills in any intelligence, which would it be? Why?

- Are there some things you are good at, but don't really enjoy? What?

Interview Card 3

- Are there some things you are not good at, but really enjoy? What?

- Are you like your parents? Why or why not?

- Do you think one intelligence is more important than others in society?

Interview Card 4

- Would the world be better or worse if everyone had the same pattern of intelligence? Why?

- Name one skill you think everyone should have.

- What intelligences does your hero have?

14 *Activity*
Journal Reflections

How I Was Smart

Describe how you used your multiple intelligences today.

Word Smart

Math Smart

Art Smart

Music Smart

Body Smart

Nature Smart

People Smart

Self Smart

A c t i v i t y 15

Timed Pair Share

Share Yourself

Pair up with a partner. Cut out the cards below, and shuffle them face down. Pick the top card and share your answer with your partner for one minute. Let your partner pick the next card and share with you for one minute.

Do you consider yourself artistic? Why or why not?	Do you respect people who are smart in different ways than you?	What do you think other people think about you?
Does the music you listen to contribute to your state of mind?	What is one goal you have to better yourself as a person?	Do you consider yourself more of a logical or emotional person?
Do you think that your hobbies reflect your intelligences?	What makes you really happy?	What does the way you dress say about you?
Are you more of an introvert or an extrovert? Why?	How are your friends like you? How are they different?	Where in nature do you prefer to be? What does this say about you?

MI Lessons, Centers, Projects, and Theme Units

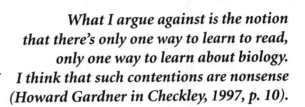

What I argue against is the notion that there's only one way to learn to read, only one way to learn about biology. I think that such contentions are nonsense (Howard Gardner in Checkley, 1997, p. 10).

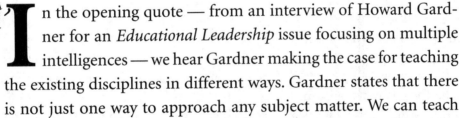

In the opening quote — from an interview of Howard Gardner for an *Educational Leadership* issue focusing on multiple intelligences — we hear Gardner making the case for teaching the existing disciplines in different ways. Gardner states that there is not just one way to approach any subject matter. We can teach students to read, teach them the content and methods of biology, and every other discipline in a number of ways.

At the root of planning MI lessons, centers projects and theme units is a very simple premise: Any topic of importance can be taught, and learned, in a variety of ways.

Then should everything be taught in eight different ways? Gardner doesn't think so:

> It is equally nonsensical to say that everything should be taught seven or eight ways. That's not the point of the MI theory. The point is to realize that any topic of importance, from any discipline, can be taught in more than one way (Gardner in Checkley, 1997, p.10).

Gardner's response reflects the essence of the MI movement. MI lessons, centers, projects, and theme units shares this simple premise: Any topic of importance can be taught in more than one way. In the process of teaching any content in a variety of ways, something magical occurs — we achieve the three MI visions!

We match how students are smart. We use a wider range of instructional strategies. Throughout the day, week, and year we use strategies that match every students' dominant intelligences and in that way make the content more accessible to each of our students.

We stretch students' multiple intelligences. As we use strategies that span the range of intelligences, we stretch students in their dominant and nondominant intelligences; we help students develop all of their intelligences.

We also celebrate MI. Some students write eloquent poems, some construct visual masterpieces, some construct infallible arguments, some create catchy jingles. Students all have the opportunity to excel in one way or another. As students engage and develop their intelligences, they gain a sense of self-worth and see the value of other students' strengths as well. Students no longer see each other as smart or dumb; they know each person is gifted with a unique profile of intelligences.

Planning and presenting MI lessons, centers, projects, and theme units involves the skillful preparation of any curriculum to be taught and learned in a number of different ways, corresponding to the various intelligences. In Chapter 7: MI Instructional Strategies, we presented a number of strategies for MI lessons, centers, and projects. This chapter describes ways to make MI come alive by using those strategies to create powerful and engaging multiple intelligences lessons, centers, projects and theme units. Many forms are provided to help you plan, present, and assess your own MI lessons, centers, projects, and theme units.

MI Lessons

We can easily transform any lesson into an MI lesson by presenting the content in a number of ways — ways that engage students' multiple intelligences. An easy way to plan an MI lesson is to generate a variety of activities, each exploring the lesson topic through a different intelligence or set of intelligences. By integrating the multiple intelligences, we match some students' intelligences, stretch the intelligences of others, and create a greater depth of understanding for all students. As we plan, present, and process MI lessons, we use the following simple five-step procedure: 1) Define MI Lesson Objectives; 2) Create MI Activities; 3) Sequence MI Activities; 4) Present MI Lesson; 5) Assess MI Lesson. See box: Steps of MI Lessons.

The process may seem a bit of a departure from your normal lesson planning routine, and the lessons which result may look, sound, and feel somewhat different. You may add musical activities to your teaching — activities that you've never tried before. You may have students work in cooperative teams to accomplish some goals. You may be stretching your curriculum. That's the power of MI — it pushes us to stretch our teaching and students' learning! The more we create MI lessons, the more natural they become, and the more lessons we stockpile to use the next time we teach the same topic. Our teaching becomes richer and the learning process becomes more fun and meaningful for students. In the process, we stretch and develop our own range of intelligences!

As an example, let's go through the five steps of lesson planning to plan an MI lesson on Christopher Columbus.

Steps of MI Lessons

1. Define MI Lesson Objectives
What do students have to learn? What do I want students to learn?
What do students want to learn?

▼

2. Create MI Activities
Generate MI activities that span the range of intelligences.
(Use MI Activity Generator.)

▼

3. Sequence MI Activities
Sequence MI activities. Consider logical sequence, developmental flow, and
elements of lesson design. (Use MI Lesson Planner.)

▼

4. Present MI Lesson
Lead students through sequence of activities across the intelligences.
Integrate authentic assessment with instruction.

▼

5. Assess MI Lesson
Assess student learning.
Reflect on lesson. (Use MI Reflection Form.)

1. Define MI Lesson Objectives

Ask yourself, "What do I want students to learn in this lesson?" We can have a very narrow, specific learning objective: I want students to learn that there is another side to the exploration coin — That this celebrated hero, like many explorers, was also a ruthless conqueror. Thus, the activities we create would all revolve around this single objective.

In contrast, we can have a more general set of learning objectives: For students to have a general background of Columbus and the relevant events leading to his discovery of America, to learn about the times in which Columbus lived including the art, music, and literature of the times. General objectives might include seeing Columbus through the eyes of the Arawaks and having students learn about the geography of

Know–Wonder–Learned

Topic _____ Name _____ Date _____

Know What I know about the topic.	**Wonder** What I wonder about the topic.	**Learned** What I learned about the topic.

the voyage. With more general objectives, the content of the activities we create will be more diverse.

Lesson objectives can also be student generated. Asking students what they are curious about or what interests them creates more personally relevant learning objectives. A Know-Wonder-Learned form works well for students to generate areas of interest. See the Know-Wonder-Learned form on page 13.4. Allowing students to direct their own learning gives students a sense of ownership; the content becomes more meaningful and motivating, and the intelligences are more fully engaged.

Another objective for MI lessons can be to enhance students' intelligences. To develop students' multiple intelligences, we may use a functional approach, strengthening intelligences in a meaningful context. In our MI lessons we can include opportunities for students to develop skills, solve problems, observe, communicate, create, acquire knowledge, and make decisions drawing on an intelligence or using many in concert. For a detailed description of the functions of intelligences, see Chapter 3: What Is an Intelligence? For an aid in planning lessons to develop the intelligences in a natural context, see the Functions of Intelligences Lesson Planning Form, page 13.6.

2. Create MI Activities

Once we have defined our objectives, the next step is to create activities across the intelligences to teach to our specific objectives. For example, one of our objectives is to give students a general overview about Columbus. We may do this using a visual/ spatial activity using the Guided Imagery strategy. We can read students a prepared script, rich in visual imagery about Columbus' voyage. With their eyes closed, students visualize the voyage. We may also reach this objective with a verbal/linguistic activity based on the strategy Round-Table. We can have students take turns reading portions of the section on Columbus.

The MI Activity Generator on page 13.7 is a form provided to help you create MI activities. In our Columbus example, we record these activities on our form, we write our objective, "Background on Columbus' voyage," in the verbal/linguistic row, "RoundRobin" as the MI strategy, and "Read Columbus passage in Chapter 3" as the content. In the visual/spatial row, we write the same objective, "Guided Imagery" as the strategy and "Read Columbus script" as the content.

For each of our lesson objectives, we generate activities across the intelligences to reach the objective. Using the MI Activity Generator stretches us to include a variety of MI activities to reach our teaching objectives. As we create activities for our lesson, perhaps we notice that we don't have a musical/rhythmic activity. Can we think of a meaningful activity to engage students' sense of rhythm in relation to the content? We can have students write and perform a song about Columbus' explorations. As another visual/spatial activity, we can have students make a Mind Map of Columbus' sea voyage. Record all activity ideas related to the topic on the Activity Generator Form. At this stage, don't worry about the sequence of activities. Brainstorm fun, creative ways to reach your learning objectives incorporating the intelligences.

Functions of the Intelligences
SSPPCCKW Lesson Planning Form

Survival
How can the lesson simulate survival?

Skills
What skills can the lesson foster?

Perceptiveness
How can the lesson enhance students' perceptiveness?

Problem Solving
What problem-solving skills can be developed through the lesson?

Communication
How can the lesson improve students' communication skills?

Creativity
How can the lesson harness students' creativity?

Knowledge
What information should the lesson include?

Wisdom
How can the lesson stretch students' decision-making skills?

MI Activity Generator

Lesson Topic _____ Date _____

Intelligence	Order	MI Strategy	Content
Verbal/Linguistic			
Logical/Mathematical			
Visual/Spatial			
Musical/Rhythmic			
Bodily/Kinesthetic			
Naturalist			
Interpersonal			
Intrapersonal			

How many activities we create for each intelligence depends on our objectives and how much time we want to spend on the lesson. If the lesson is a one day event, we may only pick one strategy from each of three different intelligences. If the topic is important, we can spend a week or month on the topic. In this case, we select several strategies from each of the intelligences; we may repeat the same strategy several times, each time with new content.

If we are at loss for a musical activity, we may pick one of the strategies in Chapter 7: MI Instructional Strategies, and ask ourselves, "How can I use this strategy to teach about…?" Often, the MI strategies spark great ideas for an activity. Another helpful resource for generating activities is the MI Activity Ideas on pages 13.9-13.12. On these pages, there are numerous ideas for activities across the intelligences.

Remember, it is not essential that we teach every lesson in eight ways. Create activities that best fit your learning objective. If a naturalist activity doesn't fit the content, don't force it. If there just isn't time for a musical/rhythmic activity, skip it. But don't forget to include one tomorrow, or sometime during the week. The eight intelligences are just helpful guidelines. It is important that we provide students the opportunity to learn through and develop all their intelligences, but definitely not in every lesson.

Also, don't feel tied to the eight intelligences. Feel free to include activities to match, stretch, and celebrate the mechanical, craft, emotional, existential, culinary, or any other intelligence you would like to validate or develop.

3. Sequence MI Activities

The next step in planning an MI lesson is to sequence the activities. What activity would create a good anticipatory set and create interest in the topic? Maybe we forgot a meaningful introduction to the lesson. Now's the time to add that activity. What would be a good closure activity? Do students need direct instruction on the content before they do the bodily/kinesthetic activity?

When sequencing activities, consider Hunter's Elements of Effective Instruction: 1) Set, 2) Input, 3) Checking for Understanding, 4) Guided Practice 5) Independent Practice 6) Closure. See Gentile (1988).

On the MI Activity Generator, there is a column titled, "Order," we may use to sequence our MI activities. Alternatively, we can write out our lesson plan on a copy of one of the other MI Lesson Planners provided on pages 13.13 and 13.14.

When our activities are ordered, we're done! We now have a powerful and engaging MI lesson with activities that span many or all of the intelligences! Well, actually we're not quite done. We still need to prepare any necessary materials, consider the type of authentic assessment we'll use in the process (see Chapter 19: Authentic MI Assessment), and then we're ready to present the lesson.

4. Present MI Lesson

Here's the fun part. We watch as our students engage in our exciting MI lesson. We can almost see their neurons stretching and making connections to the content. Be prepared to modify and adjust. Even the best laid plans sometimes go awry.

MI Activity Ideas

Verbal/Linguistic Activities

Read
- Read a book, novel
- Read a poem, essay
- Read a short story, play

Speak & Discuss
- Communicate, share ideas
- Discuss or debate
- Explain a concept
- Give a speech, impromptu
- Tell a story, tall tale
- Tell jokes, puns, riddles

Write
- Compare and contrast
- Create a slogan
- Do a crossword puzzle
- Do creative writing
- Do descriptive writing
- Keep a journal or diary
- Make a word-web
- Use the writing process
- Write a biography
- Write a book report
- Write a letter
- Write a narrative
- Write an autobiography
- Write a newspaper article
- Write a persuasive paper
- Write a play or skit
- Write a poem
- Write a research report
- Write a speech
- Write instructions

Language
- Learn a second language
- Learn vocabulary words
- Practice grammar, spelling
- Study etymology

Logical/Mathematical Activities

Logic & Higher-Level Thinking
- Analyze data
- Apply information
- Brainstorm ideas
- Classify & categorize
- Compare & contrast
- Conduct an experiment
- Decipher codes
- Discover patterns, trends
- Evaluate ideas
- Formulate hypotheses
- List or organize facts
- Make associations
- Make predictions
- Outline material
- Play pattern games
- Sequence events
- Solve logic problems
- Synthesize ideas
- Test hypotheses
- Use abstract symbols
- Use deductive/inductive thinking
- Use graphic organizers

Math
- Build answers
- Calculate probability
- Do calculations
- Make a graph
- Play number games
- Symbolize in numbers
- Solve math problems
- Solve story problems
- Use calculator, compass
- Use math manipulatives
- Use spreadsheet software
- Write an equation
- Write a proof

MI Activity Ideas
(continued)

Visual/Spatial Activities

Arts & Crafts
- Create a collage, montage
- Create a pattern, texture
- Design a brochure, logo
- Design or decorate clothes
- Design postcards, stamps
- Draw a design
- Draw a scene from the story/math problem
- Illustrate a book
- Make a mobile
- Make a poster
- Make a sculpture
- Make puppets
- Make visual aids

- Paint or draw
- Play with colors
- Practice perspective, shading, coloring
- Take photographs
- Use painting or drawing software

Visualization
- Do guided imagery
- Fantasize or visualize
- Imagine or pretend
- Mind map
- Watch films, videos

Spatial
- Build or draw in 3D
- Chart a route
- Estimate size, distance
- Make or read a map
- Play with geometric shapes
- Play with puzzles, mazes
- Use page layout software
- Use graphic organizers

Musical/Rhythmic Activities

Create Music
- Compose a melody
- Copy sounds and melodies
- Create a musical collage
- Hum, clap, click, bang, snap in tune
- Write a song, poem, jingle

Perform
- Play an instrument solo
- Play as a class
- Play as a team, band
- Sing a duo, trio, quartet
- Sing a solo, as a class

Learn About Music
- Evaluate music
- Learn about instruments
- Learn an instrument
- Learn to read notes, symbols, expressions
- Learn sensitivity to sound, rhythmic patterns
- Listen to music of different times, genres, cultures
- Study or report on a musician, instrument, era
- Use music software

Learn through Music
- Change the words to a song, jingle, rap
- Interpret lyrical meanings
- Listen to curriculum music songs
- Listen to music, background music
- Write or sing a song including facts about topic

MI Activity Ideas
(continued)

Bodily/Kinesthetic Activities

Body Expression
- Act out a role
- Act out a word, concept
- Choreograph or perform a dance, movement sequence
- Depict concepts with movement, formations
- Do a task without talking
- Learn sign language
- Perform a pantomime
- Perform a skit or play
- Play charades
- Use physical gestures

Fine Motor Skills
- Assemble/disassemble appliances, machines
- Dissect plants, animals
- Play computer or video games requiring hand-eye coordination or fine motor skills
- Use tools

Physical Exercise
- Hop, skip, jump, run
- Play sports
- Stretch, do yoga
- Work out, jump rope

"Hands-On" Learning
- Build a model
- Create projects
- Create props and crafts
- Do math with manipulatives
- Do science experiments
- Explore learning materials
- Put together a puzzle
- Touch or feel parts
- Visit places

Naturalist Activities

Observe
- Go to a zoo, farm, aquarium, forest
- Observe natural phenomena
- Observe planets, stars, comets, space
- Take a nature hike, camp
- Visit the ocean, tide pool
- Visit a river, lake, park
- Watch nature videos

Record Observations
- List characteristics
- Record changes, developmental stages
- Record color, size, form, function
- Use a log or journal

Classify & Categorize
- Classify by color, size, form, function
- Devise classification system
- Learn taxonomy system, names
- Sort & categorize natural items: seashells, leaves, animals, plants, flowers, insects, rocks, minerals
- Sort & categorize nonnatural items: buttons, pasta, nuts and bolts
- Use graphic organizers

In or With Nature
- Capture nature with photographs
- Care for classroom pet
- Collect specimens
- Grow flowers, vegetables
- Plant a tree

MI Activity Ideas

(continued)

Interpersonal Activities

Work Together
- Debate an issue
- Discuss with a partner
- Do a team presentation
- Do teambuilding & class-building
- Establish team goals
- Interview each other
- Make a team project
- Paraphrase each other
- Practice active listening
- Practice constructive criticism
- Practice taking turns
- Process interactions

- Share with others
- Take role of another
- Tutor a classmate
- Use roles
- Work on communication skills
- Write a collaborative paper or report

Solve Conflicts
- Practice compromising
- Practice mediation skills
- Reach consensus
- Role-play
- Solve problems as a team
- Solve real or simulated conflicts

Organize Others
- Assign roles or tasks
- Mediate conflicts
- Motivate others
- Plan an event

Intrapersonal Activities

Set Goals & Priorities
- Keep a "To Do" list
- Make an action plan
- Prioritize items
- Set goals and work on achieving goals

Reflection & Introspection
- Describe feelings about topic, situation
- Keep a daily log or diary
- List priorities
- Make a journal entry
- Meditate
- Observe mood changes

- Read silently
- Record, analyze dreams
- Reflect on learning
- Relate content to personal experiences
- Think about actions
- Think about thinking
- Weigh alternatives
- Work independently
- Write about thinking
- Write about actions
- Write about wants/needs
- Write an autobiography
- Write personal poetry

Values & Beliefs
- Choose between alternatives
- Defend a position
- Express likes, dislikes
- Respond to hypothetical ethical dilemmas
- Take a stance
- Write ethical code, rules of conduct

MI Lesson Planner

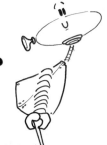

Lesson Topic _____ **Date** _____

Synopsis/Objectives

Materials

Activities/Sequence

Assessment

❑ Verbal/Linguistic

❑ Logical/Mathematical

❑ Visual/Spatial

❑ Musical/Rhythmic

❑ Naturalist

❑ Bodily/Kinesthetic

❑ Interpersonal

❑ Intrapersonal

MI Lesson Planner

Lesson Topic_____ **Date**_____

A c t i v i t i e s

Design activities for each intelligence. Write the sequence in the boxes.

Verbal/Linguistic ☐

Logical/Mathematical ☐

Visual/Spatial ☐

Musical/Rhythmic ☐

Bodily/Kinesthetic ☐

Naturalist ☐

Interpersonal ☐

Intrapersonal ☐

Resources

Spencer & Miguel Kagan: *Multiple Intelligences*

Kagan Cooperative Learning • 1 (800) WEE CO-OP

5. Assess MI Lesson

Assessment after (or in the process of) a lesson should involve some form of student assessment (Did students learn about the topic? What do students still need work on?) and reflection on the lesson (Did I reach the objectives I set out to? What worked well? What didn't work? What will I do to improve the lesson for my next class or for next year?).

Student assessment can include the traditional quiz or test to assess mastery of the basic content. Assessment can also take a more authentic format, by collecting sample work in portfolios, process-folios, using behavioral observations, recording songs and videotaping performances. Authentic assessment strives at capturing a more realistic picture of students' strengths, weaknesses and development over time. Authentic assessment engages both students and the teacher in a powerful ongoing process. See Chapter 19: Authentic Assessment of MI.

Reflection is the royal road to improvement! Taking the time to reflect on the lesson is time well spent and a wise investment in both our students and our teaching. The MI Reflections Form on page on page 13.16 is provided to lead us through thinking about our lesson and how to improve it. The perfect lesson has never been taught. There is always room for improvement.

MI Centers

MI centers engage students in each of the intelligences, each at a different physical location in the classroom. Planning and assessing MI centers is very similar to MI lessons. In an MI lesson, we direct students through a series of activities across the intelligences. In MI centers, students may do the exact same activities, but they experience them at their centers.

At each MI center, we stretch one or more intelligences, providing an activity which develops the specific intelligence(s). At the same time, MI centers match students' intelligences, delivering the content through experiences that engage the specific intelligence(s) of the center.

There are many formats of MI centers. Students may choose which center to go to, or may be assigned to the center in heterogeneous teams; the task at a center may be highly structured, or the center may be a loosely formatted exploratory center; students may work independently or cooperatively; students can progress through eight MI centers daily, or can go to one center each day during center time. For more on MI centers, see Chapter 7: MI Instructional Strategies. For MI center ideas, see Chapter 14: Creating the MI Class.

Here, we will focus on how to plan the activity for the center. As we plan our MI centers, we use the following five steps: 1) Define Center Objectives; 2) Create Center Activities; 3) Prepare Center Tasks and Materials; 4) Center Time; and 5) Assess Centers. See box: Steps of MI Centers.

MI Reflection Form

Topic_____ Date_____

+ ## What worked well?

- ## What didn't work well?

C ## What will I change next time?

Steps of MI Centers

1. Define Center Objectives

What do students have to learn? What do I want students to learn? What do students want to learn?

▼

2. Create Center Activities

Create an MI activity for each MI center corresponding to the multiple intelligences.

▼

3. Prepare Center Tasks and Materials

Prepare task, materials, and sponge activity for each center. Use MI Center Planner.

▼

4. Center Time

Students visit MI centers and engage in activities. Integrate authentic assessment with centers.

▼

5. Assess Centers

Assess student learning. Reflect on Center. Use MI Reflection Form.

Let's continue with our Christopher Columbus example to plan some MI centers. On page 13.18, there is an MI Center Planner to use when planning MI centers.

1. Define MI Center Objectives

The first step of planning an MI center is to define the objective for the center. What will students learn? The objective of each center is based on the intelligence of the center. At the Whitney Houston center, the objective is for students to explore the content through their musical/rhythmic skills. At the Leonardo da Vinci center, students

MI Center Planner

Topic _____ Date _____

Verbal/Linguistic
Task:

Materials:

Sponge:

Logical/Mathematical
Task:

Materials:

Sponge:

Visual/Spatial
Task:

Materials:

Sponge:

Musical/Rhythmic
Task:

Materials:

Sponge:

Bodily/Kinesthetic
Task:

Materials:

Sponge:

Naturalist
Task:

Materials:

Sponge:

Interpersonal
Task:

Materials:

Sponge:

Intrapersonal
Task:

Materials:

Sponge:

use their visual/spatial skills to learn the content.

2. Create MI Center Activity

The next step in planning an MI center is to create the activity for each center. Going back to our Columbus example, we can think of a number of appropriate activities for the music center: students may listen to music or play with instruments of Columbus' time, sing a song about Columbus' voyage, or use instruments to create sounds associated with events. Students enjoy creating Lyrical Lessons — putting lyrics to popular tunes. For example, they may create a song about Columbus' voyage to the tune of *Silent Night* or *When the Saints Go Marchin' In*.

At the visual/spatial center, students may make a collage representing Columbus' journey; students may create a mobile with the *Niña*, the *Pinta*, and the *Santa Maria*; draw a map of Columbus' voyage; paint a picture of the Caribbean natives used to mine gold; or build a model of a ship using tongue depressors and glue. Students might make a Mind Map of events associated with Columbus' discovery, using only pictures.

The activity for each center should be approximately the same duration. If students are to work in centers for half an hour or forty five minutes, we need to plan so students at each center will be done at approximately the same time. A trick to planning centers so students do not finish at different rates is to include a sponge activity at each at each center. Sponge activities are content-related activities which can be tacked onto any center activity. For example, at the verbal/linguistic center, when

done with their center activity, students may write a story relating to the topic. At the visual/spatial center, students may draw a picture. The MI Activity Ideas on page 13. 8 lists numerous activities for each intelligence. These activities can be easily adapted as sponge activities.

It is important that the types of activities at each center change frequently to engage and develop the wide range of skills associated with each intelligence. If we always have students draw a representative illustration at the Leonardo da Vinci center, we are not fully developing the visual/spatial intelligence. The more opportunities we give our students to engage each facet of each intelligence, the more we maximize students' learning potential and the more fully we develop students' intelligences. In Chapter 9: Developing the Multiple Intelligences, many facets of each intelligence are listed. As we plan our centers, over time, we attempt to include a range of activities that focus on a range of skills from each intelligence.

3. Prepare MI Center Task & Materials

Since centers are primarily student-directed, it is important to have the task clearly defined and materials prepared for students. Task cards work well. For example, when students get to the Albert Einstein center, they may find scissors, butcher paper, glue, a sheet of paper with sixteen events relating to Columbus, colored markers, text books, and a task card that says: "Your mission, should you choose to accept it, is to create a time line of the events relating to Columbus' discovery of America. Cut out the events, and evenly divide them among everyone at the center. Everyone is in charge of looking up the approximate date for their own event, and pasting it on the team's time line. Everyone gets a different color marker. Only you can touch your events and use your color. Make your time line as attractive as you can." Cooperative center tasks require a little extra careful structuring to ensure that all students are actively involved in the activity. Division of labor and individual accountability work well.

4. MI Center Time

As students work at their centers, we may walk around to facilitate, or may decide to sit down and work with a student or students who could benefit from individual attention. Center time is an excellent opportunity for authentic assessment. See Chapter 19: Authentic MI Assessment.

5. Assess MI Centers

Like with MI lesson plans, reflection is the route to improving MI centers. How could the center be better? The MI Reflection Form on page 13.16 is a helpful centers reflection aid.

MI Projects

MI projects activate a number of students' intelligences. There are many different formats for MI projects. The entire class may complete a project, with each student contributing in some important way. Projects may be completed by a cooperative team in small teams, or independently. Students can choose their projects from provided alternatives, design their own, or everyone may be assigned the same project. For more on MI projects, see Chapter 7: MI Instructional Strategies.

Planning and assessing MI projects will depend largely on the content of the project. Consider these general guidelines and ideas when planning and assessing MI projects: 1) Define MI Project Objectives; 2) Design MI Project; 3) MI Project Conferences; 4) MI Project Presentations; 5) Assess MI Projects.

1. Define MI Project Objectives

What do you want students to learn by doing the project? A project should be an experiential, real-life extension of the curriculum. The more the project is integrated in the topic of study, the more connected and meaningful the curriculum will be for students. Consider the intelligences you want students to use and develop as they work on their projects. A good MI project will engage students in a variety of activities that require the integration of a number of intelligences. Any single MI project does not have to address every intelligence. Some projects may target just a couple of intelligences. Over time, using a variety of projects, students will have multiple opportunities to use and develop their multiple intelligences.

2. Design MI Project

In Chapter 7: MI Instructional Strategies, a number of MI projects and strategies are described in detail. To design an MI project, we may use one of the strategies with our curriculum, or design our own project. MI project ideas include: conduct an experiment, write a research paper, create a book, build a model, write and perform a play, create a collaborative work of art, interview or survey others, train an animal, create a journal. For more MI projects ideas that focus on an intelligence, see pages 13.21-13.22.

MI Project Ideas

▼ Verbal/Linguistic Projects

- Create an audiotape
- Give a persuasive/ informative speech
- Investigate an author
- Have a debate/discussion
- Report on a book
- Report on a word smart career/famous person
- Share a poem/poet
- Teach a skill
- Write a book/story
- Write a letter/book of correspondence
- Write an essay
- Write a research report
- Write a screenplay or script
- Write a slogan/ad campaign

▼ Logical/ Mathematical Projects

- Analyze/interpret data
- Conduct an experiment
- Conduct a survey
- Create an outline
- Create a sequence of steps
- Create a time line
- Demonstrate logic/thinking
- Design a questionnaire
- Graph data
- Present statistics
- Program a web page
- Report on a logic/math smart career/famous person
- Simulate a court case
- Solve a problem
- Teach a thinking skill
- Write a computer program

▼ Visual/Spatial Projects

- Build a model
- Create a cartoon/comic book
- Create a diorama
- Create a map/blueprint
- Create a montage/collage
- Create a mural
- Create a poster
- Design a brochure/catalog
- Design a book/CD cover
- Design a logo/identity pack
- Design a poster
- Design business cards/ letterhead
- Design T-shirts/hats
- Draw/paint a picture
- Film a video
- Make a diagram/flowchart
- Make a magazine
- Make a photo album
- Make a sculpture
- Present slides

- Report on an art smart career/famous person
- Research art movement
- Teach an art skill

▼ Musical/Rhythmic Projects

- Create a musical
- Create a radio show
- Create sound effects
- Express meaning through music
- Give an instrumental performance
- Lip sync a song
- Report on a music smart career/famous person
- Research musical period
- Sing a song
- Teach a music skill
- Write a jingle
- Write an anthem
- Write a song/rap

MI Project Ideas

(continued)

▼ Bodily/Kinesthetic Projects

- Act in a play
- Act out a role
- Build a model
- Build a project
- Choreograph a dance
- Conduct a lab experiment
- Create a performance
- Create a product
- Create body sculptures
- Give a sports report
- Make a video
- Perform a pantomime
- Report on a body smart career/famous person
- Role play an event
- Teach a body skill
- Teach a fine motor skill

▼ Naturalist Projects

- Care for an animal
- Collect specimens
- Conduct a nature experiment
- Create a classification system/taxonomy
- Create an observation log
- Grow a garden

- Make a nature video
- Report on an animal/insect
- Report on flora/fauna
- Report on a natural phenomenon
- Report on a nature smart career/famous person
- Share crisis
- Train an animal

▼ Interpersonal Projects

- Conduct a survey
- Create a talk show/game show
- Do a cooperative project
- Explore sides of an issue
- Interview someone
- Make a group video
- Perform a service/help others
- Plan a public event/party
- Report on people smart career/famous person
- Solve/present a social issue
- Teach a people skill/manners
- Tutor a classmate/schoolmate

▼ Intrapersonal Projects

- Analyze dreams
- Construct a portfolio
- Create a self-portrait
- Express personal perspective on an issue
- Keep a journal/log/diary
- Make plans/goals
- Make a video on self
- Report on a self smart career/famous person
- Share uniqueness with class
- Study feelings/moods
- Teach a meditation/relaxation skill
- Write a narrative
- Write an autobiography

Let's return to our Columbus example. We are studying Columbus and want to give students an opportunity to explore the content in a self-directed, meaningful way to bring them closer to the content and to develop their intelligences.

One possible project is to have students write and present a book on Columbus' explorations. With the writing and reading normally associated with books, this may appear to be solely a verbal/linguistic endeavor. However, without too much of a stretch, we can easily design the project to integrate a number of other intelligences. We can have students work in cooperative teams as part of the project (interpersonal); include a sequence of events and dates or statistics in their book (logical/mathematical); draw illustrations, and design the layout for the book (visual/spatial); include references to flora and fauna or other natural phenomena (naturalist); and assess their contribution and presentation (intrapersonal). As students engage in projects, they acquire real-world skills in the process of creating a valued product.

In designing the MI project, there are a number of factors to consider. What resources are available to students? Will the project be completed in the class? How much time will students need to do the project? How will the projects be presented? What rubric will be used to assess the project and students' learning? After you tack down the details of the project(s), present them to the class. Assign students individually or in teams to their projects, or let students select or create their own projects and/or teams.

3. MI Project Conferences

For a basic project, where the objectives and procedures are clearly defined, a conference may not be needed. For an extended or student-generated project, a conference may be essential.

One goal of the project conference is to help students plan and present a successful project. After you assign, or students select their projects, give them some time to explore their own creative ideas. It is a good idea to have a conference early to make sure students are on the right track. If teams or individuals have their own projects, independent conferences are helpful. If the whole class is working on the same project, or all students or teams are assigned the same project, you can have a class meeting. At the introductory stage, a contract or plan can be drafted that may include who will do what research, experimentation, and presentation. Consider conferences at the various stages of the project development: introduction, planning, final preparations.

A second goal of the project conference is to help students reflect on their progress and to help them better understand their unique pattern of intelligences. Students may be asked focused questions such as: "How are you using your art smarts in the process of the project?" Or, "Which of your strengths are you bringing to work on this project?"

Conferences can be between students. Students can make appointments with other students to discuss progress and bounce ideas off classmates. In just 10 minutes every student in the class can have a five minute conference with a classmate. For the first five minutes the pair focuses on one project. Then they focus on the other student's project. If students are working in teams, teams can pair up.

4. MI Project Presentations

The culminating event of an MI project is the presentation. The preparation for the presentation and the actual presentation of the project often requires students to use their multiple intelligences at least as much as their investigation of the content. It is through the presentations that the rest of the class benefits from the team or individual's research. To the extent that the presentations are multimodal (use graphics, visual aids, video clips, music, movement), both the presenters and the students viewing the presentation are stimulating their multiple intelligences. For multiple presentation modes, see MI Project Presentation Modes on page 13.25. If all students are working on the same project, it may not make sense to spend the time to do extended presentations. However, a time to tour classmates projects may spark interest and creativity.

Presentations do not always have to be one student or one team in front of the whole class. Sometimes teams or individuals might pair up to do their presentations to each other while the teacher circulates. Simultaneous presentations save a great deal of class time and generate less anxiety among students. With simultaneous presentations, students or teams have time to present their projects more than once, improving their presentation skills each time.

5. Assess & Evaluate MI Projects

There are a number of ways to assess and evaluate MI projects. Assessment can occur in the process of the project, or after the project is complete. Evaluation almost always occurs after the project and presentation. Some different types of evaluation include teacher evaluation, peer evaluation, and self-evaluation. When introducing the project, go over the type of assessment that will be used and make it clear what is expected if the projects are to be evaluated. Students benefit greatly from having input into the form of evaluation. In some cases students can be entirely responsible for construction of the evaluation form. By allowing students to take charge of evaluation, they take greater ownership of the learning process. Student design of evaluation opens an important additional avenue for learning.

Teacher Evaluation

Teacher evaluation may be an attempt to assess the extent to which students mastered basic skills or concepts. The traditional quiz or test allows us to see if students mastered information.

Another form of teacher evaluation is a performance evaluation. How well did each student present his or her project? Or if students work in teams, how well did students contribute individually to the team presentation? Groups can be given feedback, but group performance should never feed into an individual grade (see Kagan, 1995). Individual grades should be based on individual performance or achievement.

MI Project Presentation Modes

▼ Verbal/Linguistic Presentations

• Debate/discuss topic
• Distribute article/newspaper
• Give speech
• Play audiotape
• Provide transcript
• Read writing
• Recite poem
• Tell a story

▼ Logical/ Mathematical Presentations

• Give scientific demonstration
• Have audience solve problems
• Include graphic organizers
• Make analogies/ relationships
• Outline speech/presentation
• Present sequence/order

▼ Visual/Spatial Presentations

• Display charts/graphs/ diagrams/maps/signs
• Give demonstration
• Have audience imagine/ pretend
• Incorporate visual aids

• Play movie/video
• Show slides
• Use drawings/paintings
• Use guided imagery/ visualization

▼ Musical/Rhythmic Presentations

• Include background music
• Integrate music
• Perform a musical
• Play an instrument
• Sing a song
• Show video
• Use sound effects

▼ Bodily/Kinesthetic Presentations

• Dance
• Give a demonstration
• Give audience hands-on experience
• Include audience movement
• Include gestures/body language
• Perform a drama
• Pantomime a concept
• Use manipulatives
• Use movement

▼ Naturalist Presentations

• Classify/categorize objects
• Give a demonstration
• Include observations
• Present plants/animals
• Relate content to nature

▼ Interpersonal Presentations

• Divide presentation topics
• Have audience interact with others
• Include audience participation
• Relate content to personal relationships
• Use a volunteer

▼ Intrapersonal Presentations

• Have audience write about learnings
• Relate content to feelings/ emotions
• Relate content to personal lives
• Use reflection time

Another form of teacher evaluation is product evaluation. Not all, but most projects will result in a final product. For cooperative projects, each student turns in his or her own contributions, or the project is designed so individual effort can be identified.

Peer Evaluation

Students can evaluate each other's projects. Peer evaluations are helpful information to students presenting their projects. Students can find out what peers learned, what they want to learn more about, what they liked, what they didn't understand, and how they think the project or presentation could be improved. Peers can also evaluate each other, but these evaluations should not feed into a student's individual grade. On page 13.27 there is an MI Project Peer Evaluation Form students can use to evaluate each other's projects.

Self-Evaluation

Self-evaluation is an excellent way to have students reflect on their projects and the presentation of their projects. It is also a terrific intrapersonal exercise that helps improve projects, presentations and contributes to personal development. After their presentations, when peers are filling out their evaluations, students can complete their own self-evaluation. See MI Project Self-Evaluation Form on page 13.28.

If presentations are videotaped, a useful self-evaluation technique is to have students view and critique their own presentation.

MI Theme Units

Thematic learning or integrated instruction integrates the curriculum around a central theme. Whether the theme be Apples, the Zoo, or anything in between, the content of the subject areas mirror the theme being studied. Instruction in math, language arts, science and social studies reflect the theme. Connections are made wherever possible between the theme and the subject areas.

The philosophy of integrated instruction is that by making learning integrated, the instruction builds connections for students and makes learning more meaningful. Instead of learning discrete facts, students can connect what they are learning to the larger whole. When learning is grounded in a meaningful context, students can see the rationale for learning what is being taught. Students build bridges between prior knowledge and experiences and new information and skills, and discover how the different curricular areas are intricately interwoven.

Thematic learning is compatible with current research on brain physiology. In his book, *Brain-Based Learning*, Jensen writes:

> The greater the number of associations that your brain elicits, the more firmly the information is "woven in" neurologically. This means it has more than simply a larger quantity of meanings, but it also has more associations and depth per meaning (Jensen, 1996).

Thus, grounding learning in a contextual framework builds not only greater connections among the content, but also gives the content deeper meaning.

MI Project
Peer Evaluation Form

Project Name _____

Project By_____

Evaluated By_____ Date _____

• **Overall Rating:**   1   2   3   4   5   6   7   8   9   10

• **I learned…**

• **I want to know more about…**

• **I liked…**

• **I didn't understand…**

• **Suggestions for improvement…**

MI Project
Self-Evaluation Form

Name _____ Date _____

Project _____

Teammates _____

• **Overall Rating:**   1   2   3   4   5   6   7   8   9   10

• **I learned…**

• **I want to know more about…**

• **I liked…**

• **I didn't understand…**

• **Suggestions for improvement…**

In planning MI theme units, a conscious effort is made to integrate the intelligences in the learning. Thomas Armstrong eloquently summarizes the integration of multiple intelligences with thematic instruction:

> Themes cut through traditional curricular boundaries, weave together subjects and skills that are found naturally in life, and provide students with opportunities to use their multiple intelligences in practical ways (Armstrong, 1994).

Let's return to our Columbus example. An MI lesson, MI centers, or an MI project based on Columbus is not an isolated event. Columbus is one of the many subtopics relating to our greater theme, Discovery. Students integrate their intelligences and the subject areas as they learn about a topic which is related to a larger conceptual network. With MI theme units, we build connections for students and make learning meaningful and contextual.

Planning an MI theme unit involves coordinating the presentation of MI lessons, centers and projects to revolve around the central theme. As we plan MI theme units, we use the following four general steps: 1) Select Theme; 2) Brainstorm Related Topics; 3) Sequence Topics; 4) Plan MI Lessons, Centers and Projects. Let's plan an MI theme unit together, as an example.

1. Select Theme

The effectiveness of MI theme units depends largely on the theme. A good theme must be general enough to allow for explorations across the subject areas and intelligences. If the theme is too specific, it is more difficult to make connections to the disciplines and intelligences. We can use the school's chosen MI theme, come up with our own, or use a democratic approach — have students brainstorm themes, and select their favorite. Some common themes are provided on the MI Theme Ideas on page 13.30. Notice, some themes are more general, and allow for broader connections. Our theme of Discovery is a nice broad theme that allows for exploration in many possible directions.

In his book, *The Multiple Intelligences Handbook*, Bruce Campbell (1994) outlines a number of theme topics and provides activities across the intelligences for each theme.

2. Brainstorm Related Topics

The next step is to brainstorm relevant, related topics. A helpful way to brainstorm related topics is to write the theme in the center of a sheet of paper, then make a mind map of related ideas radiating out of the central theme. We can also get the class involved by writing the theme in the center of the chalkboard. We have students or teams brainstorm related topics.

One strong approach to mind mapping ideas for a theme unit is to write the disciplines and/or intelligences around the central theme, then brainstorm ideas related to theme in each intelligence or subject area. In doing this, we stretch the content into most, if not all, intelligences and subject areas, promoting a balanced representation of the content and intelligences. The resulting mind map serves as a visual outline for students, graphically depicting the content connections.

Continuing with our Discovery example, we may write "Discovery" in the center of the page or chalkboard. Around the theme

MI Theme Ideas

(From A to Z)

Air
Animals
Apples
Art
Authors
Autumn
Balloons
Beaches
Bears
Birds
Birthdays
Bodies
Books
Careers
Celebrations
Challenges
Changes
Christmas
Circus
Clothes
Colors
Community
Computers
Colonial Times
Cooking
Cooperation
Coral Reefs
Country
Crafts
Creepy Crawlies
Cultures
Democracy
Dinosaurs
Discovery
Dragons
Ecology
Emotions

Endangered Species
Energy
Environment
Explorers
Fairy Tales
Fall
Fantasy
Families
Famous People
Farms
Folktales
Food
Friendship
Games
Growth
Habitats
Health
Holidays
Insects
Internet
Invention
Lakes
Language
Literature
Love
Movement
Music
Mythology
Native Americans
Nature
Neighborhood
Numbers
Nursery Rhymes
Oceans
Olympics

Penguins
People
Pets
Planets
Plants
Popcorn
Pumpkins
Rainforest
Recycling
Renaissance
Rivers
Rocks
Safety
School
Science
Seas
Seasons
Self-Esteem
Senses
Shapes
Spiders
Spring
Space
Sports
Stars
Summer
Technology
Teddy Bears
Television
Thanksgiving
Tide Pools
Transportation
Toys
Water
Weather
Wild West
Winter
Zoo

MI Theme Unit Mind Map

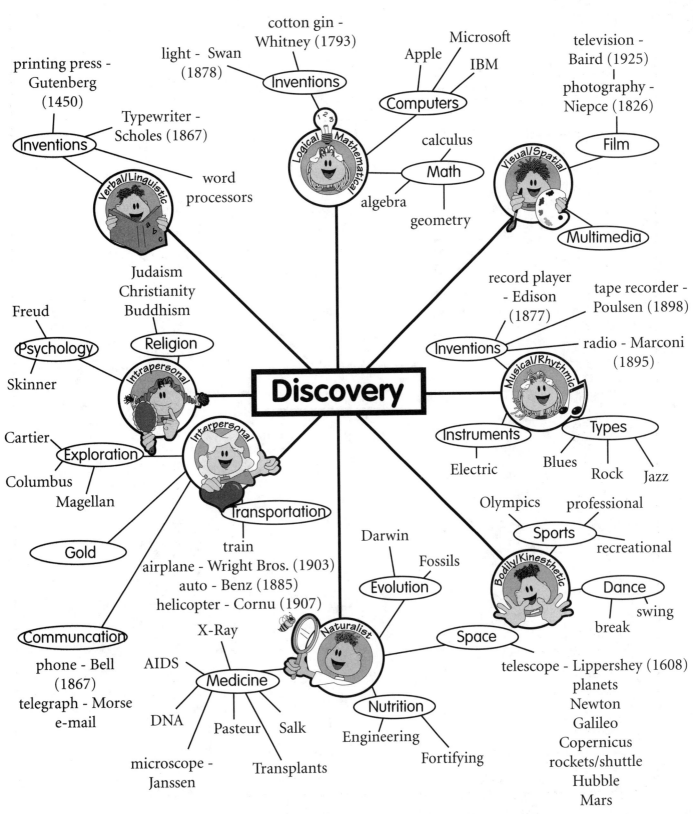

MI Theme Unit Mind Map

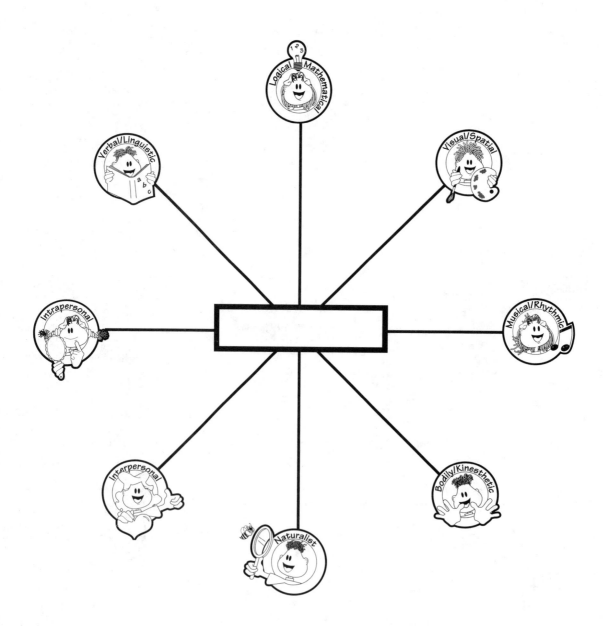

we write the eight intelligences. For the naturalist intelligence, we may brainstorm discoveries in science and nature such as: discoveries in medicine, space, nutrition, evolution. For the interpersonal subtopic, we may generate ideas on discoveries in communication, transportation and exploration. Columbus' discovery of America, Copernicus' heliocentric discovery, Edison's invention of the phonograph See MI Theme Unit Mind Map on page 13.31. A blank blackline master is provided on page 13.32.

How many related topics we cover in the theme depends again on our objectives. If the theme is very specific, we can use it for a week; if the theme is general and allows connections across the intelligences and disciplines, we might explore it for several weeks, months, or even the entire school year.

3. Sequence Topics

Once we have a list of topics we want to address, we create a sequential order for students to explore them. Alternatively, engage students in sequencing the events for study. Some topics may be developmentally or historically sequential. For example, we may decide to study discoveries in space well after we learn about Columbus. We will study the Gold Rush somewhere between.

One inherent limitation of organizing curriculum thematically is the potential lack of sequence. If we organize instruction thematically rather than sequentially or developmentally, we must be sure to ground events and topics historically and maintain developmental continuity; students need to see where events fit in and how the concepts they are studying relate to the big picture as well as to each other. Whether teaching language arts, science, math, the visual/spatial intelligence, or musical/rhythmic intelligence, learning is developmental; concepts build on concepts. As we plan our MI theme units, sequencing our MI lessons, projects, and centers is an important consideration.

4. Plan MI Lessons, Projects and Centers

After determining an appropriate sequence of learning topics, it is time to plan how students will actually receive and interact with the content. Will we direct students through MI lessons? Can students do a project addressing the content and the intelligences? Can we set up centers based on the theme, focusing on each intelligence?

Let's go back to our Discovery theme unit. Let's say the first topic we decide to study is Exploration. Columbus is our first subtopic. We choose to do an MI lesson with activities that span the range of intelligences. For the Gold Rush, we have students visit MI centers, creating celebration songs of discovering gold at the Beethoven center (musical/rhythmic), and making and following maps of hidden gold at the da Vinci center (visual/spatial). When it is time to study space, we feel a project would be a wonderful way for students to explore space. We have students research planets in teams, make models of the solar system, and share their learning with classmates.

The MI Weekly Planner on page 13.34 is a helpful tool for organizing MI lessons, projects and centers. We may use it to integrate the multiple intelligences in our class every day of the week! As we teach MI theme units, we integrate not only the curriculum and the intelligences, but our

MI Weekly Plan

Theme/Topic_____ Date_____

Intelligence	MON	TUES	WED	THURS	FRI
Verbal/Linguistic					
Logical/Mathematical					
Visual/Spatial					
Musical/Rhythmic					
Bodily/Kinesthetic					
Naturalist					
Interpersonal					
Intrapersonal					

approaches to teaching. The more ways we teach, the more students we reach, and the more ways we reach each.

Summary

MI lessons, centers, projects, and theme units spring from one simple idea: We can teach any content in a number of ways. As we expand our teaching repertoire and use a variety of MI lessons, centers and projects, teaching becomes more exciting for us and more fun and meaningful for our students. Students learn to connect the curriculum with real-world experiences and participate in intrinsically motivating activities that match their intelligences profile and stretch them in all intelligences.

As you plan and present your MI lessons, centers and projects, don't forget to take some time to reflect. Keep your plans and reflections in a three-ring binder. In no time, you will have a storehouse of MI lessons, centers, and projects you can build on and your students can enjoy every year!

References

Armstrong, T. *Multiple Intelligences in the Classroom.* Alexandria, VA: Association for Supervision and Curriculum Development, 1994.

Campbell, B. *The Multiple Intelligences Handbook. Lesson Plans and More...Stanwood*, WA: Campbell & Assoc., Inc., 1994.

Checkley, K. *The first seven...and the eighth: a conversation with Howard Gardner.* **Educational Leadership**, 1997, *55(1)*, 10.

Gentile, R. J. *Summary and Analysis of Madeline Hunter's Essential Elements of Instruction and Supervision.* Oxford, OH: National Staff Development Council, 1988.

Jensen, E. *Brain-Based Learning.* Del Mar, CA: Turning Point Publishing, 1996.

Kagan, S. *Group grades miss the mark.* **Educational Leadership**, 1995, *52(8)*, 68-71.

Creating the MI Classroom

Scratch the green rind of a sapling, or wantonly twist it in the soil, and a scarred or crooked oak will tell of the act for centuries to come. So it is with the teachings of youth, which make impressions on the mind and heart that are to last forever.
— *Henri Frederic Amiel, 1821-1881*

We, as teachers, have a tremendous responsibility. For the entire school year, we are in charge of dozens of students, each of which is entirely unique. Students come to us from diverse backgrounds, with varied experiences, with their own sets of beliefs and expectations, and with a unique profile of intelligences. We make countless decisions every day. Some decisions seem relatively small, like deciding what indoor activity to play with the class on a rainy day. Some decisions are bigger, like deciding whether to have students work independently or cooperatively on a project.

The MI classroom is an environment that matches, stretches, and celebrates all intelligences; it a fun, lively environment where all students may succeed.

Classroom decisions, big and small affect many students, often in profound ways. One student may be bored to death playing hangman on rainy day; he would much rather draw on the chalkboard than play some silly word game. The choice to work cooperatively on a project may be the impetus for tremendous excitement and involvement for a student who would otherwise be completely uninterested in a project. Others would prefer to work alone.

It is not always easy to tell how decisions we make are going to affect each student. However, we can be sure some big decisions we make regarding the curriculum, pedagogy, and class atmosphere will affect all students and their experiences with us for the year — some for a lifetime.

Every day we are faced with a multitude of decisions: What do we teach? How do we teach it? How do we arrange the classroom environment? What resources do we make available to students? How do we want students to feel in our class? What activities will allow students to know and become accepted by their classmates? These decisions are not to be taken lightly; what we do in our classroom profoundly impacts our students. Of course, we can always choose not to make a conscious decision, but we are still effectively making choices nonetheless.

One big decision we make that positively impacts our students is the decision to transform our classroom into an MI classroom. Deciding to create a multiple-intelligences friendly classroom environment — matching, stretching, and celebrating MI —is the decision to give our students a gift for life. We match MI to make learning accessible to all students of all learning styles and intelligences (see Chapters 7 and 8); we stretch MI to foster development of all intelligences in all of our students (see Chapters 9 and 10); and we celebrate MI to honor the uniqueness of each student and celebrate our shared diversity (see Chapters 11 and 12).

There are many other contextual and environmental changes we make in the class-room to transform it into an MI-friendly classroom. We bring in plants and flowers to create a more motivating classroom environment for the naturalist and use them to teach about flora and fauna — to develop the naturalist intelligence in all students. We set up an Artist Colony where students go to paint, draw or sculpt. We take our students on a field trip to a local courthouse and study how the judge uses his logical/mathematical intelligence to reach a verdict. We play with music software to create original scores and develop the musical/rhythmic intelligence. We bring in rich instructional materials and games to stimulate the multiple intelligences.

In this chapter, we look at wide array of ideas to create a motivating and meaningful MI classroom including: setting up stations or centers to develop the intelligences; decorating the classroom to make it a more MI-friendly environment; going on field trips to experience MI in action; and bringing in a rich array of classroom resources, games and computer software to stimulate the multiple intelligences.

MI Stations and Centers

One way to create an MI classroom is to set up MI stations. An MI station is a physical location in the classroom where students go to engage one or more of their intelligences. Each station has a distinct look and feel, and usually its own set of resources related to the intelligence.

Stations can be integrated well with MI centers. When it is center time, students go to one of the stations in the classroom and work on an assigned task or are free to explore the resources at the station. However, we don't need to use centers to establish MI stations in the class. We can have students visit stations while working on their projects or as a free-choice activity.

Let's look at a sample MI station: The Shop. The Shop is one of the stations we may set up to develop students' bodily/kinesthetic intelligence. The idea behind The Shop is to give students hands-on experience with assembly, disassembly and general tinkering. The Shop is constructed by students as a project in a corner of the classroom. There is a colorful sign over the cardboard door that says, "Our Shop." When we step inside, we find students working on different tasks. One student is sitting on the floor, fixing a broken tape recorder. Two students are at a desk, set up as an improvisational workbench, taking apart an old toaster with screwdrivers and a crescent wrench.

In one corner of The Shop, there is a sign that says "Tools." Underneath the sign there is a toolbox filled with screwdrivers, pliers, wrenches. Right next to the toolbox there is a storage case labeled "Materials" filled with: tape, glue, nuts, bolts, screws, wires, washers. There are two plastic milk cases on the floor labeled, "Electrical," and "Mechanical." Inside the cases we find: toasters, radios, phones, videocassette recorders, cameras, blenders, clocks, egg beaters, rainbirds, can openers, and mechanical toys.

At The Shop, students develop one facet of their bodily/kinesthetic intelligence —

fine motor skills. They also develop their logical/mathematical and visual/spatial intelligences as they discover the logic behind the construction of the clock and rainbird and explore the arrangement of parts. Students are acquiring valuable life skills through hands-on engagement with the content.

The Shop is just one of the many stations we can set up in the classroom. Unfortunately, extra space is at a premium inside the MI classroom. For that reason, we do not necessarily set up all the bodily/kinesthetic stations at once. After students have all had experiences in The Shop, we next set up the Theatre, the Dance Studio, or the Model Shop to develop other facets of the bodily/kinesthetic intelligence.

Establishing MI stations in the classroom does not have to be expensive or time consuming. Students can work in teams to design and create each station. Materials for each station can be donated, brought in by students, or can be checked out from the school's stockpile of MI resources (see Chapter 15: Creating the MI School).

For MI station and center ideas for each intelligence, see MI Stations and Centers on pages 14.4 -14.10.

Stations & Centers
To Create a Word Smart Environment

▼ The Library

The Library is an in-class library that shelves a wide variety of books including literature books, comic books, fairy tales. The books are organized by type and topics. Students can browse The Library at their leisure and check out books of interest, or they may go to the Library to do research for a project or paper. Of course, students may always go the school library if they don't find what they are looking for in the class library. School library resources on a theme may be brought into the classroom for the duration of the theme.

▼ The Periodical Area

Newspapers and magazines can be part of the Library or in a separate Periodical Area. In the Periodical Area, the magazines and newspapers are for reference, not to be cut up by students for art projects. For art projects, students use the magazines in the Image Gallery. Students visit the Periodical Area to do research, write current events, and to read about local and international events.

▼ The Reference Area

Reference books like dictionaries, thesauruses, encyclopedias, and almanacs can be part of the Library or in a separate Reference Area. Students visit the Reference Area to do research for papers and projects.

▼ The Reading Zone

The Reading Zone is a quiet, comfortable area, preferably next to the Library. A couch, rug and pillows create a nice area for students to silently browse the books in the Library. There is no talking in the Reading Zone. As a center, students go to The Reading Zone to do their reading assignment.

▼ The Listening Bar

The Listening Bar houses literature books, poems, present and historical speakers on cassette tapes and/or CD's. Students visit the Listening Bar, put on their headphones and hit play. The Listening Bar can be integrated with musical selections of different times and cultures, depending on the class theme or unit.

▼ The Writer's Corner

Create a quiet area in the classroom where students can go to write stories, poems, essays, songs. The Writer's Corner has an abundant supply of writing paper of all sizes and shapes and a variety of writing utensils including: pens, pencils, crayons, markers. One or more computers with word processing software and a printer is a nice addition to the Writer's Corner. Alternative names: Author's Alley, Steinbeck, Hemingway, or Austen Center.

▼ The Lounge

The Lounge is where students go to quietly speak to a partner, plan a project as a team, debate an issue or discuss their ever-important social issues. Alternative name: The Coffee House.

Stations & Centers
To Create a Math/Logic Smart Environment

▼ Math World

In Math World there a wealth of mathematical resources for students to manipulate, explore, build answers and build understanding. Some resources include: calculators, base 10 and fraction manipulatives, Cuisenaire rods, geoboards. As a center, students visit Math World to solve their math problems or explore mathematical concepts. Alternative names: Computation Center, Einstein Center, Numbers Nook.

▼ Measurement Center

Students go to the Measurement Center to work on a range of measurement tasks. At the center there are rulers, yardsticks, scales, cups, gallons, an other measurement materials. The Measurement Center can be integrated with Math World.

▼ The Think Tank

At the Think Tank, students put on their thinking caps and go to work on their critical or creative thinking. At the Think Tank, there are task cards with challenging problems for students to work on, brain-breaking logic puzzles for students to solve, riddles, mysteries, plexers, brain teasers and mind joggers.

▼ Sequencing Center

At the Sequencing Center, students are given the task of sequencing events, dates steps.

▼ The Lab

Students put on their white lab coats and goggles as they enter the Lab. At this science station, students find an array of hands-on science materials to freely explore. Alternatively, students lead themselves through step-by-step science experiments. Materials at the Lab include: recording sheets, beakers, safety goggles, lab coats, chemicals, magnets. Alternative names: Marie Curie Center, Science Lab, Mad Scientist.

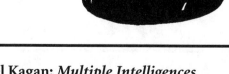

Stations & Centers
To Create an Art/Space Smart Environment

▼ The Artist Colony

Students visit the Artist Colony to work on paintings, drawings, sculptures and other art projects. In the Colony, there are lots of materials for all types of creative projects including: paper, crayons, paints, brushes, scissors, glue, glitter. The Colony is sure to get messy, so covering the floor with old carpet, drop cloths or newspapers is a must. The Colony in the primary class has aprons youngsters can wear to make sure they don't get too covered with paint, glue, or clay. The Colony is near the sink so students can easily clean up after creating their masterpieces.

▼ The Viewing Station

At the Viewing Station, students get to "see" what they are learning about. There is a television, VCR, slide projector and picture books. Students watch videos on the content, view slides, and flip through visual images. Alternative names: Movie Theater, Learning Channel, Siskel and Ebert Center.

▼ The Image Gallery

In the Gallery, students find old magazines of all types that have pictures and text they can cut out to use for their collages, montages, photo essays, books, and assorted projects. The image gallery also has lots of clip art of all types. Students pick out the art they want to use, photocopy it, and can then cut and paste it for projects. The original clip art stays in the Gallery for other students to use.

▼ Pattern World

In Pattern World, there are geometric shapes, blocks, tessellations, tangrams, and tiles of all colors and sizes. Students are free to create their own patterns and pictures with their pieces or may match determined designs or a partner's arrangement. Alternative name: M. C. Escher Center.

▼ The Space Station

At the Space Station students develop their spatial awareness skills with maps, charts, graphs, visual puzzles, pictures, 3D materials.

▼ The Electric Artist

A computer loaded with illustration, paint, drawing, and 3D rendering software makes up the Electric Artist station or center. Students work individually or in small teams to hone their visual/spatial skills at the computer. A color printer is a great way to share students' work with the class.

▼ Architect's Office

In the Architect's Office, students draft blueprints and build models. Inside, students find rulers, drafting triangles, T-squares, blocks, glue, foam board and other supplies for creative constructions.

Stations & Centers
To Create a Music Smart Environment

▼ The Music Library

Students go to the Music Library, pick out a record, tape, or CD. They put it in the player, put on their headphones and kick back and enjoy the music, fill out a worksheet in response to the music, draw a picture how it makes them feel, create a movement or dance for the song, or answer questions regarding the composition. Music from different times and cultures expands students' musical horizons and promotes an appreciation of diversity. Alternative names: Listening Bar, Music Store, Jukebox.

▼ The Symphony Station

Instruments to pluck, strum, ring, bang and blow are all found at the Symphony Station. Students work independently or in small bands to make their musical compositions. The noise may be a distraction (especially the sometimes cacophonous sounds from the musical neophyte) for other students. It is recommended that the Symphony Station is "soundproofed" with foam or even conducted outside the classroom. Alternative names: Beethoven, Mozart Center.

▼ The Recording Studio

When students have a rap, cheer, chant, song or instrumental they are ready to record, they go to the Studio. At the Studio, there is a tape recorder. Students insert their own blank tape, hit record and go to town. Students listen to their tapes, analyze them, and try again to get the sound they're looking for.

▼ Electric Musician

In the 70s it was disco. In the 80s it was rock 'n' roll, in the 90s it was alternative. What's the sound of the future? Those in-the-know predict that the next wave of music for the young generation will be "electronica." Electronica is largely synthesized, computer-generated sounds and rhythms. Much of today's music composition, sound effects and audio mastering is being done digitally. In the Electric Musician station, students compose futuristic sounds, play with the classics, tinker with sound effects, and create original songs with the aid of the computer. Alternative names: Music Machine, Digital Tunes.

Stations & Centers
To Create a Body Smart Environment

▼ The Dance Studio

At the Studio, students go to learn about dances of different times and cultures. Students create their own expressive dance movements to music or content, and choreograph a ballet or presentation. Alternative names: Fred and Ginger Center, Dance Floor.

▼ The Theater

Students go to the Theater to rehearse their skits or plays, and put on dramatic presentations and shows. At the Theater, there is a closet or box filled with costumes: shoes, hats, dresses, wigs, coats, ties, make-up; and props: briefcase, telephone, chairs, table, dishes. A mirror is a must for the Theater. A videocassette recorder is set up on a tripod next to the Theater so students can pop in their tape and hit record to capture their comedies and dramas. Alternative names: The Stage, The Playhouse, Shakespeare Center, Auditorium.

▼ Supply Room

The Supply Room is a box or closet in the classroom which houses all the sports and games equipment for students to check out for breaks, recess, snacks. The Supply Room might include: jump ropes, balls, nets, paddles, rackets, bases.

▼ Hands-On Center

There is a world of tactile experiences for students at the Hands-On Center. Students guess mystery items based on feel, build extravagant creations by hand, and explore spelling, math, and science kinesthetically. At the Hands-On Center, students work with craft materials, construction materials, letter and number manipulatives.

▼ The Shop

The Shop is where students go to do their assembly, disassembly and general tinkering. At the Shop there is an assortment of tools like: screwdrivers, pliers, wrenches; an assortment of building materials like: tape, glue, nuts, bolts, screws, wood, metal, wires, washers; and an assortment of electrical and mechanical machines like: toasters, radios, phones, camcorders, cameras, televisions, clocks, nut crackers, can openers. At the Shop you may find two students working together, taking apart a broken tape recorder, attempting to figure out how it works.

Stations & Centers
To Create a Nature Smart Environment

▼ The Zoo

Students go to the classroom zoo to learn about the animals. The Zoo can have real class pets, animal figures, and zoo books or animal reference cards describing the animals in their natural habitat. Students take turns feeding and caring for class pets. Some low-maintenance, inexpensive class pets include: hamsters, turtles, snakes, lizards, ants.

▼ Aquarium

A classroom aquarium is a wonderful way for students to explore the underwater world. A freshwater aquarium is much easier to set up and maintain than a marine aquarium. However, marine aquariums and reef tanks are unsurpassed in beauty and interest. Students learn about the myriad underwater species and their peculiarities, territoriality, biological and mechanical filtration, fish stress, disease, chemical processes, testing water. No aquarium is complete without a few books on maintenance and species selection.

▼ The Observation Station

At the Observation Station, there are a number of observational tools: binoculars, telescope, magnifying glasses, microscopes, cameras; and a number of natural items to observe like plants, animals, rocks, fossils, soil samples, leaves. Record sheets and journals allow students to write down interesting observations. Alternative name: Darwin, Muir, Goodall Center.

▼ The Classification Station

A student enters the Classification Station and picks out a large jar of buttons. She pours the buttons on the floor and starts making observations about size, shape, color, number of holes. She devises a plan and begins to sort the buttons into jars. She comes across an new button that doesn't fit the plan and she reconceptualizes the plan and starts sorting again. Other items to classify at the Classification Station include: shells, rocks, leafs, nuts, bolts, pasta, beans, minerals, insect pictures, dried flowers.

▼ The Garden

In the Garden, students plant their own flowers, vegetables, and herbs. Students record the growth stages of the various plant life. They water and maintain their plants. Supplies in the Garden include: pots, fertilizer, hand shovels, water pails, seeds.

▼ Nature Station

Entire television channels are dedicated to the species of animals with whom we share this planet. Recording and cataloging shows is a fantastic way to share the joy of the natural world with students. Students sit down at the Nature Station, put in a video of interest or one related to a topic of study, and hit play. Students take notes for their projects or papers.

Stations & Centers

To Create a People Smart Environment

▼ The Lounge

The Lounge is in a cozy corner of the classroom where students can talk quietly without disturbing others. There are two small comfortable couches seated across from each other, pillows are placed in a small circle, or around a circular table. Students sit down in the Lounge and are physically face-to-face to work together to plan projects, discuss a topic, debate an issue, rehearse a presentation. Alternative name: Coffee House, Chat Room.

▼ The Game Room

The Game Room is where students go to play together. In the Game Room, there is a shelf with many different types of games, and table or floor space for students to play. The shelves hold a wide variety of board games, puzzles, challenges across the intelligences. Pairs or small groups select a game from the shelf, play and return it to the shelf when done. Students learn to interact in a fun, playful way as they develop their multiple intelligences. Students keep Game Journals to reflect on what they learned about themselves or others while playing games.

Stations & Centers

To Create a Self Smart Environment

▼ The Concentration Station

Students go to the Concentration Station to be alone with their work or their thoughts. The Concentration Station is strategically located in the classroom to be as distraction-free as possible. It is on the opposite side of the room from the Lounge. At the Concentration Station, there are earplugs students can put on to minimize distractions even more, and little cubicles so students can be completely alone. Students can read silently, write in their diaries, explore their feelings, reflect on their learning, plan their homework, set goals for learning, or even meditate.

MI Classroom Decorations

A plain classroom with bare walls does nothing to stimulate or celebrate the intelligences. It is amazing what a little decoration can do for the classroom. A little paint here, some plants over here, some posters up here, a bulletin board there, and a banner over there can truly make the classroom come alive!

But decorating the MI classroom is more than just making it aesthetically pleasing and more interesting. We decorate the MI classroom to make it an intelligence-friendly environment, celebrating the multiple intelligences and making connections to the content. We celebrate the logical/mathematical intelligence with a poster of young Einstein standing in front of a chalkboard saying, "Do not worry about your difficulties in mathematics; I can assure you mine are still greater."

We match the intelligence of students strong in nature smarts and stretch our other students in the naturalist intelligence with a poster that identifies various types of spiders: black widow, silk spider, spiny-bodied spider, fisher spider, house spider, tarantula, garden spider, jumping spider.

A student strong in the intrapersonal intelligence studies the How Do You Feel Today? poster and says to herself, "I felt *guilty* for not preparing as much as I would have liked to for our presentation, but I was *surprised* how well we did, and *excited* when we watched our video."

In the MI classroom, we frequently change the classroom environment to provide novel stimuli. The environment never becomes stagnant. There are always new displays to check out, a new poster to study, a new masterpiece to admire. Sounds neat, but doesn't the classroom become a distraction for learning? No! In the MI class, the classroom is part of the content of learning.

Is all this decorating expensive and time consuming? No! It doesn't have to be. Say we want to celebrate the verbal/linguistic intelligence in our class. We decide some posters on some famous authors and poets would be a nice way to validate linguistic skills and teach students about the accomplishments of some famous folks. We don't have to go to the local teacher supply store. Who knows, they might not have what we're looking for anyway. As a cooperative MI project, we assign each team a famous author or poet, and have them make posters. Students learn about the authors and poets as they research them to create their posters. They use their interpersonal skills as they coordinate efforts to create the poster, their verbal/linguistic skills to write the copy for the poster, and their visual/spatial skills to design the "look" and create graphics.

In the class, we have thirty sets of helping hands that would love to decorate their own environment and learn valuable skills in the process. For purchased decorations, we can team up with other teachers to share the expense and take turns with bulletin boards, charts, displays.

For ways to decorate the MI classroom to make it intelligences-friendly, see Classroom Decorations, pages 14.12 - 14.19.

Classroom Decorations
For a Word Smart Environment

▼ The Writing Process

A poster or chart of the Writing Process describes or depicts the steps of the writing process: prewriting, writing, proofing/editing, conferring/rewriting, publishing.

▼ Proofreader's Marks

Students refer to the Proofreader's Marks poster to proofread their own and classmates' writing. Includes marks for: new paragraph, close up space, capitalize, take out word(s), add, reverse letters or words, insert a space, change word(s), add a period, move word(s), add punctuation.

▼ The 10 Steps to Become a Better Writer (or Reader)

This is a cute poster students can make that lists the 10 steps to become a better writer or reader. The ten steps for the writer poster may look like: 1. Write! 2. Write Some More! 3. Write! 4. Write About Anything! 5. Write! 6. Write About Everything! 7. Write! 8. Write Some More! 9. Write! Write! Write! 10. Write!

▼ Parts of Speech

Define the parts of speech and give samples of each: noun, verb, adjective, interjection, preposition, adverb, conjunction, pronoun.

▼ Foreign Language

Display posters in Spanish, French, German, Italian. Label classroom items in a foreign language.

▼ Types of Writing

Have students make a chart listing the different types of writing or a chart on each: Sensory/Descriptive, Imaginative/Narrative, Practical/Informative, Analytical/Expository.

▼ Phonics

Display sight words, vowels, consonants, digraphs.

▼ Punctuation Rules

Create a reference chart for: period, comma, question mark, exclamation mark, apostrophe, quotation marks.

▼ The Alphabet

Post an alphabet with manuscript and cursive letters and pictures for younger students.

▼ Famous Writers

Celebrate famous writers and their works with posters — a great project for students.

▼ Types of Poetry

Define the types of poetry frequently used, and provide samples of each: couplet, haiku, limerick, cinquain, quatrain, acrostic, sonnet.

▼ Letter Diagram

Illustrate the parts of friendly and formal letters.

▼ Book Reports

Display students' book reports where all students can read about different books, or create a book report binder.

Classroom Decorations
To Create a Math/Logic Smart Environment

▼ Tessellations
Posters are available on M. C. Escher's work with tessellations. Tessellations are also a fun mathematical and artistic activity for students.

▼ Shapes
Decorate the room with shapes of all colors and sizes for younger students.

▼ Fractals
Posters with colorful fractals are available as well as computer software for students to develop their own beautiful fractal designs (e.g. Kai's Powertools for Adobe Photoshop).

▼ Number Chart
For younger students, a number chart with physical objects is most helpful. For the number three, there are three buttons, for four, four beans. A one hundred number chart is helpful for the middle grades. A one million number chart with tiny dots representing ones illustrates the grandness of one million.

▼ Multiplication Chart
Multiplication charts usually have 1-9 on the vertical and horizontal axis and the product where the two numbers intersect. The 28 Multiplication Facts is a poster that can be easily made that illustrates for students there are only 28 facts students need to know for multiplication by deleting the ones, twos and the duplicates (e.g. 7 x 9 = 9 x 7).

▼ Measurement Conversion Charts
Charts can have distance conversions: inches, feet, yards, miles, millimeters, centimeters, meters, kilometers, miles; or capacity conversions: cup, quart, gallon, pint, liter; or weight: gram, kilogram, pound, ounce, ton.

▼ Money
Post the names and values of coins and bills for younger students. For older students, display foreign currency with conversion rates for math problems.

▼ Fractions
Create posters with fraction pieces or pizzas to illustrate fraction concepts.

▼ Roman Numerals
Make a poster with the Roman numerals and the rules for making numbers: I = 1, V = 5, X = 10, L = 50, C = 100, D = 500, M = 1,000.

▼ Telling Time
Design a large clock with moveable hands to teach time. Another poster may have many small clocks showing the time.

▼ Place Value
Base 10 blocks or manipulatives (cubes 1,000, flats 100, rods 10, units 1) can be used to show place value. Add a decimal to show decimal values.

▼ Steps to Problem Solving
Describe the steps to multiply, divide, subtract, and to approach and solve word problems.

Classroom Decorations
For an Art/Space Smart Environment

▼ Famous Artists

Celebrate the masters and appreciate their masterpieces with posters on their famous works. Van Gogh, Monet, Escher, Geddes are all favorites available inexpensively at most art supply stores. The more variety in form, content, style and period, the better. Artwork may be linked to the theme or era for greater integration.

▼ Student Masterpieces

Students proudly display their own artistic talents with drawings posted on the wall, sculptures on stands, and mobiles above their desks.

▼ Architecture

Share the aesthetics and spatial sense of architecture with students with models and posters of famous works like the Eiffel Tower, the Pantheon, the Colosseum, the Sistine Chapel, the Taj Mahal.

▼ Maps

Display local maps, state maps, maps of the United States, and a map of the world to promote students' spatial and geographical awareness. Use the maps as a bulletin board for Places We've Been, or Places We've Studied.

▼ Color Charts

Help students develop a sense of color with color wheels, value scales, and charts that name colors. Color charts are available at art supply stores. Free paint swatches are sometimes available at hardware or paint stores. Younger students can make their own color charts by writing the name of each color with the corresponding crayon or marker.

▼ Signs and Symbols

Have students make posters featuring the signs and symbols that communicate meaning: Men, women, mailbox, sports, bus, taxi, information, road signs, gas, food, high voltage, telephone, lodging, airplane, pedestrian crossing, school, money exchange, parking, no smoking, handicap, one way, baggage claim.

▼ Posters and Charts

Posters, diagrams, charts or anything that presents material in a visual format allows students to make visual connections.

Classroom Decorations
For a Music Smart Environment

▼ Musicians

Celebrate our rich musical heritage with posters or displays of famous musicians and their accomplishments — a great project for students to learn about musicians.

▼ Instruments

Display pictures, drawings, or actual instruments. Students independently or in teams can each make a miniposter of their favorite instrument, with a description of the instrument.

▼ Musical Expressions

Post a chart describing the Italian musical expressions and their translation: *presto* (very fast), *vivace* (lively, quick), *allegro* (fast), *moderato* (moderate), *andante* (walking pace), *adagio* (medium slow), *lento* (slow), *largo* (very slow) *fortissimo* (very loud). See page 10.30.

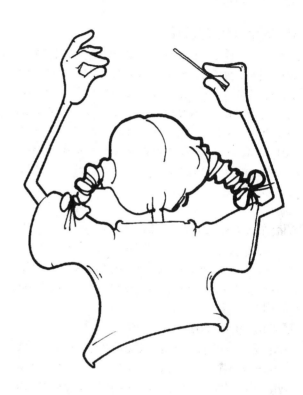

▼ Music Notes

Have students make a scale with the music notes (A, B, C, D, E, F, G) and their names for the bass and treble clefs. See page 10.33.

▼ Music Symbols

Chart the musical symbols and their translations. Some symbols include: whole note, dotted half note, half note, dotted quarter note, quarter note, eighth note, pair of eighth notes, sixteenth note, triplet, fermata, whole rest, half rest, quarter rest, eighth rest, sharp, flat, natural, treble clef, bass clef, repeat signs. See page 10.36.

Classroom Decorations
For a Body Smart Environment

▼ Sign Language

Post a chart with the sign language alphabet and easy sign language expressions for students to practice signing each other messages. See page 10.42.

▼ Anatomy Posters and Models

For young students, body smarts begins with naming the parts of the body. Older students can benefit from models the human skeleton, the digestive system, the circulatory system, the muscle system, and even more detailed anatomy.

▼ Health

The food pyramid and the four food groups are two popular posters regarding health and nutrition. Students can make their own posters by cutting out magazine clippings. The four food groups are: 1) fruits and vegetables, 2) breads and cereals, 3) meats, 4) dairy products. The USDA Food Guide Pyramid can be found on many store-bought food items including bread bags and cereal boxes.

▼ Athletic Teams

Pictures of favorite teams or game scores can be posted. One student can be selected as the classroom sportscaster to do the week in review.

▼ Famous Athletes

Pictures of gymnasts, football players, ice skaters, baseball players or dancers are posted in the class to celebrate atheleticism and great athletic achievements.

▼ Class Records

Post students' names who set class records or who are most improved on physical fitness measures such as pull ups, sit-ups, running times.

Classroom Decorations
For a Nature Smart Environment

▼ Plant Life

Bring in plants, flowers, hanging vines, trees, and palms into your classroom. The plantlife can all be gathered in the Garden or can be dispersed throughout the classroom to give it a more natural feel. Students can also grow herbs and vegetables in small containers on the window sills or outside. Assign students to care for different plants. Use the plants for science observations and experiments. Students can also make their own floral arrangements, leaf displays, and wreaths.

▼ Class Pets

Another way to liven up the classroom and make it a more naturalist-friendly environment is to have a class pet or pets. Ant farms are probably the easiest and least expensive classroom pets. Caterpillars that cocoon and turn into beautiful butterflies can be purchased inexpensively. An aquarium with fish, amphibians, snakes, lizards or turtles is a surefire class favorite. Students care for the class pet and make observations.

▼ Weather Reports

Have students make a daily weather-watching board where they can track and make predictions on the daily high and low temperatures, size and direction of the surf, high and low tides, inches of rainfall, speed and direction of wind, barometric pressure.

▼ Food Chain

Display students' food chain posters illustrating the intricate web of relationships.

▼ Rocks, Minerals & Seashells

Many posters are available that illustrate the various types of rocks, minerals, and seashells.

▼ Flora and Fauna

Posters with photographs of animals and plants can be posted in the classroom for students to become familiar with a variety of species. Post classification posters and posters with facts about plants and animals for: insects, spiders, vegetables, fruits, trees, flowers, invertebrates, fish, amphibians, reptiles, mammals, birds, leaves, ocean life, rainforest, desert, wetlands, arctic, coral reef, mountains.

▼ Environmental Issues

Help students become aware of issues concerning our environment with information or decorations regarding: recycling, pollution, hazardous waste, the ozone and the greenhouse effect, endangered species, rainforest depletion, development, water quality, landfill.

▼ Natural Phenomena

Post informational posters regarding our world's natural wonders or disasters like: earthquakes, floods, droughts, volcanoes, hurricanes, tornadoes (a great team project).

▼ Astronomy

Many great references and stunning photographs are available that pique students' natural curiosity of the wonders of the universe. Some popular posters include: planets, the sun, the moon, the space shuttle, constellations.

Classroom Decorations
For a People Smart Environment

▼ Cooperative Learning Rules

Post rules for cooperative learning. Five simple rules are: 1) Ask for and offer help; 2) Listen carefully and affirm my teammates; 3) Share my ideas and work; 4) Be prepared and give my best; 5) Be a good leader and follower.

▼ Class Rules

Class rules vary from class to class. Sometimes the rules are tied to a rigid discipline system; sometimes they are general guidelines. Here are some ideas you may consider as you or your students generate your own class rules: 1) Follow directions, 2) Respect others, 3) Listen carefully, 4) Do not disturb others, 4) Respect personal and school property, 5) Be kind with your words and actions.

▼ How to Treat Others

Have students brainstorm ideas for how to treat others and make their own poster. Some ideas are: Be polite; Take turns; Respect the ideas of others; Listen to what others have to say; Work together; Give others encouragement; Be helpful; Be caring; Use nice words and treat others nicely; Share; Care.

▼ Conflict Resolution

Conflicts come in all shapes and forms, so the more modes of resolving a conflict we have and can provide students, the better are our chances of resolving the conflict. A poster of the eight modes of conflict resolution is available: 1) Share; 2) Take turns; 3) Outside help; 4) Postpone; 5) Humor; 6) Avoid; 7) Chance; 8) Compromise.

▼ Motivational Sayings

Motivational sayings that promote interpersonal skills can be purchased or made by students. Some sayings include: TEAM-Together Everyone Achieves More; Take turns; If you want a friend, be a friend; There is no I in the word TEAM; Teamwork works; Together is better; All for one and one for all; No one can do everything, but everyone can do something; Practice random acts of kindness; We all smile in the same language; We are all one big family.

▼ Social Studies and Democracy

The United States flag and the pledge of allegiance are constants in American public education. Other decorations to honor democracy and our nation include: The Star Spangled Banner, Bill of Rights, the Preamble to the Constitution, the Emancipation Proclamation, The Gettysburg Address, Presidents, Branches of Government.

▼ Multiculturalism

Many publishers and educational manufacturers offer bulletin board sets, banners and posters celebrating diverse cultures with things like kids from around the world in their traditional clothing, greetings or sayings from around the world, flags from around the world, famous Latinos and Latinas, famous African Americans, Native Americans. A calendar posting multicultural holidays and celebrations is another way to promote multiculturalism.

Classroom Decorations

For a Self Smart Environment

▼ Motivational Sayings

Some sayings that motivate students and promote a positive self-concept include:

• I am unique
• I can do anything
• Believe in yourself
• There's no one like you
• Reach for the stars
• Every day is a new day
• Today is the first day of the rest of your life
• Don't settle for less than the best
• Be yourself
• You are in charge of your own destiny
• Life is what you put into it
• Follow your dreams
• Anything's possible
• Carpe Diem — Seize the day
• The sky's the limit
• Just do it.

Students can make up and decorate their own motivational posters.

▼ Emotions

Recognizing emotions in oneself and others is a major component of the emotional intelligence. Posters are available with students' displaying many different emotions. A favorite is one called, "How do you feel today?" which has the same illustrated boy doing all sorts of facial contortions expressing sixteen different emotions. There are also posters available, listing hundreds of emotions.

▼ Quote of the Day

A great way to get students thinking about themselves and their values is to write a quote on the chalkboard every day. Students can write their personal reactions in their journals. Excellent quotations are available in books of quotes and on the internet.

> Most of us miss out on life's big prizes. The Pulitzer. The Nobel. Oscars. Emmys. But we're all eligible for life's small pleasures. A pat on the back. A kiss behind the ear. A four-pound bass. A full moon. An empty parking space. A crackling fire. A great meal. A glorious sunset. Don't fret about copping life's grand awards. Enjoy its tiny delights. There are plenty for all of us.
> — United Technologies message

MI Field Trips

The biggest environmental change we can make is to actually take students outside of the classroom environment. We can take students on field trips to develop their intelligences in a natural setting and to witness how people use their intelligences in the real world. For example, to broaden students' musical/rhythmic horizons, we can take them to a symphony, musical, concert, festival, or an opera.

Students' parents are a great resource for field trips. Some have unique jobs they would love to share with the class. Instead of having the parent come to the class, have the class visit the parent at his or her place of work. Enlist parents' help as chaperones. Many parents are more than happy to take an active role in their child's education.

Field trips may be part of an apprenticeship or intern program. Students visit places in the community where they have an opportunity to work with a mentor or do work for the company in exchange for on-the-job experience. After the field trip students can sign up for the position if they are interested.

Schools and/or districts often compile field trip opportunities and related information. For a few field trip ideas across the intelligences, see MI Field Trips on pages 14.22 - 14.24 Field trip ideas are also listed from A to Z on page 14.25.

Field trips can break down class barriers. Multiple classes can go to the same place or can choose where they want to go. Students can go on field trips with their "Buddies," cross-age tutors.

MI Classroom Resources

The MI classroom is loaded with rich resources to stimulate the multiple intelligences. What better way to engage students' intelligences than to have students interact with a wide variety of materials associated with each intelligence? The more diverse the resources students manipulate and explore, the more we match and stretch students diverse intelligences.

For example, to fully develop students' visual/spatial intelligence, we give students opportunities to play with a wide range of instructional materials, each for developing a different facet of the visual/spatial intelligence. To develop artistic skills, students use brushes and paints to create paintings, pencils and paper to draw and sketch, clay to sculpt. Students use construction paper, scissors, markers and wiggly eyes to make creative crafts. Students build models with foam board and glue to develop their spatial intelligence. We use videos, posters and projectors to teach for and with students visual intelligence. Interacting with a wide range of resources nourishes the development of students' multiple intelligences.

Some resources that are wonderful for developing students' intelligences are games. Games? Yes, that's right, games. In Tetris, a computer game, geometric objects are dropped from the top of the screen. Students must rotate the shapes in space to fit together to clear the accumulating shapes at the bottom of the screen. In chess, students take turns moving their figures, each with its own movement pattern, along checkered gameboard in attempt to capture their opponent's king. With puzzles, students develop their analytic visual skills as they tune into the colors, patterns and shapes to successfully piece together the puzzle.

With each type of game, students develop a different aspect of their visual/spatial intelligence in a fun, challenging format. Some games provide fantastic, motivating learning opportunities that we can not easily replicate otherwise. This is not to say that we should have students come to class to play games all day. However, there is a place in the MI classroom for intelligence-building games.

Using the computer in the classroom is another wonderful way to develop students multiple intelligences in the classroom as well as to develop computer literacy skills — skills that are becoming increasingly in demand in today's technological society. In recent years there has been an explosion of computer software, across the intelligences. For the visual/spatial intelligence, there are programs for: illustration, 3D modeling and drawing, painting, collage, photo manipulation, drafting, page layout, presentation, mapping, cartooning. There are also tremendous collections of clip art and stock photography that can be used in projects and presentations.

Software is magnificent, but it can be costly. Don't despair, many computer software programs are available free over the internet. Some programs can also be shared among classes or housed in the computer lab for all students to access. With enough hard drive space, we can have a tremendous range of computer programs available for students to explore within the class and in the computer room.

On pages 14.26-14.32 there are checklists of classroom resources, games and computer software that may be used to develop the multiple intelligences. The checkboxes are provided to facilitate creating your own MI dream list or shopping list — but remember, shopping can be done by students and parents in their basements and garages. Of course, we don't need everything on these lists. These are just helpful ideas that list some of the many possibilities.

Summary

There are many things we can do to create the MI classroom to facilitate matching, stretching, and celebrating MI. Additionally, there are a number of environmental changes we can make within the classroom to transform the classroom into an MI-friendly environment. Such transformations include: establishing MI stations and centers within the classroom for students to visit and explore; decorating the classroom to activate the multiple intelligences; taking students on field trips to develop their smarts or to witness people using their smarts in a natural setting; and providing a rich array of instructional materials to develop the multiple facets of students' multiple intelligences.

MI Field Trips

Verbal/Linguistic

▼ The Library

Arrange to take students to a community library or local university library. Have the librarian give you a guided tour, and let students do some free exploration or give them assignments to find certain books.

▼ Publishing Company

Take students to a local magazine, newspaper or book publishing company. Have your guide outline the steps of what happens in the various stages from manuscript submission to distribution. Relate what happens in the publishing process to the writing process in the classroom.

Logical/Mathematical

▼ Courthouse

Millions of people were glued to the television throughout O. J. Simpson's "Trial of the Century." Will they find him guilty? Court cases can be riveting. A trip to the local courthouse is a great way for students to see our judicial system in action and learn about the logical decision-making skills lawyers and judges use so frequently.

▼ Observatory

Unlock the mysteries of the universe for your class with a trip to a local observatory. Observatories house large telescopes and other scientific equipment for students to explore. Many have wonderful educational programs established for field trips.

▼ Planetarium

Students are captivated as they sit in a dome room and watch the mysteries of the universe unfurl all around them.

Visual/Spatial

▼ Museum

Museums are a fantastic place to explore artworks of all sorts in a concentrated area. Many museums have educational programs specifically for teaching students about the artists and their works. Some museums even have places for students to create their own masterpieces.

▼ Advertising Agency

Advertisers are in the business of selling images. Take students on a tour of the place and people who create the images and some of the positions available for people with artistic talents.

▼ Architect/Engineer Office

Two common professions that use their art and space smarts are architects and engineers. Give students the opportunity to see the process involved in designing anything from towering buildings to hand-held appliances.

MI Field Trips (continued)

Musical/Rhythmic

▼ Symphony Orchestra

Stretch students' musical smarts by taking them to see the string, wind, and percussion sections playing together in perfect harmony.

▼ Recording Studio

How do our favorite bands get their music on CD? Take students on a guided tour of a recording studio. Have the guide lead students through the process and equipment involved. Students learn about the role of musicians as well as other music-related jobs.

Bodily/Kinesthetic

▼ Game or Sporting Event

A sporting event or game is usually an easy, inexpensive field trip to arrange. Local high schools and colleges have frequent games across a wide variety of sports. If you have a local stadium or professional team in your community, students can see individuals using their bodily/kinesthetic to perform amazing athletic feats. Students can write a paper, draw picture, or re-enact what they saw.

▼ Play

Actors use their body smarts to communicate great meaning through their every movement: a romantic blink of an eye; a playful pat on the back; the contorted wincing look of pain. Plays are an excellent way to see actors in action. They are especially meaningful when they are on a topic students are studying or a book the class is reading.

Naturalist

▼ Zoos and Wildlife Parks

The zoo is the next best thing to taking students on a wild animal safari in Africa. In the zoo, students can see why the lion is called the king of the jungle; they can witness the humanlike qualities of primates (or primatelike qualities of humans, depending on your perspective); and they can see firsthand just how tall a giraffe really is. Most zoos and wildlife parks have great educational programs.

▼ Aquariums

At Sea World and Marineland, students (and teachers alike) love seeing the acrobatics of the dolphins, watching the clownlike qualities of the seal, and a person kissing a killer whale. A trip to the aquarium is probably the next best thing to scuba diving the great barrier reef in Australia. Even local aquariums are usually loaded with exotic marine life.

MI Field Trips (continued)

Naturalist (cont.)

▼ Meadow, Lake, Wood and Field Trips

Any trips into a natural environment where students can observe and record nature, are not only a great break from the daily classroom routine, but also a great way to develop the skills of the naturalist and an appreciation for the natural world. A guided tour by a knowledgeable docent can open students' eyes to the wonder and beauty of our environment.

▼ Tide Pools

Tide pools are often teeming with life. Students can watch the sideways shuffle of the crab; the camouflaging and squirting habits of the sea anemone; darting fish trapped in a low tide pool.

▼ Camping

Taking students outside of civilization and allowing them to commune with nature is a great way to nurture the budding naturalist within students.

Interpersonal

▼ Police Station

The police station is a great destination to promote the interpersonal intelligence. Students can learn about people who work "to protect and serve people" and see the friendly side of law enforcement.

▼ Historical Landmark

Relive the past by visiting a historical landmark. Students learn about the people and the events that occurred at the location. Some landmarks include: missions, forts, battle sites.

Intrapersonal

▼ College or University

A great motivational field trip is to the local college or university. Students can learn about what happens in higher education and set goals for their future.

▼ Reflections

Any field trip can be turned into a intrapersonal field trip by having students reflect on their experiences. Students can keep a journal or log of the trip and when they are done write about they felt when...or what they liked most...or what they didn't like...or what it makes them think about.

MI Field Trips
From A to Z

- Advertising Agency
- Airport
- Amusement Park
- Antique Store
- Aquarium
- Architect/Engineer
- Bakery
- Bank
- Boat
- Botanical Garden
- Building
- Camping
- Capital
- Carousel
- Cemetery
- City Hall
- College
- Courthouse
- Dairy
- Department Store
- Dentist
- Doctor
- Factory
- Farm
- Field
- Firehouse
- Florist
- Gallery
- Game
- Gas Station
- Grocery Store

- Hardware Store
- Historical Landmark
- Hotel
- Humane Society
- IMAX Theater
- Lake
- Library
- Meadow
- Monuments
- Museum
- Music Store
- NASA
- Newspaper Office
- Observatory
- Ocean
- Office
- Orchard
- Planetarium

- Play
- Publishing Company
- Radio Station
- Recording Studio
- Restaurant
- Sporting Event
- Stadium
- Stock Exchange
- Symphony
- Theater
- Thrift Store
- Tide Pools
- Train Station
- TV Station
- Veterinarian
- Washington, D. C.
- Wildlife Park
- Zoo

Classroom Resources

To Stimulate the Verbal/Linguistic Intelligence

Reading
- ☐ Big books
- ☐ Bulletin and message boards
- ☐ Comics
- ☐ Dictionaries
- ☐ Encyclopedias
- ☐ Magazines
- ☐ Newspapers
- ☐ Novels
- ☐ Past-year student books
- ☐ Pocket charts
- ☐ Poetry
- ☐ ReadingBoards
- ☐ Reference books
- ☐ Sentence strips
- ☐ Thesauruses
- ☐ Word mobiles

Writing
- ☐ Bookmaking materials
- ☐ Journals
- ☐ Letter blocks
- ☐ Letter cards
- ☐ Letter stencils
- ☐ Lined paper
- ☐ Markers
- ☐ Newsprint
- ☐ Notebooks
- ☐ Paper
- ☐ Pens
- ☐ Picture story paper
- ☐ Slates
- ☐ Typewriters
- ☐ Word searches
- ☐ Writing programs

Listening
- ☐ Books on tape
- ☐ Speeches on tape

Games
- ☐ Balderdash
- ☐ Boggle
- ☐ Hangman
- ☐ Scrabble
- ☐ Spill and Spell

Computer Software
- ☐ Desktop publishing
  (Publish It!, QuarkXpress, PageMaker)
- ☐ Grammar programs
  (Dictionary, Correct Grammar)
- ☐ Spell checkers
- ☐ Typing tutors
- ☐ Word games
  (Kid Phonics)
- ☐ Word processing programs
  (Word, WordPerfect, MacWrite, TeachText,
  SimpleText, WriteNow, Nisus Writer, FullWrite)
- ☐ Writing programs
  (The Amazing Writing Machine)
- ☐ Word skills
  (Tackle English, Word Foundry)

Classroom Resources

To Stimulate the Logical/Mathematical Intelligence

Manipulatives

- [ ] Attribute blocks
- [ ] Base 10
- [ ] Bean counters
- [ ] Blocks
- [ ] Buttons
- [ ] Calculators
- [ ] Colored cubes
- [ ] Cuisenaire rods
- [ ] Dice
- [ ] Dominoes
- [ ] Fraction bars
- [ ] Fraction spinners
- [ ] Geoboards
- [ ] Geoplastic forms
- [ ] Graphing floor mat
- [ ] Legos
- [ ] Lincoln logs
- [ ] Magnets
- [ ] Microscope & slides
- [ ] Milk caps
- [ ] Mirrors
- [ ] Multilinks
- [ ] Number tiles
- [ ] Pattern blocks
- [ ] Probability spinners
- [ ] Sorting bowls
- [ ] Sorting collections (buttons, milk caps)
- [ ] Sorting trays
- [ ] Spinners
- [ ] Strategy games
- [ ] Tangrams
- [ ] Triangle flash cubes
- [ ] Two-colored counters
- [ ] Unifix cubes

Measuring Tools

- [ ] Balance scales
- [ ] Compass
- [ ] Clocks
- [ ] Graduated beakers
- [ ] Graduated cylinders
- [ ] Measuring cups
- [ ] Measuring spoons
- [ ] Meter stick
- [ ] Metric volume set
- [ ] Platform scale
- [ ] Protractors
- [ ] Rulers
- [ ] Simple scales
- [ ] Stop watches
- [ ] Tapes
- [ ] Thermometer
- [ ] Trundle wheel
- [ ] Yard sticks

Games

- [ ] Clue
- [ ] Go Fish
- [ ] Memory
- [ ] Monopoly
- [ ] Othello
- [ ] Puzzles
- [ ] Rubic's Cube
- [ ] Trivial Pursuit

Computer Software

- [ ] Math skills (Math Workshop)
- [ ] Math games (Math Blaster, Math Ace Jr.)
- [ ] Programming languages (Basic, C++, Pascal, Cobol, HTML, CGI, HyperCard)
- [ ] Logic games (Carmen Sandiego)
- [ ] Thinking skills programs
- [ ] Statistics (The Graph Club, StatView, DeltaGraph)
- [ ] Databases (Works, FileMaker, Access)
- [ ] Financial Programs (Quicken)
- [ ] Spreadsheets (Excel, Lotus 123)
- [ ] Internet site builders (SiteMill, PageMill, Dream Weaver)
- [ ] Web browsers (Navigator, Explorer)
- [ ] Online services (America Online, CompuServ, Prodigy)
- [ ] Exploration in science and math (The Ultimate Einstein)

Classroom Resources
To Stimulate the Visual/Spatial Intelligence

Arts & Crafts

- [ ] Beads
- [ ] Beans
- [ ] Buttons
- [ ] Chalkboards
- [ ] Chalk
- [ ] Charcoal
- [ ] Clay
- [ ] Collage materials
- [ ] Colored pastas
- [ ] Colored pencils
- [ ] Construction paper
- [ ] Cotton balls
- [ ] Crayons
- [ ] Drafting supplies
- [ ] Easels
- [ ] Feathers
- [ ] Felt
- [ ] Glitter
- [ ] Glue
- [ ] Hot glue gun
- [ ] Markers
- [ ] Masking tape
- [ ] Mosaic squares
- [ ] Paints & brushes
- [ ] Paper clips
- [ ] Paper mâché
- [ ] Pastels
- [ ] Paste
- [ ] Poster paper
- [ ] Q-tips
- [ ] Rubber cement
- [ ] Rubber stamps
- [ ] Scissors
- [ ] Sponges
- [ ] Stapler
- [ ] Stencils (letters, figures)
- [ ] T-Squares & triangles
- [ ] Tissue paper
- [ ] Toothpicks
- [ ] Tongue depressors
- [ ] Velcro
- [ ] Watercolors
- [ ] Wiggle eyes
- [ ] Yarn

Visuals

- [ ] Art prints
- [ ] Banners
- [ ] Calendars
- [ ] Charts
- [ ] Chart stands
- [ ] Diagrams
- [ ] Graphs
- [ ] Overhead projector
- [ ] Posters
- [ ] Slides and projector
- [ ] Slide viewers
- [ ] Stereoscopic viewers
- [ ] TV, VCR
- [ ] Video equipment
- [ ] Videotapes and player

Games

- [ ] Chess
- [ ] Pictionary
- [ ] Puzzles
- [ ] Tetris
- [ ] Win Lose or Draw

Computer Software

- [ ] 3D programs
  (Extreme 3D, Ray Dream Designer, Dimensions, 3D World, Vision 3D, Poser, AddDepth, Infini-D)
- [ ] Cards and banners
  (Print Shop)
- [ ] Cartooning
  (Comic Creator)
- [ ] Clip art & stock photos
- [ ] Computer assisted drafting (CAD)
  (Minicad, Blueprint)
- [ ] Geography
  (National Inspirer, International Inspirer)
- [ ] Illustration programs
  (Illustrator, Freehand, CorelDraw, Streamline)
- [ ] Mapping and atlases
  (U.S. Atlas, World Atlas, ZipZapMap!)
- [ ] Page layout
  (PageMaker, QuarkXpress)
- [ ] Paint & Image processing
  (Photoshop, Photostyler, PixelPaint, Painter, Photo-Paint, xRes, Collage, Dabbler)
- [ ] Presentation, multimedia, & film
  (Director, Video Craft, Premier, VideoShop, PowerPoint, SuperCard, VideoDirector)
- [ ] Type & fonts (Fontographer, Typestyler)
- [ ] Simulations
  (SimCity, SimTower)

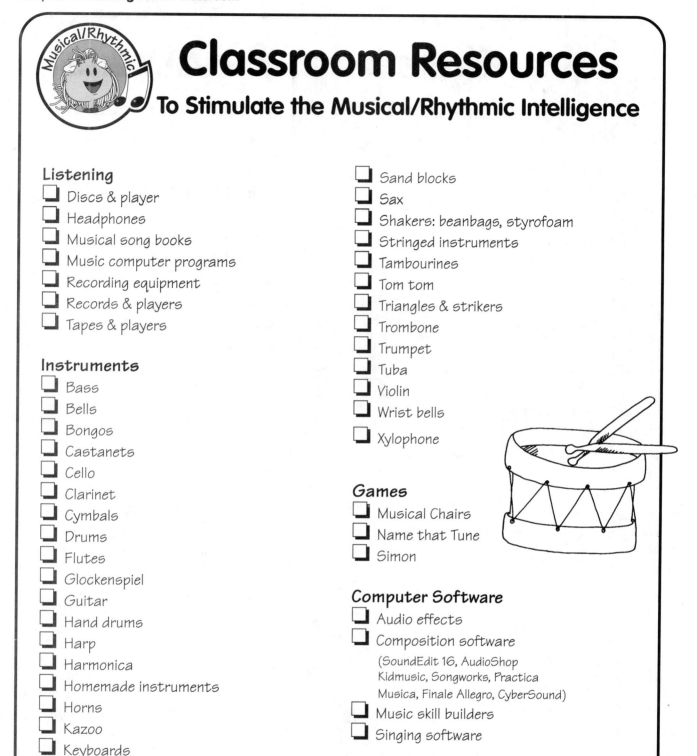

Classroom Resources
To Stimulate the Musical/Rhythmic Intelligence

Listening
- Discs & player
- Headphones
- Musical song books
- Music computer programs
- Recording equipment
- Records & players
- Tapes & players

Instruments
- Bass
- Bells
- Bongos
- Castanets
- Cello
- Clarinet
- Cymbals
- Drums
- Flutes
- Glockenspiel
- Guitar
- Hand drums
- Harp
- Harmonica
- Homemade instruments
- Horns
- Kazoo
- Keyboards
- Maracas
- Oboe
- Piano
- Recorder
- Rhythm sticks

- Sand blocks
- Sax
- Shakers: beanbags, styrofoam
- Stringed instruments
- Tambourines
- Tom tom
- Triangles & strikers
- Trombone
- Trumpet
- Tuba
- Violin
- Wrist bells
- Xylophone

Games
- Musical Chairs
- Name that Tune
- Simon

Computer Software
- Audio effects
- Composition software
  (SoundEdit 16, AudioShop Kidmusic, Songworks, Practica Musica, Finale Allegro, CyberSound)
- Music skill builders
- Singing software

Classroom Resources
To Stimulate the Bodily/Kinesthetic Intelligence

Props
- [ ] Costumes
- [ ] Hats, scarves, capes
- [ ] Mini theaters
- [ ] Puppets
- [ ] Streamers
- [ ] Umbrellas, canes

Sports Equipment
- [ ] Badminton
- [ ] Balance beam
- [ ] Balls
- [ ] Baseball bats, bases, balls, mits
- [ ] Basketballs
- [ ] Bean bags
- [ ] Cones
- [ ] Folding mats
- [ ] Frisbees
- [ ] Hockey sticks & pucks
- [ ] Inflating pumps
- [ ] Jump ropes
- [ ] Nerf balls
- [ ] Parachutes
- [ ] Paddles and ball
- [ ] Rackets
- [ ] Scooters
- [ ] Soccer balls
- [ ] Stop watches
- [ ] Volleyballs

"Hands-On" Materials
- [ ] Board games
- [ ] Building materials
- [ ] Connecting blocks
- [ ] Construction sets
- [ ] Craft supplies
- [ ] Fabric and sewing materials
- [ ] Puzzles
- [ ] Stacking blocks
- [ ] Tools

Games
- [ ] All Sports
- [ ] Jenga
- [ ] Operation
- [ ] Twister

Computer Software
- [ ] Eye-hand coordination
  (Almost all video games)
- [ ] Virtual reality
- [ ] Screen writer
  (Final Draft)
- [ ] Simple machines
  (The Way things Work)

Classroom Resources
To Stimulate the Naturalist Intelligence

Nature In the Class
- ☐ Animals/class pet
- ☐ Ant farm
- ☐ Berries
- ☐ Bushes
- ☐ Butterfly hatchery
- ☐ Flowers
- ☐ Fossils
- ☐ Fruits
- ☐ Insects
- ☐ Leaves
- ☐ Plants
- ☐ Rocks
- ☐ Sea monkeys
- ☐ Shells
- ☐ Soils
- ☐ Trees
- ☐ Vegetables

Nature Resources
- ☐ Classification posters
- ☐ Natural history books
- ☐ Nature books
- ☐ Nature videos
- ☐ Periodic table
- ☐ Science books

Science and Observation
- ☐ Beakers
- ☐ Bunson burners
- ☐ Binoculars
- ☐ Cameras
- ☐ Jars
- ☐ Journals
- ☐ Magnifying glasses
- ☐ Microscopes
- ☐ Petri dishes
- ☐ Recording logs

Computer Software
- ☐ Anatomy
  (BodyWorks, A.D.A.M., Nine Month Miracle, Life's Greatest Mysteries, How Your Body Works, The Ultimate Human Body)
- ☐ Animals
  (Noah's Ark, Zoo Explorers)
- ☐ Astronomy
  (The Planets, SkyGazer, Voyager II, The Great Solar System Rescue)
- ☐ Dinosaurs
  (Dinosaur Safari, Dinosaur Kids)
- ☐ Encyclopedias
  (Encyclopedia of Science, Encyclopedia of Nature)
- ☐ Oceanography
  (Ocean Explorers, Eco-Adventures in the Ocean, The Great Ocean Rescue)
- ☐ Science software
  (ChemOffice)
- ☐ Plants
  (Rainforest Researchers, Eco-Adventures in the Rainforest)

Classroom Resources
To Stimulate the Interpersonal Intelligence

- Biographies
- Birthday charts
- Conflict resolution
- Idea Spinner
- Multicultural books
- Role cards
- Spin-N-Review
- Spin-N-Think
- Student Selector

Games
- Board games
- Cooperative sports & games
- Team games

Computer Software
- Contact databases
  (ACT! Now Contact, TouchBase)
- E-mail
  (Eudora, Em@iler)
- Online services
  (America Online, CompuServ, Prodigy)
- Social studies
  (Timeliner, Ancient Empires, Prejudice, Feudalism, Building a Nation, Immigration, Revolutionary Wars)
- Web browsers
  (Navigator, Explorer)

Classroom Resources
To Stimulate the Intrapersonal Intelligence

- Autobiographies
- Awards
- Certificates
- Cubbies
- Ear plugs
- Feelings cards
- Feelings posters
- Journals
- Mirrors
- Motivational Posters

- Notes
- Stickers
- Self-esteem games, books

Games
- Scruples
- Solitaire

Creating the MI School

How do we educate the multiple intelligences? What would an MI school be like? And how do we get from here to there? The brief answer — and still the correct one — is that there is no recipe for a multiple intelligences education (Gardner, 1993, p. 66).

lthough, as Gardner notes in the opening quotation, there is no there is no definitive "recipe" for creating an MI school, there are many "ingredients" for creating an MI school — there are many things we as educators can do to create a school-wide atmosphere that promotes matching, stretching, and celebrating multiple intelligences. In this chapter we will explore some of those ingredients. Then, we'll take a look at Gardner's vision for the MI school, the Individual-Centered School. Finally, we'll examine some model MI schools and programs, including Project Spectrum, the Key School, Green Tree East, and New City School.

There are many things we as educators can do to create a schoolwide atmosphere that promotes matching, stretching, and celebrating multiple intelligences.

Ingredients for Creating the MI School

There are a number of ingredients we can use to transform any school into an MI school. The following ingredients can be used in

Recipe for the MI School

Start with students of every type and a visionary staff of educators
- *Add:*
  1 Cup of MI schoolwide programs
  2 Pinches of stimulating MI projects
  1 Tablespoon of schoolwide MI themes
  1 Teaspoon of alternative classroom configurations
- *Mix In:*
  A lively, intelligences-friendly environment
  Frequent staff development teaching with, for and about MI
  A few MI elective courses
  A variety pack of MI resources
- *Cook:*
  For school year at varying temperatures
- *Serve:*
When done, enjoy a fun, motivating, school environment that develops students multiple intelligences, promotes respect for self and others, and approaches academic curriculum in a multiplicity of ways.

different combinations in each school to meet a school's unique needs. The possibilities are infinite. The following ingredients, though, are among the most important to consider in creating the MI school: Sharing a common goal, staff development on MI, creating an MI friendly school environment, amassing and making available a wealth of MI instructional resources, alternative classroom configurations, MI school-wide programs, MI elective courses, MI school-wide themes, and MI school-wide projects. Let's look first at the most important ingredient.

Sharing a Common Goal

What is our goal as educators? This is a loaded philosophical question, hotly debated. In the answer lies a directive for what our schools should look like and how the schooling process should proceed. Some emphasize that our job as educators is to pass along a body of basic knowledge, a cultural literacy; students need to learn to read, write, solve math problems and know the facts that constitute our cultural heritage. Some believe our most important mission as educators is to teach students to think; the citizenry of tomorrow needs to be able to make wise, informed decisions to direct our collective democratic future. Some believe that schooling should teach respect, responsibility and relationship skills; students need to learn to get along in an increasingly pluralistic society.

We believe that all these goals are legitimate and compatible. As we see it, our goal as eductors is to provide students with the skills and knowledge needed to lead happy and productive lives — to realize their potential and make a contribution to society. Our job is to foster each students' intellectual, social, and personal growth.

Our goal as educators is to provide students with the skills and knowledge needed to lead happy and productive lives — to realize their potential and make a contribution to society.

The question then becomes, what skill or skills does each student need? What kind of information is needed? There is no single answer. None of us have a crystal ball. We don't know which students are going to be doctors, lawyers, actors, acrobats, artists, animal trainers, musicians, politicians. Even if we did, providing differential curriculum violates the most basic democratic principle of public education: equal opportunity for an equal education. Further, the change rate is accelerating so rapidly, selecting specialized curriculum for different students is more likely to limit than expand their potential.

We don't know what the world will look like in 10, 20, 50 years. And if we cannot predict the future job world with confidence, we would be foolish to prepare our students with narrow, specialized skills. As the change rate accelerates, our future success as a nation depends increasingly on the flexibility of our citizenry. And flexibility is a function of breadth of skills and experiences.

With the change rate accelerating, we need to prepare every student with as broad a range of skills as possible. Who, only a few years ago, could imagine how the job world would shift into internet-related jobs? Just a few years ago, the internet was used exclusively by an elite cadre of physicists. Today, millions of people are affected daily by the internet. People chat about topics of interest; businesses sell their wares and services over secured sites; artists design appealing, yet functional web pages; cable companies install new data-intensive lines; hardware companies develop and peddle increasingly faster modems to keep up; programmers continually update the HTML programming language and create new languages to meet the rapidly accelerating and changing nature of the web; software companies create new authoring software, and retool existing programs to make them internet-ready; students surf the web to research papers, get ideas for projects, and chat with peers from the other side of the world. Had we selected to teach typing or computer literacy to some but not other students, we would have limited the potential of a subset of our students.

As educators, we face the unprecedented task of preparing students for a future we can hardly imagine. How do we best prepare our students? Well, as MI theory and our experience as educators tells us, there are many different ways to be smart. There are many ways to learn. There are many ways to approach and solve problems. There are many different types of products valued by society. To best prepare our students for the rapidly changing future world, we must give each one a wide range of skills, a well-rounded education.

When we, as a school community, share the belief that there are many different ways to be smart, that each student can and should develop each intelligence as fully as possible, when we share the visions of matching, stretching, and celebrating MI, we have a shared goal and a common direction for creating our MI school.

As a school, we acknowledge that all students have the potential to learn and to develop all intelligences. So we look for ways to reach and teach all students and to maximize every aspect of their intellectual development. In the MI school, we institute school-wide MI programs, projects, and themes to make learning come alive and further the development of students' multiple intelligences. In the MI school, our students recognize their own strengths, as well as those of others. Students feel a greater sense of self-esteem and take pride in their unique pattern of intelligences and their schoolwork. Parents understand what's going on in the classroom and become partners in education. In the MI school, we all ask not whether someone is smart, but rather how they are smart. Sharing this vision, we see that everyone is unique and everyone has something valuable to contribute. As a community of learners and as a community at large, we are strengthened by our diversity of skills, talents, and intelligences.

How do we reach this point, where everyone shares the goal of creating an MI school? As a staff, we may have readings, meetings, and discussions examining the theoretical underpinnings of MI and the practical applications it holds for our school. We can teach our students about MI in class through discussions, activities, readings, exploration and reflection. As a school, we may have an MI assembly or assemblies. We can inform parents and local community members about MI through meetings, conferences, open house, letters, PTO or PTA meetings. We can invite parents and community members to be partners in education.

Without first establishing the rationale and sharing a common goal, any effort to transform our school into an MI school will likely meet resistance. Another teacher might ask skeptically, "Why are your students singing in your class? You're not the music teacher." Or the principal may inquire puzzled, "Why are your students so noisy and out of their seats? Don't you have work to do?" Or an uninformed parent might question, "Why is my child using manipulatives to learn math? I learned math just fine without toys."

Surely, changes can be mandated from the top down. Administrators can push for creating an MI school. However, the actual task of creating an MI school is in our hands collectively; a true MI school is created from within.

Surely, changes can be mandated from the top down. Administrators can push for creating an MI school. However, the actual task of creating an MI school is in our hands collectively; a true MI school is created from within. When we all share a common goal, and see the potential benefits MI can hold for students, our MI school becomes a reality. Motivation drives implementation. Our students are worth it!

One way we can articulate our shared vision is a mission statement. For example, see Green Tree East Mission Statement on page 15.34. Writing a school mission statement is an excellent exercise for a staff meeting. If together, as a team of educators, we can sit down and write a collaborative mission statement that captures the essence of our goal in the classroom and in the school, we will share a vision and strive together to achieve our goal. The mission statement may be posted in every classroom or in key locations in the school as a reminder of our shared goal.

Staff Development

Education is steeped in tradition. Making a concerted effort to create an MI school — effectively departing from the traditional structure — requires not only a shared goal but support. When introducing multiple intelligences and the visions it holds for education, there may be high enthusiasm. The theory resonates with our instincts as educators so well because we have regular contact with so many children; we know that each student is unique. Bringing in an MI guru for a day or so may be a great vehicle for generating initial excitement and opening eyes to possibilities,

Without continued support and encouragement from administrators and fellow teachers, enthusiasm dissipates and the class and school slips back to the default structure.

but the one-shot workshop cannot maintain long-term changes. Without continued support and encouragement from administrators and fellow teachers, enthusiasm dissipates and the class and school slips back to the default structure. Without continued support, MI can be can be a shooting star, burning brightly, but then burning out.

So how do we provide the support to sustain strides toward creating the MI school? We learned a very important lesson about sustaining changes in our experiences with cooperative learning. Let's look at this experience, then look at some ways to maintain support for teachers including in-service training, staff meetings, and peer coaching.

MI As an Additive Model, Not a Replacement Model

Not too long ago, the search for educational reform focused its attention on cooperative learning. Hundreds of lab and field studies were conducted. Cooperative learning became the most extensively researched educational innovation of all times. The results were overwhelmingly positive. Cooperative learning promoted academic gains, and improved race relations, social and affective development, and self-esteem among students. By turning their desks around and working with each other rather than independently or against each other, students learned better, liked each other more, liked school more, and felt better about themselves.

With dramatic gains in academic and social outcomes, educators across the country were thrilled. Wide-scale implementation began. Entire schools and districts began training in cooperative learning and instituted cooperative programs. Sound familiar? Teachers, principals and parents got excited, test scores went up, students started getting along. It was great. But it didn't last.

Some years after the initial wave of enthusiasm for cooperative learning, when we peeked into classrooms across America, there was little evidence of cooperative learning. Even in the same schools where cooperative learning had been thriving a few years prior, the chairs were back in rows. Education defaulted back to the traditional format. Teachers were talking; students were passively listening.

This was depressing! Was cooperative learning just another educational fad that had its time in the sun and faded away to the newest reform? How could something so positive for students not be implemented more broadly? Why was implementation not sustained? What happened?

What happened was teachers were taught to use cooperative learning as a replacement model. Teachers stayed up late, planning elaborate cooperative lessons to replace their traditional lessons. Cooperative learning was an event. It replaced prior models of teaching. In time, though, with diminished external pressure, cooperative learning events became less and less frequent until eventually, without support, they faded away.

When we analyzed what was happening, we changed our approach to cooperative learning. Instead of using cooperative learning lessons to replace what teachers were doing, our goal was, and continues be, to make cooperative learning an integrated part of every lesson. We developed "New Cooperative Learning" based on an integrated, rather than replacement model. As teachers are trained in New Cooperative Learning, we do not ask teachers to abandon what they are already doing; we provide teachers with strategies to teach what they are teaching, cooperatively, and more effectively. Teachers don't write new cooperative learning lessons, they integrate simple cooperative learning strategies into their existing lessons. Now, as we look in classrooms across the country that are trained with New Cooperative Learning, teachers continue to use cooperative strategies in their classroom as an integrated part of their daily lessons.

Of course this anecdote is an overgeneralization. Many teachers and even schools and districts have sustained tremendous success with cooperative learning from the start. We provide this example not as a condemnation of other models of cooperative learning, but rather as a caution for creating the MI school. Unless we are careful, MI can take the same path as cooperative learning and many prior educational innovations. MI can feed the replacement cycle, only to in turn be itself replaced by the next new educational innovation. If every few years, teachers are taught to replace what they are teaching with another way, a different way, or better way, resistance to innovation will build and sustained implementation is unlikely.

If matching, stretching, and celebrating MI can be integrated into existing classroom practices, rather than replacing existing classroom practices, success and long-term implementation will follow.

If we use an additive model for MI, rather than a replacement model, our goal of creating and maintaining an MI school is more likely to be realized. If cooperative learning is used successfully in the class, fantastic. Don't abandon it! See how lessons can be expanded to stimulate more intelligences. If centers are up and working successfully, great! Don't throw away the centers. See how centers can integrate MI. If matching, stretching, and celebrating MI can be integrated into existing classroom practices, rather than replacing existing classroom practices, success and long-term implementation will follow.

By integrating MI into the fabric of the classroom, we break the replacement cycle and ensure sustained implementation.

MI In-Service Training

Teachers need the practical tools to make MI a daily reality in their classrooms. The training can be led by an outside consultant, the principal, by a mentor teacher, or by teachers sharing training responsibilities. Teachers can work in small teams to explore aspects of MI which they then share with the rest of the staff.

MI staff meetings can meld the medium with the message. Staff meetings can be a model for multiple intelligences in the classroom.

Successful training in MI includes how to match, stretch, and celebrate MI. In the MI school, teachers acquire the tools to match instructional strategies to the multiple intelligences, learning when and how to use the wide range of multimodal instructional strategies to reach each intelligence. Teachers learn how to stretch MI, how to maximize the development of the multiple intelligences. Teachers learn also how to celebrate MI, how to honor the uniqueness of each student, and celebrate the diversity of students. This book has been written with these goals in mind — to be a helpful resource as you create your own unique multiple intelligences school.

MI Staff Meetings

Staff meetings can contribute to the MI school in two important ways. First, staff meetings can be used to focus on MI issues, projects, programs. Together, as a staff, we can map out the school-wide MI theme; we can plan the MI projects and decide who should lead each one; we can brainstorm MI assembly ideas; we can plan the scavenger hunt for MI resources for the school; we can schedule activities for the MI think tank; we can plan MI presenta-tions for open house night; we can talk about ways to make the physical environment more amenable to the intrapersonal intelligence; we can arrange cross-age peer tutoring for developing the different intelligences.

The second way staff meetings can contribute to creating an MI school is to have meetings which meld the medium with the message. That is, staff meetings can be a model for classroom learning. If we are asking teachers to present content multimodally, we can make our staff meeting presentations engage teachers' multiple intelligences. Staff meetings can easily incorporate many intelligences: Teachers can write their ideas down before sharing them, take turns reading excerpts, make oral presentations (verbal/linguistic); brainstorm ideas, sequence events and make schedules, make budgets (logical/mathematical); watch videos on demo lessons or on staff development (visual/spatial); discuss issues in small teams (interpersonal); have time to reflect on learning and implications for the classroom (intrapersonal). All the multimodal instructional strategies described in Chapters 7 and 8 easily can be adapted for staff meetings.

By practicing what we preach, our staff meetings become a model for classroom practice, reflecting and strengthening our commitment to the multiple intelligences.

Peer Coaching

Peer coaching is a powerful, yet underemployed tool for our development as teaching professionals (Kagan, 1994). Peer coaching — teachers pairing up to coach each other — can be a powerful tool for creating the MI school, used effectively for coaching MI lessons, centers and projects.

Coaching can create anxiety. We may be accustomed to being the only adult in a classroom. The idea of another adult in the room may be a little disquieting: we worry what she or he is thinking. Keep the goal in mind: We do peer coaching for self-improvement and to be the best teachers we can be for our students.

For peer coaching to work well, it essential to establish mutual trust and respect. Some of the best teachers make the worst coaches. Some fine teachers have gotten where they are because they are self-critical. This self-critical quality has led them to find fault with their own teaching and to seek ways to improve it. These teachers, when placed in the role of coach, however, bring to others their same critical qualities: The more self-critical a teacher, the more likely it is that he or she will be critical of others. These teachers are likely to focus on the technical aspects of coaching. Although this form of coaching is well-intended, it does not create an atmosphere conducive to experimentation, openness, and discovery. We are all put off by an observer who has all the answers. Good coaching can occur only after acceptance and support are established. During coaching, both teachers need to feel themselves as part of the same team, working together to solve problems of mutual concern.

Peer Coaching Cycle

There are three phases to the coaching cycle: 1. Planning, 2. Observation, and 3. Reflection. During Planning Time, a teacher and coach meet to discuss a lesson and to establish a contract for coaching. During the Observation Time, the coach observes the lesson, recording all the positive aspects of the lesson and making observations on specific behaviors agreed to

Peer Coaching Cycle

▼ *Planning:* Teachers meet to plan the Peer Coaching. Use Planning Form (page 15.11).

▼ *Observation:* Coach observes lesson. Use Observation Form (page 15.12).

▼ *Reflection:* Teachers reflect on lesson. Use Reflection Form (page 15.13).

by the teacher and coach. During the Reflection Time, there is a sharing of the observations and a teacher-centered discussion of the lesson.

1. Planning (Pre-Observation). The most important aspect of coaching is setting a tone of mutual trust and support. It is important that the coach know and respect the feelings of the teacher. Teaching is our profession. We are "on the line" each time we are observed. Some anxiety in such a situation is natural, especially the first time a teacher is observed by a coach. Having clear limits and structures helps reduce the

Keep the goal in mind: We do peer coaching for self-improvement and to be the best teachers we can be for our students.

risk and anxiety. Therefore, the coach and teacher must have a very clear agreement as to their roles during the observation and afterwards. Some of the most important things to establish are: what the coach will be looking for and doing during the observation session, what he or she will be sharing afterwards, and the fact that there will be complete confidentiality regarding the observation and conferences. See Peer Coaching Planning Form, page 15.11.

It is important to understand that the Peer Coaching forms provided here (pages 15.11-15.13) are not forms in the usual sense. They are not to be filled out by the person being coached. Rather these forms are scripts for an interaction. They may be filled out by the coach during the process of coaching, but the critical process is the interaction in which a safe open climate is created. Good peer coaching can occur only when the person being coached and the coach see themselves as a team.

Planning the Observation. All of peer coaching is teacher-centered. That is, the coaching will focus on what the teacher feels he or she would like to work on, not necessarily any concerns of the coach. Therefore, the coaching begins with the coach asking the teacher how she or he feels about the lesson they are going to work on.

The teacher's response sets the tone for the coaching session. If a teacher is feeling unsure about the lesson and/or the coaching process, then the coach's role should be primarily to provide support. Whatever problem solving is done, should be in a very limited domain, focusing on specific behaviors. To begin the coaching process, it is often helpful to take some very limited aspect of a lesson for observation and to make the observation relatively brief. As confidence increases, the range of behaviors observed and the length of the observation time may increase.

Confidentiality. During the Planning Stage, confidentiality between coach and teacher is established. The rule is simple: Nothing observed or discussed at any point in the coaching cycle is to be shared with anyone else. The teacher and coach may decide to waive that rule, but only for special need, and only with the teacher's approval.

Time, Place, Roles. Other aspects of the coaching contract which need to be established are exactly when the observation will take place, for how long, the role of the coach during the lesson, and most importantly, what exactly is to be observed and discussed afterwards. At first, it is probably most comfortable for the teacher and coach if it is agreed that only one specific behavior will be observed and discussed. Later, the coaching may open up to extra observations and suggestions, but only by prior agreement.

2. Observation. There are two main jobs of the coach during the observation session: Record all of the positive aspects of the lesson — the goodies list, and make the specific behavioral observations contracted for during the planning session. See Peer Coaching Observation Form, page 15.12.

The list of positive aspects of the lesson, or goodies list, is important for setting the tone during the reflection time. If we focus only on the problems, coaching fails to provide the support we all need; we need a healthy balance between problem solving and support. "One thing to grow on, ten things to glow on." Also, as indicated, the observations for problem solving must have a specific behavioral referent. The job of the coach is not to note all the aspects of the lesson which could be improved, but rather to focus on the specific behaviors agreed upon during the planning session.

3. Reflection. During reflection, teachers share their observations of the lesson.

Checking In. It is important to begin the reflection session by checking with the teacher as to his or her feelings. See Reflection Form, page 15.13. Good coaching is teacher-centered; the form it takes depends on the feelings of the teacher. If a teacher is discouraged, little or no technical feedback should occur — the coaching session should focus on motivation and support statements. If the teacher is confident, more time might be spent problem solving technical aspects of the lesson, but always there must be a balance between "things to grow on and things to glow on." Checking with feelings early can lead to some important surprises. A defensive teacher may have given what looks like a weak lesson, but want to focus only on the positive aspects of the lesson. It is very important for that teacher to know that the coach has seen and appreciated the positive aspects of the lesson and that the technical feedback be limited to only one or two items in a very supportive context. When technical feedback is given, it is absolutely essential that the feedback have a behavioral referent — that it be objective rather than evaluative.

In contrast, a very self-critical teacher may have given what the coach thinks is a great lesson, but in the coaching session may be inclined to focus only on the problems.

The most helpful thing a coach can do for a self-critical teacher is to have them focus on all the things that went right in the lesson. The highly self-critical teacher will have a hard time hearing or "taking in" his or her accomplishments. For all teachers, an early sharing of the goodies list helps set the positive, supportive context in which to do the limited and focused problem solving.

If a teacher and coach work only on those aspects of the lesson which need improvement, coaching will not provide the positive support we all need. It is very important during the reflection time that the coach has the teacher note and discuss all of the positive aspects of the lesson — the list of goodies.

Problem Solving. There should never be movement to problem solving until motivation is strong and an atmosphere of support has been established. The problem solving focuses on what the teacher wants to work on, and it is a mutual discussion and kicking around of ideas — not a time for an "expert" to tell a novice. Good problem solving is synergistic: A good test of the quality of the problem solving during the reflection time is whether solutions and ideas emerge which neither the coach nor the teacher imagined beforehand.

Good coaching is not just a pat on the back. For some teacher-coach pairs, the temptation is to just focus on what is good. But good coaching doesn't stop at support. Support is necessary to set the context for good coaching, but once there is a "we" feeling and an atmosphere of support, the teacher and coach need to take a good hard look at the lesson, examining all possible ways of improving it.

Each point on the coaching form should be taken up with an eye to how the lesson might be improved. A lesson can always be strengthened. If coaching does not increase awareness of alternatives, it is not filling an important function. If the coach and teacher don't end up feeling they took a hard look at all the alternatives for at least

Peer Coaching
Planning Form

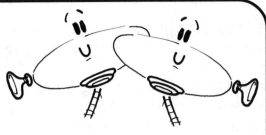

Intro

How do you feel about the lesson? _____

_____

What is the objective of the lesson? _____

_____

Describe the steps of the lesson. _____

_____

Problem Solving

What areas are you working on? _____

_____

_____

The Contract

1. What would you like me to watch for? What can I watch for or listen for that will give you useful information?

   a. _____

   b. _____

2. Observation: Date_____Time _____ End _____

3. Where would you like me? ❏ Seated   ❏ Circulating   ❏ Other: _____

4. What would you like me doing? ❏ Observation only   ❏ Talk with student or group
   ❏ Work with student or group   Which student or group?_____

5. Should I take notes?   ❏ Yes   ❏ No

6. What is our agreement about confidentiality?_____

Peer Coaching
Observation Form

1. Observations for Contract

Behavior: _____

Observations: _____

_____

_____

_____

Behavior: _____

Observations: _____

_____

_____

_____

2. Goodies List

(Think: Intelligences, Plan, Progression, Management, Student Behaviors, Creativity…)

Teacher Behaviors	Student Responses
1 _____	_____
2 _____	_____
3 _____	_____
4 _____	_____
5 _____	_____
6 _____	_____

Peer Coaching
Reflection Form

Self Analysis

How do you feel about the lesson?_____

What did you like best? Least? _____

_____

Goodies List

Some effective behaviors I observed that you haven't mentioned were…

Behaviors Observed	**Student Responses**
1_____	_____
2_____	_____
3_____	_____
4_____	_____
5_____	_____
6_____	_____

Observations for Contract

We agreed I would look for:_____
Here's what I saw:

Behaviors Observed	**Student Responses**
1_____	_____
2_____	_____
3_____	_____

Goals for Next Time

What goals would you like to set for yourself for next time?

1_____	_____
2_____	_____
3_____	_____

Positive Closure

What were the most positive aspects of the lesson? _____

_____

one aspect of a lesson, then the coaching may have been all things to glow on with nothing to grow on. The trick, of course is to work on the problem areas only within a context of basic trust and support, and for the teacher, rather than the coach, to define areas of growth and to lead the discussion. Coaching is not a time for the observer to share all that he or she knows; it is a time for the teacher to work with a coach on things of concern to the teacher.

Positive Closure. An important job of the coach is to provide a positive closure to the reflection session. Closure is provided by allowing the teacher time to restate some of the positive outcomes of the lesson and by asking the teacher to formulate some goals for next time (so the coaching cycle turns full circle and sets the stage for the next planning session). The tendency during coaching is to focus too much on the problems, to lose sight of the forest for the trees. Thus, during the "positive closure" time the coach brings attention back to the big picture: The lesson was not technically perfect (the perfect lesson has not yet been taught) but students were learning and supporting each other.

An MI-Friendly School Environment

Another ingredient for creating the MI school is making the physical environment more intelligences-friendly. Students spend a considerable amount of time outside of the classroom on the playground, in the cafeteria, in the library, in the computer lab. Can these physical locations be modified to better suit the multiple intelligences? Can some places in the school be adapted to make connections to other intelligences? Let's look at some ideas on how

the school's physical setting can help promote the development of each intelligence.

Creating a Word Smart Environment

When we think of word smart, the library is the first school building that comes to mind. The library should be filled with many kinds of books: reference books, novels, textbooks, research books, pop-up books, comic books, magazines — the bigger the variety the better. Students should all know where the library is, how to find what they're looking for and how to check out books. In general, schools do an excellent job of making linguistic resources readily available to students.

Around the school, there are some other things we do to develop word smarts. Spelling words and vocabulary words are posted in the cafeteria, on the walls or in the halls. The alphabet is painted on the blacktop near the primary classes. Celebrated authors and famous poems are posted around the school. School-wide scrap books are created featuring students' best linguistic works; the books are displayed in a central location for all students to read.

Word smarts also include foreign languages. A fairly common practice in foreign language classrooms is for teachers to label everything in the classroom with foreign words. Posters, windows, chalkboards, books, desks, walls, floors, ceilings, all get labeled with the appropriate foreign word(s). Students who tune into the words, can't help learning the foreign words for everything in the class by the end of the semester.

In the MI school, we extend this word-rich environment to the school. We label trees, the playground, the library, the field, restrooms, drinking fountains…you name it. This is a fun project for foreign language clubs. The signs may have the English word and the corresponding French, Spanish, German translations with the proper phonetic pronunciation. Little colorful, laminated signs can be taped or posted around the school. Putting words to concrete physical objects is helpful in teaching youngsters to read, and helps all students learn a foreign language. At the same time, it validates another culture and the verbal/linguistic intelligence.

Creating a Math/Logic Smart Environment

Numbers, math problems, logic problems, posters of famous mathematicians and philosophers decorate the MI school. Painting a multiplication chart on the kickboard with 0-9 on the vertical and horizontal axes and the products where the numbers meet is helpful for students learning their multiplication facts while playing handball or kickball. Posting the equations for area, volume, diameter and radius in the cafeteria makes mathematical connections at lunch. A geometric brick pattern or tile tessellation is a nice design for the new sidewalk. The MI school brings numbers and math-related topics to life around the school.

Creating an Art/Space Smart Environment

The visual appearance of the school communicates a message. Some schools are flat-out dull and dreary. These drab schools say (in a monotone voice): this is a boring place to spend your time…get outta here…go visit a hospital or prison, heck, they're more lively. Other schools are bright and vibrant, they shout: Hey you! Check this place out! This is where it's at! It's a regular party for the senses!

The drab school deadens the visual/spatial intelligence; the lively school inspires aspiring artists and provides a more aesthetically pleasing learning environment for all. To create our MI school atmosphere, we use open spaces, lots of light, bright colors, put students' art on display throughout the school, paint big colorful murals on the walls, let students draw with removable chalk on the blacktop, post famous artists and their works in the halls.

To awaken the spatial intelligence, we paint a compass on the playground that illustrates the accurate N, S, E, W directions; signs list the distances and directions of famous landmarks; students make a miniaturized map of school for display; an artistic teacher or students paint a map of the United States or the world on the playground; we hang students' 3D models from the roof, and students' architectural drawings and constructions in the library.

Creating a Music Smart Environment

In the movie *The Shawshank Redemption*, Tim Robbins plays a prisoner serving time for a murder he did not commit. Because of his accounting savvy, Robbins gets in the good graces of the Warden, and is permitted a bit of liberty, including setting up a library/resource room for the prisoners. In one scene, Robbins does the unthinkable. He locks himself in the broadcast room and plays an old opera over the public address system to the entire prison. It is a beautiful moment: We see Robbins leaning back in the chair with a smile of absolute contentment on his face as the Warden and guards pound at the locked door; then we see the prisoners in the yard, completely motionless with their jaws dropped as we hear the opera play. Morgan Freeman, a fellow prisoner and the movie narrator, says something to the effect that none of the prisoners spoke a word of Italian, and had no idea what that lady was singing, but it was the most beautiful thing they'd ever heard in their lives.

Sensory deprivation may be common in prisons, but definitely doesn't have to be in schools. School is a place the senses, and intelligences, should be activated. Music is no exception. In the MI school, soothing music or natural sounds are played in the halls, invigorating music is played during physical activities, and students' choice of music (lyric-safe, of course) is played occasionally during lunch, break, or recess.

A music room is another school-level attempt to developing the musical/rhythmic intelligence. Many schools have a music room run by the music instructor with excellent programs for teaching students about music and actually creating music as a class. Many students are intrigued by music and instruments. Allowing students free exploration of instruments and open access to the music room during breaks, lunch, and recess provides another way to support students' musical curiosity. The music teacher serves as a facilitator during free exploration and can work with students on an individual level based on interest.

Musical scales, expressions, and notes are posted in the cafeteria. Posters of musical instruments, concerts, and musicians decorate the school.

Creating a Body Smart Environment

We make our MI school a bodily/kinesthetic-friendly environment by providing students with places for student-selected physical activity (tag and juggling) and expressive movement. Many schools offer soccer and football fields; courts for tennis and paddleball; nets for volleyball and badminton; basketball courts; track for hurdles, sprints, and cross-country; jungle gyms for monkeying around; sandboxes for playing, digging and building; pools for swimming, diving and water polo; tricycles for cruising; a weight room for weight training and conditioning.

The MI school celebrates the bodily/kinesthetic with posters of famous athletes, sporting events, and student records for speed, strength, flexibility and sports.

Places for expressive movement in the MI school include a stage or theater for plays, skits, dances and other performances.

Creating a Nature Smart Environment

Have you ever been to a botanical garden, nursery, or park that has little plaques listing the names of various flora and fauna? Have you ever said to yourself, "Aha, so that's a pygmy date palm, and that's a fan palm, and that's a king palm, and that's a queen palm, and that's a sago palm." Maybe you already knew the difference. Do your students? A fun activity for the Nature Club is to make other students more aware of their natural surroundings. Club members create namecards for all the flora and fauna found around the school, and include the Latin genus and species names as well.

Nature club members lead other students through the school, pointing out the peculiarities of their natural surrounding.

To promote the naturalist intelligence, the school's physical environment is made more ecologically diverse. Climate and space permitting, a range of trees, bushes, flowers, and rocks makes for an appealing natural environment. As an afternoon project, students at Green Tree East in Victorville, California (Teele, 1997) landscaped and put in an irrigation system.

An agricultural farm, greenhouse, aviary, cactus garden, aquarium, orchid hothouse, and garden also promote the naturalist intelligence. Students raise chickens, horses, and ducks in the agricultural farm; watch sunflowers and gladioli grow in the greenhouse; and grow carrots and peas in the garden.

Creating a People Smart Environment

School provides an excellent environment for learning interpersonal skills. In the class, a diverse mix of students come together for a trimester, semester, or entire school year; some students advance from grade to grade together for several years. Outside of the classroom, even a broader, more diverse mix of students come together for breaks, recess, lunch, and school-wide programs. How students interact and the relations they establish with peers depends more on what goes on in the classroom and the school programs than the physical environment. If students work in heterogeneous cooperative teams within classrooms, and the school has cross-age programs, or implements other programs designed to create a sense of community within the school, interpersonal relations will be constructive. If the school does nothing to integrate students, left to their own devices and socialization, students are likely to self-segregate, especially along race and cultural lines.

Interpersonal relations and skills are improved in the MI school because teachers model acceptance. Some people say elementary teachers love the students; secondary students love the content. It's not true. We all genuinely care about students; that's why we are teachers! As we accept and celebrate individual differences, we let our love show through, promoting positive interpersonal relations. Students are more capable of caring and sharing when they feel accepted and loved.

The MI school is decorated to reflect our commitment to multiculturalism. Celebrating multicultural holidays, celebrations, and honoring famous individuals of many cultures is another way to make our students feel known and accepted.

The school environment also promotes appropriate behavior. There always will be the occasional tiff, quarrel, or spat. By posting a school-wide code of conduct and the consequences for inappropriate behavior, we provide consistent, fair discipline for all students.

Creating a Self Smart Environment

In our MI school, we create an environment that promotes intrapersonal development. We keep students informed about the world of future possibilities. A calendar is posted for upcoming events in which students can participate, clubs students can sign up for, apprenticeship and career opportunities. We acknowledge students for their achievement or products by displaying their work for public recognition. We motivate students and nurture self-esteem and self-worth with positive sayings, banners. Posters honor the uniqueness of every student.

For some students, accessing the intrapersonal intelligence may mean quiet reflection time. In the MI school, there are retreats where students can go to think, write or reflect in peace. Carrels or cubbies in the library, a quiet zone in the cafeteria, and a meditation garden on the playground validate the intrapersonal intelligence.

MI Resources

Having rich instructional materials available to students and teachers contributes to the MI school. Resources associated with each intelligence are described in Chapter 14: Creating the MI Class. Amassing a stockpile of MI resources does not have to be an expensive venture. Parents, local businesses, and even secondhand stores may prove to be a wonderful source for MI resources. A parent may have a garage full of old records of every genre and a record player they are more than happy to donate. A local art supply store may be thrilled to finally find a worthwhile use for their slightly damaged canvases and brushes. For less than a dollar at a thrift store, we can pick up mechanical and electrical appliances for students to assemble and disassemble (unplugged, of course).

One fun way to collect resources is to have every class brainstorm resources for each intelligence. You can also use the lists provided in Chapter 14: Creating the MI Class. Create a scavenger list from that students and teachers can use to try to locate re-

sources in the community and bring back to school. Materials can be housed in teachers' classrooms, in the library or media room to check out, or in a "Think Tank" or "Flow Room" for students to visit.

The Think Tank or Flow Room is a great idea for providing students access to a wealth of instructional resources to stimulate their multiple intelligences. In an article for *Educational Leadership's* Teaching for Multiple Intelligences issue, Jean Sausele Knodt (1997) describes a combination discovery room and lab, called the "Think Tank" that she designs and directs at Kent Gardens Elementary School in McLean, Virginia. The "Think Tank" is similar to the Key School's "Flow Room."

The Think Tank is a place where students go experience hands-on discovery projects that are based on the eight intelligences. The activities are integrated with other coursework. Below is Jean Sausele Knodt's description of the Think Tank:

> The Think Tank is a large room with a light and open atmosphere. A wall of windows lines the length of it, under which open boxes of project materials are shelved. Rugs, pillows, and plants are scattered about. Mozart or other music is often playing.
>
> Walk into a lab in progress and you see children engaged in a variety of group or individual activities. They may be working on a project at one of the round tables or at "Think It! Do It!" — our invention center. Some may be collaborating on "20 Questions," comfortably propped up on pillows. Others may be searching for objects to view under a microscope, making architectural drawings, or examining the way a door knob works. The spirit and tempo will vary from loud and active to pensive and quiet, but all the students seem to be having fun while working hard (Knodt, 1997).

A wide array of MI resources contributes to the MI school and the development of the multiple intelligences. Many resources can be obtained at little or no cost and the process of collecting MI resources may be turned into a fun, schoolwide project.

Classroom Configurations

The traditional self-contained classroom is not necessarily the best — and certainly not the only — possible classroom configuration for the MI school. In the MI school, there is room for flexible classroom and teaching arrangements that build on teachers' strengths to best meet students' needs. Within the classroom, centers, cooperative learning, and multi-age grouping are alternative arrangements that lend themselves well to MI. Across classrooms, configurations range the continuum from planning lessons together to truly collaborative co-teaching (Anderson et al., 1996) Let's look at a few options for team planning and teaching that promote matching, stretching, and celebrating MI.

Team Planning

Team planning is a step toward collegiality and collaboration. Two or more teachers, usually from the same or similar grade levels, plan MI lessons or adapt existing lessons to integrate the multiple intelligences. The combination of our strengths and ideas often leads to synergistic lessons whose sum is greater than the individual parts. Students are enriched by learning experiences which are more diverse and engage more intelligences. We benefit from the multiple perspectives and the shared work. After we present a lesson, we can meet again in planning teams to reflect on the lesson.

Expert Teachers

Another collaborative teaching arrangement is expert teachers. This arrangement recognizes that we, as well as our students, have particular strengths. Classes are combined, and we take turns teaching, each sharing with students' our expert skills or experiences. For example, three fifth grade teachers teaching a unit on the rainforest may take turns presenting a lesson, each teaching about the rainforest, but engaging a different intelligence. The first may have students list and categorize the products of the rainforest (logical/mathematical); the second may have students work in pairs to write acrostic RAINFOREST poems (verbal/linguistic); and the third who is especially artistic may lead students in creating team rainforest murals with colored construction paper, scissors, and glue.

Expert teaching frees us up to work more intimately with students who may need help or to prep our next lesson — perhaps a rainforest lesson that stimulates the bodily/kinesthetic intelligence. In the traditional cellular-class format, only a portion of the students have access to our particular skills and strengths. Expert teachers allow all students to the opportunity to learn from more than one teacher and benefit from our unique strengths and experiences.

Co-Teaching

Co-teaching involves true collaboration among teachers. Rather than the traditional compartmentalized classroom in which one teacher is responsible for the classroom, co-teaching involves shared responsibility by two or more teachers. Co-teaching can be used to teach a lesson together. For example, two history courses, both studying the Vietnam war, may be brought together for a lesson on comparing Vietnamese culture and American culture. The teachers may split the lesson, each focusing on a different intelligence or set of intelligences. The fist teacher, who recently returned from a vacation in Vietnam, may engage the visual/spatial intelligence with a narrated slide show. The second may work with students to develop their outlines for their cultural comparisons. Teachers may also teach simultaneously as when they present a debate or each give their views on an issue.

We can also use co-teaching with centers and projects. Combining classes temporarily for centers or projects allows both teachers to be present. One teacher can work with the students at the Descartes (math) center and the other at the Hemingway (language) center. During the development of a project, one teacher can work with students building their projects, and the second on presenting it to the class.

Another, more permanent, co-teaching arrangement involves actually combining two classes for a unit ore even the entire semester or year. In the elementary school, two third grade classes may be combined; mixed-grade combinations are possible too. At the middle or high school level, two same-subject classes can be combined, or even two different, but related disciplines can be combined for a more integrated approach to teaching the content. See box: On Team Teaching.

Team planning, expert teaching and co-teaching are options to consider for the MI school. Planning lessons together decreases the workload and increases the potential for more diverse lessons to reach all intelligences. Presenting lessons based on teacher strengths' gives students the oppor-

On Team Teaching

High school student on team teaching:

Team-taught classes are great. I was fortunate enough to participate in World Cultures, a combination history and English class instructed by two top-notch teachers. Together, they kept sixty of my fellow peers and myself occupied and energetic about learning for two hours straight. We were often less than willing to learn — more interested in attending to our ever important social issues — yet somehow managed to learn the material. It amazed me how sixty sophomores could learn not only as peers, but as friends. But looking back, I realize this was no accident, simply a side effect of the style in which we were taught. We usually worked in small groups — reading together, discussing together, and learning together. My thoughts were open to new ideas and points of view. In short, we learned new and better ways to think.

The lessons taught spanned far beyond English and history; we learned how to work with others as well as to think for ourselves.
— *High School Student* (Anderson et al., 1996)

tunities to receive expert instruction and to be stretched in each intelligence. Teaching together allows us to build on each other's strengths. With alternative classroom configurations, we share a sense of responsibility and a commitment to all students: They are all our students; as a team of educators we work together to do what's best for them.

MI Programs

There are a number of different schoolwide programs we can implement and coordinate to promote the MI school. Let's look at intelligences clubs, cross-age tutors, assemblies, multicultural celebrations, apprenticeships and internships.

Intelligences Clubs

Many schools have clubs that span the range of intelligences. Each teacher can be in charge of one club that meets periodically for activities, to plan events, and discuss areas of interest. Students can create their own clubs based on interest. One possible activity is for members to share their interest with the whole school, or to use their interest to improve the school. For example, the Chess Club may host chess lessons; the French Club may hold a French pastry day; the Artists Club may be in charge of creating a mural for a school wall or a hands-on art day at which art mediums of all sorts are placed about the school. See box: Intelligences Clubs.

Cross-Age Tutors

Cross-age peer tutoring, also called a Buddies program (Child Development Project, 1996) involves older students tutoring younger students. These programs stretch the interpersonal intelligence and create a caring school community. Both older and younger students benefit from having a buddy. Older students are put in the role of the teacher and learn patience, responsibility, and caring. They begin to feel important, and further master content and skills as they teach their younger buddies. Younger students benefit from the attention, feel a connection to school, feel more comfortable with older students, have a positive role model, and master skills or learn content as they work with their older buddies.

Buddies is a terrific program to develop the intelligences. Buddies activities develop the range of intelligences as students work together to: write a story, read a book, solve math problems, create art, build models, sing songs, care for a pet, plant a garden, learn an instrument, make a skit, go on field trips. The possibilities are many.

For cross-age peer tutoring, we coordinate efforts with other teachers to decide how often students will meet, who will be matched with whom, how long buddies will stay together, what buddies will work

Intelligences Clubs

Here are clubs that span the range of intelligences and content areas.

- Acting Club
- Artists Club
- Architects Club
- Book Club
- Charity Club
- Chess Club
- Community Improvement Club
- Computer Club
- Cooking Club

- Dance Club
- Environmental Club
- French Club
- German Club
- Go Club
- History Club
- Industrial Arts Club
- Internet Club
- Italian Club
- Math Wizards Club

- Mechanics Club
- Mime Club
- Music Club
- Nature Club
- Poetry Club
- Science Club
- Social Club
- Spanish Club
- Sports Fanatics Club
- Writers Club

on. Buddies can be randomly formed and changed often so students get the opportunity to work with lots of other students; or buddies can be deliberately matched: a student who needs help with math may be matched with a buddy whose forte is the logical/mathematical intelligence. Long-term matches create intimate interpersonal relations in the school. See box: On Cross-Age Peer Tutoring.

MI Assemblies

Schoolwide assemblies can be used to teach students about MI and to broaden students' horizons in all intelligences. We can have guest speakers come to the school and speak to the school about their experiences or expertise in a certain field, or we can design fun whole-school activities to promote the development of each intelligence. For example, for the verbal/linguistic intelligence, we can have a poet share her poems, a children's book writer share a book, or we can hold a spelling bee. For the musical/rhythmic intelligence, we can have talented musicians create music as the school sings and claps in harmony. For the bodily/kinesthetic intelligence, we can host multicultural dancers who recreate the dances of many lands; we can watch a play. For the intrapersonal intelligence, we can host an inspirational speaker to motivate students to reach for their dreams.

Multicultural Holidays and Celebrations

A great schoolwide program for developing the personal intelligences is celebrating multicultural holidays and events. The school can have a Mardi Gras parade in March, a fiesta for the Cinco de Mayo, and an Oktoberfest in October. Students have fun as they participate in the celebration and learn about the traditions and history of a variety of cultures.

On Cross-Age Peer Tutors

Student and Principal comments on cross-age peer tutoring (quoted in Developmental Studies Center, 1996):

I've always wanted a little sister, and now it's like I've got one. I can help her do things, and I just feel really special that I can do that for her.
— *5th Grade Student*

Our teachers have really embraced Buddies — it's been such a powerful community builder in our school. To hear the younger children refer to their buddies, and to see their faces light up when they pass in the hall — these friendships clearly make a difference. And Buddies brings out the very best in older students.
— *Principal*

Apprenticeships and Internships

Apprenticeships is one of Gardner's favored applications of the MI theory. An apprenticeship is a mutually beneficial arrangement. Students get tutelage by a skilled craftsperson or tradesperson. In return, the mentor gets the students' assistance and the opportunity to pass on knowledge and skills. An internship is usually arranged with a local business. Apprenticeships and internships can span the range of intelligences and provide students with real-world skills. Apprenticeships can occur in the school but more often take place in the community. In the school, students can work with members of the staff . Teacher's Aid is a fairly common apprenticeship. Many middle and high schools have TA's available as an elective; universities require it for graduate students. There is no reason why there can't be a principal's aid, gardener's aid, secretary's aid, janitor's aid, coach's aid and so on. Middle and high schools who have a wider range of elective courses — cooking, woodshop, metal, auto shop, graphic arts — have a range of potential apprenticeships right in the school!

Another type of apprenticeship program within the school is to bring master craftspersons or tradespersons from the community into the school. Teachers who possess special skills in an area can also serve as mentors. Students can sign up for a project of interest and receive tutelage, by a master.

With apprenticeships, we must take care not to track students into careers at an early age. By allowing students to participate in a number of apprenticeships or internships over the course of their education, students gain a well-rounded education and can explore many options of interest.

Apprenticeships and internships can be set up in the community too. Crime among school-age students is at its peak from the time students get out of school, until the early evening, usually when students' parents return. Apprenticeships and internships are a productive alternative for latch-key kids. Critical to the success of an apprenticeship or internship is creating an effective partnership between the mentor or company and the student. Some companies, if we're not careful, inadvertently take advantage of students and use them as free laborers. It must be made clear that students donate their time in effort in exchange for on-the-job training and skills.

As Gardner notes, with apprenticeships we must take care not to track students into careers at an early age. By allowing students to participate in a number of apprenticeships or internships over the course of their

education, students gain a well-rounded education and can explore many options of interest.

With apprenticeships and internships, students are immersed in contextual learning, and the barrier between learning and the real world disintegrates.

MI Classes

Another way to create an MI school is to offer a wide array of classes. In the elementary grades, we can do much to develop the multiple intelligences within the classroom and with schoolwide projects and programs. The more varied our classes, projects and programs, the more intelligences we engage and develop. At the middle, high school, and college levels, the development of the intelligences depends largely on the types of classes available to students. The greater breadth of courses we can provide for our students, the more we are providing a rounded, multiple intelligences education. Chapter 9: Developing the Multiple Intelligences provides a list of courses to develop each intelligence.

Schoolwide MI Themes

Schoolwide themes contribute to building the MI school. The faculty can settle on a school theme to focus on for a determined amount of time. For example, the theme may be Space. In our classrooms, we can integrate the curriculum and make connections to the school theme whenever possible. As a school, our assemblies, projects, and physical environment may reflect the schoolwide space theme. As a project, each class can contribute to the school's space decorations including planets, solar systems, exploration crafts; we can have a member of a space program give a talk; the Artists Club can have a space logo contest; the Writers Club can write space odysseys; we can watch *Apollo 13* as a school. The Renaissance can be the next (or the prior) schoolwide theme. Schoolwide themes contribute to the MI school because each theme can be used to focus on a certain intelligence or can be used to integrate all intelligences as well as the school community. For theme ideas, see Chapter 13: MI Lessons, Centers, Projects and Theme Units.

Over the course of one year, students in an MI school have the opportunity to participate in many schoolwide projects. Students work with classmates and with students outside of their class on a variety of projects across the intelligences. Students learn from each other and also get to see the talents and products of other students in the school. The projects create a fun, positive school tone and provide students with a well-rounded education.

Schoolwide MI Projects

There are many different types of projects we can design as an entire school to focus on the different intelligences. The projects can be integrated as part of the school theme or done as independent, fun MI projects. Some schoolwide MI project ideas are described at right (see box: Schoolwide MI Projects).

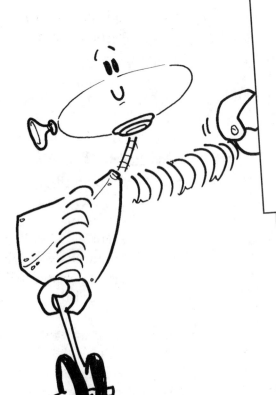

Schoolwide MI Programs

- **Intelligences Clubs**
- **Cross-Age Tutors**
- **MI Assemblies**
- **Multicultural Holidays and Celebrations**
- **Apprenticeships and Internships**
- **MI Classes**
- **Schoolwide MI Themes**
- **Schoolwide MI Projects**

Schoolwide MI Projects

Schoolwide projects develop the multiple intelligences.

Verbal/Linguistic Projects

• **Book Contest** - Students each write a book based on a certain genre or theme. Books are judged by grade level. Winners read their books to the school.

• **Poetry Reading** - Students write a poem and turn it in. Entries are formally appreciated. Poems of a range of styles and topics are shared with the school.

• **Reading Drive** - The school has a book reading goal and keeps track on a school thermometer. The school celebrates with a party when the goal is achieved.

Logical/ Mathematical Projects

• **Egg Drop** - Students design protection to keep eggs from splatting when dropped from 10 - 15 feet. Students share their designs and test them during the eggdrop. Designs are judged on a number of criteria.

• **Paper Airplane Throw** - Students research and design a paper airplane that will fly the farthest when thrown. Awards are given at each grade level.

• **Catapult Fling** - Students design a catapult to shoot a tennis ball the farthest, or closest to a target.

Visual/Spatial Projects

• **School Mural** - Students work in small teams to submit an entry for a school mural on a given topic or for the school mascot or logo. The winning entry is painted on the wall. All students contribute to the mural.

• **Art Museum** - A topic is selected for the whole school. Students display their artwork. The art is recognized along many dimensions.

• **Design Contest** - Students design a logo for a topic or theme. The best design is used as the official school design.

• **Photo Essay Display** - Students take photographs and write an essay on the topic. Photos and essays are posted in the halls.

Musical/Rhythmic Projects

• **Air Guitar/Lip Synch** - Students rehearse a song in small groups, pairs or solo. Students perform for the school in an assembly.

• **Music Videos** - Each class votes on a song. No two classes can have the same song. Classes create and rehearse their music video, then perform it for the school.

Schoolwide MI Projects

(continued)

Bodily/Kinesthetic Projects

• **Dance** - The school has a dance, or skate night based on a theme. If the school theme is Oceans, the school has an Enchantment of the Seas dance.

• **Field Day** - Mixed-grade teams are formed. Students compete in a variety of activities: tug-of-war, wheelbarrow races, potato sack races.

• **Jog-A-Thon** - Students solicit contributions for laps around track. Money is donated to a worthy cause.

• **Construction** - Students all contribute to the construction of a school facility or even possibly a structure outside of the school, such as a patio, jungle gym, or playhouse.

Naturalist Projects

• **Recycling Drives** - The school recycles used newspapers, bottles or aluminum cans. School and class goals are set and celebrated when reached.

• **Camp** - Students create or go to a nature camp.

• **Science Fair** - Each student or team of students completes a project on science or nature. Projects are based on the school's theme.

Interpersonal Projects

• **Carnival** - Every class is in charge of a different event. Students attend the carnival, and take turns working booths, games, shows.

• **Party** - Everyone brings one item: food, desserts, beverages, utensils. The school celebrates together.

• **Food and Blood Drives** - Students bring in canned food to feed the hungry, or donate blood for medical assistance. The school celebrates as it reaches different goals.

Intrapersonal Projects

• **Career Fair** - Local business set up booths and have volunteers share about careers.

• **Time Capsule** - Everyone contributes something personally meaningful — story, art, video, essay, poem — to a time capsule. The capsule is buried to give future generations a glimpse of modern times.

Gardner's Individual-Centered School

Gardner, the originator of MI theory, has provided his vision of the MI school. We will express reservations about testing designed to council students into different curriculum and/or instruction based on presumed differences in patterns of intelligences, see Chapter 16: Is MI Testing for Differential Education Desirable? If the pitfalls of differential curriculum and instruction can be avoided, the philosophy of the individual-centered school provides inspiration. In the individual-centered school, each student is encouraged to discover and develop his or her own unique pattern of intelligences — to realize fully their own individuality.

Gardner's theory of multiple intelligences was developed in attempt to describe human intelligence, a theoretical pursuit, not as a practical approach to education. Yet, in time, Gardner "began to evolve some notions about an education framed in the 'spirit' of multiple intelligences (Gardner, 1993, p. 66)." Gardner's vision for the school of the future is what he calls the individual-centered school.

To describe his individual-centered school, Gardner contrasts it with what he calls "uniform schooling." Uniform schooling is based on the idea that there is a "basic set of competencies, and a core body of knowledge, which every individual in our society should master (Gardner, 1993, p. 96)." Therefore, a uniform schooling involves uniform curriculum, teaching methods, and standardized assessment for all students. Schooling is evaluated in terms of the standards achieved.

Individual-centered schooling, on the other hand, seeks to "maximize the educational achievements of each person (Gardner, 1993, p. 96)." Gardner's rationale for the individual-centered school is two-fold: 1) Students have different minds. As MI Theory suggests, students have different intellectual profiles, so the goal of education should not be an attempt to make students more uniform, but rather maximize each student's intellectual potential. 2) Students can not master the range of disciplines and competencies. The world's knowledge base is rapidly increasing. Students can no longer be expected to master the basic set of competencies and core body of knowledge.

At the heart of the individual-centered school are three roles filled by the school staff: the assessment specialist, the student-curriculum broker, and the school-community broker.

Assessment Specialist

The assessment specialist's role is to regularly assess "strengths, inclinations, and weaknesses of the children in the school (Gardner, 1993, p. 72)." Instead of using standardized testing, the assessment specialist must use intelligence-fair measures which are developmentally appropriate and administered in a contextual setting. The findings of the assessment specialist are to be shared with teachers, parents, students and the student-curriculum broker.

Student-Curriculum Broker

The job of the student-curriculum broker is to use students' assessed strengths, inclinations and weaknesses to:

> "recommend which courses the student should elect; and in the event of a uniform curriculum, recommend how these materials are most likely to be mastered by the student (Gardner, 1993, p. 73)."

The student-curriculum broker helps students match their electives and/or the way the curriculum is presented to their intellectual profile. So, students with different profiles receive different curriculum, or are at least, presented the same curriculum differently.

School-Community Broker

This staff member uses students' assessments to "search for educational opportunities for the student within a wider community (Gardner, 1993, p. 73)." The school-community broker assembles a database of job opportunities, apprenticeships, community organizations, mentorships to help students "discover a vocational or avocational role that matches their own profile of intelligences (Gardner, 1993, p. 73)." The idea is to give students the opportunity to engage and develop their own proclivities and talents in a broader setting than in the school.

The school day for a student of Gardner's individual-centered school might look something like this: The first half of the day, students learn the traditional disciplines — reading, writing, math, social studies, science — in an untraditional way — through projects. In the classroom there is an atmosphere created for students to freely explore the content. Gardner gives the example of children's museums and apprenticeships which allow students to explore the content through engaging and

meaningful individual projects. For the latter half of the school day, students continue their explorations or investigations in the community. Students venture to museums, theaters, symphonies, aquariums. Unlike field trips, these excursions are frequent and students return to locales on a regular basis.

Gardner says the success of the individual-centered school depends on four factors: 1) intelligence-fair *assessment* of students; 2) *curriculum* that focuses on skills, knowledge, and desirable understandings; 3) *teacher education and professional development*; and 4) *community participation*.

• • • • • • • • • • • • • • •

Model Multiple Intelligences Programs and Schools

In creating the MI school, we can borrow ideas from other MI schools and programs. Let's look at a few model MI programs and schools: Project Spectrum, Key School, Green Tree East, and New City School.

Project Spectrum

Project Spectrum, a collaborative research effort between Harvard Project Zero and Tufts University, started out as a search for the indices of the original seven intelligences in preschool children. As a scientific pursuit, Project Spectrum aimed to address the questions of how early individual differences could be detected and how reliable and predictive were differences identified early. Spectrum also had a practical pursuit: Assessed differences are most helpful to teachers and parents early because students are so malleable at such a young age.

To assess the students' profile of intelligences, children were exposed to a wide range of rich materials and learning activities across the intelligences and observed in a naturalistic, intelligence-fair setting. See box: Project Spectrum Battery.

At the end of the year, the research team created a Spectrum Report to document each child's strengths and weaknesses. The practical intent of the reports was to make recommendations on what could be done at home, school or in the community to capitalize on strengths and bolster areas of weakness. The reports were compared to those of parents, teachers, and the Stanford-Binet Intelligence Scale (IQ test).

No firm conclusions have been drawn for the Project Spectrum report, but the assessments look positive. Spectrum was able to uncover strengths of which neither parent nor teacher were aware. It is interesting to note that these strengths were in domains other than language and number (such as science, visual arts, music, social) which are presumed not as easily identifiable as traditional language and math skills. However, some parents and teachers reported outstanding strengths not identified by Spectrum.

Spectrum was also able to detect areas of strengths not predicted by the Stanford-Binet test. Follow-up data on the research suggests student strengths and working styles remained relatively constant in one- to two-year follow-up period.

These are interesting results, but what does Project Spectrum tell us about creating the MI school? What started as a research project — to test how early individual differences could be detected and how reliable are the differences — evolved into a model for MI curriculum and assessment.

In Project Spectrum, the young children were given what can be considered MI curriculum — rich, stimulating content across the range of intelligences. Students received engaging tasks in movement, language, numbers, science, social skills, visual arts, and music, perhaps a broader range of curriculum than preschoolers would normally receive. This expansive curriculum serves as a model of the type of MI curriculum we should strive to provide for our students across the grade levels.

Spectrum's assessment techniques also serve as a positive model. The assessment was contextual and developmental. Instead of using standardized testing and lumping scores into an uninterpretable sum, Spectrum attempted to create a more accurate picture of student learning. Behavioral observations were used in the context of learning. Students' work was collected and documented in portfolios and by taping stories and songs. These assessments provide students, teachers, and parents a more realistic and differentiated picture of students' abilities.

Project Spectrum raises a very important question for the MI school: Even if the assessment techniques were found to effectively identify students' strengths and weaknesses, should we as educators use these assessments to stream children? Should we provide our students differential access to curriculum or remedial pro-

Project Spectrum Battery

To assess the students' profile of intelligences, children are exposed to a wide range of rich materials and learning activities across the intelligences and are observed in naturalistic, intelligence-fair settings. Spectrum's battery of assessment measures include:

▼ Movement

Children participate in creative movement activities which emphasize sensitivity to rhythm, expressiveness, body control, generation of movement ideas, and responsiveness to music; and children participate in an outdoor obstacle course for athletic movement skill including coordination, timing, balance, and power.

▼ Language

For language, students engage in a storyboard activity in which students use their range of linguistic skills to create stories. Reporter activities have students use language to report on events they experience, like watching a movie.

▼ Numbers

Mathematics activities include a dinosaur game in which students manipulate dice for small dinosaurs to escape from the large dinosaur, and a bus game in which students make calculations to keep track of how many people ride the bus as people get on and off at various stops.

▼ Science

Science activities include a discovery area (students care for animals, grow gnats and observe natural materials like rocks and shells), a treasure hunt game (students make logical inferences about which treasures are hidden under various flags), a sink and float activity (students generate hypotheses and conduct simple experiments to determine which objects sink and float, and how to make objects sink or float), and an assembly activity (students use problem solving and other skills to take apart and put together food grinders).

▼ Social

Social measures include a classroom model activity in which children are given a miniaturized model of the classroom with pictures of classmates and the teacher for students to arrange and answer questions regarding preferences and relationships. A peer interaction checklist helps teachers assess how children interact with peers.

▼ Visual Arts

Visual arts activities include open-ended projects in drawing, painting, collages, and three dimensional works, all kept in a portfolio, and structured activities in which all students create the same projects with the same materials.

▼ Music

Music activities include singing, with attention paid to the child's ability to maintain pitch, rhythm and recall a song's properties; and music perception as students discriminate pitch and identify tunes.

grams based on observed proclivities? Differential curriculum and/or instruction is a treacherous road to travel. These are serious issues, and will be explored in depth in Chapter 16: Is Testing for Differential Education Desirable?

Key School

The Key School, an elementary school in downtown Indianapolis, Indiana, is celebrated as the nation's first MI school. Approximately two years after the publication of Gardner's *Frames of Mind*, eight teachers from Indianapolis Public Schools met with Gardner and communicated their plan to open a K-6 school based in part on multiple intelligences. After a few years of hard work and regular consultation with Gardner, the Key school was born in September of 1987 (Gardner, 1993). The Key School serves as a model MI school in many interesting aspects.

MI Curriculum

The curriculum of the Key School revolves around the multiple intelligences. Gardner describes the Key School's curriculum:

> One of its founding principles is the conviction that each child should have his or her multiple intelligences ('MI') stimulated each day. Thus every student at the Key school participates on a regular basis in the activities of computing, music, and 'bodily-kinesthetics,' in addition to theme-centered curricula that embody the standard literacies and subject matter (Gardner, 1993, p. 113).

The Key School has identified what can be called MI outcomes. Curriculum is geared to achieve outcomes across the intelligences. The Key School states that upon graduation, students will demonstrate a

---

Key School's MI Outcomes

- Communicates clearly in written form
- Is verbally articulate in two languages
- Sings or plays a musical instrument proficiently
- Uses math and logic in applied areas
- Uses technology as a tool for inquiry and communication
- Recreates the three-dimensional world through the visual or practical arts
- Is physically fit
- Selects applied area for inquiry, reflection, and apprenticeship
- Participates in stewardship activities demonstrating a shared relationship with nature
- Expresses capacity to care about global issues
- Participates in groups and organizations in the larger community
- If 18, is an active registered voter

(Campbell, Campbell & Dickinson, 1996, p. 247)

---

number of specific skills across the intelligences. See box: Key School's MI Outcomes.

MI Assessment

The Key School uses alternative assessments. The assessments include progress reports, developmental performance descriptors, and video portfolios which document each student's development (Bolaños, 1997).

Progress reports (Bolaños, 1997; Lazear, 1994) are divided into the original seven intelligences. For each intelligence there are the related disciplines and the skills associated with each discipline. Students are graded on their progress, their participa-

Key School Progress Report

This is the "Linguistic" section of the Key School's progress report and the definition of terms for grading on Progress, Participation, and Performance. The progress report includes the original seven intelligences and skills associated with each intelligence.

LINGUISTIC

English:

	Progress	Participation	Performance
Listening			
Speaking			
Writing			
Reading			
Self-Evaluation			

Comments:_____

Foreign Language (   ):

Listening			
Speaking			
Writing			
Reading			
Self-Evaluation			

Comments:_____

Source: Bolaños, 1997; Lazear, 1994.

Definition of Terms

For Progress, students are given:
- **N** - Slow Progress, Needs Help
- **S** - Steady Progress
- **R** - Rapid Progress

For Participation, students are given:
- ▲ **Intrinsically Motivated** - Student shows enjoyment and involvement in the activity for its own sake regardless of external support or punishment
- ❑ **Extrinsically Motivated** - Student responds to teacher-initiated activities and rewards
- ○ **Passive** - Little or no effort to participate
- ✕ **Disruptive** - Interferes with others being able to participate.

For Performance, students are graded according to the developmental continuum:
- **UL** - Universal Level
- **CL** - Cultural Level
- **DL** - Discipline-Based Level

tion and their performance for each skill. Students also evaluate themselves for each discipline. See box: Key School Progress Report.

Pods & Apprenticeships

Each day, students work in "pods" to master a craft or real-world skill like gardening or architecture. Pods consist of students of different age levels and a teacher or skilled adult. Similar to multiage classrooms, students work at a developmentally appropriate pace. The pods provide an ap-

Key School Themes

Sets of schoolwide themes for the Key School and Key Renaissance School for 1987-1997 included:

- Connections
- Patterns
- Changes in Time and Space

- Working in Harmony: Here and Now
- Working in Harmony: In Other Cultures
- Working in Harmony: With Nature/Inventions

- Let's Make a Difference
- Heritage
- Renaissance: Then and Now

- Treasures
- Pathfinders
- Marvels

- Frontiers
- Global Perspectives
- Networks

- Relationships and Fellowships
- Mysterious Wonders
- Magical Moments

- Migrations
- Boundaries, Horizons
- Expressions

- Journeys
- Blueprints
- Quests

- Tapestry
- Illusions
- Catalysts

Source: Bolaños, 1997

prenticeship opportunity so students pick up life skills through observing and working with a mentor.

Additionally, outside specialists, usually parents or community members, visit the school weekly to demonstrate an occupation or craft. Often, the demonstrations are integrated into the theme or curriculum.

Students also can enter into long-term apprenticeships in activities like animation, journalism, and meteorology through the local Indianapolis Children's Museum.

School-Wide Themes

The Key School features three themes through the school year, approximately one theme every ten week period. The theme is selected by the school staff. Each teacher writes their own personal interpretation of the theme and designs activities, linked with a particular discipline. See box: Key School Themes.

Student Projects

Each student is required to do a project on each theme for the year. Some projects are cooperative efforts, others individualistic. Projects are often like apprenticeships in which students are guided though the various stages by a skilled mentor. Students examine the theme in detail and integrate their multiple intelligences as they plan, create, rehearse, present, and reflect on their projects.

In the presentation of their projects, students share with the class the inception, the process, details, implications; presenters answer student and teacher questions. Student presentations are videotaped. Through the succession of projects, students create a video portfolio which documents their development over time. At the end of the theme period, student projects are put on display in the school. All students interestedly examine each other's projects.

Community Resource Committee

Representatives from community businesses, cultural organizations, local government, arts, and higher education put together weekly assemblies for the entire school. The assemblies are often based on the schoolwide themes. For example, if "tapestry" is the theme, speakers might share with students the tapestry of weaving, the tapestry of mathematics and tessellations, and the tapestry of human diversity in literature.

Flow Room

The flow room is an MI resource room, designed to activate the multiple intelligences. In the flow room, there are computers, puzzles, board games, and other learning materials across the intelligences. Students have free choice in the flow room; they can participate in any of the activities alone or with other students. A teacher is present to help facilitate activities and observe students. The Key School's flow room is very similar to the think tank described earlier in this chapter.

Green Tree East

In 1992, Green Tree East in Victorville, California opened a K-6 multiple intelligences elementary school. In her book, Sue Teele (1997) describes the research she conducted at Green Tree East and provides a detailed description of how the school established a multiple intelligences environment. Green Tree East has incorporated the multiple intelligences philosophy in the

physical setting (classrooms, playground, cafeteria), school philosophy (parent involvement, mission), special programs, and the social climate (school relationships). Let's visit Green Tree East and see how they have created a successful MI school.

Physical Setting
Classrooms

As we peek inside the classrooms, we find obvious signs of MI. Colorfully displayed on the walls are posters made by the principal that describe the seven intelligences. There are also motivational posters about success and self-esteem. Student work that spans the range of intelligences hangs from the ceilings and is displayed on the walls. In most classes, round tables are used for centers at which students explore and develop their seven intelligences. Some classes have an arrangement that enables cooperative work in groups of four. From some classes, we hear music which is integrated into instruction. With lamps, pillows, rocking chairs, and stuffed animals, many classrooms create a friendly, comfortable learning environment.

Playground

On the playground, connections are made between the bodily/kinesthetic intelligence and the verbal/linguistic intelligence: Words are painted on the blacktop which teachers may use for instructional purposes.

Cafeteria

On the walls of the cafeteria, there are posters supporting the seven intelligences, vocabulary words, and musical notes for students to read and learn. Every Friday, students engage their musical intelligence and interpersonal intelligence with their "Dining In" program. Students listen to their

Green Tree East's Mission Statement

Education will be a process that encourages continual progress through the improvement of one's abilities, the expansion of one's character. Our mission is to facilitate growth through excellence in process and product (Teele, 1997).

favorite music and practice their best manners while eating at the tables covered by tablecloths and decorated with floral arrangements.

Library

The library houses books, but is also a resource center. Resources to engage the intelligences are available for teachers to check out. Some resources include: tape recorders, magnifying glasses, science kits, prisms, math manipulatives, games, puzzles, videos, books on tape, keyboards, recorders, records, record players, camcorder, televisions, parachute, hockey sticks, volleyballs. Student projects such as art work, literary work, model houses, dinosaur habitats and fossils in shoe boxes, trains made of cake are displayed in the library.

Landscape

The relatively bare landscape was transformed as an afternoon Accelerated Learning Project by students, teachers and volunteers. In class, students designed the irrigation system. They put in the water system, raked the soil, hauled the excess dirt, and tested drips. Students picked out the flowers to plant, selected kindergarten

buddies, and helped the youngsters plant the ferns and flowers. This project is a great exercise for the naturalist (although the naturalist intelligence was not explicitly emphasized). By landscaping the school, students gained a great sense of pride and ownership.

School Philosophy

Much of the success of Green Tree East can be attributed to the organizational factors including the structure and philosophy of the school and support from the district.

Before school opened, a planning team consisting of the principal, the district curriculum council, and the Director of Curriculum and Instruction met and gathered input from parents, students and the community to develop a school designed to maximize students' learning and teachers' teaching potential. Through studying MI theory as well as other theory and research, they identified a common thread: Education should focus on the individual child. The child should be the center of the educational planning.

The school held several parent workshops before the school opened and shared the school's philosophy and vision. Letters were sent home explaining the school programs and more parent workshops were held after the school opened. Teachers were interviewed to ensure they were open to the school's commitment to multiple intelligences and were aware of the commitment they were making to the students. Many of the teachers had knowledge of MI theory.

The school's dedication to the individual student can be seen in their mission statement. See box: Green Tree East's Mission Statement.

The school's belief statement is also a reflection of their educational philosophy and prizing each students' uniqueness. See box: Green Tree East's Belief Statement.

District Support

The district is supportive of the school's philosophy as it is closely aligned with that of the district, as reflected in the district's own Mission Statement:

> ...as a leader in child-centered education, to empower students to excel as contributing members of society by guaranteeing a quality educational foundation (Teele,1997).

The district provides support, but because of its commitment to helping all students learn, allows the school to remain relatively independent.

Special Programs
Morning Academic Program

The morning academic program focuses on traditional skills — reading, writing, and math — through thematic instruction and integration of the multiple intelligences. Using a variety of assessments, teachers create profiles for each student and use the profiles to design instructional strategies to help all students master the basic skills. Assessments are administered throughout each trimester to enable teachers to identify students' strengths and use their dominant intelligence to develop other intelligences. Video assessments are shared with parents and plans are established. For each student, a portfolio is created including standardized assessments, authentic assessments, parent input, student input, and student samples. The assessments are used to inform students of their progress and to help teachers identify what students still need to learn.

> # Green Tree East's Belief Statement
>
> - Every child can learn.
>
> - Quality education demands shared responsibility.
>
> - Democracy requires an educated citizenry.
>
> - Every individual has worth and merits respect.
>
> - A positive vision of the future creates a powerful learner.
>
> - Every individual is unique and has talents to contribute.
>
> - Education nurtures an understanding of individual and cultural differences.
>
> - High expectations inspire high achievement.
>
> - Children have a natural love for learning.
>
> (Teele, 1997)

Afternoon Accelerated Learning Projects

For an hour and a half in the afternoon, four days a week, students participate in cross-grade Accelerated Learning Projects (ALPS). ALPS gives students the opportunity to explore their interests and intelligences as they work on stimulating projects. Students sign up for the project of their choice and work on or investigate their project for five weeks. Some sample projects that span the intelligence gamut include cartooning, Spanish language and culture, sign language, writing and performing plays and music, science experiments, art and painting, journalism, physical fitness, field hockey, chess, pottery design and study, computers, American history and music, geometry and 3D objects, video production, cooking and history, architecture and building, geology (Teele, 1997). The sixth week is dedicated to a Celebration of Accomplishments at which students display and share with each other their art, plays, and exhibits.

When it is time to select new projects, students are encouraged to pick projects that include different intelligences. Students choose from five projects a year and in under two years complete projects that address all intelligences and a range of problem-solving skills, critical and creative thinking skills, and applications to real-world projects and products.

Social Climate

Multiple intelligences positively impacts the social climate of Green Tree East. Teachers see the unique strengths among themselves and respect students as individuals. Students feel a greater sense of self-esteem and honor the uniqueness of other students.

Staff Relations

An understanding of the theory of multiple intelligences enhances staff relations. At Green Tree East, the staff's awareness of MI theory allows teachers to identify and share each members' strengths. As the principal puts it, teachers,

> Give 110% in everything they do. They have professional respect for one another because each one has truly identified strengths of each member of the staff (Teele, 1997).

Teachers willingly share their strengths and often rotate classes to share their expertise with students. Teachers have a monthly half-day planning session with grade-level teams and cross-grade sharing to link thematic instruction to MI and integrate assessment.

The collaborative partnership between the special education teacher and regular teachers helps forge a more inclusive model for special education. Instead of pulling students out, the resource specialist comes into the classroom to work with students who need assistance, instructing them through their dominant intelligences and building bridges from their strengths to areas that need improvement.

Teacher and Student Relations

With the introduction of multiple intelligences, many teachers noted a change in focus, from looking at students' deficits and problems to seeing students' strengths. Teachers also shifted their perspective from a more narrow vision of education in which the teacher's job is to provide students with the necessary academic instruction, to a broader vision that views education as the responsibility to teach whole children (socially, academically and psychologically) and prepare them for the future. From this child-centered perspective, teachers truly take responsibility for each student. As one teacher states,

> We are a whole team of people trying to help our students. We say we will not give up on them even if they seem impossible to deal with. All of us here have the responsibility to help (Teele, 1997).

Self-Esteem and Student Relations

In Green Tree East, students have an enhanced sense of self-worth, feel good about their contributions to the esteem of their peers, and have positive relationships with students in their class as well as in other classes.

In a self-esteem survey which asked students: "Do you feel good about yourself?" 92% responded "yes," and only eight percent responded "no." The same percentages held true when students were asked: "Do you help others feel good about themselves?" One activity that helps explain such positive relations, is the use of peer praise. Several students are selected weekly for their accomplishments. Students write letters to their peers, telling them how outstanding they are for their achievements. The letters are bound as a book and given to the students to keep as recognition. Overall, students, have a very positive self-concept and are proud to contribute to each other's positive self-concept.

Students operating under the MI framework acknowledge each other's strengths. As the principal put it:

> We look for specialness. That gives pride in each student. Our students do not know who is Chapter I, SDC (Special Day Class), or other compensatory programs. They know instead that they are body smart, picture smart, or word smart (Teele, 1997).

The use of cooperative learning and cross-grade projects helps students know each other and work together in a positive context. Students working in groups have learned to share and help each other. They report learning together is easier. Cross-grade peer tutoring not only improves the reading of the younger tutors and the tutees, but also establishes a positive, helping peer norm. In the ALPS classes students work with other students in other classes and at other grade levels.

Green Tree East provides a positive model for creating an MI school on a number of levels. The physical setting of the school — from the classrooms, to the playground, to the cafeteria, to the library — supports the development of teaching with, for and about the multiple intelligences. The faculty, student body, and parents share a common vision for an education that revolves around developing the abilities and character of each individual student. From this shared vision spring many wonderful programs and benefits for all involved.

New City School

The authors gratefully acknowledge Thomas Hoerr, Director of New City School, and ASCD Network Facilitator of *Teaching for Multiple Intelligences* for his following description of New City's pursuit and implementation of MI in their school:

The New City School is an independent school of 350 students, age three through the sixth grade. Located in the City of St. Louis, we are known for our unique combination of academics, ambience, and diversity. Our use of MI helps us achieve success in each of the important areas.

The pursuit of MI at New City School began in 1988. I read *Frames of Mind* and was struck by the powerful implications that it held for our school. In defining intelligence both more broadly and more pragmatically than had been done in the past, Gardner opened a world full of educational possibilities. I shared a bit about the book with our faculty and asked who would be interested in reading the book and discussing how it might be relevant to New City School. A third of our faculty, 12 teachers, responded with enthusiasm and the MI journey began. New City has never been the same!

We read and discussed, then read and discussed some more for almost a year. As we read and talked about a chapter we created lists: *What are we already doing that supports MI? What could we be doing to support MI?* and, realistically, *What could we be doing to support MI if we had money?* Our lists grew as we talked and shared together. Indeed, although we did not know it at the time, our pursuit of MI was a wonderful example of what Roland Barth calls "collegiality:" teachers learning and growing together. Throughout, we were careful to share our newfound knowledge and excitement with the rest of the faculty.

Now, ten-plus years later, we are often called "an MI school." At an external level our success with MI is obvious. We have hundreds of educators visiting us each year to learn from our experience (more than 700 visitors in 1997-98); we have hosted two MI Conferences, attracting hundreds of educators from around the country; our faculty has published two books of lesson plans and articles about our work with MI: *Celebrating Multiple Intelligences* (1994) and *Succeeding With Multiple Intelligences* (1996); and our faculty members travel around the country presenting MI workshops and writing articles for a variety of educational magazines and journals. But those achievements pale in comparison to the real results of using MI, making a positive difference for our kids.

Our students learn — a lot — and they find school fun. Recently during spring break I talked to one of our second graders who was at school attending a break camp (we provide student coverage, for a fee, 50 weeks per year, 7 a.m. to 6:30 p.m.) and asked her if she was enjoying vacation.

"It's OK," she replied, "but I can't wait for school to start." As you might imagine, her response made my day! Similarly, a couple of years ago another student was asked how he liked being at New City School. He said, "It's great, but I can never tell when I'm having fun and when I'm learning." We have students who are disappointed when summer vacation begins. School is fun for them because they can use all of their intelligences in succeeding.

But more than just learning a great deal — our students do extraordinarily well on standardized tests (averaging years above grade level, as they should!) and excel in the secondary schools they attend after leaving New City — they are learning to be successful. They are learning to use their various intelligences to learn and to show their understanding.

For us, MI has transformed our curriculum, modified our instructional techniques, and affected how we assess our students. Students are given opportunities to use their spatial intelligence to show their understanding of the Civil War; they can use their interpersonal and bodily-kinesthetic intelligences to show their understanding of biographies by being in the "Living Museum;" they use their musical intelligences to learn fractions and to bring drama to life; T-shirt book designs and dioramas are used to show what has been learned from reading books; projects and exhibitions are created to capture a student's understanding of a unit; students learn to drum to reflect the cultures of non-Europeans in looking at the impact of slavery; a Plant Museum is created to demonstrate understanding of plants and lifecycles.

But perhaps most significantly, for us MI has been a tool to pursue developing students' personal development and character. We believe that the personal intelligences are the most important intelligences and that the intrapersonal intelligence is *the* most important. Much of what we do focuses on helping children learn to work together, with those who are similar to and different from themselves, and enabling them to reflect on their strengths and weaknesses.

Our use of MI has also had a profound effect on how we communicate with our students' parents. We understand that while our job is educating our students, we also have a responsibility to help their parents understand what we are doing and why we are doing it. As a result, our halls and walls are alive not just with student art work, but with examples and explanations to help parents understand our approach to education. We have created a rubric-based report card to show students' achievements in the linguistic and logical-mathematical intelligences. In conjunction with separate written reports from specialist teachers for art, performing arts (music, dance, and drama), physical education, science, library, and Spanish, the report gives parents a full picture of their child's growth in each of the intelligences. This is supplemented by an annual Portfolio Night in which students lead parents through the contents of their portfolios.

As exciting as our MI journey has been thus far, we are looking forward to our next steps. We are looking forward to learning and growing with our students and with one another.

Please contact us if you would like more information or want to visit the New City School.

Dr. Tom Hoerr
(TRHoerr@AOL.com)
New City School
5209 Waterman
St. Louis, MO 63108
Phone: (314) 361-6411
Fax: (314) 361-1499

● ● ● ● ● ● ● ● ● ●

Summary ▶

There is no single recipe for creating an MI school. As Gardner puts it:

> At present, the notion of schools devoted to multiple intelligences is still in its infancy, and there are as many plausible recipes as there are educational chefs (Gardner, 1993, p. 250).

Each school's interpretation and application of multiple intelligences may be as unique as the students who attend our schools. However, at the heart of any MI school is the very basic unifying, guiding philosophy that each student is a unique gift. Each student has a unique profile of intelligences. Every student can learn and deserves the opportunity to learn. Our mission in the MI school is to nurture the intellectual, social, and personal development of each student attending our school.

References

Anderson, G., et al. *Team Teaching.* York, ME: Stenhouse Publishers, 1996.

Bolaños, Pat. *Authentic Pedagogy in the Key Learning Community.* Unpublished session handout, 1997.

Campbell, L., Campbell, B., & Dickinson, D. *Teaching & Learning Through Multiple Intelligences.* Needham Heights, MA: Allyn & Bacon, 1996.

Child Development Project. *That's My Buddy!* Oakland, CA: Developmental Studies Center, 1996.

Gardner, H. *Multiple Intelligences: The Theory in Practice.* New York: NY BasicBooks, 1993.

Kagan, S. *Cooperative Learning.* San Clemente, CA: Kagan Cooperative Learning, 1994.

Knodt, J. S. *A think tank cultivates kids.* ***Educational Leadership.*** 1997, *55(1)*, 35-37.

Lazear, D. *Multiple Intelligences Approaches to Assessment: Solving the Assessment Conundrum.* Tucson, AZ: Zephyr Press, 1994.

New City School Faculty. *Celebrating Multiple Intelligences: Teaching for Success.* St. Louis, MO: The New City School, 1994.

New City School Faculty. *Succeeding with Multiple Intelligences: Teaching through the Personal Intelligences.* St. Louis, MO: The New City School, 1996.

Teele, S. *The Multiple Intelligences School: A place for all students to succeed.* Redlands, CA: Sue Teele and Associates, 1997.

Is MI Testing for Differential Education Desirable?

What the best and wisest parent wants for his own child must be what the community wants for all of its children. Any other ideal for our schools is narrow and unlovely; acted upon, it destroys our democracy. — John Dewey

What is good for the best is good for the rest. To do anything less is obscene.
— Lorraine Monroe

G iven that individuals differ in their pattern of intelligences, and therefore learn best in different ways, it is tempting to conclude that we must therefore develop tests of the multiple intelligences in order to provide different curriculum and instruction to different students, depending on their particular intellectual strengths. This approach, however, would lead education down a path we all would regret.

Testing, ultimately, has but one purpose: differential treatment. If we are not going to treat a student differently as a result of having tested the student, why bother administering the test?

Howard Gardner is unequivocally opposed to formal, decontextualized testing of intelligences:

Few practices are more nefarious in education than the drawing of widespread educational implications from the composite score of a single test — like the Wechsler Intelligence Scale for Children (Gardner, 1993, p. 176).

...America today has veered too far in the direction of formal testing without adequate consideration of the costs and limitations of an exclusive emphasis on that approach (Gardner, 1993, p. 179).

Gardner points out that scores on formal tests reflect test-taking skills, but do not necessarily represent true intelligences. He calls for abandoning formal testing in favor of ongoing assessment which occurs in the context of working on engrossing problems and projects.

> Rather than being imposed "externally" at odd times during the year, assessment ought to become part of the natural learning environment. As much as possible it should occur "on the fly," as part of an individual's natural engagement in a learning situation (Gardner, 1993, p. 175).

Testing, ultimately, has but one purpose: differential treatment. If we are not going to treat a student differently as a result of having tested the student, why bother administering the test? A critical question, then, is whether we should treat different students differently, or provide all students the same curriculum and instruction. If we come down on the side of a universal rather than differential curriculum, we can eliminate the need to test or even assess the intelligences of students. Our belief is that differential treatment of students, no matter how well-intended, almost always has drawbacks which far outweigh its benefits. We favor universal curriculum and instruction and therefore believe MI testing is not necessary nor desirable.

Gardner, while opposed to using MI tests to track students, does advocate differential curriculum and instruction based on advice from an assessment specialist and a student-curriculum broker.

> The assessment specialist shares findings and recommendations with students, parents, teachers, and the occupant of a second role called the student-curriculum broker. Based on a current view of the student's intellectual profile, this broker recommends which courses the student should elect; and, in the event of a uniform curriculum, recommends how these materials are most likely to mastered by the student (Gardner, 1993, pp. 72-73).

Thus, the question of the desirability of testing hinges in part on the how much we accept the desirability of differential curriculum and instruction. If we are to treat students differently depending on their pattern of intelligences, testing or assessment of intelligences is absolutely essential. If, on the other hand, we are to provide the same curriculum and instruction to all students, testing is unnecessary. Let's turn, then, to the issue of differential versus universal curriculum and instruction.

Differential Versus Universal Curriculum and Instruction

Because students have different patterns of intelligences, to allow each student to maximize his or her potential, Gardner feels, education should be sculpted to be responsive to individual differences in intelligences.

> ...it has now been established quite convincingly that individuals have quite different minds from one another. Education ought to be so sculpted that it remains responsive to these differences. Instead of ignoring them, and pretending that all individuals have (or ought to have) the same kinds of minds, we should instead try to ensure that everyone receive an education that maximizes his or her own intellectual potential (Gardner, 1993, p. 71).

Although it would be hard to find anyone who would disagree with the notion that each individual should be allowed to maximize his or her potential, there can be honest disagreement about how best to reach that goal. Two different approaches can be distinguished: differential curriculum and instruction versus universal curriculum and instruction. The two approaches, of course, can coexist: During some parts of the school day the same curriculum can be delivered in the same way to all students, whereas during other parts of the school day students learn different curriculum, or learn the curriculum in different ways.

The question then becomes how much of the school day should be devoted to differential versus universal curriculum and instruction.

Let's assume for a moment that we have developed an intelligence-fair MI assessment program. The program includes repeated, natural assessment of students in many engaging real-life situations as they express their various intelligences. It looks at students as they interact with and reveal their knowledge of others, express their inner life, create and solve a wide range of problems involving the various intelligences, move, find their way around, respond to and create music and visual art, study and interact with nature, and engage in various projects which include linguistic and mathematical components. We have gathered a wealth of data. The question becomes: What we are to do with the data?

As we focus on the data we have collected on any one intelligence, we find, inevitably, there are some students who score high, others average, and yet others score low. As an example, let's focus on students who score low, say on linguistic ability. We have a number of options:

Option 1: Universal Curriculum

We could ignore the results of the assessment program and create a universal curriculum attempting to teach with instructional strategies that match all intelligences and to stretch or develop all intelligences in all students without providing them different curriculum or instruction.

Option 2: Remedial Curriculum

We could develop special programs for students who score low. The programs can be administered within class (e.g., individualized study, computer assisted instruction, special reading groups), through pull-out programs, or even through special classes. In essence this approach attempts to stretch weak intelligences: It focuses on a change in curriculum for those who test low in an intelligence.

Option 3: Remedial Instruction

We could leave the curriculum unchanged and instead attempt to design special instructional programs for students who score low. The programs would allow access to the existing curriculum through intelligences of strength. The Paula case study is an example: Paula blossomed in spelling and writing when she was allowed to acquire those linguistic skills through the kinesthetic intelligence. (See Chapter 2: Three Visions for Education.) In essence, this approach attempts design special instructional programs for students low in an intelligence.

There are a number of problems with Options 2 and 3. If we choose to create remedial approaches, we would need at least eight, one for students scoring low in each of the intelligences. We would need reliable assessment methods to identify students low in one or more intelligence. Further, because many students will score low in two or more intelligences, we would have scheduling nightmares trying to get everyone into proper remedial programs without their falling down in other areas of the curriculum. And the remedial programs themselves would have to be quite differentiated, because students with a poor sense of direction would not be helped by a program which focuses on developing page layout skills or art skills. Yet another serious problem with the remedial approach is the negative self-esteem likely to develop among students in the remedial programs. Any program developed to remediate deficits produces self-esteem problems, like those associated with the negative peer and self-labeling common in remedial reading programs.

If we choose Option 3, not only are scheduling, management, and program development serious implementation obstacles, but a choice to teach with some skills is necessarily a choice not to teach with others. Thus, we may inadvertently limit exposure to instruction in nondominant intelligences, exposure which might develop those intelligences most in need of development. For example, if we identify a student as weak in verbal/linguistic skills, and therefore teach that student primarily through other modes, they may never develop the very verbal/linguistic skills they most need.

We favor use of universal curriculum and instruction as much as possible. Our preference for universal curriculum and instruction is based on a fear and a belief. We fear inevitable negative effects of labeling and differential treatment of students, and we believe that by presenting the curriculum through a wide range of instruc-

tional strategies for all students, we can ensure that each student receives the content in ways compatible with his or her intellectual pattern while at the same time developing the range of intelligences. By using a wide range of instructional strategies with all students, we can provide access to the curriculum for all students through all the intelligences. This integrated approach fosters greater development of the whole student. It is possible to match all of the intelligences and to stretch all the intelligences without providing different curriculum or instruction for different students. Universal curriculum and instruction is our best chance for validating each student and providing a truly democratic education. Movement toward providing different students different curriculum and/or instruction, is fraught with potential pitfalls so great that we should not move in that direction.

> **It is possible to match all of the intelligences and to stretch all the intelligences without providing different curriculum or instruction for different students. Universal curriculum and instruction is our best chance for validating each student and providing a truly democratic education.**

This stance is in contrast to the notion of an "individual-centered school" which provides different content and instruction to students depending on their pattern of intelligences. Although Gardner does not advocate formal testing of the intelligences, he does advocate ongoing assessment in the context of engrossing, natural problem solving. The aim of the assessment: differential treatment of students. Ongoing assessment is integral to Gardner's vision of the ideal MI school — the "Individual-Centered School."

The Individual-Centered School

Gardner's recommendation for applying MI theory to education is to create an "individual-centered school" which provides different content and instructional strategies to students depending on their pattern of intelligences.

To provide this differentiated education, in the individual centered school educators would assess the intellectual pattern of each student. Assessment, however, would not necessarily be the job of the teacher. Gardner indicates that role could be filled by someone else, an expert, whose job it is to inform the teachers, students, and others of the intelligence pattern of each student.

> A convenient way to sketch an individual-centered school is to delineate a set a roles that would be carried out within the school or school system. A first role I have termed the assessment specialist. It is his or her task to provide a regular, updated view of the particular strengths, inclinations, and weaknesses of the children in the school (Gardner, 1993, p. 72).

In the individual-centered school the assessment specialist would not rely on standardized tests, but rather on intelligence-fair, developmentally appropriate assessments which would result in concrete recommendations. The recommendations of the assessment specialist would be geared toward matching students to curriculum and instructional strategies in accordance with their patterns of intelligence.

> The assessment specialist shares findings and recommendations with students, parents, teachers, and the occupant of a second role called the student-curriculum broker. Based on a current view of the student's intellectual pro-

file, this broker recommends which courses the student should elect; and, in the event of a uniform curriculum, recommends how these materials are most likely to mastered by the student (Gardner, 1993, Pp. 72-73).

Results of the intelligences assessments would be used by educators and by students themselves to select curriculum and instructional strategies tailored to the student.

> To the extent that there are electives, it is pertinent for students to know their own proclivities. This knowledge should not be used to dictate electives (in itself a contradiction in terms!). Rather, knowledge of one's own strengths can help one to choose courses that might be particularly congenial to one's learning style. In the case of a uniform or required curriculum, such information is equally important. For even if the courses themselves are mandated, there is no reason why they need be taught in the same way to all…. A history lesson can be presented through linguistic, logical, spatial, and/or personal modes of knowing, even as a geometry class can draw upon spatial, logical, linguistic, or numerical competencies (sic) (Gardner, 1993, p. 73).

This mission of providing a differentiated curriculum and instruction to each student based on their intelligences, is facilitated by a school-community broker. "The goal of the school-community broker is to increase the likelihood that students will discover a vocational or avocational role that matches their own profile of intelligences (Gardner, 1993, p. 73)." The school-community broker would collect and organize information about apprenticeships, mentorships, and community organizations which exemplify a particular blend of intelligences.

> Of course, the information culled by the school-community broker could be drawn on by any student. In practice, however, it is particularly important for students who exhibit an unusual, nonscholastic profile of intelligences. After all, those students with a blend of linguistic and logical intelligences are likely

to do well in school, to evolve a positive self-image, and thus to feel less need for special counseling and for pursuing out-of-the-ordinary opportunities. On the other hand, for the students with unusual intellectual configurations, the school-community broker can provide the perhaps life-changing opportunity…(Gardner, 1993, p. 74).

The individual-centered school is nothing short of a redefinition of the goal of schooling. The mission of schools in this view is to help each student realize his or her unique potential. To realize this goal, teachers, counselors, and students themselves must know the student's intelligence profile. Intelligence assessment, then, is a key to success in the individual-centered school. Educators must know the intellectual profile of each student so they can create and make available learning opportunities tailored to each student's intelligences profile. Key to success in an individual-centered school, then, is frequent, and accurate assessment of intelligences:

> An individual-centered school would be rich in assessment of individual abilities and proclivities. It would seek to match individuals not only to curricular areas, but also to particular ways of teaching those subjects. After the first few grades, the school would also seek to match individuals with the various kinds of life and work options that are available in their culture (Gardner, 1993, p. 10).

Undesirable Outcomes of Differential Education

As well-intended as are these recommendations, we believe that a movement to provide individual students or groups of students with different curriculum and/or instruction based on their intelligences is

We believe that a movement to provide individual students or groups of students with different curriculum and/or instruction is a movement in the wrong direction.

a movement in the wrong direction. Students should not be matched with different curriculum nor different instruction. As noble as it is to want to help each child realize his or her unique potential, creating differential curriculum and instruction for students is contrary to the role of schools in a democracy. Let's examine six reasons we should not set up programs to assign or counsel students into different educational experiences.

Institutionalized Inequality

Students enter school with very different abilities. Some have had parents who have read to them every night; others do not have a book in their home. Some have played many number games with a grand array of manipulatives; others have never seen math or logic games. On standardized tests of linguistic and mathematical functioning, whole schools, depending on their socioeconomic status, have almost nonoverlapping distributions of achievement scores at early grades — the lowest scoring children in some high socioeconomic status schools score higher than those in the top quartile in many low socioeconomic schools. Every educator is familiar with these vast differences; they are perhaps the greatest challenge facing education in the United States today.

Even within one school in which there are socioeconomic differences among children, very large discrepancies appear. Some students come to school readers; others have never seen a book. The differences created by these very different preschool experiences do not disappear within the first few grades of school. Any testing program which assesses linguistic and mathematical functioning within the first few grades of school will reflect not just individual differences in brain structure or function, but also environmental background. Therefore differential experience can never be factored out of the equation; there is no such thing as a pure test of potential. And any program which uses assessment of any sort to track students into differential learning experiences whether they be differential curriculum or differential instruction, institutionalizes environmental differences.

In a democratic society, schools should not crystallize and exaggerate differences students bring to school based on the advantages of being born wealthy or in an enriched environment.

One of the problems with programs designed to teach through strengths is that strengths are a function not just of natural predispositions, but also experiences. For example, some students have not had exposure to text material before attending school. Others have for years had rich daily training in decoding text. If we then assess students on their verbal/linguistic skills, and design programs to teach with the verbal/linguistic intelligence for those students who score high in that intelligence, we sentence those with impoverished preschool experiences to unequal, impoverished opportunities for development. We give least to those who need most. This approach is exactly opposite the role education should play in a democracy. Schools in a democracy should level the playing field, allowing all students, regardless of preschool experiences to, over time, maximize their potential in all areas. Schools should not crystallize and exaggerate differences students bring to school based on the advantages of being born wealthy or in an enriched environment.

Admittedly, the potential of each individual in each area of the curriculum is different. But individuals will never realize their potential if we assign some to more enriched experiences than others depending on assessment of their intelligences. It is not possible to develop "intelligence-fair" tests which measure only potential and not prior experience. Functioning of any type is largely influenced by prior experience. And given that preschool experiences of students differ so greatly, any early assessment program institutionalizes preschool inequalities. Democratic schools should do exactly the opposite: Provide all students as enriched educational experiences as possible — especially in core academic areas which will determine job status — so they may reach their potential regardless of preschool experiences.

Anyone who doubts the tremendous potential of an enriched education for all students will have doubts removed if they but read two books: *Escalante: The Best Teacher in America* (Mathews, 1988), and *Nothing's Impossible* (Monroe, 1997). They tell the story of what can happen when we provide enriched education to all students.

The students Escalante taught did not come to school with the advantages of the wealthy. They would have scored terribly on any early measure of logical/mathematical abilities. In an individual-centered school they would have been assigned or counseled to courses with less rather than more math. Escalante courageously took the opposite tack, wildly confounding all expectations. He enriched the instruction and produced unbelievable numbers of students who passed advanced placement calculus. Where would those students be in an individual-centered school which was based on assessment of students and which provided enriched mathematical curriculum and/or instruction only to those thought to be high in that intelligence?

When we hold high standards and expectations for all students, a uniform instruction and curriculum works miracles. Lorraine Monroe (1997) and a dedicated staff transformed Harlem's Frederick Douglass Intermediate School. The students came mainly from central Harlem. Before a program of high standards and expectations was instituted, few students held academic aspirations and scored low on academic tests. Today, almost all are college bound. Had a program of differential curriculum and/or instruction been instituted, it is almost certain that some, but not all of the students, would be headed for college. Differential curriculum and instruction implies lower expectations for some students in some areas — expectations which institutionalize environmental inequities. Only with high expectations for all students can we realize the mission of education in a democracy.

Tracking

There are a variety of forms differential curriculum and instruction can take. In some cases assessment programs or test results would be used to match individuals to curricular areas; in other cases to particular ways of teaching those subjects. In some cases students would be assigned to certain classes; in other cases different classes would be recommended. In some cases the differential curriculum or instruction would involve only different academic assignments within the same classes; in other cases entirely different classes. In all scenarios, though, students would end up with different educational experiences depending on the results of a multiple intelligence testing program. If the tests did not result in different educational experiences, there would be no sense in administering them.

Even the best-intended tests, when used to sort students in order to provide a differentiated curriculum and instruction will relegate some students to a lower rung — first on the educational ladder, and later on the larger socioeconomic ladder.

Providing different educational experiences for students depending on their profiles on multiple intelligences measures, although not intended, would in some cases result in the undesirable outcomes of tracking. Howard Gardner has courageously stood up in opposition to tracking. It is hard to imagine, though, a program of differential curriculum and instruction which does not invite in at least some of the problems of tracking.

For some time the research results have been clear: Tracking does not help any students substantially and harms in many ways those relegated to the lower tracks.

Even the best-intended tests, when used to sort students in order to provide a differentiated curriculum and instruction will relegate some students to a lower rung — first on the educational ladder, and later on the larger socioeconomic ladder. The society will never pay or respect the mechanic as much as the engineer. For an educational system to decide early on what a student is likely to become and then create a differential curriculum to fulfill that prophecy should be outrageous to a nation built on beliefs in individual rights and potentials. The potential of students to bloom and blossom — often in unexpected directions and often late in their school career — should be sufficient in itself to inoculate us against any early form of assessment, labeling, and categorization.

The nation is struggling to rid itself of the odious practice of tracking. For some time the research results have been clear: Tracking does not help any students substantially and harms in many ways those relegated to the lower tracks. The parade of horrors for those in the lower tracks include lowered self-image, lowered self-esteem, lowered aspirations, lowered teacher expectations, diluted and different curriculum, deteriorated teacher-student and student-student relations, impoverished affective and intellectual climate, increased drop-out, increased delinquency, and increased discipline problems (See Oakes, 1985).

Probably the single most blatantly unacceptable item on the long list of unfavorable outcomes of tracking is the self-defeating resegregating of students in racially desegregated schools. The nation has spent a fortune in resources and in children's lives busing students in order to create racially desegregated schools, only to immediately turn around and undo what the courts have mandated by tracking students into racially segregated classes. This preposterous, blatantly self-defeating practice would cause us to laugh were it not so widely practiced and so clearly harmful for the nation's future.

At a time the nation is undergoing an unprecedented transformation, becoming racially integrated at an unprecedented rate, the last thing we need is any educational system which segregates students. Students today need diversity skills if they are to preserve democracy in the twenty-first century.

The roots of tracking run deep; the practice became almost universal and generally accepted in the United States for the better part of the twentieth century. Tracking was not always acceptable to a nation committed to the democratic principle of equal educational opportunity for all students. The history of tracking has been presented by Oakes (1985); there is no need to detail it here. Some key points, however, illustrate the dangers inherent in any system which after the first few grades of school would seek to match individuals with the various kinds of life and work options. In light of history, any attempt to stream students or provide them differential curriculum or instruction should sound like an echo from the past, chilling to anyone seriously committed to the belief that the primary function of education in a democracy is providing equal educational opportunity.

We ignore history at the risk of repeating it. To create different curriculum for different types of students and to counsel students into different types of courses in preparation for the different kinds of lives would be to take a path to a place we are struggling to leave behind. In 1916, Terman, a pioneer in intelligence testing, advocated the use of tests for school reorganization. Let's remind ourselves of Terman's belief in testing in order to reveal vocational possibilities:

> At every step in the child's progress the school should take account of his vocational possibilities. Preliminary investigations indicate that an IQ below 70 rarely permits anything better than unskilled labor; that the range from 70 to 80 is pre-eminently that of semi-skilled labor, from 80 to 100 that of the skilled or ordinary clerical labor, from 100 to 110 or 115 that of the semi-professional pursuits; and that above all these are the grades of intelligence which permit one to enter the professions or the larger fields of business…. This information will be a great value in planning the education of a particular child and also in planning the differentiated curriculum here recommended (Terman, 1923, Pp. 27-28).

Terman's tests lent scientific credibility to the notion that a function of schooling was to sort students and provide them different experiences in preparation for the different types of lives they were destined to live. He worked at a time schools were overwhelmed by new immigrants of diverse racial backgrounds. About eighty percent of the immigrants tested by Terman scored "feeble-minded." Rather than accepting

that as a demonstration of the invalidity of the tests, Terman chose to interpret those scores as evidence of racial inferiority. As cited by Oakes (1985, p. 36), Terman wrote:

> Their dullness seems to be racial, or at least in the family stocks from which they come. The fact that one meets this type with such extraordinary frequency among Indians, Mexicans, and Negroes suggests quite forcibly that the whole question of racial differences in mental traits will have to be taken up anew…there will be discovered enormously significant racial differences…which cannot be wiped out by any schemes of mental culture.

The nation was not entirely ready to accept the notion that not all individuals could achieve broad intellectual excellence. If we turn the clock back to 1892, Charles Eliot, president of Harvard, was chairing a Committee of Ten on Secondary Studies of the National Education Association. His

Who are we to determine early on that some kinds of curriculum are better for some students and other kinds of curriculum are better for others? Can we actually be so lacking in humility that we think that at this moment in human history we have finally come to the point at which we can early predict the course of study best suited to each child?

committee unequivocally opposed different curriculum for college-bound and non-college-bound students, recommending a high level curriculum for all students. Eliot and the committee advocated the democratic notion that all students had the potential to benefit from high-quality schooling. Eliot was opposed by Hall who accused the committee of "ignoring the great army of incapables," calling for a system of curriculum differentiation. Eliot's response to this challenge might easily have

Self-Statements of Students

"What is the most important thing you have learned or done so far in this class?"

English

▼ **High Track**

I've learned to analyze stories that I have read. I can come with an open mind and see each character's point of view. Why she or he responded the way they did, if their response was stupidity or an heroic movement. I like this class because he (the teacher) doesn't put thoughts into your head; he lets you each have a say about the way it happened.

▼ **Low Track**

I've learned how to get a better job and how to act when at an interview filling out forms.

Social Studies

▼ **High Track**

To infer or apply the past ideas to my ideas and finally to the future's ideas.

▼ **Low Track**

A few lessons which have not very much to do with history. (I enjoyed it).

Science

▼ **High Track**

I have learned to do what scientists do.

▼ **Low Track**

I can distinguish one type rock from another.

Source: Oakes, 1985, pp. 67-72.

been a response to modern calls for a differentiated curriculum. He expressed hope that Americans would refuse,

> to have its children sorted before their teens into clerks, watchmakers, lithographers, telegraph operators, masons, teamsters, farm laborers, and so forth, and treated differently in their schools according to these prophesies of the appropriate life careers. Who are we to make these prophesies (Oakes, 1985, Pp. 23-24)?

One hundred years later it is appropriate that we ask the same question: Who are we to determine early on that some kinds of curriculum are better for some students and other kinds of curriculum are better for others? Can we actually be so lacking in humility that we think that at this moment in human history we have finally come to the point at which we can early predict the course of study best suited to each child? Consider for a moment how our notion of the brain and intelligence has

evolved, from a single unified intelligence, to a split-brain intelligence, through the triune brain, to multiple intelligence, and (hopefully) toward understanding of intelligence as based on the coordination of a multiplicity interconnected modules. At any point in that history, had we tracked students based on our latest understanding of brain structure and function, we soon would have had to abandon that system in favor of another method of tracking. Can we afford to be so presumptuous as to think that at this particular point in history we have the final, best metaphor for brain and intelligence? Wouldn't it be wiser to provide every student with as rich a curriculum as possible, allowing each to find his or her level?

By now it should be abundantly clear that differential curriculum and instruction based on intelligence assessment programs

Results of Tracking for Low-Tracked Students

Decreased	Increased
• Thinking • Academic time • Self-image • Self-esteem • Aspirations • Teacher expectations • Quality of curriculum • Quality of teacher-student relations • Quality of student-student relations • Affective and intellectual climate	• Memorization • Socialization time • Drop-out • Delinquency • Discipline problems *Source: Oakes, 1985.*

would result in a different, diluted curriculum for the those with "an unusual, nonscholastic profile of intelligences," or "unusual intellectual configurations." Separate is not equal. The inequality of educational opportunity for students in high- and low-tracked classes, is evident in their self-statements, see box: Self-Statements of Students (page 16.11).

Through the mountain of evidence collected in the largest study of schools ever conducted, *A Study of Schooling,* it became abundantly clear that compared to low-tracked students, high-tracked students were exposed to more content, were expected and required to think more about what they were exposed to, and studied in classroom environments more conducive to learning (Goodlad, 1984). See box: Results of Tracking for Low-Tracked Students.

Tracking is less a response to individual differences among students than a source of those differences. Differential curriculum and/or instruction along eight dimensions would not just respond to perceived differences among students, but exaggerate those differences. At a time when increasing diversity demands students learn to relate to and work with diversity of intellectual styles and abilities, the cry should be for less rather than more segregation of every type.

Unconsciously, if not consciously, teachers in the nonacademic tracks begin to see their primary mission in very different terms than those working with students academically tracked. When asked what they most want students to learn, those teaching high-track classes were more concerned with critical thinking and self-expression; those teaching low-tracked classes emphasized low-level skills and self-control. See box: What Do You Want Students to Learn?

What Do You Want Students to Learn?

Responses of Teachers of High- and Low-Tracked Classrooms

High-Track Teachers

▼ "To think critically — to analyze, ask questions."

▼ "To be — able to express oneself."

▼ "To gain some interpretive skills."

Low-Track Teachers

▼ "Develop more self-discipline — better use of time."

▼ "Ability to use reading as a tool — e.g., how to fill out forms, write a check, get a job."

▼ "More mature behavior (less outspoken.)"

Source: Oakes, 1985, pp. 79-83.

All students, no matter what their destiny in the job world, need thinking skills — if for no other reason than that they will be the electorate of tomorrow, and how they vote will determine our future. The curriculum in the low tracks was dominated by memorization and management; higher-level thinking skills were reserved as curriculum for the higher tracks. It could be argued that in the ideal situation higher-level thinking skills would be taught within each of the intelligence tracks. The ideal situation however, is a far cry from what would inevitably result from testing and sorting students. Creating separate curriculum for the "logical/mathematical" and "bodily/kinesthetic" learners would in reality sort students along racial and so-

cioeconomic lines. The notion of separate but equal curriculum for different intelligence tracks would be half true — separate, but not equal.

Given the heterogeneity within the nation's schools it is impossible to imagine any form of tracking, no matter how well-intended, which would not result in reinforcing negative racial and economic stereotypes. As Oakes (1985, p. 91) asked,

> Could it be that we are teaching kids at the bottom of the educational hierarchy — who are more likely to be from poor and minority groups — behaviors that will prepare them to fit in at the lowest levels of the social and economic hierarchy?

Combining the lower results associated with tracking with the inevitability of non-white students ending up more often in the nonacademic tracks, any form of tracking amounts to racial discrimination, and a violation of the principle of equal educational opportunity.

The debate on tracking in any form hinges on one core issue: Whether we believe curriculum and instruction can be structured so there is success for all on a common, high-level curriculum. When our nation gave up believing in the importance of a universal, high-level curriculum it set on a course which relegated a substantial proportion of the nation's youth to an inferior education. Relegated to lower tracked classrooms, students enter what often are little more than academic holding tanks, social breeding grounds for negative self-images and antisocial behaviors.

Have we not had enough? Are we naive enough to believe that any widespread testing of intelligences and "counseling" of students into programs appropriate to their intelligences will not recreate all of the problems that were produced by IQ testing to track students. Well-intended as they might be, tests used to track students will, without fail, lead to de facto segregation and diminish educational opportunity. De facto tracking along racial and socioeconomic lines based on multiple intelligence tests, no matter how well-intended, is a price too high to pay.

Noble aspirations sometimes have ignoble results. How will differential education play out in the reality of school programs, teacher expectations, and student self-concepts? Let's listen to how noble aspirations can be misinterpreted:

> Knowledge of one's own strengths can help one to choose courses that might be particularly congenial to one's learning style (Gardner, 1993, p. 73).
> *Student to himself: I am not a logical/mathematical type, I am bodily/kinesthetic; I better sign up for shop, not algebra.*

> In the case of a uniform or required curriculum, such information is equally important. For even if the courses themselves are mandated, there is no reason why they need be taught in the same way to all…. A history lesson can be presented through linguistic, logical, spatial, and/or personal modes of knowing, even as a geometry class can draw upon spatial, logical, linguistic, or numerical competencies (Gardner, 1993, p. 73).
> *Student to herself: I am not verbally/linguistically talented; I don't want to have to write long essays; I will sign up for the personal history class, not the linguistic history class.*

Which students in our racially and socioeconomically heterogeneous schools will sign up for the logical/mathematical or verbal/linguistic classes, as opposed the bodily/kinesthetic or interpersonal/social classes? And in turn, which students will go on to college and later occupy positions of wealth and leadership? It is hard to im-

age any broad testing and tracking (through counseling or self-selection) which would operate to equalize educational opportunity. As a nation, have we not had our fill of notions that separate really can be equal? It is hard to imagine a program of broad and frequent testing of the intelligences that will not result in stig-

If we use tests of intelligences to provide students with different educational experiences, ultimately we will end up with some form of tracking. If we do not use the tests to classify and sort students, why create and use them at all?

matizing, labeling, and self-labeling, and which will not usher in through the back door new forms of tracking. Tracking is just as odious whether or not it is the unintended byproduct of noble attempts to maximize the unique potential of each individual.

If we use tests of intelligences to provide students with different educational experiences, ultimately we will end up with some form of tracking. If we do not use the tests to classify and sort students, why create and use them at all?

Let's perform a thought experiment. Let's revisit Paula. See Chapter 2: Three Visions for Education. Paula is transplanted into an individual-centered school system. It is early realized that she is a kinesthetic learner. She is placed in classes which emphasize kinesthetic content (ballet, pottery, sports, mime) and/or special classes which provide the traditional curriculum through "hands-on," kinesthetic experiences. She associates with other students so placed. Her teachers expect her to do well in areas in which there are kinesthetic experiences, less well in classes with tradi-

Like Father, Like Daughter

In elementary school my (Spencer's) daughter, Monica, was pulled out of regular classes for special education classes; each year she was considered for being held back; within her classes each year she went to the low math group and the low reading group. Near the end of elementary school she was several grades behind in reading, writing, and other basic skills. Monica was skillful in defeating my own attempts at tutoring her, as well as those of teachers and hired tutors. Monica recounts now how her late academic recovery was doubly hard because of the years being sent to the "yellow math group" which everyone knew was the dummy group, and being pulled out of regular classes for "special education" classes which left her further behind in her regular classes because of the missed time.

In seventh grade, however, Monica had a sensitive English teacher and Monica "turned-on" to literature and writing. Within a few years she made up for lost time, became the editor of her high-school newspaper, and graduated *magna cum laude* at a major university. Monica is now pursuing the goal of becoming a playwright, having written several plays, which were successfully performed at her university.

Would Monica have been better off in an individual-centered school in which her demonstrated lack of "verbal/linguistic intelligence" was recognized early and she was counseled into nontraditional classes? She would have taken classes which were linguistically less demanding. Certainly, given her early performance, she would have scored low compared to her peers on any measure of linguistic intelligence. Well-intended counseling in an individual-centered school might have deprived her of the very stimulation she most needed and have been the final blow to her intellectual identity, a blow from which she never would have recovered.

Monica's experience is remarkably similar to my own (Spencer's). In elementary school I received failing marks in spelling, was in the lowest reading group every year, and had writing skills far below average — in many cases, lowest in my class. Like Monica, for some reason my writing skills blossomed late and I became the editor of my high school newspaper. Today I support myself through my ability to give talks and write books! How would I (or students like myself) have fared in a school which early identified my lack of verbal/linguistic intelligence, and then provided me learning experiences which reinforced that limited view?

tional content and instructional methods. She forms a limited identity. She shies away from "academic" courses.

Would Paula be better off in that imaginary individual-centered school than if she was mainstreamed in a regular classroom with a teacher sensitive to the need to provide kinesthetic instruction to every student? With a sensitive teacher, Paula actually ended up mainstreamed in all classes, learning to write her spelling words without the need to dance them, performing better than average in regular classes. Do we really want to usher in a system which would result in segregation of Paula and students like her?

Testing Constricts Curriculum and Instruction

Testing drives curriculum, so the definition and measurement of intelligences amounts not just to a measure of what is, but a dictation of what ought to be. As soon as we measure eight or more specific intelligences and take on as a mission of schooling the development of those intelligences, teachers, curriculum steering committee, text book authors, and administrators will orient curriculum and instruction toward those specific intelligences. Given that teachers and administrators want their students to score well, the creation and administration of tests drive educators to redesign curriculum and instruction toward the tests. If tests include musical skills and not culinary skills, math skills and not mechanical skills, teachers and administrators will be less likely to risk spending time on culinary and mechanical activities, knowing they do so at the risk of having students score poorly compared to schools in which math and music are emphasized.

A manageable assessment program, especially if it is to be developmentally appropriate (involving different versions for different grades), frequently administered and interpreted, and intelligence-fair, (involving behavioral samples) will have to be individually administered. The specifications of such a testing program mean it will be very time consuming. To cope with the time constraints, the test will necessarily have to include some skills and not others. By excluding some skills in favor of others, the tests, in the guise of assessment, will become a very powerful force in directing students toward some types of development and away from others. By allowing a massive testing program, education will to a substantial extent hand over to testmakers the role of directing curriculum and instruction.

Testing of Intelligences Institutionalizes an Arbitrary Curriculum

As we will see in Chapter 21: Do the Eight Intelligences Meet the Eight Criteria? the eight intelligences do not meet the eight criteria of MI theory. As indicated in Chapter 5: Are There Other Intelligences? other intelligences meet the criteria as well or better than the original seven. If MI theory is to drive curriculum and instruction, if the goal of education is to develop intelligences, who is to choose which intelligences to develop?

If MI theory is to drive curriculum and instruction, if the goal of education is to develop intelligences, who is to choose which intelligences to develop?

This is no trivial question. Perform, please, the following thought experiment: imagine there are tight budgets and extra-curricular activities are under threat in many schools. There are not enough resources to fund both home economics and music classes. Who is to make the choice? Might we get a different outcome if we choose a home-economics teacher to make the choice, than if we assign the task to the music teacher? Who is to decide which intelligences are to be developed and which are to be dropped? Does physical education get more support than auto shop because in MI theory there is a bodily/kinesthetic intelligence, but no mechanical intelligence?

Are we to allow a team at Harvard University to decide? Should the decision be school-based, district-wide, or state-mandated? These silly questions point out that there is nothing within MI theory which tells us how much weight to give to each of the intelligences provided by the theory, and there is nothing outside the theory to help us weigh the accepted intelligences against alternative candidates. Thus, MI theory is a somewhat arbitrary guide for determining curriculum and instruction, and testing programs based on MI theory would arbitrarily institutionalize MI theory sanctioned intelligences (and corresponding curriculum and instruction) over other intelligences.

Testing Lowers Self-Esteem, Expectations, Effort

As soon as a student scores low on any type of intelligence test, teacher and student expectations are influenced. Often tests influence expectations far more than is realistic, because tests are designed to magnify individual differences. In the process of test construction those items which do not discriminate among students (either because most students pass them or because most students fail them) are thrown away. Even if students are very similar, the tests are designed to make them appear very different.

Testing of intelligences will lead for some students to lowered expectations which in turn will result in diluted instruction and lowered student effort in the very areas students most need help.

When teachers of low-scoring students lower their expectations they often act in ways to communicate those expectations.

Lower teacher expectations in turn lowers student effort and achievement. To the extent low-scoring students are made aware of their scores, they too lower their expectations and decrease their efforts. If there were frequent assessment, at least some if not all teachers and students would consciously and unconsciously tailor their tasks and their efforts to lowered expectations. Expectations are communicated to students even when the students are not told of their scores.

Lowered expectations can have a dramatic impact on achievement. Students whose teachers are told they are likely to bloom intellectually actually scored some 15 IQ points higher than those who did not have teacher's expectations raised (Rosenthal, 1987; Rosenthal & Rubin, 1978; Rosenthal, Baratz, & Hall, 1974). Not all teachers give more help and encouragement to those who are expected to do well; some focus the extra effort on those for whom they have low expectations; others treat all students evenly (Good, Sikes, & Brophy, 1973). Nevertheless, for many students, assessment of intelligences leads to lowered teacher expectations which in turn will result in lowered student effort in the very areas students most need help.

Picture the students who will tailor their efforts down in a math class because frequent testing has revealed they are not particular strong in the logical/mathematical intelligence. For some, repeated testing will provide a strong rationale for lowered effort, feeding a negative self-fulfilling prophecy.

Testing of any sort is a double-edged sword. For those who score high, self-esteem and pride rise along with willingness to work hard to live up to a new, higher self-image. Unfortunately, for every student who scores above the norm on a test there must be a student who scores below the norm. Tests for those other students usually lower self-image and, in turn, effort. For those who have scored low in an area repeatedly, the negative effects are cumulative. After scoring low in an area once or twice, the student may persist, trying harder. But, when the effort does not change results, the student gives up. The student begins reducing the pain of failure not by greater effort but by ego-saving rationalizations, saying things like "I don't really care about math," or "Who wants to be a nerd anyway?"

The student believes these pain-reducing rationalizations and from that point on the student has a new identity. His or her behavior falls is line with this new, lower identity. The student puts little effort into an area he or she knows is not an area of strength. Thus, the testing process actually provides an excuse for and creates diminished effort. In fact, it is psychologically adaptive for the very low achiever to quit trying. After all, it is far less painful to try hard and then fail than to be able to say, "I didn't study for that test at all." Or "I don't care about being logic smart."

Repeated testing for those below the norms often amounts to repeated reinforcement of a negative self-image; students are often punished for being themselves. One of the most poignant moments in education occurred when a whole school threw off its low self-image. Lorraine Monroe was given the opportunity to close down a Harlem school, Intermediate School 10,

and open in it's place the Frederick Douglass Academy. I.S. 10 had for years tested at or near the bottom of New York city's 179 middle schools. Dr. Monroe and her dedicated staff went to work transforming the image of the school. Not only were the burned walls and punched out ceilings replaced and repainted, a new, high set of standards and expectations were put in place for all students. Students who were performing poorly academically received special coaching and tutoring. Expectations were high for all students in all academic areas.

By mid-May the first year of test results were in. In Dr. Monroe's words, here is how they announced the results:

> We waited till 3 o'clock to tell the staff and kids over the loudspeaker, because I anticipated that they'd be loud in their joy. I was right. When they were dismissed at the door, many twirled and leaped, yelling, "We're number one! We're number one!" Their joy was mingled with disbelief. So many of them had come from failing schools with histories of low expectations. Their pride in their triumph over the tests that had so long bested so many of them made their loud celebration legitimate (Monroe, 1997).

The school and every student in it had a new identity. It was transformed — not just physically but psychologically. From out of the ashes, from the bottom of the testing heap each year, the school had risen to number one in the city! All in a year. How had it come about? Many factors were at work: a new principal with a vision; new, dedicated teachers; new students; uniforms; strict discipline; tutoring, extra help, high standards. But core to the transformation, the place from which all the changes sprang was a change in expectations. Once it was expected that the students would succeed, behavior fell in line with the new expectations. A principal who believed in her students had communicated a vision, high expectations, a vision all could see.

Just as a negative identity creates a self-fulfilling prophecy, so too does a positive identity. Once the students shook off their disbelief and realized they were attending Frederick Douglass Academy, number one in the city, they stood with more pride, they were proud to tell others where they were from, and, of course, they had to study even harder to live up to their new identity. Today almost one hundred percent of the students from Frederick Douglass Academy, students from central Harlem, go on to college! We live up to (or, unfortunately, down to) our identity — an identity formed to a considerable extent by expectations and identity set by the results of tests we take.

Early Specialization Versus Preparation for Change

The future for our students will be marked by dramatic changes in their lifetime. How we work and live will be transformed radically and repeatedly in the next century. Many of our students will be employed in many job categories over their lifetimes as the workplace is transformed at an accelerating rate. The best preparation for this kind of unprecedented accelerating change rate is a broad general education. Early specialization constricts experience and is the opposite direction from that which we should be taking in preparing students for the twenty-first century. If our goal is to prepare students for success in the lives they will live, our best hope is to increase rather than constrict their range of educational experiences.

Summary

In this chapter, we asked, "Is MI testing for differential education desirable?" Our answer to this questions is a resounding "No." Clearly, developing, administering, interpreting and applying an intelligences assessment program in order to provide students with different curriculum and instruction will lead us along a path we do not want to travel.

Where are we then? Shall we abandon the inspiring visions for education which spring from multiple intelligences theory? The answer, in our view, is again a resounding "No." The visions of broadening our curriculum and instructional strategies as well as honoring the uniqueness of each individual remain valid. They are the most inspiring and transformative visions in education today. Those visions however are best realized by enriching the curriculum for all students and using a variety of instructional strategies with all students. Only by teaching all students with a full range of instructional strategies and developing all intelligences in each student can we create democratic educational institutions which honor and allow realization of the intellectual potential of each student.

References

Gardner, H. *Multiple Intelligences. The Theory in Practice.* New York: Basic Books, 1993.

Good, T. L., Sikes, J., & Brophy, J. *Effects of teacher sex and student sex on classroom interaction.* **Journal of Educational Psychology**, 1973, *65*, 74-87.

Goodlad, J. I. *A Place Called School. Prospectus for the Future.* New York: McGraw Hill, 1984.

Mathews, J. *Escalante. The Best Teacher in America.* New York: Henry Holt, 1988.

Monroe, L. *Nothing's Impossible.* New York, NY: Random House, 1997.

Oakes, J. *Keeping Track. How Schools Structure Inequality.* New Haven: Yale University Press, 1985.

Rosenthal, R. *Pygmalian effects: Existence, magnitude, and social importance.* **Educational Researcher**, 1987, **16(9)**, 37-41.

Rosenthal, R., Baratz, S. S. & Hall, C. M. *Teacher behavior, teacher expectations, and gains in pupils' rated creativity.* **Journal of Genetic Psychology**, 1974, **124**, 115-121.

Rosenthal, R. & Rubin, D. B. *Interpersonal expectancy effects: the first 345 studies.* **Behavioral and Brian Sciences**, 1978, **3**, 377-451.

Terman, L. *Intelligence Tests and School Reorganization.* New York: World Book Co., 1923.

Are Valid MI Tests Possible?

I believe that operational definitions of each intelligence along with diagnostic procedures can be constructed, and my colleagues and I are engaged in efforts that address that objective…
(Gardner 1993, p. 41).

We must devise procedures and instruments that are "intelligence-fair" and that allow us to look directly at the kinds of learning in which we are interested
(Gardner, 1993, p. 79).

G ardner sketches in some detail his picture of how a school of the future might apply multiple intelligences theory to education. "I have in recent years devoted thought to how such an individual-centered school might be designed…(Gardner, 1993, p. 72)."

Valid measures of each of the intelligences are not possible because each of the intelligences is many things. But, lack of ability to reduce the complexity of human intelligence to any set of numbers, does not in any way prevent us as educators from realizing the powerful visions which spring from multiple intelligences theory.

He recommends the creation of individual-centered schools. The primary emphasis in individual-centered schools is to allow students to know and develop their own unique pattern of intelligences as much as possible.

Assessment is an important component of the individual-centered school:

> The general pedagogical program described here presupposes accurate understanding of the profile of intelligences of the individual learner. Such a careful assessment procedure allows informed choices about careers and avocations. It also permits a more enlightened search for remedies for difficulties.... Assessment, then, becomes a central feature of an educational system (Gardner, 1993, p. 31).

Gardner calls for the development of multiple intelligences assessment instruments; assessment, he says, determines what we teach.

> Assessment. Unless one is able to assess the learning that takes place in different domains, and by different cognitive process, even superior curricular innovations are destined to remain unutilized. In this country, assessment drives instruction. We must devise procedures and instruments that are "intelligence-fair" and that allow us to look directly at the kinds of learning in which we are interested (Gardner, 1993, p. 79).

If assessment of the intelligences is an essential component of the individual-centered school, it is critical to ask whether valid assessment of the intelligences is possible. Gardner (1993, p. 41) affirms the possibility of assessing each intelligence:

> Certainly careful articulation of each intelligence is required in the diagnostic process. I believe that operational definitions of each intelligence along with diagnostic procedures can be constructed, and my colleagues and I are engaged in efforts that address that objective.... I realize that it may be difficult to come up with precise definitions and assessment procedures for the personal intelligences and that considerable ingenuity will be required in creating formulations that are faithful to the scope of these intelligences and yet lend themselves to some kind of objective assessment.

Gardner concedes it "may be difficult" to come up with precise measures for the interpersonal intelligence and the intrapersonal intelligence — implying, remarkably, that it will not be all that difficult to come up with measures for the other intelligences. It is this assertion, that it is possible to design valid measures of the intelligences, to which we now turn.

Can we, though, after only a few grades of school with any reliability match students with life and work options. Is it possible to design assessment instruments with that kind of predictive ability? It has never been done.

Gardner indicates

> An individual-centered school would be rich in assessment of individual abilities and proclivities. It would seek to match individuals not only to curricular areas, but also to particular ways of teaching those subjects. After the first few grades, the school would also seek to match individuals with the various kinds of life and work options that are available in their culture (Gardner, 1993, p. 10).

Can we, though, after only a few grades of school with any reliability match students with life and work options. Is it possible to design assessment instruments with that kind of predictive ability? It has never been done. No one has ever been able to predict with any degree of success life work of seven and eight year old children. To even attempt such a task would be viewed by most psychometricians as enormously presumptuous.

Let's review some of the obstacles involved in developing developmentally-appropriate, culturally-fair, practical-to-administer assessment techniques for each of the intelligences which would be administered repeatedly throughout a student's school years.

Is MI Testing Practical?

Setting aside for a moment any issues of validity, let's ask if the proposed assessment program could actually be conducted. Is it practical? MI theory calls for developmentally-appropriate measures. That means that for each grade-level different assessment instruments would be developed,

> **If the assessment of each child's intelligence took only a half hour per intelligence, we would need about four hours of assessment time per pupil. Given 30 students in a class we need 120 hours of testing per class. Given six hour days, we need 20 days or one school month per class for the assessment specialist. With a school of 20 classrooms and a 9 month school year, we need two full-time assessment specialists per school to assess all the students once each year — and that does not include time to score, interpret, and design programs based on the tests!**

validated, administered, interpreted, and the results provided to each child's teacher and counselor who would then make use of them in selecting and designing curriculum and instruction for each student for each intelligence. We are talking about creating a major assessment industry and placing large demands on each teacher.

The theory demands that the measures be intelligence-fair. That probably means that only verbal/linguistic and perhaps to some extent mathematical measures could rely heavily on written answers, the other intelligences would be assessed by behaviors appropriate to the intelligence.

Tests of musical intelligence would examine the individual's ability to analyze a work of music or to create one, not simply to compare two single tones on the basis of relative pitch. We need tests of spatial ability that involve finding one's way around, not merely giving multiple choice responses to depictions of a geometric form as rendered from different visual angles (Gardner, 1993, p. 39).

To administer intelligence-fair measures of this sort would demand individual rather than group administration, taking the test administrator hours of time for each student, not just hours per class as in group-administered tests. If the assessment of each child's intelligence took only a half hour per intelligence, we would need about four hours of assessment time per pupil. Given 30 students in a class we need 120 hours of testing per class. Given six hour days, we need 20 days or one school month per class for the assessment specialist. With a school of 20 classrooms and a nine month school year, we need two full-time assessment specialists per school to assess all the students once each year — and that does not include time to score, interpret, and design programs based on the tests!

One assessment a year, however, probably would not be enough. The assessment measures need to be administered frequently because they are to be used as the basis of an "enlightened search for rem-

Is MI Testing Practical?

edies for difficulties." The magnitude of time and resources devoted to this assessment program (developing, administering, scoring, interpreting, counseling, and modifying instruction based on the tests), would be unprecedented in the history of education.

Finally, the measures would have to be culturally-fair. It is now unacceptable (unfair and illegal) to administer intelligence tests on which some racial groups score higher than others and then track those groups based on those tests (See Larry P. v. Riles in Oakes, 1985, p. 186). In the same way it would be unacceptable to use measures of the intelligences if they produced racial or other group differences — especially if the tests were then used to track or counsel students toward different educational opportunities.

The development of a multiple intelligence assessment program and placement of students in separate classrooms or separate instructional programs based on the results has excellent potential for casting new fuel on the legal fires which have blazed over IQ testing and school placement. Those fires have raged in the courts for years, a new program of multidimensional intelligence assessment would create a major industry for lawyers and the courts. There have been years of debate and numerous court cases surrounding the administration and use of single intelligence tests. What IQ tests measure, how they can be used, and whether they can ever be culturally-fair has not been established. To multiply that effort by a factor of eight or more, with the same questionable results, is a path down which education should not tread.

> **It is an oxymoron to call "manageable" a testing program which is multidimensional, developmentally-appropriate, individually-administered, culturally fair, legally questionable, interpretation intensive, frequently administered, and based on a wide range of behavioral samples involving complex behaviors across a range of representative situations.**

It is an oxymoron to call "manageable" a testing program which is multidimensional, developmentally-appropriate, individually-administered, culturally fair, legally questionable, interpretation intensive, frequently administered, and based on a wide range of behavioral samples involving complex behaviors across a range of representative situations.

• • • • • • • • • • • • • • • •
Can MI Tests Be Validated?
Multiple Intelligences and the Thumb-Jerk Reaction

It would take some time, but it would be possible to develop a valid measure of the strength of a person's knee-jerk reaction. The measure would have to involve repeated tests with varying amounts of pressure applied to a range of locations below the knee cap, probably administered in a range of contexts (by a doctor or lay person, by male or female, by surprise, and when expected). It would not be possible, however, to develop a valid measure of the strength of a person's thumb-jerk reaction. No matter where you tap, a thumb does not jerk.

Can MI Tests Be Validated?

As silly as is the idea of a thumb jerk reaction, it is important when we think about MI assessment. The evidence is very strong that there is not just one thing called linguistic intelligence, but rather a multiplicity of relatively independent linguistic intelligences. See Chapters 20 and 22. And given that there are many linguistic intelligences which are relatively independent, assessment of the strength of a single "linguistic intelligence" is more like assessment of the thumb-jerk than like assessment of a knee-jerk. We cannot validly assess that which does not exist.

Because there are a wide range of relatively independent linguistic intelligences, we cannot develop a single valid measure of linguistic intelligence which will predict linguistic functioning of many types. To the extent one believes in multiplicity theory over the theory of multiple intelligences, a community of neurons over separate frames of mind, one abandons the notion of developing a single measure of each of the eight intelligences.

Validation of the predictive power of multiple intelligences tests or assessment procedures administered in early grades in order to "match individuals with the various kinds of life and work options available in their culture" would involve an experiment of staggering proportions. Only a long-term developmental design would work. Given attrition problems and problems of representation, the study would have to be of enormous size. If we used intelligence assessment procedures as a basis of counseling students into differential curriculum and instruction, and subsequently found the students did in fact specialize in the fields suggested by the assessment procedures, we would not have established validation of the assessment procedures. Our findings might be a result of a self-fulfilling prophesy: Scores led to counseling which led to differential educational opportunities which led to the life choices. True validation of the predictive capacity of the assessments would have to include a control group in which students were not exposed to differential curriculum or instruction. We would need to know what kind of life choices the students would have made in the absence of the labeling and counseling which resulted from the testing process. We have to be convinced that multiple intelligences assessment techniques would merely discover life-directions, rather than create them.

If we believe not in the theory of multiple intelligences but rather in the existence of a multiplicity of intelligences (see Chapter 22: Beyond Multiple Intelligences — A Multiplicity!), any assessment program centered around a defined, limited set of intelligences is viewed as nonrepresentative of the range of human skills, talents, and intelligences. For example, any definition of spatial intelligence which centers around "finding one's way around" will broaden the curriculum to include those skills, but what about model building, flower arrangement, map reading, color combining, jigsaw puzzle creation, analysis and creation of depth in paintings, and the myriad other "visual/spatial skills?" To include samples of all those visual/spatial skills would make the test unmanageable, but to exclude them would make the test unrepresentative of the range of tasks and abilities in that broad domain. To produce scores for all of the great number of subskills in each of the intelligences, and then try to design educational experiences responsive to the infinite number of profiles which would result, is beyond comprehension.

Bad Tests Popping Up Like Weeds

It is hard to pick up a popular book on multiple intelligences which does not offer at least one test or assessment technique to determine the intelligences of teachers and/or students. Although, to Gardner's credit, he has indicated the need for behavioral, intelligence-fair observations and has resisted the temptation to create or endorse paper and pencil tests of the intelligences, the limits of time and resources in schools create a press for the proliferation of exactly the kind of instruments Gardner abhors. Even a glance at almost all of the available MI tests by anyone familiar with psychometrics reveals the tests ignore many basic tenants of valid test construction. In a word, the existing multiple intelligences tests are terrible. They are faulty not just because they do not involve intelligence-fair behavioral samples, but because they violate the basic principles of test construction.

Let's take a peek at some of the reasons these simple, popular multiple intelligences tests should be rejected outright.

Lack of Validity

The most fundamental principle of test construction is the establishment of validity. Let's examine three types of validity: internal validity, external validity, and construct validity.

Internal Validity

Internal validity is an issue of reliability. Will the same measure give the same results when administered a second time? Internal validity can be established in a variety of ways. Split-half reliability for a MI test would be established if half of the questions for each intelligence were randomly selected and then tested for correlation with the other half. This can be done by creating two equivalent forms which are

To establish validity for each intelligence, then, would mean creating measures which correlate substantially more highly with one intelligence than with the others. This process would have to be repeated for each intelligence, at each age group tested, to create developmentally appropriate measures — a very formidable task.

administered at different times, or simply by examining the correlation of half the items with the other half in an internal analysis. If a test has internal validity, the equivalent forms should produce similar answers just as should individual test and re-test scores. Internal validity is the easiest to establish, but internal validity of MI measures has not been established. If a test has internal validity, it may be reliable, but there is no assurance it measures what it purports to measure. The validity of what is measured is established by external validity.

External Validity

External validity is established if a test correlates well with or predicts behaviors as dictated by the theory. For example, test scores should correlate with teacher and parent observations, self-statements, and behavioral observations. In the case of a MI test, a high score in visual/spatial intel-

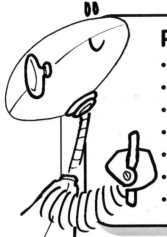

Problems With MI Tests
- Lack of Validity
- Confound of Ability and Preference
- Forced Choice
- Reactive Measures
- Oversimplification
- Normative, Not Ipsative
- Normative, Not Developmental

ligence should correlate with skill at visual/spatial tasks. A very strong form of external validity would be provided by a longitudinal study in which, for example, elementary school scores on a MI test predict career choices and successes. A mild form of validity might be the simple correlation of MI scores with choices of types of contributions to a portfolio. Again, those offering MI tests have not established any sort of external validity for their measures.

Construct Validity

The third type of validity, construct validity, is a bit harder to establish; there must be both convergent and divergent validity. Items should correlate well with those pre-

If there really are a multiplicity of intelligences rather than the eight intelligences postulated by MI theory, valid measures will not be found. Skills may simply not hang together the way MI Theory predicts.

sumed to measure the same construct (convergent validity) and not correlate well with those presumed not to be part of the same construct (divergent validity). To establish construct validity for the block design measure as a measure of spatial skills, for example, we would have to show first that it correlated highly and reliability with

other measures of spatial skills, but then also find that it does not correlate as well with measures of linguistic intelligence, mathematical intelligences and the other intelligences. Lower correlation with the other intelligences than with the target intelligence is critical if we are to establish construct validity for any multiple intelligence measure. In the case of the block design measure, if it correlated well with other measures of spatial intelligence but correlated highly also with measures of each of the other intelligences, a reasonable interpretation is that the block design is simply a measure of general intelligence, not a measure of a specific intelligence.

Construct validity is more demanding than simple internal or external validity checks. A measure could have internal consistency, and correlate consistently and highly with other measures of the same construct, but fail the test of construct validity if it did not correlate more highly with the target intelligence than with other intelligences.

None of the intelligences proposed by MI theory has obtained construct validity. Some have failed in critical tests. The block design test, for example, has good internal and external validity. It is a reliable measure and correlates well with similar measures of disembedding and spatial skills. Nevertheless, it fails the test of construct validity because it shows also a high correlation with measures of linguistic intelligence and other nonspatial intelligences. It is a good predictor of general intelligence.

To establish validity for each intelligence, then, would mean creating measures which correlate substantially more highly with one intelligence than with the others. This process would have to be repeated for each intelligence, at each age group tested, to create developmentally appropriate measures — a very formidable task. Further, the test of each intelligence would have to be cross-checked against various racial groups. If racial groups scored differently and the tests were to be used to match or counsel students toward certain kinds of curriculum or instruction, on the basis of equal educational opportunity, the assessment methods would have to be rejected.

Creating valid measures, however, is not just a matter of hard work. If an intelligence does not operate the way a theory predicts, it may be impossible to create a valid measure of that intelligence. It is almost unimaginable that strong construct validity can be established for the eight intelligences because they are so broad. For example, visual/spatial ability is presumed to relate to a wide range of diverse abilities such as finding one's way around, picturing objects rotated in space, solving jigsaw puzzles, sensitivity to and ability to create pleasing color combinations, remembering visual details, skills in drawing and painting, as well as a variety of other skills. Research with test validation reveals that validity is to a large extent a function of specificity. It is possible to get reliable and valid measures of jigsaw puzzle solving skills — those who can solve one puzzle well are likely to solve other jigsaw puzzles well — but jigsaw puzzle solving skills do not correlate well with ability to paint with pastels or navigate a sailboat. If there really are a multiplicity of intelligences rather than multiple intelligences, valid measures of the eight intelligences will not be found.

Confound of Ability and Preference

1 = Almost never; 2 = Sometimes;
3 = Often; and 4 = Almost Always

_____ Likes to read.

_____ Spells words accurately.

_____ Enjoys writing.

_____ Has a good vocabulary and uses words correctly and well.

_____ Likes to tell stories or jokes.

_____ Enjoys word games.

_____ Listens carefully and effectively.

_____ Remembers names and other verbal information easily.

_____ Speaks persuasively.

_____ Speaks clearly and well.

(Adapted from Haggerty, 1995)

Skills may simply not hang together the way MI theory predicts.

In fact, we have preliminary evidence from Gardner's own work that the intelligences do not operate in accordance with the theory. Results of intercorrelations among the Spectrum measures indicate a lack of construct validity for the intelligences: subscales of the various intelligences do not correlate any better with each other than they do with subscales presumed to measure other intelligences! The two music activities (r = -0.07) and the two science activities (r = 0.08) showed complete independence (Gardner, 1993, p. 95) indicating a complete failure to meet the most fundamental requirement of construct validity.

Confound of Ability and Preference

Let's examine a rather typical MI measure, the Student Profile (Haggerty, 1995). We take this example not as a condemnation of the book (the book is filled with great theory and practical information), but rather as an illustration of the confounding of ability and preference. Quite simply, the measure asks parents to provide helpful information about students to "help take account of his or her strengths in our teaching." Parents rate their children on a scale of 1 to 4 on a variety of characteristics for each intelligence. See box: Confound of Ability and Preference.

The problem with this kind of test is that it confounds preference and ability. In the example, we have highlighted the preferences: "Likes to read;" "Enjoys writing;" "Likes to tell stories or jokes." The other items are abilities: "Spells words accurately;" "Has a good vocabulary;" "Listens carefully." When we find what a child scores, we do not know how much that score is a function of ability versus preference.

Some children like to read, but are poor at it. Other children can spell very accurately, but spelling is one of their least favorite activities. Ability does not always predict preference. A good measure has to be clear on what it is measuring; measures which confound ability and preference make the untenable assumption that preference to perform an activity is necessarily a reflection of skill in that area or that skill leads to preference. While sometimes that is true, it is not always true. So tests which jumble preference and ability measures together provide uninterpretable results.

Gardner indicates the need to separate proclivities from skills:

> An important aspect of assessing intelligences must include the individual's ability to solve problems or create products using the materials of the intellectual medium. Equally important, however, is the determination of which intelligence is favored when an individual has a choice (Gardner, 1993, p. 31).

Unfortunately, those offering MI tests have ignored the distinction, freely mixing items of ability and preference, so the tests are uninterpretable.

Forced Choice

Many of the existing measures of multiple intelligences provide items which force a choice between two activities, such as "Would you rather read a story, or work on a jigsaw puzzle?" Choosing to read scores a point for the linguistic intelligence; choosing the jigsaw puzzle scores a point for visual/spatial intelligence. The problem with any forced choice measure is that in-

Forced Choice

Check the box you prefer. Check one box only.

Would you rather read a story? ☐

Or work on a jigsaw puzzle? ☐

terpretation is always unclear. Did the student choose the jigsaw puzzle not because the student likes or is good at visual/spatial tasks, but because the student hates to read? Did the student choose to read not because the student is particularly skilled at or enjoys verbal/linguistic tasks, but because the student is bored to death by jigsaw puzzles?

Reactive Measures

Many of the measures ask parents to rate students or ask students to rate themselves on preferences or abilities. The problem here is that students and parents know the socially desirable response and may chose the response not because it is true but because it is likely to impress a teacher. Does a student or parent say the student enjoys reading because in fact the student enjoys reading, or because they wish to make a favorable impression on the teacher?

Oversimplification

The existing MI measures almost all reduce to one score for linguistic intelligence, another for mathematical intelligence, a third for visual/spatial and so on. The problem here is that there is a multiplicity of intelligences so one score for an intelligence will always be an over simplification which will mask important individual differences. Given only one score to represent visual/spatial intelligence, a student high on mentally rotating objects in space and low on map reading might score the same thing as a student low on mentally rotating objects in space and high on map reading. Both scores would mask the underlying differences. A sophisticated approach to MI assessment would involve creating a variety of subscales for each intelligence. That approach would be more informative to

teachers and others attempting to design relevant educational experiences. The problem, of course, is that there are a multiplicity of skills within each intelligence and we run the risk of overwhelming teachers and curriculum developers.

When we reduce such a complex phenomena such as intelligence to a single score, or even to a score for each intelligence, we are always oversimplifying. In doing so, we mask important individual differences, making our scores uninterpretable. A more sophisticated and meaningful MI test would strive to accurately capture multiple facets of each

Normative, Not Ipsative

Let's assume for a moment that we have created a valid MI test and we can score every student reliably from 1 to 10 on each intelligence, with 1 being a low score and 10 indicating high development of that intelligence. We give our MI test and find Student 1 scores 5 on the visual/spatial intelligence. Student 2 scores 7. See box: Visual/Spatial Intelligence: A Normative View. Which student is stronger in visual/spatial intelligence? It is tempting to take a normative view and conclude that Student 2, the student with the higher score is stronger. This is not necessarily the case.

If we take an ipsative rather than normative approach to assessment, we do not stack students up and compare them to one another but rather look at each student's own unique pattern of skills. Taking an ipsative approach, we find Student 1's strongest intelligence is visual/spatial whereas it is the weakest intelligence for Student 2. See box: Visual/Spatial Intelligence: An Ipsative View.

Visual/Spatial Intelligence:

A Normative View

Intelligence	Student 1	Student 2
Verbal/Linguistic		
Logical/Mathematical		
Visual/Spatial	5	7
Musical/Rhythmic		
Bodily/Kinesthetic		
Naturalist		
Interpersonal		
Intrapersonal		

Visual/Spatial Intelligence:

An Ipsative View

Intelligence	Student 1	Student 2
Verbal/Linguistic	1	9
Logical/Mathematical	2	10
Visual/Spatial	5	7
Musical/Rhythmic	1	10
Bodily/Kinesthetic	2	9
Naturalist	3	9
Interpersonal	1	9
Intrapersonal	2	10

Musical Intelligence:
A Normative View

Week	1	2	3	4	5
Student 1					**6**
Student 2					**5**

Musical Intelligence:
A Developmental View

Week	1	2	3	4	5
Student 1	**6**	**6**	**6**	**6**	**6**
Student 2	**1**	**2**	**3**	**4**	**5**

The problem: Many MI measures take a normative rather than ipsative approach to assessment, looking at how students score compared to established norms or compared to classmates, rather than how they score compared to themselves — their pattern of skills.

Normative, Not Developmental

Imagine it is the fifth week of school. We have designed a program to help students develop their musical/rhythmic abilities. We also have a valid measure of musical/rhythmic intelligence on which the students can score from 1 to 10, with 10 as the high score. Two students have been assessed. Student 1 scores 6. Student 2 scores 5. See box: Musical Intelligence: A Normative View. Which is doing better in our program?

It would be tempting to conclude Student 1 is doing better. In fact Student 1 is not learning at all, and Student 2 is learning a great deal. See box: Musical Intelligence: A Developmental View.

The problem: many approaches to MI assessment take a normative rather than developmental perspective; they look at how well students are doing compared to others, not compared to themselves over time. Valid assessment must be like a moving picture of an individual, not a snapshot of a class.

Is Testing Necessary?

Given the daunting list of practical, legal, and psychometric problems associated with the development of valid and usable multiple intelligence testing programs, we have to take pause. Would the creation of assessment specialists and an expensive and time-consuming effort to create valid multiple intelligences assessment instruments and procedures be worth the price? Is testing necessary? If such programs were the only way we could realize the three powerful visions of matching, stretching, and celebrating the intelligences, we would say the investment would be worth the payoff — the visions are that precious. But, we can realize all three visions without risking all the potential pitfalls of special programs to assess intelligences.

If we simply teach all students with the full range of multiple intelligences instructional strategies, making every lesson a multiple intelligences lesson, and if we give students time to reflect on and share the cognitive processes which they are using, we can make every lesson accessible to every student regardless of their pattern of intelligences, develop all of the intelligences, and have students validate and celebrate their own uniqueness and the diversity among them.

When all is said and done, it will be concluded that valid measures of each of the intelligences are not possible because each of the intelligences is, when analyzed, many things. But, lack of valid measurement instruments for each of the intelligences and lack of ability to reduce the complexity of human intelligence to any set of numbers does not in any way prevent us as educators from realizing the powerful visions which spring from multiple intelligences theory.

In the next chapter we offer a number of MI tests. The tests, though, are not offered with the aim of facilitating differential education. Rather they are offered to make experiential this critique of MI testing. Through the tests we will experience the lack of validity of MI assessment procedures, and the multidimensionality of each intelligence.

References

Gardner, H. *Multiple Intelligences. The Theory in Practice.* New York: Basic Books, 1993.

Haggerty, B. *Nurturing Intelligences.* Menlo Park, CA: Addison-Wesley, 1995.

Oakes, J. *Keeping Track. How Schools Structure Inequality.* New Haven: Yale University Press, 1985.

The MIT and the Facet Tests

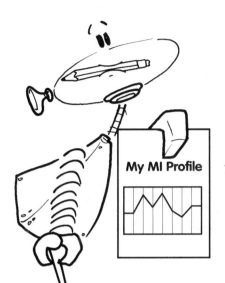

My MI Profile

The general pedagogical program described here presupposes accurate understanding of the profile of intelligences of the individual learner (Gardner, 1993, p. 31).

I n this chapter are two types of MI tests. The Multiple Intelligence Test (MIT) allows a quick assessment of the relative strength of each intelligence. The Facet Tests, one for each intelligence, allow assessment of the relative strengths of the dimensions within each intelligence. The tests, however, are not offered to score or classify students in order to provide them differential curriculum and instruction. Rather, they are offered for the opposite purpose — to illustrate why valid MI testing is not possible, and why we should not use MI tests to label students or sort them into differential educational programs. The tests are offered in hopes of furthering our understanding of the complexity and problems associated with MI testing.

It is an overgeneralization to say someone is intelligent or not based on an IQ test — there are many ways to be smart. Similarly, it is an overgeneralization to say someone is high on any one of the eight intelligences — there are many ways to be smart within each of the multiple intelligences.

The Multiple Intelligences Test

On the following page you will find the Multiple Intelligences Test (MIT). The test is designed to be taken twice, first as a forced-choice measurement instrument, and second as a free-choice measure. This produces two scores: Score 1 (Forced-Choice), and Score 2 (Free-Choice). After taking the test both ways, you will plot your scores on My MI Profile. Read the MIT instructions, then take the test. We will interpret the results after the test.

MIT Instructions

Step 1. Take the MIT Forced-Choice

The first time you take the MIT you are to choose one alternative for each item, the alternative which is most true of you. For example, read the first item: "For recreation, you like to…" Then, read the alternatives. Place a check mark (✔) in the small box **in the upper right hand corner** of the alternative that describes you best. If you cannot decide between two alternatives, choose the one you have done most recently. Remember, ✔ **just one alternative per row.** When you finish, you will have ten check marks — one for each item.

Stop! Do not read further. Take the MIT now. When you are finished, go on to step two.

Step 2. Take the MIT Free-Choice

You have taken the MIT once, as a forced-choice test. Now you will take it again, as a free-choice test. This time you will select each alternative that is true for you. For example, read the first item: "For recreation, you like to…" Then place an ✗ in the small box **in the lower left hand corner** of the same alternative you ✔ in step one. You know this alternative describes you. This time, also ✗ all the other alternatives that generally describe you. In some cases, you may even ✗ all alternatives if they all fit. Be sure, though, not to put an ✗ if you have only done something once or twice, or only thought about doing something. An ✗ in the box means the alternative is something you do repeatedly. Remember, ✗ **each alternative which is true for you.**

Stop! Do not read further. Take the MIT for the second time now. When you are done, read the instructions for scoring the test.

Spencer & Miguel Kagan: *Multiple Intelligences*

The MIT

Multiple Intelligences Test

#	Prompt	Verbal/ Linguistic	Logical/ Mathematical	Visual/ Spatial	Musical/ Rhythmic	Bodily/ Kinesthetic	Naturalist	Interpersonal	Intrapersonal
1	For recreation, you like to…	Read, write, play word games	Play logic games	Paint, draw, go to a gallery	Play an instrument, sing, listen to music	Be active, play sports, dance	Garden, attend to pets	Be with friends, family, teammates	Spend quality alone time
2	To memorize facts, you…	Create a phrase or saying	Make a logical sequence	Visualize the answer or draw it	Create a rhyme or song	Associate them with a gesture or movement	Use nature analogies	Work with a partner	Relate the facts to personal experience
3	If something breaks or won't work, you…	Read the instruction book	Examine the pieces to figure how it works	Study the diagram	Snap, tap your fingers, hum, or whistle while trying to fix it	Tinker with the parts	Examine the parts carefully	Work with someone to fix it	Weigh if it's worth fixing, fix it yourself
4	For a team presentation, you…	Write the lines	Analyze the data, present the statistics	Create the visual aids	Put words to a tune	Create movement, action	Choose a nature topic	Lead the presentation, coordinate efforts	Work alone on your part
5	In conflict, you…	Use a clever saying to make your point	Devise a winning strategy	Picture a solution	Look for a "harmonic" solution	Move, gesture	Study relations among parties	Mediate, look for amicable solution	Get away from others
6	To make the next board game move, you…	Talk yourself through the move	Weigh the consequences of each move	Visualize what the next move will look like	Keep with the rhythm of the game	"Try out" a number of moves	Think in terms of predator and prey	Analyze motives of others	Make the move that feels right
7	You like games if you can…	Talk, use your linguistic skills	Use math, analyze the possibilities	Picture the moves, draw	Have music playing	Be active, use fine motor skills	Play outside	Play with others	Play solitaire, decide your moves alone
8	To add to your portfolio, you…	Write an essay	Include math, logic	Create a picture or graphic organizer	Write or record a song or tune	Act on a video, or perform	Work with plants or animals	Perform with others	Write a private journal or evaluation
9	For a present, you like a…	A book or magazine	Logic games, logic puzzles	Art, art supplies, jigsaw puzzle	Music, concert tickets	Sports equipment	A pet, flowers, outdoor gear	Big party	Journal or diary
10	During free time, you like to…	Read or write	Solve problems	Draw, paint, make models	Listen to music, play music, sing	Work with your hands	Enjoy nature	Spend time with friends, socialize	Be alone

Top Right (✓)
SCORE 1: Forced-Choice
The Most True Alternative

Bottom Left (✗)
SCORE 2: Free-Choice
All True Alternatives

Score the MIT

At the bottom of the MIT are rows for Score 1 and Score 2. To produce Score 1, simply sum the check marks ✔ in the upper right hand corners of the alternatives in each column, and place the sum in the row for Score 1. To produce Score 2, sum the ✗ marks in the lower left hand corners of the alternatives in each column, and place the sum in the row for Score 2. See sample test on page 18.6 for an example.

Graphing Your MIT Scores

Step 1. Make a Bar Graph of Score 1

To make a bar graph representing your Score 1, forced-choice score, fill in the number of squares on the bar graph corresponding to your score for each intelligence. Use the bar graph on the My MI Profile, page 18.5. For example, if you scored two for the verbal/linguistic intelligence, you would fill in two squares. See sample on page 18.7.

Step 2. Make a Pie Graph of Score 1

Use the bar graph to fill in the pie graph representing your Score 1, forced-choice score. Continuing with our example, we would fill in two slices of the pie corresponding to the score of two for the verbal/linguistic intelligence. Label the two segments, "verbal/linguistic." Use a different color or shade representing each intelligence for your pie graph. If you did not have a check mark in a column of the MIT, simply fill in no boxes in that column of the graph and no segments of the pie for that intelligence. See sample on page 18.7

Step 3. Make a Line Graph of Score 2

Score 2, your free-choice score, is graphed only as a line graph. Draw a dot in the middle of the column of the bar graph for each intelligence corresponding to your Score 2. For example, if you scored three on the verbal/linguistic intelligence, you would draw a dot in the middle of the verbal/linguistic column, on line 3. When you have placed all the dots, connect them to form a line graph. See sample graph on page 18.7.

Step 4. Analyze Your Profile

Study the line graph and the bar graph. Do they paint the same picture. Where are they the most similar? Where are they the most different? Which administration format, the forced-choice or the free-choice, better represents your pattern of intelligences?

My MI Profile

Follow the directions to create a bar, pie, and line graph of your
Multiple Intelligences Test (MIT).

Score 1, Forced-Choice Bar Graph & Score 2, Free-Choice Line Graph

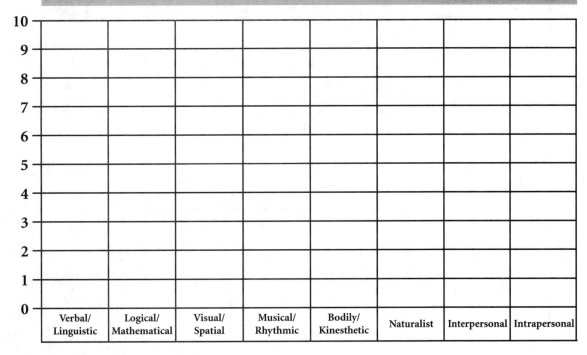

| | Verbal/ Linguistic | Logical/ Mathematical | Visual/ Spatial | Musical/ Rhythmic | Bodily/ Kinesthetic | Naturalist | Interpersonal | Intrapersonal |

Score 1, Forced-Choice Pie Graph

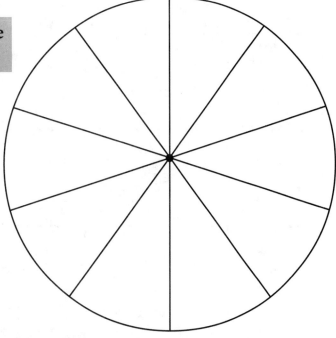

The MIT
SAMPLE

	Verbal/Linguistic	Logical/Mathematical	Visual/Spatial	Musical/Rhythmic	Bodily/Kinesthetic	Naturalist	Interpersonal	Intrapersonal
1 For recreation, you like to…	Read, write, play word games	Play logic games	Paint, draw, go to a gallery	Play an instrument, sing, listen to music	Be active, play sports, dance	Garden, attend to pets	Be with friends, family, teammates	Spend quality alone time
2 To memorize facts, you…	Create a phrase or saying	Make a logical sequence	Visualize the answer or draw it	Create a rhyme or song	Associate them with a gesture or movement	Use nature analogies	Work with a partner	Relate the facts to personal experience
3 If something breaks or won't work, you…	Read the instruction book	Examine the pieces to figure how it works	Study the diagram	Snap, tap your fingers, hum, or whistle while trying to fix it	Tinker with the parts	Examine the parts carefully	Work with someone to fix it	Weigh if it's worth fixing, fix it yourself
4 For a team presentation, you…	Write the lines	Analyze the data, present the statistics	Create the visual aids	Put words to a tune	Create movement, action	Choose a nature topic	Lead the presentation, coordinate efforts	Work alone on your part
5 In conflict, you…	Use a clever saying to make your point	Devise a winning strategy	Picture a solution	Look for a "harmonic" solution	Move, gesture	Study relations among parties	Mediate, look for amicable solution	Get away from others
6 To make the next board game move, you…	Talk yourself through the move	Weigh the consequences of each move	Visualize what the next move will look like	Keep with the rhythm of the game	"Try out" a number of moves	Think in terms of predator and prey	Analyze motives of others	Make the move that feels right
7 You like games if you can…	Talk, use your linguistic skills	Use math, analyze the possibilities	Picture the moves, draw	Have music playing	Be active, use fine motor skills	Play outside	Play with others	Play solitaire, decide your moves alone
8 To add to your portfolio, you…	Write an essay	Include math, logic	Create a picture or graphic organizer	Write or record a song or tune	Act on a video, or perform	Work with plants or animals	Perform with others	Write a private journal or evaluation
9 For a present, you like a…	A book or magazine	Logic games, logic puzzles	Art, art supplies, jigsaw puzzle	Music, concert tickets	Sports equipment	A pet, flowers, outdoor gear	Big party	Journal or diary
10 During free time, you like to…	Read or write	Solve problems	Draw, paint, make models	Listen to music, play music, sing	Work with your hands	Enjoy nature	Spend time with friends, socialize	Be alone
Top Right (✔) **SCORE 1: Forced-Choice** The Most True Alternative	2	2	0	2	1	1	1	1
Bottom Left (✗) **SCORE 2: Free-Choice** All True Alternatives	3	3	10	3	3	3	3	3

Spencer & Miguel Kagan: *Multiple Intelligences*

SAMPLE # My MI Profile

Follow the directions to create a bar, pie, and line graph of your
Multiple Intelligences Test (MIT).

Score 1, Forced-Choice Bar Graph & Score 2, Free-Choice Line Graph

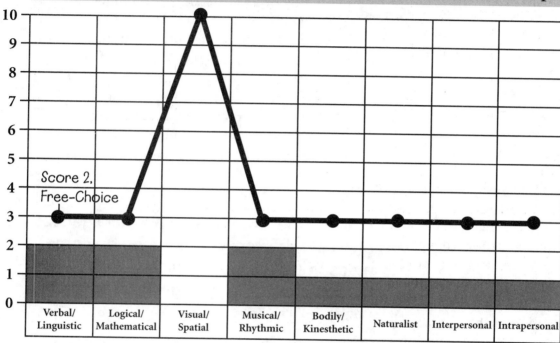

Score 1, Forced-Choice Pie Graph

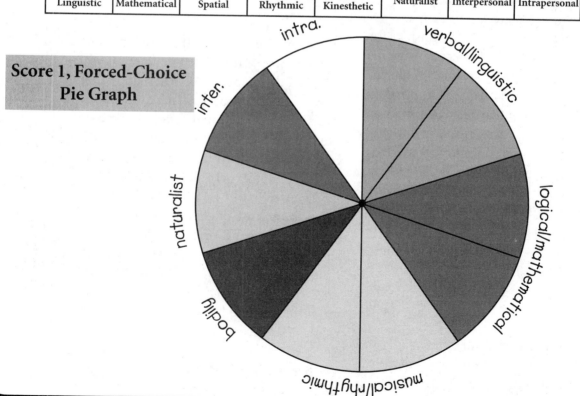

Interpretation of the MIT

Read the following comments only after you have scored and graphed your MIT.

We have administered the MIT test to thousands of teachers. In every group (but not for every individual) there are very large differences in the results when administered as a forced-choice measurement instrument as opposed to a free-choice measurement. In every group, far more people feel the free-choice format provides a more accurate picture of their pattern of intelligences, but there are exceptions.

It is not a mystery why the free-choice administration format generally produces a more accurate picture. In a forced choice situation, something which is very attractive may not be selected because something even more attractive is available. In a free-choice situation, all the attractive alternatives are selected, painting a more representative picture. Consider for a moment the scores of an imaginary individual, who always picked the visual/spatial alternative in the free-choice format, but never did so in the forced-choice format. In the forced-choice format, the strong visual/spatial orientation was not revealed because something was always just a bit more attractive. Look at his scores. See the Sample MI Test and the Sample My MI Profile on pages 18.6 and 18.7. The free-choice format revealed visual/spatial to be the strongest intelligence; the forced-choice format revealed it to be the weakest!

That the same test administered in two ways usually produces very discrepant results should be a warning. All forced-choice measures introduce artifacts.

But we cannot trust the free choice results either. By manipulating the attractiveness of the questions in the boxes of the MIT Test, we could easily make any of the intelligences appear much stronger or much weaker. This illustrates an important point: Results of any assessment technique are partially a function of the underlying construct we hope to measure, but partially a function of error variance, some of which is created by the items of the test and some of which is created by the way in which the test is administered. By choosing different questions or a different way of administering the test we can produce very different results.

Any one measure of multiple intelligences will give us a different answer than any other measure! We cannot trust any of the many available multiple intelligences tests to be valid!

Why is this important? It means that any one measure of multiple intelligences will give us a different answer than any other measure! We cannot trust any of the many available multiple intelligences tests to be valid! No existing test of multiple intelligence has gone through the very extensive process of construct validation. See Chapter 17: Are Valid MI Tests Possible? Putting a bunch of questions on a piece of paper is not valid test construction. We should not take the available tests of multiple intelligence as more than what they are — questions on a piece of paper. They are not a reliable basis for changing curriculum or instruction for students.

We believe no valid measures of the MI theory intelligences exist, and that even if they existed, they should not be used for differential treatment of students. And it is questionable whether valid measures of multiple intelligence can ever be created — the intelligences are that complex. See Chapter 17: Are Valid MI Tests Possible?

People are generally quite surprised to find the forced-choice and free-choice administration formats of the same exact questions can give quite different results. It is an important principle of test construction. Applying this principle to natural observation, we find that many of our own natural observations of our students do not allow us to accurately assess their true pattern of intelligences. Imagine for a moment that we set up two learning centers — one for reading and the other for the visual arts. Johnny always chooses the art center. We are inclined to conclude Johnny is high in the visual/spatial intelligence. Wrong. In fact, Johnny's preference has nothing to do with his ability. Johnny likes to paint, more than he likes to read even though he is far more skilled in reading than painting.

Susie always chooses the art center. We think she is high in the visual/spatial intelligence. Wrong. Her choice is not even a reflection of a preference for visual/spatial tasks. In fact, Susie hates painting — she chooses the visual/spatial center only because she hates reading more! A forced-choice assessment procedure has created an artifact.

Peter also chooses the visual/spatial center. But he could care less about painting. He is neither skilled in painting nor has a preference for visual/spatial tasks. He is attracted to Susie!

Johnny chooses the same center. He loves painting and is quite skilled in it. Can we conclude he is strong in the visual/spatial intelligence? Not at all. When we test him, we find he has the poorest sense of direction in the class! Skill or preference for one facet of an intelligence tells us little or nothing about skills and preferences for other important facets of the same intelligence.

These examples could be multiplied at length and are offered to give us pause, and a bit of humility, before concluding anything about the intelligences of our students.

The Facet Tests

Every intelligence in MI theory is a broad category encompassing many skills or facets.

On the following pages, you will find eight Facet Tests, one for each intelligence. Read the instructions and take the tests now. When done, we'll interpret the results.

Facet Tests Instructions

Circle a number from 1 to 10 corresponding to the strength of each skill for you. If you are not certain of what an item means, simply skip it. It is not critical that you score every item.

Stop! Do not read further. Take the Facet Tests now. When you are finished, continue on to the interpretation of the Facet Tests.

MI Facet Test 1
Assess Your Verbal/Linguistic Skills

Instructions: Rate your skills by circling a number from 1 to 10.
The higher number, the more highly you believe that skill is developed for you.

Grammar	1 2 3 4 5 6 7 8 9 10
Descriptive Writing	1 2 3 4 5 6 7 8 9 10
Persuasive Writing	1 2 3 4 5 6 7 8 9 10
Creative Writing	1 2 3 4 5 6 7 8 9 10
Spelling	1 2 3 4 5 6 7 8 9 10
Creating Poetry	1 2 3 4 5 6 7 8 9 10
Appreciation of Poetry	1 2 3 4 5 6 7 8 9 10
Appreciation of Literature	1 2 3 4 5 6 7 8 9 10
Reading Comprehension	1 2 3 4 5 6 7 8 9 10
Reading Speed	1 2 3 4 5 6 7 8 9 10
Vocabulary	1 2 3 4 5 6 7 8 9 10
Storytelling	1 2 3 4 5 6 7 8 9 10
Second Language Acquisition	1 2 3 4 5 6 7 8 9 10
Debate	1 2 3 4 5 6 7 8 9 10
Conversational Skills	1 2 3 4 5 6 7 8 9 10
Public Speaking	1 2 3 4 5 6 7 8 9 10

MI Facet Test 2

Assess Your Logical/ Mathematical Skills

Instructions: Rate your skills by circling a number from 1 to 10.
The higher number, the more highly you believe that skill is developed for you.

Addition, Subtraction	1 2 3 4 5 6 7 8 9 10
Algebra	1 2 3 4 5 6 7 8 9 10
Geometry	1 2 3 4 5 6 7 8 9 10
Computer Programming	1 2 3 4 5 6 7 8 9 10

Recognizing Similarities & Differences	1 2 3 4 5 6 7 8 9 10
Recognizing Patterns or Trends	1 2 3 4 5 6 7 8 9 10
Organizing, Categorizing Information	1 2 3 4 5 6 7 8 9 10
Sequencing	1 2 3 4 5 6 7 8 9 10

Evaluating Theories, Explanations	1 2 3 4 5 6 7 8 9 10
Seeking, Providing Explanations	1 2 3 4 5 6 7 8 9 10
Using Abstract Symbols	1 2 3 4 5 6 7 8 9 10
Estimating, Predicting	1 2 3 4 5 6 7 8 9 10

Accounting	1 2 3 4 5 6 7 8 9 10
Deductive/Inductive Reasoning	1 2 3 4 5 6 7 8 9 10
Analyzing Data	1 2 3 4 5 6 7 8 9 10
Determining Cause & Effect	1 2 3 4 5 6 7 8 9 10

MI Facet Test 3

Assess Your Visual/Spatial Skills

Instructions: Rate your skills by circling a number from 1 to 10.
The higher number, the more highly you believe that skill is developed for you.

Creating Mental Maps	1	2	3	4	5	6	7	8	9	10
Forming Mental Images	1	2	3	4	5	6	7	8	9	10
Rotating Figures Mentally	1	2	3	4	5	6	7	8	9	10
Reading Maps	1	2	3	4	5	6	7	8	9	10
Memory for Spatial Details	1	2	3	4	5	6	7	8	9	10
Estimating Distance	1	2	3	4	5	6	7	8	9	10
Page Layout/Graphic Design	1	2	3	4	5	6	7	8	9	10
Appreciation of Visual Art	1	2	3	4	5	6	7	8	9	10
Production of Visual Art	1	2	3	4	5	6	7	8	9	10
Creating Floral Arrangements	1	2	3	4	5	6	7	8	9	10
Color Coordinating	1	2	3	4	5	6	7	8	9	10
Appreciation of Architecture	1	2	3	4	5	6	7	8	9	10
Creating, Interpreting Diagrams	1	2	3	4	5	6	7	8	9	10
Solving Jigsaw Puzzles	1	2	3	4	5	6	7	8	9	10
Building Models	1	2	3	4	5	6	7	8	9	10
Maintaining Sense of Direction	1	2	3	4	5	6	7	8	9	10

Spencer & Miguel Kagan: *Multiple Intelligences*
Kagan Cooperative Learning • 1 (800) WEE CO-OP

MI Facet Test 4

Assess Your Musical/Rhythmic Skills

Instructions: Rate your skills by circling a number from 1 to 10.
The higher number, the more highly you believe that skill is developed for you.

Recognizing Types of Music	1 2 3 4 5 6 7 8 9 10
Recognizing Notes	1 2 3 4 5 6 7 8 9 10
Recognizing Singers	1 2 3 4 5 6 7 8 9 10
Recognizing Composers	1 2 3 4 5 6 7 8 9 10
Composing Music	1 2 3 4 5 6 7 8 9 10
Writing Lyrics	1 2 3 4 5 6 7 8 9 10
Reading Music	1 2 3 4 5 6 7 8 9 10
Playing by Ear	1 2 3 4 5 6 7 8 9 10
Singing	1 2 3 4 5 6 7 8 9 10
Sense of Rhythm	1 2 3 4 5 6 7 8 9 10
Ability to Match Pitch	1 2 3 4 5 6 7 8 9 10
Sense of Timing	1 2 3 4 5 6 7 8 9 10
Playing an Instrument	1 2 3 4 5 6 7 8 9 10
Appreciation of Classical Music	1 2 3 4 5 6 7 8 9 10
Appreciation of Rock Music	1 2 3 4 5 6 7 8 9 10
Identifying Instruments by Sound	1 2 3 4 5 6 7 8 9 10

MI Facet Test 5

Assess Your Bodily/Kinesthetic Skills

Instructions: Rate your skills by circling a number from 1 to 10.
The higher number, the more highly you believe that skill is developed for you.

Fine Motor Skills	1 2 3 4 5 6 7 8 9 10
Strength	1 2 3 4 5 6 7 8 9 10
Endurance	1 2 3 4 5 6 7 8 9 10
Coordination	1 2 3 4 5 6 7 8 9 10

Eye-Hand Coordination	1 2 3 4 5 6 7 8 9 10
Expressive Body Language, Gestures	1 2 3 4 5 6 7 8 9 10
Speed	1 2 3 4 5 6 7 8 9 10
Agility	1 2 3 4 5 6 7 8 9 10

Ability to Mimic Others	1 2 3 4 5 6 7 8 9 10
Dancing	1 2 3 4 5 6 7 8 9 10
Acting/Role-Playing	1 2 3 4 5 6 7 8 9 10
Physical Flexibility	1 2 3 4 5 6 7 8 9 10

Need for Exercise, Movement	1 2 3 4 5 6 7 8 9 10
Appreciation of Sports as Spectator	1 2 3 4 5 6 7 8 9 10
Enjoyment of Sports as Participant	1 2 3 4 5 6 7 8 9 10
Juggling	1 2 3 4 5 6 7 8 9 10

MI Facet Test 6

Assess Your Naturalist Skills

Instructions: Rate your skills by circling a number from 1 to 10.
The higher number, the more highly you believe that skill is developed for you.

Appreciation of Nature	1 2 3 4 5 6 7 8 9 10
Discriminating Fish, Ocean Life	1 2 3 4 5 6 7 8 9 10
Discriminating of Rocks	1 2 3 4 5 6 7 8 9 10
Discriminating Insects	1 2 3 4 5 6 7 8 9 10
Discriminating Plants, Trees, Flowers	1 2 3 4 5 6 7 8 9 10
Discriminating Birds, Animals, Reptiles	1 2 3 4 5 6 7 8 9 10
Knowledge of the Stars	1 2 3 4 5 6 7 8 9 10
Awareness of Stages of Moon	1 2 3 4 5 6 7 8 9 10
Love of Animals, Pets	1 2 3 4 5 6 7 8 9 10
Green Thumb	1 2 3 4 5 6 7 8 9 10
Interest in Environment	1 2 3 4 5 6 7 8 9 10
Observing Nature	1 2 3 4 5 6 7 8 9 10
Collecting Leaves or Insects	1 2 3 4 5 6 7 8 9 10
Sensitivity to Weather	1 2 3 4 5 6 7 8 9 10
Ability to Predict Weather	1 2 3 4 5 6 7 8 9 10
Attention to Detail	1 2 3 4 5 6 7 8 9 10

MI Facet Test 7
Assess Your Interpersonal Skills

Instructions: Rate your skills by circling a number from 1 to 10.
The higher number, the more highly you believe that skill is developed for you.

Resolving Conflicts, Mediating	1 2 3 4 5 6 7 8 9 10
Empathy	1 2 3 4 5 6 7 8 9 10
Tolerance, Patience with Others	1 2 3 4 5 6 7 8 9 10
Making & Keeping Friends	1 2 3 4 5 6 7 8 9 10
Enjoying Interacting with Others	1 2 3 4 5 6 7 8 9 10
Nonverbal Communication Skills	1 2 3 4 5 6 7 8 9 10
Good Team Player	1 2 3 4 5 6 7 8 9 10
Teaching Others	1 2 3 4 5 6 7 8 9 10
Leading Others	1 2 3 4 5 6 7 8 9 10
Motivating Others	1 2 3 4 5 6 7 8 9 10
Cooperating	1 2 3 4 5 6 7 8 9 10
Discerning Motives of Others	1 2 3 4 5 6 7 8 9 10
Charisma	1 2 3 4 5 6 7 8 9 10
Sympathy	1 2 3 4 5 6 7 8 9 10
Loving, Caring	1 2 3 4 5 6 7 8 9 10
Ability to Work with Diversity	1 2 3 4 5 6 7 8 9 10

MI Facet Test 8
Assess Your Intrapersonal Skills

Instructions: Rate your skills by circling a number from 1 to 10.
The higher number, the more highly you believe that skill is developed for you.

Introspection	1 2 3 4 5 6 7 8 9 10
Awareness of Own Feelings	1 2 3 4 5 6 7 8 9 10
Metacognition	1 2 3 4 5 6 7 8 9 10
Sense of Morality	1 2 3 4 5 6 7 8 9 10
Accurate Self-Perception	1 2 3 4 5 6 7 8 9 10
Enjoy, Seek Alone Time	1 2 3 4 5 6 7 8 9 10
Interpretation of Own Dreams	1 2 3 4 5 6 7 8 9 10
Transpersonal	1 2 3 4 5 6 7 8 9 10
Intuitive	1 2 3 4 5 6 7 8 9 10
Ability to Motivate Yourself	1 2 3 4 5 6 7 8 9 10
Goal Oriented	1 2 3 4 5 6 7 8 9 10
Spiritual Awareness	1 2 3 4 5 6 7 8 9 10
Ability to Control Emotions	1 2 3 4 5 6 7 8 9 10
Ability to Set Priorities	1 2 3 4 5 6 7 8 9 10
Independent	1 2 3 4 5 6 7 8 9 10
Analysis of Own Motivations	1 2 3 4 5 6 7 8 9 10

Interpretation of the Facet Tests

We have now administered the Facet Tests to thousands of teachers. We always ask the same questions:

There are three possible results: Within each test, either you came out generally high across the board on the facets of that intelligence, you came out low across the board, or you were all over the map. How did you score? Were you generally consistent, or inconsistent within each measure?

Although a few teachers score consistently high or consistently low in the skills of an intelligence, far more teachers score all over the map! This finding has very profound implications. It means that whenever we call an individual high or low in an intelligence, we are making a mistake. We are overgeneralizing. No one is high or low in all of the diverse skills of any one of the eight intelligences. We each have our unique pattern of skills within each intelligence. There is a multiplicity of intelligences.

There really is no such thing as one visual/spatial intelligence. Rather there is a large collection of skills which we subsume in the broad category called visual/spatial intelligence. Just as one IQ score cannot represent a person's intelligence because intelligence is multifaceted, one score for visual/spatial intelligence cannot represent the broad collection of skills, visual and spatial, ranging from color combining, appreciation of architecture, navigational skills, expressive painting, and ability to understand what the world looks like to another person (visual perspective role taking). Someone who can paint very expressively

may or may not be strong in representational painting or computer graphics. Each individual has a multiplicity of intelligences; no one is strong in all of the facets within any of the broad multiple intelligences categories.

Because of the multiplicity of intelligences, differential curriculum and instruction based on the presumption that an individual is high or low on a particular given intelligence may work for some students but not others. It would depend on how well the facets emphasized in the program matched the facets needed by the student.

We are probably safe in assessing a very specific skill, say ability to carry out a specific operation of a long division algorithm. But we are probably wrong if we generalize from a specific skill to speak about a "logical/mathematical intelligence." We all know a student who is strong in the algorithm, but does not really un-

It is an overgeneralization to say someone is intelligent or not based on an IQ test — there are many ways to be smart. Similarly, it is an overgeneralization to say someone is high or low on any of the eight intelligences — there are many ways to be smart within each of the multiple intelligences.

derstand the concept. We know another student who understands well the concept, but gets balled up performing the algorithm. Who has stronger "logical/mathematical intelligence?" If we use colorful, descriptive adjectives, but make many grammatical errors, are we stronger or weaker in the verbal/linguistic intelligence than someone who is grammatically perfect, but uses trite adjectives? There are myriad facets to each intelligence, so every time we describe someone as high or low on an intelligence we are over-generalizing.

It is an overgeneralization to say someone is intelligent or not based on an IQ test — there are many ways to be smart. Similarly, it is an overgeneralization to say someone is high on any one of the eight intelligences — there are many ways to be smart within each of the multiple intelligences.

One test or assessment instrument cannot measure all the facets of any one intelligence. There are far too many very specific skills within each broad intelligence. The multifaceted nature of the intelligences has profound implications for the development of curriculum and instruction. If we use MI theory's defined intelligences instead of specific skills as basis for assessing our students, and then create differential curriculum and instruction for students with different scores on the multiple intelligences, we will end up trying to place multifaceted pegs into square holes. Curriculum and instruction based on broad over-generalizations will not fit the needs of our students. Each of us is incredibly multifaceted and unique; broad categories are useful for some purposes, but not for creating differential curriculum and instruction to meet the needs of our students.

References

Gardner, H. *Multiple Intelligences. The Theory in Practice.* New York: Basic Books, 1993.

Authentic Assessment of MI

Because a student does not perform well on a written or standardized test does not mean he or she lacks an understanding of certain concepts. Not all students know, understand, and learn in the same way. We must honor these differences if we are to gain an accurate picture of students' learning and help them succeed in school. If we are genuinely concerned to reach all students and teach them things they need to succeed in the larger world, we must put an end to the assembly line approach to assessment and testing (Lazear, 1994, p. 8).

Given the undesirability of testing intelligences as part of a program aimed at differential treatment, and the difficulties or even impossibility of creating valid MI tests, there remain two questions: Is authentic assessment of the multiple intelligences possible, and, if possible, is authentic assessment of multiple intelligences beneficial? The answer to both questions is yes. We would do well to abandon attempts to test the intelligences of students, to represent their intelligences with a number, to rank students or compare them with some standard. We would do well to instead enter a partnership with our students in a process to better understand and appreciate their uniqueness; a number of important benefits result. In short, we say testing, No!; authentic assessment, Yes!

When we abandon attempts to test the intelligences of students, to rank students or compare them with some standard, and instead enter a partnership with students in a process to better understand and appreciate their uniqueness, a number of important benefits result.

In this chapter we will look first at the characteristics of authentic MI Assessment, next at a range of authentic assessment methods for the intelligences, and finally we will examine a number of beneficial goals toward which authentic assessment advances us.

Authentic Assessment of Intelligences

MI theory points out a number of problems with traditional approaches to measuring intelligence. Traditional IQ tests provide inadequate and inauthentic assessment of intelligences. Any authentic approach to assessing intelligences must avoid the pitfalls of traditional intelligence testing. Let's contrast the major pitfalls of traditional intelligence testing with the authentic assessment alternative.

Representative Assessment

Authentic assessment of intelligences must in some way reflect actual intelligences as they function in real people in the real world. Although this simple statement is obviously true, traditional tests of intelligence for the most part ignore its implications. It is possible to develop a reliable test of human intelligences which do not have much to do with actual human functioning in the real world. For example, we might develop an intelligence test based on ability to quickly arrange a given number of toothpicks to create geometric figures. As with any skill, we would find that some people are quite good at this toothpick IQ

test, some quite poor, and most average. Calling the toothpick test a measure of intelligence, however, does not make it so. To establish validity for our toothpick intelligence test, we would have to show that performance on the test predicts important intelligent behaviors. Otherwise we should not accept a score on the toothpick test as an authentic measure of intelligence. To be authentic, an assessment measure must give results that represent important, real-world outcomes. Authentic assessment is representative assessment.

The question then becomes, how much are traditional IQ measures like the toothpick test, showing reliable differences in human performance, but differences which do not represent important real-world, authentic intelligence? If our test does not represent intelligent behavior in the real world, we should reject it as inauthentic. How representative are scores on traditional IQ tests? It turns out that to a large extent scores on traditional IQ tests are not representative of intelligence as it plays out in the real world. They are not authentic measures of intelligence.

The strongest evidence we have for that conclusion is the lack of correlation between IQ test scores and actual real-world performance in real-world workplace jobs. For example, measures of cognitive ability account for only four percent of the variance in job performance in the real world (Wigdor & Garner, 1982)! Daniel Goleman summarizes the lack of relationship between IQ and real life functioning: Goleman (1995) cites the following:

> IQ offers little to explain the different destinies of people with roughly equal promises, schooling, and opportunity. When ninety-five Harvard students from the classes of the 1940's — a time when people with a wider spread of IQ were at Ivy League schools than is presently

the case — were followed into middle age, the men with the highest test scores in college were not particularly successful compared to their lower-scoring peers in terms of salary, productivity, or status in their field. Nor did they have the greatest life satisfaction, nor the most happiness with friendships, family, and romantic relations (Original Source: George Vaillant, 1977).

> **...we need far more differentiated and far more sensitive ways of assessing what individuals are capable of accomplishing. In place of standardized tests, I hope that we can develop environments (or even societies) in which individuals' natural and acquired strengths would become manifest: environments in which their daily solutions of problems or fashioning of products would indicate clearly which vocational and avocational roles most suit them (Gardner, 1993, pp. 182-183).**

A similar follow-up in middle age was done with 450 boys, most sons of immigrants, two thirds from families on welfare, who grew up in Somerville, Massachusetts, at the time a "blighted slum" a few blocks from Harvard. A third had IQ's below 90. But again IQ had little relationship to how well they had done at work or in the rest of their lives; for instance, 7 percent of men with IQ's under 80 were unemployed for ten or more years, but so were 7 percent of men with IQ's over 100. To be sure, there was a general link (as there always is) between IQ and socioeconomic level at age forty-seven. But childhood abilities such as being able to handle frustrations, control emotions, and get on with other people made the greater difference (Original Source: Felsman & Vaillant, 1987).

If IQ measures do not predict real-world smarts, they do not meet the first test of authentic assessment, that it be representative of authentic, real-world behavior.

It is not surprising that IQ measures do not predict job success. If we look at IQ test questions they involve things like repeating back meaningless digits, learning meaningless symbols to represent numbers, and using blocks to match red and white designs which may have no meaning whatsoever to the person taking the test! In the real workplace people do not repeat back meaningless strings of digits or, under time pressure, try to arrange red and white blocks to form designs that match the designs in a little booklet. We are likely to have authentic, representative assessment to the extent the assessment situations are similar to real-world intelligent functioning. When in the real world do we have to report back without error strings of numbers, or match pictures with colored blocks?

This principle can be applied to academic tests. In the real world of the workplace, employees do not sit down in rows and fill in bubbles on true-false tests. Employees are busy doing things: working with others, interacting to solve meaningful problems, creating things. The probability of our achievement tests being authentic, then, would be enhanced dramatically if they recorded behavior in the context of students interacting, solving problems, and creating things. In designing authentic assessment we will be successful to the extent our measurements are taken in the context of genuine problem solving like the kind of problem solving which occurs on the job, at home, and in other real-life situations. Authentic assessment is representative assessment.

Assessing All Intelligences

Authentic assessment of intelligences must give fairly equal weight to the various intelligences. If for example, we were to develop a measure of intelligence which assessed verbal/linguistic skills, but ignored all other ways to be smart, we would not accept that measure as an authentic assessment of intelligences. Brilliant mathematicians who happen to be weak in verbal/linguistic skills would be labeled dull. Authentic assessment of intelligences, then, must represent the range of intelligences; they must be multiple intelligences measures.

Traditional intelligence tests do a fairly good job of assessing verbal/linguistic skills (vocabulary is one subscale of traditional measures), logical/mathematical skills (there are subscales on problem solving and number tasks), and some visual/spatial skills (the block design subscale involves ability to see smaller figures within a larger figure). But for the most part traditional measures ignore the other ways to be smart. They give but little attention to interpersonal intelligence, and almost no attention to intrapersonal intelligence. Because traditional measures do not represent the range of ways to be smart, we cannot accept them as authentic measures of the full scope of human intelligence. Authentic measures assess the multiple intelligences.

Intelligence-Fair Assessment

Authentic measures of intelligence are intelligence-fair. That is, they assess each intelligence in a way appropriate to that intelligence. A true-false test about the bodily/kinesthetic intelligence, no matter how cleverly worded, tells us at best what someone knows *about* bodily/kinesthetic intelligence — not the *strength of* their bodily/kinesthetic intelligence. A person who has read a great deal about bodily/kinesthetic intelligence might pass the test with flying colors, but still not be able to perform even simple dance steps, dunk a basket, mime, or type. Someone who is quite good in all of those bodily/kinesthetic skills, and many more, might fail the test miserably. *Knowing about* bodily/kinesthetic intelligence is not the same as *having* a highly developed bodily/kinesthetic intelligence. Knowledge about any intelligence is not the same as development of that intelligence; knowledge can occur in the absence of skills. Authentic measures of bodily kinesthetic/intelligence, then, must allow the intelligence to express itself directly, not through the filter of other intelligences.

Authentic assessment allows direct, unfiltered expression of each intelligence in the mode natural to the intelligence.

Authentic measures are intelligence-fair. If we use words or paper and pencil tests to assess all the intelligences, we bias our outcomes in favor of those who are good with words and paper and pencil tests. Authentic assessment allows direct, unfiltered expression of each intelligence in the mode natural to the intelligence. An authentic measure of musical/rhythmic intelligence, then, would involve among other things recognition and production of songs, instrumental music, and rhythms; an authentic measure of visual/spatial intelligence would involve working in the visual/spatial domain, including painting, drawing, working with colors and moving objects and oneself in space.

An authentic assessment of intelligences must be facet-sensitive. It must assess all, or at least many, of the facets of each intelligence, not making over-generalizations based on sampling only one or two facets.

Authentic assessment of each intelligence involves a very different assessment format — a format fair to the intelligence. Once again we see that the principles of authentic assessment lead us to assess intelligences within the context of their natural mode of expression. The further we move from real-life expression of the intelligences, the less authentic will be our assessment.

Facet-Sensitive Assessment

Let's say for a moment that we developed a test of logical/mathematical intelligence based on ability to solve geometric proofs. If the test involved only geometric proofs and no other type of logical/mathematical functioning, Person A, who is great at geometry, but poor at outlining an essay, inductive reasoning, and designing experiments to test alternative hypotheses, would score high in logical/mathematical reasoning. Conversely, Person B who is poor in geometry, but highly skillful in outlining, induction, hypothesis testing, and a number of other logical functions, would score low in logical/mathematical intelligence. Our test would have us conclude that Person B was weak in logical/mathematical intelligence in spite of her obvious strengths in many types of logical/mathematical functioning, and that Person A was strong in logical/mathematical intelligence in spite of his many obvious weak-

nesses. Given this pattern, we would reject the test as an inauthentic test of logical/mathematical intelligence. To be authentic, a test must sample the range of facets of each intelligence.

An authentic assessment of intelligences must be facet-sensitive. It must assess all, or at least many, of the facets of each intelligence, not making over-generalizations based on sampling only one or two facets. There are a great many facets to each intelligence (See Chapter 9: Developing the Multiple Intelligences). Further, the facets are not necessarily correlated. For example, ability to recognize songs is not necessarily associated with ability to sing, ability to make pleasing color arrangements is not necessarily associated with ability to find one's way around in a city, and even extraordinary ability to make puns is not necessarily associated with ability to create a significant poem.

An authentic assessment of any intelligence must sample broadly the skills of the intelligence; to the extent it does not, it tells us about splinter skills, but not the intelligence. Given this conclusion, it becomes clear that authentic assessment is possible in the context of complex behaviors which involve many facets of an intelligence, but is less likely to the extent we sample only a few facets, as is so often the case in intelligence tests. Once again, if we want authentic assessment, we are drawn to assess intelligences within the context of real world functioning, not in the artificial context of test taking.

Affect-Weighted Assessment

To understand how someone is likely to function in the real world we need to know more than their abilities, we need to know their preferences as well. If, for example, a person is quite skilled in both mathematics and language arts, but loves language arts and has no genuine interest in mathematics, we would be safe in predicting that person will more likely gravitate to, and shine in, hobbies and jobs which are word-rich, rather than number-rich. To make an accurate prediction of real-world functioning, we need to weigh our knowledge of abilities with a knowledge of preferences. Authentic assessment is affect-weighted.

It is important, though, that we do not confuse abilities and preferences. To paint a genuine picture of someone's intelligences, we need to know both their abilities and preferences, and cannot assume that knowledge of one is knowledge of another. Most students who are strong in a subject enjoy that subject (either because easy success has led to liking, or because liking has led to effort and persistence which in turn have lead to enhanced skill). This, however, is not always the case. We all know the student who likes reading, but for whom reading does not come easily. We know the student who is quite good at reading, but who would much rather play sports, paint, or listen to music. The son of a good friend of ours always scores in the 99th percentile in reading, but almost never reads a book by choice. His ability is not associated with a preference.

A full picture of someone's intellectual pattern needs to inform us not just of abili-

ties, but also of preferences. Two students have perfect pitch and can play back tunes with little effort. Student A is passionate about music and spends all her free time playing, listening to music, and reading about the lives of composers. Student B, however, with the same musical gifts, shows no special interest in music or the lives of composers. To make a prediction about the lives of those students, or to decide how important for them it would be to teach with instructional strategies that match the musical intelligence, we must know more than their abilities — we must weigh our decisions based on a knowledge of their preferences.

A good assessment instrument can be a learning experience. But more to the point, it is extremely desirable to have assessment occur in the context of students working on problems, projects, or products that genuinely engage them, that hold their interest and motivate them to do well (Gardner, 1993, p. 178).

Authentic assessment paints a differentiated picture, telling us both about preferences and abilities, and not confusing one with the other. One of the reasons that traditional measures of intelligence fail to predict real-life career choices and success is that they are not affect-weighted; they falsely assume that skill is associated with desire.

Meaningful, Engaging Assessment

Authentic assessment cannot occur in inauthentic contexts. Two students are given the following math problem: "What is one-half divided by one-third." Student A does not produce the correct answer, and fails all similar problems. Student B gets all problems of this type correct. Later the two students are given half a candy bar and are told to divide what they have been given equally among themselves and two other students. Student A immediately, precisely divides the half candy bar into thirds. Student B is puzzled for a few moments, but then breaks the half candy bar into a number of pieces, and begins counting, "One for you, one for you, one for me, one for you, one for you, one for me…" Which student understands division better?

For student A, the abstract math problem expressed in words was not a meaningful context, but the same problem expressed in concrete manipulatives was quite meaningful, immediately engaging his logical/ mathematical intelligence. The intelligence was not engaged by the first context, but was fully engaged by the second context, partially explaining why the student failed when the problem was presented in one format, but immediately succeeded when it was presented in another. We cannot assess how fast a car can go, if the driver does not shift gears out of neutral.

Only in a personally meaningful context is potential released, and only when that potential is engaged can there be authentic assessment.

Authentic assessment depends on a meaningful, engaging context. The traditional IQ test attempts to measure intelligence in a contrived, decontextualized situation. Void of meaning, the test cannot produce an authentic assessment of intelligence. The same students who score quite low on an intelligence test, outshine high scoring students when faced with repairing a car

motor or finding a way to hustle bus money. If students with tremendous street smarts fail our IQ tests, we would do better questioning the tests than questioning whether they are really smart. A meaningful, engaging situation for one student may not be meaningful for another. Authentic assessment occurs only in meaningful contexts.

Tests for many students are not a meaningful, engaging context and so cannot produce authentic assessment. Tests introduce other pitfalls as well. Tests introduce test anxiety and evaluation apprehension. A student may score quite low when they think they are being tested, but score well when they do not think their performance is being recorded. The worry about how one will appear — anxiety associated with prior test failures — can interfere with performance. Tests are contrived and usually do not create situations similar to real-life. Traditional tests create an inauthentic context in which to assess many students. What is meaningful to one student is not necessarily meaningful to another, and what is meaningful to one culture is not necessarily meaningful to another. Intelligence test scores go up remarkably for some cultural groups when the test items are recast in culturally relevant terms.

Spencer once worked as a consultant in a school for students who were failing traditional academic classes. A tutor was having no success in producing reading gains with a young man from an extremely poor neighborhood. She could not get him to focus on the text; he would become a behavior problem whenever she tried to work with him on reading. Spencer suggested she bring in hot rod magazines, and use those as text. She had no problem at all getting him to focus on the text of the hot rod magazines, and in short order his reading scores climbed rather dramatically. In fact, for him the opportunity to read became the reward for work in other academic areas. His tutor had a hard time keeping him from sneaking out the magazines to read! The traditional text was not a meaningful context within which to assess his reading potential; the hot rod magazines provided for him a much more meaningful context. Only in a personally meaningful context is potential released, and only when that potential is engaged can there be authentic assessment.

Traditional Tests Versus Authentic Assessment

Characteristics	Traditional Intelligence Tests	Authentic MI Assessments
Goal	Rank, Grade, Evaluate Students	Know, Understand, Help Students
Reference	Norm or Criterion Referenced	Ipsative, Pattern Based
Context	Decontextualized Knowledge-Based	Meaningful, Engaging Performance-Based
What Is Assessed	Isolated Skills, A Few Facets	Interacting Skills, Many Facets
Filter	Verbal/Linguistic Test-Taking Filters	Intelligence-Fair, Unfiltered Expressions
When	After Instruction	During Instruction
By Whom	Test Administrator	Teacher and Student as Partners in a Process
How Often	One-Shot	Multiple Assessments
Type of Assessment	One-Type	Multiple Formats

Multiple Assessments

A snapshot gives us one kind of information, a video another. Two students both score 85 percent on a test of mathematical intelligence. Which is better developing the mathematical intelligence? The snapshot cannot tell us. The students, however, have been tested each month for the past five months. When we find out that over the past months Student A has scored 45, 55, 65, 75, and now 85 percent, but that Student B has scored 85 percent every month, we know which student is better developing. Authentic assessment, then, involves multiple assessments. We need a moving picture, not a snapshot.

There are a number of dimensions along which the principle of multiple assessments applies:

Time

Authentic assessments are repeated over time to produce a developmental picture, not a static one-shot picture.

Assessment Techniques

Authentic assessment uses a range of measures. One test format may not reveal the same picture as another; an authentic picture is painted only when we triangulate in on the truth, approaching it from a variety of angles. For example, a student who does poorly on the block design (a visual/spatial subtest of many IQ tests), may find his or her way around very well when placed in the maze of an unknown city. Only when we use a variety of assessment techniques can we be sure we have painted an authentic picture.

Many Contexts

Students who do very poorly in a traditional classroom, sitting in rows, often blossom when the chairs are turned around and they are allowed to work in groups. Other students do rather poorly in groups, but show rapid gains when allowed to master the same content through a computer program. To paint an authentic assessment of their potential, we must assess students in many contexts. MI theory itself facilitates more authentic assessment because it broadens the ways we teach, allowing us to observe students in a much broader range of contexts.

Different Observers

Black and white students score differently on a traditional IQ tests, depending on whether it is administered by a black or white test administrator. Students may have immediate rapport with one person, but an immediate distrust of another. Thus we paint a more authentic assessment of intelligences if we get input from many sources, teachers, parents, peers, and others. An authentic assessment considers input from many observers.

Tools for Authentic Assessment

Many approaches to authentic assessment of the intelligences have been proposed. Some involve extraordinarily complex simulations and scoring protocols which, while perhaps of theoretical value, will never become part of daily life in classrooms. Others involve rather simple observation instruments and/or even student, teacher, and parent checklists. While easier to administer, these simple measures resemble tests more than assessment approaches, and have questionable validity and questionable authenticity. If we take seriously the principles of authentic assessment, assessment of the intelligences occurs best in the ongoing context of meaningful learning situations, authentic learning situations. Creation of authentic learning situations, then, is the single most important tool for creating authentic assessment. Authentic learning provides the context for authentic assessment.

After reviewing the notion of authentic learning situations, we can then ask what kinds of observations or assessments can be made within those situations. The first, and most important question, though, is: What are some of the meaningful representative instructional settings we can create to release the intelligences? Unless the intelligences are fully engaged, we cannot assess them. In what situations are the intelligences most authentically engaged and assessed?

Authentic Learning

If we take seriously the notion that authentic assessment cannot occur in inauthentic contexts, then the prerequisite for authentic assessment is authentic curriculum and instruction. We can assess the true potential of students only as they are engaged in meaningful, motivating learning experiences. In traditional approaches to testing, there is a wide gulf between instruction and testing. First we instruct, then we test. In an authentic assessment the gulf between instruction and assessment narrows to a tiny, sometimes imperceptible gap. As we instruct, we assess. Good instruction includes ample opportunities for students to assess themselves

repeatedly, and in many different forms. In authentic assessment we enter a process in which the strengths and weaknesses of students are revealed to themselves as well as to us — assessment is part of the process of meaningful teaching, not something which occurs after the teaching is done.

To the extent that we are capable of creating learning situations in which students can work at their own, developmentally appropriate level, they will gravitate toward working in their zone of proximal development. Students have no interest in working repeatedly with problems they can easily solve, and are also not interested in repeatedly tackling problems far beyond their reach. When given appropriate support and challenge, students gravitate to the learning level which allows them to grow. They seek appropriate challenges. When they are engaged in authentic learning tasks, which are neither too easy nor too difficult, tasks which engage their intelligences, their skills as well as their limits are revealed. The problem of authentic assessment of the intelligences, then, to a large extent translates into the problem of providing appropriate support and chal-

Thus, authentic assessment must reduce the gap between assessment and real-world functioning — only meaningful, representative contexts reveal meaningful, representative intelligences. If our teaching is not relevant, our assessment cannot be.

lenge in each intelligence, and providing learning situations so students engage in authentic learning. As students encounter their appropriate level, as they engage in personally meaningful learning, they reveal their skills to themselves and to us.

The tasks which allow students to engage in authentic learning are exactly the same tasks which allow us, as teachers, to engage in authentic assessment. Tasks which do not allow authentic learning or assessment are like those of the traditional intelligence test — tasks which many students find strange, unmotivating, unrelated to real life, and which tap a very limited, externally selected set of skills. If we are to authentically assess intelligences, we must enter the world of the student — not ask the students to enter a foreign world which for them has no relevance or meaning. As we have seen, the bankruptcy of traditional intelligence testing is revealed by the lack of relation between IQ scores and intelligence as defined by the ability to succeed at the real problems of life. It is not that success on a job is unrelated to intelligence, rather, success in the real world is a function of different kinds of intelligences than those assessed by traditional measures, and the intelligences functioning in different ways. The traditional measures are inauthentic — they measure intelligences unrelated to job success or intelligences functioning in ways unrepresentative of the ways intelligences function for real world for success. Thus, authentic assessment must reduce the gap between assessment and real-world functioning — only meaningful, representative contexts reveal meaningful, representative intelligences. If our teaching is not relevant, our assessment cannot be.

Authentic learning situations allow student choice of what and how to study, they allow the intelligences to express themselves in the natural context of meaningful, mo-tivating situations, and they allow each student to exhibit his or her unique pattern of intelligences. They are not designed to compare one student with another, but rather to maximize the opportunity of each student to work on a variety of personally meaningful problems or projects in each of the intelligence areas. While the projects and problems can be solved in unique, personally challenging ways, the teacher selects topic areas which, over time, assess all of the intelligences. This is not to say that students can solve any problem, or create any project, using only one intelligence. They cannot. The intelligences always work in concert. Therefore we must define learning situations which, over time, allow students to express and develop each of the intelligences. Authentic learning situations, in which students can express and develop their intelligences, include, but certainly are not limited to, the following:

Projects and Products

Students can work alone or in groups on a wide range of engaging projects or to produce a wide range of products. As they do, we have the opportunity to assess their intelligences in action in authentic learning situations. There are innumerable projects and products which students can create such as persuasive speeches, pictures, collages, clay models, graphic organizers, inventions, physical routines, chants, new lyrics to familiar songs, surveys, interviews, autobiographies, TV ads, limericks, and outlines, to name just a few.

Authentic Assessment of Products and Projects

Sample Content: Water Cycle

▼ **Verbal/Linguistic**
Create a poem or essay about the water cycle

▼ **Logical/Mathematical**
Design an experiment to test evaporation rates under different conditions.

▼ **Visual/Spatial**
Use water colors to depict different types of cloud formations.

▼ **Musical/Rhythmic**
Create sounds to represent, a sunny day, a drizzling day, rain, and a thunderstorm.

▼ **Bodily/Kinesthetic**
Become a rain drop and act out the entire water cycle.

▼ **Naturalist**
Observe the effect of rainy and sunny days on various plants and animals.

▼ **Interpersonal**
Work in groups to create an advertising campaign to conserve water.

▼ **Intrapersonal**
Create a Raindrop Log to record times when you feel like: A raindrop falling; A rain drop being absorbed by the earth; A snowflake falling; A snowflake melting; Melting snow; Water rushing in a brook; Water falling in a waterfall; Water in a tranquil pond; Pounding ocean waves; The deep water on the ocean floor; The morning mist; Dew on a rose.

Because there are numerous possible projects and products for each of the intelligences, any given content can involve projects and products which allow authentic assessment of each of the intelligences. For example, let's take the water cycle. See box: Authentic Assessment of Projects and Products.

Any subject can be approached by projects in each of the intelligences. Cooperative learning projects are rich arenas for au-

thentic assessment. For example, in Co-op Co-op (see Chapter 7: MI Instructional Strategies) students work in teams to present a learning experience for the rest of the class, but each student on each team has a unique mini-topic. Work on the mini-topics allows individual assessment, and work as a team allows interpersonal assessment. For a variety of formats for cooperative learning projects, see Kagan (1994), *Cooperative Learning*.

Arts PROPEL is a collaborative project developed by the Pittsburgh Public School System and the Educational Testing Service (Gardner 1989; Zessoules, Wolfe, and Gardner, 1988). Arts PROPEL provides middle and high school level domain projects in a range of curriculum areas such as music composition, the use of voice in expressive writing, and composition in graphic arts. An integral part of the process in these projects is student input into the assessment measures used, and the development and analysis by students of portfolios they create. Students select the works to be entered into their portfolios and are asked to reflect on how the work reflects their development. Student reflections are entered into the portfolios along with their work, which serves as the basis for formal teacher evaluations. Emphasis is on student self-assessment. Students learn to articulate the criteria by which to evaluate a work. Student evaluations are compared to teacher evaluations. One goal: to move the locus of evaluation from the teacher to the student.

A number of MI projects are described in Chapter 7: MI Instructional Strategies. Planning MI projects, MI project ideas, and MI presentation modes are described in Chapter 13: MI Lessons, Centers, Projects and Theme Units.

Learning Centers

One of the advantages of learning centers is that students lead themselves through the tasks, freeing the teacher to circulate and spend time observing individual students. Learning centers thus are a wonderful opportunity for authentic assessment.

Engaging tasks release the intelligences of students. Learning centers can be structured so students sometimes work in groups, allowing assessment of the interpersonal intelligences. Task cards can call for sustained individual work in different mediums, allowing for individual assessment of each of the intelligences. Learning centers have a built-in authenticity — a classroom with all students busily engaged in different learning centers resembles a busy office, it creates an assessment situation which has real world authenticity. MI Learning Centers are explored in Chapters 7 and 13.

Demonstrations, Presentations, Performances

Traditionally, we have had students give occasional oral book reports, speeches, and debates. The call for authentic learning broadens the scope and increases the frequency of the performances involving all intelligences, correcting the traditional bias toward verbal/linguistic presentations. Students can demonstrate art, photo, and clay techniques they have acquired. Plays, demonstrations of math and science skills, music and dance recitals, demonstration of animal care techniques, ballet and athletic performances, and a wide range of other performances all should be a regular part of the curriculum.

In the real world, the intelligences work in concert, not in isolation. Authentic assessment of the intelligences, therefore, should be in contexts which allow the intelligences to work together. Contrived situations which attempt to assess one intelligence in isolation will not produce authentic assessment. Games are a natural form of performance which are rich in assessment possibilities. For example, the game of chess involves both logical reasoning and visual/spatial skills. As they play chess, some students may rely more on if-then logic, others more on visual/spatial skills. By observing students in a chess tournament and interviewing them about their strategies, we have a wonderful opportunity to deepen their understanding and our own understanding of their pattern of intelligences. Tasks which can be approached by many intelligences offer wonderful authentic assessment opportunities; students can reflect on and share their unique personal process — the intelligences they used during the performance.

One barrier to inclusion of more demonstrations, presentations, and performances has been the notion that they should always consist of one student or one team in front of the class. This sequential, one-at-a-time format is too time consuming. Demonstrations, presentations, and performances often can occur simultaneously: Picture this: Students are in pairs, and one student in each pair is an A, and the other a B. First all the As in the room present for two minutes to all the Bs, then all the Bs present for two minutes to the As. In four minutes every student has given their two minute presentation. Had the presentations occurred in the traditional, one-at-a-time-in-front-of-the-room format, if we include the transition times, it would have taken well over an hour for all students to make a two-minute presentation. While the students present in the simultaneous pair form, we are free to rotate, assessing different students each time a presentation

is made. A much more authentic assessment is possible as students present to a partner than as they present to the whole class — after all, in the real world we much more often work with a partner or in a small group, only very seldom do we stand in front of large groups to present. For various presentation modes, see Chapter 13: MI Lessons, Centers, Projects and Theme Units.

Reports and Exhibits

Whereas, demonstrations, presentations and performances are live, reports and exhibits can be set up for display, turned in to the teacher, posted, or circulated in the classroom. Students can get feedback from many sources on a report or exhibit. E-mailed reports can receive feedback from students in classrooms in another part of the world. Receiving feedback from a variety of sources can dramatically enhance the learning process.

Students can exhibit their knowledge in a wide range of reports and exhibits, including traditional book reports and science lab reports, but extending to recorded music performances, written music compositions, graphic organizers, student-created books, video presentations, photo displays, scrapbooks, collages, sculptures, and 4-H type exhibits of plant and animal products. Why is it that we have students report on their interpretation of a book, but not on their interpretation of their dreams? The call for the authentic assessment of all the intelligences would have us give more weight to reports evoking the intelligences under-represented in the traditional classroom, like the intrapersonal intelligence.

Compared to what happens in preparing for and taking a multiple-choice exam, in preparing various reports and exhibits, the intelligences are much more fully engaged in meaningful and authentic ways, providing contexts for authentic assessment.

Problem Solving and Experiments

Problem solving has typically been the domain of math instruction, and experiments have typically been reserved for the sciences. This does not have to be the case. Problem solving and experimentation should occur across the curriculum and across the intelligences. After all, if we are

Authentic Assessment of Experiments

Sample Content: Civil War

▼ Verbal/Linguistic
Test the effectiveness of two different antislavery essays.

▼ Logical/Mathematical
Describe the different strategies of Grant and Lee, and analyze each for its strengths and weaknesses.

▼ Visual/Spatial
Design an experiment to test effects of different colors for soldier's uniforms.

▼ Musical/Rhythmic
Analyze the tempo of different battle songs, experiment with the effects of changing tempo.

▼ Bodily/Kinesthetic
Create and test the effect of an antislavery nonverbal mime or drama.

▼ Naturalist
Describe the role of horses in the Civil War. How would you answer the question of whether they were used by either side to their maximum effectiveness?

▼ Interpersonal
Test the effectiveness of pro-Union and pro-Secession arguments presented in small group versus large group formats.

▼ Intrapersonal
Mood of soldiers determines in part their willingness to risk their lives in battle: design an experiment to test various ways of altering prebattle mood, and willingness to die for one's country or cause.

to authentically assess intelligences, and a defining characteristic of intelligence is the ability to create and solve problems, we need to do our assessment as students create and solve problems in every intelligence. Students can design experiments to test the effects of:

• *Number of descriptive adjectives on rating of a story (verbal/linguistic);*

• *Different techniques for mixing colors (visual/spatial);*

• *Perception of music as a function of prior knowledge of composer's life (musical/rhythmic);*

• *Ways of holding the ball as it effects basketball free throw success rates (bodily/kinesthetic);*

Authentic Assessment of Problem Creation

Sample problems students can generate.

▼ **Verbal/Linguistic**
• Express the critical thought in a passage in as few words as possible.
• Create new words by playing with prefixes.

▼ **Logical/Mathematical**
• Create word problems to solve.
• Create and test the effectiveness of alternative algorithms.

▼ **Visual/Spatial**
• Discover ways to rearrange toothpicks to form a different numbers of squares.
• Investigate why some colors when placed next to each other seem to stick together, while others seem to repel each other.

▼ **Musical/Rhythmic**
• Discover rules of harmony and disharmony.
• Fill in missing notes in a music sheet.

▼ **Bodily/Kinesthetic**
• Create an effective defense against a specific basketball offense.
• Test factors which contribute to making a curve ball curve.

▼ **Naturalist**
• Investigate fur thickening in animals in the winter.
• Analyze factors which cause color changes in plants.

▼ **Interpersonal**
• Test differential impact of different conflict resolution approaches.
• Test different approaches to making a person feel they are heard and understood.

▼ **Intrapersonal**
• Test the relative importance of adequate sleep in determining mood.
• Investigate the various ways to elevate self-esteem.

- *Amount of water and rate of growth of plants (naturalist);*
- *friendship as a function of similarity (interpersonal);*
- *bedtime on number and types of dreams (intrapersonal);*

The possibilities are endless.

No matter what our curriculum, students can solve problems and conduct experiments across the intelligences. For example, if we are studying the Civil War, students might design experiments across the intelligences. See box: Authentic Assessment of Experiments, page 19.15.

Problem creation is another direct expression of the intelligences, and students can be asked to create problems to solve on any academic content area, using in any of the intelligences. Students can create problems for themselves or for other students to solve. Math problems are obvious, but with some preparation students can learn to create problems in all of the intelligences. See box: Authentic Assessment of Problem Creation, 19.16.

Too often we as teachers have assumed the role of problem generators and relegated students to the role of problem solvers. Great thinkers are distinguished not just by their ability to solve problems, but also by their ability to generate new problems to solve (Csikszentmihalyi, 1989). Einstein did not just solve the problem of general relativity, he found in the existing conceptual frameworks the problems to solve. Artistic success, too, is related not just to the ability to paint or play music, but to find and focus on novel problems (Getzels & Csikszentmihalyi, 1976). As we observe students in the process of problem generation, and examine the types of problems they generate, we have another window

onto understanding their intelligences. As students engage in genuine problem solving and experimentation across the intelligences, we can come to better know and better understand each one's unique pattern of intelligences.

Assessment Instruments

While students are engaged in authentic learning, there are a number of approaches we can take to assessing and recording the development of their intelligences. Some learning tasks (such as reports) leave a record which can be collected in a portfolio which documents growth and development. Other types of learning (such as performances) in themselves leave no record, so we may create a video record, or observe or ask students to create a record of the process and/or outcomes of their learning experience. There are also formal assessment measures which have been developed by researchers to study the development of the intelligences. Let's turn first to the informal assessment approaches which open avenues for assessing and recording development while students are engaged in various projects.

Informal Assessment Instruments
Observations and Anecdotal Reporting

Observations are a primary tool in assessing the intelligences. We can record our observations in controlled, structured conditions as when we have each student work on the same task, or in uncontrolled, unstructured situations as they arise. Follow-

MI Observation Form

Student Name

Verbal/Linguistic

Bodily/Kinesthetic

Logical/Mathematical

Naturalist

Visual/Spatial

Interpersonal

Musical/Rhythmic

Intrapersonal

Comments

ing the principle of multiple assessments, a combination of both structured and unstructured observations will be most revealing. Sometimes an unsolicited spontaneous comment by a student (e.g., "the best way for me to remember is to close my eyes and see the picture on the page") reveals a great deal about the student's preferences and abilities. Keeping a three-ring binder with a place to record anecdotes about each student is a handy way to build a powerful assessment record. See MI Observation Form on page 19.18.

Structured observations are useful because they provide a basis for comparison and can be structured to reveal specific information. For example, each student in turn may be given a specific number of tinker toys and asked to build anything they wish, or be given a number of tone generating instruments (a triangle, symbols, a maraca, a bell) and be asked to create a series of sounds. Observing the students in controlled situations can be quite informative; seeing how different students cope with the same unstructured problem provides us a base rate and helps reveal the unique patterns of intelligences each student brings to a problem. The more situations in which we observe students, structured and unstructured, the more complete will be our understanding of their pattern of intelligences.

Project Spectrum researchers have developed two structured observation instruments: *Preschool Assessment Activities* and *Observational Guidelines*. Spectrum Preschool Assessment Activities include fifteen activities in seven different domains which are compatible with school curriculum.

The attempt was to create inviting, hands-on, intelligence-fair assessment situations. The measures include a score sheet and various types of quantifiable performances (Chen & Gardner, 1994). The observational guidelines include specific abilities for each intelligence, such as, for visual/spatial, "is aware of visual elements in the environment and in artwork (e.g., color, lines, shapes, patterns, detail)."

David Lazear in his book, *Multiple Intelligence Approaches to Assessment* (Lazear, 1994), provides a wide range of assessment instruments, including observation instruments. His Student Behavior Log, for example, provides five dimensions to rate for each of seven intelligences. Each dimension is rated from 0 to 4, so a student could score from 0 to 20 for each of the seven intelligences. For example, for verbal/linguistic intelligence, a teacher rates each student from 0 to 4 on questions like: "Loves talking, writing, and reading almost anything" and "Precisely expresses her- or himself both in writing and talking."

Portfolios and Process-Folios

One of the most powerful ways we have of assessing growth and development in each of the intelligences is by having students create portfolios (collections of completed work in any range of formats including essays, videos, recording, drawings) and process-folios (samples of work at various stages of completion, including student comments on their feelings about how the work is developing and their feelings about the work). Portfolios and process-folios tell a story. At some grade levels the transformation within a few months is nothing short of astounding — it is like the brain leaps to another level and we, the students, and their parents can see the transformation in vivid relief documented in the portfolio. This documentation has a wonderful impact not just on our ability to assess development, but on self-esteem of students. It is a powerful experience for a student to see that he or she can do now that which for them only a few months ago was not possible.

A portfolio may be project specific. Alternatively, students may create a portfolio which contains work from the entire school year across a range of projects and subject areas. A portfolio may have different sections for the intelligences, so sample math story problems and surveys may appear in one section, sample drawings, self-portraits, and photos of clay models in another, and sample poems, stories, and copies of journal entries in yet another. Work does not always fit neatly into one section or another (an illustrated story, for example, might appear in either the verbal or the visual section).

Students decide where things go and how the portfolio is best arranged. Students are asked to select as entries for their portfolios items of which they are particularly proud, and to comment on why they are proud of the item, or why they selected it. They are asked to reflect on what the item reveals about their development, promoting metacognitive thinking. We learn as much about students from the comments about their portfolio entries as from the entries themselves. On a regular basis the teacher schedules a time to sit with a student and review the growing portfolio, listening and observing as the student comments on the significance of the entries.

In this way the teacher comes to understanding the meaning of the work from the perspective of the child. Students may fill out the Portfolio Entry Form on page 19.21, to accompany works they submit or select for their portfolio. These entries provide us with a deeper understanding of students' portfolios and provide students with a record of their thoughts when they return to their portfolios.

At certain points, say on a monthly basis, students are asked to review the entries in their portfolios and to comment on what that review reveals. For example, they may be asked, "How has your writing changed in the last month?" Not all of their reflections need be recorded in writing. For example, they may be asked to draw something which reflects how their drawings have progressed from the beginning of the school year until the present. Students may include all manner of things in their portfolios which tell the story of the development of their intelligences. They might choose to photocopy a page from the first book they read in the school year and place it next to a copy of a page from the last book they read. They might include entries about their batting averages, photos or videos of performances, or a staff of music they played then and one they play now.

The students at Crow Island Elementary School prepare for "Portfolio Evenings" by developing and reflecting on their portfolios in response to questions like, "What would you like Mom and Dad to understand about your portfolio? Can you organize it so it will show that (Herbert, 1992)?" The teacher assigns primary students to groups of six or seven and larger groups for older students. Each group is assigned a different Portfolio Evening. That night they present their portfolios to their

Portfolio Entry Form

Name _____ Date _____

Title _____

Briefly describe your portfolio entry. _____
_____
_____

What do you like most? _____
_____
_____
_____

What do you like least? _____
_____
_____
_____

What would you change if you were to do it again? _____
_____
_____
_____

What does this entry say about you? _____
_____
_____
_____
_____

parents for about an hour and a half. The teacher and principal circulate, visiting each student, highlighting particular milestones. The teachers, however, for the most part attempts to remain in the background to allow children run their show.

Videos & Tapes

Videos of students creating and presenting projects and presentations create a permanent record which later can be assessed along any number of dimensions by students, teachers, parents, and even assessment specialists. At the Key School, an elementary school in Indianapolis, students create projects on a school-wide theme several times a year, and the student presentations along with interviews of the students are captured on videos which become a permanent record of each student's progress throughout their entire stay at Key School. The videos can be assessed from any number of perspectives including, ways in which the student reveals his or her unique pattern of intelligence, how the student conceptualizes the project, and the technical and aesthetic skills revealed by the project. (For more details on the Key School, see Olsen, 1988).

Self Evaluation

Student self-evaluation engages students in metacognition and is a learning process in itself. If self-evaluation is a frequent process it becomes internalized. Becoming a skillful self-evaluator is one of the most important processes leading to excellence in any field. In working with students at the elementary, middle and secondary levels, Carol Rolheiser (1997) and associates identified a four-step process of self-evaluation

which can be applied to any content. First, students are involved in defining criteria. Next they are instructed in how to apply the criteria. Students engage in self-evaluation and receive feedback on their self-evaluations. Finally, students use their self-evaluations as a basis for developing action plans for improvement.

Student Response Forms

Students can be asked to respond to their own work or the work of classmates in a variety of ways. The Smart in Many Ways form on page 19.24 works well for students to reflect on their own use of their intelligences for an MI project. It also allows classmates and the teacher to assess multimodal presentations.

For example, after a team or independent presentation, each student may fill out a Smart in Many Ways form; presenters may do a self-assessment. The form allows the assessors to comment on what they liked/learned for each intelligence and how they think the presentation could be improved for each intelligence. There is also room for an overall evaluation. Completed forms can be turned into the teacher and/or to the presenters. This is a more differentiated approach to critiquing projects and presentations. Students look at each other's work from multiple perspectives.

Students can also respond to each other's writing, projects, presentations using the Peer Response Form on page 19.25. On this form, students answer questions about what they learned, what they would like to learn more about, what they liked, ideas for improvement, and overall evaluation on a scale of 1 to 10.

A Reflection Response form is provided on page 19.26. On this form, students write reflections on their own work such as a paper, drawing, experiment, performance, video. Students give the form to a classmate or to the teacher along with their paper or after a presentation for a response to their work and/or to their reflections. This Reflection Response form can create a dialog among students and/ or the teacher in a non-threatening way. For example, a student reflects: "I felt a little nervous doing the dance. How did it look?" The respondent writes: "I could tell you were a little nervous, but it didn't subtract from the performance. It was great! Besides, I would be a little nervous too."

A simple PMI, a form developed by Edward de Bono (1983), may be used for student reflection and feedback. Students write what they like (**P**lus), what they don't like (**M**inus) and what's **I**nteresting about their own work or that of classmates. See PMI Form on page 19.27.

The Dialogue Journal can be adapted as an assessment measure. This, too, allows us to engage students in a dialogue over their own work. See Dialogue Journal blackline on page 19.28.

Students can use the Was It Easy? Did I like it? form on page 19.29 to assess their own work on an MI project or presentation. It is a simple two-by-two matrix that allows students to reflect on what was easy and hard and what they liked and did not like. This can be quite revealing, providing insights not only to students' strengths and weaknesses, but to their preferences as well.

Formal Assessment Instruments
Project Spectrum

Project Spectrum is designed to determine the intelligence profiles of children as young as four or five. The tasks of Project Spectrum are designed to be intelligence-fair. For example, mathematical intelligence is assessed by number games, spatial skills by assembly task involving mechanical objects, and interpersonal intelligence is assessed as students talk about dolls representing real people. Guidelines and checklists are designed to document children's interest and development, and detailed scoring systems have been developed for many of the activities. Spectrum reports are generated to help parents and others understand children's strengths and weaknesses. A Modified Spectrum Field Inventory is being developed which can be administered in two one-hour sessions in a home or classroom (Hatch & Gardner, 1990).

The results of Project Spectrum measures reveal that all the Spectrum Tests except the numbers activities do not correlate significantly with the Stanford-Binet IQ test, and that different measures of the same intelligence do not correlate significantly with each other, except the math tests. For example, the two music measures (singing and music perception) do not correlate significantly with each other. This pattern of results indicates that we need to be very cautious when attempting to assess the intelligences; any one measure or observation cannot tap the richness of a domain as broad as "musical intelligence," or "visual/spatial intelligence." There are a multiplicity of ways to be smart within each intelligence. Any conclusion that a student is strong or weak in an intelligence is likely

Smart in Many Ways

Title _____

Created/Presented By _____

Assessed By _____ **Date** _____

 **Verbal/Linguistic** What I liked/learned: Ideas for improvement:	 **Bodily/Kinesthetic** What I liked/learned: Ideas for improvement:
 **Logical/Mathematical** What I liked/learned: Ideas for improvement:	 **Naturalist** What I liked/learned: Ideas for improvement:
 **Visual/Spatial** What I liked/learned: Ideas for improvement:	 **Interpersonal** What I liked/learned: Ideas for improvement:
 **Musical/Rhythmic** What I liked/learned: Ideas for improvement:	 **Intrapersonal** What I liked/learned: Ideas for improvement:

Overall Comments _____

_____

_____

_____

_____

_____

Peer Response Form

Title _____

Created/Presented By _____

Assessed By _____ Date _____

I learned...

I would like to learn more about...

I liked...

I didn't understand...

Ideas for improvement...

Other comments...

Overall evaluation... (circle one)

1   **2**   **3**   **4**   **5**   **6**   **7**   **8**   **9**   **10**
Needs Work   Satisfactory   Couldn't Be Better

Reflection Response Form

Instructions: Write your reflections about your work in the "My Reflections" column below. Give this form to the teacher or a student to respond to your reflections and/or project or paper.

My Reflections	Response
Name_____	**Name**_____

PMI Form

Instructions: In the space below, record what you like (plus), what you don't like (minus) and what you find interesting.

Name _____ **Date** _____

Plus

Minus

Interesting

Dialogue Journal

Name_____ **Date**_____

Topic_____

Journal Entry_____

Comments

Spencer & Miguel Kagan: *Multiple Intelligences*
Kagan Cooperative Learning • 1 (800) WEE CO-OP

Was It Easy? Did I Like It?

Name _____ Date _____

Topic _____

	Parts I Liked	Parts I Didn't Like
What Was Easy		
What Was Hard		

Other Comments: _____

_____

_____

_____

_____

to be an over-generalization — most of us are strong in some facets of an intelligence, but weak in other facets. See Chapter 18: The MIT and the Facet Tests.

Lazear's Assessment Instruments

There are many test instruments which have been designed to assess the strength of each of the intelligences. David Lazear in his book, *Multiple Intelligence Approaches to Assessment* (Lazear, 1994), provides a wide range of assessment instruments, including measures of focus (on what kind of stimuli do students focus) problem-solving assessment forms, and ways to assess students' intelligences as they play games, respond to television, and invent things. Lazear is to be commended because he has created a wide range of ways to assess intelligences in the context of authentic learning situations. Lazear's work represents the broadest array of MI assessment instruments as well as the attempt to look at the intelligences from the greatest number of angles.

The Rub: Intelligence-Fair Versus Facet-Sensitive Assessment

There is a trade-off between two critical dimensions of authentic assessment. On one hand we have very intensive, intelligence-fair performance measures like those of Project Spectrum. On the other hand we have paper-and-pencil measures which assess a broad array of skills within each intelligence, like many of Lazear's checklists and observation sheets and Kagan's Facet Tests. The intensive, time-consuming performance instruments cannot set up assessments for each facet of each intelligence; they take hours to produce measures of but a few facets of each intelligence. So the performance tests are

not Facet-Sensitive: A scores on a Spectrum Test does not represent the strength of an intelligence, but rather the strength of, at best, a few facets within each intelligence. The lack of correlation among the subscales within an intelligence reported by Spectrum reveal that each subscale reflects not the whole intelligence, but just a facet of that intelligence. On the other hand, we have the broad observation checklists, some of which are Facet-Sensitive. But those paper-and-pencil measures are not intelligence-fair. A teacher, student, or parent rating a student's behavior may or may not reveal what a performance measure would reveal.

So there is a trade-off between intelligence-fair measures and facet-sensitive measures. As teachers we need both. We need the facet-sensitive measures to keep us from making over-generalization, but we need the intelligence-fair measures to keep us from viewing one intelligence through the filter of another. The solution: authentic assessment must involve multiple measures. If there is a skill we wish to assess, we need to examine that skill in-depth with intelligence-fair performance measures, probably in the context of authentic learning. On the other hand, we would do well to administer facet-sensitive tests as well for they remind us that any one skill within an intelligence is not necessarily a reflection of the general strength of that intelligence.

Practicality of Authentic Assessment

Authentic assessment, as we have seen, can be as simple as listening in as two students discuss which intelligences they used as they solved a problem. It can be, however, as complicated as setting up, observing, and scoring time-consuming simulations for specific facets of each intelligence.

In working with teachers for years, we have found that time-consuming programs which involve complicated set-up may be greeted with initial enthusiasm, but they do not last. Teachers burn out on methods which add burden to teaching. Teaching is challenging enough. In the long-run only assessment approaches which are administered in the context of teaching are likely to endure. The other approaches will come and go.

So our recommendation is to focus on authentic assessment methods which further the teaching process. For example, student journals and logs and student portfolios enrich almost any topic, they would be worthwhile even if they were not used as part of the authentic assessment process. They provide added value to curriculum and instruction. Paper and pencil tests and complex simulations and observations schedules, in contrast, are used exclusively for assessment — usually they are subtractive rather than additive with regard to teaching and learning.

Focusing on those assessment approaches which provide added value in the instructional process finds justification in the ra-tionale for authentic assessment. Over and over as we reviewed the principles of authentic assessment at the outset of this chapter we saw that authentic assessment is best achieved in the context of authentic learning. Thus authentic assessment, to be practical and to be authentic, should be integrated assessment — it should occur in the process of instruction, not as an added event.

Necessity of Authentic Assessment

All three MI visions, matching, stretching, and celebrating the multiple intelligences, can be realized without any assessment. As we use an MI strategy in our classroom, teaching with a visual/spatial strategy, for example, we reach students strong in the visual/spatial intelligence. At the same time we are developing the visual/spatial intelligence, stretching that intelligence for all students. And if we use a range of MI strategies, representing the range of intelligences, we match and stretch all the intelligences. Further, if on a regular basis we pause to have students reflect on, discuss, and appreciate how they used their various intelligences, we celebrate the range of intelligences — students learn MI theory experientially. *All of this can occur without an ounce of assessment!* We do not need assessment, even authentic assessment, to realize the three visions. Why, then, have we spent time exploring authentic assessment? It turns out that while assessment is not a necessity, it can add considerable richness to curriculum and instruction, and help us reach the three visions more fully. It is to this final topic, then, that we turn: What are the aims of authentic assessment of the intelligences.

Aims of Authentic Assessment

What do we do with the results of authentic assessment? If we can match, stretch, and celebrate MI without assessing our students, why bother? Authentic assessment provides added value to the teaching process in a number of ways, including the following:

Self-Assessment Skills

Authentic assessment approaches engage students in the process of self-assessment. Self-assessment skills are important throughout life. No matter whether we are working at a job or to improve a relationship, to the extent that we pause and assess our progress on a regular basis we will be more successful. Self-assessment leads to reevaluation of the tactics we are employing and even of our goals. After we pause to reflect on what we have accomplished and what we have not accomplished, we return to our task with renewed focus and/or a different type of effort. If self-assessment occurs often in the classroom, it will become habitual, and our students will develop the habit of self-assessment — a tool for life. To the extent that authentic assessment leads to developing self-assessment skills, it provides added value to our students.

Metacognition

One of the surest ways to improve thinking is to think about the way one is thinking. Metacognition puts our thinking processes in perspective. A student may be tackling a problem in one way and will persist in that way until she stops and thinks about how she is thinking. At that point, she realizes that she is approaching the problem from but one of many possible ways, and may decide to approach the problem in other ways.

Metacognition enriches our sense of ourselves. It allows us to become more aware of our own particular ways of thinking and our own unique pattern of intelligences. Metacognition, then, is a powerful tool in reaching the third MI vision, celebrating the intelligences.

Refinement of Learning Process

As a student is learning any topic, reflecting on the intelligences which he is using and not using, refines the learning process. Not only does the student become more aware of his strengths and weaknesses, but he become aware of how best to solve different kinds of problems, how best to accomplish certain kinds of tasks. When confronted with a similar task in the future, the student is more likely to be successful because he has reflected on which kinds of intellectual processes have served him well in the past in dealing with that type of task. The student has learned not just to solve the problem, but to intelligently select from the range of problem solving strategies. Thus the learning process is refined and deepened by the self-assessment and metacognitive components of authentic assessment.

Self-Knowledge

The authentic assessment process involves metacognition and self-assessment, and both of these lead to self-knowledge. As students reflect on their own thinking and assess their own products and progress, they come to know themselves better. A more realistic picture of oneself increases not only the probability of success (if a student knows her limits, she does not bite off more than she can chew), but also the probability of growth (a student who knows her strengths and weaknesses, is more likely to work in her own zone of proximal development). Self-knowledge of one's own cognitive preferences and abilities ultimately allows a person to lead a happier and more successful life — the better we know ourselves the more likely it is that we will choose a career and social activities which fit our interests and abilities.

Self-Acceptance, Self-Respect, Pride

If a student knows there are eight or more ways to be smart and that each of us is strong in some and weak in others, that student is more likely to accept and respect himself or herself. For example, failing in a visual/spatial task, the student can take comfort in knowing the failure is not a reflection of his or her general intelligences, but just one of many aspects of intelligence. The student says to him or herself, "I may not be great at that type of task, but there are other types of task at which I shine." It is easier for a student to persist in the face of failure if the student does not interpret a failure as a reflection of low general intelligence, but rather as only a reflection of one aspect of intelligence. Knowing our unique strengths, we take pride in ourselves. Self-knowledge leads to self-acceptance, which in turn is the basis for self-respect and pride.

Student Empowerment

As we allow students to engage in the process of self-assessment, we empower them. The locus of evaluation is no longer centered entirely outside each student. As students take charge of evaluating themselves, they are less likely to feel dependent on the evaluations of others and feel empowered to take control of their lives. To the extent a student is the ultimate evaluator of his or her own performance, the student fears the evaluation of others less, and is more willing to take risks and take charge of his or her life. Authentic assessment empowers students.

Improved Instruction

Authentic assessment improves instruction in a number of ways. As we, as teachers, obtain better knowledge of what our students can and cannot do, we can better plan lessons appropriate to the skill levels of our students. When we have authentic assessment of the intelligences of our students we better know which intelligences they are strong in (and so which intelligences to match) and which intelligences they are weak in (and so which intelligences to stretch). As we know the intelligence pattern of each of our students, we are better equipped to help each student in knowing and celebrating his or her own unique pattern.

To some extent, each of us teaches our classroom of students as if they all had the same pattern of intelligences as ourselves. For example, if we are very strong in visual/spatial intelligence, we naturally create more interesting and colorful three dimensional bulletin boards, use graphics on the overhead and on worksheets, and arrange our classroom in a way appealing to visually/spatially sensitive students. As we engage in authentic assessment, we become sensitive to the range of intelligences among our students and naturally begin to attempt to meet the needs of all students. Authentic assessment counters our unconscious bias toward students with a pattern of intelligences similar to our own. In this way authentic assessment encourages us to stretch our own intelligences, to experiment with and become proficient with instructional strategies which match our weaker intelligences. The paradox: the strategies we most need to learn are those with which initially we are least comfortable.

Improved Curriculum

Knowing the intelligences of our students helps us to better select curriculum appropriate to their needs and developmental level. It helps us know which curriculum they are likely to gravitate toward and which curriculum they are likely to resist. Knowing initial levels of motivation, we are better prepared to devote appropriate time and energy to creating a set for a lesson. Similarly, ongoing authentic assessment allows us to determine when it is safe to move from guided to independent practice. Authentic assessment can allow a teacher to design or modify a learning experience to better meet the needs of a particular student. Finding a student weak in the naturalist intelligence but strong in logical mathematical intelligence, the teacher might attempt to stretch the naturalistic intelligence through the mathematical intelligence. For example, the word problems or survey content may include animals as a possible content.

Authentic Assessment and the Three Visions

By using the range of MI strategies we can match, stretch, and celebrate all the intelligences without assessing our students. Authentic assessment, however, provides an enriching dimension to teaching and learning. In the process of authentic learning we take time to know our students, and they take time to know themselves and others. As a student interacts with someone who knows and accepts their unique pattern of intelligences, they come to know and accept themselves more. They better understand their own uniqueness, and in turn are positioned to better understand the diversity among us. Authentic assessment methods engage students in metacognition and self-assessment and so directly facilitate Vision Three: Celebrating the intelligences. To the extent we know the intelligence patterns of our students, we can better select appropriate instructional strategies to match their intelligences, and better design learning experiences to stretch their intelligences. Thus authentic assessment, while not necessary for reaching the three visions, facilitates our realization of each.

There are pitfalls associated with assessment. To the extent we use assessment techniques to sort, rank, or label our students we are doing them more harm than good. Any label is limiting — limiting both to how we see our students and how they in turn see themselves. Sorting students into differential curriculum or instruction crystallizes limits. If for example, a student is weak in an intelligence and so we decide to teach that student primarily through other intelligences, we limit the opportunity of that student to surprise us and himself by blossoming in the weak intelligence. By teaching all students in all intelligences, we maximize the opportunity for all students to reach their full potential and we minimize the chance of creating a harmful self-fulfilling prophesy. Any assessment oriented toward differential curriculum and/or instruction runs too high a risk of lowering expectations in teachers and students, of creating exterior and self-imposed barriers to the full development of all intelligences.

The second pitfall associated with assessment of the intelligences is that it can be subtractive rather than additive to the teaching/learning process. To the extent that assessment is not an integral part of authentic learning, it probably is not as authentic as it should be, but also takes time from teaching and learning. Authentic assessment to be authentic must be in the context of meaningful, authentic learning. External tests, questionnaires, and simulations imposed on students steal time from learning and will at best provide information about how those students respond to situations not directly relevant to the course topic. Relevant authentic assessment, then, occurs within the context of teaching for the course objectives; it can occur without losing a minute from instruction and learning.

References

Chen, J. & Gardner, H. *Alternative Assessments for a Multiple Intelligences Perspective.* In D. F. Flanagan, J. L. Genshaft, & P. L. Harrison, **Beyond Traditional Intellectual Assessment: Contemporary and Emerging Theories, Tests, and Issues.** New York: Guilford Publications, 1994.

Csikszentmihalyi, M. *Motivation and Creativity.* **New Ideas in Psychology.** 1989, *6(2)*, 159-76.

de Bono, E. *The direct teaching of thinking as a skill.* **Phi Delta Kappan.** 1983, *64(1)*, 703-708.

Felsman, J. K. & Vaillant, G. E. *Resilient children as adults: a 40-year study.* In E. J. Anderson and B. J. Cohler, eds., *The invulnerable child.* New York: Guilford Press, 1987.

Gardner, H. *Multiple Intelligences. The Theory in Practice.* New York: Basic Books, 1993.

Gardner, H. *Zero-based arts education: An introduction to ARTS PROPEL.* **Studies in Art Education.** 1989, *3(2)*, 71-83.

Getzels, J. W. & Csikszentmihalyi, M. *The Creative Vision.* New York: Wiley, 1976.

Goleman, D. *Emotional Intelligence.* New York: Bantam Books, 1995.

Hatch, T. & Gardner, H. *If Binet had Looked Beyond the Classroom: The Assessment of Multiple Intelligences.* **International Journal of Educational Research**, 1990, *14(5)*, 415-429.

Herbert, E. A. *Portfolios Invite Reflection — From Students and Staff.* **Educational Leadership,** 1992, *49(8)*, 58-61.

Kagan, S. *Cooperative Learning.* San Clemente, CA: Kagan Cooperative Learning, 1994.

Lazear, D. *Multiple Intelligences Approaches to Assessment. Solving the Assessment Conundrum.* Tucson, AZ: Zephyr, 1994.

Olson, L. *Children flourish here: 8 teachers and a theory changed a school world.* **Education Week**, 1988, *18(1)*, 18-19.

Rolheiser, C., (Ed.) *Self Evaluation... Helping Students Get Better At It.* Ontario, Canada: Ajax, 1997.

Vaillant, G. *Adaptation to life.* Boston, MA: Little, Brown and Co., Inc., 1977.

Wigdor, A. & Garner, (Eds.) *Ability Testing: Uses, Consequences, and Controversies.* Washington, DC: National Academy Press, 1982.

Zessoules, R., Wolf, D., & Gardner, H. *A better balance: ARTS PROPEL as an alternative to discipline-based art education.* In J. Burton, A. Lederman, & P. Landon (Eds.), **Beyond discipline-based art education.** University Council on Art Education.

Is MI Theory Brain-Based?

Given the desire of selecting intelligences that are rooted in biology...(Gardner, 1993, p. 16).

The unquestioning general acceptance of MI theory among educators is in part based on the belief that MI theory is a logical conclusion from brain science. Much of the language used in presenting the theory aligns the theory with biology and neuroscience. In describing the theory, Gardner (1993) talks about having "uncovered (p. 9)," seven intelligences. The theory presents "intelligences rooted in biology (p. 16)," which have "biological validity (p. 38)." Gardner (1983, p. 63) indicates that he considers "evidence from neuropsychology" to be the ultimate test of any intelligence. Gardner indicates that the extent to which a particular faculty can be destroyed or spared in isolation as a result of brain damage "may well constitute the single most instructive line of evidence regarding those distinctive abilities or computations that lie at the core of a human intelligence (Gardner, 1983, p. 63)."

Intelligent functioning is characterized not by the exercise of separate intelligences but by incredible integration.

To evaluate this claim of "biological validity," and the potential of "isolation" of human intelligences, we will take a trip into the structure and function of the brain. Our tour reveals that the brain is not structured in a way which supports the notion of separate intelligences. Intelligent functioning is characterized not by the exercise of separate intelligences, but by incredible integration. Thus, we are confronted with a metaphor war: The brain does not consist of separate "Frames of Mind;" but rather is an interactive "Community of Neurons." The metaphor we adopt impacts in fundamental ways on how we conceptualize the brain and intelligence and, in turn, how we design curriculum and instruction.

Mini-Tour: Brain Structure and Function

The human brain is the most complex known entity. It weighs only three to four pounds, but contains a trillion cells, some 100 billion of which are neurons. About 30,000 of these tiny neurons fit into the space of the head of a pin. Each neuron has about a meter of DNA when unraveled, and different types of neurons respond to different subsets of the genetic instructions encoded in the DNA. Brain neurons have a great range of structural variety — some look like highly branched trees, others like spiders; some have but a few sources of input, others reach out to receive signals from over 1000 other neurons. Because of the fantastic number of synaptic connections, every neuron in the brain is connected to every other neuron within the span of only a few neurons.

Neurons are organized in a unidirectional network: they receive input along highly branched extensions, called dendrites, and send it out along a single unbranched extension called an axon. The neurons are structured as if they are hungry, reaching out for many sources of input. The organization of this web of neurons is hierarchical: those close to sensory input receive few inputs; those at successively removed areas receive successively greater numbers of inputs — the neurological underpinnings of the difference between low level, perception-bound (concrete) and higher level, concept-oriented (abstract) thought.

All parts of the brain are functioning at different rates all of the time, making the brain the most active part of the body — weighing only two percent of the body's total weight, it consumes almost a quarter of the body's oxygen! Neurons are constantly, rapidly firing — up to 200 times a second. Neural impulses or action potentials travel only a millimeter or two and then must be recharged, leading to a very

The human brain is the most complex known entity.

slow rate of transmission (100 meters per second — a millionth the speed of an electrical signal in copper wire). There are scores of distinct chemical neurotransmitters. Different neurons respond to quite different neurotransmitters (explaining our very different reactions to Valium, Prozac, cocaine and nicotine). Some neurotransmitters act only locally, causing the passage of an action potential from one neuron to another; other neurotransmitters facilitate the firing of whole modules of neurons. Some remain active for only milliseconds; others for weeks (underpinning short and long-term memory).

Neurons Form Connections

Neurons develop along predetermined channels, but many more neurons develop than eventually survive. A process of neuron budding and later pruning rids the brain of those neurons which make inappropriate or unneeded connections. The brain is actually reshaped by experience. For example, in the somatosensory cortex of the brain, larger portions are devoted to parts of the body which have greater sensitivity (lips take up more area than our legs). Experience, though, can change the portion of the brain dedicated to input from a sensory area. Michael Merzenich of the University of California, San Francisco, demonstrated specific structural changes in the somatosensory cortex as a function of specific training: a monkey was trained to touch a wheel using only the three middle fingers of its hand. After three months of training for one hour a day the somatosensory cortex area corresponding to those three digits had grown dramatically at the expense of the lesser used digits (Kandel & Hawkins, 1992).

Early experience is more important than later experience in the organization of neurons. Researchers reported,

> In the brains of nine string players examined with magnetic resonance imaging, the amount of somatosensory cortex dedicated to the thumb and fifth finger of the left hand — the fingering digits — was significantly larger than in nonplayers. How long the players practiced each day did not affect the cortical map. But the age at which they had been introduced to their music did: the younger the child when she took up an instrument, the more cortex she devoted to playing it (Begley, 1996, p. 57).

Neurons Learn

The probability of transmitting an impulse is determined not just by impulses a neu-

The brain is actually reshaped by experience.

ron has received, but also by the response of other neurons to the impulses it has sent.

Short-term synaptic changes are associated with short term memory; middle and longer term memory is associated with different types of structural changes.

Neurons Compute

Neurons are constantly firing. To determine the intensity (action potential frequency) of their output, each neuron must continually integrate up to 1,000 synaptic inputs. Each neuron does not fire as a simple linear function of the amount of input received, rather, it weighs the input to determine its output, actually acting as a miniature computer! The brain consists of 100 billion interacting, networked mini computers, each firing 200 times a second. Given this community of networked neurons, it is an over simplification to say there are eight discrete relatively autonomous human intelligences.

Neurons Cooperate

In many areas of the brain, neurons are organized in cooperative, interconnected modules. A typical module in the visual cortex includes about 100,000 neurons; it responds to a line of a particular orientation. The module measures approximately one tenth of a millimeter. The cells within the module are specialized so each participates in local circuits devoted to a particular function. Damage to or lack of development of that module can result in a very specific deficit (like the inability to recognize horizontal lines while maintaining the ability to recognize vertical lines).

Information is processed hierarchically. For example, one module may respond to horizontal lines, another to vertical lines, and yet others to lines of various angles. Recognition of an object as a specific type of triangle is a result of a module responding to simultaneous stimulation from independent modules responding to one horizontal line and two vertical lines in a specific relation to each other. Information is assembled in higher and higher increments by neuron groups which receive input from greater and greater numbers of other modules. Our contact with reality is in this way "assembled." Paradoxically, the truest picture of reality is the one generated by neuron groups furthest from sensory contact. (For a fuller and far better presentation of these ideas see Calvin, 1996).

Intelligent behavior is the ability to integrate the functioning of many separate modules. Let's take a simple example: Catching a red ball. The simple act of catching a ball thrown to us involves the action of many discrete parts of the brain all acting in extraordinary coordination. As we see the person about to throw the ball we make estimates about its probable velocity and direction. Before we even move in the direction of where we think the ball will be, specific neurons fire — they are the underpinnings of intention. If we decide to move in one direction, a certain set of neurons fire; if we decide to move in a different direction, other neurons fire. These "intention" neurons do not lead to movement. It is yet other neurons which activate actual movement.

As we view the approaching ball, one part of the brain processes its color, another its shape, another its relative distance, another its velocity, and yet another, the feeling of the ball as it hits our hand. Specific brain lesions would mean the loss of some of these functions, but not others. Other sets of neurons reach down to connect to all of these diverse sources of input, to create an integrated experience of catching the ball. Yet different neuron modules are responsible for translating this experience into a memory. The memory is stored locally in those different parts of the brain responsible for different functions, and there are neuron systems responsible for storing and recalling all this information in an integrated way, so that we can remember it as a unified experience.

Every experience of a feeling, every intention, every action, and all learning is a product of incalculable cooperative coordination of neurons.

In the face of this incredible coordination of functioning in the simple act of catching a ball, it does not fit actual brain functioning to conceptualize skill in catching a ball as an example of a separate "bodily/kinesthetic intelligence." Catching a ball is an incredible miracle of integrated brain function. This miracle of integrated brain function is repeated for every act we perform, for everything we learn, for every act of memory.

Every experience of a feeling, every intention, every action, and all learning is a product of incalculable cooperative coordination of neurons. As Robert Sylwester (1995, p. 2) emphasizes,

> A neuron may connect to thousands of other cells, so the chemical information in a neuron is only a few neurons away from any other neuron.

As we stand in awe at the wonder of integrated brain function and the very existence of consciousness, we must feel more than a little uncomfortable with any attempt to conceptualize human intelligence as the functioning of a relatively small number of discrete "intelligences" operating in relative independence. The whole structure of the brain is organic, complex, integrated, and interdependent. To claim "brain-based" for a theory which postulates relatively independent intelligences, is to ignore the strongest message of brain study.

The notion that the intelligences fall out of a study of brain structure is not supported by surprising research indicating functions we think of as quite distinct are actually governed by the same areas of the brain such as mimicking facial expressions and speaking language:

> There are two major lines of evidence that suggest that the lateral language area above the left ear also has a lot to do with nonlanguage sequencing. The Canadian neuropsychologist Doreen Kimura and her co-workers showed that left-lateral stroke patients with language difficulties (aphasia) also have considerable difficulty executing hand and arm movement sequences of a novel sort, a condition known as apraxia....

> The Seattle neurosurgeon George Ojemann and his coworkers further showed, using electrical stimulation of the brain during epilepsy operations, that much of the left-lateral language specialization is involved with listening to sound sequences.... The big surprise was that these exact same areas seem heavily involved in producing oral-facial movement sequences — even nonlanguage ones, such as mimicking a series of facial expressions (Calvin, 1996).

If brain isolation is the single most important criterion of an intelligence, and if the skills of any intelligence cannot be isolated, MI theory faces a major contradiction.

What falls out of these studies of brain science is the primacy of sequencing. What is secondary is the content — whether what is sequenced is words or movements. To define a separate bodily/kinesthetic intelligence and a separate verbal/linguistic intelligence is fine for many purposes, but it is not consistent with their co-dependence on common sequencing structures and certainly is not a necessary or even logical consequence of brain science.

When Gardner first published *Frames of Mind* he was aware of the modular nature of the brain and that complex actions involve a coordination of different parts of the brain. Gardner wrote about the modular and even mini-modular organization of brain (Gardner, 1983, p. 50) and provided numerous examples of how the functioning of one intelligence could not be isolated. He wrote,

> in the case of freehand drawing, certain left-hemisphere structures prove crucial for the providing of details, while right-hemisphere structures are equally necessary for the mastery of the overall contour of the depicted object (Gardner, 1983, p. 54).

Gardner well understood that different kinds of impairment in freehand drawing depend on which half of the brain is injured. This observation flatly contradicts the notion of the intelligences as being capable of brain isolation.

If brain isolation is the single most important criterion of an intelligence in MI theory, and if the skills of any intelligence cannot be isolated, the theory faces a major contradiction. Why was Gardner comfortable speaking about a single very broad "visual/spatial intelligence" — which includes freehand drawing as well as a vast number of other very different types of functioning, each of which involve very different parts of the brain? Gardner simply chose to look at brain functioning from a more molar perspective. This was a practical decision based on what would be useful, not one rooted in brain biology.

> A list of 700 intelligences would be forbidding to the theoretician and useless to the practi-

Localizing Broad Intelligences — A Contradiction in Terms

Broad intelligences can never be localized in the brain because they do not reside in one place in the brain. In fact, they do not reside in many places. They have no place.

A person is not a thing onto themselves. Who we are depends on with whom we are interacting. We are a different person when we talk to our spouse or loved one, quite another person when we talk with a sibling, and yet another person when we interact with a son or daughter. We do not exist independent of those around us. We exist in interaction.

Nothing is a thing unto itself.

Yes, without a specific module of neurons, a certain kind of intelligent functioning cannot happen. But, no, that module is not semi-autonomous. That module functions differently depending on what is happening in and between thousands of other modules. Each module is necessary, but not sufficient. No intelligence resides in specific sets of neurons;

> **"Things derive their being and nature by mutual dependence and are nothing in themselves."**
> — Nagarjuna, second-century Buddhist philosopher

intelligence resides in the interaction among the billion members of the community of neurons. Intelligence has no place, it is a by-product of millions of simultaneous interactions.

This realization encourages us to focus on the whole, unique student, not his or her separate intelligences. It is a realization for brain science parallel to those which enlighten ancient philosophy and modern physics.

> **"An elementary particle is not an independently existing, unanalyzable entity. It is, in essence, a set of relationships that reach outward to other things."**
> — H.P. Stapp, twentieth-century physicist

tioner. Therefore MI theory attempts to articulate only a manageable number of intelligences that appear to form natural kinds (Gardner, 1993, p. 45).

But this was a choice Gardner made, not a logical conclusion from brain isolation studies. MI theory is useful as a taxonomy of intelligences, but the eight intelligences are not an inevitable result of brain science. Broad categories of intelligence are created, not discovered; they are not a necessary conclusion from the study of brain structure and function.

Any truly brain-based notion of intelligence must account at once for the incredible number of discrete functions of the brain and simultaneously their integration to create unified consciousness and action.

Any truly brain-based notion of intelligence must account at once for the incredible number of discrete functions of the brain and simultaneously their integration which creates unified consciousness and action. The metaphor of a community of neurons better captures the structure and function of the brain than does a metaphor of independent frames of mind. The 100 billion neurons in our brain do not come with a few discrete labels; we create those labels for different types of behavior in an attempt to make sense of the enormous complexity of the human experience. The neurons and the modules they make up are best understood in terms of their interconnectedness, not by their separateness. Notions about a small number of separate intelligences help us categorize behavior, but they are not an objective finding of brain science.

Music on Our Minds

Another way of approaching the issue of brain localization and whether separate intelligences can be discovered by the study of the brain is to take one MI theory intelligence and examine it in some depth. In a remarkable book, *Music, The Brain, and Ecstasy*, Robert Jourdain (1997) provides an in-depth summary of what we know about how music is processed in the brain. What he demonstrates is that we cannot locate the musical intelligence in any one spot in the brain, and that we must give up the notion that intelligences can be isolated. As we move to higher level intelligent functioning of any sort, more and more different parts of the brain are involved, many of which are involved in very different types of intelligences as well.

Musical Intelligence Can't be Located

Results from brain scans and from cases of brain damage reveal that different portions of the brain are dominant for different musical skills. *Amusia*, a general loss of musical function, may result from damage to any of many different parts of the brain.

> It seems that there can be as many origins of amusia as there are brain regions that participate in perceiving or making music. Low-level skills tend to favor the right temporal lobe; higher-level skills, the left. But highest-level musical skills may make use of structures on either side of the brain, structures applied sometimes to music, sometimes to language, and sometimes to a host of other undertakings (Jourdain, 1997, p. 292).

Because musical skills are located in different parts of the brain, Amusia can take many forms: a person may have some combination of *receptive amusia* (inability to process musical input), *expressive amusia* (inability to perform music), *amelodia* (loss of skills with melodies), or *arrhythmia* (loss of rhythmic skills). Brain scans confirm separate locations as dominant for processing different facets of the musical intelligence.

> This dichotomy is clear in left-right preferences for music processing. …harmonies tend to be better recognized by the right hemisphere and …rhythm is favored by the left. Both skills are roughly centered in the same areas of temporal cortex, although harmony is much more strongly localized than rhythm (Jourdain, 1997, p. 281).

The parts of the brain dominant for processing different facets of music, however, are not static. Localization depends to an important extent on experience, learning, and training.

> We've also seen that formal music training encourages analytical perception of music, analysis in which musical elements are related through a hierarchy of sequences. This sort of analysis is the speciality of the left brain. So it is not surprising that professionals tend to be left-dominant for tasks that non-expert listeners handle mainly in the right brain (Jourdain, 1997, p. 281).

The part of the brain which is dominant in processing music depends not only on which facet of the musical intelligence we are looking at and the training of the listener, it differs also for different aspects of the same facet. Short melodies are processed in the right hemisphere, but long melodies are processed in the left.

> Interestingly, dominance in melody processing goes to the right hemisphere, despite the fact that melodies unfold across time and thus might be considered just the sort of serial process for which the left hemisphere is specialized. The right brain is not unaware of temporal relations, but merely inept at modeling them in complex hierarchies. It can compare a melody's relations for the fraction of a minute needed to trace the shape of a melodic contour. But when melody appears as a long thematic development spanning many minutes, it is the left brain that dominates (provided it is well enough trained to know how.) (Jourdain, 1997, p. 281).

Further, harmonic and nonharmonic melodies are processed primarily in different parts of the brain:

> Even with simple melodies, the right-brain advantage disappears when non-harmonic melodies are encountered, as in some contemporary music. Nor does the right brain show any particular talent for melody when it encounters an unfamiliar harmonic system, such as Indian sitar music (Jourdain, 1997, p. 282).

Given that the skills underpinning musical intelligence are located in quite distinct parts of the brain and that similar findings exist for each intelligence, it is not meaningful to speak of "brain localization," as a criteria for an intelligence. Musical intelligence fails any test of brain localization because musical intelligence does not reside in any one place in the brain.

One could argue that localization of an intelligence does not have to be in just one area. One could pose a looser criteria for brain localization, saying an intelligence passes the test of brain localization if we can find brain activity associated with exercise of the intelligence, regardless of whether the activity is located in one portion of the brain or not. If we take this looser criteria, however, then the meaningfulness of brain localization as a criteria of an intelligence is cast in doubt. Every intelligent behavior is associated with brain activity in at least some places in the brain, and so all intelligent behaviors would pass the looser test of brain localization.

Musical intelligence is not only inextricably intertwined with logical, sequential skills; it is intimately connected to the spatial/relational and emotional intelligences as well.

The whole point of brain localization for cognitive skills becomes questionable when we realize that all higher level skills do not reside in any one location, but rather in the interaction of many modules of neurons, each of which may provide input for any number of skills. Jourdain (1997, pp. 282-283) is his comprehensive analysis of how the brain processes music states it eloquently:

> …most of the cognitive skills of which we are most proud and most want to understand are hardly localizable in any sense. They are achieved by momentarily bringing together various brain modules designed for low level processing of various sorts, modules that a moment later may be assembled in a different way for different ends. We can point at a scan of a brain analyzing simple chords and say, "There!" But there is no lone brain center for following counterpoint or phrasing or large-scale form.

Musical Intelligence Can't Be Separated

Studies of people who have lost musical skills through brain surgery or brain damage reveal the inability to separate musical intelligence from other intelligences. Jourdain cites the case of a musician who had a cingulotomy (removal of parts of the cortex surrounding the bridge between the two hemispheres). The musician did not lose any of the lower-level component musical skills, but could no longer put them together. She could not learn new pieces, improvise, compose, read scores, or listen in a meaningful way to music. But she lost also the ability to perform sequences across all the intelligences, losing, for example, the ability to follow stories, play sequential logic games, and even follow the thread of a conversation. "Her case demonstrates how music can require our highest intellectual abilities, and how music must share parts of the brain with other activities (Jourdain, 1997, p. 289)."

Musical intelligence is not only inextricably intertwined with logical, sequential skills; it is intimately connected to the spatial/relational and emotional intelligences as well. Jourdain cites a case study of a professor of music who suffered a stroke in the right hemisphere. Following the stroke he was able to conduct music, but the loss of right hemisphere spatial/relational skills proved to be disastrous for the musical intelligence as well.

> To make matters worse, the damage extended into parts of the right parietal lobe essential for spatial reasoning. The professor could no longer use perspective when drawing, and he constantly became lost in his hometown. Similarly, he had trouble laying out music on a page, and he couldn't manipulate musical devices that many composers conceive spatially, such as complex meters and elaborate interplay of voices. The professor found that his musical experience was trivialized, that his brain could no longer model high-level musical relations. He wrote,

> *The compositional process for me at this time seems to lack a Gestalt. Notes are correct, orchestration skills are very much intact and show no diminution. Content, however, is dull, lifeless (soulless). Since the compositional process has for me been one of working at several levels of*

the on-goingness of the melodic, harmonic, rhythmic flow simultaneously and keeping track of the various factors, I find that I am not able to maintain a thread of continuity and must work in small segments which, while appropriate and significant in themselves, do not interrelate with each other (Jourdain, 1997, p. 290).

Overall, the evidence accumulating from a variety of sources indicates the musical intelligence cannot be located in one place in the brain because higher order intelligent musical functioning does not occur in one place in the brain. Areas of the brain which serve logical, emotional, and spatial intelligences are essential also for the musical intelligence. Although we might then be tempted to conclude that the musical intelligence fails the most important criteria of multiple intelligences theory, brain localization, we would find that so too do each of the other intelligences. Intelligent behavior of any sort is a function of an extraordinarily large community of interacting neurons. Ultimately, then, we are led to reject not the musical intelligence, but the first of the eight criteria of multiple intelligences theory—brain localization. Localization of higher level intelligence in the brain is an oxymoron.

PET Scans are Misleading

The conclusion that we cannot locate the intelligences in the brain would seem to fly in the face of the apparently clear pictures painted by positron emission tomography. PET scans show one part of the brain glowing while someone is hearing music, a very different part when they are performing math problems, and so on. The pictures produced by PET scans do show extreme localization of function, but they overestimate tremendously the amount of lateralization and localization occurring during any type of function. The brain does not function the way the PET scans make it appear. In fact, the PET scans themselves are not what they seem to be. PET scans are not pictures of the brain; they are computer generated composites which depict activity across trials compared to resting base rates.

Ultimately, then, we are led to reject not the musical intelligence, but the first of the eight criteria of multiple intelligences theory — brain localization. Localization of higher level intelligence in the brain is an oxymoron.

To understand why these composites exaggerate tremendously the extent of localization, we need to consider how a PET scan is produced. To produce a PET scan a bit of radioactive material is injected into the bloodstream so that the flow of blood can be traced. The brain scans we see are not photographs of the brain, but rather computer generated images which are composites of many trials. The computer is instructed to subtract out background noise and show only the parts of the brain which are more active than usual. This leads to a misrepresentation of what is really going on at any one moment in the brain. Whereas the scan would have us think that the whole brain is at rest except the part pictured in red (or whatever color the computer is instructed to draw the parts of the brains which are more active than usual), the reality is that the whole brain is enormously active all the time. The brain consumes nearly one fourth of all calories we eat. All the neurons are firing hundreds of times a second. With only a slight increase in activity in one hemisphere or one location over usual levels of functioning, the brain scan image shows up as if just that one hemisphere or one location is active. Nothing could be further from the truth. The community of neurons are constantly coordinating their actions, exchanging information. Every complex act is a by-product of many modules, in different parts of the brain, each of which consist of millions of neurons.

> Lacking any entirely suitable technique for observing the brain in action, all mappings of brain function should be taken with a grain of salt. To point to a crimson patch on a PET scan and say, "Grammar is here," or "Absolute pitch is here," is like pointing to China on a globe and saying, "Buddhism is here." Buddhism is indeed centered in China, but so is acupuncture and scroll painting (Jourdain 1997, pp. 285-286).

To fully understand Buddhism we must travel outside China. To fully understand any intelligence, we must examine many parts of the brain. Because one part of the brain is more active than usual while we exercise a particular intelligence does not mean that other parts of the brain are not absolutely essential for high-level functioning of the intelligence, and those other parts may well be absolutely essential for high-level functioning of other intelligences as well.

Computer analogies to the brain are fraught with problems, but they can be instructive. There are low level components of our computers which are dedicated to specific functions. Letters are input through the letter keys, numbers through the number keys, pictures through the scanner, and voice and music through the recorder. Yet as we move to higher level manipulation of that input, store and transform it in various ways, the same memory and processor components are involved across a range of content. If we looked for those parts of the computer which "light up" most are uniquely associated with a specific input, say when words are being processed, we would discover the letter keys; but that does not mean that processing words in the computer is located in the keyboard. Processing words, or any other higher function cannot be located, because many parts of the computer are involved with any complex action. Many parts of the brain are involved with any intelligent action. Brain localization is not the key to understanding intelligence.

A Coda

Different aspects of musical functioning, like the different facets of each intelligence, are located in many parts of the brain. There are simple abilities such as tone recognition which can be localized, but as we move up to higher level integration which is the essence of intelligence, simultaneous integration of input from many parts of the brain is essential. Further, musical intelligence is dependent on the very same brain structures as are other intelligences. We cannot localize musical intelligence apart from other intelligences because the intelligences operate in concert and aspects of various intelligences are dependent on the very same parts of the brain. In short: musical intelligence, like all intelligences, cannot be located in the brain.

● ● ● ● ● ● ● ● ● ● ● ● ● ● ● ● ●
The Metaphor War

If the brain does not come with eight neat locations for the intelligences, and any concept of "mind" or "intelligence" is an abstraction, rather than a discovery rooted in brain science, how should we best conceptualize brain structure and function? We can create notions of "frames of mind" and think of the brain as housing separate intelligences, but that is but one of many possible ways to conceptualize brain functioning and intelligence. Recent brain research is more consistent with a very different metaphor. Intelligent behavior is not the functioning of relatively independent intelligences, but rather harmonious integrated functioning of many neurons working together within many distinct neuron modules which in turn function together in a highly coordinated ways. The brain is not a set of relatively independent Frames of Mind, but rather a Community of Neurons.

Metaphors Drive Curriculum and Instruction

The battle for a metaphor for mind is not trivial; our metaphors determine how we view our students. The metaphors we live with determine whether we resonate to integrated instruction or separate disciplines, whether and how much we emphasize teaching music, teaching about music, teaching through music, or integrating music as part of a holistic learning experience. The brain metaphor we as educators adopt will determine to some extent how comfortable we are with tracking students or pushing for full inclusion.

As brain researchers have labored toward a model of the brain, there has been a parallel battle among educators for a metaphor for mind. In historical terms it was only very recently that we educators fell in love with the right-brain/left-brain di-

chotomy. At that point in our evolution we actually began to speak of our students as "right-brained" or "left-brained." Later, of course, we were forced to abandon that metaphor in the face of advancing knowledge. This recent adoption and embar-

As brain researchers have labored toward a model of the brain, there has been a parallel battle among educators for a metaphor for mind.

rassed abandonment of one metaphor for mind has not prevented us from adopting with renewed fervor the new MI metaphor: Teachers now speak of bodily/kinesthetic learners and visual/spatial learners! Apparently educators are hungry for a metaphor of mind, and hunger knows little caution.

The metaphor for the brain and intelligence we adopt has profound implications for what we do in our classrooms. For example, if we accept the view there are distinct intelligences and that "musical intelligence" is a core intelligence and "mechanical intelligence" is not, we will be more likely to teach music and teach with musical instructional strategies, and relatively less likely to teach mechanics and with mechanical instructional strategies. We will be likely to have our students take music classes and sing songs about the American Revolution during their history lessons; we will be less likely to have them take shop classes and during their history lessons, make and use the tools of the colonial times.

If we accept the Community of Neurons metaphor and think in terms of a multiplicity of interacting intelligences rather than a few relatively separate intelligences, we are more likely to create learning experiences with tools, music, and many more dimensions, integrating our curriculum and instruction. Whether we view intelligences as working primarily in isolation or in coordination, determines to some extent how we view our mission as educators — as attempting to develop separate intelligences or as developing whole students. We will prepare very different learning experiences for our students if we accept the separate intelligences metaphor as opposed to the integrated brain metaphor.

To the extent we adopt a metaphor which emphasizes the integrative functions of the brain, we will be more likely to integrate our instruction, creating more brain-compatible learning. If we see all aspects of the brain acting in concert during formative learning experiences, we will be less likely to attempt to develop the intelligences in isolation or develop teaching strategies

> **Whether we view intelligences as working primarily in isolation or in coordination determines to some extent how we view our role as educators — as attempting to develop separate intelligences or whole students.**

which engage but one intelligence at a time. We will be more likely to favor integrated instruction — creating personally meaningful learning experiences which integrate emotional, perceptual, and cognitive experiences of every type.

To the victor in the metaphor war goes the impact on both curriculum and instruction. We need to be mindful of our metaphors because, consciously or unconsciously, we mind our metaphors. Our tour of brain structure and function has thrown into question the very existence of separate intelligences. How, then can MI theory, make a claim for eight intelligences? It is to this question that we now turn.

● ● ● ● ● ● ● ● ● ● ●
References

Begley, S. *Your Child's Brain.* Newsweek, 1996, February 19, 55-62.

Calvin, W. H. *How Brains Think. Evolving Intelligence, Then and Now.* New York: HarperCollins, 1996.

Gardner, H. *Frames of Mind. The Theory of Multiple Intelligences.* New York: Basic Books, 1983.

Gardner, H. *Multiple Intelligences. The Theory in Practice.* New York: Basic Books, 1993.

Jourdain, R. *Music, The Brain, and Ecstasy.* New York: Avon, 1997.

Kandel, E. R. & Hawkins, R. D. *The Biological Basis of Learning and Individuality.* **Scientific American,** 1992, **267(3)**, 78-86.

Sylwester, R. *A Celebration of Neurons. An Educator's Guide to the Brain.* Alexandria, VA: Association for Supervision and Curriculum Development, 1995.

Do the Eight Intelligences Meet the Eight Criteria?

…how does one actually identify an "intelligence (Gardner, 1993, p. 16)?"

We cannot doubt that there are many ways to be smart. But are the ways described by MI theory the most important ways? Is there something special about the eight intelligences? MI theory sets forth eight criteria for determining what constitutes an intelligence. MI theory claims the original intelligences meet enough of those eight critical criteria to be considered "bona fide intelligences."

Teachers are adjusting what and how they teach to align curriculum and instruction with the specific intelligences proposed by MI theory. Is there something special about those intelligences?

It is this selection of specific intelligences which most directly impacts on curriculum and instruction. If, for example, the educational community accepts the existence of a musical intelligence, but does not accept a culinary intelligence as a bona fide intelligence, teachers will be more likely to have students singing and playing musical instruments, and less likely to have them growing, selecting, storing, preparing, cooking, and presenting foods. Teachers around the world have begun assessing their students along the dimensions dictated by MI theory. They have students assessing themselves along those same dimensions. Teachers are adjusting what and how they teach to align curriculum and instruction with the specific intelligences proposed by MI theory. Is there something special about those intelligences?

To answer that question we need to examine how intelligences are selected in MI theory. The original presentation of MI theory specified eight criteria for an intelligence, but did not specify a specific number of criteria a "candidate intelligence" must meet to qualify as a selected intelligence, or how many criteria an intelligence must fail to meet to be disqualified. The theory simply indicated that meeting only one or two criteria is not sufficient for inclusion, and failing to meet just one criterion is not sufficient for exclusion;

> the effort is to sample as widely as possible among the various criteria and to include within the ranks of the chosen intelligences those candidates that fare the best (Gardner, 1983, p. 62).

In later work Gardner (1993, p. 16) specified the selection process a bit more:

> Only those candidate intelligences that satisfied all or a majority of the criteria were selected as bona fide intelligences.

For something that is becoming the basis for transforming the nation's, and to some extent the world's, curriculum and instruction, this "including in the ranks of the chosen," intelligences which "fare best" has a pinch too much subjectivity. If we are to select some, but not all sets of human skills as "bona fide intelligences," who is to decide which fare best? Who is to choose the "candidate intelligences" from which we select the "chosen intelligences?" Should we accept MI theory conclusions, each adopt our own, or appoint a national or international committee to do the selecting? Should we set tough or easy standards to determine if a candidate intelligence should be included among the ranks of the chosen, bona fide intelligences? Why exclude any intelligence?

Let's examine the eight criteria and how well the eight intelligences meet the MI theory criteria.

The Eight Criteria of an Intelligence in MI Theory

1. Potential isolation by brain damage.
2. The existence of idiot savants, prodigies, and other exceptional individuals.
3. An identifiable core operation or set of operations.
4. A distinctive developmental history, along with a definable set of expert "end-state" performances.
5. An evolutionary history and evolutionary plausibility.
6. Support from experimental psychological tasks.
7. Support from psychometric findings.
8. Susceptibility to encoding in a symbol system.

Criterion 1.

Potential Isolation by Brain Damage

As we have seen in Chapter 20: Is MI Theory Brain-Based?, MI theory is part of a continuing evolution toward a progressively more differentiated view of the brain and intelligence. Brain science is in it's infancy; only 100 years ago Santiago Ramon Y Cajal, father of modern brain science, began staining neurons with silver salts. He discovered the brain was made of discrete units, nerve cells — it was not one unified organ as previously thought.

MI theory's first and most important test of an intelligence is if it can be isolated (destroyed or spared) by brain lesions.

With time and research, our views of the brain have become progressively more differentiated: When it was discovered by Sperry and others that the two hemispheres had different functions (right-brain — relational, emotional; left-brain — analytic, logical) the split brain view gained sway.

The right-brain/left-brain dichotomy gave way in 1978 to Paul MacLean's model of a triune brain with hierarchal layers for survival, emotion, and rational thought. More recently, Gazzaniga (1985) emphasized neurons were organized into many interconnected, semiautonomous modules. We now know there are several hundred million of these tiny neural networks, each about three times the size of the head of a pin, containing about 100,000 neurons, and each responsible for a very small seg-

ment of brain functioning. Each of these modules of neurons sends its impulses to other modules, which deal with progressively more complex input. Every conscious act in normal people involves integrated actions between both hemispheres and many parts of the brain.

Gardner places brain function as most important among the criteria for intelligences, indicating

> …every researcher has a bias; and in my own case, I believe that the most valuable (and least misleading) information is likely to come from a deep knowledge of the nervous system: how it is organized, how it develops, how it breaks down. Findings from the brain, in my view, serve as the court of last resort, the ultimate arbiter among competing accounts of cognition (Gardner, 1983, p. 30).

To the extent that a particular faculty can be destroyed, or spared in isolation, as a result of brain damage, its relative autonomy from other human faculties seems likely. In what follows I rely to a considerable degree on evidence from neuropsychology and, in particular, on that highly revealing experiment in nature — a lesion to a specific area of the brain. The consequences of such brain injury may well constitute the single most instructive line of evidence regarding those distinctive abilities or computations that lie at the core of a human intelligence (Gardner, 1983, p. 63).

It may seem, for example, that the capacity to process auditory sequences is a strong candidate for an intelligence…. However, studies of the effect of brain damage have repeatedly documented that musical and linguistic strings are processed in different ways and can be compromised by different lesions. Thus, despite the surface appeal of such a skill, it seems preferable not to regard it as a separate intelligence (Gardner, 1983, p. 67).

Thus, MI theory's first and most important test of an intelligence is if it can be isolated (destroyed or spared) by brain lesions. At times Gardner comes close to suggesting each of his intelligences will be found to correspond to concrete neuronal systems. For example, in his speculative voyage forward to the year 2013 Gardner indicates that in the future,

> Without question, neuroscientists will have established far more firm knowledge about the organization and development of the nervous system. After years of observing mental processes as they actually occur in the living brain, they will be able to describe the neural structures that are entailed in the conduct of various intellectual activities…(Gardner, 1993, p. 249).

There is no doubt that future technology will increase our ability to observe neuronal functioning associated with specific mental events, but that technology will never reveal separate sites for the separate broad intelligences of the MI theory. Each act of intelligence is the by-product of an incredibly complex, unique set of interacting neurons acting in coordination. Intelligence does not reside in specific places in the brain, it is a by-product of a community of neurons interacting.

As support of the independence of the intelligences, Gardner (1993, p. 23) contrasts the effects of Alzheimer's disease (which is associated with deterioration of posterior portions of the brain) with the effects of Pick's disease (which impairs frontal lobe functioning). Alzheimer's patients lose spatial, logical, and linguistic functions, but remain socially proper; Pick's disease patients lose social graces.

Although this differential loss of functions as a result of the two diseases might suggest an independence of spatial, logical, and linguistic skills from interpersonal skills, the pattern of function loss in

Alzheimer's and Pick's disease patients poses major problems for MI theory: Alzheimer's patients lose a wide range of intelligences, not a specific intelligence, hardly evidence of the independence of intelligences. Similarly, Pick's patients do not suffer only from loss of social graces. As Gardner (1993, p. 25) notes, the frontal lobes are involved in intrapersonal intelligences, not just interpersonal intelligence. Alzheimer's and Pick's diseases then, do not support the notion that intelligences are independent; they are not lost or spared in isolation.

A single "linguistic intelligence" fails the test of brain isolation: there are many discrete linguistic intelligences, each of which can be destroyed or spared in isolation depending on the site of a lesion.

An even more serious threat to the claim of brain isolation is that each intelligence does not reside in one place in the brain. All broad intelligences are a by-product of interconnected functioning of different neurons in different parts of the brain. As we saw in Chapter 20: Is MI Theory Brain-Based?, the simple act of catching a ball involves an incredible coordination of neurons from many parts of the brain. Many discrete neuron modules act in coordination to produce all intelligent behavior.

Let's examine one aspect of the presumed "visual/spatial intelligence" — response to color. It turns out that very different parts of the brain deal with different aspects of color and that different lesions create selectively different disabilities regarding color (Damasio & Damasio, 1992). A lesion in the temporal segment of the left lingual gyrus causes anomia; patients with anomia experience color normally, but

Color Can't Be Localized

Lesion Site	Function Lost
Temporal segment of the left lingual gyrus	Anomia: Inability to name colors correctly
Left posterior temporal and inferior parietal cortex	Inability to pronounce color words
Occipital and subcalcarine portions of the left and right lingual gyri	Achromatopsia: Inability to perceive or imagine colors.

they lose the ability to consistently name colors correctly (patients will call something "blue" that most of us call "red" even though they function well in color chip experiments, matching blue to blue and red to red). A lesion in the left posterior temporal and inferior parietal cortex, in contrast, leaves patients impaired in their ability to pronounce color words (patients

The notion of one visual intelligence is far too broad to correspond to brain structure and function.

might say "buh" rather than "blue," but they do not attempt to call a color by a different name, and they function fine with noncolor words and with other nonverbal color tasks). A third type of lesion, in the occipital and subcalcarine portions of the left and right lingual gyri, causes achromatopsia — the inability to perceive or even imagine colors (these patients live in a gray world, even though their eyes and optic nerves function normally).

Thus, each of these color functions involves quite different parts of the brain and "can be destroyed, or spared in isolation." The notion of one visual/spatial intelligence is far too broad to correspond to brain structure and function. This same pattern is revealed with each intelligence: a multiplicity of functions can be isolated. See, for example, the sites for linguistic skills described in the box on page 22.3

Different abilities even within the very narrow domain of color each fit the first criterion of an intelligence — each can be isolated. But, of course, it would be absurd to speak of a color naming intelligence, and a color word pronouncing intelligence, and a color visualization intelligence. Or would it be? We are faced with a multiplicity of intelligences. Any attempt to group them and name them will be arbitrary; there simply is no one visual/spatial intelligence which meets the criterion of brain isolation.

Let's take another example, this time from the interpersonal domain. There are very specific cells in primates (and presumably in humans as well) dedicated exclusively to face recognition. They respond to the sight of a face, but do not respond to any other type of stimuli. In humans, it is possible to lose the ability for face recognition in isolation, without losing any other interpersonal skills (Fischbach, 1992). Other parts of the brain are associated with recognition of emotion in others, yet other parts are associated with memory and storing proper names of individuals, and yet other parts of the brain are associated with remembering details of personal histories. A lesion can destroy or spare any one of these functions without affecting the others. In light of the modular structure of the brain, how meaningful is it to speak of a single "interpersonal intelligence" passing the test of brain isolation?

This distinction is not trivial for education. Whether we think of the brain in terms of multiple intelligences versus a multiplicity of intelligences will translate into comfort or discomfort as we hear teachers and educators speaking of students as "people smart." It is an overgeneralization to speak of anyone as strong in "interpersonal intelligence." Brain science indicates we should not be comfortable with such broad generalizations. If we accept that there is a multiplicity of ways to be smart, we reject the term "people smart," and ask instead how strong the student is in each of many distinct interpersonal skills. We stop asking how strong is a students' interpersonal intelligence and start asking how the student is strong in interpersonal intelligence.

This examination of brain structure and function reveals that each intelligence is far too broad to meet the most important first criterion: Brain Isolation. Each broad intelligence consists of many skills, each of which can be compromised independently by different brain lesions. Although a single verbal/linguistic intelligence cannot be isolated in the brain, many mini-linguistic intelligences can. But not one of these separate mini-intelligences can, in isolation, produce intelligent behavior; intelligence is a function of all of these mini-intelligences interacting as a cooperative community. The cooperative/modular organization of the brain means none of MI theory's broad intelligences can be isolated. **They do not reside in a single location. They all fail MI theory's most important test — potential brain isolation.** Intelligent

behavior is a fantastic cooperative effort among many parts of the brain.

Gardner himself, in at least one place, appears to deny the physical existence of the intelligences, stating:

> These intelligences are fictions — at most, useful fictions — for discussing processes and abilities that (like all of life) are continuous with one another; Nature brooks no sharp discontinuities of the sort proposed here.... I must repeat that they exist not as physically verifiable entities but only as potentially useful scientific constructs (Gardner, 1983, p. 70)."

Intelligences do not reside in a single location. They all fail Gardner's most important test — potential brain isolation.

But if these intelligences do not exist as physically verifiable entities, does that not mean they fail the first and most important criteria of MI theory? How can something which has no physical existence meet the test of brain isolation?

• • • • • • • • • • • •
Criterion 2.

Idiot Savants, Prodigies, and Exceptional Individuals

In MI theory the existence of prodigies, exceptional individuals, and savants is taken as support for the existence of separate intelligences. A prodigy shows early very strong development in one or more areas, but is normal or above normal in others. Exceptional individuals do not show the precocious development of a prodigy, but may attain extraordinarily high levels of skill in one or more areas with normal skills in other areas. Grandma Moses was an exceptional individual, but not a prodigy; she became a great painter, but began late in life. Savants develop extraordinary skills in one or more areas, but manifest extremely underdeveloped skills in most.

Prodigies, exceptional individuals, and savants all provide very strong support for MI theory's claim there is not one general intelligence; if there were just one general intelligence, individuals exceptional in just one area, but normal or below average in other areas, would not exist. If there were but one intelligence, individuals would be high or low in all areas, not very high in some but normal or retarded in others.

Whether we view intelligences as working primarily in isolation or in coordination determines to some extent how we view our role as educators — as attempting to develop separate intelligences or whole students.

MI theory, however, takes the existence of savants not just as counter-evidence against the notion of general intelligence, but also as evidence for the existence of separate, definable intelligences. In fact, though, a deep look into the performance of savants provides very strong evidence against the existence of separate intelligences. A deeper look into autism demonstrates that intelligent behavior depends on ability to integrate a multiplicity of intelligences and that one mathematical or one linguistic intelligence does not exist.

Gardner indicates the claim of a specific intelligence is enhanced if the condition of

the savant can be linked to "specific neural regions" (1983, p. 63). Gardner interprets the behavior of savants as manifestations of the intelligences operating independently:

> In the case of the idiot savant (and other retarded or exceptional individuals, including autistic children), we behold the unique sparing of one particular human ability against a background of mediocre or highly retarded human performances in other domains. Once again, the existence of these populations allows us to observe the human intelligence in relative — even splendid — isolation.

In fact the existence of savants demonstrates the opposite: human intelligences do not operate in isolation. To understand this, we must take a second tour — a tour through the world of autism and savants. Let's start with some basic distinctions: Autistic savants are rare. Autism is found in only 2 to 5 of every 10,000 children, depending on the strictness of the definition. Savant behaviors occur in fewer than one in ten autistic children, making autistic savants among the rarest of individuals. There is disagreement among experts regarding the relation of autism to savant behaviors. Some theorists consider all "savants" to be autistic; in this view idiot savants are autistics who have extraordinary skills in one or more areas (See Rimland 1978; Treffert, 1989). Given this view, Rimland argues that "autistic savant" is a more polite term than "idiot savant," and should be substituted for "idiot savant." Others, taking a stricter definition of autism, claim only half of all "idiot savants" are autistic (See Frith, 1989, p. 84). We will sidestep that debate here, simply using the term "savants" for those individuals with extraordinary abilities in one domain who manifest below normal abilities in most. Savants have demonstrated a

Skills of Savants

Documented skills of savants include the ability to...

Music

▼ Recognize and sing hundreds of melodies at a young age.
▼ Play complex songs after hearing them but once.
▼ Make extraordinary auditory discriminations.

Memory

▼ Remember at a glance all the dots on dominos scattered at random.
▼ Recall over thirty random digits stated quickly or shown briefly.
▼ Recall a full day's conversation and repeat it verbatim — including tone and cadence of the various participants.

Math

▼ Perform astonishing calculations.

Visual/Spatial

▼ Remember complex routes from maps or from experience.
▼ Rapidly construct jigsaw puzzles with the pieces turned face down.
▼ Sculpt or draw astoundingly realistic figures or pictures from a fleeting glance at an object or picture.

Time

▼ Tell the precise time without a clock.

Clairvoyance

▼ Describe events they have not seen.
▼ Predict events.

Kinesthetic

▼ Spin and balance objects in the air, and stack objects in intricate balanced formations that others cannot.

Sources: Rimland, 1978; Treffert, 1989.

wide range of extraordinary skills, see box: Skills of Savants.

Some of the skills of savants stretch believ-ability. Consider the retarded man who could give the square root of any 4 digit number in an average of 4 seconds and the cube root of any 6-digit number in about 6 seconds! He was asked the number of grains of corn in any one of 64 boxes if one grain was placed in the first box, two grains in the second, 4 in the third, 8 in the forth, and so on. He gave answers for the fourteenth (8,192), for the eighteenth (131,072), and the twenty-fourth (8,388,608) instantaneously. By six seconds he was able to state (140,737,488,355,328) was the number of grains in the forty-eighth box. By forty-five seconds he correctly announced the total in all 64 boxes — 18,446,734,073,709,551,615 (Treffert, 1989, p. 59)!

At first glance one might be tempted to interpret the astounding performances of savants as does Gardner, as intelligences acting in "splendid isolation." As one learns of the savant who can stack quarters on edge it is tempting to attribute the skill to an extraordinary kinesthetic intelligence. Math feats can be ascribed to an exceptional logical/mathematical intelligence. Jigsaw puzzle skills can be viewed as a manifestation of a highly developed visual/spatial intelligence. And so on.

Savants do not demonstrate any of the eight intelligences, but rather isolated skills.

Closer examination, however, reveals savants do not demonstrate any of the eight intelligences, but rather isolated splinter skills. Savant twins who could swap prime numbers for entertainment could not count to thirty. The same savant who can stack quarters cannot reliably catch a ball or ride a bike. Savants show splinter skills rather than general mathematical or kinesthetic intelligences, and this pattern holds across domains, so, for savants a skill in any one of the eight intelligences does not predict strength in other skills in that same intelligence. The pattern of isolated skills among autistic savants is evidence against intelligences like those postulated by MI theory: If a single mathematical intelligence existed, we would expect individuals to be generally high or generally low in mathematical skills, not manifesting the extreme discrepancy among math skills displayed by savants. Thus, we must conclude the skills of savants are not manifestations of an underlying intelligence.

If the feats of an autistic savant were support for the existence of a "mathematical intelligence" rather than isolated mathematical skills, we might expect the mathematical savant to produce higher order mathematical equations or pose mathematical questions. They can't. This same pattern of isolated splinter skills among savants holds for the various intelligences. Savants who can produce the dictionary definition of almost any word do not grow up to write original essays in a way we would expect from someone gifted in a "linguistic intelligence." Alonzo, a well-studied savant who produces remarkable, true-to-life sculptures does not manifest a general "visual/spatial intelligence." His ability to sculpt is unrelated to other visual/spatial skills. Alonzo will never develop skills in chess or become an architect. Savants are generally incapable of abstract thought; their skills are most often concrete, often related to memory and/or extraordinary perception.

Experiments reveal savants lack the normal preference for and memory for coherent and patterned stimuli over incoherent and random stimuli (Frith, 1989). They process information without normal regard to patterns or meaning. In contrast to normal individuals, for example, they remember nonsense items as well as meaningful items whereas normal people remember the meaningful items far better. For savants, this tendency to ignore context, pattern, and meaning and to focus instead on discrete elements holds true across the multiple intelligences. It does not matter if the items are sounds, words, or colored counters (Frith & Baron-Cohen, 1987).

These findings are in stark contrast to Gardner's suggestion that there are distinctive processes for memory in each intelligence (Gardner, 1993, p. 42). The pattern of memory among savants illustrates a common information processing approach crosscutting the multiple intelligences. Within all intelligences, savants show specific skills which are manifestations of a general tendency toward concrete, detached, perception-bound cognitive functioning. They focus on the trees and fail to see the forest. No matter what kind of information they are processing, autistics have as Frith (1989, p. 174) so eloquently put it, "a weak drive for central coherence of all information." Because this pattern of cognitive functioning holds true across all types of information — it is not intelligence-specific — it is strong evidence that the intelligences do not operate in isolation.

Some autistic children read quite well. Although they score as well as nonautistic readers of the same mental age on tasks of grammatical competence, they fail terribly on tasks which depend on context. For example, unlike nonautistic children, they are not surprised or disturbed while reading a factual nature story when they come across a sentence like, "The hedgehog could smell the scent of the electric flowers." Similarly, when the context of a story clearly reveals the proper missing word is "beaver," unlike normal children of the same mental age, autistics are content with the word "horse" (Frith, 1989, p. 128). While the sentences are grammatically correct, they are incorrect in the context of the passages. Once again, the focus is on the elements, without regard to the context. Autistics demonstrate that a general tendency to ignore the broader meaning or context manifests itself across all eight MI theory intelligences. The intelligences do not operate in isolation.

This concentration on discrete elements rather than the meaningful whole among autistics manifests itself also in interpersonal exchanges (presumed "interpersonal intelligence"). Three fourths of all speaking autistic children show at least some

In all intelligence areas, savants show specific skills which are manifestations of a general tendency toward concrete, detached, perception-bound cognitive functioning. They focus on the trees and fail to see the forest.

echolalia — in response to a request like, "Bob, please say hello" they may respond by simply saying back, "Bob, please say hello." This communication failure may be interpreted as a function of a focus on words as sounds rather than words as conveyed meaning. It is consistent with a general failure to move beyond sensory input toward cognitive processing of that input; a failure to interpret stimuli in their broader context.

Autistics almost all show a failure in the pragmatics of language. A normal person at a dinner table, when asked, "Can you pass the salt?" will understand the question in the context of the situation, and will respond by passing the salt. This response depends on linguistic pragmatics, the ability to interpret words in the context of the communicative situation in which they are uttered. Autistics score low on pragmatics compared to nonautistics matched for mental age. The autistic, when asked at the dinner table, "Can you pass the salt?" instead of responding by passing the salt, might well simply respond, "Yes" (Frith, 1989, p. 120). This response is not an intent to frustrate the person making the request. The autistic innocently responds to the question without regard to context, giving a response which would be perfectly appropriate in a different context. The communication failure occurs because the autistic fails to interpret the words in the context in which they were spoken.

Failure to respond to context leads to literal comprehension. The autistic boy intently searches a room after he hears that someone in that room has "cried their eyes out." He is looking for the eyes! A ten-year-old autistic girl (IQ 100) manifests catastrophic anxiety when the nurse wishing to do a simple blood test says "give me your hand." The girl must be assured that the nurse is not asking her to cut off her hand and give it to the nurse (Coleman & Gillberg, 1985)! Literal comprehension can lead to drastic miscommunication. Consider the able autistic young man who often did shopping and who was trusted with money:

> One day, as his mother was mixing a fruit cake, she said to him: "I haven't got any cloves. Would you please go out and get me some?" The son came back a while later with a carrier bag full of girlish clothes, including underwear, from a High Street boutique (Frith, 1989, p. 177).

The tendency to ignore context actually places autistics at an advantage in "disembedding tasks" — tasks which demand that the individual ignore context or pattern of stimuli which normal people spontaneously organize into a coherent whole. Among the subtests of standard IQ tests, autistics score strongest on the block design in which success depends on focusing on separate segments of a design rather than seeing the design as a whole. With no hints autistics spontaneously focus on the

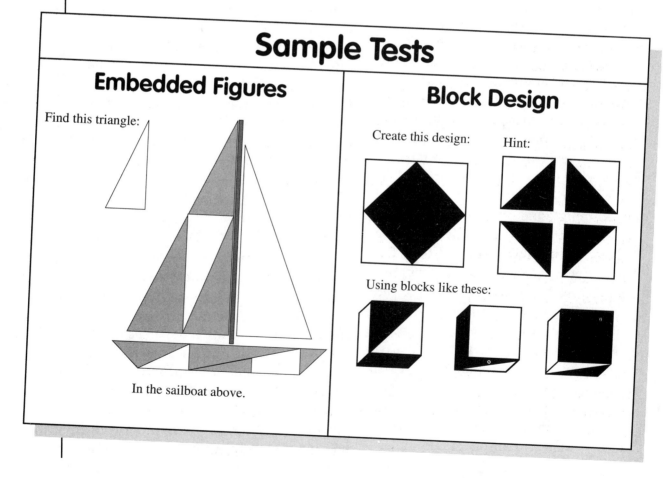

Sample Tests

Embedded Figures

Find this triangle:

In the sailboat above.

Block Design

Create this design:

Hint:

Using blocks like these:

components of the design rather than the design as a whole. Autistics also do very well relative to other tasks on hidden pictures tasks in which an individual must ignore the whole picture, concentrating on its elements out of context (Frith, 1989, p. 99). See box: Sample Tests.

> The red thread running through all the results is the high performance of autistic children on tasks requiring isolation of stimuli, favoring detachment, and their low performance on tasks requiring connection of stimuli, favoring coherence. In contrast, for young normal children, retarded children, and also unschooled older children from a different cultural background, the balance goes entirely in the opposite direction. Therefore, we assume that a central cohesive force is a natural (and useful) characteristic of the cognitive system. But we also assume that is significantly impaired in autism (Frith, 1989, p. 102).

Further support for the notion that the feats of savants are not a manifestation of intelligences operating in isolation, but rather a general process operating across "intelligences" comes from the frequency of savants who show extraordinary skills in more than one splinter skill, crosscutting the intelligences. Among savants, it is often noted that their extraordinary skills cut across different types of intellectual functioning. One of many possible examples illustrating this point is a savant we will call Billy. Billy was subject of an intense five-year case study (Scheerer, Rothmann & Goldstein, 1945). Billy could perform lightening calculations, play the piano, sing with perfect pitch, sing operas in several languages, spell words with ease forwards or backward, recite long speeches, and sing complex arias. Unfortunately, these feats were not manifestations of intelligence in any meaningful sense of the word — Billy had absolutely no understanding of the operas he sang or the mathematical meaning of even simple concepts like why three quarters equal seventy-five cents!

Savants do show extraordinary skills, but not intelligence — at least not in the usual sense.

A review of the potential biological explanations of the extraordinary skills of savants is beyond the scope of this book. When applied to understanding autism, the new brain imaging technology will almost certainly reveal a relative lack of activity in those areas of the brain responsible for integrating diverse sensory input. Compared to normals, savants probably also will show greater activity in areas closer to sensory input.

How the ability to focus so narrowly (or inability to focus broadly) comes about is not well understood, but genetic factors cannot be doubted: 82 percent of identical twins of autistics show intellectual impairment in contrast to 10 percent of fraternal twins (Folstein & Rutter, 1977). Prenatal and birth complications are also indicated: a full 37 percent of autistic children have experience with complications such as neonatal convulsions, delayed birth, and delayed breathing (Kolvin, Ounsted & Roth, 1971). Treffert (1989) has proffered an intriguing, integrated theory of savant behavior as development which is compensatory for very early damage to certain parts of the brain. However they come about, the skills and deficits of savants involve a narrowing of attention and a tendency to focus on elements to the exclusion of their context. This tendency to intently focus of some things to the exclusion of others is often noted by those working with autistics. This tendency is manifest across the multiple intelligences, as in the tendency to see the earring and miss the face; to not hear someone shouting their name, but rush to the faint sound of a candy wrapper being torn open; to recognize a person only if they are wearing a specific pair of glasses. Selective, prolonged, narrow attention, of course, is a double-edged sword, allowing fantastic feats of perception and recall, but preventing integration, higher-level thinking, and the creation of meaning.

Savants do show extraordinary skills, but not intelligence — at least not in the usual sense. Savants calculate answers, but they do not create problems — they are calculators, but not mathematicians. In speech, many echo rather than converse. In music, many play back with perfection, some can play a piece in a variety of styles, a few improvise, almost none create. In sculpting, savants replicate with amazing precision, but they do not interpret reality or create original styles. In movement, they mimic but do not choreograph. Savants do kinesthetic tricks, but do not become acrobats or athletes.

Just as MI theory argues against the notion of a general intelligence because an individual can be high in math but low in language arts, autistics provide excellent evidence against the notion of a mathematical intelligence (or any broad MI theory intelligence) because they can be extraordinary high in some math skills while phenomenally low in others.

If there were a single mathematical intelligence or a single linguistic intelligence the skills for each would likely correlate. Just as they are not found in one place in the brain, those skills do not correlate in savants. Savants are living proof of the independence of different types of skills within the linguistic intelligence, within the mathematical intelligence, and within the other intelligences. Savant behavior in one skill does not predict savant behavior in another skill — within the same presumed intelligence. This pattern of discrete splinter skills within intelligences holds for each of the eight intelligences.

Just as MI theory argues against the notion of a general intelligence because an individual can be high in math but low in language arts, autistics provide excellent evidence that each of the eight intelligences is too broad — an individual can be extraordinarily high in some math skills while phenomenally low in others. To speak of a single mathematical intelligence or any other intelligence is to paper over the complexity of human functioning and individual differences.

The performance of savants is consistent with the modular view of brain functioning. They demonstrate that true intelligence takes a community of neurons interacting harmoniously, not separate neural structures working in isolation. The feats of savants are not, as claimed in MI theory, a manifestation of an intelligence working in "splendid isolation." The skills of savants demonstrate there is not one general mathematical intelligence or a single linguistic intelligence or visual/spatial intelligence. There are separate mathematical, linguistic, and spatial skills. When these skills operate in isolation, they do not result in intelligent behavior. Intelligence depends on a cooperative community of neurons all functioning in harmony.

The existence of savants does give us a special window through which to view human intelligence. The insight we gain, however, does not support the conclusion that human intelligences operate in isolation. Rather, to understand autistic savants is to understand that intelligence in part is a drive for coherence, a drive to integrate a wide range of stimuli into a meaningful whole. We live in an interactive world. The same stimuli have a very different meaning when they occur in different contexts. Intelligence is not just the ability to see the individual trees, but to see the forest as well. This drive for coherence is not intelligence-specific. It is not an accident that great thinkers like Einstein apply their skills to math, science, religion, philosophy, and politics. It is also not an accident that autistic individuals engage in autistic thinking in many domains. Splinter skills are not intelligences. An understanding of the savant clarifies the nature of intelligence, but at the same time demonstrates the inadequacy of any theory which suggests that there are separate human intelligences which operate in isolation.

● ● ● ● ● ● ● ● ● ● ● ● ●
Criterion 3.
An Identifiable Core Operation or Set of Operations

The third criterion for an intelligence in MI theory is that it depends on an identifiable set of "core operations." Unfortunately for MI theory, there is no established independent set of "core operations," against which to check a candidate intelli-

gence. This places MI theorists in the position of choosing both the intelligences and the core operations upon which they depend, so it is hard to avoid circular reasoning. One might find "core operations" for any intelligence one wished to "include within the ranks of the chosen intelligences," and then, to complete the circle, take the existence of those core operations as evidence for the existence of the intelligence.

Thus, intelligence is not the result of a few separate core operations applied to different information or problems. If we are to speak in terms of "core operations" at all, we would conclude all behavior can be analyzed for it's "core operations" and intelligent behavior integrates a multiplicity of "core operations."

Let's take a silly example. First, we create a new intelligence, say tinker toy assembly. Next we analyze that "intelligence" for "core operations" and come up with two core operations, say, 1) identification of tinker toy parts, and 2) ability to fit them together. Finally we say, because tinker toy assembly was found to depend on core operations (ability to identify tinker toy parts and fit them together), we have provided support for the existence of that intelligence. Using this process, we could find support for any candidate intelligence we wished to include within our group of "chosen intelligences."

MI theory provides an information-processing approach to defining core operations associated with each intelligence. For example, sensitivity to pitch is the core operation for musical intelligence, and an ability to imitate movements of others is a core operation for bodily intelligence. This process of identifying "core operations" associated with an intelligence would allow us to support any number of intelligences. For example, we could propose an olfactory intelligence with the core operation of sensitivity to smell; a touch intelligence with the core operation of sensitivity to tactile stimulation; and a humor intelligence with core operations of sensitivity to unexpected outcomes, human foibles, and exaggeration to the point of absurdity.

The criterion of core operations poses a problem also for the independence of interpersonal and intrapersonal intelligences. A core operation of interpersonal intelligence is sensitivity to the feelings of others; a core operation of intrapersonal intelligence is sensitivity to one's own feelings. But these sets of skills are two sides of the same coin. Can we be sensitive to a feeling in another, if we are not sensitive to that feeling in ourselves? Can we recognize the full range of our own feelings, if we cannot identify them in others?

The notion that intelligent functioning in different domains is based on distinct core operations leads to odd ways of conceptualizing behavior. Is it more accurate to conceptualize the performance of an Olympic gymnast as the product of core operations of a kinesthetic intelligence, or the result of an extraordinary act of integration of many visual, spatial, kinesthetic, and logical skills functioning in harmony?

Guided fantasy, visualizing successful performance without actually moving, enhances athletic performances. Is it meaningful, then, to speak of a kinesthetic intelligence which operates in isolation of the visual intelligence or intrapersonal intelligence?

Any intelligent behavior involves many core operations. Is it meaningful to say that assembling models, arranging flowers artistically, parallel parking, reading maps, color coordinating one's clothes, and navigating sailing ships are reflections of the same core operations? It would be nice if as teachers we could teach a few core operations and improve such diverse skills as writing poems, interpreting literature, debating, and understanding the discourse of others. If only a few core operations provided the basis for all math and logic, our jobs as teachers would be so much easier! Unfortunately, there are not just a few core operations which underlay any of the broad MI theory intelligences.

Thus, intelligence is not the result of a few separate core operations applied to different information or problems. If we are to speak in terms of core operations at all, we would conclude all behavior can be analyzed for it's core operations and intelligent behavior integrates a multiplicity of core operations.

● ● ● ● ● ● ● ● ● ● ● ●
Criterion 4.

A Distinctive Developmental History, Along with a Definable Set of Expert "End-State" Performances

MI theory states that during the course of development, normal as well as exceptional individuals pass through identifiable stages of development in each intelligence, reaching and passing identifiable milestones, stretching toward exceedingly high levels of competence.

In a number of the eight intelligences, individuals do pass through identifiable stages. In language, we develop from one word utterances, to simple phrases, to fluency, including sophisticated syntax and abstract figures of speech. In math, we develop from concrete operations to abstract formal operations. In spatial relations, we develop from inability to distinguish our own point of view from that of others, toward decentration and differentiation. In interpersonal skills, too, we progressively decentrate — both in our ability to separate our own feelings from those of others, and in the ability to follow disinterested rather than egoistic moral principles.

All of these stages, however, are not necessarily a demonstration of unique, intelligence-specific developments toward intelligence-specific end-states. In fact, a strong argument can be made that they are manifestations of a general development toward an intellectual end-state which crosses all the multiple intelligences. The developments in each case, while occurring at different chronological ages, are remarkably parallel, suggesting a general process of cognitive development. The development in all of these presumed separate intelligences is a development from simple, perception-bound, egoistic cognition toward complex, abstract, decentrated cognition. The ability to differentiate and balance one's own point of view with that of others is dependent on the ability to simultaneously juggle and integrate greater

amounts of information — movement from simple perception-bound cognition toward higher level abstraction. The developmental pattern in speech is away from a word-to-object and a word-to-act correspondence, toward words which express increasingly abstract concepts and experiences. In math, too, the movement is from the concrete toward the abstract.

Given the parallel nature of development in all areas, Gardner's claim of "unique developmental histories" for the different intelligences is at least open to question. The alternative interpretation seems very attractive — that the development of intelligence in all areas is a function of general cognitive development associated with movement from concrete to abstract, reaching toward integration of progressively greater amounts of stimuli.

Thus, development in all of the intelligences is toward the ability to integrate increasing amounts of information. When my (Spencer's) son, Simón, was a toddler I took him for a walk in the park. He watched me take a drink from the water fountain. He then walked to the fountain, turned the handle, and was delighted to see the water turn on. The fountain had the kind of handle with a spring so that when it was not held, the water turned off. After turning on the water, Simón moved his mouth toward the spigot to take a drink, but as he concentrated on positioning himself to take a drink, he released the pressure on the handle so that just as his mouth was in position to receive water, the water turned off. Simón was surprised and disappointed. He looked again at the handle, turned it on, and saw the water go on again.

He looked pleased. He again moved to take a drink, but again the concentration on taking a drink led him to release the handle, and once again the water turned off just as he was about to get his drink! For a second time Simón was surprised and disappointed. He repeated this process five, count them, five times before turning to me indicating he wanted help. He simply was not at a developmental stage to master coordinating both things at once. Within a few weeks, with no additional contact with the drinking fountain or instruction from me, when we returned to the park Simón was able to coordinate his efforts, operating the drinking fountain, taking a drink by himself.

We share the story of Simón and the water fountain not just because it is amusing; we share it because it is a symbol of a great deal of development. During late infancy, in the second postnatal year, connections are made in the brain between the brain stem where emotional responses are generated, the cortical centers for analysis of sensory input, and the frontal lobes. These connections are associated with dramatic

> **These dramatic developments are not manifestations of distinct developmental end-states in separate intelligences. A common rather than intelligence-specific underlying developmental process explains much of development.**

spurts in learning in diverse areas such as problem solving, voluntary control of behavior, language acquisition, and understanding others. Many of the dramatic transformations which occur at that age have to do with the ability of the child to attend to and integrate input from more than one thing at a time. Children negoti-

ating this passage are for the first time able to understand quantity of objects does not change when their form does (the liquid does not become more when poured into a taller, skinnier beaker), objects can belong to more than one category, objects can represent more than one thing, other people have different visual perspectives than oneself, others have different intentions than oneself, and the meaning of a word or phrase may be different for others than for oneself.

All of these transformations are best characterized not as separate development in the kinesthetic, interpersonal, visual/spatial, and linguistic domains, but as manifestations of a general intellectual development. These dramatic developments are not manifestations of distinct developmental end-states in separate intelligences. A common, rather than intelligence-specific, underlying developmental process explains much of development.

Given the parallel nature of development in all areas, MI theory's claim of "unique developmental histories" for the different intelligences is at least open to question. The alternative interpretation seems very attractive — that, to a very important extent, the development of intelligence in all areas is a function of general cognitive development associated with movement from concrete to abstract, reaching toward integration of progressively greater amounts of stimuli. These remarkably similar developments crosscutting all of the intelligences parallel the increasingly higher-level neuronal connections which allow the integration of progressively greater amounts of information and the development of increasingly abstract thought.

The end state toward which we strive in each area of functioning is not best captured by a tendency to develop separate intelligences, but rather by a tendency to integrate experience. The brain is structured to make successive abstractions, to integrate otherwise dissociated perceptual stimulations, striving for integrated experience. The metaphor of a community of neurons functioning in harmony fits well with the development in all domains — development toward higher and higher levels of integration of experience. Exclusive focus on distinct, intelligence-specific developmental end-states ignores important evidence from both behavioral studies and studies of brain organization and development.

• • • • • • • • • • • • • • • •

Criterion 5.

An Evolutionary History and Plausibility

The criteria of evolutionary plausibility is met to the extent we can locate an intelligence's evolutionary antecedents or existence in other species. Gardner (1983, p. 65) indicates this criterion is one in which we find "firm facts especially elusive."

Gardner suggests a possible link between bird song and human song. Evolutionary biologists would find this a very strange suggestion indeed. The primary function of bird song is to define and defend mating territory. Human song expresses a variety of intense emotions — human males do not generally burst into song when another male begins to flirt with their mate or invade their territory. A link between bird song and human music seems strange also from an evolutionary perspective: in terms of evolution, chimps are much closer relatives to us than are birds, and chimps do not sing. To support a link between bird song and human song, we would have to assume evolution plays leapfrog! What then is the evolutionary basis of human song? Perhaps human opera does not find its roots in the behavior of lower animals; perhaps it is an expression of intense integrated perception, cognition, and feeling unparalleled in other species.

The criterion of evolutionary plausibility creates some other problems: It is doubtful that lower animals spend much time in introspection. If we could make the case that the intrapersonal intelligence has an evolutionary basis, is there any intelligence for which we cannot argue the case of evolutionary plausibility? To all but creationists, it goes without saying that every identifiable set of skills involves the activation of a set of brain structures and so has an evolutionary history. But if all skills have an evolutionary origin, this fifth criterion turns out to be not very discriminating; a criterion which filters out none, provides no support for those included.

To all but creationists, it goes without saying that every identifiable set of skills involves the activation of a set of brain structures and so has an evolutionary history. But if all skills have an evolutionary origin, this fifth criterion turns out to be not very discriminating; a criterion which filters none out, provides no support for those included.

● ● ● ● ● ● ● ● ● ● ● ●

Criterion 6.

Support From Experimental Psychological Tasks

The sixth criterion of an intelligence in MI theory is support from experimental tasks. Gardner (1983, p. 65) points to three main types of studies: interference, transference, and intelligence-specific memory and attention. As we saw when we analyzed criterion 2, studies of autism reveal that memory and attention systems operate in a crosscutting pattern across all of the intelligences, failing to support the independence of the intelligences. As we have seen, autistics attend to and remember the trees,

Task interference is more a function of attention than of similarity of input.

but not the forests, regardless of the intelligence with which they are dealing. If this incredible focus on detail were unique to one intelligence, we would have support for the independence of intelligences. Because perceptual gating and selective memory of autistics occurs across intelligences, the evidence contradicts the claim of intelligence-specific memory and attention.

The other two types of experimental tasks taken as support of the independence of the intelligences, interference and transference, also provide questionable support.

Studies of Task Interference

Certain kinds of input interfere or fail to interfere with different types of performance. For example, experimental studies show lack of cross-interference between linguistic and musical input, but presence of cross-interference between two linguistic tasks. For example, as we write this, music is playing and it does not distract us, but if the music had lyrics, it would interfere with our writing. MI theory takes this lack of interference between words and music, but presence of interference between words and words, as evidence for the separateness of the intelligences. We could, however, demonstrate lack of cross-interference between a number of skills within each of broad multiple intelligences. For example, the processing involved in creating a geometry proof is quite different than that involved in simple addition. Hearing random digits would interfere considerably with an addition task, but far less with the solution of a geometry problem. A modular view, rather than an interpretation of broad intelligences, is again supported. Task interference is more a function of attention than of similarity of input. It is hard to distract a child intent on succeeding in a video game, whether you use lights or words or numbers. It is easy to distract the same video game addict, though, with just about any kind of stimuli if you are trying to distract him or her from a boring math calculations worksheet.

Studies of Transference

If a person receives training in one skill, it may or may not facilitate performance of others. Gardner (1993, p. 8) poses the rhetorical question: "…does training in mathematics enhance one's musical abilities, or vice versa?" The presumed answer: no. But in fact there is evidence of transfer of skills across Gardner's intelligences: Children early trained in music perform better in math.

> At UC Irvine, Gordon Shaw suspected that all higher-order thinking is characterized by similar patterns of neuron firing…. So Shaw and Frances Rauscher gave 19 preschoolers piano or signing lessons. After eight months, the researchers found, the children "dramatically improved in spatial reasoning," compared with children given no music lessons, as shown in their ability to work mazes, draw geometric figures and copy patterns of two-color blocks. The mechanism behind the "Mozart effect" remains murky, but Shaw suspects that when children exercise cortical neurons by listening to classical music, they are also strengthening circuits used for mathematics. (Begley, 1996, p. 57).

Remarkable examples of "transference" across intelligences have been documented. For example, groups of high school students trained in chess (Steinem, 1992) or calculus (Mathews,1988) later performed better across the curriculum. These kinds of transformations, however, are best interpreted as mediated by a change in self-concept or self-esteem, rather than "transference" in the usual sense.

Lack of transference within the intelligence is just as much a threat to MI theory as existence of transference across the intelligences. Any teacher can cite plenty of examples of lack of transference within the broad intelligences: Training in classification does little for computation in long division; training in spelling does not improve oracy; mastery of the basketball pass does little for the football tackle; training in flower arrangement does not improve map reading.

The experimental evidence, in general, indicates the independence of human skills and is consistent with the conclusion that there is a multiplicity of distinct human skills, each depending on coordination of a different set of the neurons in the community of neurons.

Criterion 7.

Support From Psychometric Findings

The results of psychological tests form the basis of the seventh criterion for intelligences in MI theory.

> "To the extent that the tasks that purportedly assess one intelligence correlate highly with one another, and less highly with those that purportedly assess other intelligences, my formulation enhances its credibility (Gardner, 1983, p. 66)."

Psychometric research and theory indicates the eight intelligences are far too broad to meet these conventional tests of psychometric validity. It would be possible to cite hundreds of references to research

From a psychometric perspective, to lump independent skills into one category simply makes no sense.

demonstrating independence of measures of psychological variables which fall within the same intelligence. The Spectrum test results revealed tests of the same intelligence did not correlate in ways they would have to if the facets of an intelligence were subcomponents of a single intelligence, see page 17.8.

Let us cite a few examples from our own work: Within the presumed interpersonal intelligence, affective-role taking, empathy, and prosocial development all show inde-

Each of the eight intelligences consists of many discrete skills. Calling them all examples of one or another intelligence does not change reality; each of those discrete skills may or may not correlate with each other, and almost certainly shows a different pattern of intercorrelations within different populations.

pendence and a different developmental course (Kagan & Knudson, 1982; Knudson & Kagan, 1982; Kagan & Knudson, 1983). This independence and differential pattern of development of interpersonal skills means that lumping them all in one category and describing them all as a reflection of a single interpersonal intelligence, is inconsistent with the psychometric data. In a parallel set of findings, reliable and valid measures of affiliation do not correlate highly with reliable and valid measures of cooperativeness (Kagan & Knight, 1981). The psychometric data reveals there is a multiplicity of interpersonal skills or intelligences, not one general interpersonal intelligence.

Similarly, when we turn to the other intelligences, the psychometric data is more consistent with a multiplicity of intelligences, not the existence of a relatively few broad intelligences. For example, two of the most extensively studied visual/spatial skills are field-independence and visual perspective role-taking. These fundamental visual/spatial skills, though, are independent (Knudson & Kagan, 1977), not correlated in the way we would expect if there were one broad visual/spatial intelligence which encompassed both sets of

skills. The psychometric findings reveal there is not one visual/spatial intelligence, but many. (See the Facet Tests in Chapter 18.)

Psychometric findings do not support the existence of one general visual/spatial intelligence or any of the other broad MI theory intelligences. The psychometric data, like the brain research, supports the existence of many visual/spatial intelligences or skills. Calling all those discrete skills examples of one visual/spatial intelligence does not change reality; each of those discrete skills may or may not correlate with each other, and almost certainly shows a different pattern of intercorrelations within different populations. Each of the intelligences consists of many discrete skills.

It follows that to describe a student as high or low in visual/spatial intelligence would not be as helpful in designing developmentally appropriate learning experiences for each of the separate skills in the visual/spatial domain. Common experience, psychometric evidence, and the demands of a differentiated curriculum all indicate we would be better off with the multiplicity metaphor rather than one which gives us a few broad categories. Broad categories mask the fantastic complexity of human skills and experience.

Lumping and Splitting

So far we have been pointing out that MI theory fails to meet the test of psychometric validity because it lumps too many discrete skills under each of the eight broad categories of intelligence. It is lumping when it should be splitting; the theory needs to be more discriminating if it is to correspond to reality. Oddly, MI theory, overall has us focus on the separation of the intelligences and ignores their interrelations. In this regard, the theory overemphasizes splitting, when a bit of lumping might better conform to reality.

Interpersonal and Intrapersonal Intelligences

Particularly questionable is the claim that interpersonal intelligence and intrapersonal intelligence could meet the psychometric test of divergent validity. Gardner lumps the two into a chapter called "Personal Intelligences" and states,

> In the course of development, these two forms of knowledge are intimately intermingled in any culture, with knowledge of one's own person perennially dependent upon the ability to apply lessons learned from the observation of other people, while knowledge of others draws upon the internal discriminations the individual routinely makes.... Under ordinary circumstances, neither form of intelligence can develop without the other (Gardner, 1983, p. 241)."

Empathy is the ability to recognize and feel that in others which one has experienced. To the extent a person is blind to a feeling in oneself, that person will be insensitive to that feeling in others. One of the primary tools of every depth psychologist is the ability to analyze the feelings the patient invokes in oneself (countertransference). If, as Gardner admits, understanding of oneself and understanding others are inextricably intertwined; they fail to meet the psychometric criterion of divergent validity.

MI theory is based on the assumption that the separate intelligences are relatively independent. Gardner does not deny general intelligence, but denies the importance of

general intelligence for real-world functioning, and makes the claim that it is largely artifactual, a function of short answer paper and pencil tests which are dependent on linguistic and logical test taking skills (Gardner, 1993, Pp. 39-40).

There is almost universal agreement, however, on the importance of an overriding factor or factors beyond the separate intelligences or skills. Different theorists call it by different names ("executive function," "positive manifold," "central integrative function," "general intelligence") and interpret it in terms of different neurological and psychological theories (speed of reaction time, number and type of dendrites, general differentiation, amount and type of neural transmitters).

MI theory, in contrast, would have us believe in the relative independence of the intelligences; that they do not depend on some common property or properties (Gardner, 1993, Pp. 42-43). This view is in

MI theory is lumping when it should be splitting; the theory needs to be more discriminating if it is to correspond to reality. Oddly, the theory also does some splitting when a bit of lumping might better conform to reality.

direct contradiction with a great deal of psychometric evidence that different measures of intelligence and different subscales of intelligence correlate positively (Anastasi, 1958; Cronbach, 1970; Guilford, 1982). As Sternberg states,

> One could easily fill a book as long as Gardner's with counter evidence to the theory's claim of independent multiple intelligences, which, unfortunately, is the central claim of the theory as it now stands (Sternberg, 1983, p. 221).

Gardner dismisses that contradictory evidence as due to the fact that traditional psychometric data is based on paper and pencil tasks which favor linguistic and logical functioning. In fact, however, nonpaper and pencil tests such as the block design of spatial ability, the Draw-A-Person Test, and Raven's Progressive Matrices consistently reveal strong correlations with purely verbal tests of intelligence such as the vocabulary and comprehension subscales of the WISC or WAIS, as well as paper and pencil tests of logical and mathematical functioning. The correlation between spatial and linguistic intelligence subscales while not as high as between spatial and logical/mathematical subscales is still quite substantial.

The community of neurons is complex — not only are there a greater number of distinguishable subdivisions of specialized neurons than accounted for by MI theory, but those subdivisions are more intimately interrelated than accounted for by MI theory.

The psychometric data which demonstrates the interrelation among intelligences is consistent with what we saw when we examined the physical structure of the brain and with the breakdown of function across intelligences in autism. The community of neurons is complex — not only are there more independent subparts than accounted for by MI theory, but those subparts are more intimately interrelated than accounted for by MI theory.

Criterion 8.
Susceptibility to Encoding in a Symbol System

MI theory indicates symbol systems evolved to represent and communicate knowledge, stating

> a primary characteristic of human intelligence may well be its "natural" gravitation toward embodiment in a symbolic system (Gardner, 1983, p. 66).

We have words, math symbols, gestures, and musical notation. These are neat examples of the ability to encode four intelligences into distinct symbol systems. But where are the neat symbol systems for the intrapersonal, naturalist, spatial, and interpersonal intelligences? Can we seriously suggest that maps capture the range of skills which fall into the category of visual/spatial intelligence? Is interpersonal intelligence fully expressed in the ability to encode and decode facial expressions and gestures? Leadership skills do not reduce neatly to encoding facial expressions. Only half of the MI theory intelligences have a neat symbol system which captures or expresses the range of activities presumed to be manifestations of that intelligence.

"Meeting the Eight Criteria"

In this chapter we have encountered the eight criteria of MI theory. We found many of the eight intelligences fail to meet the

Problems with the Eight Criteria

1. Brain Isolation

Brain study reveals each intelligence is not located in one place in the brain; there are a multiplicity of intelligences which can be isolated.

2. Exceptional Individuals

Exceptional individuals can be found in every field and so can be taken as support for any proposed intelligence; savants show splinter skills, not "intelligences." They demonstrate high and low performance within the same intelligence.

3. Core Operations

There is no single set of operations per intelligence; operations are common across intelligences; "core operations" can be defined for every human skill.

4. Developmental History

Development is marked by common features across the intelligences: ability to integrate progressively more information, and movement from concrete to abstract processing, occur in all areas. Intelligence specific end-states could be defined for any candidate intelligence.

5. Evolutionary Plausibility

Chimps show leadership, but they don't sing. Genetic fitness argues against separate, semi-autonomous intelligences in favor of the ability to integrate information across domains.

6. Experimental Support

Perception, attention, and cognition show common patterns across intelligences, not unique patterns within intelligences. Transference and interference studies are often not supportive: transference is often absent within intelligences; interference can occur across intelligences.

7. Psychometric Support

The multiple intelligences are far too broad to receive psychometric support. Project Spectrum provides multiple measures of each intelligence, but the lack of correlation of measures of the same intelligence supports a multiplicity interpretation; measures of the same intelligence don't correlate with each other. Intelligence-fair visual-spatial performance measures like the block design (which use no words), correlate highly with linguistic measures of intelligence, and with general intelligence.

8. Symbol System

Music, math, language, and the body all have their symbol systems, but there is no adequate symbol system to express the range of skills for the naturalist, interpersonal, intrapersonal, and visual/spatial intelligences.

criteria. More critically, we found the criteria themselves to be faulty. Some criteria (brain isolation, exceptional individuals, core operations, definable end-states, evolutionary plausibility) admit a multiplicity of intelligences. Other criteria (symbol systems, experimental support, psychometric validity) admit only a few or none of the intelligences proposed by the theory. In sum, many of the intelligences fail to fit many of the MI theory criteria, and there are serious flaws in the criteria themselves. For a summary, see box: Problems with the Eight Criteria.

Brain research and the analysis of the eight criteria suggest there are a multiplicity of ways to be smart. Intelligent behavior involves an ongoing interaction among a multiplicity of intelligences. It is to that theory, then, multiplicity theory, that we now turn.

● ● ● ● ● ● ● ● ● ●

References

Anastasi, A. *Differential Psychology: Individual and Group Differences in Behavior (3rd Edition).* New York: Macmillian, 1958.

Begley, S. *Your Child's Brain.* Newsweek, 1996, February 19, 55-62.

Coleman, M. & Gillberg, C. *The biology of autistic syndromes.* New York: Praeger, 1985.

Cronbach, L. J. *Essentials of Psychological Testing (3rd Edition).* New York: Harper & Row, 1970.

Damasio, A. R. & Damasio, H. *Brain and Language.* **Scientific American**, 1992, **267(3)**, 89-86.

Fischbach, G. D. *Mind and Brain.* **Scientific American**, 1992, **267(3)**, 48-57.

Folstein, S. & Rutter, M. *Infantile autism: a genetic study of 21 twin pairs.* **Journal of Child Psychology and Psychiatry**, 1977, **18**, 297-321.

Frith, U. & Baron-Cohen, S. *Perception in autistic children.* In D. J. Cohen, A. Donnellan, & R. Paul (eds.) Handbook of Autism and Pervasive Developmental Disorders, New York: Wiley, 1987.

Frith, U. *Autism: Explaining the Enigma.* Blackwell Publishers, Ltd. Oxford: 1989.

Gardner, H. *Frames of Mind. The Theory of Multiple Intelligences.* New York: Basic Books, 1983.

Gardner, H. *Multiple Intelligences. The Theory in Practice.* New York: Basic Books, 1993.

Gazzaniga, M. *The Social Brain: Discovering the Networks of the Mind.* New York: Basic Books, 1985.

Guilford, J. P. *The Nature of Human Intelligence.* New York: McGraw-Hill, 1967.

Guilford, J. P. *Cognitive Psychology's Ambiguities: Some Suggested Remedies.* **Psychological Review**, 1982, **89**, 48-59.

Kagan, S. & Knight, G. P. *Social motives among Anglo American and Mexican American children: Experimental and projective measures.* **Journal of Research in Personality,** 1981, *15,* 93-106.

Kagan, S. & Knudson, K. H. M. *Differential development of affective role-taking ability and prosocial behaviors.* **The Journal of Genetic Psychology,** 1983, *143,* 97-102.

Kagan, S. & Knudson, K. H. M. *Relationship of empathy and affective role-taking in young children.* Journal of Genetic Psychology, 1982, 141, 149-150.

Knudson, K. H. M., & Kagan, S. *Differential development of empathy and prosocial behavior.* Journal of Genetic Psychology, 1982, 140, 249-251.

Knudson, K. H. M., & Kagan, S. *Visual perspective role-taking and field-independence among Anglo American and Mexican American children of two ages.* **Journal of Genetic Psychology,** 1977, *131,* 243-253.

Kolvin, I. Ounsted, C. & Roth, M. *Studies in the childhood psychoses. V. Cerebral dysfunction and childhood psychoses.* **British Journal of Psychiatry,** 1971, *118,* 407-414.

Mathews, J. *Escalante. The Best Teacher in America.* New York: Henry Holt, 1988.

Rimland, B. *Inside the mind of the autistic savant.* **Psychology Today,** 1978, *12(3),* 68-90.

Scheerer, M., Rothmann, E., & Goldstein, K. *A case of "idiot savant": an experimental study of personality organization.* **Psychology Monographs,** 1945, *58,* 1-63.

Steinem, G. *The Royal Knights of Harlem, In Revolution from Within: A Book of Self-Esteem.* New York: Little, Brown & Co., 1992.

Sternberg, R. J. *How Much Gall Is Too Much Gall? A Review of Frames of Mind: The Theory of Multiple Intelligences.* **Contemporary Education Review,** 1983, *2(3),* 215-224.

Treffert, D. A. *Extraordinary people. Understanding "Idiot Savants."* New York: Harper & Row, 1989.

Beyond Multiple Intelligences — a Multiplicity

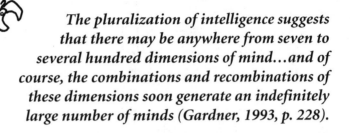

The pluralization of intelligence suggests that there may be anywhere from seven to several hundred dimensions of mind…and of course, the combinations and recombinations of these dimensions soon generate an indefinitely large number of minds (Gardner, 1993, p. 228).

Everything should be made as simple as possible, but not simpler. — Albert Einstein

If the brain is a community of neurons rather than housing separate frames of mind, we should find not one linguistic intelligence or one spatial intelligence, but rather many discrete linguistic intelligences and many discrete spatial intelligences all of which coordinate their efforts. This is not a trivial distinction. If there is one linguistic intelligence, it makes sense to speak of someone as "word smart" or "linguistically talented". If we recognize there are many discrete linguistic intelligences, we recognize a label such as "word smart" as a dangerous overgeneralization. The great orator might be a poor reader; the biblical scholar who, for hours on end takes great pleasure in finding subtle nuances in words and phrases,

mul•ti•ple
Having, relating to, or consisting of more than one individual, element, part, or other component.

mul•ti•plic•i•ty
The state of being various; a large number.
Source: American Heritage Dictionary

might have no interest at all in puns or rhymes. Educators have begun to speak of someone who is "visually/spatially intelligent." But does map reading ability really predict skill or delight in color combining? Does ability to mentally rotate something in space have the least bit to do with picking socks, slacks, and shirt with colors which do not clash? Does the ability to estimate one's grocery bill before being rung up at the check stand correlate with skills in syllogistic logic? Is there just one logical/mathematical intelligence, or would we better off thinking in terms of many discrete logical and mathematical intelligences?

We make here the same argument against the multiple intelligences that MI theory makes against the IQ Test. MI theory advanced education by arguing it is more useful for educators to think not in terms of one general intelligence; it demonstrated the usefulness of thinking in terms of many intelligences. A similar advance for education can be made by thinking not in terms of one linguistic, or one mathematical, or one spatial intelligence, but many. Just as one general intelligence was far too broad and encompassing to survive the test of advancing brain science and usefulness for educators, each of the intelligences of MI theory are also far too broad. We are in the process of developing more differentiated models of intelligence.

As we have seen, MI theory uses eight criteria to determine the existence of an intelligence. Here we will use the eight criteria to ask a simple question: Is it more meaningful to speak of a single linguistic, mathematical, or spatial intelligence, or is it more meaningful to speak of many in-

telligences in each of those domains? Are we in closer approximation to reality thinking in terms of multiple intelligences, or a multiplicity of intelligences? Can we count our intelligences on the fingers of both hands, or do we need all the hairs on a young man's head, plus some?

● ● ● ● ● ● ● ● ● ● ● ● ● ● ●

1. Brain Isolation:
Boy Kisses Girl

MI theory claims that if an intelligence can be destroyed (or spared) in isolation by a specific lesion, that is evidence for the independence of that intelligence. It turns out that if we use this criterion, we have very strong evidence for many linguistic intelligences, not one linguistic intelligence.

MI theory advanced education by arguing there is no such thing as one general intelligence, claiming there are many. A similar advance for education can be made by claiming there is no such thing as one linguistic or one mathematical or one spatial intelligence, but many.

Let's analyze brain structures which are the foundation of linguistic functioning. Using brain isolation as our criterion, we find concepts, words for concepts, and ability to pronounce the words for concepts are all separate intelligences — any one can be destroyed or spared independently, depending on the site of specific lesions (Damasio & Damasio, 1992). Many linguistic intelligences may be lost without losing other linguistic intelligences, depending on the site of a lesion. See box: Specific Lesions Produce Specific Losses.

1. Brain Isolation:

Specific Lesions Produce Specific Losses

Depending on the site of a brain lesion, patients lose some linguistic skills while retaining others. Linguistic skills are not located in one site in the brain. If brain localization is our criterion, there is not one verbal/linguistic intelligence but many! The following are specific skills which can be lost due to a brain lesion — while other verbal/linguistic skills are retained:

▼ Proper Nouns vs. Common Nouns

Patients may lose the ability to recall or use proper nouns while retaining a use of common nouns. For example, the patient has no problem talking about cars, but cannot say "Chevrolet" or "Ford."

▼ Nouns vs. Syntax

Patients may lose the ability to use both proper and common nouns correctly, while maintaining excellent syntax and fine use of adjectives, verbs, prepositions, and conjunctions. The patient tells us of something large and gray lumbering through the forest, but cannot say the word "elephant."

▼ Animals vs. Tools

Patients may lose the ability to recall the names of specific classes of nouns (animals) while retaining the ability to recall other specific classes of nouns (tools). A patient of this sort might recognize a raccoon and readily describe details of its behavior, but be unable to name it. The same patient has no trouble naming tools or items from other classes of nouns.

▼ Selecting Words

Patients may lose the ability to assemble phonemes into words, and lose the ability to select entire word forms. These patients might say "lolipant" for "elephant" or "headman" instead of "president."

▼ Grammatical Processing & Production

Patients may lose the ability to speak with or interpret proper grammar. Patients with damage in the anterior perisylvian sector speak in flat tones, take long pauses between words, leave out conjunctions and pronouns, and have problems with grammatical order. With this type of lesion, grammatical processing as well as production is compromised: given sentences like "The boy was kissed by the girl," these patients get confused as to who kissed whom! They function fine with many other dimensions of language.

Source: *Damasio & Damasio, 1992.*

What are the implications of these many discrete, brain-based linguistic skills? They point away from any notion of a single brain-based linguistic intelligence. The same type of evidence argues against each of the eight intelligences. There is a multiplicity of intelligences, not just eight. There is no one brain location for a linguistic intelligence which can be spared or destroyed in isolation. Linguistic intelligences do not reside in one place in the brain; they fail the test of brain isolation. Or, better put, each discrete linguistic intelligence passes the test of brain isolation too well. If we accept brain isolation as the criterion, we need to abandon the concept of a unified linguistic intelligence in favor of many linguistic intelligences.

Brain structure and function is consistent with our everyday experience with students: We all know students who are great poets, but poor essayists, and vice versa. We know students who give a great flowery speech, but are poor at punctuation.

We align ourselves with reality and do ourselves and our students a favor when we stop talking about students who are either high or low in linguistic intelligence. By abandoning the notion of unified intelligences, we will design and deliver a more differentiated curriculum and instruction.

● ● ● ● ● ● ● ● ● ● ● ● ● ● ● ●
2. Exceptional Individuals:
"37, 37, 37...111"

Savants are a second powerful demonstration that the multiple intelligences are too broad. Let's take a peek at a pair of twins in action:

Before, sadly, they were forcibly separated from each other and as a consequence lost their fantastic powers, George and his identical twin brother Charles could announce the day of the week of any given day over a span of 80,000 years, 40,000 forward and 40,000 backward. They could beat a computer in naming the years Eas-

> **We align ourselves with reality and do ourselves and our students a favor when we stop talking about students who are either high or low in linguistic intelligence. By abandoning the notion of a single linguistic intelligence, we will design and deliver a more differentiated curriculum and instruction.**

ter will fall on March 23. They amused themselves by trading 20-digit prime numbers. They could rapidly factor with ease almost any number. In an amazing feat immortalized in the film *Rainman*, when the twins saw a box of matches fall from a table and the matches scatter on the floor, George and Charles simultaneously called out "37, 37, 37" followed by "111." Later, when the matches were counted there were exactly 111, which, of course, is three sets of 37 (Sacks, 1985; Treffert, 1989).

MI theory takes the fantastic skills of the savants as evidence of the independence of intelligences because savants who are fantastic in math may be subnormal in all other areas; musical savants may be incapable of a conversation. While the savants do demonstrate there is no one general intelligence, the existence of a musical savant does not demonstrate there is one musical intelligence, and the existence of mathematical savants does not demonstrate the existence of a single mathematical intelligence.

In fact, the general pattern of skills among savants are a powerful demonstration of the lack of existence of any single intelligence of the type postulated by MI theory. Consider this: George and Charles could remember 30 digit strings and astound people by immediately answering questions like, "What day of the week will June 6th fall in year 91260?" At the same time, they could not count to 30, add simple numbers, or give correct change from a ten dollar bill following a six dollar purchase! Clearly, if there were one general mathematical intelligence, we would not observe such extreme independence of math skills among savants.

There is a multiplicity of intelligences within each of the broad multiple intelligences categories; excellence in one type of performance within an intelligence does not predict excellence in another.

This pattern of isolated skills is common in all types of savants. For example, savants who can give the dictionary definition of thousands of words verbatim cannot write. Others who have photographic recall of the directions from one place to another from just one look at a map, or from just one car ride, demonstrate no special abilities in art, sculpture, color discrimination or other skills presumably associated with the "visual/spatial intelligence." There is not a single visual/spatial intelligence, a single linguistic intelligence, or a single mathematical intelligence. There are many. There is a multiplicity of intelligences.

● ● ● ● ● ● ● ● ● ●
3. Core Operations:

Geometry and Algebra

The core operations associated with geometry are distinct from those of algebra (many who do quite well in geometry fail algebra). The core operations in singing a song are distinct from those in playing a musical instrument; the core operations in writing a coherent essay are a world apart from those of carrying on a conversation. This is additional evidence in support of multiplicity theory: it is more meaningful to speak of many mathematical intelligences, not a single mathematical intelligence, many verbal/linguistic intelligences, not a unified verbal/linguistic intelligence.

● ● ● ● ● ● ● ● ● ● ●
4. End-States:

The Drummer and the Diva

The expert performances of the popular drummer and the opera diva are no more similar to each other than each is to the orator. The drummer and the diva each have a very different course of development, and each, when fully developed, will have an entirely different set of end-state skills. There is not one end-state that characterizes all the very diverse skills within the category of the musical/rhythmic intelligence or any of the other eight intelligences. It is absurd to speak of excellent map reading and excellent oil painting as achieving excellence or full maturity in the "visual/spatial intelligence." The various skills within each intelligence are not manifestations of a striving toward a common set of developmental end-states. Excellence in one type of performance within an intelligence does not predict excellence in another because there is a multiplicity of intelligences.

5. Evolutionary Plausibility:
Advantage for Multiplicity

There is a selective advantage in diversification. Imagine two types of brain organizations, one in which all kinesthetic skills were narrowly located in one place in the brain; the other in which a variety of kinesthetic skills existed, but were more dispersed. With a specific lesion or lack of development in a specific part of the brain, the brain with diversification of types and locations of skills would survive, the one with a single location or single set of skills would not. With regard to evolutionary plausibility, diversification gets the nod. Thus evolutionary plausibility stacks strongly against the single skill, single location scenario. Multiplicity theory is far more plausible from an evolutionary perspective than the notion of a relatively few discrete intelligences. With a multiplicity of intelligences the brain can combine and recombine skills within and across intelligences in an infinite number of ways. A portion of the brain now used to sequence a musical string is later used to sequence a linguistic string. This affords flexibility, and flexibility is the foremost consideration in granting evolutionary plausibility.

6. Experimental Tasks:
Keyboarding and Tackling

Perform a thought experiment: Train up a group of students at keyboarding. After weeks or months of training, they are all extremely skilled at keyboarding. Now take the whole bunch out on the football field. Will their new keyboarding skills improve their ability to make a good football tackle? No transference occurs. It is just plain silly to lump specific fine motor skills with gross motor skills and say they are both manifestations of a single bodily/kinesthetic intelligence. Similarly, different fine motor skills, like printing and typing, do not transfer. As we became better at typing, our printing became worse.

The rod and frame test measures ability to determine the true upright. It is perhaps the most extensively researched spatial test. Success does not correlate with sensitivity to or ability to paint a still-life or a host of other skills presumed to be a reflection of a single visual/spatial intelligence.

MI theory takes transference (training in one skill improving another) as evidence of the skills being manifestations of the same intelligence. Anyone who has coached a sport knows how unlikely it is to get transference: Learning to pass well does not improve dribbling. Holding general conditioning constant, improving the freestyle stroke does not improve the breaststroke. Transference is difficult: learning spelling words from a list, for many students does not transfer to use of those same words during free writing. Again, support falls on the side of a multiplicity of intelligences.

7. Psychometric Findings:

Creative vs. Athletic Movement

The most fundamental tenant of psychometric validity is construct validity. For a construct to be validated psychometrically, it must have convergent validity and divergent validity. That is, different measures of the same construct must correlate well with each other (convergent validity) and not highly with measures of other constructs (divergent validity). For example, if the construct of a kinesthetic intelligence were to receive validity, creative movement and athletic movement activities would have to correlate better with each other than with subscales of other intelligences.

The psychometric pattern of results completely fails to support the notion of one general musical intelligence, or any of the other broad intelligences proposed by MI theory.

Gardner recognizes the need for intelligences to obtain construct validity.

> There is every reason to expect that each natural kind will have several (or more) subcomponents. For example, linguistic intelligence clearly entails several dissociable elements, such as the capacities to conduct syntactic analyses, to acquire literacy, and to learn languages by ear. However, it is also likely that, in most normal human behaviors, the several subcomponents of an intelligence should cluster together, while they should show little inclination to correlate with subcomponents of other intelligences. This claim could and should be tested empirically (Gardner, 1993, p. 45).

In Project Spectrum Gardner and his associates designed a battery of intelligence-fair tests to measure the profile of intelligences of young children. Project Spectrum was initiated to find the early indicators of the seven intelligences. Several activities were included in a number of the intelligences including two in math, four in science, two in music, two in language, two in movement, and two in social skills (Gardner, 1993, Pp. 91-92). Results of intercorrelations among the Spectrum measures indicated a lack of construct validity for all of the eight intelligences, save math. Subscales of the various intelligences do not correlate any better with each other than they do with subscales presumed to measure other intelligences! Of all the activities tested, only the two numbers activities correlated quite highly ($r = 0.78$), consistent with the conclusion they are measures of one underlying dimension. All of the rest of the activities showed no significant correlations. The two music activities ($r = -0.07$) and the two science activities ($r = 0.08$) showed no correlation at all, indicating complete independence (Gardner, 1993, p. 95).

Overall, he psychometric pattern of results completely fails to support the notion of one general musical intelligence, or any of the other broad intelligences proposed by MI theory. Although the two Spectrum math activities did correlate, without much effort, it would be possible to design a variety of math activities which do not correlate. To speak, then, of one kinesthetic intelligence, one musical intelligence, or even one mathematical intelligence is not consistent with the general pattern of psychometric data.

Anecdotal evidence is also consistent with the conclusion that reality is better described by speaking of linguistic intelligences rather than a single general linguistic intelligence. Consider a child from the Spectrum classroom (Gardner, 1993, Pp. 104-105):

> ...a child who had been an outstanding storyteller was very reluctant to start writing, and experienced difficulty both with his fine-motor coordination and sound-letter connections. At the two-year follow-up, he was reported still to love listening to stories and performing in class plays.

Skill at telling stories and joy in listening to stories do not predict skill or joy in writing. There is not one linguistic intelligence, but many. Both anecdotal evidence and the psychometric data align well with the view there are not a limited number of discrete intelligences, but rather a multiplicity of intelligences.

● ● ● ● ● ● ● ● ● ● ● ● ●
8. Symbol Systems:
A Multiplicity of Symbols

There is no single symbol system to encode or process activities which are a reflection of the interpersonal intelligence because there are many discrete interpersonal skills. There is no single interpersonal intelligence. Similarly there is no single symbol system which captures a sense of self-esteem, an inner knowledge of strengths and weaknesses, and the ability to control impulses. All of those skills are conceptualized best not as manifestations of one intrapersonal intelligence, but rather as discrete skills or different intrapersonal intelligences. The various intrapersonal skills cannot be symbolized by a common symbol system because they are manifestations of different discrete abilities, not a single intrapersonal intelligence. With a stretch, we might think of the peri-

odic table as a symbol system of the chemist, but it has nothing to do with the ability to distinguish or understand animals. There is no single symbol system for the naturalist intelligence because there is no single naturalist intelligence. Once again, we have support for a multiplicity of intelligences.

● ● ● ● ● ● ● ● ● ● ● ● ●
Multiplicity Theory Gets the Nod

Just as there is no one general intelligence, there is no one general linguistic intelligence and no one general mathematical or musical intelligence. All of the MI theory intelligences break down under scrutiny. Individuals cannot easily be pigeonholed. We have a multiplicity of intelligences — far too many to be captured by a small number of simple labels.

There are important advantages for education in thinking in terms of a multiplicity of intelligences, rather than a relatively small discrete number of intelligences. If we think of one kinesthetic intelligence, we might fall into the trap of labeling a student as strong or weak in kinesthetic intelligence. A more differentiated view is that the student is strong in certain kinesthetic skills and weak in others. The multiplicity view supports a more differentiated view not just of our students, but of our curriculum. The teacher who thinks in terms of one kinesthetic intelligence might be satisfied if a lesson includes some movement. Adopting the multiplicity view, the teacher would be more likely to ask if the lesson would be enriched by inclusion of mime, manipulatives, dance and a host of other kinesthetic activities.

Multiple Intelligences vs. Multiplicity of Intelligences

Multiple Intelligences Theory	Multiplicity Theory
Number of Intelligences	
Manageable number	
	Too many to count
Impact on Teachers and Students	
Teacher friendly	
Stereotypes likely	Intimidating
Student self-labeling likely	Stereotypes not likely
Social comparison likely	Self-labeling unlikely
	Social comparison unlikely
Impact on Curriculum & Instruction	
Less differentiated	
	More differentiated
Relation to Brain Science	
Less brain-based	
	More brain-based
Psychometric Support	
Not supported	
	Supported
Evolutionary Plausibility	
Implausible	
	Plausible

Assessment, too, is enriched by multiplicity theory. We need to assess multiple dimensions of each intelligence, providing a far more differentiated road map for curriculum and instruction.

Yet another advantage of multiplicity theory is its consequences for student self-perception. MI theory shows that thinking in terms of several intelligences, rather than one general intelligence, makes students less likely to stack themselves up against each other using one yardstick.

Spencer & Miguel Kagan: *Multiple Intelligences*

Self-understanding and acceptance would be furthered far more if students did not think of one general linguistic or one general mathematical intelligence. Students need to think of themselves in more differentiated ways.

An argument against multiplicity theory is that it is not practical for schools to assess and design curriculum and instruction for a huge number of intelligences.

It turns out, though, as we have seen, we can teach with and develop a multiplicity of intelligences without designing different learning experiences for each student. Matching, stretching, and celebrating a large number of intelligences is not dependent on assessment, and not dependent on identifying any fixed number of intelligences.

It is liberating to abandon a fixation on any limited number of intelligences and think in terms of fostering development among students in a multiplicity of directions. Consider the Key School approach. In the Key School there are a dozen pods in a variety of areas ranging from architecture to gardening, from cooking to "making money." Over time, pods are added, deleted, or transformed. There is no reason students can not rotate through a fantastic number of pods throughout their educational careers, as we match and stretch a fantastic number of intelligences.

The possibilities are limitless. Given the multiplicity of intelligences it would be wise for us as educators to greatly broaden our curriculum and instruction. It is this gift to education, the broadening of curriculum and instruction in a multiplicity

Just as a movement away from thinking in terms of several intelligences rather than one general intelligence makes students less likely to stack themselves up against one other using one yardstick, self-understanding and acceptance is furthered even more when students do not think of one general linguistic, or one mathematical intelligence. Students need to think of themselves in a more differentiated way.

of ways, that is the greatest contribution of MI theory. The more ways we teach, the more students we reach.

• • • • • • • • • • ▶

References

Damasio, A. R. & Damasio, H. *Brain and Language.* ***Scientific American***, 1992, ***267(3)***, 89-86.

Gardner, H. *Multiple Intelligences. The Theory in Practice.* New York: Basic Books, 1993.

Sacks, O. *The Man Who Mistook His Wife for a Hat.* New York: Perennial Library, 1985.

Treffert, D. A. *Extraordinary People. Understanding "Idiot Savants."* New York: Harper & Row, 1989.

Contributions of MI Theory

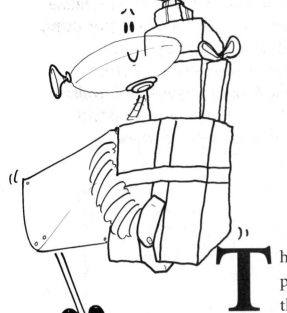

*You see things, and you say "Why?"
...I dream things that never were,
and I say "Why not?"*
— *George Bernard Shaw*

T he evaluation of MI theory cannot be complete if we examine only how well the theory meshes with brain science, or furthers our knowledge of brain functioning. The evaluation of a theory must consider, as well, its impact. From this latter perspective, the contributions of multiple intelligences theory are spectacular. Education has never seen a more transformative theory. Education will forever be transformed in the wake of MI theory — transformed in positive ways along many dimensions.

MI theory is sparking powerful visions of what education can be. It invigorates thought, hope, and experimentation. It is revitalizing the search for more authentic, student-centered approaches to curriculum, instruction, and assessment.

MI theory is touching a nerve in education. It is a catalyst, releasing a tremendous amount of energy. The theory offers a simple idea: there is not one but many ways to be smart. Educators worldwide are finding in that simple idea a stimulus to transform classrooms. MI theory is sparking powerful visions of what education can be. It invigorates thought, hope, and experimentation. It is revitalizing the search for more authentic, student-centered approaches to curriculum, instruction, and assessment. It shifts our attributions: A slow student is not dumb, just smart in ways we need to find.

It shifts our direction: let's not teach only facts, let's teach the various ways to be smart. It transforms how we look at students, ourselves, and our mission as educators.

Juxtaposed against these powerful, positive results of MI theory are the potential negative consequences it can foster: a too narrow, over simplified view of intelligences, and well-intended but socially irresponsible assessment techniques which would produce the predictable pitfalls of labeling students and pigeonholing them into different classrooms with differentiated curriculum — tracking which would limit the range of educational experiences for all students. The father of MI theory, Howard Gardner, has urged that we must remain vigilant against the pitfalls of tracking which can result from misapplication of the theory.

The question, then, becomes: Can we harness the powerful spirit and energy of the positive MI visions without becoming entangled in the traps of testing, labeling, and sorting students? The answer is yes. To harvest the fruits of MI theory we do not need to test or even assess students, and we do not need to shunt them off toward different educational experiences. We can throw out the bathwater while saving the baby.

The powerful MI visions are simple. Vision 1. Matching our instruction with the ways students learn: Teaching in more ways, we reach more students and reach all students in more ways. Vision 2. Stretching all intelligences: Elevating the development of the multiplicity of intelligences to a central position in our curriculum, we more fully prepare our students for success in the varied work and social situations they will encounter in our fast-changing world. Development of the intelligences becomes a guiding light for curriculum development for the twenty-first Century. Vision 3. Celebrating the intelligences: By appreciating the individuality of each student, the multiplicity of ways each is smart, and allowing each student to understand and celebrate his or her own uniqueness and that of others, we transform in positive ways each student's self-concept and their social perceptions and social relations. Students find in themselves and others intellectual strengths to celebrate, strengths which were masked by IQ-style thinking. The three visions are as noble as any in education.

The three visions are as noble as any in education.

Realizing these visions is not served by testing and labeling students, nor by segregating students into different courses of study or into classes which use different instructional strategies. It is not served by developing tests of the intelligences. It is not even dependent on sensitive assessment, although sensitive, authentic assessment can facilitate the realization of the goals. The visions are most easily and directly realized by inclusion of a range of instructional strategies which match and stretch the multiplicity of intelligences.

●●●●●●●●●●

Matching:
Teaching in Many Ways

MI theory reminds us there are many possible instructional strategies, and if we use a greater range of strategies, we will capture the attention and motivate more students. By using a large assortment of strategies we deliver the academic curriculum for more students in intelligence-compatible ways. Some students are intrigued by an abstract logic problem, others love to manipulate objects, yet others love to put new words to an old tune. Any one way of teaching will not capture as many students as using a broad range of teaching techniques.

By using a variety of MI strategies, we match our instruction to how students are smart. We build multiple bridges onto our curriculum, giving our diverse population of students equal access to the learning material. We make learning more meaningful and engaging for all students.

We do not need brain localization studies to tell us that movement invigorates the class; the Total Physical Response (TPR) has been working for educators for some time. Teachers who include movement as one of their instructional strategies respond to the primary needs of more students, and respond more completely to each student, than teachers who do not.

Every student has all of the intelligences — far more than we can name. To broaden our repertoire of instructional strategies is to include links between the curriculum and additional intelligences, providing more ways for students to relate to and understand the curriculum.

MI theory has given us a simple checklist with which to guide ourselves as we teach any content. Are we including music? Is there movement? Can we approach this content with numbers? Can it be drawn? What part of the content shall the students write about? Have students interacted over these ideas? Have students linked the content to an inner state, such as a feeling or value? Our teaching will be better, the more we teachers ask ourselves these questions — and a multitude of additional questions like them. The questions should become an unconscious mantra for every teacher so that at any moment, any teacher, at any grade level in any content area, will draw from a wide range of instructional strategies.

There are a variety of ways teachers can match the multiple intelligences without ever assessing students. Learning centers can be used which engage the different intelligences. Multiple intelligences bulletin boards are easy to make. Parts of the room can be dedicated to interpersonal interaction while other parts of the room are set aside for quiet, introspective work. At times in the day students can gravitate to those parts of the room which best suit their needs at the moment. Having more ways to connect to the content through their strengths, students will perform better, and enjoy class more.

We enrich our curriculum and instruction to promote the development of students' multiple intelligences. We help students become smarter in many ways.

Stretching:
Teaching Students to Be Smarter

If our goal is to stretch all students, to develop all of their intelligences as fully as possible, we do not want to leave the choice of learning centers or projects entirely to choice. We need to teach all students in all ways. At times students might rotate from a mathematical, to a linguistic, to a visual/spatial learning center, and so on. If we believe there are a multiplicity of intelligences, we will regularly rotate the content of the learning centers, and the content of our instruction, designing activities to develop the many ways to be smart in each intelligence category. Our potential chefs, childcare workers, mechanics, magicians, entrepreneurs, entertainers, theorists, theologians, naturalists, novelists, painters and pianists can all be served well, if we design learning experiences to match, stretch, and celebrate the multiplicity of ways to be smart.

As we match a given intelligence, using a musical instructional strategy, if we require all students to participate, the curriculum is more engaging and attractive to those strong in the musical intelligence, while those less talented in that intelligence get a stretch, increasing their opportunity to develop a nondominant intelligence. In the heterogeneous class, instruction which matches any intelligence motivates learning of the content for students strong in that intelligence, but stretches that intelligence for students weak in the intelligence. An instructional strategy which engages an intelligence realizes Vision 1 for students strong in the intelligence while at the same time realizing Vision 2 for those weak in the intelligence.

Celebrating:
Honoring Uniqueness & Celebrating Diversity

As we enter the twenty first century, we face increasing diversity. Depending on how we handle diversity in our classrooms we will create a future society enriched by diversity or one torn apart by diversity. As educators, on a daily basis we determine if the future will be marked by harmonious racial relations or strong racial cleavages.

We have available a number of ways to reach the third vision, to have each student understand and appreciate his or her own unique pattern of intelligences and that of others, and to understand, appreciate, honor, and celebrate the diversity among us. Among our most powerful tools in fostering mutual understanding and honoring diversity are reflection and interaction. Simply having students think about and discuss with each other which facets of their intelligences they have used during different activities, how they differed in approaching a given problem or project, goes a long way toward bringing home the understanding that we are all different and that we all bring different strengths to a task. Each of us brings a different information base to a given problem. Students need to rediscover in their own experience that "Two heads are far better than one," and that "All of us are far smarter than any one of us."

If we engage our students in metacognition on the intelligences before, during, and after they work on problems and projects, we make progress toward the goal of having each student better understand himself or herself and others as well. The third vision is best reached in a heterogeneous classroom in which students are exposed to the range of intelligences. The third MI vision is undermined by any attempt to sort students and send them away from each other for different content or instruction. Diversity is best understood and appreciated only when interacting in the full range of diversity. Diversity skills are acquired in the context of diversity.

The miracle of these MI strategies is that a strategy which matches an intelligence, stretches it as well. Further, each additional strategy provides an additional window through which students can view and understand themselves and others, creating a knowledge of and respect for diversity.

At times, students can be given choices as to types of projects to make, each based on different intelligences. At times students may make choices of types of entries to make in their portfolios, or types of learning centers in which to work — each stimulating different intelligences. When

they are allowed to reflect on how they made their choices and how they approached problems and projects, students come to understand better their own unique pattern of intelligences, their self-understanding is enhanced. When they are allowed to hear and understand the basis for different choices made by others, they grow in their social understanding.

Breaking the Replacement Cycle

The use by teachers of simple, content-free MI strategies is, in our view, the greatest hope we have in realizing the three powerful visions which spring from MI theory. Too often education has been faced with recurring replacement cycles. A new innovation appears on the educational horizon, and educators jump on the bandwagon to replace old methods with the new. Those who have been through a number of these replacement cycles grow skeptical and weary. How much energy, they ask, should I put into retooling to teach with this year's new thing when I know it will soon be replaced with next year's new thing?

MI lessons and centers which involve replacing old methods with new run the risk of feeding this replacement cycle. In contrast, simple strategies which can be incorporated as part of any lesson promote a building of competencies rather than a replacement of old methods with new. Effective strategies can be integrated into next year's new thing, so that MI will endure rather than become just one more passing educational fad.

There are a number of simple instructional strategies to match and stretch each of the intelligences. The miracle of these MI strategies is that a strategy which matches an intelligence, stretches it as well. Further each additional strategy provides an additional window through which students can view and understand themselves and others, creating a knowledge of and respect for diversity. For example, a simple Team Interview, in which each student in turn is interviewed by his or her teammates, makes learning attractive for those strong in the verbal/linguistic and interpersonal/social intelligences (matching those intelligences) while at the same time it develops those intelligences for all students. The gregarious and loquacious student finds links to the curriculum when he can talk and interact in a Team Interview; the shy and laconic student in the same structure comes out a bit, and becomes a bit more fluent. And as they interact, all students come to know their own pattern of intelligences more and understand and appreciate their differences.

Some of the strategies match and stretch many intelligences at once. Match Mine engages students in arranging game pieces on a game board. Students each have their own game board and game pieces, but a barrier prevents them from seeing their partner's game pieces or game board. After the sender arranges her pieces, the object is for the receiver to make a perfect match. To be successful, the students must describe the location of their game pieces on their game boards, but they cannot peek at each other's pieces. The game develops the visual/spatial, verbal/linguistic, and interpersonal intelligences. While playing,

The decision of how to teach is a decision also about what we teach. Teaching with an intelligence is teaching also for the intelligence. As teachers, then, we cannot afford not to use a full range of instructional strategies.

students hone their verbal communication skills (describing the game pieces), their visual/spatial skills (locating pieces in a two- or three-dimensional area), and their interpersonal/social skills (learning to take the role of the other, seeing the world through the eyes of someone else). The game is content-free and can be played at any grade level: high school biology students arrange the parts of a cell on a game board in the shape of an animal cell; middle school students arrange geometric shapes; first grade students arrange animals on a game board which depicts a barnyard scene.

Match Mine is but one of dozens of simple multiple intelligences strategies. Some strategies involve music, others movement, others verbal skills, yet others logical skills. Over time, by teaching with strategies which match each intelligence, the multiplicity of intelligences can be engaged, stretched, understood, and celebrate. As we teachers broaden our repertoire of instructional strategies we match, stretch, and celebrated the multiplicity of intelligences. By using a full range of instructional strategies, all MI visions are realized. Over time, all students, regardless of their pattern of intelligences, find the curriculum more accessible and have ample opportunities to develop and appreciate all of their intelligences.

It is not possible to separate curriculum from the instructional strategies used to deliver it. Embedded in each instructional strategy is a curriculum. As we hear a lecture about the Civil War we engage and develop the linguistic intelligence; as we build a model of a Civil War cannon, we engage and develop the mechanical intelligence; as we interview each other in role as historical characters, we develop, among other things, our interpersonal intelligences. The decision of how to teach is a decision also about what we teach. Matching an intelligence also stretches that intelligence. As teachers, then, we cannot afford not to use a full range of instructional strategies. If we truly believe there are many ways to be smart, then we must have many ways to teach. Our goals are to reach and teach students with every possible pattern of intelligences, stretching all of their intelligences to their fullest potential, and validating their unique intellectual gifts. A rich set of MI instructional strategies is our greatest asset as we restructure to realize the powerful MI visions.

The contribution of MI theory to education is nothing short of a complete reevaluation of what and how we teach as well as a new vision of who we are, who our students are, and how we can best serve them. MI theory is guiding us toward new visions of what is possible. The theory leaves us empowered, with a renewed sense of our mission. Nobler visions for education do not exist.

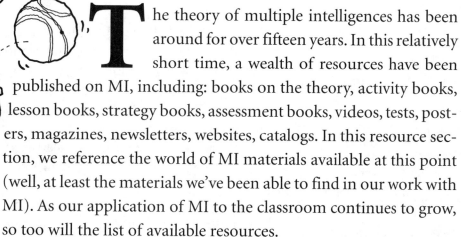

MI Resources

The theory of multiple intelligences has been around for over fifteen years. In this relatively short time, a wealth of resources have been published on MI, including: books on the theory, activity books, lesson books, strategy books, assessment books, videos, tests, posters, magazines, newsletters, websites, catalogs. In this resource section, we reference the world of MI materials available at this point (well, at least the materials we've been able to find in our work with MI). As our application of MI to the classroom continues to grow, so too will the list of available resources.

Many fine MI resources have also been created specific to each of the intelligences. Some are based on MI; many aren't, but are fantastic resources for developing the intelligences, nonetheless. Since there are so many resources available for each intelligence, we provide our abridged "authors' pick," a short list of some of our favorite resources from our personal library. At the end of this resources chapter, you will find Internet links for exploring MI and the intelligences via the Internet.

We provide this section in hope that we may facilitate your journey of matching, stretching, and celebrating multiple intelligences.

I. MI Theory and Practice

Armstrong, T. *Multiple Intelligences in the Classroom.* Alexandria, VA: Association for Supervision and Curriculum Development, 1994.

Armstrong, T. *7 Kinds of Smart: Identifying and Developing Your Many Intelligences.* New York, NY: Plume, Penguin Group, 1993.

Berman, S. *A Multiple Intelligences Road to A Quality Classroom.* Arlington Heights, IL: IRI/Skylight Training and Publishing, Inc., 1995.

Bolanos, P. J. *From theory to practice: Indianapolis' Key School applies Howard Gardner's multiple intelligences theory to the classroom.* **The School Administrator**, 1994, *51 (1)*, 30-31.

Campbell, B. *The Multiple Intelligences Handbook. Lesson Plans and More...* Stanwood, WA: Campbell & Assoc., Inc., 1994.

Campbell, L., Campbell, B., & Dickinson, D. *Teaching & Learning Through Multiple Intelligences.* Needham Heights, MA: Allyn & Bacon, 1996.

Chapman, C. & Freeman, L. *Multiple Intelligences Centers and Projects.* Arlington Heights, IL: IRI/Skylight Training and Publishing, Inc., 1996.

Chapman, C. *If the Shoe Fits...How to Develop Multiple Intelligences in the Classroom.* Arlington Heights, IL: IRI/Skylight Training and Publishing, Inc., 1993.

DeAmicis, B. *A Daily Dose: Integrating MI into Your Curriculum.* Tucson, AZ: Zephyr Press, 1997.

Fogarty, R. & Bellanca, J. *Multiple Intelligences. A Collection.* Arlington Heights, IL: IRI/Skylight Publishing, Inc., 1995.

Fogarty, R. & Stoehr, J. *Integrating Curricula with Multiple Intelligences. Teams, Themes & Threads.* Palatine, IL: IRI/Skylight Publishing, Inc., 1995.

Fogarty, R. *Problem-Based Learning & Other Curriculum Models for the Multiple Intelligences Classroom.* Arlington Heights, IL: IRI/Skylight Training and Publishing, Inc., 1997.

Gardner, H. *Creating Minds.* New York, NY: Basic Books, 1993.

Gardner, H. *Frames of Mind. The Theory of Multiple Intelligences.* New York, NY: Basic Books, 1983.

Gardner, H. *Leading Minds.* New York, NY: Basic Books, 1995.

Gardner, H. *Multiple Intelligences. The Theory in Practice.* New York, NY: Basic Books, 1993.

Gardner, H. *Reflections on Multiple Intelligences: Myths and Messages.* **Phi Delta Kappan**, 1995, *(Nov.)*, 200-209.

Gardner, H. *The Unschooled Mind. How Children Think and How Schools Should Teach.* New York, NY: Basic Books, 1991.

Guilford, J. P. *The Nature of Human Intelligence.* New York, NY: McGraw-Hill, 1967.

Haggerty, B. *Nurturing Intelligences.* Menlo Park, CA: Addison-Wesley, 1995.

Jasmine, J. *Multiple Intelligences Activities (5-8).* Huntington Beach, CA: Teacher Created Materials, Inc., 1996.

Jasmine, J. *Teaching with Multiple Intelligences. Professional's Guide.* Huntington Beach, CA: Teacher Created Materials, Inc., 1996.

Kagan, L. & Kagan, M. *Creating the Multiple Intelligences Classroom.* San Clemente, CA: Kagan Cooperative Learning, 1998.

Kagan, S. & Kagan, M. *Multiple Intelligences: The Complete MI Book.* San Clemente, CA: Kagan Cooperative Learning, 1998.

Korff Wilkens, D. *Multiple Intelligences Activities (K-4).* Huntington Beach, CA: Teacher Created Materials, Inc., 1996.

Lazear, D. G. *Teaching for the Multiple Intelligences. Fastback number 342.* Bloomington, IN: Phi Delta Kappa Educational Foundation, 1992.

Lazear, D. *Intelligence Builders for Every Student: 44 Exercises to Expand MI in Your Classroom.* Tucson, AZ: Zephyr Press, 1998.

Lazear, D. *Seven Pathways of Learning: Teaching Students and Parents about Multiple Intelligences.* Tucson, AZ: Zephyr Press, 1994.

Lazear, D. *Seven Ways of Knowing.* Arlington Heights, IL: IRI/Skylight Training and Publishing, Inc., 1991.

Lazear, D. *Seven Ways of Teaching: The Artistry of Teaching with Multiple Intelligences.* Arlington Heights, IL: IRI/Skylight Training and Publishing, Inc., 1991.

Marks-Tarlow, T. *Creativity Inside Out. Learning through Multiple Intelligences.* Menlo Park, CA: Addison-Wesley, 1996.

McGrath, H. & Noble, T. *Seven Ways at Once, Book 1. Classroom Strategies Based on the Seven Intelligences.* Melbourne, Australia: Longman Australia Pty. Limited, 1995.

McGrath, H. & Noble, T. *Seven Ways at Once, Book 2. Classroom Strategies Based on the Seven Intelligences.* Melbourne, Australia: Longman Australia Pty. Limited, 1995.

New City School Faculty. *Celebrating Multiple Intelligences: Teaching for Success.* St. Louis, MO: The New City School, 1994.

New City School Faculty. *Succeeding with Multiple Intelligences: Teaching through the Personal Intelligences.* St. Louis, MO: The New City School, 1996.

O'Connor, A. T. & Callahan-Young, S. *Seven Windows to a Child's World: 100 Ideas for the Multiple Intelligences Classroom.* Palatine, IL: IRI/Skylight Publishing, Inc., 1994.

Sternberg, R. J. *How Much Gall is Too Much Gall? A Review of Frames of Mind: The Theory of Multiple Intelligences.* **Contemporary Education Review**, 1983, *2(3)*, 215-224.

Teele, S. *The Multiple Intelligences School: A place for all students to succeed.* Redlands, CA: Sue Teele and Associates, 1997.

Weber, E. *Roundtable Learning: Building Understanding through Enhanced MI Strategies.* Tucson, AZ: Zephyr Press, 1997.

Wilson, L. O. *Every Child, Whole Child. classroom Activities for Unleashing Natural Abilities.* Tucson, AZ: Zephyr Press, 1994.

• • • • • • • • • • • • • •
II. MI Teacher Resources

Bruetsch, A. *Multiple Intelligences Lesson Plan Book.* Tucson, AZ: Zephyr Press, 1995.

Kagan, M. *Multiple Intelligences SmartCard.* San Clemente, CA: Kagan Cooperative Learning, 1997.

Kagan, S. & Kagan, L. *Colorful Multiple Intelligences Transparencies.* San Clemente, CA: Kagan Cooperative Learning, 1998.

Kagan, S. & Kagan, L. *Multiple Intelligences Binder.* San Clemente, CA: Kagan Cooperative Learning, 1998.

Kunzler, D. *Kid Smart Posters.* Tucson, AZ: Zephyr Press.

Lazear, D. & Margulies, N. *Tap Your Multiple Intelligences Posters.* Tucson, AZ: Zephyr Press.

Skylight Training and Publishing. *Have You Used Your Eight Intelligences Today? Poster and MI Tasks.* Arlington Heights, IL: IRI/Skylight Training and Publishing, Inc., 1993.

• • • • • • • • • • • • • •
III. MI Assessment

Bellanca, J., Chapman, C, & Swartz, E. *Multiple Assessments for Multiple Intelligences.* Arlington Heights, IL: IRI/Skylight Training and Publishing, Inc., 1994.

Chen, J. & Gardner, H. *Alternative Assessments for a Multiple Intelligences Perspective.* In D. F. Flanagan, J. L. Genshaft, & P. L. Harrison, **Beyond Traditional Intellectual Assessment: Contemporary and Emerging Theories, Tests, and Issues.** New York: Guilford Publications, 1994.

Hatch, T. & Gardner, H. *If Binet had Looked Beyond the Classroom: The Assessment of Multiple Intelligences.* **International Journal of Educational Research**, 1990, *14(5)*, 415-429.

Lazear, D. *Multiple Intelligences Approaches to Assessment. Solving the Assessment Conundrum.* Tucson, AZ: Zephyr, 1994.

Teele, S. *Teaching and Assessment Strategies Appropriate for the Multiple Intelligences.* Riverside, CA: University of California, Riverside, 1992.

Teele, S. *The Teele Inventory of Multiple Intelligences.* Redlands, CA: Sue Teele and Associates.

Terman, L. *Intelligence Tests and School Reorganization.* New York: World Book Co., 1923.

Torff, B. *Multiple Intelligences and Assessment.* Arlington Heights, IL: IRI/Skylight Training & Publishing, Inc., 1997.

• • • • • • • • • • • • •
IV. MI Videos

Armstrong, T. *Multiple Intelligences: Discovering the Giftedness in All.* Port Chester, NY: National Professional Resources, Inc., 1997

Gardner, H., with Lazear, D. *Discovering the Seven Intelligences.* Sandy, UT: The LPD Video Journal of Education, 1997.

Gardner, H., with Lazear, D. *Enriching Students' Intelligences in the Classroom.* Sandy, UT: The LPD Video Journal of Education, 1997.

Gardner, H. *How Are Kids Smart? Multiple Intelligences in the Classroom. Teachers' and Administrators' Versions.* Gloucester, MA: National Professional Resources, Inc., 1995.

Jennings, Peter. *Common Miracles — the Revolution in Learning. ABC News Special.* Orland Park, IL: MPI Home Video.

Kagan, S. & Kagan, L. *Cooperative Learning and Multiple Intelligences, Middle School.* Sandy, UT: The LPD Video Journal of Education, 1998.

Kagan, S. & Kagan, L. *Cooperative Learning and Multiple Intelligences, High School.* Sandy, UT: The LPD Video Journal of Education, 1998.

Kagan, S. & Kagan, L. *Cooperative Learning and Multiple Intelligences, Elementary.* Sandy, UT: The LPD Video Journal of Education, 1998.

Kagan, S. & Kagan, L. *Multiple Intelligences. Part of Every Lesson.* San Clemente, CA: Kagan Cooperative Learning, 1998.

Lazear, D. *MI in Action: Your School and the Multiple Intelligences. 5 Video Set.* Tucson, AZ: Zephyr Press, 1995.

V. MI Catalogs & Organizations

ASCD
Teaching For MI Network
Alexandria, VA
1 (800) 933-ASCD
www.ascd.org

Kagan Cooperative Learning
San Clemente, CA
1 (800) WEE CO-OP
www.KaganCoopLearn.com

The MI Company
San Clemente, CA
1 (800) 939-4648

The New City School
Saint Louis, MO
www.NewCitySchool.org

New Horizons For Learning
Seattle, WA
www.newhorizons.org

Project Zero
Cambridge, MA
617-495-4342
http://pzweb.harvard.edu

Skylight Training and Publishing
Arlington Heights, IL
1 (800) 348-4474
www.iriskylight.com

Teaching Technology
Austin, TX
1 (800) 579-5836
www. teachtech.com

Video Journal
Sandy, UT
1 (800) 572-1153
www.videojournal.com

Zephyr Press
Tucson, AZ
1 (800) 232-2187
www.zephyrpress.com

VI. Verbal/ Linguistic

Bromley, K. *Journaling.* New York, NY: Scholastic Inc., 1993.

Curran, Lorna. *Language Arts and Cooperative Learning: Lessons for Little Ones.* San Clemente, CA: Kagan Cooperative Learning, 1994.

Daniels, H. *Literature Circles.* York, ME: Stenhouse Publishers, 1994.

DeBolt, V. *Write! Cooperative Learning & the Writing Process.* San Clemente, CA: Kagan Cooperative Learning, 1994.

DeBolt, V. *Write! Mathematics: Multiple Intelligences and Cooperative Learning Activities.* San Clemente, CA: Kagan Cooperative Learning, 1998.

DeBolt, V. *Write! Science: Multiple Intelligences and Cooperative Learning Activities.* San Clemente, CA: Kagan Cooperative Learning, 1998.

DeBolt, V. *Write! Social Studies: Multiple Intelligences and Cooperative Learning Activities.* San Clemente, CA: Kagan Cooperative Learning, 1998.

Kessler, C. (Ed.). *Cooperative Language Learning.* Englewood Cliffs, NJ: Prentice Hall Regents, 1992.

Krashen, S. *The Power of Reading: Insights from the Research.* Englewood, CO: Libraries Unlimited, Inc., 1993.

Stone, J. *Cooperative Learning and Language Arts.* San Clemente, CA: Kagan Cooperative Learning, 1994.

Stone, J. *Cooperative Learning Reading Activities.* San Clemente, CA: Kagan Cooperative Learning, 1995.

Stone, J. *Cooperative Learning Writing Activities.* San Clemente, CA: Kagan Cooperative Learning, 1995.

Strunk, W. & White, E. B. *The Elements of Style.* New York, NY: Macmillan Publishing Co., Inc., 1979.

Zinsser, W. *On Writing Well.* New York, NY: Harper and Row, 1988.

McCracken, R. A. & Marlene, J. *Stories, Songs and Poetry to Teach Reading and Writing.* Winnipeg, Canada: Peguis Publishers, 1987.

VII. Logical/ Mathematical

Andrini, B. *Cooperative Learning and Mathematics.* San Clemente, CA: Kagan Cooperative Learning, 1996.

Burns, M. *A Collection of Math Lessons (K-3).* White Plains, NY: Math Solutions Publications, 1987, 1987, 1990.

Burns, M. *A Collection of Math Lessons (3-6).* White Plains, NY: Math Solutions Publications, 1987.

Burns, M. *A Collection of Math Lessons (6-8).* White Plains, NY: Math Solutions Publications, 1990.

Candler, L. *Discovering Decimals through Cooperative Learning.* San Clemente, CA: Kagan Cooperative Learning, 1997.

Curran, Lorna. *Mathematics and Cooperative Learning: Lessons for Little Ones.* San Clemente, CA: Kagan Cooperative Learning, 1994.

de Bono, E. *Lateral Thinking: Creativity Step by Step.* New York, NY: Harper and Row, 1973.

Erickson, T. *Get It Together: Math Problems for Groups (Grades 4-12).* Berkeley, CA: Equals, 1989.

Erickson, T. *United We Solve: 116 Math Problems for Groups (Grades 5-10).* Oakland, CA: eeps media, 1996.

Fogarty, R. & Bellanca, J. *Patterns for Thinking: Patterns for Transfer.* Palatine, IL: Skylight Publishing, 1989.

Fogarty, R. & Opeka, K. *Start Them Thinking: A Handbook of Classroom Strategies for the Early Years.* Arlington Heights, IL: IRI/Skylight Training and Publishing, Inc., 1998.

Fogarty, R. & Bellanca, J. *Teach Them Thinking: Mental Menus for 24 Thinking Skills.* Arlington Heights, IL: IRI/Skylight Training and Publishing, Inc., 1986.

Goodman, J. *Group Solutions. Cooperative Logic Activities.* Berkeley, CA: Lawrence Hall of Science GEMS, 1992.

Goodman, J., with Kopp, J. *Group Solutions, Too!* Berkeley, CA: Lawrence Hall of Science GEMS, 1997.

Martin, H. *Multiple Intelligences in the Mathematics Classroom.* Palatine, IL: IRI/Skylight Training & Publishing, Inc., 1996.

Robertson, L. *Fraction Fun through Cooperative Learning.* San Clemente, CA: Kagan Cooperative Learning, 1993.

Wiederhold, C. *Cooperative Learning and Higher-Level Thinking: The Q-Matrix.* San Clemente, CA: Kagan Cooperative Learning, 1995.

•••••••••••••••••
VIII. Visual/Spatial

Barry, J. *Draw, Design and Paint: Projects Designed to Foster Individual Expression in the Visual Arts.* Torrance, CA: Good Apple, 1990.

Bellanca, J. *The Cooperative Think Tank.* Arlington Heights, IL: IRI/Skylight Training and Publishing, Inc., 1990.

Bellanca, J. *The Cooperative Think Tank II.* Arlington Heights, IL: IRI/Skylight Training and Publishing, Inc., 1992.

Bromley, K., Irwin-De Vitis, L., and Modlo, M. *Graphic Organizers.* New York, NY: Scholastic, Inc., 1995.

Edwards, B. *Drawing on the Right Side of the Brain.* Los Angeles, CA: Jeremy P. Tarcher, Inc., 1989.

Evans, E. & Moore, E. *How to Teach Art to Children.* Monterey, CA: Evan-Moor Corp., 1992.

Gardner, H. *Zero-based arts education: An introduction to ARTS PROPEL.* **Studies in Art Education.** 1989, *3(2)*, 71-83.

Hume, H. D. *American Art Appreciation Activities Kit.* Englewood Cliffs, NJ: Prentice Hall, 1996.

Jenkins, S. & Foote, M. *Adventures with Art.* Glenview, IL: GoodYear Books, 1993.

Kagan, S. *Same-Different: Holidays.* San Clemente, CA: Kagan Cooperative Learning, 1997.

Kagan, S. *Same-Different: Fairy Tales.* San Clemente, CA: Kagan Cooperative Learning, 1998.

Langer, S. K. *Problems of Art.* New York, Charles Scribner, 1957.

Margulies, N. *Mapping Inner Space. Learning and Teaching Mind Mapping.* Tucson, AZ: Zephyr Press, 1991.

Mason, K. *Going Beyond Words: The Art and Practice of Visual Thinking.* Tucson, AZ: Zephyr Press, 1991.

McKim, R. H. *Experiences in Visual Thinking.* Belmont, CA: Brooks Cole, 1972.

Parks, S. & Black, H. *Organizing Thinking, Book I.* Pacific Grove, CA: Critical Thinking Press & Software, 1992.

Parks, S. & Black, H. *Organizing Thinking, Book II.* Pacific Grove, CA: Critical Thinking Press & Software, 1990.

Seymour, Dale. *Visual Thinking.* Palo Alto, CA: Dale Seymour Publications, 1983.

Swerdlow, J. L. *Vincent van Gogh: Lullaby in Color.* National Geographic, October 1997, 101-129.

Zessoules, R. Wolf, D., & Gardner, H. *A better balance: ARTS PROPEL as an alternative to discipline-based art education.* In J. Burton, A. Lederman, & P. Landon (Eds.), **Beyond discipline-based art education.** University Council on Art Education.

IX. Musical/ Rhythmic

Campbell, D. *The Mozart Effect: Tapping the Power of Music to Heal the Body, Mind, and Unlock the Creative Spirit.* Avon Books, 1997

Campbell, D. *The Mozart Effect: Music for Children.* The Children's Group, 1997.

Danes, E. *First Book of Music: A Complete Introduction.* London, England: Usborne Publishing, Ltd., 1993.

Gardner, H. *Keynote Address. Is Musical Intelligence Special?* Verna Brummett, (ed.) Ithaca Conference '96: Music as Intelligence. A Sourcebook. Ithaca, New York: Ithaca College, 1997.

Hart, A. & Mantell, P. *Kids Make Music.* Charlotte, VT: Williamson Publishing Co., 1993.

Klose, C. & Wolfe, L. *Lyrical Lessons for American History, Language Arts, Math, Multiple Intelligences, Natural Science, Plants & Animals, School Community, Science, Social Studies.* San Clemente, CA: Kagan Cooperative Learning, 1997.

Mandel, M. & Wood, R. *Make Your Own Musical Instruments.* New York: Sterling Publishing Co., 1978.

Meyer, C. & Pickens, K. *Sing and Learn: Songs and Activities Using Familiar Tunes.* Parsippany, NJ: Good Apple, Inc., 1989.

Troxel, K. *Song Kits for Addition, Geography, Grammar, Multiplication, States and Capitals.* Newport Beach, CA: Audio Memory Publishing, 1996.

Wallace, R. R. *Rappin' and Rhymin': Raps, Songs, Cheers, and SmartRope Jingles for Active Learning.* Tucson, AZ: Zephyr Press, 1992.

X. Bodily/ Kinesthetic

Arnold, C. *Pele: The King of Soccer.* New York: Franklin Watts, Inc., 1992.

Asher, J. *Learning Another Language through Actions.* Los Gatos, CA: Sky Oaks Productions, Inc., 1993.

Benzwie, T. *A Moving Experience: Dance for Lovers of Children and the Child Within.* Tucson, AZ: 1987.

Brennan, J. L. *Duke: The Life Story of Duke Kahanamoku.* Honolulu: Hu Pa'a Publishing Inc., 1994.

Campbell, D. G. & Brewer, C. *Rhythms of Learning: Creative Tools for Developing Lifelong Skills.* Tucson, AZ: Zephyr Press, 1991.

Gilbert, A. G. *Teaching the Three R's through Movement.* New York, NY: MacMillan, 1989.

Gregson, B. *The Incredible Indoor Games Book.* Torrance, CA: Fearon Teacher Aids, 1982.

Gregson, B. *The Outrageous Outdoor Games Book.* Torrance, CA: Fearon Teacher Aids, 1984.

Krull, K. *Lives of the Athletes.* San Diego: Harcourt Brace & Co., 1997.

Orlick, T. *The Cooperative Sports & Games Book: Challenge Without Competition.* New York: Pantheon Books, 1978.

Orlick, T. *The Second Cooperative Sports & Games Book: Over Two Hundred Non-competitive Games for Kids and Adults Both.* New York: Pantheon Books, 1982.

Patterson, M. N. *Every Body Can Learn. Engaging the Bodily-Kinesthetic Intelligence in the Everyday Classroom.* Tucson, AZ: Zephyr Press, 1997.

Rohnke, K. *Silver Bullets: A Guide to Initiative Problems, Adventure Games and Trust Activities.* Dubuque, IA: Kendall/ Hunt Publishing, 1984.

Sobel, J. *Everybody Wins: 393 Non-Competitive Games for Young Childen.* New York: Walker and Company, 1983.

Spolin, V. *Theater Games for the Classroom.* Evanston, IL: Northwestern University Press, 1986.

XI. Naturalist

Brooks, F. (Ed.) *World Wildlife.* Tulsa, OK: EDC Publishing.

Candler, L. *Cooperative Learning & Hands-On Science.* San Clemente, CA: Kagan Cooperative Learning, 1995.

Candler, L. *Cooperative Learning & Wee Science.* San Clemente, CA: Kagan Cooperative Learning, 1995.

Cornell, J. *Sharing Nature with Children.* Nevada City, CA: Dawn Publications, 1979.

Darwin, C. *The Origin of Species by Means of Natural Selection or the Preservation of Favored Races in the Struggle for Life.* New York: The Modern Library, (originally published in 1859).

Masson, J. M. & McCarthy, S. *When Elephants Weep. The Emotional Lives of Animals.* New York: Dell Publishing, 1995

Goodall, J. *In the Shadow of Man.* London: Collins, 1971.

Horsfall, J. *Play Lightly on the Earth.* Nevada City, CA: DAWN Publications, 1997.

Roberts, M. *The Man Who Listens to Horses.* New York: Random House, 1996.

Roth, K. *The Naturalist Intelligence: An Introduction to Gardner's Eighth Intelligence.* Arlington Heights, IL: IRI/Skylight Training and Publishing, Inc., 1998.

VanCleave, J. *Play and Find Out about Nature: Easy Experiments for Young Children.* New York: John Wiley & Sons, Inc., 1997.

VanCleave, J. *200 Gooey, Slippery, Slimy, Weird & Fun Experiments.* New York: John Wiley & Sons, Inc., 1993.

VanCleave, J. *201 Awesome, Magical, Bizarre & Incredible Experiments.* New York: John Wiley & Sons, Inc., 1994.

VanCleave, J. *202 Oozing, Bubbling, Dripping & Bouncing Experiments.* New York: John Wiley & Sons, Inc., 1996.

Watt, F. *Earth.* London, England: Usborne Publishing, 1992.

XII. Interpersonal

Bellanca, J. *Building a Caring, Cooperative Classroom: Integrating Social Skills Through the Language Curriculum.* Palatine, IL: IRI/Skylight Publishing, Inc., 1991.

Child Development Project. *That's My Buddy!* Oakland, CA: Developmental Studies Center, 1996.

Cowan, D., Palomares, S., & Schilling D. *Teaching the Skills of Conflict Resolution.* Spring Valley, CA: Innerchoice Publishing, 1992.

Craigen, J. & Ward, C. *What's This Got To Do with Anything: A Collection of Group/Class Builders and Energizers.* Canada: Jim Craigen & Chris Ward, 1996.

Developmental Studies Center. *Ways We Want Our Class to Be: Class Meetings That Build Commitment to Kindness and Learning.* Oakland, CA: Developmental Studies Center, 1996.

Drew, N. *Learning the Skills of Peacemaking: A K-6 Activity Guide on Resolving Conflict, Communicating, Cooperating.* Carson, CA: Jalmar Press, 1995.

Duvall, L. *Respecting Our Differences: A Guide to Getting Along in a Changing World.* Minneapolis, MN: Free Spirit Publishing, Inc., 1994.

Elias, M., et al. *Promoting Social and Emotional Learning. Guidelines for Educators.* Alexandria, VA: Association for Supervision and Curriculum Development, 1997.

Gibbs, J. *Tribes. A New Way of Learning and Being Together.* Sausalito, CA: CenterSource Systems, 1995.

Johnson, D. W., Johnson, R. T., & Johnson-Holubec, E. *Circles of Learning: Cooperation in the Classroom.* Edina, MN: Interaction Book Company, 1993.

Kagan, S. *Cooperative Learning.* San Clemente, CA: Kagan Cooperative Learning, 1994.

Kagan, M., Robertson, L., & Kagan. S. *Classbuilding.* San Clemente, CA: Kagan Cooperative Learning, 1995.

Kagan, L., Kagan, M., & Kagan, S. *Teambuilding.* San Clemente, CA: Kagan Cooperative Learning, 1997.

Kohn, A. *No Contest: The Case Against Competition.* New York, NY: Houghton Mifflin, Co., 1992.

Kriedler, W. & Furlong, L. *Adventures in Peacemaking: A Conflict Resolution Activity Guide for School-age Programs.* Cambridge, MA: Educators for Social Responsibility, 1995.

Kriedler, W. *Creative Conflict Resolution: More than 200 Activities of Keeping Peace in the Classroom.* Glenview, IL: Good Year Books, 1984.

Lickona, T. *Educating for Character: How Our Schools Can Teach Respect and Responsibility.* New York, NY: Bantam Books, 1991.

Rice, J. A. *The Kindness Curriculum: Introducing Young Children to Loving Values.* St. Paul, MN: Redleaf Press, 1995.

Sharan, Y. & Sharan, S. *Expanding Cooperative Learning through Group Investigation.* New York, NY: Teachers College Press, 1992.

Shaw, V. *Communitybuilding in the Classroom.* San Clemente, CA: Kagan Cooperative Learning, 1992.

Slavin, R. E., *Cooperative Learning: Theory, Research, and Practice.* Needham Heights, MA: Allyn & Bacon, A Simon & Schuster Company, 1995.

York, S. *Roots & Wings: Affirming Culture in Early Childhood Programs.* St. Paul MN: Redleaf Press, 1991.

XIII. Intrapersonal

Borba, M. *Esteem Builders: A K-8 Self Esteem Curriculum for Improving Student Achievement, Behavior and School Climate.* Carson, CA: Jalmar Press, 1989.

Canfield, J. & Siccone, F. *101 Ways to Develop Student Self-Esteem and Responsibility.* Needham Heights, MA: Allyn and Bacon, 1995.

Fogarty, R. *How to Teach for Metacognitive Reflection.* Palatine, IL: IRI Skylight, 1994.

Goleman, D. *Emotional Intelligence.* New York: Bantam Books, 1995.

Kostick, D. P. *The Biography of Me: A Journey of Self-Discovery.* Parsippany, NJ: Good Apple, Inc., 1992.

Lickona, T. *Character Education: Restoring Respect and Responsibility in our Schools. Video.* Port Chester, NY: National Professional Resources, Inc., 1996.

Mayer, J. D. & Salovey, P. *What is Emotional Intelligence?* In P. Salovey & D.J. Sluyter, Emotional development and emotional intelligence: Educational Implications. New York: Basic Books, 1997.

● ● ● ● ● ● ● ● ● ● ● ● ● ● ●
XIV. Internet Links

These Internet links are provided courtesy of Brian Maas and Dave Sanders of **The Multiple Intelligences Company**. They have compiled and provided Internet sites dealing with MI resources, MI books and articles, and some "best picks" for teachers and students to explore the intelligences via the Internet.

These Internet links all can be accessed directly from the *Kagan Cooperative Learning* home page:
www.KaganCoopLearn.com

The plan is to continue updating these links, so if you know of additional MI links, or great sites for any of the intelligences, please let us know. At the *Kagan* site you will find a bulletin board as well as an E-mail link.

Please note that the Internet is in constant flux. Some of the sites below may not exist by the time you attempt to access them. We'll keep updated links on the *Kagan* home page. You will also find a place to vote for your favorite sites. Those sites receiving the most votes will be placed at the top of the list.

MI Resources Links

Educational Leadership: Teaching for Multiple Intelligences
ASCD advertises their Educational Leadership magazine special issue on MI. Two articles *The First Seven…and the Eighth: A Conversation with Howard Gardner* by Kathy Checkley and *Variations on a Theme -- How Teachers Interpret MI Theory* by Linda Campbell are available to read.
http://www.ascd.org/pubs/el/sept97/sept97.html

EdWeb: Exploring Technology and School Reform
Provides an overview of multiple intelligences theory and resources for technology and school reform.
http://edweb.gsn.org/edref.mi.intro.html

The Key Learning Community
The Key Learning Community is a model application of multiple intelligences involving students, teachers, administrators, researchers and parents.
http://www.ips.k12.in.us/mskey/

Multiple Intelligences for Adult Literacy and Adult Education

Oriented toward applications of MI methods toward adult education, you will find strategies, case studies, and assessment suggestions valuable at all grades.
http://literacynet.org/diversity/home.html

Project Zero

Visit this site to obtain information on Harvard's Project Zero projects and publications. You can order MI books and articles by Howard Gardner and colleagues and for a fee subscribe to their online publication, LEARN@PZ.
http://pzweb.harvard.edu/

The Tool Room: About Howard Gardner — Theory of Multiple Intelligences

You will find information about teaching and learning through MI, an article by Bruce Campbell on the naturalist intelligence, and information about Linda Campbell, Bruce Campbell, and Dee Dickinson's book, *Teaching and Learning Through Multiple Intelligences.*
http://www.newhorizons.org/trm_gardner.html

MI Books & Articles Links

Barkman, R. *Patterns and the Eighth Intelligence.* **Mindshift Connection.** Tucson, AZ: Zephyr Press, Spring, 1997.
http://www.newhorizons.org/trm_mipattern.html

Campbell, B. *Multiplying Intelligence in the Classroom.* **On the Beam,** Vol IX, No.2, Winter 1989, 7.
http://www.newhorizons.org/art_miclsrm.html

Campbell, B. *The Research Results of a Multiple Intelligences Classroom.* **On the Beam,** Vol XI, No.1, Fall, 1990, 7.
http://www.newhorizons.org/art_mireserch.html

Campbell, L., Campbell, B., & Dickinson, D. *Teaching and Learning Through Multiple Intelligences.* NY: Allyn & Bacon, 1996.
http://www.abacon.com/books/ab_0205163378.html

Dickinson, D. *Learning Through Many Kinds of Intelligences,* 1994.
http://www.newhorizons.org/art_lrnthrumi.html

Durie, R. *An Interview With Howard Gardner.* **Mindshift Connection.** Tucson, AZ: Zephyr Press, Spring, 1997.
http://www.newhorizons.org/trm_duriemi.html

Gardner, H. *Intelligence in Seven Steps.* From: **Creating the Future: Perspectives on Educational Change.** Dee Dickinson (Ed.) Aston Clinton, Bucks, UK: Accelerated Learning Systems. 1991.
http://www.newhorizons.org/crfut_gardner.html

Gardner, H., Kornhaber, M. L., & W. K. Wake. *Intelligence: Multiple Perspectives.* NY: Harcourt Brace, 1996.
http://www.the-bac.edu/wake/intellig/

Gardner, H. & Hatch, T. *Multiple Intelligences Go To School: Educational Implications of the Theory of Multiple Intelligences.* **Educational Researcher** 18,8 (November, 1989): 4-9. EJ 369 605.
http://www.edc.org/CCT/ccthome/reports/tr4.html

Hoerr, T. R. *The Naturalist Intelligence.* **Mindshift Connection.** Tucson, AZ: Zephyr Press, Spring, 1997.
http://www.newhorizons.org/trm_hoerrmi.html

Oddleifson, E. *A Fifty School Arts Education Demonstration Project.* Boston, MA: Center for the Arts in Basic Curriculum, Fall, 1989.
http://www.newhorizons.org/art_fiftyscharts.html

Unger, C. *Teaching for Understanding — Questions to ask yourself and your students.*
http://www.newhorizons.org/restr_unger.html

Veenema, S. & Gardner, H. *Multimedia and Multiple Intelligences.* **The American Prospect** no. 29 (November-December 1996): 69-75
http://epn.org/prospect/29/29veen.html

Wahl, M. *Multiple Intelligences Power Up Math Teaching.*
http://www.newhorizons.org/restr_wahl1.html

Weber, E. *Curriculum for Success.* **On the Beam.** 1992.
http://www.newhorizons.org/article_weber92.html

Intelligences Links

These Internet resources open a wonderful world of exploration: Teachers and students can visit a cyberworld zoo, manipulate words to create poetry, experience and interpret visual illusions, and explore a multitude of incredible, intriguing, interactive Internet intelligence inventions.

Verbal/Linguistic

Book Nook
(*Teachers & Students, Primary - High School*)
Book reviews by kids, for kids. Reviews are arranged according to grade level (or age group). Allows Search by Titles, Authors, Publishers, or ANY words.
http://i-site.on.ca/booknook.html

Hang Person
(*Students, Elementary - Middle School*)
This Java version of the word game hangman lets you play in real-time. It even keeps score.
http://www.parkmaitland.org/staff/wellshangman.html

Human-Languages Page
(*Teachers*)
A comprehensive catalog of language-related Internet resources, including over 1700 links. Whether you're looking for online language lessons, translating dictionaries, native literature, translation services, software, language schools, or just a little information on a language you've heard about, the HLP probably has something to suit your needs.
http://www.june29.com/HLP/

Kid's Word Jumble

(Teachers & Students, Elementary - Middle School)
Three sets of jumbled words are given each week. The answers are posted the following week.
http://www.countryfriends.org/KWJumble.html

Number and Word Puzzles

(Teachers, Elementary - High School)
This site features 54 monthly entertaining and educational puzzles for all ages. Most are crossword puzzles that are formatted to be printed.
http://www1.tpgi.com.au/users/puzzles/

Poetry Post

(Students, Elementary)
Poems submitted by students from around the world. Grahamwood Elementary 5th and 6th grade CLUE students invite their global classmates to participate in this uni'verse'al expedition.
http://www.mecca.org/~graham/Poetry_Post.html

Virtual Verse

(Students, Elementary - Middle School)
Students have access to many words that they can drag to rearrange into poetry. Inspired by the Magnetic Poetry Kit © Dave Kapell.
http://freezone.com/tmf/magnetic/

Visualizing Verbs and Voices

(Teachers)
This teacher-created site demonstrates how to employ the visual/spatial intelligence to help teach language skills. Includes links to other more general MI resource pages.
http://www.cypress.ne.jp/schwindt/tesol/vtnvs.htm

Word a Day

(Teachers & Students, Middle - High School)
Use this site to subscribe to the mailing list A.Word.A.Day (AWAD) which mails out a vocabulary word and its definition (with occasional commentary) to subscribers every day.
http://www.wordsmith.org/awad

Young Writer's Clubhouse

(Students, Elementary - High School)
For students who are considering being writers. Resources include FAQ, E-mail newsletter, online chat, and critique group.
http://www.realkids.com/club.shtml

Logical/Mathematical

A+ Math Flashcards

(Students, Elementary - Middle School)
Students receive quick math problems in a flashcard format. Includes: addition, subtraction, multiplication, division, reducing and multiplying fractions. Play three Games: Math Bingo, Hidden Picture, and Concentration.
http://www.aplusmath.com/

Card Trick Central

(Teachers & Students, Middle - High School)
A collection of card tricks and instructions on how to perform them.
http://web.superb.net/cardtric/

Grey Labyrinth

(Teachers & Students, Middle - High School)
Tough puzzles designed to change perceptions. Some are mere mental calisthenics. Others require sitting back and trying to gain a new perspective on a problem.
http://www.greylabyrinth.com/puzzles.htm

Math Forum
(Teachers & Students,
Elementary - High School)
Features include: "ASK DR. MATH," "Elementary Problem of the Week," and an "Internet Resource Collection" complete with ability to browse by level or subject.
http://forum.swarthmore.edu

MegaMath
(Teachers & Students,
Elementary - High School)
Includes an online "workbook" filled with all sorts of different interactive math activities.
http://www.c3.lanl.gov/mega-math/menu.html

Mind Breakers
(Teachers & Students, Middle - High School)
More puzzles and riddles, labeled by their difficulty and coolness.
http://leden.tref.nl/mhulsman/files.htm

Shack's Page of Math Problems
(Teachers)
Over 100 Math and logic problems and puzzles, rated by type and difficulty. Contains links to other Math and puzzle pages.
http://www.charm.net/~shack/math/

Spacetime Wrinkles
(Teachers & Students, High School)
An extensive visual investigation of relativity, Einstein, and black holes.
http://www.ncsa.uiuc.edu/Cyberia/NumRel/NumRelHome.html

Views of the Solar System
(Teachers & Students,
Elementary - High School)
In addition to animations of every planet, this site features a great Educator's Guide to Eclipses as well as a separate Educator's Guide for each of the following: moon phases, impact craters, micrometeorites, convection, eclipses, and sunspots. Includes chronologies of exploration of the Sun, Venus, Mars, Jupiter, Saturn, and Uranus.
http://www.hawastsoc.org/solar/eng/homepage.htm

Visual/Spatial
ArchKIDecture
(Teachers & Students, Middle - High School)
Architecture described for kids. Focuses on the architecture of buildings from the past and present, and even one from the future.
http://www.solidprint.com/julieweb/page1.html

Coloring Book
(Teachers & Students,
Primary - Elementary)
Black and white line artwork that can be printed for a coloring project.
http://www.countryfriends.org/KWColorBook.html

Favorite Art Lessons
(Teachers & Students,
Elementary - High School)
A collection of teacher's art lessons.
http://www.artswire.org/kenroar/lessons/lessons.html

Illusion Works
(Teachers & Students,
Elementary - High School)
The most comprehensive collection of optical and sensory illusions on the world-wide web.
http://illusionworks.com/

International Child Art Foundation
(*Students, Elementary - High School*)
Art contest information; an "add to me" list of events; links to drawing sites, galleries, and contests.
http://www.icaf.org/

Maze Man
(*Teachers & Students, Elementary - High School*)
Large collection of downloadable mazes to print and solve.
http://users.aol.com/themazeman/index.html

Planning from the Visual Art Curriculum Guide
(*Teachers*)
A page with references on the education section from the Government of Saskatchewan. Includes recommendations for transforming ideas into visual form.
http://www.sasked.gov.sk.ca/docs/artsed/g7arts_ed/g7vplaae.html

Rubik Online
(*Teachers & Students, Middle - High School*)
A few challenging visual puzzles. By the maker of the rubik's cube.
http://www.rubiks.com/

Visual Understanding in Education
(*Teachers*)
A nonprofit education orginization committed to conducting developmentally based educational research.
http://www.vue.org/

Musical/Rhythmic

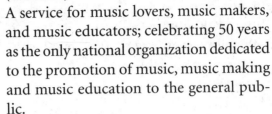

American Music Conference Internet Service
(*Teachers*)
A service for music lovers, music makers, and music educators; celebrating 50 years as the only national organization dedicated to the promotion of music, music making and music education to the general public.
http://www.amc-music.com/

Computers in the Music Discipline
(*Teachers & Students, Middle - High School*)
This site is a part of a large "humanities" page that deals specifically with music. Highlights include pages on "Music Composition for Beginners" and "Looking at Different Cultures of Music."
http://www.humanities.mcmaster.ca/~hccrs/ssmusicwebpage/titlepg.htm

International Lyrics Server
(*Teachers & Students, High School*)
Find the lyrics to 77221 songs! Extraordinary resource!
http://www.lyrics.ch/

Kit Eakles' Virtual Music Classroom
(*Teachers & Students, Primary - High School*)
Students learn, listen, and play on this site; teachers following different links to find strategies for teaching music.
http://cnet.unb.ca/achn/kodaly/koteach/

REI Institute
(*Teachers*)
The REI Institute is a MusicMedicine research organization and therapy provider focusing on the effects of musical rhythm on the central nervous system.
http://www.reiinstitute.com/

Rhythm: The Long and the Short of It

(Teachers & Students, Middle - High School)
An introduction to rhythm and music.
http://www.neiu.edu/~jalucas/muscon/
lectures/rhythm/index.htm

School House Rock

(Teachers & Students,
Elementary - Middle School)
Audio files and lyrics of the school house
rock television shorts.
http://genxtvland.simplenet.com/
SchoolHouseRock/index-hi.shtml

Bodily/Kinesthetic

Bauman Theatre Forums

(Teachers)
Explores the varied connections between
physical training for the actor and its application in performance with an emphasis on Physical Theatre.
http://www.geocities.com/Broadway/
1723/

Hands-On Technology Page

(Teachers & Students,
Primary - Middle School)
Science experiments and other hands-on
activities to generate excitement among K-
8 students. All of the activities are done
with everyday, inexpensive materials. Many
pages are designed to be photocopied and
used directly by your class. Includes
teacher's notes and materials lists.
http://www.galaxy.net/~k12/

Learn How to Juggle

(Teachers & Students, Middle - High School)
A community of jugglers post information
to learn different types of juggling.
http://www.juggling.org/help/

Sports Illustrated for Kids

(Students, Middle - High School)
http://www.pathfinder.com/SIFK/

World of Mime Theatre

(Teachers)
An international resource for mime theatre education, information and contacts.
Sections include a library, calendar,
clickable index, and an information and
resource guide about the art of mime theatre.
http://www.geocities.com/Broadway/
5222/

WWW Virtual Library: Dance Page

(Teachers)
A very comprehensive listing, allowing you
to browse dance related sites by type, or
alphabetically, as well as a list of dance resources.
http://www.artswire.org/Artswire/www/
dance/dance.html

Naturalist

Astronomy for Kids

(Teachers & Students,
Primary - High School)
Features include "Sky Maps", "The Plan-
ets", "How do they Know?", and "Star
Links".
http://www.dustbunny.com/afk/

Cyber Zoomobile

(Teachers & Students,
Primary - High School)
Enter an interactive realm where you are
able to bring many of the world's most
exotic species into your home or school for
viewing, study or research. The educational
commentary is combined with hundreds
of hyper-links, transforming ordinary text
into visual images of animal behavior.

Learn about classification, distribution, individual characteristics, life cycles, endangered/threatened species status and many other interesting aspects of life on planet earth. Information "buttons" provide worldwide links to search engines; zoos and wildlife parks; animal related educational materials; scientific research; veterinary medicine; recreation and eco-tourism; mammals; birds; fish; invertebrates; microbes; primates; dinosaurs; wildlife rescue and rehabilitation; evolution and creationist theories and State and Federal Agencies.
http://www.primenet.com/~brendel/

Environmental Research Laboratories
(Teachers & Students,
Elementary - High School)
Resources for dealing with oceanographic and atmospheric issues. An "Earth Day" page features the following headings: Weather/Natural Phenomena; Climate and Global Change; Air Quality/Water Quality; Looking at the Sun; Oceans, Great Lakes, and Coastal Environments; Education/Outreach; and a large list of related links.
http://www.erl.noaa.gov/

Grand Canyon Explorer
(Teachers & Students,
Elementary - High School)
Provides geographical and historical information about the Grand Canyon.
http://www.kaibab.org/geology/
gc_geol.htm

Lindsay and Megan's Zoo On Line
(Teachers & Students,
Elementary - High School)
An entire zoo on the Internet! Pictures, sounds, and information about the animals and their classifications.
http://www.rnet.net/linds_megs_zoo/
zoo_cover.htm

Sea World
(Teachers & Students,
Elementary - High School)
Developed by the educational department at Sea World, this site provides extensive information on many animals, including scientific classification, habitat, physical characteristics, eating habits, reproduction, birth, and care of young. Includes many activities for classroom use.
http://www.seaworld.org/infobook.html

United States National Arboretum
(Teachers & Students, Middle - High School)
The mission of the U.S. National Arboretum is to conduct research, provide education, and to conserve and display trees, shrubs, flowers, and other plants to enhance the environment. Includes a "plant hardiness zone map", "Horticulture FAQs and Facts" and "Research Activities."
http://www.ars-grin.gov/ars/Beltsville/
na/index.html

Volcano World
(Teachers & Students,
Primary - High School)
Active on the Web for over three years, this site features: Volcano info, pictures, movies, games, and an A-Z listing of major points of interest in Volcano World.
http://volcano.und.nodak.edu/

Yuckiest Site on the Internet
(Teachers & Students,
Elementary - Middle School)
Teaches students how their bodies work and additional information about bugs and worms.
http://www.nj.com/yucky/index.html

Interpersonal

Graffiti Wall
(Students, Elementary - Middle School)
A place where kids can write to each other on an interactive wall.
http://www.kidscom.com/orakc/
GraffitiWall/wallright.html

Human Communication Research Centre
(Teachers & Students, High School)
This site brings together theories and methods from several formal and experimental disciplines to understand better how people communicate and process information. The focus is on spoken and written language, but they also study communication in other media — visual, graphic, and computer based.
http://www.hcrc.ed.ac.uk/Site/
site_home.html

Lemonade Stand
(Students, Middle - High School)
Practice running a lemonade stand to test and develop your entrepreneurial skills.
http://www.littlejason.com/lemonade/
index.html

Social/Cultural Anthropology Internet Guide
(Teachers)
This subject guide is designed to help the user by reducing the mass of social and cultural anthropology resources that exist on the Internet to a manageable level of complexity. It is arranged alphabetically and separated into different areas of social and cultural anthropology to guide the user to their topic of interest. It provides a mixture of text and directories that contain links to additional resources.
http://www.ualberta.ca/~slis/guides/
canthro/anthro.htm

Yahoo's Chat Site for Kids Only
(Students, Elementary - Middle School)
This provides students a fully monitored chat room with topics like "Homework Help Chat" and "Advice Chat."
http://chat.freezone.com/

Intrapersonal

Famous Philosophers and Discussions about Them
(Teachers & Students, High School)
A site setup by the IUPUI University Library, these pages contain links to many other philosophy related sites (Ethics, Logic, Philosophers, etc...).
http://www-lib.iupui.edu/subjectareas/
philos/famous.html

Goal Setting
(Students, High School)
Articles on how to set goals and achieve them.
http://www.mindtools.com/page6.html

Meta-Programming: Discovering the Higher Self
(Teachers & Students, High School)
Meta-Programming is a set of analytical procedures which you apply to yourself, in order to differentiate the spiritual part of your being - the higher self - from the mental and physical.
http://www.trans4mind.u-net.com/
meta.htm

Motivating Moments
(Teachers & Students, High School)
An ever-growing online collection of motivational, inspirational, positive and success-oriented quotations.
http://www.selfgrowth.com/index.html

Personality Online
(Teachers & Students,
Middle - High School)
Provides many personality tests including:
The Enneagram, The Colour Test, Keirsey
Temperament Test, Maykorner Test, and
the Personality Profile. Also features a chat
area to discuss with others your results and
reactions.
http://www.freshy.com/personality/

Tests, Tests, Tests
(Students, Middle - High School)
Online personality tests, intelligence tests,
attitude and emotional health tests.
http://www.queendom.com/tests.html

Emotional
Get Your Angries Out
(Teachers & Students,
Elementary - High School)
Website with articles on controlling anger
grouped in sections for adults, students,
and parents.
http://members.aol.com/AngriesOut/
index.htm

Nonverbal Communication Clues
(Teachers & Students, High School)
A single page that lists many aspects of
body language.
http://www2.egr.uh.edu/~lab17654/
bodyl.htm

Tools for a Happier Life
(Teachers & Students,
Elementary - High School)
A page dedicated to bringing more happiness into people's lives and decreasing unnecessary emotional suffering, this site includes essays, inspirational quotes and stories, self-help overviews based on the
teachings of Jesus Christ, Kahlil Gibran,
O'Henry, Tony Robbins, James Michener,

Barry Neal Kaufman, I Ching, Tao Te
Ching, The Art of War and Deanna
Cummins.
http://www.lollie.com/

Working (and playing) with Dreams
(Teachers & Students, High School)
Provides numerous ways to derive meaning from dreams, an essay on the meaning
of dreams, and links to dream-related sites.
http://www1.rider.edu/~suler/
dreams.html

Culinary
Cookbook.com
(Teachers & Students, High School)
Over a million recipes online!
http://www.cookbook.com

Feeding Frenzy
(Teachers & Students,
Middle School - High School)
Contains recipes for different meals of the
day. From FreeZone's kid website.
http://freezone.com/fun_games/cuisine/
intro1.html

Kid's Food Cyber Club
(Teachers & Students,
Primary - High School)
A spectacular site with separate areas for
Kids, Parents, and Teachers. Plenty of re-
lated links to satisfy your hunger for more
information.
http://www.kidsfood.org/

Kitchen Link
(Teachers & Students, High School)
A master index to almost 8,000 food and
cooking related links on the net.
http://www.kitchenlink.com/

Nancy's Death by Chocolate
(Teachers & Students, High School)
An entire site devoted to chocolate, and how to prepare chocolate desserts.
http://www.geocities.com/Paris/2177

Nutrition Facts about Fruits and Vegetables
(Teachers & Students, High School)
http://www.dole5aday.com/nut_center/NUTINFO.html

Mechanical/Crafts

Brad Shute's Wicked Good Handmade Glass WebSite
(Teachers & Students, Middle - High School)
A site devoted to sharing information about handmade glass, glassblowing, lampworking, and glassmaking.
http://members.aol.com/bshute36/index.html

Crafters Network
(Teachers)
A virtual community for artists, crafters, collectors, and hobbyists worldwide. Access a great number of resources dealing with handcrafts, including chat and message forums, and a "top 100 craft sites" listing.
http://www.crafters.net/

Mechanical Toys Page
(Teachers & Students, Elementary - High School)
A website with toys that you can make yourself. Instructions included.
http://www.nfra.nl/~mgoris/mechtoys/

Simple Machines
(Teachers & Students, Middle - High School)
A collection of links, explanations, and demonstrations on how different simple machines work.
http://www.ced.appstate.edu/whs/goals2000/projects/machines.htm

Existential

Existentialism Hideout
(Teachers & Students, High School)
Dedicated mostly to the philosophy of existentialism, contains articles, ranging from introductory to very complex.
http://www.geocities.com/Athens/6510/

Mary's House O' Philosophy
(Teachers & Students, High School)
Provides an overview of existentialism and famous existentialists.
http://shrike.depaul.edu/~mchasen/

Meaning of Life
(Teachers & Students, Middle - High School)
Asks the visitor first to explore their reasons for seeking the meaning of life, then presents some answers in essay format.
http://www.aristotle.net/~diogenes/meaning1.htm

Meaning of Life Home Page
(Teachers & Students, High School)
Discusses human origins, purpose, and spirituality. Many articles and links to other sites focused on the meaning of life.
http://www.intrepid.net/~hollyoak/lifehp.htm

Psychology, Prophecy, and Philosophy
(Teachers & Students, High School)
A collection of papers written by Bill Kvasnikoff.
http://www.lookup.com/Homepages/77711/home.html

Categories of Intelligences

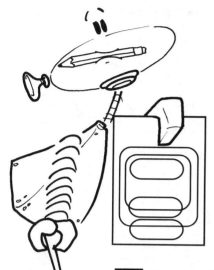

If as educators we are to match, stretch, and celebrate the multiple intelligences, it behooves us look at the intelligences from as many perspectives as possible. By asking how the different intelligences are similar and different we gain insight into the nature of human intelligences — and hints about how best to create and use intelligence-compatible instructional strategies and how to foster the development of the various intelligences.

Although each of the eight MI theory intelligences involves attraction to and skill with different kinds of stimuli, the intelligences differ, so each shares some characteristics with other intelligences and fails to share other characteristics. Thus, it is possible to categorize the intelligences. In what follows, we propose one way to categorize and conceptualize the eight intelligences. There are surely many alternatives. The categories that we propose are overlapping (some intelligences fit into several categories) and each category contains some gray areas (some intelligences just "sorta fit" into a category, or fit into the category in a different way than the other intelligences). See Categories of Intelligences on the following page.

No category system for the human intelligences will be completely satisfying because each intelligence is so complex and multifaceted that none can be placed neatly into just one box. Nevertheless, it is instructive to attempt to categorize the intelligences — it deepens our understanding of their essence.

Spencer & Miguel Kagan: *Multiple Intelligences*

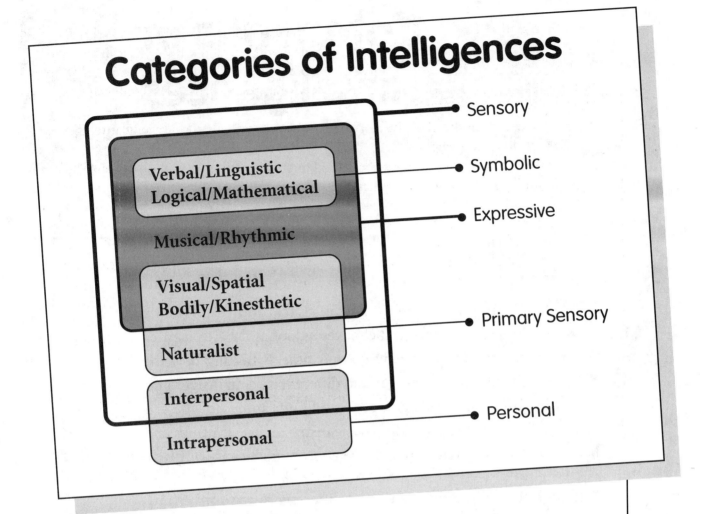

Categories of Intelligences

- Sensory
- Symbolic
- Expressive
- Primary Sensory
- Personal

Verbal/Linguistic
Logical/Mathematical

Musical/Rhythmic

Visual/Spatial
Bodily/Kinesthetic

Naturalist

Interpersonal

Intrapersonal

Personal Intelligences

The intrapersonal and interpersonal intelligences deal with people — self and others. There is an intimate relation between these two intelligences because we cannot know others fully without knowing ourselves. If we have never experienced a feeling, we cannot relate fully to a person who is experiencing that feeling.

Morality has its roots in not wanting to cause for others an experience we do not want for ourselves. To the extent we are empathic and can identify with others, it hurts us to hurt others.

Conversely, observing and interacting with others allows us know and develop parts of ourselves we might not otherwise. As we observe and identify with others, we find our potential. The smile of a mother allows the infant to try on a smile; those who see empathy or anger displayed by another more fully identify with their own empathy or anger. As Dr. Gardner pointed out, the development of the two personal intelligences are intimately intertwined.

Expressive Intelligences

Without a stretch, more than half of the intelligences can be categorized as "languages" we use to express ourselves. We can express our thoughts and feelings easily through words (verbal/linguistic), mime and gesture (bodily/kinesthetic), playing or composing a piece of music (musical/rhythmic) and painting a picture (visual/spatial). Math too is a language, but of a different sort. It expresses not feelings, but our thoughts about relations among abstract symbols which may stand for quantifiable external reality. The naturalist intelligence, too, can be used as a way to express one's feelings (picking a flower to present to a friend, planting a certain kind of garden, grooming one's pet a certain way), but that is perhaps too much of a stretch to qualify the naturalist intelligence as an expressive intelligence.

Sensory Intelligences

Intelligences as defined by MI theory are not linked to the senses, yet as we categorize intelligences, a "sensory intelligences" category is provocative. We make a division within the category of sensory intelligences, distinguishing primary sensory intelligences from sensory intelligences.

Three of the intelligences almost certainly evolved primarily to help us know immediate, concrete external reality. Clearly, knowing reality has great adaptive advantages. The sensory intelligences function to allow us to know the objective world; they deal with stimuli which are independent of the self — stimuli to which anyone can have access. Visual/spatial intelligence deals with colors, shapes, and locations among objects; the bodily/kinesthetic intelligence deals with the "feel," texture, and weight of objects; the naturalist intelligence helps us recognize and categorize flowers, plants, and natural phenomena such as rocks and clouds. These primary sensory intelligences have their roots in our need to maintain awareness of an objective, external reality and are in contrast to intelligences which are oriented toward internal stimuli generated by the self (intrapersonal intelligence) and intelligences which have their roots in our need to express our reactions to, impressions of, and generalizations about reality (verbal/linguistic and logical/mathematical intelligences).

A point is made in MI theory to distinguish the senses from intelligences, yet it is interesting to note that the theory deals quite well with two of our five senses: sight, the visual/spatial intelligence, and touch, the bodily/kinesthetic intelligence. MI theory, however, does not acknowledge an intelligence or intelligences that deal specifically with the other three senses: smell, taste, and sound. If, as MI theory claims, intelligences evolved to deal with specific stimuli, what do we make of the fact that the theory fails to directly address three of the most important sensory stimuli present throughout our evolutionary history?

This simple notion makes the case for a culinary intelligence even more compelling. The culinary intelligence directly integrates two other important sensory stimuli: taste and smell.

Thus, we are left with sound, the last of the senses. MI theory accommodates auditory stimuli, not with a specific intelligence, but across the intelligences. Sounds from nature are processed by the naturalist intelligence, spoken words by the verbal/linguistic intelligence, and rhythmic sounds and music by the musical/rhythmic intelligence. We have already accepted the naturalist intelligence as a primary sensory intelligence as it deals so much with understanding our external reality — the natural environment we inhabit. The musical and verbal/linguistic intelligences, however do not qualify as primary sensory intelligences.

Both words and music are created by humans and are not otherwise found in nature, with the exception of bird song.* Logic therefore dictates that music and language were first expressive and second sensory — how could we sense something that did not yet exist? Thus the musical/rhythmic intelligence probably has its roots most deeply in our need to express ourselves, rather than to grasp a reality beyond. Music expresses relationships, rhythms, harmonies, counterpoints, patterns, flow, mood, and the creation and resolution of tension. Music is the natural language for making statements about relations among internal states, just as math is the natural language for making statements about the relations among external objects or abstract symbols. Music is not, in its origins, a sensory intelligence but an expressive one.

Naturally, though, the music, words, and math composed, spoken, or expressed by one person as self-expression becomes sensory input for another. So the musical/rhythmic, verbal/linguistic, and mathematical/logical intelligences each have an expressive and a receptive side. Brain research indicates a basis for this "receptive / expressive" distinction. Thus, in this category system we include music, words, and math as both expressive and sensory. We simply do not categorize them as primarily sensory, because we do not believe their primary function is to maintain contact with the external reality.

The behavior of others, their facial expressions, actions, dress, posture, words also all provide sensory input; it is that input which particularly attracts the person strong in interpersonal intelligence. Thus, we include the interpersonal intelligence among the sensory intelligences as well.

In the broad category of sensory intelligences we exclude only the intrapersonal intelligence. Clearly our thoughts, dreams, aspirations, feelings, and internal sensations provide sensory input. But the stimuli with which the intrapersonal intelligence deals is internal. The intrapersonal intelligence is oriented toward knowing the internal world, not sensing the world beyond ourselves. We include in the broad category of sensory intelligences only those oriented toward sensing the world outside ourselves. Otherwise all intelligences would be sensory intelligences; all intelligences have as a basis attraction to some kind of stimuli.

Because the sensory intelligences allow us to perceive reality, composing with the elements of sensory intelligences allows us to communicate with others. The sensory

---

* If we consider the musical/rhythmic intelligence to encompass all sounds, or consider rhythm outside of the auditory domain (the rhythm of naturally occurring patterns and repetitions) the musical/rhythmic intelligence would qualify as a primary sensory intelligence. This, however, seems to be stretching the definition of the intelligence.

intelligences provide powerful mediums with which to express ourselves and to communicate with others as we create dances, paintings, and sculptures.

Although we are not classifying language and music as primary sensory intelligences — they do not appear to have evolved primarily to sense the world external to ourselves — they too are among our most powerful mediums of expression. As we work with the sounds and meter of words or the tones and rhythms of sounds, we compose and convey powerful messages. Concerts and poems communicate the deepest of human feelings and perceptions.

Symbolic Intelligences

Two human intelligences are completely dependent on symbol systems. The verbal/ linguistic and logical/mathematical intelligences appear to have their root in our need to discover and express patterns and generalizations beyond single concrete experiences. The symbolic intelligences allow us to deal at a level removed from specific concrete experiences; they express generalizations about sets of experiences. To do so they use symbols which stand for sets of experiences. In this respect the symbolic intelligences are metasensory — their primary function is not to perceive or manipulate sensory stimuli, but rather to make statements about those stimuli.

It can be argued that paintings, sculpture, music, mime, and dance are all symbolic, standing for perceptions, inner states and even expressing generalizations. This is true. But the symbol systems of the sensory intelligences are qualitatively different from those of math and language. This becomes perhaps most clear when we leave our own culture and tour. As we visit different cultures we find different kinds of music, art, sculpture, architecture, dance, language, and math. But there is a qualitative difference in how the music, art, and dance differ across cultures compared to how languages and math systems differ. As we experience the music, art, and dance of a different culture, with no instruction we are powerfully impacted, we get much of the message. In contrast, when we listen to the language or look at the math symbols, we are lost, completely baffled. Why?

Music, visual art, and dance communicate even very abstract thoughts through concrete experiences. A sculpture stands as an object onto itself; a word does not. A word is a symbol for something else. It is a code. To understand the word we need to understand the symbol system; we need the key to the code so we can translate the language. We need no key to get the message of music or to understand a painter's mood. We may understand math quite well using Arabic numbers, but when first confronted with Roman numerals, we may not get the message. We need the key — we need to know for what the symbols stand. Language and numbers are symbol systems unlike those used for any of the other intelligences. Thus it is meaningful to speak of the verbal and mathematical intelligences as the symbolic intelligences.

Let's peek for a moment at how the symbolic intelligences come to rely on symbols representing nonspecific experiences, generalizations based on specific experiences. If every time a very young child sees a chair they hear the word "chair," eventually the child will associate the word "chair" with the object. Upon seeing the chair, they will say "chair." Only later does the child learn that the word "chair" is not the name of one specific object, but rather the name given to all objects which meet certain criteria. Over time the word "chair" comes to be an abstract symbol for a whole set of things which are used to sit on and which, often but not always, have four legs, a seat, and a back.

In the same way, a child learns that "2 + 2 = 4" does not stand only for combining two marbles with two other marbles, but rather it represents combining two of anything with two of anything else. The statement "2 + 2 = 4" comes to mean a set of two when combined with another set of two becomes a set of four, regardless of what the 2's stand for. The 2's of the equation can be hands or lamps or stars or tears. But in an important sense, they are none of those things. The equation does not stand for specific objects. It is a statement about how things in general combine. The symbols of the equation are abstract, with no one-to-one correspondence with concrete objects. Math, like language, at core is symbolic.

As we "put something into words" we are translating from experience, trying to capture with words the essence of an experience. The words stand for something else. In the same way the symbols of a geometry proof stand for relations among things, they are abstractions from concrete experiences, attempts to capture the general rule. The Pythagorean theorem holds for any right triangle on a plane. In contrast, the notes in a tune or the colors on the canvas are not in the same way abstract symbols standing in a one-to-one relation for other experiences. The notes and the colors in and of themselves create a mean-ingful experience. Whereas they may be symbolic of other experiences, their symbolism is very subjective and may mean something quite different to each observer or may not be symbolic at all. The notes and the colors stand on their own, have meaning and impact on their own. The words and numbers have meaning only to the extent that they stand for something else.

Words and numbers are a natural way to make statements which are abstract generalizations, symbolic of sets of experiences, removed from any single specific experience. The formula "2 + 3 = 5" can refer to notes of music, players on a football field, rocks on the ground, or words on a page. They are abstract symbols removed from specific sensory experiences. The colors and forms in a painting are not in the same way intended to stand for a wide range of different stimuli, they are not a natural medium to express generalizations. With language and math we express relations *about* sensory experiences, with music, the visual arts, and dance we express ourselves *with* sensory experiences. Because the symbols of language and math are abstractions from reality, they are uniquely capable of communicating generalizations.

Language and math are symbols qualitatively different from paintings, musical notations, and choreographic notations. Each note on a staff of music stands in a one-to-one relation with a piano key to be played or a guitar string to be plucked. The musical notation does not talk about the music, it represents the music. The colors on the canvas and the moves of the dance do not each stand for something else, they are components of the composition, gaining their meaning within the composition.

Although the painting or dance may be a symbol for a set of life's experiences, we do not have to look beyond the dance or the painting to find meaning. In contrast, when we use the number "2" or the word "bird" the meaning is completely lost if we do not know the external experiences for which they stand. Further, the symbols of language and math often do not stand for specific experiences, but rather sets of experiences. We do not have in mind a specific bird or a specific set of two, we use those symbols to express something true about all birds or about all sets of two. Language and logic systems are the natural medium for expressing generalizations; the arts convey feelings and universal experiences, but have difficulty with generalizations. How do you paint the idea "All birds have feathers?" The arts express themselves through the concrete. They do a far better job of expressing the "featheriness" of a bird or even of many birds, but cannot with precision convey anything about all birds. Language and math are metasensory intelligences, they are uniquely capable of expressing our experience not of specific sensory experiences, but of sets of sensory experiences.

To the extent numbers and language are used to stand not just for specific, sensory experiences, but to express generalizations about those experiences they are abstract symbol systems. Because they are not limited to specific sensory experiences, and because they make use of symbols for sets of experiences, it is meaningful to call them the "symbolic intelligences" in contrast to the "sensory intelligences" that more directly deal with perceiving or creating specific sensory experiences.

Perhaps the traditional bias for associating the linguistic and mathematical intelligences with intelligence as a whole, is that the symbolic intelligences are a natural medium to convey the general rules one has managed to induce from experience. Intelligence, however, is much more multifaceted than inducing rules, and MI theory provides a needed corrective to the overreliance on the symbolic intelligences.

It is the symbolic nature of language and math, not their abstractness that distinguishes them from the other intelligences. Not all language and math are abstract (we talk about and count specific objects), but all language and math is symbolic (we use symbols to stand for those objects). Language has both concrete and abstract functions: We have proper nouns which correspond in a one-to-one relation to specific external objects, and common nouns which represent abstractions from a class of objects. Importantly, ability to understand proper and common nouns are dependent on different parts of the brain; in brain injury we can lose either ability without losing the other. The words "John Smith" are representative of a specific concrete person; the word "man" refers to any one of the class of things which have certain characteristics. In either case, though, the words are symbols, standing for a concrete or abstract reality. A painting or sculpture can be representational (painting John Smith), or can be abstract (attempting to express the essence of humankind). But in both cases the painting stands on its own, expressing itself by what it is; we need no key to decode it. Nor do we need a key to decode music. Whether the painting is abstract or representational, it does not use a symbol system like language or math. It may be symbolic, representing a range of experiences and symbolic in that it talks about humans and not John Smith, but it is not symbolic in the same way that language and math are —it is not a set of symbols which derive their meaning only when we understand them as a code to represent an external reality.

It is perhaps important to note that one aspect of the intrapersonal intelligence is completely dependent on a symbol system. Our dreams, as Freud and Jung demonstrated, are symbols for events, feelings, premonitions, and thoughts. The symbol system of dreams, though, is qualitatively different from the symbol system of language or math. It is an idiosyncratic and completely contextual symbol system. A car may stand for one thing in someone's dream and another in someone else's, or one thing in one dream and something completely different in the context of a second dream. Further, dreaming is but one aspect of the intrapersonal intelligence which includes plans, values, emotions, self-perception. Thus, we do not place the intrapersonal intelligence in the category of a symbolic intelligence.

Music in one sense is the most abstract of the intelligences. It is also symbolic, representing and expressing a great range of human experience, especially internal experiences such as rhythms, harmonies, counterpoints, patterns, flows, moods, and the creation and resolution of tension. In this sense music is symbolic. In the more limited sense of using a symbol system which stands for something else, though, music is not symbolic. We do not need to translate music to understand it. The notes of music, unlike the words of language, do not each represent an external reality; they are a reality. It is in this limited sense that language and math are unique as symbolic intelligences.

Language is a universal symbol system; math a more limited symbol system. Language can express relations about the range of human experience, both inner and outer experience: we talk about our feelings and about the number and type of people who attended the party and about our place in the universe. Math is more limited. It is a symbol system limited to expressing relations about the external world. We use language to express all experiences; it feels quite natural to talk about a painting, a symphony, or a dance. It feels strange (but probably is instructive) to paint a conversation or dance an essay. Language quite naturally expresses itself about the other intelligences whereas the other intelligences do not generally make statements about language. Language is the universal symbol system.